How They Built the Settle-Carlisle Railway

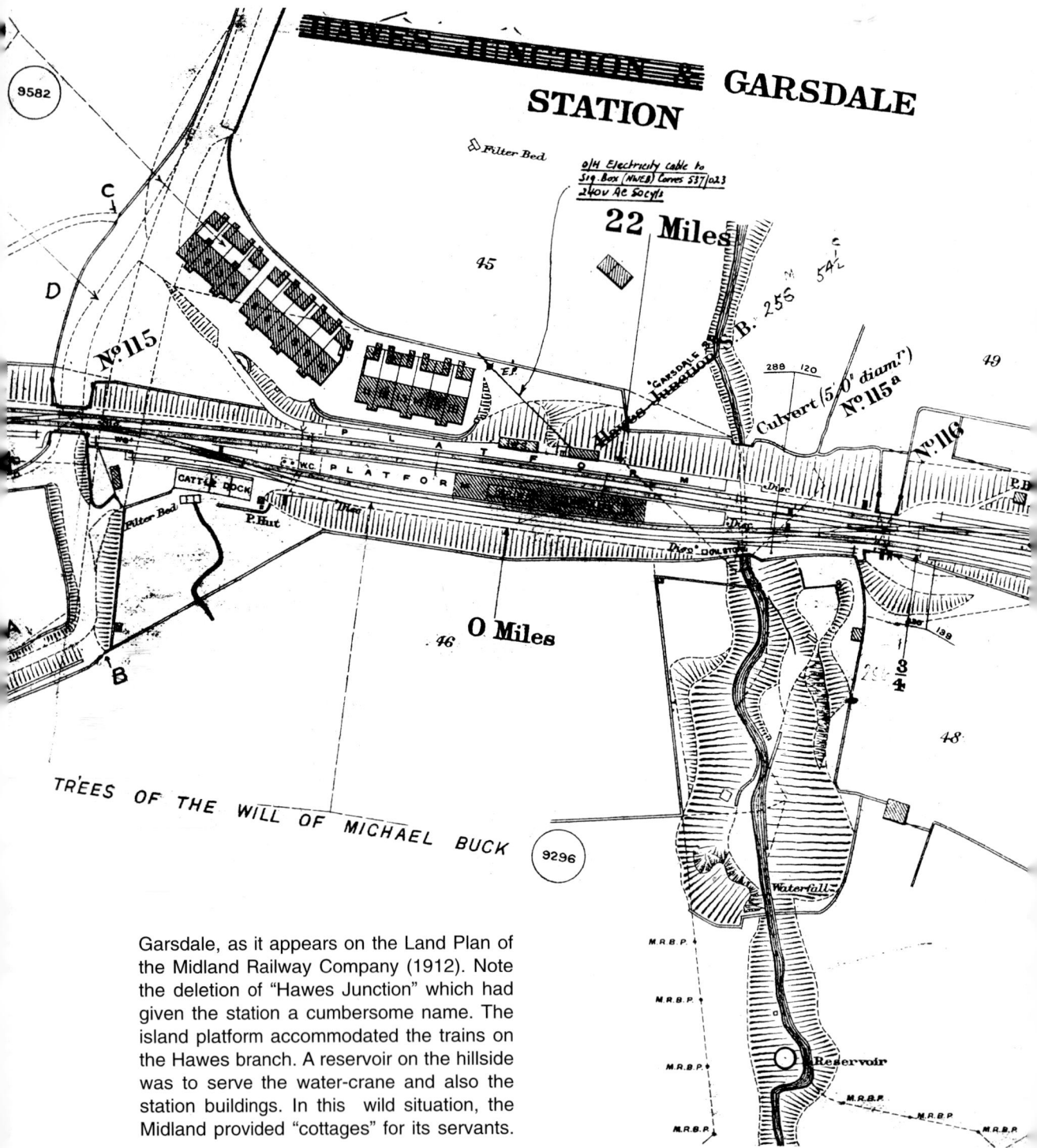

HAWES JUNCTION & GARSDALE STATION

Garsdale, as it appears on the Land Plan of the Midland Railway Company (1912). Note the deletion of "Hawes Junction" which had given the station a cumbersome name. The island platform accommodated the trains on the Hawes branch. A reservoir on the hillside was to serve the water-crane and also the station buildings. In this wild situation, the Midland provided "cottages" for its servants.

How They Built the Settle-Carlisle Railway

**Compiled by
W. R. Mitchell**

**Visuals:
Peter Fox**

James Allport (pictured above) was the General Manager of the Midland Railway from 1860 until 1880. He presided over the company's affairs during the protracted and expensive construction of the Settle-Carlisle line, a grand scheme through which the Midland was able to secure a direct share in the lucrative Scottish traffic. Pictured below is the mightiest of the viaducts—24-arch Ribblehead—as the first six arches were being turned. Note the timber scaffolding and steam-powered lifting equipment.

CASTLEBERG

Contract No:

CARLISLE

SCOTBY

CUMWHINTON

COTEHILL

ARMATHWAITE

LAZONBY

LITTLE SALKELD

LANGWATHBY

CULGAITH

NEW BIGGIN

LONG MARTON

APPLEBY

ORMSIDE

CROSBY GARRETT

KIRKBY STEPHEN

GARSDALE/ HAWES JCT.

DENT

HAWES

RIBBLEHEAD

HORTON-IN RIBBLESDALE

SETTLE

SETTLE JUNCTION

M.R.

4

3

2

5

1

LEVEL   1 IN 100

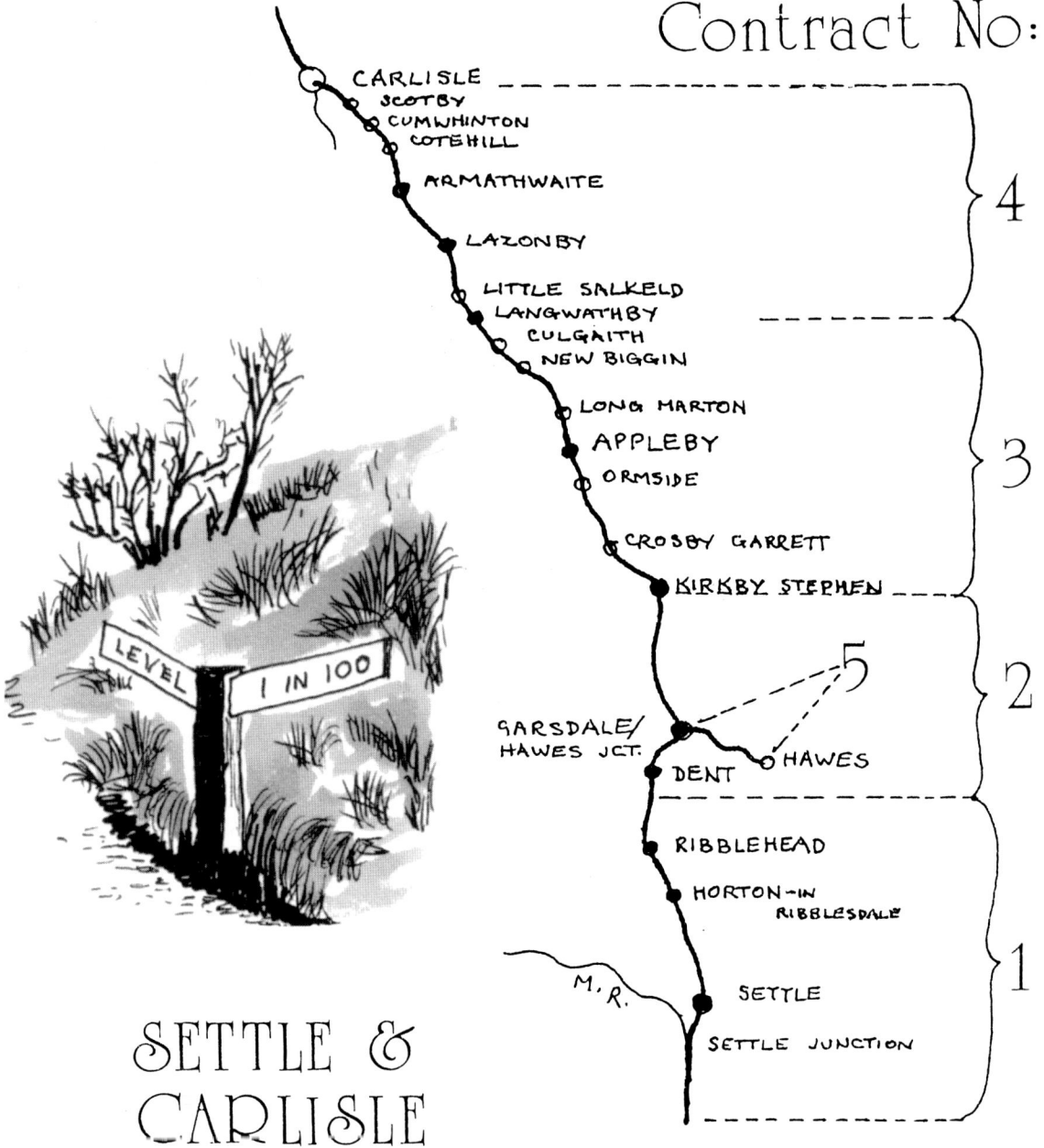

SETTLE & CARLISLE

Printed by Lamberts Print & Design, Station Road, Settle, North Yorkshire, BD24 9AA.
Published by W.R. Mitchell, 18 Yealand Avenue, Giggleswick, Settle, North Yorkshire, BD24 0AY.

© Compilation, W.R. Mitchell, 1989. Re-printed 1992, 1996, 2001, 2005.

ISBN: 1 871064 03 1.

Contents

Foreword 6

A Victorian Enterprise 7

Contract No. 1 11

Contract No. 2 26

Contract No. 3 37

Contract No. 4 41

Contract No. 5 44

All Speed to Scotland 45

Initials in the text:

C.J.   – Chambers's Journal.
C.W.A. – Cumberland and Westmorland Advertiser.
L.G.   – Lancaster Guardian.
M.R. – F.S. Williams's "Midland Railway" 1877.
W.A. – Wildman's Almanac (Settle).
W.G. – Westmorland Gazette.

Illustrations:

Front cover, top – John Crossley, Chief Engineer of the Midland Railway, who delayed his retirement so that he might supervise the Settle-Carlisle. *Left* – "Leander" and her driver pose at Appleby (Peter Fox). *Bottom* – The northern end of Ribblehead viaduct in the course of construction (British Rail).

Back cover, top – Steam Special 5305 climbs after a blizzard near Ais Gill, 1980 (Peter Fox). *Bottom* – Mossdale viaduct, on the Hawes branch (from the Midland Company's Land Plan, 1912).

This page, above – Crosby Garrett viaduct (110 yards long, 55ft high) nearing completion. Note the workman's huts. The line has 18 viaducts along the route.

Peter Fox contributed the line drawings appearing on pages 4, 6, 8, 16, 17, 22, 23, 27, 28, 31 (top), 34, 39, 40 (top), 45. Also the photographs appearing on pages 7, 20, 34 (bottom), 36.
Rowland Lindup: sketches on page 1, 4 (top), 10, 11, 26, 37, 41.
Contract Maps by R.W. Swallow. Land Maps from the archives of British Rail (courtesy of the Chief Civil Engineer, Preston).
British Rail: 3 (bottom), 5, 9, 18, 19, 25, 44 (right), 46.
Isaac Hailwood: 40 (bottom).
W.R. Mitchell: 14, 29, 32, 33, 38.

CONTRACTOR'S LOCOMOTIVE.

Foreword
by Alan H. King
C.Eng.FICE
(formerly Deputy Regional
Civil Engineer, LMR)

MY INVOLVEMENT with the Settle and Carlisle Railway started in 1976 when I became British Rail's Divisional Civil Engineer at Preston. Part of my duties included maintaining and repairing the line's infrastructure, a job which had been passed from Engineer to successive Engineer since the line was first built.

Bill Mitchell illustrates the remarkable story of the line's construction in a readable and easy to understand format. His book is not a reference book for the shelf, but a guide book which provides a source of information and enlightenment for the traveller who makes a journey through history along one of the outstanding civil engineering ventures of Victorian times.

There is a significant national interest in the Settle and Carlisle Line, which was summed up for me in a _Sunday Observer_ Colour Supplement article on _Britain by Stopping Train_ and where the line was described, and I quote: ''It is the King Lear of Railroads, an epic route conceived in a fit of rage and driven recklessly across the kind of country that the S.A.S. might choose for endurance training!''

This is a fair comment. It was built during the worst winters of the 19th century and it is in these harsh and demanding conditions that my staff maintained the track and structures for British Rail. I would like to pay tribute here to the Supervisors and men who keep the Settle and Carlisle route operating throughout the winter, often, as in 1979, in the most arduous conditions in England and with good humour and dedication.

I hope that the book will inspire readers to visit the ''magical'' viaducts and enjoy the atmosphere and delight that personal experience can give.

In 1876, when the Settle and Carlisle Railway became fully operational, no one could have imagined that 112 years later it would be passing through the most eventful period in its history. The proposed closure of the line has raised a lot of emotion during the last few years. However, change on British Rail is inescapable and the drastic revision of commercial and operating practices now in hand are as full of incident as those met in the first decades of railways existence. To my mind, the possible privatisation of the Line is as full of promise, within a more limited sphere, as when the Settle and Carlisle Railway was first unveiled.

Let us hope that passengers have many more years in which to enjoy the Line.

"DUCHESS OF HAMILTON" AT MOORCOCK VIADUCT.

A Victorian Enterprise

WHEN THE Settle-Carlisle railway was opened in 1876, a writer in "The Westmorland Gazette" urged his readers to stand back and look at the structures. "The traveller over the line will miss some of its greatest beauties by his inability to see the bridges and viaducts on which it is carried . . . Nearly all these are remarkable for their great height; and, although they are extremely simple in design, the tapering upwards of their lofty piers adds a very pleasing elegance to their simplicity. They have all been designed by Mr. Crossley and constructed under his immediate superintendence."

This book, a companion to *Shanty Life on the Settle-Carlisle Railway (1988)* takes the newspaper scribe's advice. The compiler then rummaged among the records of the 1870s to recreate the story of its construction, using extracts from contemporary reports.

Navvies by the thousand were mustered in the north-south valleys of Ribble and Eden, and in the high fell country lying between, and much hard physical toil went into the enterprise. Making the Settle-Carlisle also called for specialists in civil engineering and for equipment that was somewhat more complicated than a shovel. The Settle-Carlisle, being among the last of the great British railways to be built, could benefit from technological advances that had been made since the pioneering days of the 1840s.

This book was written for all who find delight in this bold Victorian concept and who enjoy visiting the bleak but attractive landscapes through which the trains operate. A visitor of the 1870s had a somewhat unusual view of a viaduct when he canoed in the Eden. He described one adventure in *The Field* in 1872: ''I paddled towards the new viaduct of the Midland line to the south of Appleby. The buttresses of the viaduct were completed and I was loudly hailed: ''Ye canna get through!'' ''Why not?'' ''T'water drops foor or foive feet.'' ''But there's lots of it, isn't there?'' ''Oh aye, there's lots on it,'' came back his final reply, and pulling myself together I ran at my first weir; away shot the bow into the air, followed by a plunge, and in a moment I was careering down a rapid stream. . .''

Not all the devices used by the Victorian engineers were complex. One—the bog cart—was based on an idea that pre-dated railways. In Williams's history of the Midland Railway, published in 1877 (though dealing with Settle-Carlisle experiences in the previous year) we read: ''At Settle, we stood in front of a 'machine' that consisted of a huge barrel, over which was a light cart-body and shafts, so arranged that as the horse pulled, the barrel would turn round underneath like a gigantic garden roller . . . 'We used to fill it,' said our informant, 'with victuals, or clothes, or bricks, to send to the men at work on the line, across bogs where no wheels could go. I've often seen . . . three horses in a row pulling at that concern over the moss till they sank up to their-middle, and had to be drawn out one at a time by their necks to save their lives'.''

Every book needs a hero. *How They Built the Settle-Carlisle Railway* has one readily at hand in J.S. Crossley, the Midland Railway Company's engineer-in-chief, who delayed his retirement so that he might supervise the building of this fell-top railway. When Mr. Allport, a top Midland man, retired, and a presentation was made to him of a painting of himself with Blea Moor in the background, he recalled: ''Mr. Crossley and I went on a voyage of discovery—'prospecting'. We walked miles and miles; in fact, I think I may safely say, we walked over a greater part of the line from

Frenzied activity in a cutting during the construction period. Much of the work depended on men with pick and shovel.

Settle to Carlisle, and we found it comparatively easy sailing till we got to that terrible place, Blea Moor. We spent an afternoon there looking at it . . . If I have had one work in my life that gave me more anxiety than another, it was this Settle and Carlisle line.''

John Crossley had to oversee a major engineering project and send soothing reports to the Midland directors at Derby, to whom the project was a considerable drain on their financial resources in a difficult, inflationary period. On the Settle-Carlisle, things were never quite as they seemed. The aforementioned Mr. Williams recorded that in sinking the foundations of Smardale viaduct an unexpected difficulty appeared. The river seemed to be running clear immediately over the solid rock, which appeared to supply an excellent foundation.

"We began to sink," said the engineer, "but not a bit of rock was to be found. The limestone rock and the 'brockram' were gone; and we had to go down 45 feet through the clay till we came to the red shale, and upon it we built.''

This story of railway-building is presented in five main sections, each representing the extent of a Contract awarded by the Midland. (The fifth Contract was for the Hawes branch). The initials following each note relate to the periodical in which it appeared; refer to the list of abbreviations for further details. The co-operation of British Railways in providing some contemporary documents is warmly acknowledged.

I have presented the quotations as they were originally written, which means there are variations in the spelling of place names and in punctuation.

The first pioneer sent into this remarkable country on behalf of the Midland Company was a young engineer named Sharland. A Tasmanian by birth, he had been for some time professionally engaged on the Maryport and Carlisle Railway, and had become familiar with this entire district. Immediately on his appointment he started off to find the best route for the proposed line and in ten days walked the whole distance from Carlisle to Settle.

M.R. (1876)

The line is now being constructed in Sectional Contracts, under the superindendence of—

John H. Crossley, Esq., as Engineer-in-Chief of the Midland Railway Co; John Thomson, Consulting Resident Engineer.

Contract No 1—Resident Engineers, R.E. Wilson and Edgar O. Ferguson; Contractor, John Ashwell; Contractor's Agents, James Hope, W.H.Ashwell. (The Contract No. 1 is now being carried on by the Midland Co., A. Terry being the agent assisted by W.H. Ashwell).

Contract No. 2—John S. Storey, Resident Engineer; Assistant Engineer, Frank Lynde; Contractors, Benton and Woodiwiss; Contractors' Agent, James Hay.

Contract No. 3—Resident Engineer, Jesse Drage; Contractor, Joseph Firbank; Contractor's Agent, J. Throstle.

Contract No. 4—Resident Engineers, John Allis and Samuel Paine; Contractor, John Bayliss; Contractor's Agents, J. Lambert, E. Williams.

Contract No. 5 (Hawes branch)—Resident Engineer, Edward Newcome; Contractors, Benton and Woodiwiss; Contractor's Agent, James Hay.　　　W.A. (1873)

From the Ribble to the Eden

All the engineering works have been completed in a most substantial manner and steel rails have been laid along the whole length from Settle to Carlisle. The line will accommodate a rich agricultural district in Westmorland and Cumberland but its main object is to afford a new and additional route for the traffic between England and Scotland.

W.G. (1876)

The strata passed through on the whole Line is Limestone, Gritstone, Shale, Clay, Washing and Boulders, Red Sandstone, Sand and Marl.

W.A. (1873)

Mentioning navvies to a man with soiled clothes, he quickly replied: ''Do you call me a navvy?'' Though the honest labour of the lowest scale of workers on the line is honourable, still as a miner he felt his honour was impeached by being classed with navvies.

L.G. (1873)

A list of head and hand workers connected with railway making may be interesting to the curious. Directors, engineers-in-chief, resident engineers, contractors and sub-contractors, inspectors, clerks, cashiers, gangers, time-keepers, masons, brickmakers, masons' and brickmakers' labourers, carpenters, minders, platelayers, horsekeepers, carpenters, engine drivers, stokers, tippers, saddlers, mechanics, sawyers, quarrymen, cement burners, mortar grinders, engine tenters, and navvies. Lawyers and doctors have a share in the conern, but as one did not know which niche to give them, prudence directed a separate recognition.

L.G. (1873)

How easily in railway construction could money be wasted or spent to misuse if the head direction were faulty; for one day on this line if every man did work that was of no use we reckon the amount of wages alone would equal about £1,200. This is calculating 6,000 men at four shillings per diem.

W.A. (1874)

If the line had been simply a branch line, quicker curves and steeper gradients no doubt would have been adopted and a comparatively light line secured on the sidelong hills, twisting and twirling in and out to avoid cuttings and embankments; but the Settle to Carlisle is to be a trunk link on which the traffic will be of great dimensions and in this case flat curves and as good gradients as possible must be adopted. And when one thinks by the means of curves and inclines the number of routes that could be selected it shews a masterly mind to be able to conquer all the various obstacles and difficulties that retard the way.

W.A. (1874)

From Settle Junction to the termination of the second contract there is not a cornfield on either side of the line. Near Smardale Viaduct is a field of turnips.

L.G. (1875)

Contract No. 1:

Settle Junction to Dent Head

The map shows the railway route with the following labelled features (north indicated):

Dent Head · Blea Moor Tunnel · 2419′ ▲ Whernside · Chapel Le Dale · B 6255 · Ingleton · Ribblehead · 2373′ ▲ Ingleborough · Beecroft Quarry · Horton in Ribblesdale · 2273′ ▲ Penygent · Clapham (junction) · To Lowgill and Lancaster · Taitlands Tunnel · Craven Quarry · Settle · Settle Junction · N

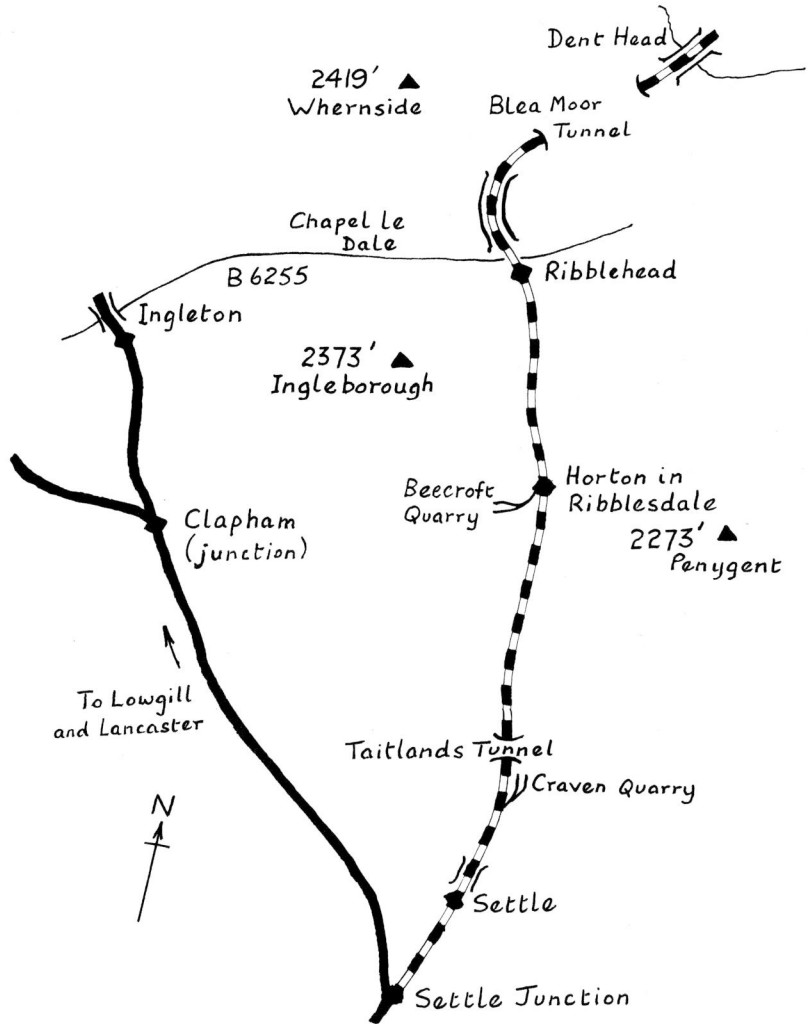

The Railway commences by a junction with the present line, 1½ miles south of Settle Station, 125 feet above sea level, where there are temporary sidings in connection with the tramway for the receipt of materials from the main line destined for the works.

W.A. (1873)

The junction of the new line with the *Little North Western* is at a point little short of two miles south of Settle, and at an elevation of 425 feet above sea level. The bridges between the junction and Settle are a skew girder bridge of 62 feet span, and an arched one of 39 feet span. They are of excellent material, are well finished, and to passers on the road they have a very neat appearance. No. 1 or Anley Cutting is a very long and deep excavation, through very hard grit, which proved very serviceable for bridges and other works of masonry. Many men were employed in dressing the batters with excellent soil, which gave the batters a garden-like apearance.

L.G. (1873)

At Settle Junction, an exchange station is being built and the platform and necessary siding are nearly completed. The station will be approached from the Settle and Long Preston turnpike road, which has been slightly diverted and improved. A close paling is nearly erected to prevent the engines from being seen from the road, a nuisance which has for a long time made this road very dangerous.

W.A. (1876)

At Settle we notice a large quantity of land enclosed, at present a busy scene of importance, occupied by temporary buildings, stables, sawing machine, mortar mill, etc. The mortar is composed of lime from Leicestershire known as "Hydraulic"; it is ground here by steam power, and carried in trucks to the various bridges.

W.A. (1873)

A large quantity of earth has been removed on the west side of the line nearly opposite Ingfield, to fill up the embankments. The Settle station ground is being filled up gradually to nearly the level of the rails and will make a station yard of considerable area.

W.A. (1874)

At Settle new station, several buildings have been constructed. The station house, the stationmaster's house, a large goods warehouse, a water tank for supplying the engines, and a weigh-house have all been erected by Mr. Israel Horton, of Bradford, under the superintendence of Mr. James Gray, his foreman. The Goods Warehouse will accommodate five trucks at once; platforms for unloading cattle, carriages and horses have also been built. Six cottages for signal-men, porters, etc., have been finished and are inhabited. All the buildings are of the gothic order of architecture, and built in stone from Shipley . . . The Water Tank holds 200 tons of water and is about 27ft above the level of the rails. The water gravitates into it from up the line, using the waste water in the cuttings.

W.A. (1876)

Marsh Field viaduct, which crosses the road near the Friends Meeting House, Settle, is a neat structure of 23 feet in height, with four arches of 30 feet span. Not far from this, a more massive viaduct crosses the turnpike road near the church, a large portion of the viaduct standing in the beautiful grounds of Mrs. George Hartley.

L.G. (1873)

The railway shortly passes Barrel Sykes, the residence of G.W. Perfect, Esq., where there has only been just sufficient room to get an easy curve without pulling down the house. The line crosses Langcliffe road south by a neat bridge, 25ft span, of the same material as the viaduct. A wooden hut nestles itself behind it from the biting east winds, and on the left of the line shortly after passing this road is a garden of some notoriety. It is a piece of severance caused by the railway that has been dug and planted with such success that many of the prizes at the local horticultural shows have been taken by its produce.

W.A. (1874)

The line [near Langcliffe] enters a solid blue limestone cutting at the entrance of which a pretty light iron girder bridge is finished for the footpath leading from Langcliffe to Langcliffe Place and Mills: it is also spanned in two places by "fly-arches" which start from the solid rock and are about 42ft span. In this cutting are a few spar lodes charged slightly with copper, and we should think it looks a likely place for lead if a shaft was sunk to a greater depth.

W.A. (1874)

At Willy Wood or the "Stainforth Sidings", as it is called on the signal box, all the necessary sidings are in for the accommodation of the Craven Lime Company and Mr. Thomas Murgatroyd, both of which firms are sending off large quantities of Lime and Limestone, and they keep a great many men employed.

W.A. (1876)

Near Willy Wood, north of Langcliffe, the Craven Lime Company is erecting extensive limeworks on Hoffman's patent. The chimney, which is to be 204 feet in height, is more than half of its height, and as such a lofty brick structure needed a good foundation, it is built on chisled limestone six feet below the surface. Mr. George Dawson, of Leeds, is the contractor for the chimney, which will take about 200,000 bricks.

L.G. (1873)

Further on at Sherwood Brow a pretty peep is had of the Ribble and two handsome bridges are nearly finished over the river. This part of the line is an ingenious piece of engineering,

A group of Horton-in-Ribblesdale quarrymen photographed in late Victorian times. In their manner and clothing they would be similar to the men who built the Settle-Carlisle line.

the peculiarity of the district involving crossing the river twice. The first bridge is built to an angle of 34 degrees, and the wing walls are of great length, to prevent the embankment falling into the river.

W.A. (1873)

A mile beyond Stainforth we for the first time pass over the wide rocky bed of the Ribble by a three-arched bridge. Here the engineers had great difficulty in selecting the best route to be taken. Should they cross and re-cross the river, or by two very heavy cuttings, and perhaps

tunnels, to take the line further to the east. The bridge is built at an angle of 34 degrees, and the long wing walls that sustain the embankment are of ingenious construction, though they were not liked by the builders on account of the number of ''quoins'' or corners they required.

M.R. (1876)

Elworth (Helwith) Bridge is a fine new structure seven yards wide, and is considerably higher than the old narrow bridge which is not yet taken down. Near this bridge, on the south side of the stream, a lucky workman just commencing business for himself, built a small sawmill for flags on the land through which the railway would run, but as he, in the multiplicity of business, had been overlooked, report says that he secured £700 as compensation.

L.G. (1873)

Helwith or Elworth Bridge is to be entirely rebuilt on a fresh site. The road has to be raised to enable the railway to pass underneath it, and involves a viaduct of five arches. The site of an ancient tarn has evidently been crossed by the line near here, as we are told the foundations of some of the bridges are twelve feet below the surface through silt and washings. . . The locomotive from Settle now runs as far as Row End for Horton.

W.A. (1873)

Dressed Stone, Ribblehead.

From Selside to Dent Head about 1,050 men are employed. Mr. Crossley, of Derby, is the engineer-in-chief. Mr. Wilson, of Settle, is resident engineer for No. 1 division of No. 1 contract; Mr E.O. Ferguson, resident engineer for No. 2 division of contract No. 1. Mr. A. Terry is chief agent for the company who now carry on the works of No. 1 contract, Mr. John Ashwell having given up his contract. Mr. W.H. Ashwell is agent or manager of the northern end of this contract, under Mr. Terry.

L.G. (1873)

At half a mile south of Selside the ''pot hole'' has been filled up and adds largely to the size of the field. The filling in this hole prevented all possibility of the embankment slipping. A tip waggon lies buried at the bottom as it accidentally slipped over, and it would have been more expense pulling it up than what it was worth.

W.A. (1876)

At the Ashes (between Selside and Ribblehead) the level crossing has been abolished and a bridge built over the railway and approach made from it. This is a great improvement as the level crossing, if made, would have been a very objectionable one. The Railway crossed the road at a considerable angle and would have been in a district where a large quantity of cattle are driven to and fro, near the line.

W.A. (1876)

''I have known the men,'' remarked Mr. Crossley to us the other day, ''blast the boulder-clay like rock and within a few hours have to ladle out the same stuff from the same spot like soup in buckets. Or a man strikes a blow with his pick at what he thinks is clay, but there is a great boulder underneath almost as hard as iron, and the man's wrists, arms and body are so shaken by the shock that, disgusted, he flings down his tools, asks for his money, and is off. . .

M.R. (1876)

One of the dwellings in this little wooden town is differently constructed from all the rest, as from its appearance, it must have served as a caravan. It was said that it was brought all the way from London, and that it was the first human dwelling fixed on Batty Green.

L.G. (1870)

After tea, Mr. Pollen entertained me with a historical account of Batty-wife-hole, from his first appearance in a van on its soil, exactly three years previous. Shortly afterwards, he said, "some chaps came down to make experimental borings, and they had to bide wi' us in the wan, for there were nowheres else to bide. All that winter there were ten of us living in that van, and a tight fit it were, surely. Of a night I used to have to stand by it for half an hour with a bull's-eye as a guide to the men homecoming through the waste. Sometimes one would stick, and his mates would have to dig him out; there were two chain o' knee-deep water four times a day for the fellows atween their meat and their work.

C.J. (1872)

Making one's way to Batty Green, one could not but look with astonishment at the numerous huts which dot the moor, and are known as Batty Green, Sebastopol, Jericho, Jerusalem and Tunnel huts. At the first mentioned place there are a mission room, day and Sunday Schools, a public library, post office, and shops for the sale of a variety of merchandise, a new and neat looking hospital with a covered walk for convalescent patients. All is life and bustle at this moorland town of huts, potters' carts, traps and horses for hire, drapers' carts, milk carts, green grocers' carts, butchers' carts, bakers' carts, and brewers' drays in addition to which may be seen numerous pedestrian hawkers plying from hut to hut their different trades. The company's offices, yard, stables, store rooms, shops etc. take up a large space of ground at Batty Green.

L.G. (1873)

Batty Green is a very wild and bleak spot; although many of the men have seen rough and foreign countries, railway making there, still they all agree that they were never in such a wild place before. The wind up the Ingleton

valley is of a most piercing nature and on many days the bricklayers on the viaduct have been unable to work from fear of being blown off.

W.A. (1874)

The railway crosses the turnpike road to Ingleton [at Batty Green] by a handsome arch bridge, on the "skew", span 39 ft., in very massive masonry of blue limestone. We notice blocks of stone eight feet in length. One hundred yards from this bridge, towards the tunnel, an embankment is being tipped, which will contain 280,000 cubic yards of earth when finished. There still remains a large proportion of this to be done, although as much as 800 cubic yards can be "tipped" per day.

W.A. (1873)

The greatest quantity of men employed on Contract No. 1 is about 2,300 and about 130 horses.

W.A. (1873)

After taking some refreshment at Ingleton . . . the journey to Batty Green had to be performed on foot. Carts laden with coal and railway material were numerous, but there were no public conveyances for passengers... The little chapel in the dale, with its much improved appearance, its enlarged burial ground, and the snug parsonage adjoining were a fine relief in the centre of rocks and mountains.

L.G. (1871)

The population at Batty Green at the present date is from 250 to 300. It is here where all the operatives at Dent Head, Sebastopol, Batty Wife Hole and Selside are paid. It is said that last Saturday night their wages amounted to about £1,500. This was exclusive of ''sub'' money and the large sums paid to tradesmen and farmers and others who cart materials to the works. The number of men employed on the works between Batty Wife Hole and Dent Head is about 700. Upwards of 100 horses are also employed in this division of the contract.

L.G. (1870)

A tramway is being laid between Batty Wife Hole and the south end of the tunnel, which is at the distance of two and a half miles. This iron road, which will be a great saving of horse flesh, is within a few hundred yards of being completed. An engine of twelve-horse power is in daily use on this tramway.

L.G. (1870)

The brick-making establishment (at Batty Green) is under the management of Mr. Rixon.

The brick works cover a large space of moorland and consist of extensive drying sheds, ovens, a large patent brick-making machine by Porter and Co., of Carlisle, a crushing machine, and a traveller seventy yards long to deliver the bricks in the shed above the ovens where they are dried by the waste heat. Porter's machine when in full work will make about 20,000 bricks a day. At present, as only half of it is at work, it makes from 11,000 to 12,000 a day. There are ten ovens with two fire holes to each oven. An oven holds from fourteen to fifteen thousand bricks, and it takes about a week to burn them. The quantity of fuel consumed at these works is only half the quantity used at an ordinary brick kiln.

The bed of clay which lies under a thin strata of peat is a mud deposit and much of it on account of its sandy nature is thrown aside. A crushing machine is employed to grind shale which, being intermixed with the clay used at the works, yields bricks of such a superior quality that when thrown out of the ovens they ring like pots. From 26 to 28 persons are employed at the works. Two girls were busy carrying bricks from the never-ceasing traveller. The large quantities of bricks made at these works are used for lining and arching the tunnel.

L.G. (1871)

Below: Artist's impression of an early goods train crossing Ribblehead viaduct.

Completing a viaduct. The contractor's engine and trucks carries the coping stones to the masons.

Batty Moss Viaduct, is under the superintendence of Mr. Hurst . . . This immense structure, when finished, will consist of twenty-four arches, each arch of 45ft span and 18ft rise. The piers, which are being built of black marble dug out of a quarry on Mr. Farrer's estate, will terminate at springing with a thickness of 6ft, the batter on the face being 1 inch in 32. The north abutment and the piers for the first six openings are already raised to heights varying from 10 to 25ft. The foundations for the next six piers are put in and built up to the level. The foundations are taken down to solid rock, which is mountain limestone . . . The lime used at the works is Barrow lime, brought from the neighbourhood of Leicester. The limestone of which the viaduct is built burns to a very good hydraulic lime.

The staging for a quarter of the length of the viaduct is to the height of within 20 feet of springing. A steam crane is employed to unload the stone, and two hand cranes and their travellers to turn the stone and for setting it. The whole of the stone is brought from two quarries under Whernside, at the distance of one and a quarter miles, by a locomotive. The stone requires much labour to dress it . . . A ten-horse power engine is constantly employed for mixing mortar. About sixty masons and labourers are employed on this work; the number of workmen varies much, for though good wages are paid some of them generally leave after every pay day; sometimes as many as eight fresh hands are set on the works in a day. According to the opinion of the foreman it will be two years at the present rate of progress before the viaduct will be finished.

The work hitherto has been attended with many impeding difficulties — such as the hardness of the stone, the flooding of the quarries by a mountain stream, and the wetness of the moor. The black marble, which is capable of a fine polish, is dug out in blocks . . . It is in mind to use additional mechanical forces so that double the number of workmen may be employed. A steam pump will be used at the quarry, and two steam travelling cranes on the gantry.

As the foundations of the piers and abutments are laid so deep, a cursory observer will not see the full extent of the progress made. Mr. Ashwell, the contractor, has done much to make the workmen comfortable. On the gantry, the men have boxes to shelter them from the weather and on the ground there are sheds for the comfort of the masons. The wages on these works average from 1s. to 1s. 6d. per day higher than the wages in Lancashire and Yorkshire; many of the masons get 6s. 6d. per day.

L.G. (1871)

The masons of Batty Moss Viaduct, Dent Head Viaduct and some other portions of the Settle and Carlisle . . . have been on strike for more than a week. For 9 hours per day theyhad 6s. 3d. and as the contractors required them during the summer months to work 10 hours per day, with the addition of 8d per extra hour, they have struck work. It is not reported whether there is any prospect of a speedy agreement between the men and their employers. For the sake of the completion of the new line, the sooner the dispute shall come to the end the better.

L.G. (1872)

It [Batty Moss Viaduct] will contain 30,000 cubic yards of masonry, besides 3,000 cubic yards of concrete, six feet of which is under nearly all the piers. The foundations were sunk 25ft in depth through peat, clay and washings before the solid rock could be met with, on which the viaduct stands . . . At the foot of the viaduct is a network of tramways, passing round the sharpest of curves, and up inclines as steep as 1 in 18, used for bringing stones, mortar, and other materials to the viaduct. There are also mortar mills, brick-making machines, drying sheds and kilns . . . We are shown the quarries for the Viaduct, which are formed by damming and altering the course of the river. The beds of rock are then taken out. Peat in this district seems to abound. Some we saw was 9 feet deep, but it is not used at all, coal being carted instead, as much as 600 tons a month being used on Contract No. 1.

W.A. (1873)

Batty Moss viaduct, of 24 arches, will be perhaps the finest piece of masonry on the new line. The first stone of this massive structure was laid by Mr. William Ashwell, October 12th, 1870. There are 23 piers and two abutments. The piers which stand 45ft apart are 13ft wide at the base and 6ft at the top. Eleven of the piers are finished. The centres are in for six arches and the turning of them in brick was

Ribblehead viaduct in course of construction. Notice, on the right, some Midland workshops and shanty huts.

begun on the 9th inst. Twelve piers are nearly at the top and the rest are at plinth level, 43ft below springing. Every sixth pier is as wide again as the others, so that were an accident to take place all the arches could not fall at once.

The viaduct is 1,328ft in length and about 100ft to the level of the viaduct. The blocks of black limestone, some of which contain two cubic yards and weigh from four to five tons, are dug from a quarry in Little Dale beck. It is said this structure will, when finished, contain 30,000 cubic yards of masonry and 3,000 cubic yards of concrete. About 100 men are employed on this viaduct and as the weather has been for some time remarkably fine, the works under the able management of Mr. Charles and Mr. Walter Hirst have made great progress. The viaduct when completed will be the admiration of all lovers of imposing and massive masonry, and no doubt generations unborn will look upon it with wonder, and think how clever were their forefathers to rear such a structure . . .

L.G. (1873)

The arches (of Batty Moss Viaduct) are covered with concrete and then asphalt is laid over to ensure the bricks from getting saturated with water.

W.A. (1875)

When leaving the viaduct, my guide hailed an engine driver who was about to return with a train of empty wagons to one of the cuttings in the direction of the tunnel; after mounting the engine and taking our position, so as to support ourselves by the brass rail on its side, the snorting steed started off at a tolerably quick speed.

No one can imagine the queer sensation which comes over one from the rolling and pitching motion of the locomotive caused by the unevenness and crookedness of the tramway excepting a novice in such a mode of transit. Up and down, heaving on one side and anon on the other, slackening its speed at curves and then accelerating it when they were past, was

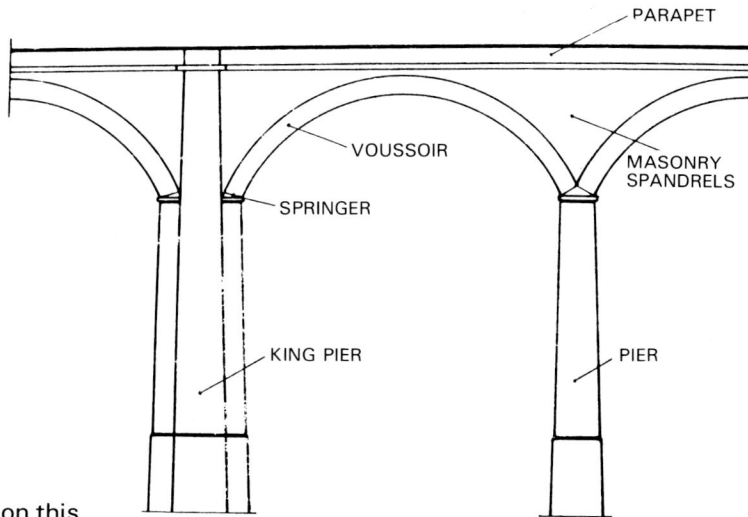

RIBBLEHEAD VIADUCT—PART ELEVATION.

enough to make a nervous person giddy and to relax his hold.

It was a relief when the locomotive had accomplished its journey to alight safe and sound on terra firma.

L.G. (1871)

Engines are being fixed upon the southern and northern summits of Bleamoor, which is 1,753ft high. The heavy material is drawn up a steep tramway on the northern side of the moor by means of three "crabs" placed at different distances on the route, and platelayers' trollies. A similar tramway will shortly be laid on the south side of the moor when crabs will be superseded by the engines now in course of erection. Donkeys are employed on the south side for carrying coals and other light materials in sacks. The water and debris are now drawn from the shafts by horses, but shortly engines will be employed for that purpose at all the shafts except No. 4, which is on the north side of the moor.

L.G. (1870)

The cuttings on this (South) side of Blea Moor Tunnel are well opened up, the gullets being well driven in advance. About 150,000 cubic yards have been taken out. Two locomotives are employed in conveying the excavated earth to the bank and about 150 men are employed at these cuttings. The number of men fluctuates very much. At present there is ample room for double the number. Most of the work on this part of the line is let to Batty Moss gangs and the men divide their earnings equally among themselves, or in proportion to the hours they work. The men, on account of this co-operation, earn good wages and they might do well but for drink. Drink meets them at every step and they appear to be powerless to resist the British workman's greatest foe.

L.G. (1871)

At the south end of Blea Moor Tunnel all appeared to be life and activity. The chatter of machinery, the noise of children and men indicated that no ordinary work was going on. As we reached the south end of the tunnel a train of trollies was about to ascend the steep tramway to the summit of Blea Moor. This mountain line is worked by a wire rope and a fixed engine on the hill. Most of the trollies were laden with coal, which were crowned with bags of flour and other domestic commodities. Before an engine was erected, coals were carried up the mountain by donkeys, and heavy railway material was drawn up by ''crabs''.

L.G. (1871)

Shaft A, sunk at the proposed entrance to the south end of (Blea Moor) tunnel, is 35 yards deep. About 100 yards have been driven or tunnelled northwards. The lining of the arch with brickwork varies from 1ft 6 inch to 2ft 3inch in thickness completed. At this shaft, a 12-inch winding engine is employed, which also works an 8 inch pump and a Blow George to supply the men below with air.

No. 1 shaft is a permanent shaft which has been sunk to the foundation level. About 40 yards from this shaft have been tunnelled each way, and the arching of the top has been completed as at A shaft. A 12 inch winding engine is used to draw the debris from the tunnel. A 16 inch engine is employed to pump the water and blow air to the men at the bottom.

No. 2 shaft is also a permanent shaft and it has been sunk to foundation level, a depth of 127 yards, and lined throughout with brickwork so that operations will soon be in full force for taking out the tunnel and driving headings. A 16-inch winding-engine is used to draw up the debris from the tunnel and a 20 inch engine is fixed for working the pump, which is a 10 inch one, the same as No. 1. The water met with varies from 80 to 100 gallons per minute. Engine power is laid down to raise 450 to 500 gallons per minute.

The heading from the north on Dent Head end has been driven a distance of 750 lineal yards, or nearly half a mile, into the hill and is fast approaching the summit. It has been driven under No. 3 shaft, which has been standing for some time.

Below: Steam-hauled express leaves Ribblehead viaduct on a sharp winter's day.
Huge embankments buttress the viaduct from north and south.

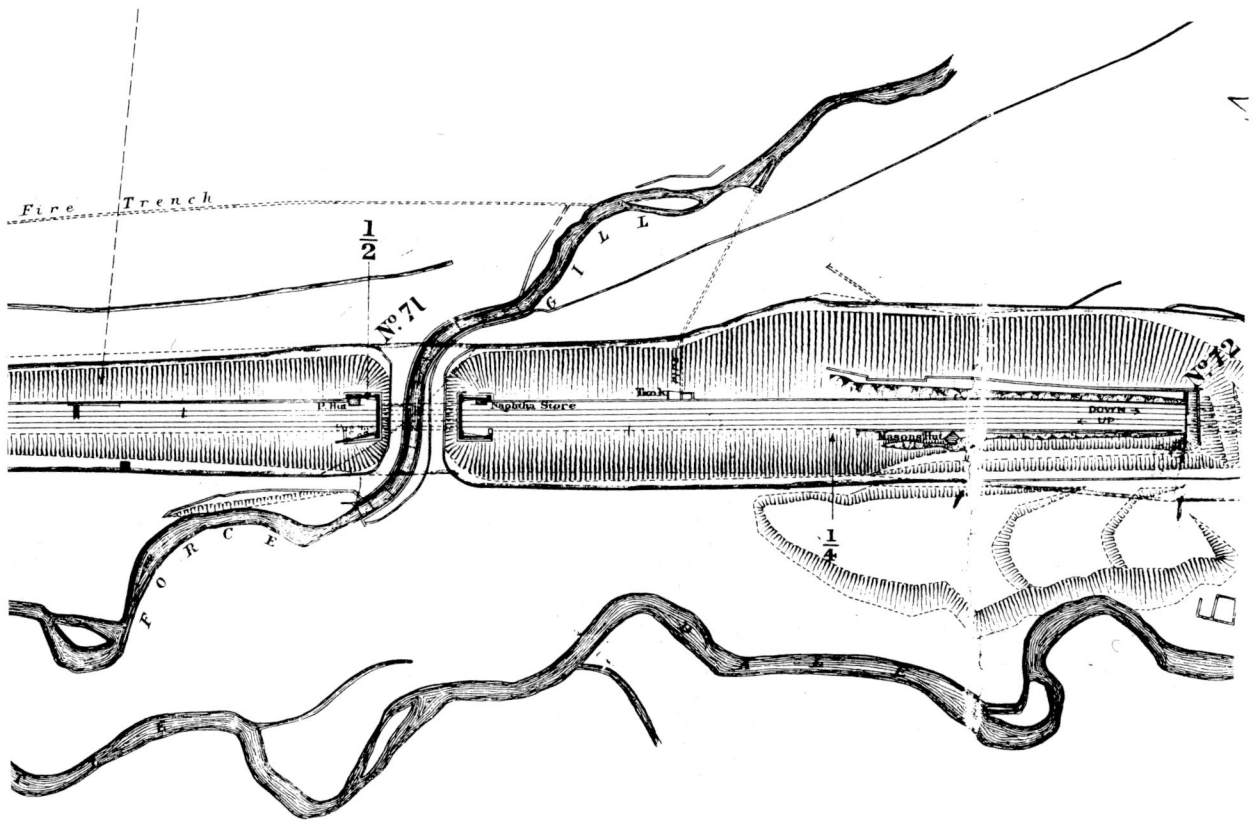

Acqueduct and South Portal of Blea Moor Tunnel
(from the Midland Railway's "Land Map").

At this end, the air is supplied to the workmen at the face of the heading by a simple and effectual contrivance, viz. a long column of water in a wrought-iron pipe, which has its outlet through a rose fixed on the tip. The column of water has a pressure of 120lb per square inch. Consequently, the rush of water drives the air up a pipe 11 inch by 9 inch to the face of the heading. The force of the air is so strong it will blow a candle out two or three yards from the end of the pipe.

The whole of the tunnel, with very little exception, is hard rock, such as limestone and grit. The average speed of driving at a face is about four yards per week. Though there are about 160 miners at work in the tunnel, still there is sufficient room for twice that number.

L.G. (1871)

For about 350 yards the Tunnel is on a curve; it is then straight for the rest of the distance. At No. A Shaft, the level of the railway is 1,151ft above the sea, the incline for 11½ miles being nearly 1 in 100 for the whole distance.

There are seven stationary engines on the Tunnel, two for winding materials up the incline planes from each end, the rest for pumping and winding the excavations up and for lowering bricks and mortar down the shafts. The miners also use this means to get to and from the Tunnel. At the top of the Tunnel there is a self-acting incline. The loaded trucks coming down draw the empty ones up to a millstone grit quarry which is used for obtaining stone for concrete and sand. The absence of the latter material has greatly increased the expense of mortar.

W.A. (1873)

The Tunnel is in a great state of forwardness and in most places the arches are turned. Some of the side walls are of brick, while in other places the arches are turned on the solid rock... The tunnel for the greater proportion of its area is driven in solid rock, and the difficulties met with in some part of the operation arise from spontaneous combustion of the rock after the advanced headings have been driven. As this is a source of much danger to the workmen, great care is needed while carrying on mining and other operations. The works on many occasions have thus been retarted, and even now, though some of the faces are in the hardest rock, it is necessary to use timber to protect the workmen.

There are about 300 miners, bricklayers and labourers employed in the tunnel and the works are being pushed on with considerable force. The entrance to the south end of the tunnel is at present barred by a stout piece of cutting, which it is hoped will be taken out by August, when there will be a communication from one end of the tunnel to the other without descending any of the shafts. The strata met with in the tunnel is black limestone and gritstone, with a few beds of shale.

Only one fatal accident has happened in the tunnel, and that was to a horse-driver who unfortunately slipped and fell in front of a loaded wagon. The horses used in the tunnel are sleek in their skin and in fine condition. As a rule, the horse-drivers on the whole line pride themselves on their horses, and decorate their heads with showy ribbons.

In the tunnel there are two bricklayers for each side, who have each one labourer, and there are two mortar carriers for the whole of the bricklayers. These bricklayers with their

THE BOG CART.

servers will lay about 35,000 bricks in three days. About 70,000 bricks are used in the tunnel weekly. Ten locomotives and 18 portable and stationary engines are in constant use on No 1 Contract and about 1,800 men are employed.

No person can walk in the tunnel for an hour or more and listen to the thundering reports and reverberations of blasting, see the miners wielding with terrible force their sledge-hammers when drilling the hard rock, and breathe the thick smoke of the exploded dynamite, without feeling sympathy for those employed in such mining operations, and of seeing what a privilege it is to travel by rail at the rate of a penny per mile.

In Little Dale, at a short distance from the south entrance to the tunnel, there had been a slip of earth, containing 20,000 cubic yards, which is nearly cleared out . . .

The distance between Settle Junction and where the line crosses the Ingleton road at Batty Green is 12¾ miles within 110 yards, and from there to the south end of the tunnel is nearly two miles. Nearly nine miles of permanent way, single line, between Settle Junction and Ingleton road, is laid, and half a mile between there and the south face of the tunnel. Wagons with coal and other material now run from Settle Junction to the top of Bleamoor.

L.G. (1873)

The temperature of the Headings before they were joined was 80 degrees; when the passage was through, the thermometer read 57, showing a difference of 23 degrees.

W.A. (1873)

The Headings have met correctly, within 3 inches we are told, a distance of 924 yards having been driven from the two ends. The strata is Limestone, Gritstone, Gritstone beds, and shale. In some parts the tunnel requires no lining; in others the roof only is lined and in places it is lined throughout. The lining is of brickwork and varies in thickness from 1 ft 6 inches to 3 ft . . . Black damp has been met with in the Heading, and also an explosive stone. It is supposed that there is compressed air in the hill which forces the stone outwards when partly excavated.

W.A. (1873)

In the Tunnel, the work never stops from Sunday night at ten, until Saturday night at the same time; relays of men relieving one another at 6 a.m. and 6 p.m. It is formed by hand drilling, filling the holes with gun-cotton or gunpowder, and then igniting by means of a time fuse. The debris is then cleared away, either up the shafts in "skeps" or in waggons at the open end; the brick lining follows as soon as possible. The light is obtained by means of tallow candles, and has a pretty effect. About 16 yards of tunnel are done in a week, although here and there we see water dripping and the engines pumping.

W.A. (1873)

Before we taken leave of the [Blea Moor] Tunnel we will explain to our readers the new explosive material called "Dynamite", which is a safer and much stronger agent than gunpowder or guncotton. Dynamite looks very much like potted lobster; it will not explode, we are told, unless heated to 420 degrees Fahrenheit. If a match is placed against it, it burns like fat or grease. The extra heat required to make it explode is obtained by a cap of "Fulminating Powder".

Dynamite can be carried about, and is carried about, to bring it to the required temperature, if frozen, in one's trousers pocket, as it will not explode if exceedingly cold. Railway companies in England will not carry it, and all that is brought on to this [Settle-Carlisle] Railway has to be carted from either Carlisle or Newcastle. Its cost is about £200 a ton, or more than five times that of gunpowder.

W.A. (1874)

In Blea Moor tunnel [entered from the north] a few men were working. When about half-way through, a fog signal made the driver of the light engine greatly diminish his speed. Shortly we came to a number of workmen whose dimly burning candles only made the deep excavation look all the more gloomy. The sounds of the shrill whistle of the engine were so loud and discordant that one was glad to weaken the sensation by putting one's fingers in the ears.

L.G. 1875)

NAVVIES WITH PICK AND SPADE.

The double line has been laid from the Junction to Batty Green, and a goods engine makes regular journeys, with materials, to the Tunnel about four times a day.

W.A. (1875)

At Blea Moor there are sidings for shunting in goods trains to allow quicker trains to follow, also two cottages for the use of signalmen and platelayers, a water tank for supplying the engines and a signal box. At this point the line is 680 ft higher than at the junction and is close against Little Dale beck which runs to Weathercote and thence to Ingleton. Little Dale Beck has been lowered about 12 feet to enable it to be bridged across, and to keep the water from going into the cuttings. The line crosses under Force Gill, a tributary of Little Dale beck, by means of a short tunnel.

W.A. (1876)

After leaving Blea Moor tunnel at the north end, the Dent Valley opens to view and is crossed by a pretty Viaduct of 10 arches, the same span as the Batty Moss Viaduct, with one thick pier in the centre. The height is 100 feet above Fell End Gill. This Viaduct, the road bridge, with the farmhouse at its foot, and the road winding down by the side of the hill, form altogether a most picturesque scene. There are two large quarries on this side of the hill, for supplying this Viaduct with stone.

W.A. (1873)

Black 5 at Ribblehead

Ribblehead and Dent Head Viaducts

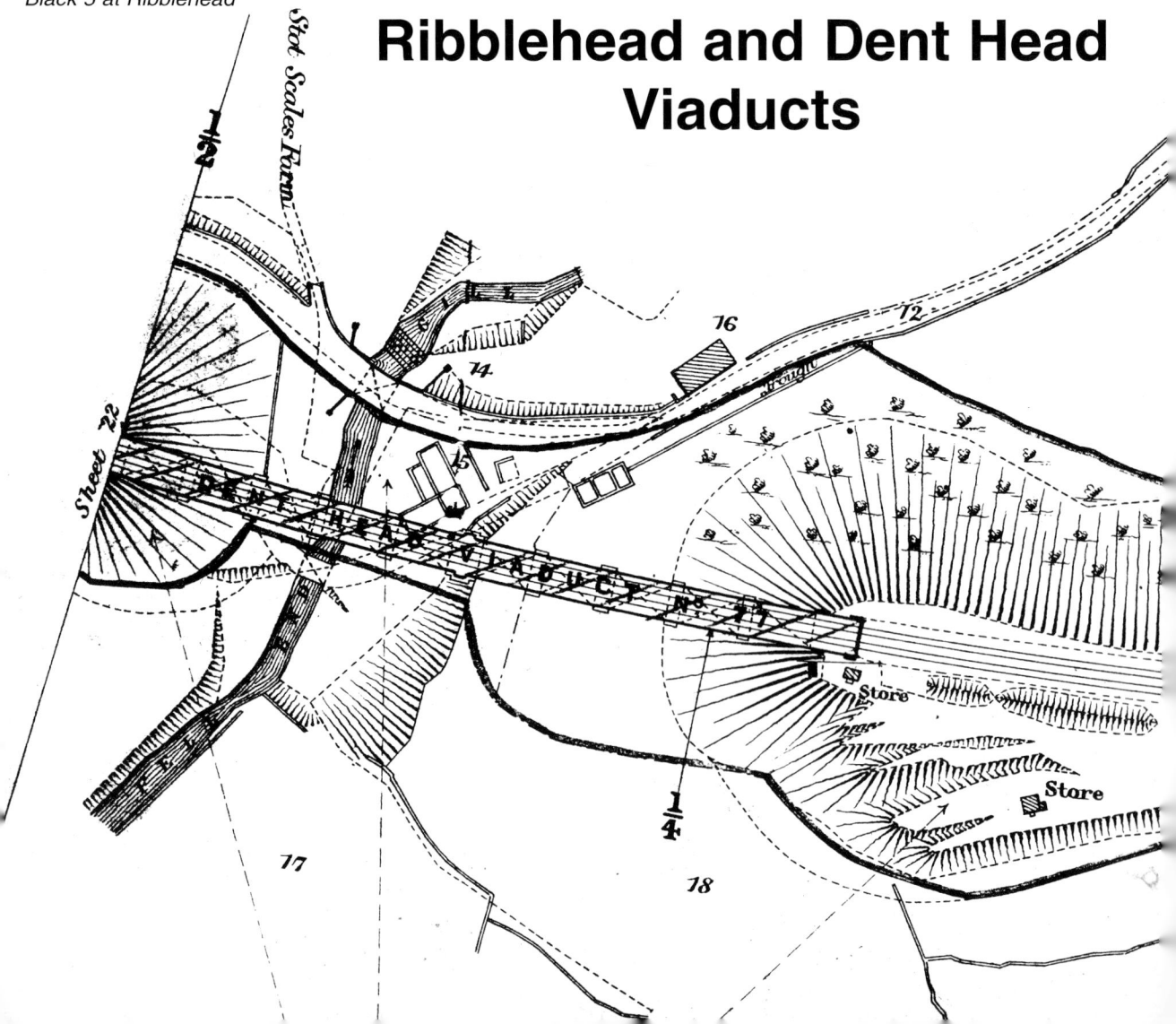

Wooden Scaffolding on the piers.

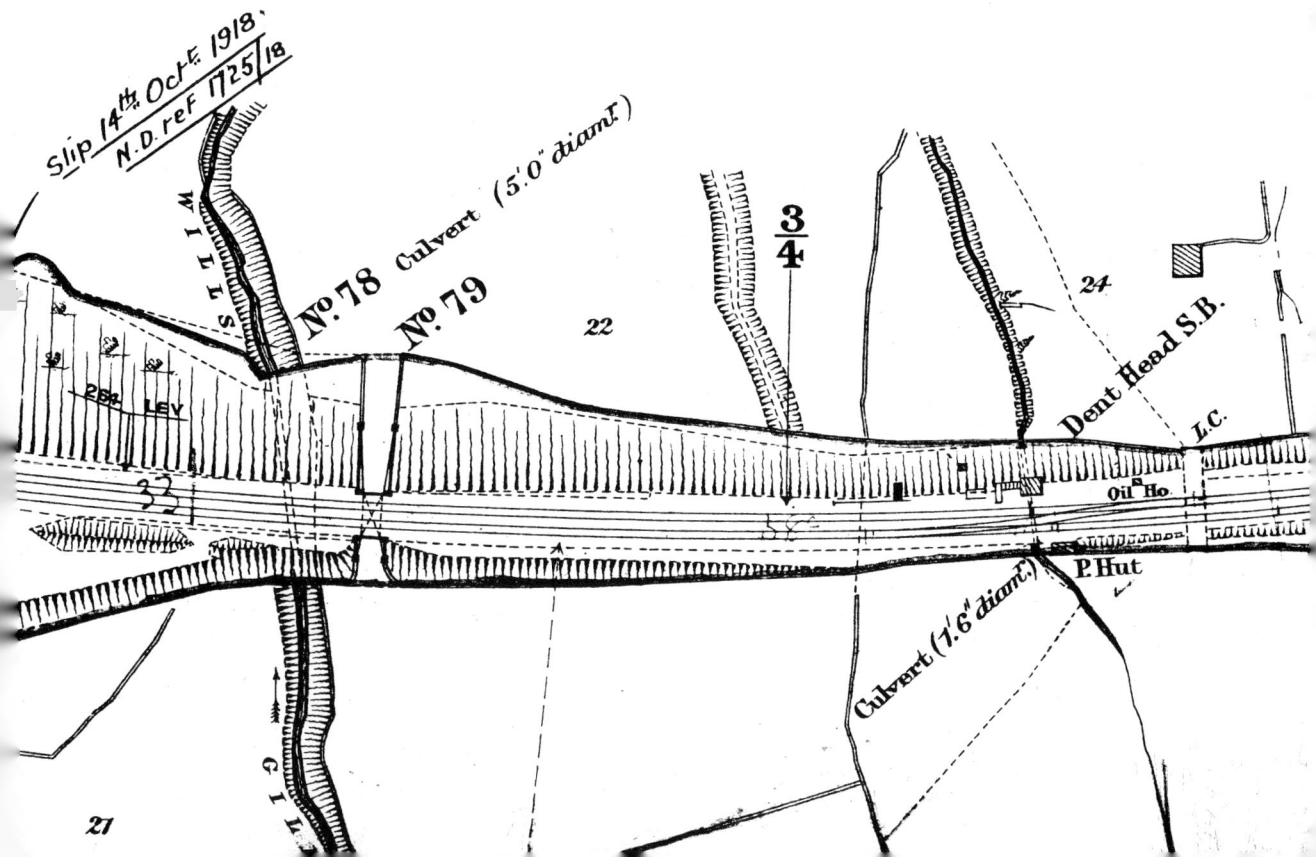

to Dent

Slip 14th Octr 1918.
N.D. ref 1725/18

WILLS

No. 78 Culvert (5'0" diamt)

No. 79

22

GILL

28¼ LEV

33

21

$\frac{3}{4}$

24

Dent Head S.B.

L.C.

Oil Ho.

P. Hut

Culvert (1'6" diamt)

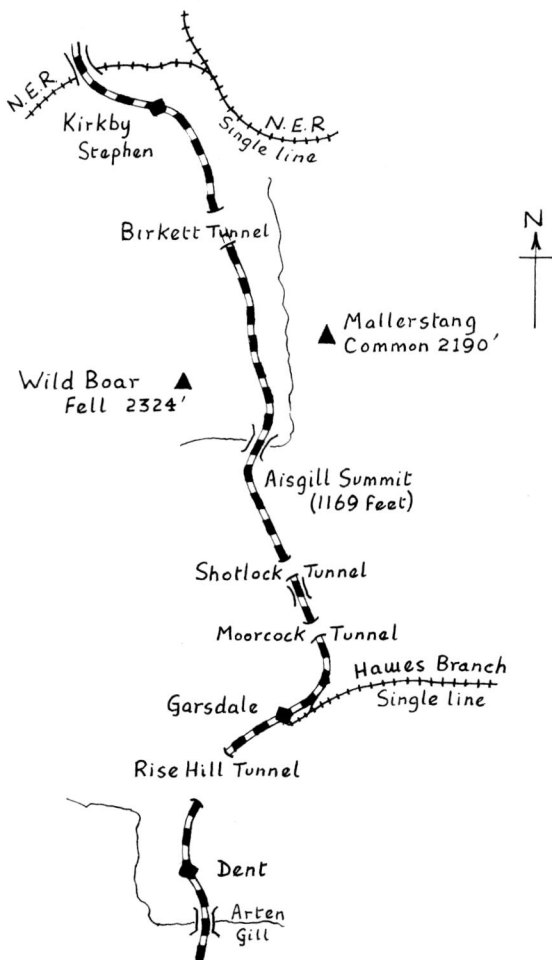

Contract No. 2:

Dent Head to Kirkby Stephen

Contract No. 2 commences in the midst of Yorkshire hill scenery. It was let to the contractors in September, 1869. The strata is chiefly boulder clay, which accounts for the works being in their present unfinished state. The material is so hard that blasting is necessary to sever it, but in wet weather it turns to mud and slurry. The rain of 1872 greatly retarded this contract.

W.A. (1874)

According to report, the rain which fell at Dent Head in 1872 was 92 inches and at Kirkby Stephen 60 inches. The excessive wet of that year retarded the works seriously by driving many of the workmen from that high moorland district, diminishing the number of working days and rendering much of the material for the embankments so soft that it could not be tipped until the return of fine weather. On the same account many of the

large cuttings had to be deserted for a time.

L.G. (1873)

Arten Gill Viaduct is the first great work on Contract No. 2 and consists of 11 arches, the same size as those of Batty Moss Viaduct, but 120 feet high in the deepest part: by diverting the line the viaduct was made 50 feet less in height, as it now crosses over the top of a waterfall instead of the bottom.

W.A. (1873)

At a short distance from Dent Head Viaduct, Messrs Benton and Woodiwiss's contract begins, and one of the heaviest works on their line is Artengill Viaduct. This is a work of considerable difficulty, and it has been carried on under many disadvantages. The works of late had been much retarded through the breaking of the machinery for lifting stone. The gill is very deep and rugged, and its sloping banks on

A steam-powered crane lifts a block of dressed stone.

each side are very steep. Before the viaduct was begun there was a waterfall of 60 foot descent, which is now partly filled up with debris.

The viaduct is 235 yards in length, and consists of ten piers and two block piers. The block piers at their base are 42ft by 28ft, and the smaller piers are 38ft by 15ft. The piers are 45ft apart, and the highest is 103ft to springing, and 26ft above that will be rail level. The foundations are all on rock, and some of them are 60ft below the surface.

L.G. (1872)

The stone used for the work (Artengill Viaduct) is dug from a quarry at the bottom of the gill and the immense blocks are conveyed by bogies to the staging and fitted to their places by a steam traveller. This machine on account of its perpendicular, transverse and longitudinal motions is a very handy apparatus.

As no sand could be found in the neighbourhood, Mr. Crossley, the head engineer, to overcome this difficulty, suggested that burnt clay should be ground up with the lime. This compound is found to be an excellent plastic substance, which in a short time becomes almost as hard as cement. The lime and clay are burnt on the spot, and a steam engine is employed to grind and mix the mortar.

No serious accident to life or limb has occurred on this undertaking; though the man who has charge of the steam traveller a short time ago had a marvellous escape. When lifting a stone from 6 to 7 tons weight, the sling chain broke, when, in consequence of the concussion, one of the uprights was knocked from under the staging. As the horizontal beam through the pressure of the engine was gradually giving way, the engine man made his escape from a small window, and walked on a side beam to a safe standing. He was but just out of harm's way when the steam traveller and its tackle fell with a terrible crash into the bottom of Artengill.

While we were on the staging, a stone about 5 tons weight was lifted by this machine a height of 70ft in 2½ minutes. To lift the same stone by a hand traveller would have taken 6 men an hour.

L.G. (1872)

All the foundations are laid but one, and that is in progress. While on the staging, a block of black limestone was lifted for one of the block piers which measured 14ft by 6ft, and one foot thick, containing 84 cubic feet, and weighing over 6 tons. One accident, fatal to life, had happened from a stone in the quarry at the foot of the viaduct falling upon a workman who, after lingering some time, died from the effects of the injury.

L.G. (1873)

By diverting the line, the height of Artengill Viaduct was reduced more than 50 feet, as it crosses a waterfall at the top side instead of the bottom, as originally intended, and this without any decrease in the radii of the curves. It is built in blue limestone obtained from a quarry in the side of the hill close by; the same class of stone is cut and polished at Mr. Nixon's marble works in the valley and is used for mantel-pieces and such like articles . . .

Great difficulty was met with in getting foundations for the piers. Some are more than 55 feet below the surface of the ground, the timbering and strutting to support the ground looking quite a mass of wood in all directions. At a short distance from the Viaduct is an occupation bridge which was also the cause of much expense in the foundations, for after sinking 30 feet deep, piles were obliged to be driven another 25 deeper into the ground.

W.A. (1874)

Between Artengill Viaduct and Rise Hill or Black Moss tunnel, there are some very heavy works. An occupation bridge to the high moors, though as a rule a matter of little difficulty, in this case proved, on account of the nature of the soil, a serious undertaking. After sinking the foundations 30ft it was found necessary to rear the superstructure on piles driven 25ft deeper. A little futher on the line there is a deep cutting containing 95,000 cubic yards.

L.G. (1873)

Kell Beck culvert was, owing to the state of the ground, built in steps, and as there are from 20 to 30 breaks in the descending underground watercourse, the repeating falls of the mountain stream have a pleasant effect on both the eye and the ear. On the east side of this culvert a number of men were employed getting stone from an immense quarry, out of which rocks had been dug for most of the bridges and culverts in the neighbourhood.

The next cutting is one of considerablelength and depth, containing 150,000 cubic yards, and over which the coal road from Lea Yeat runs by Helmsike Hill and Alick's Fold to the coal pits, which are at an elevation of more than 1,700ft above sea level. Shortly beyond this cutting there is a very large embankment over Cowgill containing 160,000 cubic yards of filling.

At the bottom of the gill is the largest culvert on the contract, measuring 540ft in length,

Arten Gill, whose slender and tapering piers achieved a high standard of design and craftsmanship.

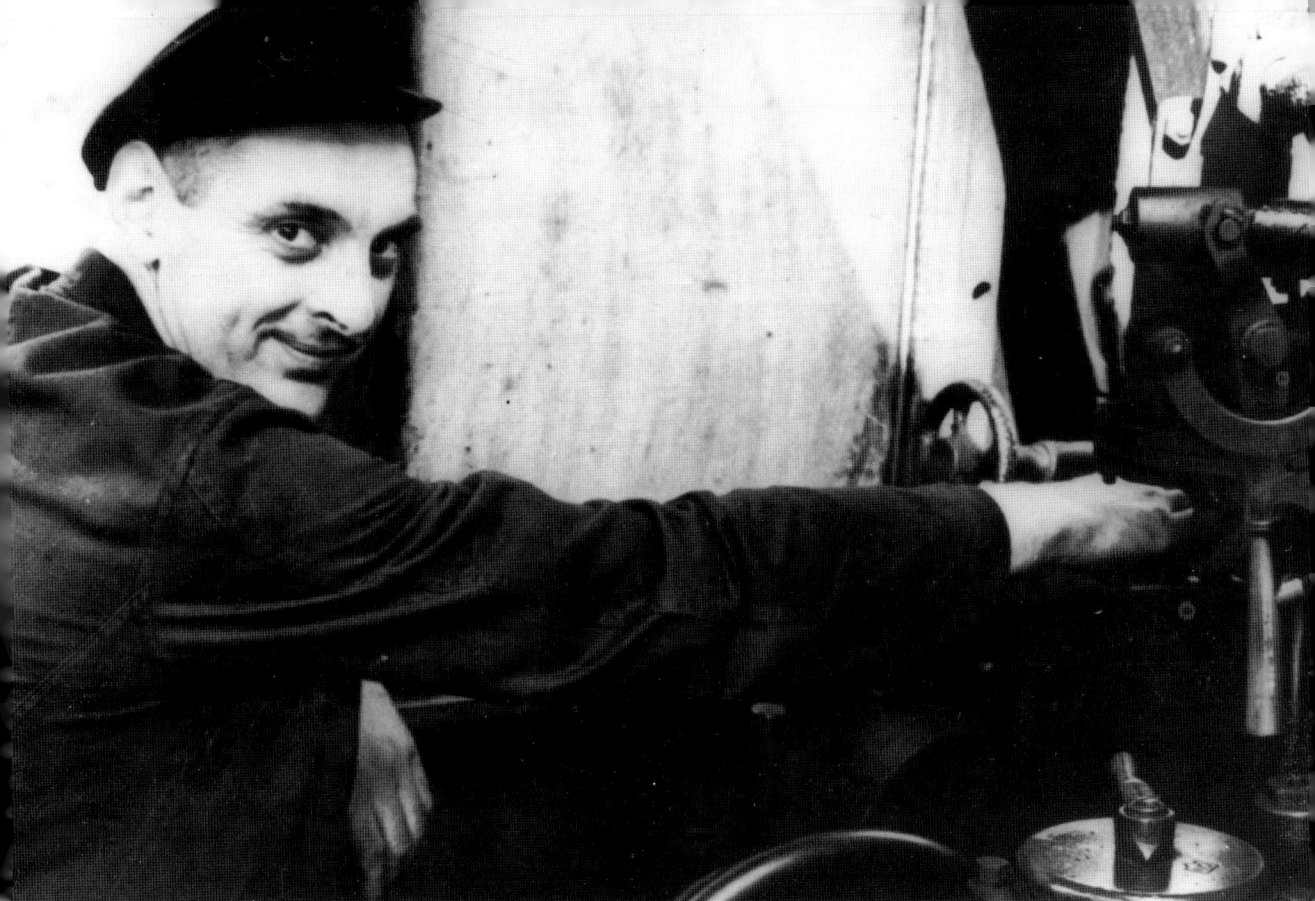

The driver of a goods train on the Long Drag. The days of steam began with the diminitive contractors' locomotives.

and the opening for the stream, which is a pointed or Gothic arch 16ft by 10ft in width. The mason work of this culvert is of great strength, rendered necessary by the superincumbent matter and the immense quantity of water which will flow through it in heavy rains. The height of the embankment in the centre of the stream is 80ft, and at the south west of it about 100ft. Workmen were building on this side of it an immense dry breast-wall, 50ft high, to prevent the embankment from slipping away.

L.G. (1873)

Cow Gill [south of Dent] is crossed by an embankment about 100ft in height. The culvert is a gothic arch in shape and 540ft in length. The embankment has to be dry packed with stones for 50ft in height to prevent it slipping away. In this Gill stones full of iron pyrites were discovered.

W.A. (1874)

It is supposed that a station will be made near the Cowgill coal road. At one time it was in contemplation to make it at Dent Head. Whichever site may be fixed upon, the ascent to it will be steep and difficult.

L.G. (1875)

At the bottom of Rise hill or Blackmoss we came to a deep and wide gully, through which runs Cowgill beck. Many disasters of a nature to retard operations have occurred during the progress of the work on account of the frequent rains and floods. At times it was impossible to go on. As it was impracticable to divert the stream in consequence of the gully on both sides being so steep, the staging and other materials were frequently washed away.

The filling up of this gully will be a great and a difficult operation on account of its great depth, and the miry nature of the earth in the immediate district. Although it was calculated that it would take about 200,000 cubic yards of earth to fill up this gully, now it is thought that it will take 155,000 cubic yards more.

At these works there are a mortar mill and two powerful steam cranes. The stone, as at Artengill Viaduct, is laid in Crossley cement.

L.G. (1872)

There are now about 1,400 men employed on No. 2 contract, and since the works were begun about 17,000 men have "jacked up" as it is called. It is true that some of the 17,000 were discharged from the works, but the great bulk left of their own accord.

L.G. (1872)

A deal of plant in this locality [above Dentdale], which was conveyed from Kirkby Stephen on to the line at a great cost, has not only been useless for want of workmen, but has fallen to decay. Indeed, there is such a lack of men, that four could be employed where there is only one.

L.G. (1872)

Being curious to see what was going on in Black Moss [Rise Hill] tunnel, I descended with two of the men into number one shaft. The gloom in the rocky excavation, the hammering of drills, the voices of the men and the dim lights of candles gave to the murky scene a novelty that will long be remembered... Some idea may be formed of the hardness of the rock when it is stated that thirty-five drills have been blunted with 18 inch boring. The atmosphere is so close in the tunnel that the men have to strip to their flannels. In blasting the rock it requires more than ordinary care as sometimes pieces of 15cwt fly to the distance of 20 yards.

L.G. (1872)

The cutting at the entrance of [Rise Hill] tunnel is attended with numerous difficulties; consequently the progress is very slow. The side of the hill is breaking away in many places, and the excavated matter is little else but what is called in railway parlance "slurry" or slush. One of our informants remarked that it was nothing but slurry and boulders and that the slurry stuck to the tools like treacle. Some of the water-marked boulders are three tons in weight. The slurry is chiefly removed by grafting tools and water buckets.

L.G. (1872)

At No. 2 shaft [Rise Hill tunnel] there are a blacksmith shop, eight huts, miners' cabin, store-room and engine-house. The engine is a double cylinder one, of twenty horse power, and used for blowing air into the tunnel and lifting the debris from the excavation. At No. 2 shaft there are a steam engine of twenty-five horse power, and a double cylinder of twelve horse power, for drawing up the steep ascent from Garsdale coals, provisions and railway material. There are also a blacksmith shop, a general store-house, a mortar mill and five huts...From the summit of Rise Hill, we descended the steep incline at a quick rate in bogies. It was a trial of a man's nerves who was not accustomed to such a mode of locomotion. At the bottom of the hill were numerous huts, a weighing machine, stabling for ten horses and a blacksmith shop.

L.G. (1872)

Black Moss or Rise Hill tunnel, one of the heaviest on the line, is mined from two shafts 170ft deep, and at the headings of the south and north entrances. The excavation is through solid and hard rock, some of the pieces weighing more like iron than stone. The tunnel is 1,230 yards in length and 26ft in width and 20ft in height. In the middle of it about 500 yards had been mined, in addition to a large heading of 250 yards, which had been driven beyond this point. About 120 miners are employed in the tunnel. Descending No. 2 shaft in an iron skip one was soon down at rail level, when the mining south and north was examined, until one felt an ardent longing to see the brighter world above.

To a stranger there is something unearthly in the sounds and appearances of mining operations so far beneath the surface of the earth. Dimly burning candles, uncouth looking wagons standing on the rails or moving to and fro, men at the facings, some above and some below, with their numerous lights like twinkling stars in a hazy night, the noise of the twirling drills beneath the terrible force of big hammers wielded by stalwart men, and the hac-hac or

Above: Mossdale Head, the only tunnel on the Midland branch from Garsdale to Hawes.

Below: An ex-Midland Railway Class 2P 4-4-0 locomotive stands near the water tower, and refreshment coach for local dances, in this 1930s study.

half sepulchral groan at each stroke, the murky vapour, the chilling damp, and the thick breathing make a novice to such scenes feel a thrill of more than ordinary pleasure when he ascends to breathe the unpolluted mountain air.

It will be necessary to arch the tunnel with masonry, as the rock is so full of backs and joints it is not possible to mine the roof to the shape required. In some places, large pieces of rock have fallen and left the roof for 20 yards quite flat.

L.G. (1873)

Rise Hill Tunnel unites the Dent Valley with Garsdale and is under the superintendence, as well as Blea Moor Tunnel, of Mr. William Thomson.

W.A. (1874)

Rise Hill or Black Moss Tunnel was finished with the exception of about 239 yards of arching. About two-thirds of the arching is of brick and stone, and the rest solid rock. At intervals, the arching is strengthened by iron ribs. In different parts of the tunnel one passed under stages where the bricklayers were quietly performing their daily task.

L.G. (1875)

Telegraph equipment.

Between the north end of [Rise Hill] tunnel and the junction with the Hawes line there is a long culvert in Cotes gill where the water on the Garsdale side falls 30 feet. The bank over this gill, on the low side especially, was made with difficulty, and it was necessary to buttress it with a stone wall containing 6,000 tons of stone. As the gill on both sides of the line is lined with trees, it gives an ornamental appearance to this portion of the moorland route.

L.G. (1873)

As an indication of the inaccessibility of this spot [head of Garsdale], we may mention that every tip wagon here used by the contractor had to be brought by road up from Sedbergh and that the carriage of them cost a guinea each.

M.R. (1876)

With Dandry Mire Moss embankment, which is near Moorcock, the miry state of the ground has given the contractors and managers an inconceivable amount of trouble and labour. Tipping went on for more than two years, and instead of a solid embankment being formed, the peat yielded to the weight of the filling to such an extent that it rose on each side of the line in the form of a high bank—in some places 15ft.

Shotlock Hill Tunnel. The Midland Railway used this method of surface water drainage on many of the tunnels.

Finding after more than 250,000 cubic yards had been tipped that the bog would not sustain the weight of the clay and stone used for filling up, it was decided to make a viaduct in the deepest part of the moss—a viaduct of six arches, each of 45ft span. The greatest depth is 53ft, and for nearly the whole length it will average from 45ft to 50ft from foundation to top of the peat. The peat varies from 5ft to 15ft, the greater portion of which had to be dug out before the embankment which is to join the viaduct could be formed.

L.G. (1873)

Messrs. Benton and Woodiwiss, the contractors for making the line from Dent Head to Kirkby Stephen, requiring the services of a locomotive engine for earth work, received one by rail at Sedbergh on Monday last, named the *Lorne,* which was conveyed to Garsdale Head by about 20 horses. One or two slight mishaps occurred on the road owing to the great weight of the engine, but by the patience and perseverance of the men in charge they were overcome without much difficulty.

C.W.A. (1873)

Near the moss is the Moorcock bridge which skews at an angle of 70 degrees. This fine and massive-looking bridge which crosses the Hawes and Sedbergh road contains about

"Hawes Junction and Garsdale."

3,000 cubic yards of masonry. The structure, which is finished, with the exception of the coping stones, has a span of 35ft and it is 36ft in height. At the foot of the bridge on the Moorcock side is the boundary stone which divides the North and West Ridings.

L.G. (1872)

There are a few dreary cuttings before the summit of the railway is met with at Ais Gill Moor. The level of rails at the summit is 1,167ft above the sea. Near this spot, three rivers take their rise, the Eden, the Ure and the Swale. The railway follows the first-mentioned to Carlisle. W.A. (1874)

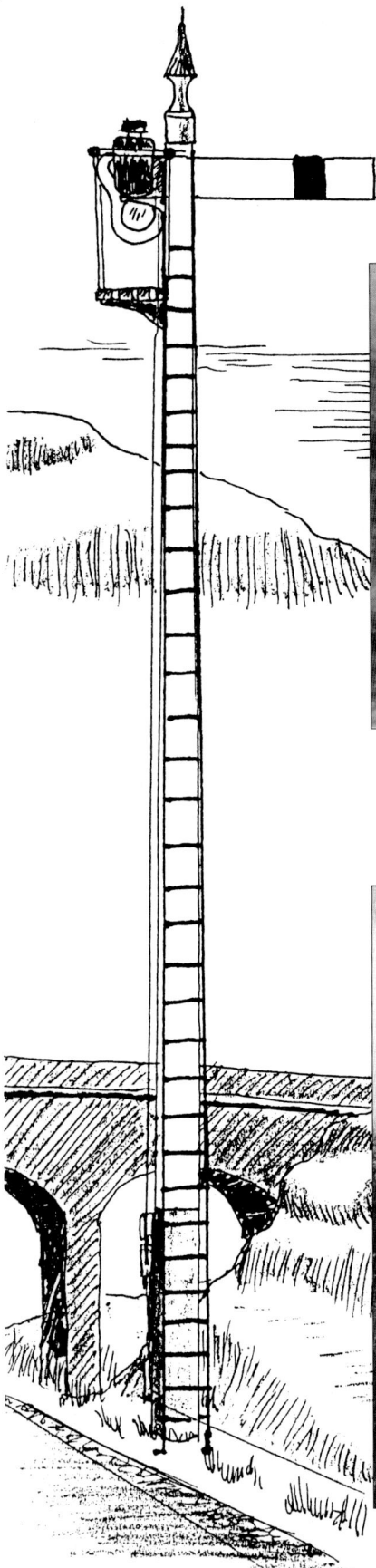

Drawing shows a typical Midland Railway signal, this one being erected near Aisgill summit. Photographs: Ex-Midland Railway 2P 4-4-0 passing the scene of Aisgill railway disaster of 1913. The carriages of the train have the Midland clerestory roof arrangement.

''Cumbrian Mountain Express'' of the 1980s almost at the summit of the line at Aisgill.

Good progress is being made at Aisgill Viaduct, which consists of 4 arches 66ft high and 45ft span. The breadth of the piers at the base is 33ft, which taper to 29ft at the top. The length of the viaduct is 99 yards. The gill on the south side is very romantic and on account of its overhanging rocks it presents to the eye a very bold appearance. The stone which is dug from the gill on the high side is lifted to the viaduct by a steam jib crane.

L.G. (1872)

No. 19 bank down Mallerstang is 20 chains in length and 80ft in depth. The workmen on this bank have been tipping on the same metals for 12 months without getting the bank any higher on the top. The material is of such a loose and soft nature and made more slushy by the constant rains, so that instead of forming a permanent way, it spreads itself out in the valley.

L.G. (1872)

On the 10th December, William Ridley, a driver 23 years of age, was following his ordinary employment, and driving a waggon at Aisgill Moor, on the line, when he was accidentaly run over, and had his right leg severely crushed. Dr. Harrison of Hawes attended him and amputated the leg on Tuesday, the 13th, but Ridley sank and died last Sunday. The coroner did not think it necessary to hold an inquest.

C.W.A. (1870)

After passing through a heavy cutting [in Mallerstang], the line is carried along the Intake Bank, about 100 feet high. At this point an extraordinary circumstance occurred; the tipping proceeded for twelve months without the embankment advancing a yard. The tip rails, during the whole period, were unmoved, while the masses of slurry . . . rolled over one another in mighty convulsions, persisting in going anywhere and everywhere, except where they were wanted.

M.R. (1876)

The first sod of the Settle and Carlisle Railway (in the county of Westmorland) was cut on Monday, the 24th ult, in the township of Mallerstang, on the property of Sir Richard Tufton, of Appleby Castle, by Mr. Parkin Blades (Sir Richard's agent). Mr. Blades said he should be glad to give Messrs. Benton and Woodwiss, the contractors, every facility in carrying on their operations through the property.

C.W.A. (1870)

A terrible accident happened in Birkett tunnel, near Kirkby Stephen, on May 18, between four and five a.m. Among the miners at work at this early hour were John Roberts and Caleb James, known as "Birmingham Bill". The miners are frequently cautioned not to meddle with any holes in the rocks in which there may be unexploded dynamite. From report, the two men were attempting to drill a hole containing dynamite, and that while in the act of drilling it exploded, and so injured James that he died shortly afterwards. The explosion knocked out the eye of the other man, and it is likely that the sight of the other eye is destroyed.

L.G. (1874)

Birkett Tunnel, the Burleigh Rock Drill is being used with good effect. This drill makes a hole a foot deep in five minutes, the same depth taking two men at least 40 minutes.

W.A. (1874)

At the south end of the Birkett Tunnel in the cutting, a very fine vein of lead ore has been cut and a Company are now driving levels underneath the Railway to work it out.

W.A. (1876)

Intake Embankment which for two or three years caused so much trouble and extra labour, on account of the slushy character of much of its tippings, is now an unyielding bank, equal to any on the line.

L.G. (1875)

In passing through Kirkby Stephen railway yard, we noticed the hospital for accidents, stabling for 25 horses, saddlers, blacksmiths, and carpenters' shops, and an engine for sawing wood, cutting hay and crushing beams and oats for 100 horses.

L.G. (1872)

A machine for excavating the boulder clay lies near here [Kirkby Stephen Station]. The machine is patented by two gentlemen engaged on the railway, but we hear diversity of opinion exists as to its capabilities. Being a trial machine many improvements are already seen in it, but the ''modus operandi'' is entirely new in construction and ingenious in design.

W.A. (1874)

Kirkby Stephen Station was in an advanced state and shortly it will be finished. A four-wagon goods shed was being roofed in. Six cottages and the station-master's house were finished. The station, which is a smart building, is built of freestone from Bradford and dressings from Barnard Castle. A good many men were employed in making cattle docks and by-sidings.

L.G. (1875)

Being at Kirkby Stephen, and having twice previously walked over the whole line, one naturally felt a wish to take a ride on an engine to Settle. With Mr. Hay, manager for Messrs. Benton and Woodiwiss, I mounted one of the engines going south, and though the day was cold and cloudy, still the ride was a very pleasant one . . . At Mallerstang Sidings, a pilot engine was attached to ours and we had to follow in its wake to the other side of Cowgill Embankment . . . After passing over the highest elevation of the line, which is something over 1,100ft, the rate of speed was much accelerated.

L.G. (1875)

The staging [at Smardale Viaduct] is up and many of the piers are being raised. One of the arches will span the South Durham line at an elevation of 38ft. The view down the deep and wooded glen with Scandal beck winding its course between the rugged banks, will have charms for sight-seers both in summer and winter.

L.G. (1872)

Smardale Viaduct consists of 12 arches, 45ft span, and will be 130ft high above the stream to rail level. It is built in grey limestone of most excellent quality from off the South Durham and Lancashire Union (North Eastern) Railway, about half a mile further up Scandal Beck. A complete absence of sand also in this Contract has added a large item to the expense, burnt clay being used instead of it, by permission of the Engineer-in-Chief, and it has been a most complete success.

W.A. (1874)

On Tuesday, the completion of Smardale Viaduct was celebrated by an interesting ceremony. The ''last stone'', on which was inscribed the following words — ''This last stone was laid by Agnes Crossley, 8th June, 1875'' — was well and truly laid by the lady.

Below: The ''Thames-Eden Pullman'' coasts through the Eden Valley towards Carlisle.

Contract No. 3:

Smardale to Crowdundle

The Third Contract ends a little on the south side of Crowdundle beck, which divides Westmorland and Cumberland. The Company's resident engineer is Mr. Drage; contractor's engineer, Mr. Phillips; contractor, Mr. Firbank; manager, Mr. Throssel. On the Contract there are four locomotive engines, 17 portable engines and steam cranes, 1,400 men, 111 horses, 500 earth wagons, 2,000 tons of contractor's temporary rails in use, and several miles of permanent way laid.

L.G. (1873)

Crosby Garrett Tunnel is through solid rock, which is a mixture of limestone and grit, and at the heading, which was within 20 yards of the south entrance, the rock is mixed with flint, and is so hard that it is very difficult to excavate. The tunnel is 176 yards in length, and from the nature of the rock it will be necessary to line it throughout with brick. Nearly one hundred men are employed at this undertaking.

L.G. (1873)

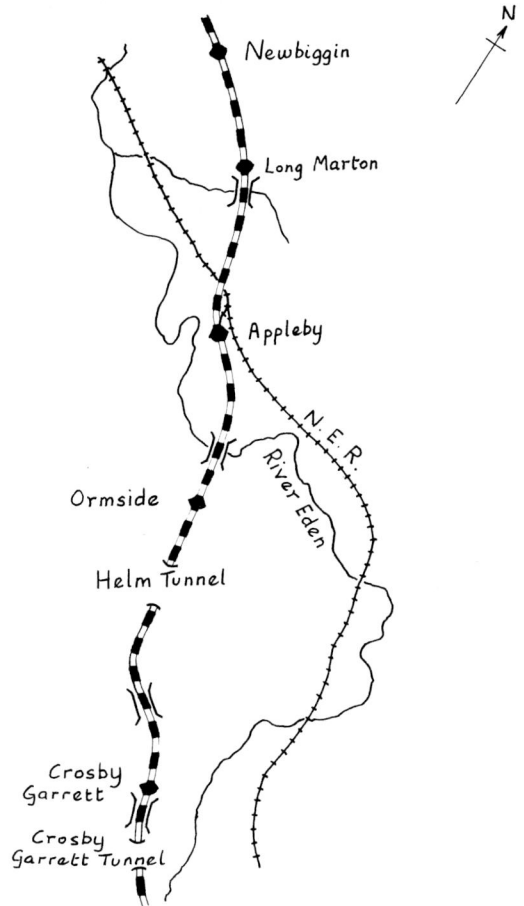

At a short distance from Crow Hill, the Helm Tunnel begins, which is nearly 600 yards in length, 26ft wide and over 20ft in height. The sides are stone finished, and the arches are turned with brick. The entrances to the tunnel are faced with excellent freestone from a quarry in the neighbourhood. Though the interior of the tunnel has been finished some time ago, the last stones of the facing of the north arch were put in place on the 19th of June, before breakfast. At the Helm, not far from the tunnel there is an extensive hut village where brickmaking and various kinds of employment connected with the railway are carried on.

L.G. (1873)

Ormside Viaduct, which is the first over the Eden, consists of nine piers and two block piers, and ten arches. The piers are of freestone and the arches will be turned with brick. From the bed of the river to the top of the parapet will be 100ft. The viaduct is at a short distance above the Clint rock, which stands

Crosby Garrett signal box and the staff of the station.

Below: The newly-completed station at Crosby Garrett.

out very prominently on the north side of the Eden.

L.G. (1873)

At Ormside Viaduct, John Payne and another man were raising about two tons of lime by means of a travelling crane. When it had been raised to the proper height, Payne's companion let the handle on his side go before the crane was locked or ''spanged''. The lime went down again. The handle being held by Payne was forced round with such ferocity he was struck on the arm, which was broken in several places and he also received a severe blow on the head. He was taken to Appleby to be attended by Dr. Armstrong. His injuries are of a serious nature.

C.W.A. (1873)

At Long Marton, one of the largest villages in the county, and at a distance of three miles north east of Appleby, there is a neat viaduct over Troutbeck. It consists of four piers and two block piers with five arches of 45 feet span. The height to rail level is 60ft. The arches are turned with brick and faced with red and white sandstone alternately. The quoins are red sandstone. This viaduct was all finished except one parapet.

L.G. (1873)

A sad accident befell a young man of the name of Donaldson, a native of Carlisle. He was employed carting stones from Dufton Quarry to the railway works at Appleby. He was on his way to Dufton with a heavy wagon and two horses, riding in front, and on turning a corner at Gallows Hill met a cart laden with wood, at which his horse shied, and he was thrown from his seat and the wheels of the wagon passed over one of his thighs and arm, both of which were broken and the poor fellow sadly crushed. He was conveyed to Belgravia Buildings, within a short distance, and attended by Dr. Armstrong, and now lies in a very critical state.

C.W.A. (1872)

On Boxing Day, the mechanics and other officials in various departments engaged under Mr. Joseph Firbank, the contract for the

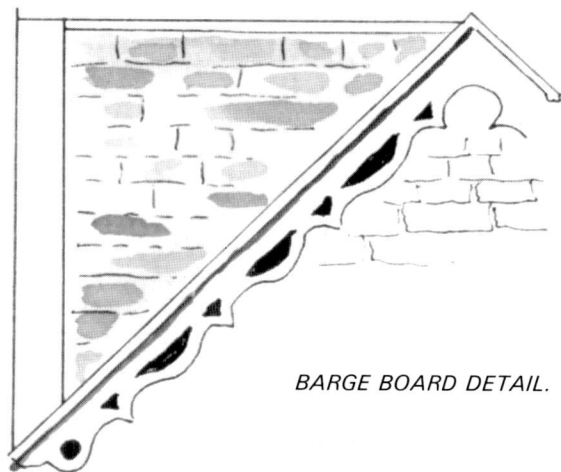

BARGE BOARD DETAIL.

Appleby section No. 3 of the Settle and Carlisle Railway Extension, met according to their annual custom—in whatever part of the world they may be engaged—to celebrate Boxing Day by a public dinner and entertainment. It took place at the *Crown and Cushion Hotel.* An excellent and substantial repast was prepared by the hostess, Mrs. Longrigg, to which between 40 and 50 did full justice to the good things provided. Mr. Brown Firbank occupied the chair. A number of toasts were interspersed with songs, recitations, etc. An agreeable and pleasant concert was accompanied by violin, concertina and banjo.

C.W.A. (1872)

On February 13, the ceremony of fixing the last brick in Helm Tunnel was performed by Mr. W.S. Fulton, of the Cumberland Union Bank, Appleby, in the presence of a large number of officials. The tunnel, which is about 600 yards long, was brilliantly lighted up for the occasion. A stage being erected in the centre, round which the company assembled, Mr. Fulton proceeded with trowel in hand to the top, and, having duly fixed the brick in the aperture, amid ringing cheers, intimated the successful completion of ''The Helm Tunnel''. He proposed in succession three cheers for Mr. Firbank, the contractor, Mr. Throssle, the representative of Mr. Firbank, and other officials connected with the works. Mr. Drage, the Company's engineer, said it was nearly two years since the first stone was laid in Helm Tunnel, which had been completed without loss of life or any serious accident.

L.G. (1873)

Snow was a hazard during construction and continued to raise many problems during the operating period. Above: An impression of a small snow plough fitted to the buffer beam. The locomotive has an over-sized tender cab to protect the footplate men. Below: A snow plough as used in the 1960s takes water at Blea Moor. It was attending to a line blockage at Dent.

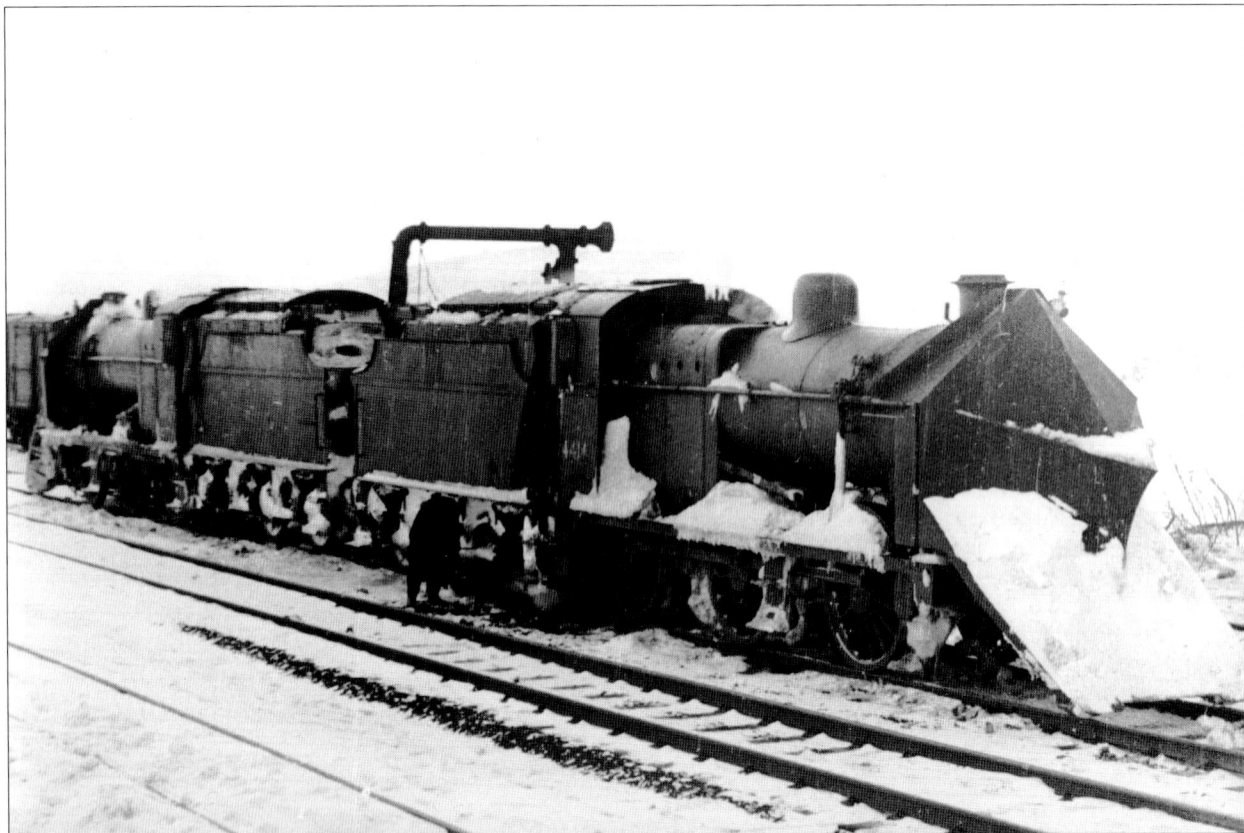

Contract No. 4:

Crowdundle to Durranhill

On the line there are over 1,000 men, 70 horses, 4 locomotives, and 12 station engines. Mr. Allis is contractor, Mr. Lambert is head manager over the contract, Mr. Williams is manager and engineer of the south end of the contract, Mr. Stewart is resident engineer.

L.G. (1873)

In the deeply-wooded gill at Crowdundle Beck, about a quarter of a mile from Temple Sowerby. . .all was life and work and noise. The rattling of steam cranes, the puffing of engines, the clang of masons' and carpenters' tools, and the din of tongues and the singing of birds, were like life from the dead. . .The viaduct over the gill consists of three piers and two abutments, and four arches of 45ft span. The arches will be turned with red sandstone. To the coping stones from the surface is about 50ft. Some of the stones which were dug from Crowdundle quarry were of massive size.

L.G. (1873)

At Culgaith. . there is a tunnel through a high bank in a forward state towards completion. It is 800 yards in length, 700 yards of which are completed. . .the sides and arches are of brick. The facings at the entrances of the tunnel are of blue Staffordshire brick, with string courses and coping of freestone. The excavation was through hard red marl.

L.G. (1873)

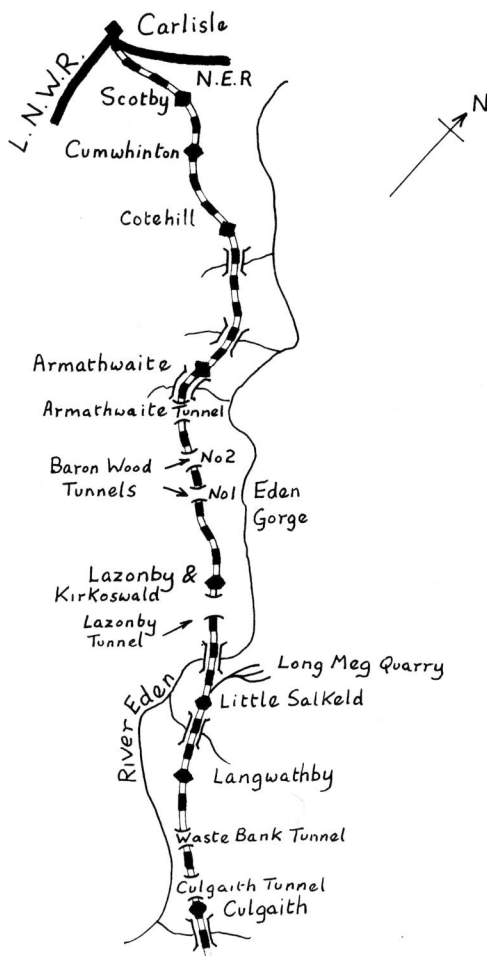

All the foundations at Eden Lacy Viaduct are in, and some of the piers are at springing, and the remainder are within 15 feet of springing. About a quarter of a mile from this viaduct a three arched ornamental bridge spans the line as an occupation way for Col. Sanderson of Eden Lacy House to pass from one part of his park to the other. This bridge is the finest piece of masonry on the Settle and Carlisle line, and its workmanship is a credit to both architect and workmen. The piers and arches are faced with rustic quoins, and the spring courses, parapets, and coping are all tooled and diamond hammered on the outward surfaces. The bridge, which was nearly finished, is built of old red sandstone, which with the superior workmanship gave it a unique appearance.

L.G. (1873)

At Eden Lacy viaduct, some difficulty was experienced by the engineers in getting a

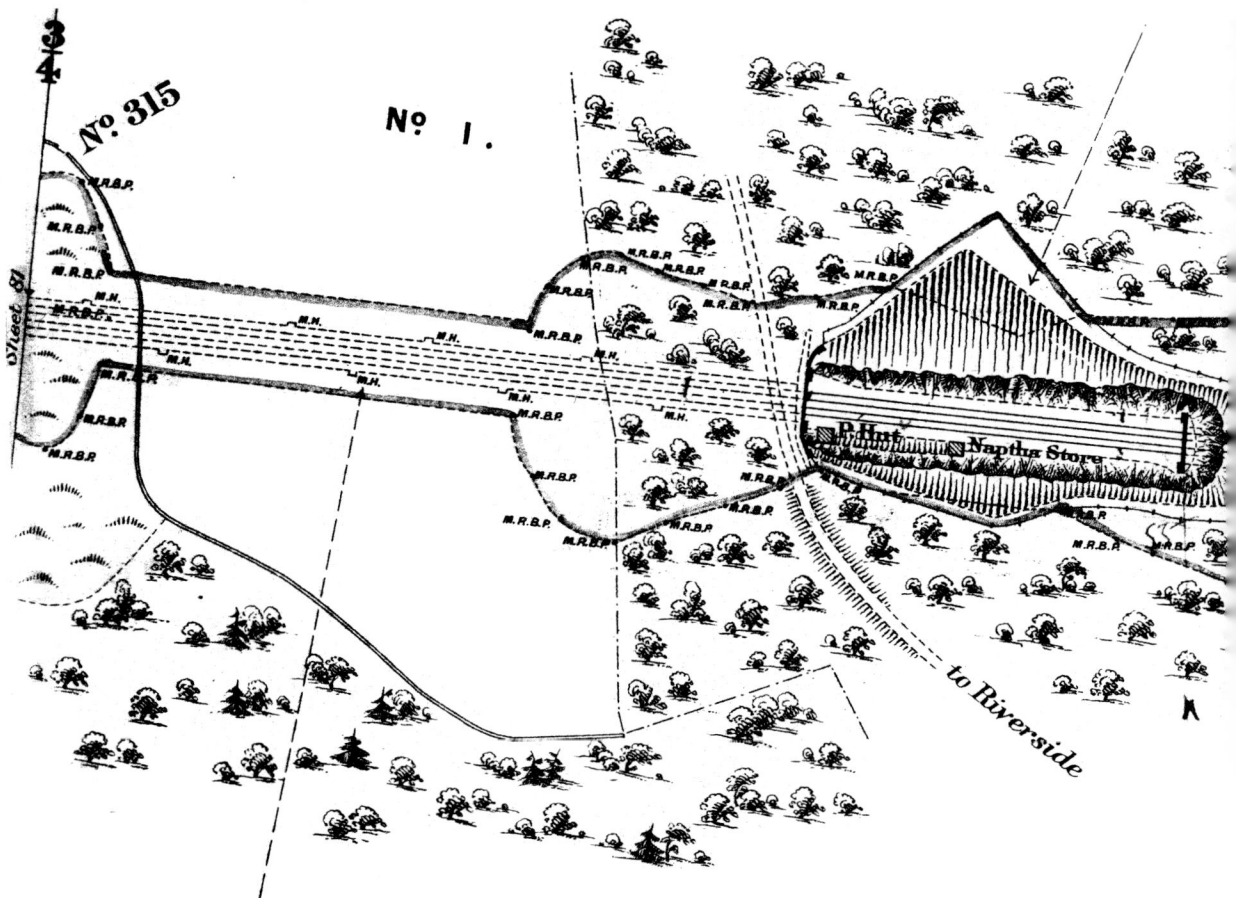

Above: Baron Wood Tunnels No. 1 and No. 2 (from the Midland Railway Land Plan).

foundation down on the red sandstone, in consequence of the gravel that had accumulated in the bed of the river; and it became necessary to make a coffer dam. Accordingly, a double row of piles was driven into the bed of the river so as to form an oval; ''puddling'' was put between the two series of piles, to keep the water from running in; the water inside the oval was then pumped out by engines, and the foundation excavated and cleared.

M.R. (1876)

Shortly before entering Baronwood there is a heavy cutting through red sandstone, 660 yards in length and 50ft in depth. Some splendid blocks of stone had been dug from this cutting and used for many of the bridges and viaducts on the line. Though the cutting was finished, still on account of the excellent

character of the rock a number of men were quarrying stone from the east side of the line for railway purposes.

L.G. (1873)

The Barren Park Cutting through red sandstone is a very heavy undertaking, as it is 42ft in its deepest place and nearly a mile in length. Just on the north side of Samson's Cave the line is cut out of the edge of a high bank, so that the west side of it has the appearance of a deep cutting while that on the east has the appearance of an embankment sloping down to the brink of Eden.

L.G. (1873)

After passing [southwards from Carlisle] under Duncowfold Bridge, a large tract of ground has been taken for ballast. The railway

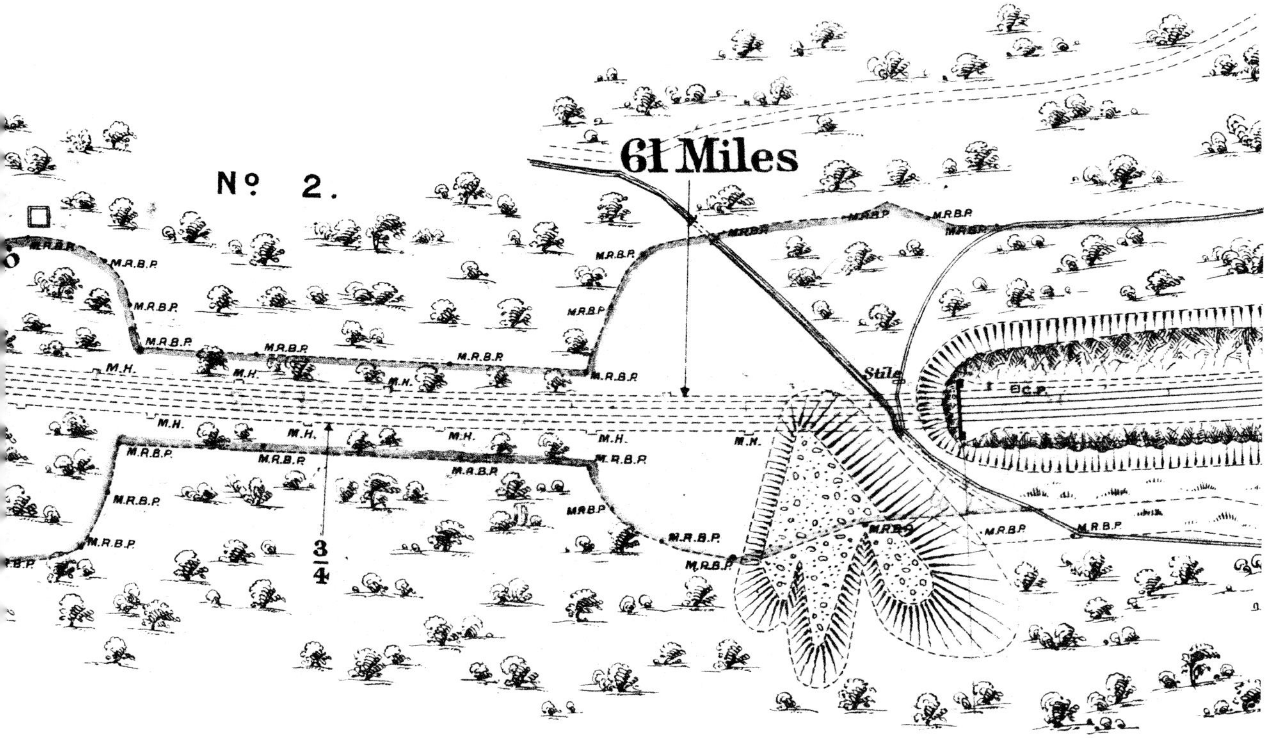

61 Miles

from this point to Armathwaite, along the rugged banks of the Eden, must have been very heavy work. After half a mile of filling there is a gorge over which the scaffolding is being erected in order to throw a small viaduct of three arches, in height sixty feet from the bed of the brook. Crossing this deep defile with some difficulty, three quarters of a mile brings us to what is known by the name of the slip at Eden Brows, and which the gangers say has been the heaviest part of this expensive line.

The railway rises here 120 feet above the bed of the river, and this deep gorge had to be filled in with earth. After many months' tipping it was found that the foundations were slipping—that is the earth was moving en masse towards the river. Growing plantations shifted their position in this direction, and trees may now be seen growing 40 yards from the place in which they stood a few years ago, while the breadth of the river has been reduced apparently about one half.

Two years ago at this spot the men were tipping earth—to the number of 15 or 20. They are still tipping and the work is not yet complete, although very nearly so.

C.J.

At Carlisle a large area of land, perhaps 50 acres, is being prepared for the building of station, offices, goods warehouses, station yard., etc.

L.G. (1873)

The goods station at Carlisle covers 80 acres of land and comprises Engine Sheds, Goods Warehouses, Cattle Docks, Marshalling Sidings, etc. The present joint Carlisle passenger station is being enlarged and remodelled to admit of the new traffic.

W.A. (1876)

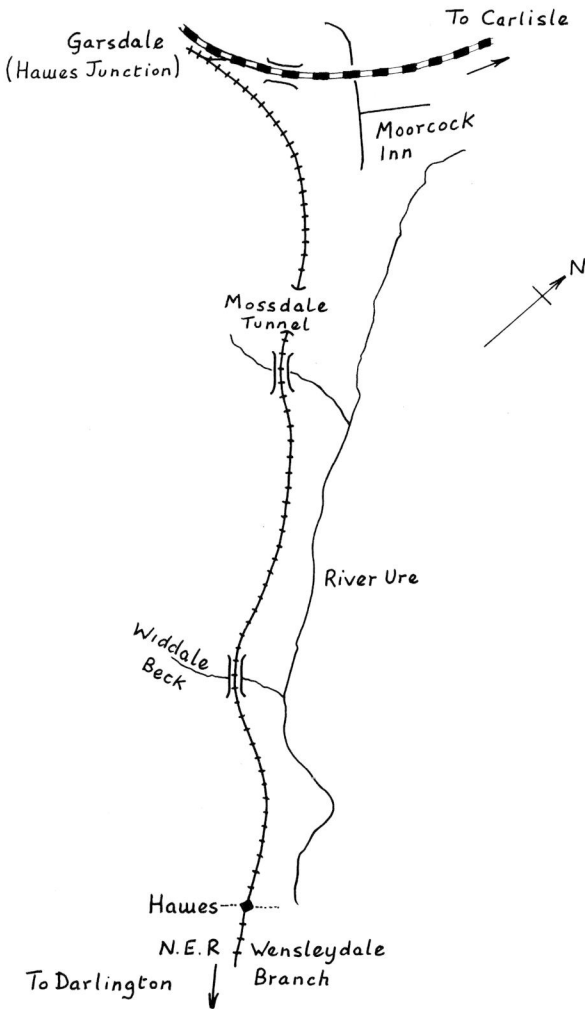

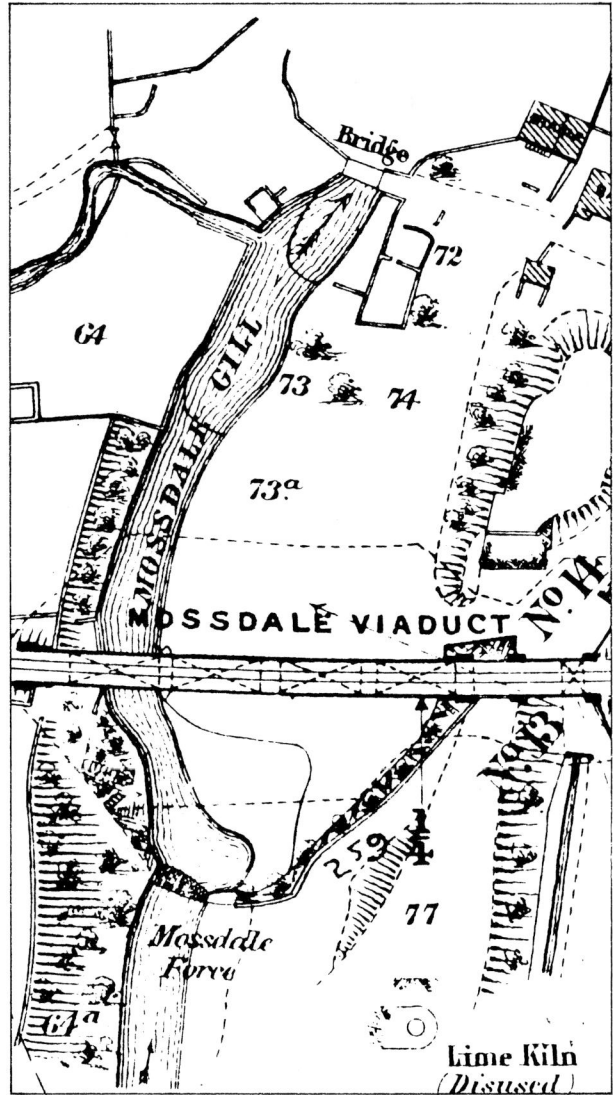

FROM THE MIDLAND LAND PLAN (1912).

Contract No. 5
(the Hawes branch)

This branch line is 5¾ miles in length and will be a single line...Mr. Story is the resident engineer and Mr. Crossley the head engineer ...The cutting at the junction is finished, and for two miles from the terminus at Hawes the line is railed off. Two cuttings on the Hawes side are finished and three more cuttings are commenced. A road approach from Hawes to Moorcock and two occupation bridges and several culverts are finished, and a girder bridge is nearly finished.

Hawes Junction with the Midland is at Garsdale Head, where considerable works are to be erected. The platform walls were in progress and a number of cottages were being built. The works, when completed, will form a small village. There will be over twenty houses and an engine shed, besides a number of sidings for the exchange of traffic. It is reported that a large reservoir will be made to supply the engines and other places with water.

L.G. (1875)

A smallpox hospital has been built at Appersett for the men working in the North Riding district.

L.G. (1872)

With all Speed to Scotland

1st. MAY **1876**

On Thursday last, a party of the engineers and contractors went over the northern part of the Settle and Carlisle extension, making a preliminary inspection prior to the visit of the Midland directors, who are to pass over the whole of the new line—Settle to Carlisle—on the 29th inst, without change of carriage. The whole of the works are being pushed forward, now that the weather is so favourable, with all speed, the men being allowed to work all the hours they possibly can in order to effect the opening of the line for goods and mineral traffic by either July or August 1st.

W.G. (1875)

We understand the line is laid through with steel rails, and the station accommodation which has been provided for passengers leaves nothing to be desired.

R.T. (1875)

The first sod of the new line was cut near Anley, in November, 1869; and by the time of our visit, skill, energy and money had brought the work nearly to its completion.

M.R. (1876)

For the purposes of the public sale of contractor's plant, which commenced on Monday forenoon, a special train was run from Leeds, stopping on the way at Shipley, Keighley and Skipton. Upon their arrival at Settle, the company (numbering about 200 passengers) found large quantities of working "plant" arranged in no fewer than 1,200 lots on both sides of the line for a distance of nearly a mile from the new station. The collection, as may be supposed, was a heterogeneous one, including a locomotive, boilers, engines, upwards of 70 wagons, 400,000 bricks, nearly 400 tons of contractor's rails, more than 100 tons of scrap

45

iron, and 800 tons of firewood, as well as other articles less known to the general public, and variously described as "Goliaths", "overhead travellers", etc.

The whole of this accumulation belonged to what is distinguished as the first contract, and its sale is expected to realise something like £10,000. The auctioneers are Messrs. Oliver, Son and Appleton, of Leeds, who will continue the sale during the week.

L.G. (1875)

After five years' hard work and immense outlay of capital, the making of this important new railway is now practically completed. Owing to the somewhat rough state in which portions of it still remain, the line is not yet quite ready to be thrown open for ordinary traffic. It may, however, be inferred that the time for this is not far distant, the fact being that a special train of saloon carriages has passed over the entire length of seventy-two miles from Carlisle to Settle, with the directors of the Midland Railway Company, and that the auction sale of contractors' plant (another unmistakeable sign of the finished of work) was commenced on Monday. This news will be welcomed by the travelling public, and still more by shareholders, many of whom have long been impatient for some return from the enormous cost of the undertaking.

L.G. (1875)

When opened for passenger traffic, the celebrated Pullman Cars will be run from London to Scotland, and vice versa, so that at night passengers will be able to retire to rest at one terminus, and alight refreshed at the other in the morning.

W.A. (1876)

The permanent way is laid throughout with 82lb steel rails, and adapted for heavy traffic and high speed . . . The line is fitted with block signalling apparatus and interlocking points and levers, and the wires to the distant signals are connected with an ingenious compensating apparatus which takes up any slackness due to stretching or expansion, and keeps them always taut. The officials believe that signals so fitted could not be overpowered by snow, as were those on the great Northern Railway on a recent occasion.

W.G. (1876)

Taking the brake apparatus and the signalling together, it may fairly be said that the new line has been rendered as secure as it is possible for appliances to make it. Nor is it only the safety of passengers which has been considered, for in the moorland country, the telegraph wires have been arranged with special reference to the grouse—in some places in a horizontal row, instead of the usual vertical one; in others in a single rope of such thickness as to be easily seen.

W.G. (1876)

On Monday, the stations along the new line were crowded and the trains, as they passed through, were loudly cheered. At Appleby, there was a demonstration in the shape of athletic sports, dancing on the green and a ball at night.

W.G. (1876)

Below: Ormside viaduct shortly after completion.

The Midland introduced the Pullman cars, of American origin, to Britain and they were soon operating on the Scotch expresses using the Settle-Carlisle.

When the workforce had dispersed, local people took over the operation of the line. Several generations of well-known Dales families served as porters, gangers and signalmen. The signal box shown here was constructed at Aisgill and our picture shows a vigilant signalman with a Class 4F freight locomotive "waiting for the road". Above the levers can be seen a string of detonators to be placed on the line to warn traffic of danger. Notice also the lamps on the shelves above. This signal box is now to be seen at Butterley, in Derbyshire.

Where are we going, boys…? Weston-super-Mare, July 1963

Contents

Introduction 7

Part I :
Blue Suburban Skies 19

PART II :
Show Me That I'm Everywhere 145

PART III :
The Beatles: Carry That Weight 311

Bibliography 425

Thanks 427

Introduction

It remains the Fabbest Story Ever Told. How four teenagers from a port in the North of England, in pursuit of girls and avoidance of a day job, unwittingly changed the world. As if the music they fashioned on record in eight years wasn't enough, it was their demeanour, their style, their attitude which reached out far beyond their birthplace and from an otherwise anonymous building on a north-west London street.

No one in popular music will ever be able to equal their achievements; no one will be able to match that incredible, unrepeatable career arc, from 'Love Me Do' to 'Strawberry Fields Forever' in under five years. No one will ever equal their accomplishment of occupying the entire Top 5 – with nine other simultaneous hits – in one week on the American Hot 100. That was when people had to leave home, go out to a store and physically purchase the disc. To buy those records, to own those records, required a cash commitment rather than an idle online graze.

Of all the millions of words written about their achievements, one element I feel which is under-appreciated was the long, long trail a-winding: from Liverpool to Germany to London to Sweden to France and then, the ultimate prize, the United States. It was the Beatles' conquest of America which raised them to a different plateau. That most lucrative and emulated musical entertainment stronghold had proved largely indifferent to transatlantic traffic.

Certain British acts had indeed established a foothold on the American charts, but not one – not Vera Lynn, Acker Bilk, Cliff Richard, the Tornadoes nor Laurie London – had *sustained* a career there. They did. The Beatles did. And in their wholesale assault on the American music industry, they opened the floodgates for what has rightly been called 'The British Invasion'. Every single one of the groups associated with that term owed their success to the pioneering work of the Beatles, and the persistence of their driven manager Brian Epstein.

The wonderful thing with the Beatles is that their reach *did* exceed their grasp. At a time when studio technology, class divide, economics, popular culture, the music industry and the Establishment could be seen to be working against them, they not only competed, but triumphed. Overcoming all obstacles; challenging all that was put before them, laughing at adversity, they steered a path and cut a swathe through their times. And beyond.

The music they created over, effectively, 12 LPs and a dozen or so stand-alone singles, has stood, and will stand the test of time. Here was lightning caught in a bottle. Again and again… Every aspiring boy band, each 'pop phenomenon', every YouTube or TikTok sensation are hailed as "the new Beatles". As fresh technology and a palpable sense of immediacy increases, Andy Warhol's oft-repeated dictum that "in the future everybody will be famous for 15 minutes" grows increasingly redundant. A quarter of an hour suddenly seems like an *awfully* long time in the full glare of 21st-century celebrity culture.

Once the four became Fab, there was no stopping them. The estimate is that they had clocked up 10,000 hours of performance prior to their even entering a recording studio. That undeniably stood them in good stead. But it was so much more than the opportunity to pump out 30-minute versions of 'What'd I Say'. Once cemented, the songwriting partnership of Lennon and McCartney eclipsed all around. Steadied by the unwavering managerial hand of Brian Epstein, steered by the production skills of George Martin, within 12 months of beginning their professional recording career, they were fully formed, and unstoppable.

The coming together of all the elements was fortuitous. But it was genuine, not manufactured. More than half a century since the four recorded together, the Beatles occupy an elite place in the pop firmament. As the years go by, and as the actual group recede further into history, their achievements, their accomplishments, their legacy remains unparalleled.

It is a truth, universally acknowledged, that the Beatles changed *everything*. Generation Z may cavil, but try and imagine a world without them: the UK's parochial, hidebound record industry... The Establishment ruling the roost, looking down on provincial arrivistes... men's fashion, sexuality, youthful endeavour and ambition... The tumbling of social mores and class barricades... For those that did experience it firsthand, or live through those turbulent years 1963–70, yes, it must be very frustrating to hear what you missed. To have the same old tropes trotted out. Chafe if you will, but what you cannot deny are the building blocks of the group's greatness. Their music.

I still find it extraordinary that one group over an eight-year period could produce music which is not only enduring, but so diverse. From simple love songs to anthems which challenged the status quo; children's sing-alongs to meditative ballads; psychedelic excesses to music hall pastiche; long ones, short ones and everything in between...

My conviction remains that the true Beatle greatness lay in their songwriting partnership; it was the Lennon and McCartney material which elevated them above their peers. It gave them a self-contained stronghold, which meant they had no need to rely on any outside source. Not for the Beatles fighting for first dibs on American hits or squabbling over Adam Faith rejects. Couple that with the willingness to experiment, their inability to stand still. Marry that with the steadying hand and the production zeal of George Martin, and that for me, helps explain their enduring appeal.

As the 21st century progresses, and we move further away from the Beatle times, what is apparent is that what survives of them is their music. Of all their songs, at least half have inculcated their way into the culture. The singalong favourites echo from football terraces; the lingering ballads fill out karaoke evenings. The odd experimental ones still provide a way forward for those who came in their wake. Open any music periodical of the past half century and read of bands citing their new work as "our *Sgt Pepper*". Except, of course, it isn't. And while that much cited LP is not necessarily the best Beatle album, it is the one which drew a line in the sand. Pre-*Pepper* it was 'pop'; post-*Pepper* I would argue was when it became 'rock'. It was the first pop album to feature lyrics on the sleeve... the first to be called a "concept album"... to link songs together... to fashion a collection of songs as a cohesive whole... to dazzle from the outside cover in...

It came, lest we forget, in a year begun by what many still consider the greatest 45 rpm single ever, 'Strawberry Fields Forever' / 'Penny Lane'. It continued with the most widely-*seen* pop single of all time, 'All You Need Is Love'. The year steamrollered on with the wondrous 'Hello Goodbye' and concluded with the visually flawed, but eminently listenable *Magical Mystery Tour*. Over two dozen original songs! All that in just 12 calendar months.

Leaving aside their manager's untimely death, their dabbling in Eastern mysticism and investigating a Greek hideaway, by their standards, 1967 was a relatively *idle* year. For a frantic four years before, they had existed, indeed thrived, against a maelstrom of TV appearances, radio shows, live gigs, pre-motorway travel, photo sessions, drug experiments, personal appearances, film shots, press interviews, business meetings, relationships, parenthood…

It is, and remains, a fascinating story, a fairy tale which bears up under repeated listening, viewing and reading. Even leaving aside that extraordinary body of work, just look at them – the facial hair, the changing fashions; the forward looking "Beatle suits", the retrospective fondness for Victoriana; the psychedelic foppery, the sombre mundanity of their last photo session.

Or re-view those early, infectious encounters with the press – their wit, their wide-eyed enthusiasm, their zeal… "Never such innocence again". Now, everyone in the public eye, be they a blogger, a reality star, an influencer, a TV talent contest winner … all *expect* that level of fame and attention. Immediately. Now!

The Beatles just simply couldn't believe their luck. After all those years of hometown basements, or seedy Reeperbahn dives; of hammering up and down the B-roads of Britain, they had made it. Big Time. All those cups of tea at Lime Street, waiting for Brian Epstein to bring them news of the latest record company rejection. They had paid their dues, in spades. It wasn't the blink of an eye, it was a long, hard look, and they made the most of it.

For anyone alive during The Beatle Years, even looking in from the outside, it was a whirling, exhilarating rollercoaster ride. You never knew what the next single would sound like. Or what excitement could be found on their new Christmas-present LP. Like archaeologists sifting through the remains of ruined civilisations, you'd chance upon a precious artefact… The song they chose to introduce themselves to on American television, 'All My Loving', was 'only' an album track… The haunting, driving folk of 'Things We Said Today', negated to a B-side and album filler. And 'Yesterday', that most recorded song in the history of popular music, familiar to UK fans only as a song on side two of the soundtrack to their second film!

It was the best of times. And … it was the best of times. Only when the sorry split was announced, came a feeling of momentary sadness and reflection. That tempestuous decade had effectively begun with them, and now it was over, and so were they. If there was pause for consideration, it was symbolic. But in the hurly-burly pop world of the early 1970s, plenty more came along to replace them as we swapped our pile-'em-high Dansettes for stylish Garrard turntables… Like most fans of the time (did we really think of ourselves as 'heads'?), I defected to Caravan, Led Zeppelin, Pink Floyd, King Crimson, Yes, Roxy Music. But not Genesis. Never Genesis. I adhered to sensitive singer-songwriters (Dylan, of course) but also what one critic called the other "cry babies" – Al Stewart, James Taylor, Don McLean, Leonard Cohen…

And besides, no pop group ever stayed apart, not *forever*. Whenever one of the four broke cover, *the* question was inevitably addressed. There were sporadic reports of a Beatle Reunion – courtesy of Sid Bernstein, or for Bangla Desh or Concerts for Kampuchea… But somehow the moment came, and went, and the pop and rock firmament carried on hurling around. Today, with the Beatles cemented into UK history, with theirs the canon, the yardstick by which every rock trajectory is measured, during the dog days of the 1970s my memory is that they had been, and were now gone. If their records were played it was as a simple, occasional nostalgic reverie.

Their solo releases were charted with a modicum of interest. The general consensus was that, yes, together there was a chemistry, but was there any *real* lasting enthusiasm for *Mind Games*, *Ringo the 4th*, *Extra Texture* or *London Town*?

Then one cold December day in 1980, it became apparent that there would be no Beatle reunion. And we mourned. Lennon's murder was a JFK, Apollo 11, 9/11 moment. After the sadness, came the appreciation that there was, and would remain, the music. And that the one reunion which we all had quietly, enviously hoped for, could not, would never be.

With the expiry of their EMI contract in 1976, they were poorly served by compilations such as *Reel Music* and *The Beatles Ballads*. In time, with a drink taken, we all played "Let's make up the best Beatle LP from the best tracks of their solo albums"… Or with the introduction of compact discs, reformatting familiar albums to make up your own personal playlist – coming up with the original track sequence for *Sgt Pepper*; inserting 'Her Majesty' into its proper place on *Abbey Road*; skipping 'Revolution #9' on *The White Album*… (I was reminded of Sir Thomas Beecham's response when asked if he'd heard any Stockhausen? "No, but I think I've trodden in some").

Then came the memoirs, the biographies, the fly-on-the-wall accounts; the critical analyses; then came the bootlegs. Then, when Apple could stand it no more, came the BBC sessions, the *Anthology* releases, the remasters, the box sets… On and on, and all providing the opportunity to marvel and wallow once again at the grandeur and majesty of that incredible music. All fashioned in a miraculous seven-year burst, that extraordinary body of work, which shows no signs of diminishing or disappearing.

When it comes to trying to grasp and comprehend a career, writers frequently search for 'The Big Bang'. This is taken as the explosive moment when the most significant achievement is realised. One reason why the Beatles continue to fascinate is when was *their* Big Bang? Homegrown Beatlemania, and the frenzy of 1963? The conquest of America? *Revolver*? *Sgt Pepper*…? The final flourish of *Abbey Road*? There are few comparisons: Picasso and his creative mood spins… Miles Davis and his peripatetic odysseys… Bob Dylan's freewheeling switch from folk into rock and morph into country… However, for the impact on a wider culture and society, the Beatles and their achievements occupy an unassailable place.

*

During 40-odd years as a professional music writer, I have been lucky enough to write about and meet those whose music has played such a formative part in my life. Many of those close encounters (Bruce Springsteen, Art Garfunkel, Lou Reed, Van Morrison…) have provided something memorable. But it is when you are in the presence of a *Beatle* that the hair on the back of your neck does a tango and the heart starts pumping just that little bit faster.

I have been lucky enough to sit and talk and interview Paul McCartney, George Harrison and Ringo Starr. That would be three of the Beatles then. All, of course, keen to discuss their latest work. They want to talk up the album they have spent the previous year fashioning, not the work they undertook many years ago. For magazine articles or press kits, usually only a small percentage of the interview winds up being used, so I am pleased to say that many of the quotes from those three appear here for the first time. They may have gone on to repeat the anecdote in later interviews, but when I say it was told to me, that was *me* sitting opposite the bass player, lead guitarist and drummer of that legendary group as they reminisced.

Whether it was hotel room, recording studio, office boardroom, rehearsal space, rock star mansion, I sat, spellbound, by the still-strong Liverpool accent of George; fascinated by Ringo's fascination for a long-forgotten blues singer; enthralled by Paul's fondness for skiffle... But it is when those talismanic names pepper the conversation that your heart goes into overdrive: "John" ... "Beatle" ... "Pepper" ... And the – shall we call it 'carapace' – of what you hope to project as an outwardly professional journalist goes out the window... And you are reminded of a plump schoolboy drawing guitars in his exercise book as you are taken through Latin conjunctives and the summer sun shines on... Of the gawky adolescent too shy to ask a pretty girl to dance to 'Ticket to Ride'... Or the cousin of a best friend preferring to linger over *Rubber Soul* than listen to my ardent devotion. Or the teenager exploring the secret chambers of *The White Album* on headphones. Or the sixth-form singalong to 'Carry That Weight' in the Arts Room...

Alas, my close encounters took place in the days before selfies or smartphones. I was there to meet them, usually in a professional capacity. To have asked the magazine photographer for "Just a quickie" shot would have been unprofessional. I did, however, have the common sense to bring along my Christmas 1963 present of the *Please Please Me* LP which Paul, George and Ringo dutifully signed. (I remember reading that George could "do" John's signature, and was almost tempted to say, "Oh, while you're at it George, could you do a quick John for me?") But, again, no ... unprofessional.

*

I cannot claim the fly-on-the-wall closeness of Michael Braun or Hunter Davies. Nor the breathtaking research of Mark Lewisohn. Nor the academic discipline of Ian MacDonald. Nor the first-hand Merseyside diligence of Spencer Leigh. I have tried not to draw *too* directly on their works, only quoting where I felt their words eclipsed mine. Those uber-fans who can recite the words to the Quarry Bank school song may find my chronology a bit wonky. Those admirers who can quote catalogue numbers and chart positions could well find fault with my song analysis. Loyalists who have sat through every take of every Beatle song may find my impressionistic take debatable. Those who side with John Lennon may take issue with my fondness for his former songwriting partner.

From my point of view, I do believe it is such a great story which is worth re-telling. So many of the recent volumes obsess with the minutiae, but the story of the Beatles needs a

Author's autographed copy

bigger canvas. A 20th-century fairy tale, of how four lads from Liverpool left their native home and conquered the world.

Over the years, I have interviewed three of them; I have been in the *presence*. I spent time with Linda McCartney and George Martin. Talked to musicians who worked with them. I have visited Abbey Road and Apple, been to the Cavern, stood at the gates of Strawberry Field (and the Reeperbahn) and sat in the chairs they sat in at Forthlin Road and at Mendips. I witnessed the hysteria a Beatle can still arouse, first-hand, accompanying Paul in Spain. I was a member of their fan club. I grew up in the UK when they were a functioning act. And I wanted to communicate something of the enduring and life-affirming qualities of the band.

I also felt that there was a book which needed to celebrate their *Englishness*. John, after all, took his middle name from England's wartime Prime Minister, while George was named after the country's ruling monarch. They were all born while a world war raged; they grew up hemmed in by rationing, in a landscape rutted by bomb sites. These were the *real* Blitz kids.

You can never exaggerate the importance of *The Ed Sullivan Show* or Shea Stadium. By 1964 they had gone to the world, but getting there was from an England of ... boiled cabbage, hard Izal toilet paper, fish and chips, outside toilets, double-decker buses, warm beer, spotted dick, press button A, the Salvation Army, Bonfire Night, poppy sellers, the NHS, bob-a-job day, stiff upper lips, allotments, Brylcreem, cricket, £sd, crazy paving, the X-Certificate, 10/- notes, school milk, Rupert the Bear, K-E-Y-N-S-H-A-M, queueing, Littlewoods pools, pickled onions, belt and braces, licensing hours, television licences, Kiss Me Quick hats, Giles cartoons, 11+ exams, Marmite, Vaseline, the cane, Lucozade, waltzers, helter-skelters, Dunkirk spirit, Shakespeare, knickers, skiffle...

Oh, and the music they fashioned during that kaleidoscopic decade which they came to epitomise. In life, their achievements were only matched by Bob Dylan and the Rolling Stones. But neither of their peers had their discipline when it came to recorded music – not for the Beatles was there a risible *Satanic Majesties* or wayward *Nashville Skyline*... Even the on-the-run fourth LP, or the flawed *Let It Be* shone by comparison. Both Dylan and the Jagger & Richards partnership came up with individual songs which matched those of the Beatles. But not their consistency on disc. On record, and tip of the hat to Sir George Martin, they had no equals. And it is to the music each generation is drawn.

The music will never die or fade away. But it is the mesmerising, cabalistic power of "The Beatles" which still exerts an enduring and compelling fascination to all and sundry.

For all the millions of words written about them, about their philosophies, musical instruments, legal battles; their lyrics, hairstyles, merchandising, auction house sales, day-to-day activities ... there are surpassingly few biographies of the band. And those there are tend to end the story on a windy London rooftop in 1969, or in 1970 with the group's bitter break-up. What fascinated, *fascinates*, me is their durability, how the Beatles *brand* carries on well into the 21st century. Not simply the anniversary reissues of *Sgt Pepper*, *Yellow Submarine*, *The White Album* or *Abbey Road*, but rather the way they have become embedded into the consciousness of their homeland, and branded across the world.

When the National Trust announced it had bought, and was opening to the public, Paul's home in Forthlin Road, I sense it was the magical, mysterious connection with the word

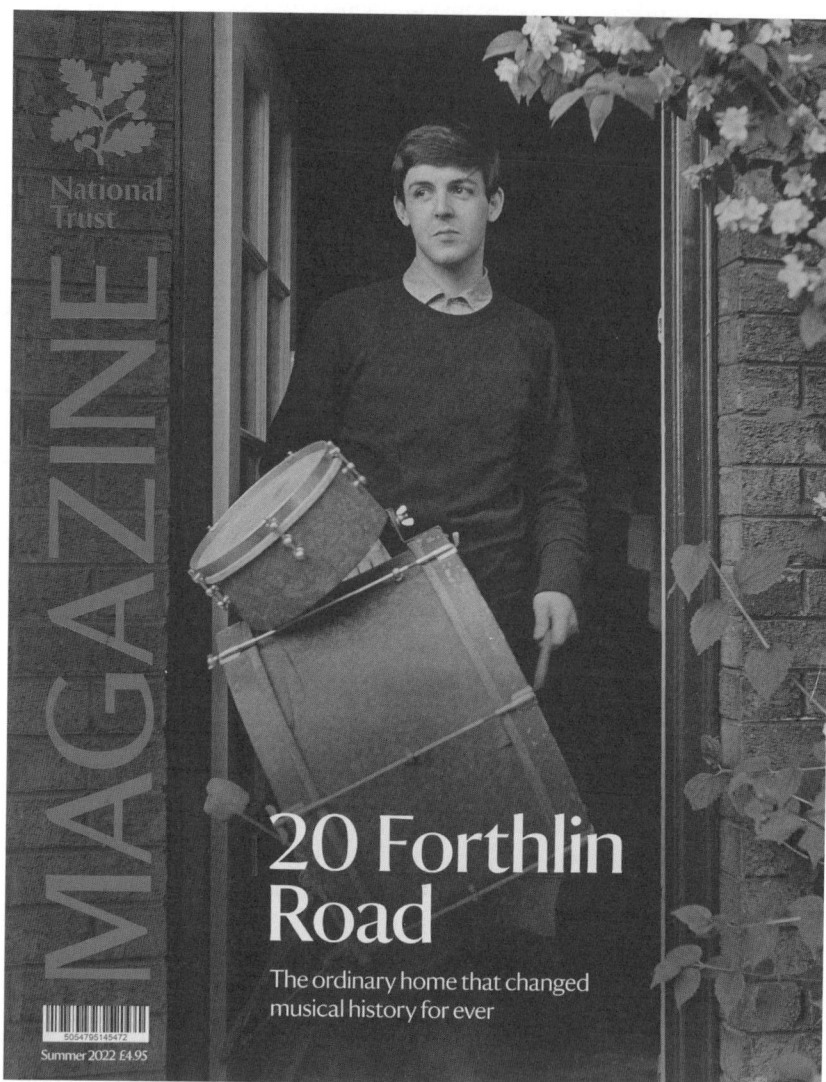

National Trust Magazine, summer 2022

"Beatle" which propelled the decision. It was a testament to the living, breathing legacy of a pop group which broke up in 1970. On into the 21st century, the Beatles are the paradigm by which every pop act is measured. But, while largely based on that incredible arc of seven years of recorded music, that appeal has transcended simply the music. The Fab Four are commemorated in every medium, in every language, in every conceivable context.

They are now more than a mere 'group' or 'band'. Their influence and impact spreads from philately to newspaper headlines; from government discussions to cover versions; from a cultural yardstick to tabloid gossip; from boardroom struggles to tribute acts; from one-off references to entire films devoted to a world *without* the Beatles... During the 2020 Covid-19 pandemic, once again the Beatles were called in to do their bit. Locked down across the globe, Beatles songs were a unifying force. *The Times'* rock critic Pete Paphides (born the same year as their last gig) compiled an exercise tape to go running with and his words found echo in many people's thoughts: "Just when you think you've listened to them one too many times, they blindside you with their brilliance".

It is estimated that a new book on the Beatles is published somewhere in the world every fortnight. Individual biographies of John, Paul, George and Ringo dutifully chronicle their solo work, but tend to err heavily on their earlier group. Alan Partridge opined: "Wings? Only the group the Beatles could have been". Barring McCartney's stellar post-Beatle career, and odd individual tracks from the others, you are inevitably drawn back to the eight years which bracketed their recorded career, 1962–70.

With increasing regularity, Beatle anniversaries allow for fresh reflection on that extraordinary career. Correspondence revealed at auctions; alternate takes on box sets; the diligent perseverance of Mark Lewisohn... all have combined to spread fresh light on the group and their achievements.

Certainly, every generation comes fresh to the music, endeavouring to replicate that unrepeatable odyssey which saw them fashion rock's most enduring and influential back catalogue. For me, one of the greatest debut albums in UK rock history remains the Stone Roses. It took them *six years* to follow it up with the desultory *Second Coming*. *Music Week* in October 2012 noted that "The Beatles' 12 studio albums were issued in a period of just seven years and two months. That is shorter than the years that have elapsed since the last George Michael studio album came out...!" While Portishead laboured for eleven years between albums, the Beatles did it all in eight. Twelve LPs, 220-odd tracks which indelibly, irrevocably, altered the face of popular music.

No doubt about that. But how does that explain the magnetic hold the Beatles still exercise? Their image, their influence ... their legacy. Every week appears to offer a fresh anniversary seized upon by Apple or the media. Every group of 15-minute-fame junkies spawned by TV shows who manage a Top 20 follow-up to their debut hit are routinely labelled "the new Beatles". My grumpy response is, "Well, when *one* group occupies the entire Top 5 of the US charts, has 14 entries in the Hot 100 simultaneously and accounts for an estimated 60% of singles sold in America in one year ... *then* we'll have that whole 'new Beatles' conversation!"

The only-ever authorised Beatles biographer, Hunter Davies, once estimated that there are around 5,000 people making a full-time living around the world out of the Beatles. Careers ranging from tribute bands to museum staff; record label executives to studio engineers; biographers to auction houses; tour guides to acrobats.

Every new format battles for the rights to Beatle music. Use of a Beatle song in an incongruous context pricks up ears. A previously unseen photo guarantees coverage. The death of a Beatle sends shock waves, and generates front-page news across the world.

I was lucky enough to interview three of the Fab Four. I missed John by a few months. The late Ray Coleman was my mentor, as Editor of *Melody Maker* he employed me on the weekly in 1980. Ray had a long relationship with the group. Soon after I joined the *Maker*, Ray was planning to go to New York to interview John about his new LP, *Double Fantasy*. He had been talking to him on the phone, and Lennon told Ray he was planning a private visit to the UK early in 1981, "to see if anyone remembers me". Ray promised me he would get me to meet John when he came over. Tragically, of course, events on a cold New York street in December 1980 made that impossible.

I had to wait a further 20-odd years for my close encounter. I had a brief and inglorious spell in PR with the firm Rogers & Cowan, one of whose clients was Paul McCartney. I had written a release about MPL's yearly 'Buddy Holly Week' which Paul had seen and liked and wanted to talk more about.

Once admitted, *everyone* is tongue-tied in the presence… Presidents and pop idols stand with their eyes widening and jaws dilating as Paul or Ringo stands before them making small talk. But how do you make small talk to a Beatle? How can you talk about tube delays; white or black coffee or standing in the English rain when you are a handshake away from the hands which originated 'Hey Jude' or propelled 'Helter Skelter', or any one of half a hundred songs which have literally been the soundtrack to one's life?

They are of course aware of your nerves. They have been doing this since Harold Macmillan was Prime Minister. They have been shielding the same questions since John F. Kennedy was a living President. You are aware that you have but a brief window to impress a Beatle. You do *not* do this by citing session dates from 45 years before, or querying alternate takes of long-ago LPs. Yet you have to convince this Beatle you are familiar with the group's work and, more importantly, their subsequent solo activities. You must demonstrate a sweeping knowledge of their life and oeuvre which will impress, particularly their life *after* the Beatle phenomenon. You must convey enthusiasm. You must impress with cool professionalism. You must not come across as a stalker.

The problem invariably is that the Beatle in question wishes to discuss the work which has pre-occupied him the preceding eight months in an airless, windowless recording studio. You, however, want to go over a recording session in a different century, when the four convened in Abbey Road under the watchful eye of George Martin fashioning yet another timeless masterpiece.

They will put you at your ease, and you will endeavour to convey suave confidence, an almost offhand blitheness in your dealings in the limited time you have. But niggling away, all the time, like toothache, is the pounding insistence, "Fuck me. I am sitting here talking to a Beatle. One of the *Beatles*…" It's a feeling you never forget. Because they have *literally* provided half a hundred songs lodged in your DNA – from school dances to stadia; from scratchy 45s to Christmas-present LPs; from shiny 1980s CDs to lavish 6-CD birthday box sets; from short-trousered puberty to grey-haired maturity. And, as long as there is electricity to fuel those songs, they remain there still.

In a quiet London street in the fashionable area of Knightsbridge lies a smart, affluent, tree-lined square. Even as a lifelong London resident, I am still struck when chancing upon such a location, so quiet, so perfect in its period details that it looks like a film location.

Only a small gold plaque announces the location of a company which primarily exists to conduct business on behalf of a group who effectively went out of business in 1970. While 50% of their members are dead, and given that the last time they performed together was when Harold Wilson was Prime Minister and the financial dealings of their currency were conducted in pounds, shillings and pence, there is not the same abiding interest in, say, Brian Poole & the Tremeloes. However, more than half a century on, there remains an enduring, abiding fascination with that other group who almost shared a label.

Going up the two steps, as you enter to your left is a boardroom overlooking the square. But it is the entry atrium and just beyond which stops you in your tracks, and lets your gaze sweep round 360 degrees and up to the glass dome high above… For every inch of wall surface is covered in gold. Framed gold records; floor to ceiling, from across the known world, gold glitters. On a sunny London afternoon, the effect is literally quite dazzling.

Here is the financial testament to the enduring popularity of the world's most fabled and influential band of all time. Timeless in their appeal, as testified by the sales, many of them awarded long after they ceased to exist as a working group. Of course, what cannot be measured is the impact they had on each subsequent generation: on the clothes, language, lifestyles, politics, fashion, music, philosophy, technology… What cannot be framed and wall-mounted is the inspiration and devotion which still adheres to them and their legacy, like limpets on an old Liverpool liner.

What makes you stand and marvel still is the box of treasures that they opened, a Pandora's box – not unleashing all the ills of the world, rather, once opened, spreading joy, happiness, love and, still, a sense of wonder…

"Presently, as my eyes grew accustomed to the light, details of the room within emerged slowly from the mist, strange animals, statues and gold – everywhere the glint of gold… When Lord Carnarvon, unable to stand the suspense any longer, inquired anxiously: 'Can you see anything?' it was all I could do to get out the words, 'Yes … wonderful things.'" These were Howard Carter's memories of opening Tutankhamun's tomb on 26 November 1922. It was how I felt when visiting Apple.

The "wonderful things" the Beatles brought to the world began differently for everyone: a chance listen to 'Love Me Do', then on to *the* British Beatle year of 1963, tied in with great train robberies, sex in high places and a Presidential assassination. In America, one night in February 1964, when a nation was transfixed by a quartet of entertainers. Or on a chill London street in 1969 as sounds from up on the roof were carried on the wind over London's tailoring hub.

We all have our favourite Beatle records, our unforgettable Beatle moments. We all remember where we were when John was shot, forever robbing the world of the one reunion which really mattered. Or reading of the brutal assault George suffered before fucking cancer took him.

For most who were there on the public journey from its real beginning, in the autumn of 1962, the memories begin at *their* beginning, in a faraway place of which little was known prior to 1963. A place that might as well be on the dark side of the moon, a place where no motorway reached; a land which to effete Southerners might well be off the map, a place called Liverpool.

"The time has come, the Walrus said
To talk of many things ..."

Lewis Carroll, 'The Walrus and the Carpenter'

Part I: Blue Suburban Skies

Writing of the impression the UK made on the post-war Windrush immigrants, Peter Ackroyd conjured up an "England to which they had come [as] hag-ridden and worn. The proud imperial nation of rumour … could be discerned with difficulty in a small, cramped island, still gasping from the blows of war… The promise of 'diamond streets' was belied by ones that seemed paved with lead, gashed by bomb sites besides grey houses … and a population which seemed so old".

And that was the impression the nation's *capital* made. The prosperous South was more than just economically isolated. As a UK resident, you forget just how remote Liverpool was. To anyone outside the North in January of 1962, Liverpool probably only meant *Z-Cars*, the popular BBC TV police drama which had just begun. It was gritty television, far removed from the cosy familiarity of *Dixon of Dock Green*. A year before the Beatles broke, the best-known music out of Liverpool was an old Scouse skipping song, 'Johnny Todd' which was used as the *Z-Cars* theme ('Johnny Todd' itself was later recorded by Bob Dylan and The Band on *The Basement Tapes*).

When 'Love Me Do' made its chart entry in October 1962, Alan Smith in *New Musical Express* explained to the weekly's readers that "the Beatles [were] a vocal-instrumental group who hail from Liverpool, the birthplace of such stars as Billy Fury, Frankie Vaughan, Norman Vaughan and Ken Dodd". While playing with the Chris Barber Band in the early 1950s, Alex Revell told me: "They were horrendous, those pre-motorway journeys – 13 hours back from Liverpool in an unheated coach".

The first time I visited Liverpool was in the mid-70s. It was terribly run-down, bomb sites still littered the city 30 years after it was blitzed. Whole streets consisted of boarded-up shops and derelict houses. The Cunard liners had long gone, the docks were running down. The pubs, by and large, depressing beer halls. For sustenance, long before they could spell 'gastro', the bars boasted pickled onions in jars, like medical specimens. The ceilings were mahogany brown after years of cigarette smoke, the clientele appeared to be mainly toothless smokers.

Nineteen seventy-three, and the Beatles were a memory. A 1970 book, *Portrait of Liverpool*, only mentioned the Beatles twice. We did go down Matthew Street, but there was nothing to indicate the location of the world's most celebrated rock & roll venue. There was a bedraggled statue dedicated to the 'Four Lads Who Shook The World', and the pub opposite where the unlicensed Cavern stood, The Grapes, seemed remarkably unchanged. It retained that inimitable aroma of pub toilets, even in the 'posh' Saloon Bar.

Yet even on that first visit, long before the National Trust, Beatle City and John Lennon Airport, there remained something magical about our mystery tour. To stand outside the gates of Strawberry Field (and wonder where the 's' was); to go down Penny Lane, and then see the names on the buses that were as alien to Londoners as the cities of Middle Earth – Speke, Knotty Ash, the Dingle…

Love's Arthur Lee spoke eloquently: "Years later I went up to Liverpool and looked all over for the places those beautiful songs came from. And I couldn't find them anywhere. I came to the conclusion that they wrote them in their minds". Like Ray Davies at his best, those Beatle songs managed to make the mundane universal.

Many, many years later, thanks to the wonderful Talking Pictures TV channel, I chanced upon the Frankie Vaughan film *These Dangerous Years* (1957). Banking on his chart hits ('Green Door', the No.1 'Garden of Eden') the film was a vehicle designed to put the Liverpool-born singer into the Elvis league.

Known as *Dangerous Youth* on its American release, Frankie played a lippy rock & roller (with the suitably rebellious surname 'Wyman'). Incongruously, it was produced by Anna Neagle, and directed by her husband, the sedate Herbert Wilcox, whose oeuvre was more at home in Mayfair salons than the gritty streets of Liverpool. The accents were more Manchester than Mersey, and 'Scouse' was used as a term of insult by Frankie's National Service opponents.

What made me sit up was the rather apt opening credit: "The Cast Iron Shore 'The Cassy' is a desolate backwater of Liverpool's prosperous river front, a world of crumbling hulks … an unsupervised world where boy is king, where the shining waters of the Mersey breed the germs of crime, failure *and sometimes success*" [my italics]. The Cast Iron Shore was, of course, one of the retrospective locations Lennon conjured up on 'Glass Onion'.

Another film of the era which revelled in the city's rebellious nature was *Violent Playground* (1958). Stanley Baker played a detective consigned to Liverpool's juvenile delinquent division, in the hope that "some of the children grow up less anti-social than their ancestors". Those anti-social Teds Lennon and Starkey would no doubt have enjoyed the film for all the wrong reasons. It was not released in America until the mid-60s, to cash-in on the fact that its location was the Beatles' hometown. And also that the film's leading delinquent was David McCallum, then enjoying similar popular appeal on TVs *The Man From UNCLE*.

To drink in the same Liverpool pubs and breathe the same air as *they* had once breathed even in 1973 was still quite intoxicating. By then, with all four still alive and functioning, the Beatles were a brand condemned to legend. The *Red* and *Blue* releases not yet totemic. We had our fond memories, but they were allied to childhood, as we nudged out of our teens, the Beatles were already tied to a nostalgic past. The music of today was steamrollering Led Zeppelin; cosmic-expanding Pink Floyd; identity-challenging David Bowie… not a quartet of Scousers trilling about luv.

The port was in decline, and the inner-city misery which would explode in the early 1980s was evident. Yet there remained something magical about that first visit, it was somehow tangible, a link with the group. Even if their status was not as elevated as it would become in the aftermath of Lennon's murder, or re-invigorated by CD releases, here was a connection with the Beatles. They had simply been there throughout the kaleidoscopic, capering 60s. It was, genuinely, a decade they underlined (a debut single in 1962, when the Edwardian Conservative Harold Macmillan occupied No.10 Downing Street, to a final gig in 1969, played out under Harold Wilson's Labour premiership).

So synonymous had the group become with the social changes the nation had undergone during the period, that the first (and best) book to look back on "the revolution in British life in the fifties and sixties", *The Neophiliacs* by Christopher Booker, placed them centre stage: "The upper class father image of Mr Macmillan himself had acted as a catalyst for all the aggression that was to unleash the New England of Mr Wilson and the Beatles".

Throughout it all, the music of the Beatles synchronised with the events of the era. And the base for that music, for those lives, was their home city of Liverpool. They are linked as closely to the city as Elvis is to Memphis. But prior to the Beatles the remote Northern outpost was barely famous as the birthplace of comedians Ken Dodd and Arthur Askey. For successive generations though, the city exuded an almost spellbinding power; Binns Road, Liverpool was the HQ of Hornby train sets and those mysterious, metallic Meccano sets which offered "a real story of a boy's journey into a sunny land where all is happiness and fun; where dullness is never known". Tony Bramwell told me how he and childhood chum George Harrison used to bunk over the factory wall and sift through the bins for rejected Meccano bits – "I had twelve Eiffel Towers".

So many of the current batch of 21st-century Beatle books marvel at their mortality – "They ate chip butties" – which overlooks just how 'normal' they were at the beginning of the madness. They quickly acclimatised to what was the norm, and their aspirational backgrounds were very much part of that. But soon the madness overtook them; I remember asking one of the girls who worked at Brian Epstein's NEMS and used to go along to the Cavern regularly, when she thought Liverpool had lost the Beatles? "In 1962, Paul said his favourite food was egg and chips; in 1963, it was crepes suzette...!"

Tea featured prominently in their lives; it was the British staple, it saw us through the war. A French critic felt the underlying message of *Brief Encounter* was "make tea, not love". There is even, I kid you not, a fanzine *The Teatles Book*. And I loved the immaculately typed itinerary Brian prepared for their 1964 trip to Paris, flying from Manchester to London, and prior to their departure to the French capital, 90 minutes was allowed for "afternoon tea".

There's a fascinating 1963 TV documentary, *Beat City*, which looks at the city in the aftermath of the Beatles. It was hosted by the epicene Daniel Farson, normally seen propping up the bar in Soho's Colony Room. Farson was fascinated by the "vitality, so characteristic of Liverpool", even if he speculated "if one was to make a film of Jack the Ripper, this city would be the setting".

Of particular interest are the locations so familiar from Beatle books – the Jacaranda, the Blue Angel. And, of course, the Cavern. You can find it on YouTube, poor black and white quality, but offering priceless contemporary footage of groups performing at that historic venue. A pounding Faron's Flamingoes, 15-year-old Chick Graham and Rory Storm & the Hurricanes, featuring the fabulously named Johnny Guitar. A blonde girl is interviewed talking about dating Rory "but he left me at Woolton Cemetery".

The Cavern is inextricably linked to the story of the Beatles. It is where they played somewhere in the region of 300 gigs. And linked to the Cavern were their earliest, loyal fans. It was the lunchtime gigs they enjoyed the most – the opportunity to get up close, to shout and requests and enjoy a bit of Beatle badinage. And all for a bob (5p).

Those lunchtime gigs posed a problem for the office workers who attended, that distinctive Cavern aroma clung to suits and skirts and informed their bosses of the low dive they had attended in their lunch hour. That proximity forged a bond with the band. Long before London, Llandudno or Los Angeles, the Beatles were *their* group. Ron Watson saw them over 100 times, and maintains "People say they saw the Beatles live, but it was only about 3,000 people around Merseyside who saw them as they really were".

A significant Cavern gig occurred on 19 February 1963 – opening the show were the Lee Curtis All Stars with their new drummer, Pete Best. It was the last time that any of the four Beatles ever saw their hapless drummer. It was also the occasion when DJ Bob

Wooler made an announcement to what he anticipated would be a delighted audience: the Beatles' second single 'Please Please Me' had reached No.1. They were, by nationwide, record-buying acclaim, the country's top act. The news was greeted with stony silence. The audience shiver wasn't from the cold of the Big Freeze outside; it was the certainty that the group, *their* group, now had to be shared. It was time for The Leaving Of Liverpool.

"To a great extent it was the innovations of The Beatles which hastened Merseybeat's demise", wrote Paul Du Noyer in his comprehensive biography of the city. "Having ascended to some higher realm of pop existence, they pulled the ladder up behind them". Indeed, it is hard to imagine, say, the Fourmost at the feet of the Maharishi.

Back then, it was a different century, a different world. A world without the Beatles. But it was Liverpool which formed and fashioned them. It was Liverpool they knew, and Liverpool they needed to get away from. Yet it was Liverpool which remains the birthplace of the four men who caused the most seismic event in the entertainment industry, but who also sent shockwaves through the English establishment, engineering social changes they could never have imagined when Hitler's bombs rained down on the city which gave them all birth...

*

While none of their childhoods could be called 'Dickensian', some of the most interesting parts of *Anthology* were hearing the group talk about their growing up. It acts as a forceful reminder of just what a bridge the Beatles provided between the austere, immediate post-war, heavily rationed, black and white world of their adolescence. Contrast that with the vivid, hedonistic, technicolour landscape which accompanied their stratospheric rise.

These were streets which echoed to the sound of horse-drawn deliveries of coal; of rag and bone men and their knackered mares clacking along the cobbles. Motor cars were a rare sight. Few television aerials pockmarked the sky. Trips were frequently to outside toilets. The electric clang of the electric trams and clamour of the docks was the city's soundtrack.

Long before a note was heard of the blues or rock & roll music which would later inspire them, Liverpool had a connection with the Mississippi Delta. It was the state's cotton which lubricated its wheels of commerce. To get the cotton picked, the antebellum South relied on slaves, four million of them.

As the Civil War raged, one of the few locations for an Embassy for the Southern Confederacy was located in Liverpool. And it was cotton which bound Liverpool and the American South, long before W.C. Handy heard the blues in Tutwiler, Mississippi. Long before Elvis recorded at Sun Studios in Memphis. Even before Paul's dad Jim found employment ... cotton was the umbilical cord between the USA and Liverpool. And it has even been suggested that the last official lowering of the Confederate flag in the Civil War era was on CSS *Shenandoah* on the River Mersey.

For those freed slaves not content with 40 acres and a mule in the post-Civil War South, there was one way out of the Delta. Highway 61 was the blues highway, snaking out of Mississippi and to the industrial heartlands of Chicago and Detroit. It carried on, and up through the Midwest until it hit the Canadian border, pausing only to thread by Duluth, Minnesota, the birthplace of Bob Dylan...

A thriving seaport, Liverpool always regarded itself as one step removed from the UK. There was something intriguing and slightly illicit about its inhabitants, not for them the flat adenoidal drawl of Birmingham or the Geordie lilt of Newcastle. There was something hard and indomitable about the Liverpool accent. Liverpudlians prided themselves on their lippy, chippy, chip on their shoulder.

Scousers[1] were proud of their city. But for years, Liverpudlians were notorious for their free and easy ways. Winston Churchill was fond of repeating a joke from his old friend, the Liverpool MP, F.E. Smith: Saint Peter is at the gates of Heaven to greet a group of Liverpudlians. He disappears to check their credentials with God. God agrees to admit them and Peter goes to relay the news, only to return looking shocked. God asks what's wrong? "They're gone," says Saint Peter. "What, the Scousers?" "No, the Pearly Gates!"

All four of the group were wartime children, growing up in an age of austerity – in the UK rationing was not lifted until nine years after war's end and the year Elvis began recording. Great Britain was a country which had famously won the war, but lost the peace. The old certainties were wavering and during the uncertain 1950s, a new sound was heard. While the 1960s have been endlessly chronicled and documented, for me, the preceding ten years is 'The Lost Decade'.

Churchill's 1945 election defeat came as a shock, as much for the new Prime Minister, Labour's Clement Attlee: "I think the general feeling was that [the electorate] wanted a new start. We were looking towards the future. The Tories were looking towards the past". It was Attlee's immediate post-war Labour government which laid the foundations for the Welfare State, under which our four heroes prospered.

The best-selling Beveridge Report, made available in 1942 even while the war raged, aimed to "eliminate Poverty, Disease, Ignorance, Squalor and Idleness". It was intended to banish the misery of the 1930s. Of benefit to them, and to the entire country, a National Health Service was founded in 1948. They too benefitted from the Butler Education Act of 1944, which raised the school-leaving age to 15 and introduced the 11+ exam which allowed working-class children access to the up-market grammar schools, as well as providing free, bone-enriching milk. Sweeping changes were intended to abolish fee-paying public schools, but for Lennon and McCartney the retention of the lower-down-the-pecking-order grammar schools ensured them an education, which would gradually filter into their songs.

As schoolboys, they watched spellbound on television as a young Queen was crowned, within days of the tallest place on earth being scaled by citizens of her Commonwealth. They read of motorways linking the country, watched the aeroplanes jet in and out of the city's airport. Heard the mournful wail of the Cunard liners as they sailed from the port. They could only imagine the Promised Land to which the liners sailed...

It would be inaccurate to say that without Liverpool there would have been no Beatles, but the hard-edged, port city played a formative part in their early years. Even today, I am struck by how – Ringo aside – they retained their accents. (Indeed, John's Aunt Mimi was

---

1 Scouse itself was a particularly indigestible beef and potato pie made popular in the city when it was introduced by Scandinavian sailors in the 19th century.

shocked when she heard him being interviewed, emphasising his Liverpudlian accent.)

It was the Second World War which cannot be ignored when considering the birth of the Beatles. Following the outbreak of war in 1939, there was a period of seven months known as "the Phoney War", until Hitler unleashed his Blitzkrieg, and within two months, all of Europe, from the Arctic to the Mediterranean, was under Nazi occupation.

When it became apparent that invasion was impossible, the Nazis turned their wrath onto the cities of the United Kingdom. For four days at the end of August 1940, Liverpool became the first city to suffer sustained bombing from the Luftwaffe, when every night 150 bombers pounded the city and its docks. After London, Liverpool was the next heavily bombed city in the UK. At the beginning of May 1941, the city suffered eight successive nights of bombing. In the suburb of Bootle, only one out of every ten houses escaped bomb damage. So sustained was the blitz a rumour surfaced that the population were rioting, and martial law had been declared. Volunteer fireman, Paul's father Jim McCartney, witnessed that May blitz which left 1,300 dead and an estimated two thirds of the city's houses damaged.

Liverpool was where the merchant ships mustered for the North Atlantic convoys. For 200 years the city's port had seen cargoes from around the world pass through. By 1941, what kept Britain in the fight against Hitler were the supplies issuing from the land of the brave and the home of the free, across the U-Boat-infested Atlantic, and into Liverpool. That was why Liverpool became a target for the Luftwaffe bombs, and it is quite possible that the oldest Beatles who were born in 1940 could have come into the world to the sound of bombs exploding.

Of the four, Richard Starkey (7 July 1940) was the real working-class hero, his childhood home of the Dingle was defiantly proletarian. Yet it was the middle-class Lennon who happily rewrote his childhood history.

Ritchie was a sad, solitary child, plagued by illness – pleurisy, peritonitis. Prolonged spells in hospital meant Ritchie missed out on crucial years of schooling and education. No wonder he always looked so mournful and found sanctuary in music. Who could have thought that a brightly coloured drum could have provided such a future for the lugubrious youth with the prominent nose?

Despite having an absent father, Ritchie benefitted from a loving family. He was the perfect age when rock & roll kicked in: a 16-year-old with limited horizons. But like Lennon, before being captivated by Elvis, Ritchie was lured in by a homegrown music. Lonnie Donegan's skiffle explosion of the mid-50s was a precursor of punk. A brand of music which anyone could have a go at, whether it was on cheap Spanish guitars or, particularly popular in Liverpool due to its busy port, a tea-chest bass. Just get an empty tea chest, stick on a broom handle, tie string to the top, attach to the chest, and bingo, the bass foundation, complete with echo chamber.

Years later, Ringo reflected on Lonnie for a TV documentary based on my Lonnie Donegan biography, and came out with the best quote on the influence of the King of Skiffle: "It was Lonnie who got us out of the factories".

In a patriotic gesture he was to reject as an adult, John Winston Lennon (9 October 1940) was named after the defiant wartime leader. A few months younger than Ringo, much has been made of John's fractured childhood, and certainly growing up without a father left an indelible impression. But his mother Julia was giving in her love, and her network of sisters provided John with a flurry of affectionate aunts. Of them all, the most celebrated was Mary 'Mimi' Smith. It was Mimi who took the errant John under her maternal wing, and her husband George provided a stability the boy appreciated until George's untimely and premature death in 1955 when John was only 14.

That event sent Mimi into the middle-class universe of taking in lodgers. Her house Mendips was ideally suited to the purpose. Visiting it today, it requires little imagination to picture it as it was during the time John occupied it. From inside the hall, you turn to the immaculately tidy lounge, kept for special occasions (ours was known as the "best back"). Upstairs the Lennon bedroom is like he's just left – the pin-up posters of Brigitte Bardot and Juliette Greco (unattainable sirens for a Liverpool schoolboy), the record player, the bookshelf.

Pride of place went to Richmal Crompton's 'Just William' books, which John was particularly fond of. William Brown remains one of childhood literature's great characters. His rejection of smug, middle-class values struck a chord with the young Lennon. William's gang also numbered four, with him as the leader, and Ginger, Henry and Douglas in thrall. The first William book appeared in 1922 and carried on until the author's death in 1969. Bill Harry believes John asked for a picture of the author for the *Sgt Pepper* sleeve, but for whatever reason, she never made it. William's nemesis, the lisping Violet-Elizabeth Bott, in one of the later books, was very proud of her "beatleth wig".

Whether Lennon knew it, one of the last William books was 1965's *William and the Pop Singers*. It featured a group called the Argonauts. William chances upon 'Chris', the "leader … the life and soul of us … the brains of us…" who has walked out on the group. "I should have been a troubadour, a jongleur, a strolling player… I have the soul of a poet, a dreamer, a dramatist". William is told that Chris is "wasting his life singin' pop songs and he's got to work it out of his system". With William's encouragement, Chris returns invigorated with his song about his "moon girl", and its insistent chorus "Yeah! Yeah! Yeah!"

The most distinguished visitor to Mendips after it opened to the public was Bob Dylan. In 2009, Bob paid his £16 and sat hooded and unrecognised on the coach, but he was later granted a 40-minute private tour with curator Colin Hall. Dylan was apparently struck by the similarities between the teenage Lennon bedroom and his own in Hibbing. He was particularly interested in John's bookshelf, and spent time peering at the 'Just William' titles after Colin explained John's fondness for the timeless outlaw.

The Mendips dining room remains, surely as spotless as Mimi would have left it. And the kitchen, stocked with brands which every post-war baby boomer would recognise from their childhood – Daz, Brillo, bars of green Fairy soap, Bisto, tins of Spam, Camp coffee…

Then out into the garden: the lawn trim, with neat, orderly borders. And in the far corner, a tree the young John was always climbing. From the top of the tree he could be a pirate captain surveying a distant ocean from his topsail. He could be Jim Hawkins on the rigging of the *Hispaniola*. He could be a commando about to parachute behind enemy lines. He could be Davy Crockett on the mission walls of the Alamo. He could be Lancelot looking down from the ramparts of a Norman castle. He could be Edmund

Hillary tackling his own Everest. No one ever accompanied the young John up that tree. With his glasses on he could peer into the gardens of the Salvation Army home which lay behind Aunt Mimi's. It was called 'Strawberry Field'.

Visiting the Lennon home at Mendips is like entering the middle-class, suburban comfort of Just William rather than that of angry young man Joe Lampton. "The only claim [Lennon] had to be a working-class hero was on the sheet music", Liverpool musician Howie Casey told Bob Spitz.

From the comfortable, suburban avenues like Menlove, only a few miles away, the McCartney family home still exudes working-class confidence, a spick-and-span council house. As the crow flies, only a mile separates the McCartney home from Mendips in Menlove Avenue. Cosy and safe, 20 Forthlin Road is pinched by comparison.

Like two of his future bandmates, James Paul McCartney (18 June 1942) came from a close and loving family. Like John, the McCartney family roots stretch back to Ireland. It has been suggested that the family began as McCarthy, and as part of the 90,000 who fled to Liverpool to flee the potato blight which caused the Irish Famine of the 1840s, 'McCarthy' was either misheard by customs officials on arrival, to become 'McCartney'.

Able to patronise a younger brother, Michael, Paul inherited a love of music from his father Jim and relatives that he would later name in song. Because of his mother Mary's esteemed position as a district nurse, the McCartneys were inched up the housing ladder and settled in Forthlin Road. Such was Mary's standing and importance in the community, the family were even accorded the status symbol of their own telephone, rather than having to juggle cumbersome old bronze pennies and the challenging buttons of A and B in the bright red public phone boxes.

Built at a cost of £1,369/9s/1d the McCartneys moved into the property in 1955. Once again, you can easily evoke the home as it was when occupied by the McCartneys. The National Trust have lovingly, and accurately, preserved the house in all its early 1960s aspic. The intention was to conserve the property as a prime example of post-war council housing. It was in such perfect condition, as the family who were housed there immediately after the McCartneys left in 1964 preserved it perfectly until they left over 20 years later. So, what is left at 20 Forthlin Road was a perfect specimen of 1940s architectural and social history. Undeniably it also helped that the property had once been occupied by the nation's most successful songwriter.

The National Trust bought the property in 1995 and opened it to the public in 1997. Julian Gibbs was the Historic Buildings Representative of the Mercia Region: "I'd have been very disappointed if we hadn't had some letters threatening to resign in protest," he laughed, recalling the Establishment protests which greeted the Beatles' MBEs.

The day I visited, over 40 years after Paul had left, there was that eerie sense of deja vu. *There* was the fireplace in front of which Paul and John were photographed as they inched their way to completing 'I Saw Her Standing There'. The custodian thought it unlikely that the front room piano was the one from the McCartney occupation, but it was the same model, and purchased from the same store from which Jim McCartney had originally bought it, Harry Epstein's North End Music Stores.

There was something affecting and rather touching in visiting the home; what drew me there was the McCartney connection. But here was a place built in the immediate aftermath of the Second World War by a Labour government, determined to eradicate the poverty, squalor, ill health and ignorance which were familiar to all Beatle parents. Such a property was the foundation of the Brave New World which gave the United Kingdom universal education and its greatest peacetime achievement, the National Health Service.

As with all the Beatle sites in Liverpool, the span of visitors was broad and striking. Asked if anyone played the piano, a teenage American volunteered and sat down to play. 'Let It Be' echoed round the McCartney family home: the song a bearded Paul wrote as a tribute to his late, lamented parent who died in 1956, barely a year into their new home. To hear the song Paul wrote for "mother Mary", played on a piano she would have recognised, in the last home she was ever to know, was an emotionally overwhelming experience.

On view were copies of Paul's favourite childhood reading – *The Rupert Book*. Every Christmas, like millions of his contemporaries, the annual brought something comforting to the young Paul. In the red pullover and yellow check trousers the little bear was no stranger to adventures. But they were not the adventures favoured by William and his rebellious Outlaws. 'Rupert and the Blue Moon' found him flying through the coloured air to a land inhabited by "a perfect little boy and girl. They are always polite and always clean and tidy, and never late…"

Of all the men who would be Beatles, George Harrison (25 February 1943) was born into a family which was wider travelled and drew in more outside influences. George was the youngest in a family of four children. His eldest brother Harold lost his late teenage years to National Service, a fate which the Beatles narrowly avoided. When looking back, Paul enviously recalled Harold arriving back from Christmas Island "with a gorgeous tan in his army uniform and we thought 'My God, he's been made a man of…'"

The Harrison family home at 12 Arnold Grove was closely knit, and unlike Lennon's, was traditionally stolid working class, a typical two-up, two-down, with outside toilet. Of them all, George had the widest references as an adolescent: elder brothers and their girlfriends helped alert him to a world outside the family home. George's fondness for his family years and the home he occupied for his first six years came to light later, when he used 'Arnold Grove' as an occasional pseudonym to ensure his anonymity.

The Harrisons were a close-knit family, and George's mother Louise was the Beatle mum closest to the fans. As the group's fame grew, nothing was too much trouble for her. It was Louise who dutifully replied to fans' correspondence, an estimated 3,000 letters a month. Callers would be received with tea and a tour where her son's sleeping arrangements were proudly displayed. Louise even helped out with a lyric for her youngest son's 'Piggies'.

But it was the oldest Harrison sibling, Louise, who acted as a bridge between worlds. A GI Bride, Louise (1931–2023) married Gordon Caldwell and emigrated to America in 1954, aptly the year that Elvis made his first recordings at Sun.

By the time of George's birth, the German bombing of Liverpool had ceased. Soon after, the Nazis suffered their first substantial defeat at Stalingrad and plans were underway for the invasion of Europe, which would follow on D-Day, 6 June 1944.

It is worth underlining that all four were war children. All were born while bombs were falling on their homeland; whose parents "did their bit", as fire watcher, soldier or merchant seaman. They all would have grown up with blitzed buildings as their playgrounds. All would have been brought up to "waste not, want not". What might later be perceived as "penny pinching" had been ground into them as children.

By 1945, the war was won, and Attlee's Labour government set about building the New Jerusalem for families like the Harrisons, Starkeys and McCartneys. But crippled by war debts, and with 1947 the coldest winter on record, it was a slow and agonising climb out of the chasm. By the time John and Ritchie entered their teens, nationwide rationing was still in force (I was two when it was finally abolished in 1954). As they watched the economies of the vanquished Germany and their American allies boom, they, like their parents must have asked just who had won the war.

While the cliched image of the United Kingdom during the 1950s is of pinched austerity, a black and white world of hardships undergone by a grim population whose finest hour was in the long-gone wartime years. A nation draped in pervasive smog … like all cliches, there is more than a grain of truth in it.

Growing up, the boys who would be Beatles would have celebrated Empire Day, which was only abolished in 1958. In his history of the British Empire, Jeremy Paxman wrote: "Anyone who has grown up or grown old in Britain since the Second World War has done so in an atmosphere of irresistible decline, to the point where now Britain's Imperial History is no more than the faint smell of mothballs in a long-unopened cupboard".

The world in which the Beatles grew up was one of deference, with the class barriers rigorously reinforced. There was little to look forward to: boys graduated from short to long trousers, and tried to emulate their parents. Girls may have been allowed a brief detour to the typing pool, but marriage and motherhood was the only ambition their mothers handed down. The concept of a teenager lay over the horizon.

Imagine you are a testosterone-filled, mid-50s teenager turning on the radio, sulking over the washing up or mowing the lawn for your paltry £sd pocket money. None would have had the pleasure of cleaning the family car in anticipation of its weekly "spin". Buses and trams were how the bulk of the population got around Liverpool. There were barely 3,000,000 cars throughout the entire United Kingdom.

In its strictly limited needle time allowance of popular discs, the BBC Light Programme graciously allowed you to hear Alma Cogan's 1955 'Where Will the Dimple Be'. Surly at the possibilities life offers, sulking at the restrictions placed upon you, you listen to a record whose sole reason for existence is trying to imagine where the first-born's dimple will appear. The suspense is almost bearable.

Much of the problem was economic. For communities in Liverpool, refrigerators, motor cars and television sets were the stuff of unattainable dreams. Fourteen million people a week religiously did their football pools. Tenaciously, they persevered, with little prospect of a way out, short of boxing or crime. For a century, the city of Liverpool only lagged behind Glasgow in its violent reputation. ("What do you call a Scouser in a suit?" the old gag ran. "The accused".)

*

Both John and George attended Dovedale Primary School. Lennon carved his initials into one of the school desks with a pair of compasses. Legend had it if you sat in *that* desk you were guaranteed good fortune.

Bookish and unremarkable, as he entered his teenage years, John benefitted from the strengths of both Smith sisters: Mimi instilled responsibility and the importance of education. It was Mimi and her husband George who steered John through his all-important 11+ exam. Had he failed, he would have disappeared into the gulag of the comprehensive school system and, likely as not, never be heard of again. With sullen diligence, John persevered, and thus qualified for Quarry Bank, the grammar school.

On the other hand, he was drawn to his mother's rebellious nature. Her home provided a bolthole. Julia was everything Mimi was not – flighty and irresponsible, flirty and capricious. She injected John with an irreverence which made Mimi's role as disciplinarian even harder.

Slacking at school, resentful of the petty impositions imposed by the well-meaning Mimi, embarrassed by his clunky glasses and frustrated by his myopia, pining for an absent father, at one remove from his mother… All the while adolescent hormones were working overtime, it needs no more than a bargain basement Freud to see where the seeds of John Lennon's later rebelliousness came from.

Perhaps the stern hand of a father might have steered the errant teenager. But Fred Lennon had long gone. The boy only got to know his birth father during adulthood. Fred's own childhood was not trouble free, he was farmed out to the Bluecoat Orphanage, where he formed a friendship with a man who would later teach his son, 'James Bond'.

A school detention report from June 1955 found comments on the 14-year-old John's "complete idleness", his "chewing in class" … "making "silly noises during an examination" … having "just no interest whatsoever" and, intriguingly, "sabotage". On that evidence, the future looked bleak for John Winston Lennon.

His absentee father Freddie worked the transatlantic liners. The big ships owned by Cunard and White Star may well have departed the port and gone down south when the companies merged in 1934. But a vestige remained of those glamorous Blue Riband days of the 1930s, when cocktails were taken by dinner-jacketed passengers as the sun sank over the Atlantic, and Cole Porter melodies swelled up from the first-class lounge.

The night before boarding one of the luxury liners, Cunard passengers would be put up at Liverpool's leading hotel, the Adelphi. Designed to mirror the seaboard luxury they would soon encounter, the Adelphi was the city's most exotic location. You can get a flavour of the times in the TV version of *Brideshead Revisited*, the shipboard scenes were filmed at the Adelphi – ironically, one of the series' stars was Jane Asher.

Paul McCartney, meanwhile, meandered happily along. He too passed his 11+, and became a pupil of the Liverpool Institute, another grammar school. He was lucky to learn English on the watch of Alan Durband (1927–93). It was his English teacher who instilled a lifelong love of language in the youngster – Professor John Sutherland recalled meeting McCartney in 2019 and was surprised when the ex-Beatle "loosed a volley of Chaucer (word and accent perfect)". It was all down to 'Dusty' Durband, who Paul remembered fondly in his 2021 *Lyrics* book. Although at the time he was less encouraging to his pupil. When Paul announced he was going to Hamburg with his group, Durband advised, "Go to Teachers' Training College. We can't all be Tommy Steele, you know."

A lifetime later I was interviewing Paul and we were talking about influences and he said: "There's some Dryden line that I haven't remembered, God, in 20 years: 'Madness and genius are near allied / Thin partitions do their bounds divide'". Not bad, and a testament to his teacher. I couldn't recall *any* poetry from my schooldays.

Paul enjoyed escaping the restrictions of the city, revelling in the freedom of the Cheshire countryside, or visiting relations on the Isle of Wight. In another life, McCartney told Barry Miles that, with university an unlikely destination, he had a simple ambition: "I wish I was a lorry driver, Catholic lorry driver. Very, very simple life, a firm faith and a place to go … in my nice lorry I envied the innocence".

A chance encounter in July 1957 put paid to that ambition.

Paul was a happy child, polite and respectful to his elders, with a keen ear for the songs his father Jim picked out on the family piano. For his 22nd post-Beatle album, McCartney's 2012 *Kisses on the Bottom* was a delightful return to "some of the old songs that my parents' generation used to sing at New Year's Eve do's," he told Paul Du Noyer. "Us kids would arrive at the do, the carpets would get rolled back, all the women would sit around on chairs with their little drinks of rum & black, gin & it, Babycham… Someone would play the piano, all these old songs – 'Bye Bye Blackbird', 'Paper Moon', 'I'm Gonna Sit Right Down and Write Myself a Letter'".

It was of course his dad Jim's dance band influence which percolated into the McCartney subconscious. It was those old, pre-rock & roll era songs which later infused such Beatle favourites as 'When I'm 64', 'Your Mother Should Know', and 'Honey Pie'.

I interviewed Paul when he released his *Run Devil Run* album of rock & roll favourites, and it sparked some fond memories: "'Fabulous' by Charlie Gracie, it's a little known thing I remember from a day at the Sefton Park Fair, when I had on a blue fleck jacket with a flap on the top breast pocket… We thought we were looking cool, walking round the fair, and I remember hearing this playing off the waltzer…"

But as with John, the darkness soon drew in, and when he was barely 14, his mother, Mary, was taken by cancer, and Jim was left to bring up his two sons alone. Paul was bereft, and like John, his mother's death at a young age corroded his adolescence. However, like John, Paul was about to find solace, somewhere over the rainbow…

Ironically, following a childhood dogged by illness, Ritchie Starkey entered his teenage years content and optimistic. While his own father had left when he was seven, when his mother Elsie remarried, he was close to his stepfather Harry Graves. It was Harry who bought the boy a drum kit, which he nobly transported all the way back from London to Liverpool.

When I last visited Liverpool, Ringo's birthplace in Madryn Street was under threat, with all the houses boarded up. But those cosy, comfortable working-class dwellings were saved following a successful petition. Even boarded up, they conveyed a sense of community, little Coronation Streets. At the top of the road, and nestling next to Admiral Street, is The Empress, where Ringo's parents used to sup, and where he returned to shoot the cover of his first solo LP *Sentimental Journey* in 1970.

Ritchie Starkey had left school when he was 15 and with no formal qualifications, scuffed around as a delivery boy, barman, joiner… But like his soon-to-be compadres, he too heard the clarion call… When I interviewed him, Ringo told me: "I'm from Liverpool. I just wanted to be a drummer from 13. From the age of 13, I only wanted to play the drums. And I wanted to be in a band. I wanted to play with great musicians. That's the dream. And the dream's still going on.

"Drums are the instrument I love. I don't know what it is. We had a piano, which did nothing for me. My grandparents played mandolin and ukelele – nothing! My grandfather bought me a harmonica – nothing! I only wanted the drums. I was born to be a drummer!"

George had passed his 11+, thereby gaining admission to the Liverpool Institute. He hated his time at senior school, and took any opportunity to skive off. George claimed he knew at an early age that the teachers were only there to hammer a little knowledge into pupils destined for apprenticeships, the docks or the factories. The one thing George took away from the Liverpool Institute was forging a friendship with a boy in the year above him, Paul McCartney.

With its tongue firmly in its cheek in 1963, the Liverpool Institute school magazine noted that "Mr G. Harrison (1956) and Mr P. McCartney (1956) have found success as members of 'The Beatles' singing group and have made a number of television and local stage appearances. They recently made their second record to top the national Hit Parade".

By 1956, the stars were aligned and what it took was not a plea to keep off blue suede shoes or register at Heartbreak Hotel. Rather an invitation to climb aboard a railroad train that ran out of far, far away New Orleans. It was a song, improbably sung by a Glaswegian cockney, culled from the songbook of Leadbelly. Before Elvis there was Lonnie Donegan. The impact on the youth of the United Kingdom with his DIY music was seismic. It was called skiffle…

*

In hindsight, Lonnie Donegan's 1956 hit 'Rock Island Line' was an odd song to spark a musical revolution. Squeezed into a traditional jazz session two years before and forgotten, its belated release came as much of a surprise to its singer as the world. Much of its two minutes and 31 seconds are taken up with a (frankly, tedious) spoken list of contents of a freight train. It is only halfway through that the song picks up momentum, and it is those fiery, frenzied last 90 seconds which kickstarted rock & roll in the United Kingdom.

Lonnie is all but forgotten now, but as a musical pioneer he should be esteemed and venerated. For without Donegan's energetic, homegrown, anyone-can-do-it-style of skiffle, it is highly unlikely that the Beatles would exist.

Skiffle originated in the poor black quarters of the American south, at rent parties on homemade instruments, and the name was first used on record in 1928. While playing in Ken Colyer's Trad Jazz band, Donegan used to lead a small ensemble during breaks so the horn players could go off for a cigarette break or a hit of the lethal Merrydown cider. Drawing on blues, folk and country, the resultant acoustic music was easy to emulate. And it was that ease of access which appealed to the lazy John Lennon. The very first record John ever bought with his own money was Lonnie's 'Lost John', and it was Lonnie Donegan who inspired John Lennon to take his first faltering steps on the road which would lead to the wider world beyond Menlove Avenue.

John loved 'Lost John', he loved altering the lyrics ("if anybody asked you who sung the song, tell 'em John Lennon's been here and gone"). He loved the rambunctious, freewheeling Donegan repertoire of the hits which followed – 'Cumberland Gap', 'Bring a Little Water Sylvie', 'Puttin' On the Style'. Infectious songs, strong melodies, vibrant choruses, and easy to master on his cheap Gallotone guitar.

All across Liverpool the skiffle boom, led by Donegan, spread like wildfire. Paul McCartney was smitten: "Skiffle was great for getting us started, and Lonnie was a great live act to watch. I just loved it, used to go to a lot of his shows…"

It was the easy-to-master element of skiffle which appealed to the teenagers, but there was still a necessity to conquer the basics. "It became like a quest to find chords and records," Paul remembered for *Anthology*. "It was like looking for the Holy Grail. We would hear of some guy in Fazakerley – was *that* a long way away! It was like going across the world for us: this guy knows B7! We must all go on a journey".

In 2003, a few months after Lonnie Donegan died, I asked our premier rock knight to tell me a little more about Lonnie's influence on his music. "Well, there was a real primal energy to Lonnie's stuff back then," McCartney enthused. "He was great: 'Rock Island Line', 'Lost John' – I mean, you hear that in the middle of all those Dickie Valentines … and it's just very, very good! It was like hearing Elvis for the first time – only before. Lonnie was a giant!

"I don't remember entering any skiffle contests though. We entered talent contests but always lost! My mate was into skiffle, Cass (of Cass & The Casanovas) was a guy from our school, and we went along to support him. I remember going along to 'Jim Dale's National Skiffle Competition' to support Cass.

"The Quarrymen wasn't quite skiffle by the time I joined, it was a bit more Eddie Cochran, which I'd like to think was my influence. But John was certainly doing skiffle, it was all skiffle at the Woolton Village Fete, he even skiffle-ised 'Come Go With Me' by the Del-Vikings. He didn't have the record, so he didn't know the lyrics… it was 'Come, come, come, go with me, down, down, down, down, to the penitentiary'. He skiffle-ised that: 'penitentiary' is certainly not in that song.

"I ran into Lonnie in clubs sometimes, and I'd always go up and have a chat: 'You were it, man! You were the one!' I paid homage! I remember 'Footsteps in the Snow', Johnny Duncan & The Bluegrass Boys! Lonnie … Skiffle, man…!' And he shook his head… And for a moment, the man with the world at his feet was hurled back to a wide-eyed teenage enthusiast, his future uncertain."

Another Beatle was also spellbound; George's sister-in-law took him to see Lonnie in concert, during a week-long residency at the Liverpool Empire, in November 1956. George Harrison's brother Harry remembers 13-year-old George travelling to Speke to get Lonnie's autograph. And Arthur Kelly also remembered his friend George being utterly beguiled by 'Rock Island Line' and playing him the single. As he later told Beatle biographer Bob Spitz: "By the end of the afternoon, we said: 'let's get guitars!'"

A rare mention of Donegan in the wake of the groups he inspired came in the *Melody Maker* of 10 May 1964, bulging, as you would expect, with the Beatles. The report was from the set of *A Hard Day's Night* boasting the incongruous headline 'Lonnie Donegan Was My Idol'. As George Harrison explained: "Right in the very beginning, there was just

Lonnie Donegan. I suppose he really started most of the groups… It was hearing him that made me want to play the guitar…"

Lonnie was sanguine about the mantle being passed on ("The Beatles arrived on the scene, and I went out. It was as simple as that," he told me). In a symbolic shift, in 1962 Lonnie's last chart entry (the apt 'The Party's Over') was descending the UK charts just as 'Love Me Do' was making its ascent. The baton had been passed.

For a further 40 years, Lonnie persevered until his death in 2002. He carried on a career in cabaret, pantomime and toward the end, gained recognition from his peers like Van Morrison, Elton John, Mark Knopfler, Brian May, Eric Clapton and Ronnie Wood.

While the first records Ritchie Starkey remembered were by the Four Aces and Frankie Laine, it was Lonnie and skiffle which really registered. Ringo told me: "Lonnie? Oh yeah. He was great… I feel he influenced Liverpool. A lot of us thought: skiffle, wow. I was in skiffle groups, and the guy did have the tea-chest bass. And I'm in the band because I had a snare! And the guitarist who lived next door, Eddie, he could play a guitar. We just went on and did it. We had no sense of time or anything. But we were skiffling away.

"Lonnie was very influential in this country. And the big thing about Lonnie also was that he had a hit in America. And that was like wow, he's had a hit in America, he must be the great Lonnie Donegan now."

Interviewed for the Lonnie TV documentary, Ringo remembered:

"Lonnie opened all the doors to all of us because we could *do* that. Then
when we got a washboard player … yeah it was so simple, so popular, you
know, half of Liverpool started playing stuff, playing something every
street, it was huge, hundreds of bands".

As the skiffle craze exploded, in 1956 every aspect of UK society, art and politics shifted – nothing was ever quite the same again. The 12 months that made up 1956 really were cataclysmic. Changes do not always fall conveniently into calendar months. A period of 365 days is not always conveniently linked into its 12 months, but on occasion, its impact and repercussions spread far beyond these calendar restrictions.

In the UK, it was a year in which you can carbon-date the birth of the teenager. As well as Lonnie's first hits and the skiffle boom, Elvis Presley and Little Richard registered their first UK hits. *Giant*, the final film of the late James Dean, was released. And in London, John Osborne's play *Look Back in Anger* premiered, and announced the arrival of the Angry Young Men. On the world stage, the botched invasion of Suez marked the decline of Great Britain as a world power, and saw the mantle pass to America. The iron fist of the USSR was revealed as Russian tanks rolled in to crush the rebellion in Hungary.

On the home front, it was Lonnie's infectious personality and singalong anthems which fired up a generation. And it was that skiffle music which led John Lennon to push his education even further behind him as he formed his first group, the skiffle outfit which came to be known as the Quarrymen.

By 1957, Skiffle was everywhere: the *Daily Herald* was 'Calling All Skifflers' and offering £175 in 'cash prizes' to Donegan devotees, as part of a joint promotion with Butlin's. Meanwhile, the most ambitious skifflers queued up to audition for television shows like *The Carroll Levis Talent Show* and Hughie Green's *Opportunity Knocks*. Carroll Levis, aka 'Mr Star Maker', held an audition at Liverpool's Empire Theatre in

June 1957, in which local skiffle group the Quarrymen were beaten by the Sunnyside Skiffle Group from Speke.

And it was the formation of that group which led to the historic getting-together of Lennon and McCartney, which is where the story of the Beatles really begins. The catalyst for the historic fusion between Lennon and McCartney, and one of the unsung heroes in the Beatle story was Ivan Vaughan (1942–94). Paul McCartney told me while reminiscing on the skiffle era, "I never played a tea-chest bass! I played guitar. Always guitar even in the skiffle era. My friend Ivan (Vaughan) did the tea-chest bass, so there was never any call for me to".

In truth, Ivan Vaughan was much more than just a tea-chest bass player; he was a crucial catalyst in the history of the Beatles. Because he was the guy who thought that his mate Paul would get on well with his mate John, and then effected that historic introduction at the Woolton Village Fete in 1957.

It is fruitless, but fascinating, to speculate if that introduction had not been forged that day. I think it unlikely John would have sought Paul out; Ivan might have persevered at putting his two friends with so much in common together. But anything – scout camp, girlfriends, academic results – could have kept them apart. None of the Quarrymen could have filled the McCartney shoes. And Menlove Avenue was more than just geographically distant from Forthlin Road. Lennon and McCartney, feted to be apart, were joined by a simple twist of fate.

Many years later, I interviewed Ivan Vaughan. He was a courageous man, who had written a book about his battle with Parkinson's Disease, and how he had rejected medical orthodoxy and reliance on medication, choosing instead to wage his own solitary battle against the crippling disease. We went to a little pub in Cambridge for a drink, and talked about John, Paul, the Quarrymen, the boys, the men, the Beatles… Ivan said that when he first discovered he'd contracted the disease one of his first thoughts was to contact John.

It was during Lennon's half-decade away from the limelight; when he was holed up in the Dakota building, happy being a New York house-husband further removed than ever from Liverpool and the Quarrymen. Somehow though, Ivan told me, he managed to obtain a number for his teenage friend. He rang it tentatively and, when a voice answered, identified himself. "Well, if you're Ivan Vaughan," the voice from New York said, "what did you have written on your tea-chest bass?"

Casting his mind back over 20 years, to those teenage skiffling days, Ivan answered: "Jive With Ive; Your Ace On The Bass!" "That's right!" laughed a delighted Lennon, and the two set about repairing a friendship sundered by Beatlemania. In typical Lennon fashion, Ivan was delighted to receive a crate from New York after the phone call, full of everything his teenage friend could find on Parkinson's Disease. John died ten weeks later.

With the arrival of Elvis, Lonnie was on the verge of being swept away, and Lennon's schooling had slipped even further behind. To Mimi's constant despair, John locked himself away in his bedroom, mooning over pin-up pictures of his fantasy heroines. Or practising his guitar, his fingers fumbling round chords. Or like a freedom fighter, ear pressed against the radio, waiting for musical signals pulsing from far, far away to which he would respond. BBC radio policy on broadcasting rock & roll was about as sympathetic as its views on airing Communist propaganda. Occasionally though, Elvis would break through the static with one of his seven UK hit singles during 1956.

With his saturnine good looks and throbbing energy, Elvis was The King, overshadowing poor old Bill Haley, though the young Paul McCartney ("in short trousers…!") has memories of going to see the 'Rock Around The Clock' man. He told me: "Vic Lewis was on for the whole first half, and I thought fucking hell, 24 bob for this, and there's 12/- worth of Vic Lewis!" He laughed, then enthused, "Then the lights darkened for the second half. And it's 'One, two, three o'clock…' And it's 'Whooargh' … I was just *gone*. Tingles, goosebumps everything. And they were *great*. Tartan jackets, Rudy Pompilli, all the guys we'd seen on record covers, there they were".

Rounding up similar-minded schoolfellows for what from the beginning was *his* group, Lennon cajoled the Quarrymen into putting on shows wherever they could in and around Liverpool. Quarryman banjoist Rod Davis remembered that fateful day in 1957: "It was a village fete, a thing called the Rose Queen, and every year the church, some dignitary crowned the Rose Queen and we'd all travel around the village on the back of a lorry.

"So on Rosemary Street down in Liverpool 8, and just after that,
the local toughs from the street next door decided they were going to get
Lennon, so we dived into the house and stayed there, hoping they would
go away, but they didn't. So, we phoned for the police and a solitary
policeman came along and escorted us to the bus stop, so that's the first
incident of Beatlemania, you could say".

Throughout that year, Lennon's loyalties had been split between Lonnie Donegan and Elvis Presley. Elvis had liberated Lennon; he marvelled at Elvis, and admired him from afar. But Lennon had purchased all Lonnie's singles – and he knew that Lonnie was the one he could emulate.

All of Lonnie's hits made their way into young John's record collection. And early in 1957 he persuaded his long-suffering Aunt Mimi to stump up for a Gallotone Champion guitar – because it was like the one Lonnie Donegan played. By July, Lennon had mastered the essential skiffle chords E, A and B, and was well on his way to C and G. Years later, that same six guinea guitar would be sold again, this time at auction – for £155,000.

The Woolton Village Fete was a big event for the schoolboy musicians, and as the day wore on the Quarrymen started running through their jiving repertoire. The bulk of the teenagers' material that afternoon was skiffle: 'Midnight Special', 'Cumberland Gap', 'Bring a Little Water Sylvie', 'Rock Island Line' and 'Puttin' On the Style' – all of them learned by listening to Lonnie.

On the evening of 6 July 1957, Lennon's skiffle group the Quarrymen were booked to play their biggest gig to date. The Grand Dance in St Peter's Church Hall, marked the finale of that day's Woolton Parish Garden Fete – with the Quarrymen second on the bill, behind the older George Edwards Band.

In another of those you-couldn't-make-it-up moments which percolate Beatle history, a souvenir of that performance survived. 'Puttin' On the Style' is one of only two songs that still survive from the Quarrymen's performance on that long-ago summer evening. Recorded at the time, and miraculously having survived the intervening decades, the tape was sold at auction some 40 years later for £78,000.

In 1994, when the tape came up for auction, its owner Bob Molyneux was interviewed by Mark Lewisohn. He recalled lugging his 82 guinea GrundigTK8 around Liverpool ("and was rather popular for it"). He was in the same youth club as Lennon, and knew fellow Quarrymen Pete Shotton (1941–2017) and Rod Davis. That afternoon he remembered as being "just a typical summer's afternoon suburban garden fete, with lots of different stalls and people wandering around listening to the music as they went".

Where the event entered history was later that same evening. Bob returned ("after I'd gone home and had my tea"). He got to the hall where the regular Saturday night youth club events were held about eight. The Quarrymen appeared between sets by the George Edwards Band ("playing waltzes and foxtrots"). He remembered John as "clearly the leader of the group". Symbolically, as the evening sky grew dark, a thunderstorm fused the lights, thwarting Bob and his Grundig, plugged into the mains.

As a working journalist, I was allowed to hear snippets of the tape prior to its sale at the Sotheby's auction; and what was so odd was that, yes, it was undeniably John Lennon. The very same Lennon five years before his professional recording debut.

Besides being a genuine slice of 1950s skiffle, the tape offers a poignant taste of pre-Fab, pre-fame innocence. Because, of course, what really made that Quarrymen gig on 6 July 1957 so special, was what happened in the church hall afterwards. That was the moment *they* met for the first time… When 14-year-old James Paul McCartney of Allerton made the acquaintance of 16-year-old John Winston Lennon of Woolton. What happened to those two teenagers subsequently, would make the Quarrymen the best-known skiffle group in the world…

Bob Molyneux later joined the Liverpool Police in 1963, and remembers mentioning the tape to Ringo, who expressed no interest in the six-year-old recording. He would have been happy to give it to John, but no one got back in touch, so it remained in a bank vault until it came under the hammer.

That historic day inspired an entire book, Jim O'Donnell's *The Day John Met Paul* (Penguin, 1996). It is flawed ("The teenage Paul is a helter-skelter of raw emotions after his mother's death. The event sets an ocean liner of doubt adrift in the heretofore navigable waters of his life"). However, it is a testament to the author's zeal that you keep turning each page. You *know* how it all ends. But that meeting is evocatively constructed in a history that has the pace of a thriller. This is *The Day of the Jackal* of rock biography.

Sixty years after that gig in Woolton, the Quarrymen's washboard player Pete Shotton, still had no doubts about the group's major inspiration: "Lonnie Donegan was the Messiah," he told *Record Collector*. "Up to then, you had to have professional tuition and had to learn the chords. Lonnie comes along and says 'You can all play music. Get a drum and bang on it, get a tea-chest bass and twang the string, get a washboard, it doesn't matter whether you're good or bad, just enjoy it.' He took the music from the professionals to grass roots, street-corner stuff, which was brilliant."

Years later, in the Beatles' ever-desperate search for a drummer, Rod Davis popped up when he bumped into John who offered him a return to the group, this time on the drum stool. But Rod's mother chided, "He's not going to Hamburg with *that* Lennon". The chippy, lippy "that Lennon" was the teenager that worried parents did *not* want their children to become. A rebellious teenager, a seat-slashing Teddy Boy.

While it was two of the Quarrymen who went on to become legends, in another of those extraordinary coincidences which pepper the Beatle history the Quarrymen's banjo player Rod Davis later re-appears. While studying at Cambridge, Rod jumped on the Trad Jazz bandwagon. His university group the Trad Grads released a single ('Rag Day Jazz Band Ball') in 1964, on Decca, the label which had earlier declined the services of the Beatles.

Then, rather eerily, in another of those extraordinary moments, Rod was in London pursuing a lead in his travel expedition business early in 1969: "I found myself walking down Savile Row", he told Hunter Davies. "I heard the unmistakable sound of The Beatles coming from the rooftops. They were playing what turned out to be their last live performance. I stood there listening to them in the cold, until I had to leave for my appointment. It was", the Quarry Man recalled, "the only time I ever heard The Beatles play live…!"

Back when the Quarrymen were still together, Lennon's drive and enthusiasm overcame any doubts he may have had about his own musical abilities. Too idle to pursue his school work, too lazy to adhere to artistic discipline; too feeble for boxing; too rebellious to join the army or police force, and not hard enough for a life of crime – music was to be Lennon's 'out' of provincial Liverpool.

It was with the arrival of the younger McCartney, obviously possessed of a musical knowledge far superior to that of the Quarrymen's leader, that a new phase began. Paul joining John's group also coincided with the waning of the skiffle phenomenon.

By the time of that historic Quarrymen gig in July 1957, Elvis had enjoyed his first UK No.1 single, while Gene Vincent and Little Richard had also left their mark. In the wings, Buddy Holly, the Everly Brothers, Jerry Lee Lewis and Eddie Cochran were revving up. Now, British teenagers no longer wanted to travel down the Rock Island Line. They had a new clarion call: "Awopbopaloobopalopbamboom…!"

Barely into his teens, George Harrison had been equally mesmerised by the cannon blast of rock & roll and, with a diligence which later characterised him, came to master the guitar that an elder brother had passed down. George was not a 'joiner', and it was only a chance encounter with school acquaintance Paul McCartney on one of those long bus journeys to school which later brought him into the Quarrymen's orbit.

On the other side of town, as the Quarrymen switched allegiance to Elvis, Ritchie Starkey remained enamoured of the skiffle craze. But with his schooling virtually non-existent due to all his childhood illnesses, Ritchie drifted through a succession of dead-end jobs.

But, running from the tough gangs in Garston and the dreariness of the future in Liverpool, Ritchie was determined to cast his net wider. He told me: "I tried [to emigrate to America], at 19. We went down to the Consulate and got the papers. The first set were fine, we filled them up, my friend John and I, and we were going to Houston, because Lightning Hopkins lived there, and I wanted to be where Lightning Hopkins was – because he's my all-time blues hero. So we were gonna go to Houston. Then we were given another set of forms, and it was pretty difficult in the 50s. I was the teenager who wouldn't fill that form in – ah fuck it, go to the pub! So we never got there!"

The drums remained a constant though, and with the skiffle boom still clinging on,

Ritchie got his first gig with the Eddie Clayton Skiffle Group, then moved on to the Raving Texans, who morphed into Rory Storm & the Hurricanes. Ritchie was happy with Rory, who he recognised as a great front man. By all accounts, Rory was the most charismatic of all the Merseybeat singers, but like so many was swept aside by the all-conquering Beatles.

Talking to me about the skiffle period, Ringo remembered: "My first kit of drums I went to Hessy's to look at these drums and in '58 could just

about afford to get them on the HP … It was

going to be like eleven quid extra on the hire purchase and I went and asked me

grandad for the money, and he gave me … 'Ah, where am I gonna get that

sort of money.' Anyway, next day he got it and so I paid him back a pound a week.

So, yeah, I had a kit, but I couldn't take it anywhere,

you know. You'd be helped to a gig, but you're on your own after the gig because

everyone's pulling (laughs), and so I just ended up taking a snare drum".

Even with those few-and-far-between Quarrymen shows, John Lennon's schooling was in a parlous state. Contemptuous of the authority offered by the school from which his group took their name, he sloughed through his last years. Predictably, at a time when exam results mattered and counted for steady employment in the future, Lennon failed every one of his all-important O-Levels. Lazy and surly, Lennon was heading for the dole.

Very little of what was taught the recalcitrant Lennon registered. In later years though, Lewis Carroll remained – I think one reason why I was so drawn to Lewis Carroll in this book is that *Alice* … would have been familiar to all four of the group. And there was something familiar but dissociative in her Adventures which to me captured the dislocating turbulence of the *Pepper* period. For John, at Quarry Bank, as well as Alice, something registered: Edgar Allan Poe on 'I Am the Walrus', and J. Milton Hayes' 'The Green Eye of the Little Yellow God', which cropped up many years later on 'Nobody Told Me'.

It was only the prescience of John's head teacher, the Dickensian-sounding Mr Pobjoy, who recognised an elusive something in the surly teenager. It is to William Pobjoy's eternal credit that he intuited an artistic bent in his reluctant pupil. It was at his teacher's insistence that John managed to gain an entrance to the heady world of Bohemia. Liverpool Art School was where John began in September 1957. Like so many of his peers, Lennon found the atmosphere liberating – you could smoke! There were girls! Beginning in the style of a Teddy Boy, John soon switched to the more Left Bank look of the art student, and revelled in the freedom. Bonding with like-minded pupils of his own age, the Quarrymen took a back seat.

Lennon fared no better at Art School. He was lazy and inattentive; his teachers discerned no real talent. The little work he bothered with was derivative and unoriginal. His second-year report found him ninth out of a class of 13. Predictably he lounged and slacked, a teacher's report gave the reason why: "Give up your guitar, otherwise you will never pass your exams".

In keeping with the arty image which he was busy cultivating, and with the Quarrymen occupying less and less of his time, John finally left the comfort of Mendips and moved into a student flat. The Gambier Terrace apartment was legendary in its squalor. "It was an art student's flat", Paul remembered when we spoke in 1999, "very bare, very empty, no furniture, but there was a mattress on the floor, a candle by the bed, ashtray and a record player and a little stack of records. Kind of all you needed.

"Me and George, because we were a bit younger, that was the first time I'd ever stayed out at someone's flat. And we stayed up all night, beer and ciggies mainly… most dangerous we got was to undo the Benzedrine inhalers and sniff 'em… I remember waking up, burning eyes job, and one of the guys just put on Johnny Burnette's 'Honey Hush' … a real favourite place and memory".

It was in the freedom at the Gambier Terrace flat that John also found a soulmate in his art school buddy, Stuart Sutcliffe. Musically, Stuart played a peripheral role in the Beatles story. His friendship with John, however, was perhaps the strongest of Lennon's life. It was John's prompting which enrolled Stuart in the Beatle orbit, although one in which he was never fully at home. But it did give the talented painter the opportunity for love to blossom during his short life in distant Germany.

While still schoolboys, Paul and George used to skive off at lunchtime to John's artistic paradise next door. For the young Harrison it made a strong impression. "It was unbelievably relaxed," he said in *Anthology*. "Everybody was smoking or eating egg and chips, while we still had school cabbage and boiled grasshoppers. And there'd be chicks and arty types, everything… We could go in there and smoke without anyone giving us a bollocking".

Six months before the Quarrymen's gig in Woolton, a crucial location was introduced into the Beatle story. Latterly, the bourgeois Abbey Road and Savile Row became indelibly linked to their history. But long before any of them had ventured south to London, a Liverpool cellar was to prove formative.

*

By the mid-1950s, Paris was the condition that everyone aspired to. It led the field in fashion, food and philosophy. Strong French cigarettes were painfully inhaled to a soundtrack of sultry chanteuse Juliette Greco. Pin-up posters of Brigitte Bardot filled teenage walls… Yves Saint-Laurent and Pierre Cardin led from the front in fashion in the 50s. Ambitious and black-clad teenagers around the world cultivated a disillusioned, existential air over Gitanes and black coffee.

It was at Parisian cafes like the Deux Magots, where Sartre and de Beauvoir smoked and existentialised, that 'cool' was contained. Left Bank bars became magnets for disaffected youth in search of that elusive 'something' in the period of liberation. All around Saint-Germain, wraith-like, intense existential drifters existed on a diet of coffee, cigarettes, vin ordinaire and baguettes while they grappled with the real issues of the day.

American rock & roll was slow making its mark in the French capital, jazz was the soundtrack to the city. Paris provided a home for black American musicians. They had grown tired of the institutionalised racism at home, persecuted by the red-hunting hounds of the McCarthy witch hunts and were welcomed by the jazz-crazy zazous of the French capital. Sidney Bechet, Dexter Gordon and Bud Powell were only some of the jazz emigres who made their home in Paris. Miles Davis, the king of cool, enjoyed a long affair with Juliette Greco in the City of Light.

And to play host to 'le jazz hot', clubs opened as frequently as bottles of vin rouge. The best known was the Tabou on the Rue Dauphine, the template for the subterranean club which was to provide the Beatles with their Liverpool platform. One visitor described, "A tunnel of a room, some 15 metres by eight, with bare brick walls curving into a low vaulted ceiling … a bar, an ill-tuned piano, a gramophone and a few tables and chairs".

It was precisely the sort of place that jazz lover and Francophile Alan Sytner (1935–2006) had in mind when he visited Paris. But could it work on Merseyside? The young son of a GP, and part of the city's Jewish community which also numbered Brian Epstein, Alan had first been to Paris as a teenager: "I could go to jazz clubs and see the Bohemian life," he told Spencer Leigh. "I was dazzled by it and it was all part of the glamour of Paris after the war". It was a subterranean descent to Caveau de la Huchette which flicked the switch.

Using the money that had matured on his 21st birthday, Alan had run a jazz club in suburban Croxteth but, chancing upon a vacant cellar in a narrow street not far from the docks, Alan had found his own ideal venue: "Matthew Street looked like a little narrow street in the Latin Quarter in Paris, so I felt I was bringing the Left Bank to Liverpool".

The Cavern opened with a jazz gig by the Merseysippi Jazz Band on 16 January 1957, and remained primarily a jazz venue. As well as it being his music of choice, Alan's musical policy coincided with the Trad Jazz boom, although Alan Sytner's doctrinaire policy did allow skiffle, as the genre could trace its roots back to jazz. The first Beatle to play the Cavern was Ringo Starr on 31 July 1957, when he took the drum stool with the Eddie Clayton Skiffle Group.

Infamously the second Beatle to take the Cavern stage was John Lennon. Three weeks after that historic meeting with Paul McCartney, John was performing at the Cavern. But the young Paul was not with him, outdoor activities held more allure. Lennon led the Quarrymen through their skiffle set, which by the time they took to the stage in August 1957 was edging more towards rock & roll. And that was one thing the Cavern owner would not countenance. As the Quarrymen launched into their fledgling Elvis repertoire, John gleefully announced, "We've had a request". Over the years, the actual wording used may be in dispute, but Quarrymen drummer Colin Hanton said it was from Alan Sytner and read succinctly: "cut out the bloody rock & roll."

The Cavern had an absolute capacity of 300, and played a key role in the history of all the Liverpool groups who played there. It was unlicensed and the over-riding memory of fans and bands alike was the smell. Unappealingly, body odour, urine; the stench of decaying fruit and vegetables from the Matthew Street market and disinfectant all mingled in an unappealing miasma. An unanswered key question in the history of Merseybeat remains: was it Dettol or Jeys Fluid which was used to kill the rats at The Cavern and provide that lingering aroma?

While the drive of Lennon and McCartney has been flagged many times, I always found it touching and symptomatic that Paul did not officially join the Quarrymen until October 1957 – the delay due to his schoolboy enthusiasm to attend scout camp. Mind you, he was not alone. It has been estimated that Baden-Powell's *Scouting for Boys* is the fourth most popular book in the world, after the Bible, the Koran and Mao's *Little Red Book*.

Having dib-dib-dibbed, and once back on board, the Quarrymen locked together. But it was the stellar partnership of Paul and John which drove them forward. Talking to Quarrymen guitarist Len Garry many years later, he admitted that for the rest, it was a schoolboy thing, a lark, but that the two principals were *really* motivated. For the others it was little more than a distraction. Being in a group helped you meet girls, got you free drinks. Being onstage elevated you above your contemporaries. It wasn't all fish & finger pies & brown ale though, pity poor Colin Hanton, having to drag his drum kit across town – by bus.

Thanks again to the diligence of Mark Lewisohn, we can chronicle those glamorous Quarrymen gigs – the Cavern! The Conservative Club!! Stanley Abattoir Social Club!!! It wasn't the London Palladium, or indeed, the Liverpool Empire, but the venues provided stage room for teenagers to show off, and topped up their pocket money by a few bob.

While Lennon idled his days away at art school, for Paul and George next door at "the Inny", the music was becoming even more important during their formative years. Following the death of Paul's mother, the older McCartney persevered with his music, even fashioning his own songs, an unheard-of accomplishment. George too put his head down and mastered the fingering on his guitar neck. Even before he was 15, George had mastered relatively complex guitar parts from the hit records of the period.

The shock of Julia's death under the wheels of a car driven by an off-duty policeman when John was only 18 infused the boy with an anger and carved a deep groove on the teenager's shoulder. It was that tragedy which further bonded the Lennon and McCartney partnership. The death of a parent is always upsetting, to a teenager it marks the final severing of adolescence. When Julia died, 18-year-old John Lennon put away childish things.

College left Lennon unengaged, and back at home, he was chivvied by Mimi. It was his general attitude, his surliness, his unwillingness to conform, his reliance on the guitar... There was Mimi's famous advice, "The guitar's all right for a hobby, John, but you'll never make a living out of it" (rather sweetly, years later, some American fans had it made into a plaque and presented to her).

Lennon was capable of pulling the wool over Mimi's eyes. On his return from Hamburg in 1960, John somehow convinced Mimi he had re-enrolled at Art College, but her suspicions were aroused when she "heard that John was being seen playing with the Beatles at this cave place".

It was getting out of that stifling atmosphere at Mendips which drew John closer to Paul and, with Jim out at work, the McCartney family home offered the art student and the truant schoolboy a sanctuary. In a moment of teenage rock & roll reminiscence, Paul told me: "I didn't know I was going to be a musician, it just filled my brain all that stuff... And when I met John, it filled his brain too, so we'd just sit around in his bedroom or my bedroom, or the front vestibule, sometimes if Aunt Mimi wouldn't let us in the house ... it had a good echo I often think that got me through a lot of misery – John and I both losing our mothers when we were teenagers. I'm sure the cradling of the guitar, and the holding of this beautiful shape to you... It's certainly very satisfying for me".

While John had a chip shop full of frites on his shoulder, from an early age, Paul had shown a determination to write his own material, something which not even the ambitious

Lennon had fully realised. Lazy and always going for the easy option, learning other people's songs was less hard work. Creating something original required more effort.

Talking about the early days of that crucial partnership, Paul told me: "We went to the pictures, that's the only other thing we did; we went to the pictures, or sat at each other's house doing music. So these are the soundtracks to that period of our lives. So to me it's all walking down Menlove Avenue or Mather Avenue, guitars over our backs, walking through the golf course, or Calderstones Park, playing – walking along, playing like a couple of minstrels. We just loved it so much. So that's where it all came from".

We now know that Paul's first ever composition was 'I Lost My Little Girl', which he wrote when he was 14, soon after the death of his mother Mary. In tandem with John, the teenagers persevered – Paul thought that the first in that blue-lined school notebook was 'Too Bad About Sorrows'. Others included 'Keep Looking That Way', 'Just Fun', … Though how many of them actually developed beyond titles after nearly 60 years remains unclear.

When I spoke to him he grew endearingly nostalgic about one of those early 'lost' songs 'Thinking of Linking': "My greatest memory was George remembering this song that only he and I, in the whole universe could have known. It was at the Gaumont in Allerton where I used to live. He'd come up and we'd go to the pictures and there was an advert on for Link Furniture. It said, 'Thinking of linking? Getting married? You'll need some furniture'. It was all that terrible G-Plan, brown shiny stuff.

"We used to have a laugh about that, but I thought – you know me – not a bad one, 'Thinking of Linking'… a bit Buddy Holly-ish so we did this 'Well I've been thinking of linking my love with you, thinking of linking a love so true, thinking of linking can only be done by two…' and George did these lovely little Buddy guitar riffs.

"Years later we're doing this thing for *Anthology* and George starts playing that riff. And it was like fucking hell. It was like whipping the curtain back. I hadn't heard that song in 40 years – nobody could've. And if George had not remembered it, it would just have gone, because I'd forgotten it completely".

Just prior to his death, John told *Playboy* that he remembered his first song as 'Hello Little Girl' (later dispatched to the Epstein-managed Fourmost for their debut hit). "It was a play on that song from the 30s or 40s, 'it's delightful, it's delicious'… It was probably connected to my mother, she used to sing that one".

I love the later picture of what would become rock music's most influential and widely imitated partnership at the beginning of their career, huddled together by the Forthlin Road fireplace, one long-ago afternoon in the last century. Thanks to Paul's left-handed ability, their mirror image guitars sweep over a notebook of "Lennon & McCartney Originals", little knowing that the song visible ('I Saw Her Standing There') would open their debut LP and allow them to leave Liverpool and all their teenage anxieties behind.

What is so intriguing is just how many of those pre-Parlophone, Forthlin Road songs did eventually make their way into the Beatle repertoire: among them 'One After 909', 'I'll Be on My Way', 'When I'm 64', 'I'll Follow the Sun'…

While Paul was bonding with John, George was also finding fellowship with his schoolboy chum. Together, Paul and George would share the long bus journeys to school then, when Paul felt the time was right, Paul introduced his young friend to the older, intimidating John. While looking his age, George's playing belied his youthful exterior. He recalled it was the sight of Slim Whitman playing the guitar which had a profound influence on him. George remembered his dad Harold bringing back a record player from his days in the merchant navy. "He'd also brought some records from America," George remembered for *Anthology*, "including one by Jimmie Rodgers, 'The Singing Brakeman'. He was Hank Williams' favourite singer and the first country singer that I ever heard… My dad had 'Waiting for a Train', that led me to the guitar".

But it was his mastery of Link Wray's 'Raunchy' which persuaded John to let him join the Quarrymen.

With much of his formal education spent drawing guitars, or trying to slip past teachers in his modified Teddy Boy school uniform, George eased out of school with minimum qualifications. The future stared bleakly ahead and, with Quarrymen gigs guaranteeing little in the way of a regular income, 16-year-old George began his first job as a trainee electrician. "Always carry a screwdriver in your top pocket" was sound advice the trainee received. As was the way with the world back then, George undertook a five-year apprenticeship. If he had persevered, it would have ended in 1964. But by then, 21-year-old George Harrison had already taken another career path.

George's youth was always a factor, he was patronised by Lennon, with all the wisdom and experience the three-years-older John could bring to bear. Yet he seemed somehow worldly-wise: bearded and mysterious, while recording *Sgt Pepper*, George was a mere 24. When I reflect upon myself in my twenties, I still find it hard to credit that George was only 26 when he *left* the Beatles.

As teenagers, all were keen to escape a future which could, at best, be described as 'unpromising'. They pined for smart suits, the latest singles and LP records. They dreamed of motor cars, the lure of London, the far-away Shangri La of the USA. In the chill northern port, all four Beatles pressed their noses against shop windows, drooling over guitars, shiny drum kits and amplifiers. Located in the main shopping street of Whitechapel, just along from the North End Music Stores, Hessy's was the cynosure for all the Liverpool musicians. With its windows full of the latest gleaming guitars and dazzling drum kits, the store was the ideal stopping-off point for every wannabe Shadow.

With the wide post-war availability of Hire Purchase (HP, nicknamed 'Live Now, Pay Later') even those previously dreamed-of but unattainable instruments were within reach. That was, provided a responsible adult signed the forms, which is what Mimi Smith did when she splashed out £15 for her nephew's first guitar. Years later, Hessy's still exuded its magnetic power, when a young D.P. MacManus (better known as Paul McCartney's writing partner, Elvis Costello) purchased a Rickenbacker there "formerly owned by George Harrison".

Hessy's was where they stood and coveted. It was the window of dreams. And they dreamed… They all dreamed. Long and hard, they all dreamed. Of course, then they had no way of knowing that those teenage dreams would be realised. At one meeting with Paul McCartney at his Central London HQ, we were interrupted because a guitar manufacturer wanted to present him with a custom-made, Paul McCartney model. He rolled his eyes, "I've *got* guitars; when I needed guitars was 20 years ago!"

Once again, at another meeting, the rock & roll of his youth came back to haunt him.

Drive my car… the first fruits of fame

I was interviewing Paul in his Sussex studio, and on the way out remarked on the double bass standing in the corner. "Linda bought it for me," he smiled, "it's the one Bill Black played on 'Heartbreak Hotel.'" I mouthed, "Oh. Wow!" The world's best-known left-handed bass player then twirled the instrument and plucked out the first notes of the Elvis hit. Then leaned it reverently back. We both stood, united in a brief reverie, then shook hands, and went our separate ways, to our different worlds.

*

"George and I hitch-hiked to Wales, and we had *Elvis Golden Records: Volume 1* that whole week," Paul McCartney told me in 1999. "'Trying to Get to You', I still get goose pimples thinking about that – I was at Scout Camp for that one!"

By the summer of 1958, the skiffle boom had peaked and, while Elvis still reigned as King of Rock & Roll, there were now the other contenders for the crown. And the one which connected directly with the Quarrymen was a singer-songwriter, barely in his 20s, whose hiccupping vocals and shuffling rhythms they were eager to emulate. For the myopic Lennon, there was also the image of Charles Hardin Holley, a rock & roll star confident enough to sport black-rimmed glasses like his own.

It was the vulnerability of Buddy Holly which found such appeal in teenagers of the period. Gawky and bespectacled, barely older than the audience he was addressing, Buddy was accessible and easy to emulate, unlike the remote, alluring Elvis, described as a "delicious hunk of forbidden fruit".

Buddy Holly was a man ahead of his time, one of the few legends whose tragically premature death robbed rock music of a talent which could only have developed. On the evidence of the final solo tracks he recorded in his Greenwich Village apartment in January 1959, a few weeks before his death, a strong case can be made for Buddy Holly as a fledgling singer-songwriter, a bridge from the rocking 50s to the folk-singing early 1960s. Buddy was the first artist of the rock era to use strings on a record, and he was a fine interpreter of other people's material – Paul Anka's 'It Doesn't Matter Anymore'; Sonny West's 'Rave On'; Chuck Berry's 'Brown Eyed Handsome Man'.

But it is as a rock & roll pioneer and with his own material that his reputation was built – the bracing 'Peggy Sue', 'Well… All Right', and, particularly, 'That'll Be the Day'. Not enough credit has been given to that 1956 John Wayne film *The Searchers*. It gave a name to the second- best group to come out of Liverpool, and Wayne's catchphrase gave Holly the title for his first hit. And perhaps most significantly, 'That'll Be the Day' marked the first-ever recording of John Lennon, Paul McCartney and George Harrison. Apt then that one of cinema's enduring masterpieces should also provide a starting point for the world's most influential band.

Accompanied by drummer Colin Hanton and, occasional Quarryman, pianist John 'Duff' Lowe (1942–2024), the quintet made their way to a recording studio in the Liverpool suburb of Kensington. Abbey Road it wasn't … but the 15 square foot ground floor of Percy Phillips (1895–1984) property did have thick curtains, microphones, a tape recorder and the equipment to transfer the tape to a vinyl acetate. For 17/6d (87½p) 'That'll Be the Day' was committed to disc. Even Mark Lewisohn cannot confirm the *actual* date of the session, but it is likely to have occurred around the time of Holly's sole UK tour in the spring of 1958. As well as the Holly homage, the boys tackled 'In Spite of all the Danger', a unique McCartney/Harrison composition.

It was not the quality of the material which makes the 10", 78 rpm Percy Phillips' recording the single most valuable in rock & roll, but the fact that it marked the precious beginning of something so substantial which none of those taking part could have conceived. However obvious, it is worth emphasising that none involved had a 'career' in mind when they exited Percy Phillips' property. That disc was a lark, something to wow girls with, maybe even land them a few more bookings.

Each of the group were allowed ownership of the precious piece of disc, to play to parents and impress girlfriends, proof positive that there was something in their decision to pursue music. Here was the evidence.

The acetate was thought lost for decades, until Duff Lowe, who had been the last of the group to take it home to play, contacted Paul many years later and, for considerably more than 17/6d, sold it to him. Paul ran off vinyl copies, leased it to Apple for *Anthology 1* and hung on to the original. And that is what makes 'That'll Be the Day' by the Quarrymen what *Record Collector* called "the most valuable record in the world". Kept in a sock drawer for years by Duff, it is now valued at £150,000.

Duff's musical career rather dwindled on quitting the Quarrymen in 1959. He was headhunted by Ricky Tomlinson, later a stalwart of British TV, for his group Hobo Rick & the City Slickers. And that was that.

The Quarrymen missed Buddy's Liverpool show, as they had a gig that night. But like virtually every British teenager of the period, at least three of the Beatles, Mick Jagger, Richard Thompson, Keith Richards, Pete Townshend, Bruce Welch, Hank Marvin … all hunkered down to see Buddy Holly in action on television. Buddy made his UK TV debut on the popular *Sunday Night at the London Palladium* on 2 March 1958. Sheridan Morley told me that it was his father, the actor Robert Morley who actually introduced Buddy as "an act who has a nice festive feel to his name … Buddy *Holly!*"

As well as seeing and hearing Buddy, the generation who would come to dominate the 1960s music scene were as spellbound by Buddy in action with his distinctive Fender Stratocaster. Huddling close to the pinched black and white television set, the likes of Lennon, McCartney and Harrison were mesmerised by Holly's hands on the neck, trying to figure out how he fingered those chords.

Perhaps because he is tied in to so many of their teenage memories, Buddy Holly occupies a special place in the Beatles history. Many years later, on learning that song catalogues could be bought and profited from, Paul's MPL company snapped up the Buddy Holly catalogue. And when four LPs of Buddy's complete recordings were re-released in 1968, four sets made their way to Apple's HQ.

Holly's 'Crying, Waiting, Hoping' was in their repertoire, and appeared on *The Beatles at the BBC;* 'Words of Love' of course helped pad out *Beatles for Sale.* And during the dog days of the *Let It Be* sessions at the end of their career, the Beatles busked Buddy's 'Mailman, Bring Me No More Blues' (it eventually appeared on *Anthology 3*).

For a Buddy Holly Week event, Paul spoke to me about the young American's influence: "There was the approachability of his stuff, because they were just three chords, which was the stage we were at – A, D and E. Maybe C, F and G7, if pushed… Also he was one of the first people to play his own instrument. We were learning to play our own instruments and play at the same time, which was very un-Elvis, very un-Cliff…"

When pushed for his favourite Buddy song, Paul told me: "'That'll Be the Day' because it was the first… 'Think It Over' because I have a particular memory of me, John and George going to do the *Carroll Levis Discoveries* at Ardwick Green in Manchester, a big ABC cinema, where he was holding his auditions. We didn't have a full line-up, had to borrow guitars, and John just stood between us with his arms around me and George singing 'Think It Over', which is a cute memory, even if we didn't win".

One can only speculate at the influence Buddy Holly could have exerted had he lived beyond the tender age of 22. Certainly those last solo tracks (notably 'Crying, Waiting, Hoping' and 'Learning the Game') indicate a confidence in his own material and a willingness to try something new and switch direction. We shall never know. I would take issue with biographer Philip Norman that Buddy Holly was "the century's most influential musician", but I certainly agree that he was taken too soon, and with so much more to offer. 3 February 1959 wasn't the day the music died, but it did mark the end of an era. And those who were about to inherit the Holly mantle were in the wings, crying, and certainly waiting, and hoping…

Another American who held an equal place in teenage Beatle hearts was Eddie Cochran, who played a residency at the Liverpool Empire in 1960. It was Paul's confident cover of Eddie's '20 Flight Rock' which convinced John to let him join his group. Eddie not only looked cool, he sounded great. Again, one of the few rock & rollers whose early death left a tantalising 'What If…?' over a career cut short. Eddie, with girlfriend Sharon Sheeley, wrote and played much of his own material. Barely out of his teens, he had mastered studio technology; technically, he was way ahead as a guitar player. And he looked like James Dean.

Eddie's songs soon found their way into the early Beatle repertoire, and I would cite his 'Somethin' Else' as perhaps the quintessential 50s rock & roll record. Cochran's tragic death in 1960 was a bookmark on an era: Elvis came out of the Army muted and tamed; Jerry Lee Lewis had been hounded out of the UK; both Carl Perkins and Gene Vincent had been seriously injured in car crashes; Little Richard had denounced rock & roll; Buddy Holly and Eddie Cochran were dead…

White bread rock & roll was the mood of the moment. But fledgling Beatle ears were open to every musical nuance. "We normally hated Pat Boone," Paul told me, "but he did one 'Friendly Persuasion' from the movie. I trekked all the way out to Aintree to see it, and it was just the title song. It was really just a movie about the Amish people … but I still find it a very tender song, beautiful melody".

Anything and everything American was venerated – cars, movies, hamburgers, refrigerators, Coca Cola, 45s… "We all got this big turn-on from America," Paul laughed, "those people, ever so exciting records, much better than Dennis Lotis, who was for the Mums and Dads. Dickie Valentine, he was massive 'spit on me Dickie', that was what the girls used to shout… I remember that, clear as a bell".

Following the death of John's mother, the absence of anything approaching a regular income from shows, together, with parental disapproval, the loose aggregation of

Quarrymen almost ceased to exist. Drummer Colin Hanton quit after a row, and George Harrison found their absence of gigs alarming, so sided with the Les Stuart Quartet. But when they failed to honour a booking at a newly-opened club, George called in Paul and John, and Les Stuart's bassist Ken Brown, who had been a Quarryman for only six weeks.

So, for a spell during the late summer of 1959, the Quarrymen came close to something approaching a residency when the Casbah Coffee Club opened in West Derby. Such was the promise, that the opening night even made it onto the front page of the *West Derby Reporter*.

Another peripheral but nonetheless crucial figure in Beatle history was Mona Best (1924–88). Born in India when it was still part of the Empire, Mona married an English army officer with whom she had two sons, Peter and Rory. With independence looming, the Best family left India and in 1945 settled in Liverpool. Moving to a large family home on the outskirts of town, Mona always encouraged her children and, seeing that Pete particularly enjoyed music, bought him a drum kit.

Between the end of skiffle and the birth of Merseybeat, there remained a thriving scene for the city's teenagers. While the Cavern adhered to its jazz policy, Mona Best recognised that another venue for youngsters to sit and sip Coke through straws or get a milky lip with cappuccino would be welcome. Mona's favourite film was the Charles Boyer weepie *Algiers*, boasting the immortal line "Come with me to the Casbah…" (although, like many mythical Hollywood lines, it was never uttered in the film). But the very name suggested mystery, romance and exoticism, so the basement of the Best home at 8 Haymans Green was transformed.

The 15-room house, formerly home to the West Derby Conservative Club, came into the Bests' possession after Mona had put a bet on a 33–1 outsider in 1957; 'Never Say Die' was ridden to victory by an unknown Lester Piggott. While never rivalling the Cavern, over its three-year span, as well as the nascent Beatles, the Casbah hosted the Remo Four, the Searchers and Gerry & the Pacemakers. The club closed in 1962, soon after Pete was dismissed from the group who used to play there. It reopened in 2002, and in 2006 was granted Grade II listed building status.

Through interlocking and circuitous roots, the Quarrymen landed a residency at the new club, and it was only a row over fees which led to them leaving. "Residency", "repertoire" and "concert" are too fanciful to describe the teenagers' turn during those Saturday night shows. John, Paul, George and … Ken played a run of gigs there in late 1959. They were still effectively a schoolboy band, whose repertoire was covers of the day's hits. The transatlantic magic of Buddy Holly, Gene Vincent, Little Richard, Chuck Berry, Carl Perkins, the Coasters, Fats Domino and Eddie Cochran held sway.

Bill Harry, who was especially close to the group during their formative years, later wrote: "The Casbah Club played an important part in the career of the Beatles. If it had not opened, the Quarrymen would probably not have re-formed, and there never would have been any Beatles".

Blundering into the history of the Beatles around this time came energetic hustler Allan Williams (1930–2016). Never quite the Svengali figure he would later cast himself as, he was older and, his beard masking a gritty determination, he soon took the Quarrymen under his wing. Williams was an ineffectual organiser. He kept too many balls in the air and switched loyalties as the mood took him. But his was another of those links in the chain, rungs on the ladder, which led a bunch of snotty schoolboys to become *the* entertainment phenomenon of modern times.

As well as helping them decorate his Jacaranda club, Williams got the group prestige bookings, such as backing Janice the stripper. Crucially, more by luck than judgement, it was Allan who got them their first trip abroad. However, prior to that, and tired of waiting, two of the group made an epic pilgrimage south…

Were you perhaps drinking in Berkshire's Fox & Hounds in Caversham the last weekend of April 1960? Would you have been struck by the performing brilliance of 'The Nerk Twins'? Or Paul McCartney and John Lennon as they were better known to themselves. The pub was run by Paul's cousin Betty, and in exchange for helping out behind the bar, the two future Beatles sat on bar stools and played to customers on Saturday night and Sunday lunchtime. The only known song performed was Les Paul & Mary Ford's 'The World Is Waiting for the Sunrise', although 'Be-Bop-A-Lula' was rumoured. It marked the first ever 'Beatle' performance outside Liverpool.

Back on their home turf, while running the Casbah, Mona Best recognised a nascent something in the early Beatles, and began organising bookings for them in and around Liverpool. Only much later was it revealed that the Bests' lodger, and Beatle roadie, Neil Aspinall, had an affair with Mona, siring a son, Roag. And that surely must have further muddied the waters when Pete was fired by Brian Epstein in 1962.

In the first months of the first year of the new decade, something happened to the Quarrymen… They were offered a professional engagement, but for that they needed a drummer. Spinal Tap had more luck than the Beatles with drummers. Long before Ringo there was, infamously, Pete Best, before him: Quarry Man Colin Hanton, the hapless Tommy Moore, Norman Chapman, Paul McCartney(!). The subsequent dismissal of Pete Best would have had a familiar ring to Quarryman Eric Griffiths (1940–2005), summarily dismissed by the group's 'manager' Nigel Whalley, on the say so of John, Paul and George, none of whom had the bottle to tell him to his face.

A McCartney letter was auctioned in 2011 in answer to an ad in the *Liverpool Echo*, offering the applicant "an audition for the position of drummer… You will, however, need to be free soon for a trip to Hamburg (expenses paid £18 per week (approx.) for 2 months". Neatly written, smartly punctuated, and communicating via the "Jacaranda Club (ROYal 6544) and ask for either a member of the 'Beatles', Allan Williams, or else leave a message…"

On a 1962 tour with Joe Brown, Brian Epstein approached drummer Bobby Graham asking him if he'd like to replace Pete Best? "Why would I want to join a band in Liverpool nobody's ever heard of?" George Harrison and Joe Brown were later friends and neighbours in Henley and it was Joe's rendition of 'I'll See You in My Dreams' which memorably concluded the *Concert for George* in 2002. One of my favourite pre-fame Fab photos is George proudly clutching Joe's guitar. George had nipped into the headliner's dressing room and was snapped by Mike McCartney in 1962 while Joe was in the toilet. It was following that show that made Joe switch his career options. In his autobiography he remembered: "The band we followed was the Beatles, and it was pandemonium… The place was alive. All I can say is we managed to hold the stage with a good set. But I knew that was it. I'd seen the writing on the wall. It was a time to start looking in new directions or I wouldn't just be a fading pop star, I'd be back firing engines".

Billy Fury was only a few months older than John and Ritchie Starkey, but by 1960 was already established as a strong competitor to Cliff Richard. His manager was the legendary Larry Parnes, famous for transforming teenage wannabes into hip-swivelling rockers. Thus, shy Ronnie Wycherley became moody Billy Fury.

Whether out of homage to his native Liverpool, or, more likely, because Parnes knew that the beat-hungry groups would work for less than their London contemporaries, the pair travelled to Liverpool in May 1960 to hold auditions for groups to back Fury on his UK tour.

Every Scouser with a pulse and instrument turned up for the audition, and the Quarrymen were down on two counts: their terrible name, and absence of drummer. Tommy Moore had been inveigled along, but couldn't get off work, so the Big Three's Johnny Hutchinson (who had little time for the art school antics of Lennon, McCartney, Sutcliffe or Harrison) sat on the circular stool. For years, that one photo of that audition tells it all: Stuart hiding shyly at the back, while the front line of Lennon, McCartney and Harrison are evidently in rock & roll heaven: John's drop-kneed Elvis homage; Paul's looking like he's trying to imagine a future if they passed the audition and a blissfully young George stares tenaciously at his fingering on the guitar neck. And there on the drum stool is their drummer, Johnny Hutchinson, in a grey windcheater, making no effort to mask a glazed look of indifference.

As a drummer and personality, Johnny Hutchinson was highly thought of in the Merseybeat firmament, maybe because he cut an intimidating figure. When Pete Best was dismissed, Brian asked Hutchinson to replace him. "I wouldn't join the Beatles for a gold clock," he told Epstein.

The enthusiasm of the group did not translate into paid employment. Parnes took his protege back to London, while the rejected and dejected Quarrymen licked their wounds. They spent some time rehearsing, but like all groups without a record deal, more time arguing about what to call themselves.

John dipped back to his childhood reading for one group name – Long John Silver was the fearsome pirate from Robert Louis Stevenson's *Treasure Island*; Johnny & the Moondogs, the Silver Beetles, Beatals ... before Lennon tinkered with the spelling to arrive at the name the world would know them by. [With all the name changes, I have stuck to 'The Beatles' for consistency].

Whatever they were called, musically they were, at best, lacklustre, but they were cheap. So, a week after the failed Fury audition, Allan Williams received a phone call from Larry Parnes asking if his group would back another of his stable on a short tour of Scotland? We now know that the Silver Beetles were the fourth choice for the tour, after groups like Derry & the Seniors and Gerry & the Pacemakers declined.

John and Stuart had no trouble bunking off art school, George was happy to ditch his apprenticeship for a shot at showbiz glamour. It was at a crucial time for Paul McCartney, swotting hard for his A-Levels, which could lead to university and the prospect of a proper job as a teacher if he persevered. Somehow, Paul managed to persuade his father that, rather than spending his time studying for those all-important, life-changing exams, he would be far better served touring Scotland with an amateur rock & roll group.

For their first step on the professional ladder, and in the tradition of Larry Parnes' acts, the group all decided on pseudonyms to give their act the gloss it so desperately needed. James Paul McCartney was transformed into 'Paul Ramon' ("because it sounded really glamorous, sort of Valentino-ish"). Little was he to know that that off-the-cuff pseudonym would later be adopted by another bratty quartet as an homage – when in 1974, John Cummings, Douglas Colvin, Thomas Erdelyi and Jeffrey Hyman became … the Ramones.

As a testament to the influence of Carl Perkins, George became "Carl Harrison". Sticking true to his art school roots, Stuart took the name of the Russian painter and answered to "Stuart de Stael". The group's drummer did not bother with a pseudonym. Thirty-six-year-old Tommy Moore had little in common with the bratty teenagers he found himself touring with. Moore's experience of the seven dates he undertook as the fledgling Beatles' drummer did little to make him want to quit his day job permanently.

Soon after the publication of his *The Beatles: An Illustrated Record* in 1975, legendary *New Musical Express* journalist, the late and genuinely lamented Roy Carr, was surprised to receive a letter from New York. Following the release of his *Rock & Roll* LP, John Lennon was beginning his purdah. In the book, Roy and co-author Tony Tyler remarked that during that Johnny Gentle tour, Lennon appeared under his pseudonym "Johnny Silver". "I was never", the letter ran, "repeat never known as Johnny Silver. I always preferred my own name". He even included a clipping of a 1960 Beatles gig namechecking 'John Lennon'.

I always found it rather touching that towards the end of his life, the contentious, argumentative and defiantly un-nostalgic Lennon had surrounded himself with memorabilia from his early life. Endearingly, promoting the release of his final album, he regularly took to wearing his Quarry Bank school tie. Throughout his life, much as he hated his time there, Quarry Bank occupied a place. While in the USA, Lennon was a keen collector of Beatle bootlegs and had obviously accrued a considerable collection of Beatle press cuttings in a big box marked 'Liverpool'. At the end, is my beginning…

In 1967, Stephen Bayley, a student at the school, wrote to the Beatles asking if the Billy Shears on the group's new LP was named after the school's Head of History? Somehow the letter got through the Praetorian Guard surrounding the Beatles and Lennon replied with memories of his schooldays. John was also keen to debunk the "the mystery and shit" which was building up around Beatle lyrics. He sounded off about "smashing" that sort of speculation; 'I Am the Walrus' and 'Glass Onion' came not long after…

Those 1960 engagements in Scotland, the first professional dates the group undertook, were little short of a disaster. Johnny Gentle (1936–2024) was, even by Parnes' standards, a second-rate act, and the venues were hardly better than their familiar Liverpool haunts – church halls and ballrooms with audiences hungry for Cliff or Billy or Adam. But "Johnny Gentle and his Group", as one contemporary advert had it, hardly set the woods on fire. Poor food, shabby rooms, little salary, long journeys in a battered old van with tempers fraying between the drummer and a Lennon bitter at the squalor and palpable lack of opportunity.

As a footnote, the tour did allegedly account for John Lennon's first contribution to a recorded song. 'I've Just Fallen for Someone' was released as a single by Darren Young on the Parlophone label in August 1962. 'Darren Young' was actually Johnny Gentle, the singer who the Beatles had backed on his 1960 tour of Scotland – he claimed that Lennon wrote the song's middle eight, although he is not acknowledged on the finished single.

A nice little item came up for auction in 2004. Following a van crash which saw drummer Tommy Moore lose his front teeth, the group waited around for assistance just outside Banff. A teenage fan approached 'The Beatals' and got the signatures of John Lennon, 'Paul Ramon', 'Carl Harrison', Stuart Sutcliffe, Tommy Moore and Johnny Gentle. In return, she supplied them with dinner from the local chippie.

After their return from their desultory Scottish dates, Allan Williams hustled some local gigs for the quartet, who were downcast, and remained drummer-less. Tommy Moore pitched in, but his heart was never in the Silver Beetles. Perhaps my favourite anecdote which Mark Lewisohn unearthed back in his pioneering 1986 book *The Beatles Live!* has Paul and John searching Tommy Moore out to fulfil a gig at the Grosvenor Ballroom. Recognising the mettlesome teenagers, Moore's girlfriend screamed down from an upstairs window: "You can go and piss off! He's not playing with you anymore, he's got a job at the Garston bottle works on the night shift!" (It is the specific detail ['the Garston bottle works'] which to my mind lends the encounter such poignancy.)

While the Silver Beetles reeled from their Scottish defeat, Ritchie Starkey was high on the hog. After a spell as a skiffle pioneer and trainee joiner, Ritchie was enlisted by Rory Storm for his group the Hurricanes, reckoned by many to be the best in town. Ritchie's rise was far removed from the situation of his future bandmates: while they struggled with silly pseudonyms for a week, 20-year-old Ritchie Starkey became "Ringo Starr". And the Hurricanes were lucky to be locked into a summer residency at Butlins, Pwllheli.

From the Pier Head, Liverpool, all the city's teenagers dreamed of the Promised Land of America, way beyond the horizon. Or, enviously onscreen, they watched the dolce vita lifestyle of the Italians: a permanent fug of Peter Stuyvesant swirling over their Cinzanos to a roar of Vespa scooters, and throbbing teenage energy exercised on screen goddesses like Gina Lollobrigida and Sophia Loren.

If they were lucky, those self-same, envious teenagers settled for something closer to home. It is hard to envisage the excitement and glamour that Butlin's holiday camps exerted on post-war English holidaymakers. Before the advent of cheap foreign travel, a fortnight at Butlin's was very heaven. And once they had paid, everything was *free* – all the grub, rides, attractions and entertainments. Even if it rained, there were indoor pools and cheery young Redcoats to cajole and encourage you into having Fun with a capital 'F'.

A recently-discovered letter came from Paul to Redcoat Mike Robbins who was married to his cousin, Betty. It was a request from the teenage McCartney for "any kind of work" at the holiday camp for himself and two friends, one un-named (presumably John) and "Len", likely to be Quarryman Len Garry.

Parents could witness Glamorous Granny and knobbly knees contests. For those at the older end of teenage, Butlin's was synonymous with sex. Young girls who could escape the parental eye found themselves in boys' cabins where their initiation went beyond a fumble and squeeze. Certainly, one of the attractions Rory offered Ringo was the opportunity for simple, uncomplicated sex without ties. And the fact that he was elevated in the holidaymakers' eyes by being up on stage certainly did Ringo's love life little harm during their three-month residency. "A new coachload of girls would arrive every week at Butlin's," Ringo remembered for *Anthology*. "And we'd be like, 'Hi, I'm with the band, you know'. It was paradise for that. There'd be tears at the end of the week, and then a new coach".

It was a period Ringo remembered with great affection, and went on to recreate in the 1973 film of Ray Connolly's 1950s cinematic memoir *That'll Be the Day*, a far more cynical and bitter UK version of the contemporaneous *American Graffiti*. It saw Ringo effectively cast as the sort of Teddy Boy he was always too ill or too shy to actually *be* at the time. In a further irony, the character of 'Stormy Tempest', based on that of Rory Storm, was played in the film by the man who turned down the nascent Beatles as his backing band – Billy Fury. There's a great cameo from Keith Moon as Stormy's manic drummer who gets to deliver the line which was to elevate Ringo's next group: "It's Americans who write the songs, isn't it?"

So, while the newly-baptised Ringo Starr philandered in Pwllheli, John, Paul, George and Stu relied on Allan Williams to stir up interest. With Liverpool proving increasingly barren, the ever-ingenious Williams had set his sights further afield.

By one of those incredible coincidences which litter Beatle history Allan Williams had made a lightning trip to Hamburg in January 1960 where he had chanced upon the Kaiserkeller Club, and fallen into conversation with its owner, one Bruno Koschmider. A hard-bitten war veteran, Bruno was always on the lookout for groups to play at his Hamburg club, to keep up a steady throb of American rock & roll to make the visiting US and UK servicemen dance, work up a sweat and drink more.

A few months later, Koschmider made a beeline for Soho, and to the best-known of all the Soho coffee bars. The 2i's had been opened by a couple of Australian wrestlers in April 1956, and named after the Irani brothers who owned the site at 59 Old Compton Street. The 2i's became a mecca for aspiring skifflers and rock & rollers and, over the years, the 250 square foot cellar played host to every major British rock & roll star. Cliff Richard, the Shadows, Marty Wilde and Tommy Steele were just some of the acts discovered in Old Compton Street. Ironically, the skiffle king Lonnie Donegan never played the club – by the time it opened, he was just too well known.

Adam Faith was another who started out at the 2i's, although success didn't come as quickly as he'd hoped. The Vipers' Wally Whyton once told Spencer Leigh: "I remember Adam Faith saying to me when he was still Terry Nelhams, 'I've been playing the 2i's for three months now, and I'm still not a star!'"

In his desperation to find the next Lonnie, Cliff or Adam, Parlophone executive George Martin told the *Daily Mirror*: "I make a regular visit to Soho. Six months ago I wouldn't have dreamed of going there but now it has become a breeding ground for talent".

Bruce Welch of the Shadows told me: "Soho was unbelievably exciting for two kids from Newcastle – which in the 50s was all bomb-sites, shipyards, the pits, grey places… If we'd stayed there, we could have ended up down the mines. London was colourful, although it had bomb-sites; but Soho – the Italian restaurants, the coffee bars. Every second shop was a coffee bar, with the frothy coffee, the Gaggia machine, we'd never seen a chrome coffee machine!… The bright lights, the hookers down there in the doorways".

A further coincidence occurred when Bruno conveyed to Williams in his sparse English that he was looking for groups to take back to Germany. Through a convoluted period of cancelled bookings, Williams brought one of his acts down to London to meet Herr Koschmider. So, Derry & the Seniors were packed off to Hamburg, but Herr Koschmider confided in Williams that he wanted to open another club, and would need another of these top quality British acts of whom Herr Williams appeared to have such an inexhaustible supply.

With Rory Storm & the Hurricanes having a high old time at Butlin's, with Gerry & the Pacemakers reluctant to quit their hometown, Allan Williams pitched the opportunity to his third choice. And thus opportunity knocked, and the Beatles made their way to Hamburg… Not everyone was enchanted. Derry Wilkie (of Derry & the Seniors) reckoned the Hamburg pitch could be seriously queered if Williams sent over "a bum group like the Beatles".

Grotty gigs around town had done little to buoy the group up, so any offer was welcome, particularly one which involved exotic foreign travel. But as ever, the lack of a drummer confounded them. An August 1960 letter from Paul to a fan (which surfaced at auction in 1996) found him enthusing about "a couple of bookings at £1 each a night. I'm on the drums now you know, till we find a good reliable drummer".

With Stu's manifest incompetence on bass, the lack of a pounding drum sound left them sounding limp. And to keep Herr Koschmider's crowds happy, at what no doubt would prove to be a glamorous night club, a drummer was essential. In Liverpool, Tommy Moore grudgingly came on board for a couple of gigs; picture framer Norman Chapman hit the skins temporarily for the group, Paul McCartney reluctantly quit the front line to do a Sandy Nelson… But it was all touch and go, until the group drifted back to Mona Best's Casbah Club one Saturday night in August 1960, where they caught her son's group, the Blackjacks in action.

So, famously before he was asked to leave, Pete Best *joined* the Beatles in 1960. Knowing what was to follow, perhaps we read too much into Pete's image. From the photos at the time, Pete never did seem to smile, but then that could be something he learned from Elvis, ("You can't be a rebel if you smile," he said before his first film role). From those photos, Pete always appeared an outsider, refusing to fashion his hair like those of his bandmates. But during his spell with the group, Pete undeniably had his own fanbase. It was Cavern DJ Bob Wooler who coined the "mean, moody and magnificent" tag for Pete. Borrowed from the hype surrounding Jane Russell 20 years before, Pete was also compared to the now long-forgotten 50s film star, pin-up Jeff Chandler.

What really opened the eyes of the Quarrymen though was Pete's gleaming Premier drum kit. The loose aggregate had moved on from washboards and tea-chest basses. But their three guitars were just not enough. To keep the rhythm, and mask the inadequacy of Stuart Sutcliffe's bass playing, and meet the requirements for their Hamburg commitments, a drummer was urgently required.

So, after a brief but redundant rehearsal, Pete Best joined John, Paul, George and Stu as their first full-time drummer. If they were expecting a more glamorous trip than their freewheeling caper round Scotland, the group were to be disappointed.

As if the five Beatles weren't enough for his tiny van, Allan Williams, his wife Beryl, and his brother-in-law and man about Liverpool Lord Woodbine set off on their awfully big adventure. Briefly stopping in London to pick up the guy Allan had roped in as Bruno Koschmider's Soho translator, Williams' battered van made it to Harwich for their ferry across the Channel.

For the first time ever, in August 1960, the Beatles set foot on foreign soil. You cannot escape the sheer, powerful, overwhelming symbolism of the first photo taken of the Beatles abroad: stopping at the war memorial in Arnhem, to commemorate the servicemen who died in the 1944 "bridge too far" fiasco. Allan and his wife Beryl; Lord Woodbine along for the ride, Pete savouring the moment. In a photo taken by Beryl's brother Barry, with John refusing to leave the van, there sit, Paul and George... One summer morning in 1960, within earshot of the cataclysmic changes they would bring to that new decade, under the inscription that Rudyard Kipling had selected when he joined the Imperial War Graves Commission following the loss of his only son in the carnage of an earlier war. He chose the biblical phrase inscribed on many British war memorials... 'Their Name Liveth For Evermore'.

In his honeymoon period as a Beatle, Pete grins next to George while, standing in shades, Stu gives it his best James Dean. Paul occupies centre stage. John couldn't be arsed to get out of the van. And so the caravanserai continued through Holland, until, just as the evening sky grew dark on 17 August 1960, the van pulled up onto Hamburg's Grosse Freiheit.

Leaping free, their feet clicked and clacked on the cobblestones as their heads turned. The neon night was brightly alive. From the ships in the nearby harbour the sirens wailed, like primeval monsters, echoing over the run-down district of St Pauli. They were here. They had arrived. For this motley crew, a new chapter was about to begin...

*

In 1914, a guidebook was published for visitors to Germany. Author Henry J. Hecht enthused: "Hamburg is a city bound to appeal to every Englishman; the inhabitants are extremely English in their tastes and in their love of sport". In later years, the city boasted a thriving Anglo-German Club. It was Hamburg that provided a launch point for the diaspora which helped inhabit the New World. An estimated five million Europeans left the port between 1850 and 1939 to begin their new life in America.

Like the Beatles' home city, Hamburg suffered during the War. In what was seen as revenge for the two years of Blitz the UK had suffered, on the night of 27 August 1943, RAF Bomber Command unleashed 'Operation Gomorrah'. A firestorm engulfed the city with temperatures in excess of 1,000° centigrade, killing 42,000 occupants. Over 40,000 houses, 24 hospitals, 58 churches, nearly 300 schools and a zoo were destroyed. As Max Hastings wrote: "In one week, Bomber Command had killed more people than the Luftwaffe had achieved in the eight months of the blitz in England during 1940/41..." The scale of the destruction paved the way for Dresden and Hiroshima. It was to Hamburg that the Beatles came 17 years after the firestorm, to a city which still bore the vivid sears and scars of that dreadful week.

But with typical German efficiency, Hamburg was rebuilt. On her first visit to Liverpool, future Beatle acquaintance and Hamburg resident Astrid Kirchherr was shocked at how bomb-scarred the English city still was. The similarities between the two cities are marked – clustered around the docks, like flies round a corpse's mouth, are the bars and brothels. Here are the ports, in their heyday, into which the liners steamed and the vessels disgorged their cargoes.

Today the Hamburg streets are largely tarmacked but, just occasionally, the cab will clatter over cobblestones as an aural throwback to the city the young Beatles would remember. Back then, the better-paid groups lodged at the Hotel Pacific, located right near the Dom; this was the fairground where the fair pitched up quarterly, and where Astrid would photograph those leather-clad teenagers, all those lifetimes ago. St Michael's Church looms over the disreputable St Pauli district. Through the trees you can just glimpse the statue of Bismarck, the Iron Chancellor who unified disparate states into the German nation, and whose family came from nearby.

In the Book of Genesis, God destroyed the cities of Sodom & Gomorrah for their wickedness. The RAF had unleashed their own Gomorrah, by the time Allan Williams' van drew up, the wide-eyed Beatles had arrived at their very own Sodom. This time, the young Brits were visiting as entertainers, but that could all have been so very different. I have long been fascinated by just how close the Beatles came to National Service, and manifestly, how that would have affected not just their career, but all of us…

One of the reasons National Service was introduced was to ensure that the British Army On The Rhine (BAOR, referenced on the 1965 Beatles Christmas record) was sufficiently strong to keep an eye on the subdued Germans, whilst also countering any threat from Stalin's Russia. Reeling and bankrupt from six years of war, Britain still needed to maintain an army, so in 1948 a peacetime National Service Bill was introduced. Every male between 18 and 26 years of age was liable for two years compulsory National Service. From that moment on, until the last National Serviceman was discharged, around 160,000 youngsters each year would quit home for a draughty Army barracks. The more fortunate were sent to Hong Kong, Malta, Vienna, Gibraltar, Jamaica, Cyprus or Germany; while the less lucky conscripts were in combat in Egypt, Malaya, Kenya or Korea.

Over two million National Servicemen went through the ranks between 1948 and 1963. In passing, it is worth noting that the final National Serviceman to be discharged (Lieutenant Richard Vaughan) was freed on 16 May 1963, the night the Beatles were making their second BBC TV appearance. It is always revealing to watch feature films and documentaries of the period, and be aware of the number of army personnel in transit, clogging up the railway platforms.

Just in time for our heroes, the ruling came in that those born on or after 1 October 1939 would not be required to serve King, Queen or Country. Reflecting years later, Paul told *Radio Times*: "A couple of years earlier, we would have been in the Army, and it's very doubtful that the Beatles would have formed. We would have been at Aldershot, or wherever, in various camps and might not even have met".

Later, talking to Jon Wilde, McCartney confirmed the relief: "Our parents had all had to join the army, as National Service had been compulsory. Growing up we were all looking at that as a grim possibility. To say the least, it wasn't the cheeriest of prospects… The end of National Service was [the turning point]. Without that there would have been no Beatles. To me that was like God opening the Red Sea for Moses and the Israelites to come pouring through". (In later years, John Peel ruefully reflected that "the rock festival was the post-war generation's substitute for National Service".)

Army conscription also applied in the States, the Everly Brothers did their bit, but the most famous recruit was called up at the peak of his fame. Elvis famously served as PFC 53310761 between 1958 and 1960, and was sure he'd be forgotten while on Army service. While serving in Germany, Elvis was convinced Roy Orbison would steal his thunder. In the same way, if the timing had been different, Mark Lewisohn believes McCartney was convinced Gerry & the Pacemakers would overtake the Beatles in popularity if they were called up. In the UK, rock & roller Terry Dene was called up, but suffered a nervous breakdown, and was discharged. Bill Perks (later Wyman) enjoyed his stint as a serviceman. Much was made of a pop star undergoing National Service in Anthony Newley's *Idol on Parade* (1959), as 'Jeep' Jackson and his lacklustre brand of 'rockaboogie'. Those who came just a few months before weren't so lucky. National Service was responsible for most of the skiffle groups breaking up.

As it happens, the Beatles avoided National Service by a whisker. One can only speculate, though with some certainty, on how the rebellious Lennon would have coped with 'square bashing'. Or how George's karmic philosophy would have jarred with screaming regimental sergeant majors. You sense Paul could have managed okay. Ever the diplomatic Beatle, he looked quite comfortable in uniform behind a desk in *Magical Mystery Tour*, and his well-known charm would probably have seen him through. And with such a disturbed background, the easygoing Ringo would no doubt have coped, perhaps securing a space in his regiment's marching band.

But with a war over, the Damocles sword of military service removed, and with new territories to conquer, the Beatles spilled out of Allan Williams' van and took their first bleary look round the city which would be their home on and off for the next two years.

In Britain, in Philip Larkin's oft-quoted chronology, sexual intercourse did not begin until 1963, marked by the Lady Chatterley ban "and the Beatles' first LP". However, by the time the fledgling Fab Four arrived in Hamburg, sex was well into its stride. In Liverpool, sex was fully clothed and limited to fumbling forays in cinema back rows. In Hamburg, it was in the air with pants around the ankles.

When I visited in 2000, a half-hearted attempt had been made to 'clean up' the St Pauli district, but even as you passed through the gates of Herbertstrasse still on neon display were *World Of Sex… Sexy Heaven… Vegas World… the Pascha Erotic Palace… Kino Homo…* The sign denied entry to "men under 18 and women prohibited".

I was expecting St Pauli to be like a sprawling film set, but the clubs are all cloistered close by, barely a city block off the seething city streets. It nestles near the Chinese quarter. The area was long synonymous with sin. The Nazis destroyed the quarter in the 1930s, and all the indigenous inhabitants, the "Unter menschen", were shipped off to concentration camps. You pass the 'Polizei' station where the Liverpool youngsters were banged-up for their later teenage conflagration, the site of the first Beatle bust. In the safety of daylight you proceed along the Reeperbahn. It is a long, straight street, the reason for its unbending length is, according to Richard Thompson (who knows these things), that it was used to lay the long ropes for the sailing ships which filled the bustling harbour in the 19th century. A brightly-lit sign boasted 'Radeberger', a popular German beer brand; it blinks nervously in the sunshine over where the Top Ten Club was – a name redolent of ankle-deep lager, switch-blade knives, Benzedrine and lechery.

Then here's Grosse Freiheit, a tiny, narrow street, room for one car and a pedestrian. It takes little imagination to picture the prellied-up Scousers, reeling along, boots clattering on the cobbles. A beer shop, not an unusual site in Hamburg, marks the location of the original Star Club. As with Liverpool and the Cavern, a replica Star Club has been recreated nearby. Originally a cinema (the Stern-Kino), the short alley was lined with glamorous photos of film stars.

Over the crossroads and a gold plaque on the Indra Club boasts of its Beatle connections. The area was so compact, few of the musicians felt the need to quit St Pauli, they knew the food and beer were cheap, they knew who to know, and were known by.

Back on the Reeperbahn is Ertman's, still standing, where the groups bought all their leather gear. Turn right, just by Burger King and opposite McDonald's (brands unknown to the Beatles then) is Herbertstrasse, another narrow street, where the prostitutes sit in windows, displaying their wares. This was the magnet, when the huge American battleships berthed in the bustling docks and disgorged thousands of US sailors in an injection of pure testosterone onto the Reeperbahn. That's what it was then: a gigantic prophylactic for early 60s priapism.

It remains still shamefully, but quite enticingly ... seedy.

Perhaps too much has been made of the influence of Hamburg on the Beatles; Bob Wooler, for one, doubted the transformative power of the city – if it worked its magic on them, why not Faron's Flamingoes? The Undertakers? Kingsize Taylor? Rikki & the Red Streaks? Dean Devlin & the Dynamites? What is certain is that, prior to their exhausting stints in the city, fate might not have fingered the Beatles in an identity parade of 'The Next Big Thing'. But, following those endless nights effectively rehearsing in public, they *were* ready for anything.

The importance of Hamburg might just have been geographical; one's first time abroad, particularly when full of youthful fervour, is always memorable. I think Hamburg's similarities with their home port played a part in their envelopment. But it remains the city where the Beatles went from being emulators to inspirers. From the Harwich ferry they looked forward; from Hamburg, they never looked back.

*

The head-turning, eye-swivelling opportunities were brazenly on offer on Grosse Freiheit as the teenagers took their first tentative steps into Hamburg's notorious red-light district. Their location was not the relatively swish Kaiserkeller but, rather Herr Koschmider's new club, the more off-the-beaten-strasse Indra Club. Half-heartedly transformed from a strip club to a rock & roll venue, within a day of their arrival, the group began their gruelling residency of all-night shows. All night. Every night. It was their apprenticeship. It was their transition from the boys ... to the men ... to the Beatles.

Hamburg marked the transformation from a bunch of teenagers who, although three years into a 'career', were basically putting off the moment they had to sit at the grown-ups' table and get proper jobs… They became a professional outfit, brimming over on the cusp of a new era, with the prospect of a real career as musicians. It was a long, hard slog, yet it marked, as Churchill famously remarked some years before, "the end of the beginning…"

"1, 2, 3, 4…" it could be any of the multitude of songs on any one of the hundreds of Hamburg nights. Freed from all responsibilities, liberated by the licentiousness on offer, fuelled by the pep pills and unlimited lager, delighted at the opportunity at being paid to play … the Beatles *exploded* in Hamburg.

For all the grottiness of their accommodation, the run-down venue and its boisterous audience, it was the gruelling apprenticeship at the Indra which laid the foundations for the greatness which was to follow. Though anyone in the audience of that shabby strip club would be hard pushed to perceive any future at all for the five youngsters bopping the night away. They were clearly enjoying themselves on the shabby stage. They were simply there to provide a backdrop to intoxication and sexual intercourse. The thumping, floor-shaking music was a wall of sound; little clarity was expected, just a constant, pounding riff.

If the venue in which they made their European debut was tawdry, their accommodation at next door's Bambi Kino cinema was even worse. But at that age, liberated from their Liverpool homes and free of parental disapproval, they poured everything into their performances.

Bruno Koschmider's contract was brutal: every weekday night required 270 minutes of music, while each weekend a punishing six hours every night was required. Within hours of arrival (one account has Koschmider putting them onstage the very night they arrived after their 36-hour continental journey) they soon appreciated that their limited Quarrymen repertoire would soon be exhausted.

A few nights in, there was little room for lightweight skiffle, and their familiar rock & roll repertoire had been plundered to death. To cater to the baying crowds, hungry for authentic American rock music pumping out of jukeboxes or on the American Forces Network radio, the Beatles dipped deeper and deeper into shared memories. They plundered B-sides, LP tracks, other groups' material, their own tentative songwriting efforts just to keep the beat going throughout those endless nights.

"We were always looking for material that the other bands couldn't get," Paul told me. "So we had to look for other ways, and the two ways we did it was that John and I started writing, and that was the sole reason we started writing, which is a great thing to remember… And the other thing was we accessed B-sides… where there were strange tracks".

The debate still rages about the Beatle repertoire prior to their own professional songwriting career commencing. For many years it was believed to be 'the Cunard Yanks' who supplied the Liverpool groups with records which were hard to obtain in Great Britain.

A few years before rock & roll hit the UK, 'Geraldo's Navy' had set sail. Geraldo was a popular pre-war bandleader, and also a talent-spotter for the Cunard Line, finding musicians to play aboard their liners plying the transatlantic route. When the *Queen Mary* made her first post-war voyage to New York in 1947 – after a wartime spent serving as a troopship – she took with her a posse of musicians. Jazz-starved musicians like Ronnie Scott and John Dankworth, who were happy to blow for diners throughout the Atlantic crossing, just so they could finally get to pay homage to Bird and Diz on New York's 52nd Street.

The next generation were believed to have had their musical ears opened by the Cunard sailors bringing back rare and unreleased rock & roll records from the States. But the assiduous Spencer Leigh found "around 350 cover versions by Liverpool groups. In almost every case the original version *had been* [my italics] released in the UK on such labels as Top Rank, Oriole, London American and Pye International". Spencer also highlights Radio Luxembourg's freewheeling playlist policy compared to the stodgier BBC Light Programme which provided further opportunities to hear those B-sides and hard-to-find 45s. He also cheekily points out that "the Eppy-centre", where many of the records were stocked, was Brian Epstein's NEMS store in Liverpool's Whitechapel. Mark Lewisohn too is also dismissive of the oft-repeated Cunard Yanks theory: "they had little or none of the influence on the Beatles' music that commentators have always suggested".

During those Hamburg nights, onstage they roamed far and wide – film themes, ballads, even tentative Lennon & McCartney originals. The Beatles were also early advocates of Motown... *Mersey Beat* editor Bill Harry remembers being told that Merseyside was the biggest source of sales for Berry Gordy's label in the UK. When the Beatles began including Motown material on their own albums, Gordy returned the favour on the Supremes' third LP. *A Bit of Liverpool* was released in 1964, intended as a testament to the city's fondness for the label, but it was – geographically – a bit wide of the mark including 'Bits & Pieces' (Tottenham); 'House of the Rising Sun' (Newcastle') and 'Do You Love Me' (Detroit).

Onstage in Hamburg, George could display his penchant for country & western and even the reluctant Stuart was coaxed into the limelight to croon 'Love Me Tender'. Teenage favourites Chuck Berry, Fats Domino, Buddy Holly, Gene Vincent, Eddie Cochran, Carl Perkins, Little Richard, Lloyd Price and Fats Domino were all harvested. And, of course, *everyone* within the Liverpool postal district knew Ritchie Barratt's 'Some Other Guy'.

In Hamburg, while Bruno Koschmider stinted on accommodation for his new act, he did splash out on a group photo to display outside the Indra. And there they are, in the first professional 'Beatle' photo: you are drawn to John, Paul and George, all coming out of their Teddy Boy phase; Pete's saturnine good looks appear to emphasise his Indian heritage. But it is Stuart, giving it his best James Dean, who stands out – quiff in excelsis while the mean and moody element is emphasised by the sunglasses.

"There was this one bar in Hamburg we used to go to," Paul remembered, "it had a pool table and a great jukebox... Every time I went there I always used to put on Little Richard's 'Shake a Hand' and 'Smoke Gets in Your Eyes' by the Platters... Always takes me back to that bar, the pool table, Derry & the Seniors, Howie Casey, all the lads, little half a pint, you know, playing the snooker and having a chat".

During those early nights at the Indra, the quantity was as important as the quality. The five boys poured their hearts into their material, fired up by pep pills and their thirst quenched by steins of beer left onstage by grateful punters, the fledgling Beatles gave everything they had on that shabby stage those summer nights.

In a sense it didn't matter what was being played, as long as Pete pummelled out a 4/4 beat and the keen boys clustering round the microphones let the lingua franca of rock & roll be heard. From early on it became obvious that to earn their paltry salary (30 Deutsche Marks per week, about £10 by 1960 standards, to be split among the five) they just had to keep playing.

Rock & roll, show tunes, gospel, film themes… "John used to do 'Somewhere over the Rainbow' for Christ's sake," Paul told me. "And he used to do 'Up a Lazy River'… The 'Harry Lime Theme', John used to play that, his little party piece". Novelty numbers and the odd ballad, effectively they had to keep up a barrage of loud music. A particular favourite was Ray Charles' call and respond 'What'd I Say', which could be stretched like elastic, then snapped back again as it wove into a version which could stretch into a 15-minute marathon.

Pepped up by Preludin, the Beatles were literally playing their hearts out. "'What'd I Say' was always the one that really got them," Paul remembered for *Anthology*. "That was one of our big numbers. It became like trying to get into the *Guinness Book of Records* – who could make it last the longest. It has the greatest opening riff ever… you could keep that riff going for hours".

Their nights fully occupied with performing, the days were their own. Paul wrote to his brother Mike about the food "Potatoes with salad, cold tomatoes… sausages are extremely long and are made with fish and meat. Ugh!" Jim Hawke ran the Hamburg Mission and recalled the five-man Beatles blinking into the daylight. Occasionally clustered round the piano or playing draughts or just quietly devouring their egg and chips, "I'd look over from the bar and see the five of them", Hawke told Philip Norman, "always around the same table, not talking – just staring into space. I've seen the same look on men who've been away at sea in tankers for a long time…"

Grosse Freiheit literally translated as 'Great Freedom', and here were the eye-popping sights for the teenagers to absorb. The dock area of St Pauli was where the Reeperbahn became a magnet for sailors with bulging pockets. To cater to them were prostitutes of every hue. They paraded their wares along a nearby street which was barred at both ends to keep juveniles out. You had to carry an identity card to prove your age. Once over 18, you were free to ogle the girls on display in the red-lit windows or teetering on high heels along the gleaming, sex-sodden strasse.

"In Liverpool the girls all wore very rigid girdles," Paul said in *Anthology*. "It was medieval. In Hamburg, they were almost flashing it… They were great looking girls too, so it really was pulling the birds time".

To keep order in the clubs, bars and brothels, tough security was employed. These were not the dinner-jacketed bouncers of home, these were ex-Nazis, mercenaries, gangsters. For all that has been written (and exaggerated) about the Beatles' transition from men to boys during their Hamburg residencies, one consistent, abiding memory from the four principals was the pall of violence which accompanied their performances.

Armed with truncheons, coshes, knuckle-dusters, these were hard men. "Gangs of fucking British servicemen [would] try to stir things up," John was quoted in *Anthology*. "When we could smell Senior Service in the audience we knew there would be trouble… after a few drinks they'd all be lying there half dead after they'd tried to pick a fight with the waiters over the bill… The waiters would get out their flick-knives or their truncheons, and that would be it. I've never seen such killers".

When Derry & the Seniors' contract at the slightly lusher Kaiserkeller ran out at the beginning of October 1960, Bruno Koschmider was impressed enough to move the Beatles upmarket from the Indra. They alternated sets with another Liverpool group, Rory Storm & the Hurricanes, where they struck up a rapport with Rory's drummer, the bearded and grown-up Ringo Starr.

"I still think of Ringo as a very old person", Paul told *Anthology*, "because he is two years older. He was the grown-up of the group when he came to us, he had a beard, he had a car and he had a suit. What more proof do you need of grown-upmanship?"

For Ringo, the Kaiserkeller was Butlin's writ large. Hamburg was Liverpool on the Elbe, so naturally the Scouse groups all clustered together. There was an immediate bond, strangers in a strange land. The visiting Ringo and Rory were stunned at the transformation from the amateur Silver Beetles to the Beatles who invaded the Hamburg stage. They were brash and exuded a cocky confidence which only increased every night they consolidated their turf.

In another of those coincidences which percolate Beatle history, 15 October 1960 was the very first time that John, Paul, George *and* Ringo played together on disc. A version of George Gershwin's 'Summertime' was cut on a 78 rpm disc near Hamburg's railway station, accompanying the Hurricanes' Lou Walters. Pete was out and about. Ringo was there fortuitously because he was a bandmate of Lou's, and the others, well in the words of one of their heroes Lloyd Price, 'Just Because'…

Lou fancied himself as a singer and paid for the session. Acetates were pressed up. "No one knows where the five acetates have gone," Bob Wooler told Spencer Leigh, reflecting on the first time the Fab Four recorded together. "Allan Williams had one, but he left it in a pub in London! Whoever has it now has one of the most valuable records in the world".

All through the night, on a stage that literally collapsed beneath their feet, on they played, ransacking song catalogues, competing with themselves, their peers, insulting and endearing themselves to audiences… It was an unparalleled apprenticeship, but not the sort which they had envisaged as apprentice electricians or trainee teachers a mere few months before.

The audiences grew increasingly fond of the reckless swaggering boys on the Kaiserkeller stage. As if casting aside the bitter, bloody memories of the war, here they let their hair down. The audience's pleasure was made real by the endless trays of foaming beer and lager which made its way onstage. Flouting authority with every irreverent gesture, pounding through the latest American rock & roll, parading a look culled from big screen idols … the Beatles were by all accounts simply mesmerising.

What they learned was perhaps too chaotic to be called 'stagecraft', but it was honing and improving an act fashioned in Liverpool which developed and then, due to the eye-wateringly wearing demands made by the club's owner, matured. Between the grinding all-nighters, after the knee-tremblers in back alleys and snatched moments of sleep, they watched. They listened. They learned…

The one performer of the period to whom all the groups deferred was a youth they called 'The Teacher'. Tony Sheridan. Only 20 years old, Sheridan had crammed a lot of rock & roll into his tender years. He had spells backing Conway Twitty, Brenda Lee, Chubby Checker in the UK. But it was the time he spent on the fatal 1960 Eddie Cochran and Gene Vincent tour which left its mark on Sheridan. Like anyone who saw Cochran in action, either onstage or from the audience, Sheridan was spellbound. Cochran had the look, the flash, he was also a supremely talented guitarist, and everyone (Joe Brown as well as Sheridan) picked up what they could from him while he was in the country.

Sheridan had appeared on TVs *Oh Boy*, had been a regular at the 2i's in Soho. And, with the Jets, opened the door to British rock & roll when they began a residency at the Kaiserkeller in June 1960 – the first British group to play there. Only a few months older than John Lennon, Sheridan had accrued stagecraft and television experience by the time he had got to Hamburg.

As a point of interest, in another of those historic rock & roll What Ifs … by hanging out at the 2is, Tony Sheridan had almost made it into Cliff Richard's backing group the Drifters (later the Shadows). But he had missed out on that opportunity, as he was to later do with the Beatles.

George Harrison in particular was enchanted to learn guitar tricks from Sheridan, which Sheridan himself had got direct from the Master, Eddie Cochran himself, only a few months before. Years later, Jimmy Page commented: "the only English guitarist who was any good during that time was Tony Sheridan". Looking back, George told me: "I think I really would have benefitted [from] a couple more years in the clubs, that would have helped me, working places like Hamburg, where you were resident in a club and you could just play".

The few pictures of the Kaiserkeller from the era that survive show buxom hausfraus letting their hair down and burly boyfriends out for a night of boisterous dancing with the promise of more to follow as they staggered out into the brash, enveloping Hamburg night.

Of all the visitors who witnessed the Beatles in action during those heady autumn nights of 1960, a trio of German teenagers were spellbound. Klaus Voormann, Astrid Kirchherr and Jurgen Vollmer were fashionable beyond their years. Their earlier love of all aspects of American culture had been superseded by the fashionable philosophy, style and chanson wafting over from Paris.

In truth, the existentialist movement which swept over post-war Europe was more a fashionable attitude than a strict philosophical discipline. Existentialism was defined as emphasising "individual uniqueness, freedom and responsibility in opposition to various forms of determinism… human choices are not dictated by a determining essence or fixed human nature… Much of [the] writing is characterized by disillusionment".

It was probably more a response to the post-war disillusion, the shadow of the H-Bomb and the opportunity to go around dressed in black, moaning that "nobody understands me" which propelled the teenage existentialists of the period. They tried to make sense of a world which had survived a holocaust and which now sheltered under satellites and the chill horror of the Hydrogen bomb. What was the point of anything if, at the press of a button, a weapon could be unleashed a *thousand* times more powerful than that which had levelled the Japanese cities of Hiroshima and Nagasaki only 15 years before?

Stylish and iceberg-beautiful, 22-year-old Astrid Kirchherr (1938–2020) was an art student. She and her boyfriend, the striking-looking Klaus Voormann had been an item since meeting at art college. One evening, following a row, Klaus had stormed out into the Hamburg night and was drifting along Grosse Freiheit when he heard subterranean rock & roll drifting up. Curious, he made his way to the basement and was greeted by a stage full of the exis' sworn enemies – rockers!

Nervous but exhilarated by what he heard, Klaus brought Astrid along to the club where she witnessed the Beatles in action, and found her attention drawn to the shy bass player, so unsure of his ability that he often stood with his back to the audience. Stuart, shielded by his sunglasses, was so at odds with his exuberant bandmates that immediately Astrid felt a kinship. It was the beginning of a beautiful, doomed friendship.

As a photographer Astrid was equally struck by how the group looked as how they sounded. And so, to her eternal credit, she tried to capture some of that magnetism in those first compelling photographs of the group in Hamburg. There is that famous shot in the Der Dom park of the five-man line-up. Endlessly scrutinised, there they are, the embryonic Beatles, all proudly clutching their instruments, all a long way from Beatle fringes, still defiant Teds in winkle-pickers and leathers. Those shots of the leather-clad Beatles in Hamburg further reinforced the gang mentality, the Wild Bunch in black leather and cowboy boots.

None smile, the photo is at once at odds with the cheesy 'showbiz' snaps of the period. This is stern, moody monochrome. Pete and George look into the camera. Behind his shades you would guess that Stuart was looking at his new girlfriend through her lens. But John and Paul are staring to the left of the lens, Paul unimaginably boyish, John firmer, older. Is it too fanciful to imagine the two of them looking to the future…?

On a diet of slimming pills and beer, fried food and cornflakes, the Beatles blitzkrieged their way into Hamburg legend. We can only speculate on how they sounded as no tapes exist of that first visit. But we can close our eyes and imagine the piledriving enthusiasm and loutish exuberance. Lennon castigating the crowd as "fucking Nazis". The constant cries of "mach shau" to stop the energy level dipping. Even the ruthlessly un-nostalgic Lennon looked back fondly at the period – on the sleeve of his 1975 *Rock 'n' Roll* album, the Teddy Boy is pictured leaning in a Hamburg doorway. As if to convey the frenzy of the period, the remaining Beatles pass by in a blur. It is a photo snatched from oblivion, the leather-clad Lennon on the verge of becoming more than a myopic, surly, art-school dropout. And to his post-Beatle audience he wrote simply, "You should have been there…"

That photo had been taken by Klaus and Astrid's pal Jurgen Vollmer. The image is of a laconic Ted barely out of his teenage years, leaning in a seedy doorway off Wohlwillstrasse in an unremarkable North German port. Yet that doorway has become another destination on what appears to be a never-ending list of Beatle locations. My friend Jeremy Taylor visited the location one day, over 60 years since the photo was taken, to find himself in a queue behind visitors from Croatia, South America and Japan, all keen to replicate the pose and location.

"I had a very precise image in my mind. Of all the Beatles, John was the perfect model for my image of the tough rocker, the young Marlon Brando type in *The Wild One*," the photographer explained. To get the shot he wanted, Jurgen had Paul, George and Stuart walk past in a blur. The original photo displays the pointed shoes Vollmer was keen to emphasise, "but unfortunately they cropped it in a way you don't see the artistic effect of the shoes! It's my most famous picture – from my first year in photography. It went downhill from there!" (Not strictly true, the Smiths used a Jurgen photo for the cover of their *The World Won't Listen*).

It was Jurgen who also played another key role in the Beatles' developing history. It was to Paris that John and Paul had made a beeline in October 1961 as a gift to mark John's 21st. To get a flavour of the French capital at the time, look at Tony Hancock's *The Rebel*, and its take on Bohemia. Haunting the Left Bank, the Liverpudlians were impressed by the chic style of the women and the cafe society which Liverpool was so lacking.

There was a tantalising excerpt from Paul's 1961 diary shown at his 2023 *Eye of the Storm* exhibition. I was drawn to him and John witnessing Vince Taylor in action. Touted as "the British Elvis", Taylor is best remembered today as a prototype for Bowie's Ziggy Stardust and his 'Brand New Cadillac', which the Clash covered on *London Calling*. For McCartney though he is repeatedly, bafflingly referred to as Vince ("come back Ron") Taylor.

A more lasting impact of that first French visit was the change in their appearance fashioned by their Hamburg friend, Jurgen, who was then living in Paris as a photographer's assistant. ("I first had what they called the moptop haircut back in 1955 when I was 15 years old," Jurgen told Jonathan Wingate. "One day after I had been swimming at school I didn't comb my hair, so I just let it hang over my forehead when it was still wet".)

Surging ahead of the competition they were wowing everyone who came to see them. But as the autumn turned to bitter winter, following the destruction of the Kaiserkeller stage under the combined weight of Beatles and Hurricanes, Bruno Koschmider was furious. But he was even angrier when he learned that the Beatles were breaching their contract by appearing onstage at the more upmarket Top Ten Club with Tony Sheridan.

Koschmider got his revenge by fingering the group's guitarist. To be around the red-light district of Hamburg, you needed an identity card to say you were over 18. Seventeen-year-old George Harrison was reported to the police and swiftly deported. Offered accommodation at the Top Ten, Paul and Pete returned to the grotty Bambi Kino to retrieve their belongings. Either in an act of defiance to Bruno, or to illuminate their grisly unlit surroundings, they pinned condoms to the wall and lit them. On hearing of the damage to his property, Koschmider alerted the police, and the two teenage Beatles found themselves banged up overnight.

They too were deported, and in their wake, with no group behind him, came a bitterly disillusioned Lennon. Stuart stayed on to be with Astrid but, just before Christmas 1960, he too was back home in Liverpool.

On their return, their tails between their legs, widely ignored by the city that had spawned them, it is perhaps worth further reflecting on the Beatles before they became, THE BEATLES.

Just how good were they? "We were pretty bad at the beginning. I mean, we weren't that good. But with all the time we had in Hamburg, we just got good" (Paul told Dylan Jones). With Pete Best's pedestrian but alright-on-the-night drumming; Stuart Sutcliffe's plodding bass; without the magic wealth of Lennon & McCartney material; without the imaginative production sheen of George Martin... If you stacked them up against a hundred other Liverpool bands of the period… Litres of heady German beer inside, head throbbing with music, a blonde on the make, would you, *really*, hand on heart, have singled out the Beatles?

They were certainly committed to Making It, but more as an Out from the dead-end Liverpool rather than any other aspiration. Make no bones, for all the highfalutin stuff written about the band, the reason the Beatles got together was to meet birds. To avoid the dread apprenticeships, to keep out of the factories and dockyards, to bypass the inevitable treadmill Albert Finney's Arthur Seaton found himself on in *Saturday Night and Sunday Morning.*

The songs which were to change the world, the class barriers they helped tumble, the barricades they broke down… all that came much later and quite inadvertently. At the beginning there was simply the simple joy of being paid to get up onstage, play the music they loved and have a laugh. Then offstage, realising it attracted the opposite sex, they made of that what they would. At the dawn of the 1960s, the resilient Quarrymen were glad to have avoided National Service and were just about managing to scrape a living. Playing at the Cavern, the Kaiserkeller, the Knotty Ash Village Hall … got you out of the bottle works or a five-year electrical apprenticeship. None appreciated that this, this crazy capering magic, could actually be a career.

As Paul told Paul Du Noyer, his ambition to be a musician came as much: "to get out of having a job and to pull the birds" as it was with any musical ambition. Or George: "Our original intention was just to be in a band as opposed to having a job. The goals were quite small, really".

Dave Mattacks was recording with George the day they heard John was shot. "We talked a bit about Beatlemania," he told Graeme Thomson, "and then George said the phrase that really stuck with me… 'All I really wanted to do was to be in a band'…"

Of course, timing had a lot to do with it. As the 1960s dawned, rock & roll was all but dead – Elvis sequestered in the Army; Eddie Cochran and Buddy Holly dead and buried; Gene Vincent a broken man; Little Richard a religious fanatic, Chuck Berry banged up on morals charges and Jerry Lee Lewis railroaded out of the UK with his teenage bride… Well, he just didn't give a cuss and carried on being Jerry Lee.

On the UK charts, Cliff Richard, Adam Faith and Tommy Steele were edging towards the middle of the road which was already comfortably occupied by Frankie Vaughan, Michael Holliday and Craig Douglas. Johnny Kidd fought a valiant rearguard for real rock & roll with the stuttering guitar riff which ushered in 'Shakin' All Over'. I feel the sheer awfulness of pre-Beatle Britpop can be epitomised by the Avons' 1959 'Seven Little Girls…' faux American accents; trite automotive imagery… Even through the warm glass of nostalgia, it remains slim, charmless, safe and predictable. There is nothing wrong with 'easy listening', nothing pejorative about the term, whether it's Perry Como or Cliff taking his foot off the pedal and switching to become an all-round entertainer. I have fond memories of the music of the period. It was safe. It was unchallenging. It was what the BBC rationed and spoon-fed you. You didn't know any better, so you took what was on offer.

But by 1960, it was recognised that the teenager had arrived: a 1960 survey had over 5,000,000 UK teenagers, accounting for a healthy percentage of disposable income.

So they became a target for advertising – in the UK, advertising expenditure doubled between 1955 and 1960. As the critic Alexander Walker reflected: "Youth [was endowed] with a corporate identity and going a long way to wiping out the more obvious social distinctions. Aspirations were on the way up; pride and even consciousness in belonging to a particular class was growing blurred as the economic boom brought more and more consumer goods within everyone's range…" That meant television sets, motorcycles, hi-fi stereos, guitars, amplifiers … all to fuel the new decade of the 1960s.

Such was the background against which the Beatles returned to their Liverpool home. Their Hamburg absence had left a void which was now filled by dozens of groups. In February 1961 a poll by John Cochrane marked Liverpool's groups on Personality, Showmanship, Singing, Musical Ability, Beat, Originality of Numbers and Originality. He even included his own group, the fabulously-named Wump & the Werbles along with the Thunderers, Topspots, Cimarrons, Pressmen… the Beatles came equal second (after the Dominoes) and were only awarded 3/5 for Originality of Numbers.

The gloomy pre-Christmas days of 1960 were a low point in their existence. After three years of sporadic gigging locally, they had beefed up their craft onstage in Hamburg all-nighters. They had learned licks at one remove from the late, great Eddie Cochran. They had demonstrably expanded their repertoire. They had fashioned a new image. They were coiled, and ready. Unfortunately, by and large, Liverpool wasn't. Paul and George didn't even know John had slinked his way back to Mendips and Mimi's withering welcome.

Broke and broken down, as 1960 wound down, the Beatles were all but busted. But thanks to the championing of Pete Best's mum and encouragement from a British Rail employee there was some light at the end of the tunnel…

*

Allan Williams had all but washed his hands of the band. George hung around home depressed, he had been convinced that his bandmates would remain in Hamburg and carry on without him. It led to Paul taking his only 'proper' job (trainee coil-winder at Massey & Coggins, with his apprenticeship scheduled to finish in 1966 – happily circumstances intervened, "I wasn't a very good coil-winder").

Pete was also at home, a location which also happened to provide a basement for teenagers to relax in… So before long, the Beatles were back at the Casbah. For once they had a regular drummer, but with Stu still exiled in Hamburg and cementing his relationship with Astrid, Pete's mate Chas Newby took over on bass. So, locked and loaded, in the dog days of 1960, a local DJ took a hand.

Bob Wooler (1926–2002) was a fascinating character, and another whose role in the subsequent success of the group has been under-appreciated. Mind you, much of that was due to Wooler's conflicting personality. He could switch anecdotes as efficiently as the discs he flipped. The British Rail clerk was a frustrated songwriter, with a penchant for classic pre-Beatle songwriters – Cole Porter, Johnny Mercer, Irving Berlin, etc. Yet it was Bob Wooler who was undeniably one of the moving forces in the whole Merseybeat phenomenon. (Many years later, Bob Dylan confirmed it, on one of his *Theme Time Radio Hour* shows: "I hope I can be as good a DJ as Bob Wooler".)

Wooler had a way with words – Faron (of Faron's Flamingoes) he christened "the Panda-Footed Prince of Prance". Paraphrasing *The Maltese Falcon*, Wooler called the Beatles "the stuff that screams are made of". On the back of the first 007 film, when Bob was fed up inveigling Brian to get more dates for the group at the Cavern, the DJ eventually christened him 'Dr No'. Talking to Bob in a Liverpool pub a few years before he died, after some reluctance, I chided him into repeating his famous Cavern announcement, which he made an estimated 274 times: "Hi there all you cave dwellers, and welcome to the best of cellars… Turn the hi-fi high and the lights down low, and welcome to the fabulous … Beatles show!"

Bob Wooler's knowledge of the latest American recordings, his network of contacts on the burgeoning beat scene of Liverpool and as an occasional getter-of-gigs for groups, all made him a key player in the city. As for the Beatles, it was thanks to a Wooler booking, on 27 December 1960 that the tide turned in their favour. It took a lot of persuading from Bob to promoter Brian Kelly to have the Beatles on the show at Litherland's Town Hall Ballroom. Despite the posters which have turned up at auction houses over the years, as Bill Harry pointed out, they were forgeries. The group's addition to the bill was too late for the posters to be printed including their name.

Mark Lewisohn has written of their gig at Litherland's Town Hall Ballroom on 27 December 1960: "If any one live performance … could be described as the turning point it was this… the group never looked back after this night".

For years, and with memories of the sort of crowd a group might attract at the time, I have tried to picture the scene… As a hormone-fuelled teenager with a few bob in your pocket to burn… You could stay in to watch BBC (that night's highlights included the London Festival Ballet, the film of *Albert RN* – plucky POWs baffle gormless Goons – and concluding with *Ar Yr Aelwyd* "Welsh light entertainment").

Obviously, you would rather stick needles in your eyes… So it is off to a council-run ballroom. Toppin' up in the pub beforehand, once inside you light up and make do with coke in a bottle as you scan the talent. The boys are all beefed up, six years off the ration, and sweaty from manual work, their Elvis quiffs are beginning to wilt. A dapper appearance is required, 'Mod' is too strict a discipline; too southern; too queer, and lies in the future.

Merseyside boys are neat, but not too neat, you don't want to get blood on the old Montague Burton. Those early Beatle shows in Liverpool were marked by an air of menace. It could simply be the testosterone firing up as a casual glance at 'your' bird sparked up a fight. Or it could be territorial, a gang straying into another group's turf. The ground for these gladiatorial combats was often the dance halls the Beatles played. To keep things in order and on the straight and narrow, hard-eyed bouncers scanned the crowd.

Too often the trouble came from the girls. Squeezed into silk skirts, they were as territorial as their boyfriends. Even though it was an age before the Pill could guarantee guilt-free sex, it didn't stop lubricated, lustful thoughts. All bopping like Chuck Berry's 'Sweet Little Sixteen' with "the grown-up blues, tight dresses and lipstick".

Sipping coke through a straw, seated around the ballroom, the Scouse Sophia Lorens are as steely-eyed as their dinner-jacketed protectors. Through a fug of Nelson smoke and as their blood-red lips ceaselessly chew gum, they too scan the competition. Squeezed into bras to make them more Jayne Mansfield, willing to let a hint of slip show and wagging to the beat as they wonder if a stray hand will make contact with stocking top before evening's end.

Clutching close, the couples manoeuvre round the dance floor, stray hands caressing silk-clad buttocks before being moved back up. Earthy promises whispered below beehive hairdos. Nicotine-breathed pledges as lips lock. Held close, each looking forward, to a future just four days ahead, a future which could take them outside and away from Litherland and into the New Year of 1961.

Bob Wooler spins his discs professionally – that week's No.1, Elvis' immediate post-Army, light operatic 'It's Now or Never' would almost certainly have featured, as would current hits from Cliff, the Drifters, the Shadows. If there is a sense that the crowd is still in a sentimental, post-Christmas mood, seasonal hits like Nina & Frederick's 'Little Donkey' or Adam Faith's 'Lonely Pup' might be slipped in…

To build the anticipation, the live acts are screened from the dancers by curtains. They float above the crowd on the stage. Bob Wooler mutes the 45s, and announces the headliners as "direct from Hamburg". Certainly as the curtains part, and the leather-jacketed, cowboy-boot-stomping group are revealed, no one associates them with the skiffle outfit who had been limping round Liverpool for years.

Leather spelled trouble, it implied motorcycle gangs, rockers; tough types who wielded their bicycle chains to resolve an argument, then talk about it in the bloody and bleeding aftermath. These Germans onstage had that hard-edge look to them, an arrogance which had taken the world to war only 20 years earlier. Thriller writer Dick Francis confirmed the menace in his 1965 *For Kicks*. To transform into a 'good' character "a black leather jacket [completed] what sideburns begin. Wearing both you won't have any character to speak of. They are regulation dress for delinquents".

Just look at the group: the doe-eyed singer comes across as positively unhinged as he tears into Little Richard's 'Long Tall Sally'. The rhythm guitarist's myopia lends itself to a steely stare – unable to see the crowd, he comes across as an arrogant, leather-clad lout. An image he did little to dissuade onlookers from. The other guitarist (little distinction was really made between "lead" and "rhythm" at a dance) brought little in the way of showmanship or stagecraft. His head bobbed to the song's rhythms, but his eyes were locked on to the spider fingers working their way up and down the guitar's neck. Their temporary bassist kept his head down. And at the back, unsmiling, thumping away, the drummer, hammering the beat so you could feel it on the undulating dance floor.

What emanated from that stage was a power, an energy which even Bob Wooler's specially selected Hit Parade discs couldn't match. Battle-hardened by Hamburg, the Beatles could draw on hundreds of songs culled from Preludin-powered nights in Germany.

That night in Litherland, they took no prisoners. As the New Year dawned, word of mouth spread about the Beatles. Chas Newby's short spell as a Beatle was finished when he returned to college, which left a vacancy on the bass. Over the years, conspiracy theorists have had McCartney filling the bass slot as a deliberate move to shift the balance of power in the group. With Stuart out of sight, Paul on bass could edge closer to John. But looking back he told me it was a professional decision, made out of necessity: "I have *always* been a guitar player, that's a big central thing with me, a big core thing… I started off on trumpet, then guitar, then played guitar with the Beatles for a year, then I got lumbered with the bass really. I was the only one who'd do it, nobody else would.

"There's these stories that have come up about me trying to shove Stuart out of the group and get the bass spot. But it was the spot nobody wanted! There are these strange barnacles of stories that cling over the years".

Looking back on those pre-fame shows in and around Liverpool years later, Paul still shivered when he recalled the menace of the Teddy Boys. Out to damage anyone who looked like muscling in on their birds. And the prime target was the group, elevated onstage and the cynosure of all attention.

The Liverpool gangs were legendary for their toughness, literally stamping on anyone who raised their ire. They would come equipped with flick-knives, bicycle chains, knuckle dusters. The Garston Baths was a regular venue, known locally as 'the Blood Baths'. The Grafton Ballroom, aka 'The Grafton Brawlroom'.

"The Grosvenor Ballroom in Wallasey was one of the worst places," Paul remembered when we spoke: "There would be a hundred Wallasey lads squaring up to a hundred lads from Seacombe and all hell would break loose… There were fists flying everywhere. One Ted grabbed me and said, 'Don't move, or you're bloody dead'. I was scared for my life but I had to get my Elpico amp".

Bob Wooler was the Godfather of the Merseybeat explosion. It was the pedigree of his musical knowledge, his vast and comprehensive collection of recorded music allied with his unmitigated enthusiasm for the music filling the air of his native Liverpool which fuelled that enthusiasm. It was following that pivotal, powerhouse Litherland performance that Wooler took on the challenging task of finding the Beatles more paid gigs in and around town.

Thanks to pioneering investigation by Mark Lewisohn, we can trace those early 1961 hometown shows as the arc of the Beatles' progression – the Aintree Institute, Bootle's St John's Hall, Seaforth's Lathom Hall, the Merseyside Civil Services Club, with Mona Best's Casbah Club as a default setting. On occasion, the bigger ballrooms took them in. Advertised as 'Direct from Hamburg', the group were frequently amused by overhearing fans remarking on how good their English was.

Eight weeks later, it was to be another date at an otherwise inauspicious venue which marked a further notch. The Beatles cemented with the club that was to be linked to their rise like a Siamese twin. By the time they first came to play the Cavern, at a lunchtime session in February 1961, rock & roll was allowed, with the Trad Jazz boom, which had succeeded skiffle, close on its heels.

Accountant Ray McFall (1926–2015) bought the Cavern in 1959, and for the next couple of years, it had been the Trad Jazz acts who pulled the punters in: Kenny Ball, Alex Welsh, Humphrey Lyttelton, Ken Colyer, Acker Bilk, Chris Barber, Mick Mulligan (with singer George Melly) and at least 30 other ensembles were gigging up and down the country. They happily pillaged the music of New Orleans from half a century before.

As well as his bibular onstage antics, and his avowed fondness for surrealism, until his death in 2007, George Melly was an astute commentator on the pop culture scene. Writing in 1966, looking back a mere half decade, Melly remembered an early 60s gig at the

Cavern when he appreciated that the writing was on the wall for his type of music: "The Mick Mulligan Band ... played the Cavern, and we noticed that the management was no longer hiring a local jazz band to play during our interval. Instead, we returned from the pub to find the small stage cluttered with amplification, in place of the three-piece front line playing the reassuring if stereotyped Negro dance music of the 1920s, there were these young men with electric guitars playing and shouting the modern Negro urban blues at what seemed to be a quite unnecessary volume".

(For a colourful idea of Bohemian life and the 50s jazz scene in pre-Beatle Britain, Liverpool-born George Melly's *Owning-Up* is unbeatable.)

The impact of the Trad Jazz boom on the pre-Beatle British music scene of the 1960s is frequently overlooked. Skiffle, which provided the nascent Beatles with a beginning, grew out of the music popularised by Ken Colyer and Chris Barber. The first No.1 single that George Martin produced was the Temperance Seven's nod-of-the-head to Trad 'You're Driving Me Crazy'. Beatle chums the Bonzo Dog Doo-Dah Band flowered under the Trad umbrella. *Hard Day's Night* director Richard Lester cut his teeth on the cash-in 1961 quickie, *It's Trad, Dad*. As well as the usual suspects (Ball, Barber and Bilk) the film included incongruous performances from Gene Vincent, Chubby Checker and Del Shannon.

Acker Bilk, the bowler-hatted clarinetist from Somerset, merits a mention. With his beguiling instrumental 'Stranger on the Shore', Bilk became the first British act of the rock & roll era to reach No.1 on the American singles charts. 'Stranger on the Shore' hit the top in May 1962, a full 20 months before the Beatles stormed the citadel. And as if that wasn't enough Acker ... many years later, on 31 March 1976, the Sex Pistols made their debut at Oxford Street's 100 Club. A poster of the period showed the punk pioneers squeezed between the Black Bottom Stompers and Mr Acker Bilk & His Paramount Jazz Band.

While Ball, Barber and Bilk carried on chart success way into the 1960s, the new Cavern club owner Ray McFall knew that rock & roll was where the future lay. Witnessing the excitement generated by the Beatles during their lunchtime sessions in the first couple of months of 1961, McFall lost no opportunity to get them along at every opportunity. It had been McFall who introduced the popular lunchtime sessions, primarily to attract the secretaries from the nearby offices. Thus it was, around lunchtime on 21 February 1961, that the Beatles made their debut at the club which was to become indelibly linked to both them and the entire Merseybeat phenomenon.

In recognition of his championing of the group, McFall accompanied the Beatles on that historic first trip to America in February 1964 – he's the dazed looking chap in the Russian hat. Alas, unable to provide funds for a fire exit and to refurbish the toilets, McFall was declared bankrupt in 1966, and the original Cavern closed down.

Over the years, as well as its place in Beatle legend, the club had had its moments: Paul McCartney roared with laughter when he told me that, while recording *Run Devil Run*, the Pirates' guitarist Mick Green recalled playing there with Johnny Kidd: the highlight of the piratical purblind rocker's act was to hurl his cutlass onto the wooden stage; unfortunately the trick backfired and the sword bounced off the concrete stage and nearly decapitated an audience member who immediately ran off with the sword. It was from the Cavern stage that a tired and emotional Jet Harris took a tumble on occasion when the Shadows played there.

It was reopened later in 1966 by Prime Minister Harold Wilson and soldiered on for three more years. Among the names who appeared on the stage until its final shutdown were Jimmy Page, Family, Edwin Starr, Ben E. King, Chuck Berry, Status Quo, Vinegar Joe (with Robert Palmer and Elkie Brooks), Brinsley Schwarz (watched from the audience by Elvis Costello), Supertramp, Suzi Quatro and Tim Rose (with John Bonham on drums). The new Cavern (still on Matthew Street) opened in 1984.

McFall was determined to keep the Cavern as smart and as reputable as he could, instilling a dress code ("we kept out the jeans brigade", he told Mark Lewisohn). Intriguingly, when I visited Elvis' birthplace of Tupelo, I learned that jeans were what the poor white trash wore in rural Mississippi, testifying to their humble status. When he became famous, Elvis refused to wear jeans for any film role or public appearance.

The Beatles came to the Cavern, buoyed and cocky from their Hamburg nights. One regular fan compiled a list of the 90-odd songs the Beatles played at the Cavern (interestingly neither 'Love Me Do' nor 'I Saw Her Standing There' was included). With a bulging German repertoire, they came and played with a fire and fervour which was literally 'in your face' at the Cavern. On a stage that was barely elevated from their audience, the group swapped and switched roles: Paul and John as front men, with shy George occasionally stepping forward. At the back, Pete kept up that floor-pounding rhythm. Intimidating in their leathers, in-jokes filled the air between numbers, dog ends were flicked, fag ash dropped. It was the Cavern which gave them a base. It was a long way from the London Palladium and Carnegie Hall, but it was the Cavern which gave them their grounding. It was the Cavern which witnessed the first, fledgling signs of Beatlemania.

Cavern founder Alan Sytner was convinced the club played a key role in the subsequent success of the group which came to be so closely allied to the club. Talking to Spencer Leigh, Sytner attested: "Without me, no Cavern; without me, no Beatles… Obviously Lennon and McCartney were geniuses, but would they have flourished without the Cavern? If they had been playing in church halls in Maghull, would anyone have taken any notice?"

*

Then it was back to Hamburg for a far more successful and substantial second visit. Much has been written about the Beatles' German activities, but Sin City certainly welcomed them with open arms. Amidst the sweltering all-night sets, the pounding rock & roll, the visit passed in a blur of pill-popping Preludin excitement. Like a pied-piping William Brown, Lennon led his priapic Outlaws in a frenzy of French letter, knee-trembling bacchanalia.

"The Germans like mainly rock tunes", Paul wrote back to Liverpool, "we've learned 'Peppermint Twist' for over here". The tune provided a rare showcase for Pete Best, who kept the all-important beat going onstage, but rarely socialised with the group members offstage.

Stuart Sutcliffe had made a brief return to Liverpool but was back in Hamburg, drawn deeper into his relationship with Astrid. By now, committing himself wholeheartedly to his art, Stuart effectively quit the group, leaving Paul as the full-time bassist. It was in Hamburg that McCartney bought his signature Hofner violin bass. It was on one of his rare forays outside the St Pauli district, to the more up-market Colonnade 29, where the Steinway showroom was located.

Rarely has one musician been so closely associated with one instrument: while I was watching him rehearse in 2003 I found myself standing by a rack of his onstage instruments. And there it was, *that* bass: I tentatively touched it, and confirmed that, yes, still sellotaped to it was the set list from the Beatles' last ever concert before a paying audience. Tour photographer Bill Bernstein was happy for me to be photographed holding it aloft, and as I reached out to grasp the bass by the neck I halted. Knowing my luck, what must surely be the world's most valuable piece of rock memorabilia, would have come apart in my hands... So I let it be, with a soft caress of that neck...

On their second visit to the German city, the group had moved up a notch, with a residency at the Top Ten Club. It was a plusher, less raucous environment than previous residencies. And there to welcome the Scousers were their regular Hamburg compadres – Astrid, with Stuart, Klaus and Jurgen. Tony Sheridan was happy to have them as his backing band as well as them having to play their own marathon sets, six nights a week. Scholars (alright, the indefatigable Mark Lewisohn) estimate that during their second Hamburg stint, the Beatles played for a total of 535 hours.

Cosy, hot meals with Astrid's mum; better accommodation; the beginnings of a dedicated audience; a repertoire far wider than that of their contemporaries... second time around, Hamburg gave them a home from home. Even with Stuart largely absent from the performing group (he would still on occasion join them for his crowd-pleasing 'Love Me Tender') it was Stuart's offstage life which was to have a lasting impact.

Somehow sensing that the James Dean quiff was so 1950s, Astrid fashioned Stuart's hair into the comb-forward fringe popular with the pseudo-existentialists. All succumbed except the drummer. Whole books, films and two autobiographies have been written about Pete Best's departure from the Beatles. But, conspiracy theories aside, what was evident from early on is that... He Just Didn't Fit In. In his *Drummed Out! The Sacking of Pete Best*, Spencer Leigh doggedly lists 13 reasons why he was dismissed, the most evident being George Martin's dislike of his drumming. But that was just the tinder for the flame the producer lit on something which had been simmering for some time.

Leaving aside his qualities as a drummer (to my mind, nowhere near as bad as made out and, hell, at that stage, it *was* only rock & roll) Pete was the outsider. Reluctant to indulge in their offstage antics, rarely mingling once offstage from the Top Ten or even in their shared accommodation, Pete was the drummer who didn't belong.

In one of the few mentions in *Anthology*, George remembered: "Pete would never hang out with us. When we finished the gig, Pete would go off on his own, and we three would hang out together, and then when Ringo was around it was like a full unit, both on and off stage. When there were the four of us with Ringo, it felt rocking".

The one who rocked was still with Rory Storm, and living the high life at Butlin's, Ringo surely thought life couldn't get any better than this? Birds on tap, and changing

BEATLES CHANGE DRUMMER !

Ringo Starr (former drummer with **Rory Storm and the Hurricanes**) has joined **The Beatles**, replacing **Pete Best** on drums. Ringo has admired The Beatles for years and is delighted with his new engagement. Naturally he is tremendously excited about the future.

The Beatles will fly to London to make recordings at E.M.I. Studios. They will be recording numbers that have been specially written for the group, which they have received from their recording manager George Martin (Parlophone).

THE BEATLES TO PLAY CHESTER

As a result of the phenominal Box Office success of The Beatles during their 4-week season of Monday nights at the Plaza Ballroom, St. Helens, the directors of Whetstone Entertainments, controllers of the ballroom, have engaged The Beatles for a series of four Thursday night sessions at the Riverpark Ballroom, Chester, which commenced on 16th August.

PETE BEST

Mersey Beat Shock! Horror!

every week! His own Ford Zodiac! Sailing past 21, Ringo had avoided the Army, and could sign his own HP agreement. He occasionally crossed paths with the Beatles in Liverpool and in Hamburg. And I hadn't realised that Ringo had drummed with the Beatles at the Cavern on at least three occasions, once when Pete was in court for a driving offence.

There was little real rivalry between the groups, aside from odd arguments about who did the best version of a Gene Vincent number, or the longest 'What'd I Say'. Otherwise, it was the usual audience of hookers, gangsters and rock & roll-starved Germans who welcomed the Beatles back with open arms. "'Be Bop A Lula' was the first record I bought," Paul told me. "I remember going to a place near Penny Lane for the afternoon, as we often did. Have a ciggy and just listen to records – 'Blue Jean Bop' was always one of my favourites".

The Beatles got to know Gene Vincent during those hazy, crazy Hamburg days. "He was a crazy man, a Marine, and he had the injury on his leg, and he really liked his Scotch," Paul told me. Repairing to his hotel, "Gene said, 'My girlfriend Margy's in there you know'. We never knew about girlfriends, could have been a groupie, we were so respectful – gosh, an older man's girlfriend (we thought the girl Johnny Gentle had on tour was his wife!).

"She eventually comes to the door alone … and there's some trousers on the bed and he says, 'Those Henry's trousers?' She says, 'No, they're yours Gene'… So Gene goes to the little table between the twin beds and pulls out a gun! And we're going, 'Oh fuuuck!' You know, we're just kids, we don't wanna die now. And he's going, 'Where's Henry?' So we just said, as soon as the gun came out, 'Listen Gene, we gotta go'."

As well as Gene, the German city also managed to attract big name American acts like Jerry Lee Lewis. Paul wrote to Liverpool fans while the group were in Hamburg, "Little Richard is a laugh", improbably adding, "we have some great Bible meetings with him".

Fortuitously, the city provided the location for the Beatles to cut what became their first vinyl release. Soon after arriving at the Top Ten, the group had been seen by record producer Bert Kaempfert (1923–80). The fact that Kaempfert's 'Wonderland By Night' had knocked their idol Elvis' 'Are You Lonesome Tonight' off the US No.1 spot would have impressed the group, even if the mild middle-aged (he was 37) man didn't. Even less impressive was the location Kaempfert chose for that all-important first recording, a civic hall on the outskirts of town.

That first professional Beatles record was 'My Bonnie', recorded in Hamburg with singer Tony Sheridan in June 1961, credited to them as 'The Beat Brothers' because 'Beatles' sounded too much like the German for 'penis'. 'My Bonnie' was eventually released in the UK on 5 January 1962, credited to Tony Sheridan & the Beatles, a good ten months before the group's official debut, 'Love Me Do'. Lennon took lead vocals on another song from the Hamburg session, 'Ain't She Sweet', while the punningly-titled instrumental 'Cry for a Shadow' only became officially widely available on *Anthology 1*.

Also included on that session, the Beatles backed Sheridan on Hank Snow's maudlin 'Nobody's Child', a song which George returned to many years later with the Traveling Wilburys. To his credit, in February 1962, following a request from Brian Epstein, Kaempfert released them from his contract. "I do not want to spoil the chance of the group getting recording contracts elsewhere…" One can only speculate on their future if the gentlemanly Kaempfert had said 'Nein!'

Until then, and in the wake of worldwide Beatlemania, those Kaempfert recordings were a footnote in Beatle history. Had they been solely by Tony Sheridan, or had Kaempfert been happy enough to let Kingsize Taylor loose in the studio, would whole books have been written about those records?

'My Bonnie' was first copyrighted in 1882, and although frequently credited as 'Traditional' it was written by the 19th-century songwriter and band leader Charles Pratt. It was based on a traditional Scottish folk song, dealing with the flight of Bonnie Prince Charlie after the 1745 Battle of Culloden. The Beatles' version, with Sheridan on lead vocal, was typical of the rocked-up versions of popular standards – it was a habit the rockers couldn't leave alone, just listen to Conway Twitty's revved-up take on 'Loch Lomond'.

Like haruspical soothsayers sifting through the entrails, in 'the birth of the Beatles', those rudimentary Hamburg recordings have been endlessly sifted and analysed. In truth they are footnotes to the bigger picture: some nice Beatle harmonies on 'My Bonnie', which includes a competent George solo; an energetic John singing on 'Ain't She Sweet'; a nice Hank Marvin tribute on 'Cry for a Shadow' with some Bruce Welch flourishes from John on rhythm guitar… But, hand on heart, there is little of real substance or indication of their momentous future.

Tantalisingly, again not until *Anthology 1*, these fledgling releases were the only official opportunity to hear how Pete Best sounded with the Beatles. And in fairness, he's fine, providing a substantial beat, locking behind Paul's solid bass.

The record's later place in the group's history, of course, came in the wake of their UK and US triumphs a few years later when both 'My Bonnie' and 'Ain't She Sweet' achieved respectable chart placings in the wake of the Beatles' American triumph. Significantly and, however disputed the legend has become, it was that Polydor recording of 'My Bonnie' which led to a teenage fan inquiring of its availability in a Liverpool record store a matter of months later…

Brian Epstein was recognised as a successful player in the UK record retail trade of the time. A colleague of Brian's accompanied him on a trip with other UK record salesmen to Hamburg soon after the Beatles arrived on their second visit to the city. Graham Pauncefort told Mark Lewisohn that he was "fairly certain" he and Brian had stuck their heads into the Top Ten club while a group was performing onstage. That group could, of course, have been the Beatles and if so, Brian would have seen them in action some months before Raymond Jones made his historic inquiry at Brian's record counter.

In another of those You Couldn't Make It Up moments, a diary entry of 7 June 1961 finds former *Punch* editor, TV pundit and later Commissioner of Light, Malcolm Muggeridge[2] in Hamburg. His diary entry reads: "Dropped into a teenage rock-and-roll joint. Ageless children, sexes indistinguishable, tight-trousered stamping about, only the smell of sweat intimating animality. The band were English, from Liverpool, and recognised me. Long-haired, weird feminine sounds; bashing their instruments and emitting nerveless sounds

---

2   American historian Thomas E. Ricks points out that Muggeridge "in his long and varied life was the only person to converse with all three of the great 'Winstons' of twentieth-century England – Churchill, Orwell (1984's 'hero' was *Winston* Smith) and Lennon".

into microphones. In conversation rather touching in a way, their faces like Renaissance carvings of saints or blessed virgins. One of them asked me 'Is it true you're a communist?' No, I said; just in opposition. He nodded understandingly; in opposition himself in a way. 'You make money out of it?' he went on. I admitted that this was so. He, too, made money. He hoped to take back £200 to Liverpool". (A footnote adds "This was probably John Lennon".)

Rare political discussion in German basements aside, the Beatles finished their second Hamburg stint. Tearful farewells to Stuart and Astrid, then they were homeward bound. As well as their Liverpool peers like the Searchers, Gerry & the Pacemakers and the Remo 4, in the Beatle wake into the Hamburg furnace came the next generation – Steve Winwood, the Move, Dave Dee, Ritchie Blackmore, Cliff Bennett, the Jaybirds (later Ten Years After), Dave Berry … all made their bones in the clubs along the Reeperbahn.

On their return to Liverpool in the summer of 1961, the Beatles made a beeline to the Cavern. Back in its comforting subterranean grottiness, they harmoniously resumed their onstage joshing and closeness to their loyal Liverpool audience. Loyal fans besieged Bob Wooler with requests to be played. Each Beatle had their own fervent following. And that included Pete Best.

As an aside, John Lennon began contributing to the newspaper *Mersey Beat*, which was first published by his art school contemporary Bill Harry. To his credit, Harry recognised that something was happening in and around Liverpool. It was too far from London for any of the music weeklies to notice. Bill equated it to the birth of jazz in the Storyville district of New Orleans 60 years before. Even if any publication had noticed, they would not have seriously equated the beat music pounded out by pop groups with the musical symmetry of Louis Armstrong or Kid Ory. So Harry decided to start his own magazine to convince the sceptics.

The best-known of all Lennon's contributions to the magazine came in Issue 1, 'On the Dubious Origins of the Beatles, Translated from the John Lennon'. Written in cod nursery rhyme, with a nod to the Old Testament, it's a humorous account of heavy German policing and the group's beginnings. A lifetime later, Paul McCartney called his 1997 album *Flaming Pie* after a John mention in that magazine debut.

Those prose scraps formed the basis of Lennon's first book; *In His Own Write* was published at the height of Beatlemania. He was accorded the distinction of a Foyle's Literary Lunch – the London literary landmark received more requests for tickets since they had honoured George Bernard Shaw. Lennon was accompanied by Brian Epstein and Lionel Bart, and would have been delighted to have seen Goon Harry Secombe in the audience. But was clearly overwhelmed by the event. Hungover and unaware he had to address the audience, his 'speech' consisted of "Thank you. God bless". Turning to the walrus-mustachioed cartoonist Osbert Lancaster to his left, Lennon remarked: "You've got a lucky face".

In the convoluted early years of the group it was obvious they were honing their craft and edging ahead of the competition. But it was all done (in the case of the Cavern quite literally) on a small stage. They needed someone to act on their behalf, to arrange contracts, sort bookings strive for that all-important record deal. Bill Harry was too busy with his *Mersey Beat* magazine; Cavern owner Ray McFall and local Liverpool promoter

Sam Leach were not really on their wavelength. One person they looked to declined: "The Beatles wanted someone who could further their career in a very positive way," Bob Wooler told Spencer Leigh. "They wanted somebody with nous, somebody with clout, somebody with cash and somebody who drove a car".

While the Cavern was effectively a home from home, it also gave the group an income. Historically, it provided them with a platform on which they would be witnessed by a shy shopkeeper who would, in a few short years, transform their lives, his own and, as an afterthought, the world in which we live.

The timing was impeccable: by the end of 1961, the Beatles had effectively been together for four years and remained a Merseyside phenomenon. They had done all they could do oop North. They were chafing to get out of Liverpool. The career of the man who would alter their fortunes and shape their future was running on parallel lines. Call it what you will – fate, kismet, chance, que sera sera … the combination would prove to be world-beating.

*

For many years, the story of how Brian Epstein (1934–67) chanced upon the Beatles has been almost as fiercely debated as the authorship of Shakespeare's plays. History has a customer's query alerting him to the group's existence. But as a Liverpool record shop manager with his finger firmly on the pulse of what his customers wanted, Brian must *surely* have heard of the Beatles? As a contributor to Bill Harry's *Mersey Beat* magazine, he must have seen their name in print. But I like to adhere to the authorised version of the story, because it fits so neatly into those fantastic conjunctions and connections which litter the early part of the Beatle story…

Another name in Beatle history who has long fascinated me is that of Raymond Jones, a key player in one of the great What Ifs of rock history; in the Beatle story, he is the unwitting instigator of unanticipated historic forces… Raymond Jones is the Gavrilo Princip of rock & roll.

The teenager had been blown away while having seen the Beatles play the Cavern and heard that, while in Germany, they'd cut a disc… Where else to inquire but Brian Epstein's NEMS record department? Which is what took Raymond Jones there on Saturday 28 October 1961.

I like to picture the boy, bored with the prospect of Saturday afternoon *Grandstand*, maybe buoyed by a few pints of beer, drifting in to inquire about a 45 rpm single. And it was that inquiry which irked Brian Epstein, because he couldn't locate 'My Bonnie' and that led the dapper young bachelor a few hundred yards along the road to the Cavern that fateful day a few weeks later.

But such are the twists and turns of Beatle history that, in later years, word went out that Raymond Jones never even existed! That he was a figment of the imagination of Brian's assistant Alistair Taylor, who made the name up in order to square NEMS' paperwork.

Such historical rewriting takes away the role of a key player in Beatle history. After years of silence and anonymity, Raymond Jones was tracked down by the tenacious Spencer Leigh, and was grateful to have his place in pop history assured: "No one will take away from me", said the real Raymond Jones modestly to Spencer, "that it was me who spoke to Brian Epstein and then he went to the Cavern to see them for himself. I didn't make them famous, but Brian Epstein made them famous and things might have been different without me".

Bob Wooler too confirms the existence of this key player – even giving his address (48 Stonefield Road, Liverpool, 14). "He worked at KB Print… He was an attractive boy and I'm sure that, had the record been requested by a girl, Brian would not have been interested. Nothing transpired between them, of course, but it made Brian want to seek out the group that Raymond Jones liked so much".

At 27, bachelor Brian Epstein was restless, chafing to escape the retail trade. In the same way that Elvis needed a Colonel Parker to elevate him from a word-of-mouth novelty south of the Mason–Dixon line, the Beatles needed Brian Epstein to lift them out of Liverpool. Over the years, the manager's relationship with his prime clients has been the subject of endless fascination and fruitless speculation. Hindsight has revealed that Epstein was not the best manager in rock history – his eager acceptance of low royalty rates from EMI and, significantly the substantial loss of merchandising income during the American blitzkrieg of 1964/65, revealed his naivety and managerial feet of clay.

In fairness, as Paul Du Noyer wrote: "Epstein's was … a world without signposts. Nobody had ever faced the sort of decisions he did, because The Beatles were reinventing the very nature of things, on a scale unimagined". He was also scrupulously honest. Unlike his peers – the Searchers' manager allegedly had at least two sets of books, one for the group to see, and one for him, which told the true story (there were even rumours of a *third* set, for the Inland Revenue).

I feel that, at the end of the day, and if for nothing else, it was Epstein who liberated them from Liverpool. It was Brian Epstein who got them to London; it was Epstein who secured them auditions for record labels and, crucially, it was Brian Epstein who secured them that vital recording contract. For those reasons alone, he stands supreme in the history of pop management. Unwittingly, he occupies a place in our island's history.

Urbane, charming, Jewish, homosexual, cultured … Epstein was everything his proteges were not. And indeed, it is still mystifying about what drew Epstein to the Beatles. Early biographers perforce had to shy away from any homosexual attraction; later ones sometimes appeared to concentrate on little else.

Musically they were miles apart – Brian erred towards classical music and what might be called 'easy listening' pop. Culturally and socially, the divide was equally wide. Yet something in the group's brash, ebullience connected with this reserved businessman. Perhaps it was through them that Brian could realise his ambitions, they could do all the things he only dreamed of; their outspoken, extrovert nature a realisation of his reserved introspection.

Born into a prosperous Jewish family in September 1934, Brian drew artistic impetus from his mother, Queenie and a strong business sense from his father, Harry. It was while at school as a teenager that Brian first became aware of his homosexual leanings, the illegality of which conflicted him for the remainder of his life.

He also had to cope with routine anti-semitism, although the UK had said No to Fascism in 1936, when the East End stood up to Mosley's Blackshirts. But the sacrifices made during WWII, and the horrific details of the Holocaust tempered much of the hostility. The occasional lyrics of Noel Coward and the novels of Dennis Wheatley portrayed the Jews as scheming, money-lovers. But, by and large, their financial astuteness was recognised. When Paul McCartney's father Jim heard that Brian Epstein was to manage his son's group he approved, like many of his generation he appreciated that Jews had "a good head for business".

Brian's Jewishness was as discreet as his homosexuality, however. A magazine report (*London Life* November 1966) had Brian and his new business partner, Vic Lewis, bringing the Oberammergau Passion Play to London. Strident protests from the Board of Deputies of British Jews saw Epstein issue the statement: "Under no circumstances did I wish myself or my organization to give offence to Jewish communities here or anywhere else in the world", and the project was dropped.[3]

The Beatles were lucky to have Brian as manager. Crucially, he got them a recording contract, which got them out of a provincial backwater and to London, the beating heart of the entertainment industry. I can understand Brian's snatching at the Parlophone offer, a recording contract was crucial to the group's future. In retrospect though, Brian's manifest failings became apparent: he could have, *should* have, fought harder over film advances and crucially all those lucrative merchandising opportunities. But within barely over a year Brian Epstein had gone from managing a furniture store to representing the biggest entertainment phenomenon in the country's history. Brian was sailing into unknown waters. Amateur he may have been, but that naivety was matched by a scrupulous honesty.

Too often fledging pop stars were taken advantage of – "What is this strange, Svengali power you have over me?" pop idol Anthony Newley asks scheming manager Sid James in *Idol on Parade*. "It's all under the stamp on your contract, boy". Such was Brian Epstein's integrity, he never even signed his first contract with the Beatles, the one with Pete Best's signature. A contract *was* signed, on 1 October 1962, by which time Ringo was on board. Such was their tender years, that Paul and George's signatures had to be endorsed by their fathers as the boys were under the legal age of 21.

On leaving school, the highly-strung, restless Brian reluctantly entered the family business, as a furniture salesman. It was a long way removed from any artistic ambitions he harboured. But dutifully, Brian wanted to please his parents, and he found that he was good dealing with the shop's customers. Unlike his later charges, the National Service net swept the 18-year-old Epstein up in 1952. His two-year army service at least gave him the opportunity to be based in London. But it was not to last… In Brian's account, he was discharged early for inadvertently impersonating an officer. In fact, he was discharged 'on medical grounds', a euphemism for a psychiatrist's discovery of his homosexual tendencies.

Back in Liverpool, Brian returned to the family firm, but a brief taste of the capital's high life had only reinforced what a stultifying future lay ahead in his pinched and parochial hometown of the mid-1950s. In the first Epstein biography, the fair-minded

---

3 In Germany in 1945, Billy Wilder had to authorise German theatrical productions. On learning that the Oberammergau Passion Play was about to be performed, with an ex-SS man playing Jesus, Wilder okayed the production, "As long as they use real nails".

Ray Coleman chronicled the subterranean but quite wide-ranging network of pubs and clubs where Liverpool's gay community could gather. The Asnett, the Magic Clock, the Spinning Wheel, the Old Dive… all were known to Brian.

For all the 9–5 limitations Brian was a dutiful son and he immersed himself in the family's furniture business. But he was still drawn to his artistic side, happily mingling with actors from the bustling Liverpool Playhouse, which led to his applying to, and being accepted by, the prestigious Royal Academy of Dramatic Art (RADA) in London. Fortuitously, Brian began his foray into the London theatrical world in the autumn of 1956, the same time that John Osborne's play *Look Back in Anger* premiered at Chelsea's Royal Court Theatre and, with the force of a hob-nailed boot, kicked in the French windows of English theatre.

As a student, Brian was diligent, and as a performer, there was an indication that, if he persevered, a career on the stage could have beckoned. His reports singled out his "Very pleasant personality… glimpses of latent power and breadth, which augur well…" But by now, the 'confirmed bachelor' was fully aware of his homosexuality. By his early 20s, Brian had already become involved in Liverpool's subterranean gay locations and, now resident in London, he could take full advantage of the capital's queer scene.

Any plans he may have had for remaining in London at RADA were thwarted when he was arrested for soliciting, following a police sting at a public toilet in Swiss Cottage. Back then, a full decade before its legalisation, police persecution of homosexuals was a regular element of the Met's crime-busting activities. Brian was caught, arrested and tried.

Confiding in his diaries, Brian looked through "the wreckage of my life by society… the lying criminal methods of the police in importuning me and consequently capturing me leaves me cold, stunned and finished". Epstein's self-loathing was apparent. One senses he would love to have been, as society saw it at the time, 'normal'. You appreciate the pleasure it would have given him to have presented his beloved mother a happily married son and daughter-in-law, with the prospect of grandchildren.

Following his arrest, Brian was allowed to return to his studies, and by all accounts, displayed a real potential for the acting world. But with his evident butterfly tendencies, Brian dropped out during his second year. For all his fondness for the theatre and its environs, RADA marked another flop on the Epstein trajectory.

So it was back up North to a despairing family, concerned about just what would occupy the attention of their eldest son and heir. When he took over the management of North End Music Stores (NEMS) in the city centre in 1958, the family breathed a sigh of relief. Here was something which could, and did, occupy Brian, and he soon even began enjoying the supervision of the store's record department. Brian's artistic flair was soon manifest in the store's window displays, while he displayed an ingrained business sense when it came to stocktaking.

Like EMI's later idea to keep classical music from contaminating with pop, Brian had the store's classical department to greet you on the ground floor. That ghastly, noisy 'pop' which attracted such scruffy customers was consigned to the basement. Of course, NEMS was not the only place to buy records in the city. A number of department stores had their own departments – Rushworth & Draper's was only a few doors along from Brian's store in Whitechapel. Often to be found behind the record counter was Elvis Costello's mum

Lillian. It is tantalising to think of her selling records to Quarrymen, but she had gone down South by then.

On the surface, Brian had it all: self-confident, quietly handsome, a secure job with a prosperous future... But there was a restless dissatisfaction. Beneath the surface was his sexual orientation, that alone made Brian 'different' in the stilted, stultifying north of England during the complacent Conservatism of the 1950s. A taste of London life, an appreciation of good food and fine wine, a fondness for foreign travel, all marked Brian out, but at his core was the guilt he felt over his sexuality. By all accounts, it was a leaning towards 'rough trade' which attracted Brian, and which inevitably left him open to violence and blackmail.

A second court appearance, this time in Liverpool, led to the blackmailer being jailed, his victim escaped without his being named, but the threat of prison had hung over Brian. An intriguing letter from February 1962 came to light from Brian's solicitors. At the Kardomah café, a teenage boy spoke to "two members of 'The Beatles'... 'I believe Brian Epstein is managing you, which one of you does he fancy?'" It continued that the "unwarranted innuendo [was one] which our client takes the gravest possible exception". The shocked teenager duly apologised. But this was the shadow life Brian had to lead.

One senses that it was that element of 'feasting with panthers' which appealed to Brian. But he never let it overshadow his efficient management of NEMS' record department. It was the organisation of the records, not the music it sold which appealed to him. Brian's tastes erred more towards West End musicals, classical music, ballads... Not for him the revolutionary rock & roll of Elvis or the teenage frenzy of Gene Vincent and Eddie Cochran. But Brian knew what the kids who flocked into NEMS and filled the listening booths to hear the latest pop sounds liked. By their standards, at the age of 27, with his smart suits and tie, his carefully cut hair and fastidious style of speaking, Mr Epstein was old.

Ironically, though he may not have 'got' the music, Brian knew a hit when he heard one – his assistant Alistair Taylor ordered five copies of John Leyton's 'Johnny Remember Me'. On hearing the song, Brian demonstrably increased the order. By the summer of 1961, it was the UKs No.1 single. True to his word 'Mr Brian' would obtain any record a customer requested: a teenage Spencer Leigh remembers a man in front of him asking if his record of Hitler's speeches had arrived!

Much as he enjoyed the work which kept him occupied at the family store, Brian also relished the opportunities to escape – dining out in posh restaurants in the Cheshire countryside or regular theatre visits. More prosaically, he holidayed in Italy and his beloved Spain. He enjoyed a business trip to Germany. These escapes only seemed to fuel that Epstein restlessness. With NEMS established and running smoothly, there was little to keep him occupied. There was nothing to challenge him... Until liberation came in the unlikely shape of a teenage Ted one afternoon in October 1961...

Brian became frustrated at his inability to supply this customer's request, and his search for a copy of 'My Bonnie' became something like a crusade. Half a century on, it was evident that Brian Epstein *must* have known of the Beatles – the Liverpool grapevine alone should have alerted him to their existence. But Raymond Jones' inquiry was the catalyst. In his methodical way, Brian wrote in his memo pad on that otherwise unremarkable Saturday, "The Beatles. My Bonnie. Check on Monday".

An innocent inquiry liberated Brian from the family firm and saw him established as the Svengali behind the nation's biggest-ever entertainment phenomenon. It took him from Liverpool to the world, and to a tragically early death. Barely six years after Raymond Jones inquired about a pop record, Brian Epstein was dead. He was 32 years old.

*

Every great journey begins with a single step. The single step which set Brian Epstein off on his unimaginable trajectory was actually 18 steps, down to the grungy murk of the Cavern during the lunchtime of 9 November 1961. In typical Epstein fashion, the trip was planned with a military efficiency his Army superiors would have appreciated. Uncertain as to how he would be received, Brian asked his assistant Alistair Taylor to accompany him. He also asked Bill Harry to clear it with the club's owner Ray McFall to allow him access. It was as if he was booking guinea tickets for an Olivier performance at the Old Vic rather than a bob on the door to see a bunch of teenage rockers in a Liverpool cellar.

We shall never really know the thoughts and images which flitted across Brian Epstein's imagination the very first time he witnessed the Beatles in action that autumn. Erotic fantasies of the leather boys? A liberating, escapist vision? A painful reminder of how buttoned-up he was? Or simply – recalling his failed Army spell, his failed run as an actor, his dead-end future at NEMS – were they an opportunity for him to escape a humdrum future?

By all accounts, it was a typical Beatle performance at the Cavern. Pumping out a loud, brash style of rock & roll which Brian would have been unfamiliar with, would certainly have struck him as sounding different to the polite pop he sold over the counter during the day. Clad in leather jackets and jeans, they certainly looked different from the current pop idols like John Leyton, Jess Conrad or Eden Kane. Smoking, joking amongst themselves, clowning between numbers, they obviously had a rapport with their adoring audience.

Dapper as ever, Brian made his way to speak to the group between sets. George recognised the shop owner. "What brings Mr Epstein here?" inquired the laconic Beatle (Note the respectful "Mr"). A brief chat, perhaps obtaining more details of the availability of 'My Bonnie', a polite inquiry into where they might be performing next... And he was gone.

Realistically, what was it that drew Brian Epstein to the Beatles? What *was* it? A homoerotic fantasy? Drawn by the guitarist's hard stare, suggesting a welcome brutality (actually John's myopia)? Or the engaging cuteness of the boy playing bass? To Brian's comfortable, middle-class world they suggested ... menace. And was the only way to get close to them was to pose as a manager, convince them that he was the one to liberate them?

Or simply the buttoned-up shop manager responded to their energy. They evinced a couldn't-give-a-damn attitude at odds with Brian's reserved mien. A mental coin toss made him decide to persevere. One thing is certain, the performance provided an immediate incentive for Brian. Alistair Taylor recalled the fateful trip, primarily his descent into the Cavern ("a ghastly place"). Intriguingly he conjured up a moment which *may* have been the reason to alert Brian's interest. Prior to the set ending, Paul introduced 'Hello

OPERATION BIG BEAT

TOWER BALLROOM, NEW BRIGHTON

FRIDAY, 10th NOVEMBER, 1961   7-30 A.M.—1-0 A.M.

JIVING TO MERSEYSIDE'S TOP 5 GROUPS

THE BEATLES————————GERRY AND THE PACEMAKERS
RORY STORM AND THE HURRICANES————————THE REMO FOUR
KINGSIZE TAYLOR AND THE DOMINOES

LATE TRANSPORT (LIVERPOOL, WIRRAL, CHESHIRE) TWO LICENSED BARS (until 11-30 pm.)   BUFFET
TICKETS 5/- from Rushworth's, Lewis's, Crane's, Strothers and Tower Ballroom. Transport details from Agencies and Crown Coachways and Tower. Coaches leaving Mersey Tunnel, Manchester Street from 7-0 p.m onwards

ENTERTAINMENTS GUIDE

The entertainments guide is now a regular feature in "Mersey Beat" and contains information of the entertainments available. Proprietors are invited to send the name and address of their establishments. Further information can be included at the rate of 4d. per word.

JIVE HALLS

AINTREE INSTITUTE. Every Friday and Saturday.
BEAT ROUTE CLUB. Crawford Avenue. Friday, Saturday and Sunday.
BLAIR HALL. Every Saturday and Sunday.
BLUE PENGUIN CLUB. St. John's Hall, Bootle. Every Friday.
BURTON CHAMBERS. Walton Road. Saturday and Sunday.
COLUMBA HALL, Widnes. Every Thursday and Saturday.
CARR MILL, St. Helens. Every Friday.
DAVID LEWIS. Every Monday and Friday.
EMPRESS CLUB, New Brighton.
GROSVENOR BALLROOM, Wallasey. Friday and Saturday.
HAMBLETON HALL. Every Wednesday and Sunday.
HOLYOAKE HALL. Every Friday and Saturday.
JIVE HIVE. St. Luke's Hall, Crosby. Every Wednesday and Saturday.
LA MYSTERE, Maghull. Every Saturday.
LITHERLAND TOWN HALL. Every Monday and Thursday.
LOCARNO, West Derby Road. Monday and Tuesday.
ORRELL PARK BALLROOM. Friday, Saturday, Sunday, Monday.
PLAZA BALLROOM, St. Helens. Thursday, Saturday and Sunday.
QUAINTWAYS Chester.
RIVERPARK, Chester. Saturday and Monday.
IVARMAR CLUB, Skelmersdale. Every Saturday, Sunday and Monday.
KNOTTY ASH HALL. Every Friday and Saturday.

ST. BARNABAS HALL, Penny Lane. Every Saturday.
SPRINGWOOD HALL, Mather Avenue.
TOP HAT CLUB, Lockerby Road.
WEST DERBY VILLAGE HALL. Saturdays.

JAZZ CLUBS

BLACK CAT CLUB, London Road. Country and western, folk and rock and roll. Yearly membership 5/-.
THE CAVERN. 10 Mathew Street. Yearly membership 1/-. Traditional jazz rock and roll.
DOWNBEAT, Victoria Street.
KRAAL JAZZ CLUB New Brighton.
STORYVILLE JAZZ CLUB, Temple Street. Yearly membership 2/6. Traditional jazz.

COFFEE CLUBS

BASEMENT. Mount Pleasant.
BLACK ROSE. South Castle Street. For membership apply to the secretary.
EL CABALA. Bold Street.
HEAVEN AND HELL. Opening shortly.
JACARANDA. Slater Street. Members only.
KON TIKI. Wood Street.
LANTERN, Aigburth Road. Open until 4 a.m.
LA LOCANDA, Duke Street. 10 p.m. until 2 a.m.
MASQUE. Clarence Street.
ODD SPOT. Bold Street. Opening shortly.
PINK PARROT, Duke Street.
PHOENIX, Mount Pleasant. New members welcome.
NEW SHAKESPEARE, Wilde Street.

CLUBS, GENERAL

MANDOLIN CLUB, Warwick Street. Now open.
MARINA CLUB, Scotland Road.
NEW PALM COVE. 237 Smithdown Lane.
TUDOR CLUB, Upper Parliament Street.
WALTON LANE SOCIAL CLUB, Walton Lane.
COLONY CLUB, 80 Berkley Street.

RESTAURANTS

CAPTAIN'S TABLE/CHEFS CORNER. Lord Street.
CHANTICLEER, Tarleton Street.
JOE'S RESTAURANT. 139 Duke Street.
NEW CHANTICLEER, Tarleton Street.
OCEAN RESTAURANT, Lord Street.

CABARET SHOWS

BLUE ANGEL, Seel Street.
CABARET CLUB, Duke Street.
NEW ROYAL RESTAURANT, Hanover Street.
SPEKE AIRPORT HOTEL.

THEATRES

BLUECOAT CONCERT HALL
CRANE THEATRE, Hanover Street.
EMPIRE THEATRE, Lime Street.
PLAYHOUSE THEATRE.
PHILHARMONIC HALL, Hope Street.
ROYAL COURT THEATRE, Roe Street.

BINGO CLUBS

CAPITOL, Overton Street.
PAVILION, Lodge Lane.
PLAZA BINGO CLUB, Plaza Theatre, Borough Road, Birkenhead.
RIALTO, Upper Parliament Street.
GRANADA, DOVECOTE

Gig the day after Brian Epstein first saw the Beatles

Little Girl' as "one we've written". Could that have prompted Brian to act as a Svengali to the next Rodgers & Hammerstein? Taylor also remembered the hasty lunch following that momentous introduction, where Brian was already excitedly mulling over the future. ("They *are* awful but I think they're fabulous… What do you think about me managing them?")

The group were at a point where they needed someone. Paternal advice from Bob Wooler, lackadaisical management by Allan Williams, encouragement from Bill Harry, bookings from local promoter Sam Leach… the Beatles were trickling along. But like Brian, they too felt the same churning urgency to leave Liverpool. They had the raw talent. They had the experience. They had the energy and the drive. They needed someone to translate that ambition into hard cash. Could the soft-spoken store manager really provide that drive? Over the next couple of weeks, Brian witnessed more performances in different venues; sounded out friends, relatives and colleagues about the group's possibilities. But none shared his belief in their talent and potential. No one shared his *vision*.

Perhaps the appeal was the escape which pop group management offered Brian. His future was drearily laid out: a shy bachelor, managing the family store in a dreary, run-down, provincial, north English port. Diversion lay in illegal fumbling encounters in the dark. Or the occasional dinner in a Wirral restaurant endeavouring to match the sophistication of its peers down south.

Paul McCartney remembers being impressed by Brian's suave charm and his car ("a big Zephyr Zodiac"). Also, Paul's dad Jim "thought Jewish people were very good with money". This was the common wisdom. Early on, Brian appreciated where the power lay. Diplomatically, whenever he visited John's intimidating Aunt Mimi at Mendips, Brian always arrived bearing either chocolates or a pot plant.

Less than a month after that first Cavern visit, Brian invited the group to NEMS, to discuss their future on his watch. Brian's father had allowed his son use of office space above the family store, so he wouldn't be too far from the shop counters. On being told he was undertaking a managerial role, Harry Epstein was also encouraged by his son's guarantee that managing the Beatles would only occupy him two afternoons a week.

Bevved up with a few pints before the meeting, and with Bob Wooler hauled along for moral support, John, George and Pete listened as Mr Epstein made his pitch. Paul was absent, preferring a bath to a meeting.

Keen to get something formally agreed prior to the Christmas rush at NEMS, Brian consulted a couple of solicitors, before drawing up the document which appointed him Beatles manager. Once legally committed, Brian was bubbling with enthusiasm about his new project as the old year faded. The actual, binding contract wasn't signed until early in 1962, but by then Brian had taken the group under his wing.

While Brian began his new, part-time career, on behalf of the Beatles, the group made their first disastrous foray south. Promoter Sam Leach had booked them to play in Aldershot, an army town, miles from London at a 'Big Beat Session'. Due to a technical hitch, there was no promotional material or advertising, so only 18 people witnessed the Beatles – Live at the Palais Ballroom. No legendary gig this, no I-Was-There-When (delete where applicable) Bob Dylan was at the Singers' Club, Marylebone; Jimi Hendrix blew the roof off Blaises; the Sex Pistols played the 100 Club… For the Beatles, 9 December

1961 was a tail-between-the-legs catastrophe. Barely a week before they had enlisted Brian as manager, yet here they were playing to the proverbial three men and a dog. Years later, McCartney called it "the night we couldn't get arrested". Such a catastrophic engagement must surely have weighed in Brian's favour.

Many years later, that night, Admission 5/-, an "historically rare" poster for The Big Beat Session, the Beatles versus Peter Jay & the Jaywalkers, was sold at auction for an eye-watering £20,000. Following the fiasco, the Beatles quit Aldershot and made their first visit to the capital. They whiled the night away at a Soho club, then it was back to home turf.

They played out the rest of the year on the usual circuit, with the Cavern as their default setting, while Brian – still promising his parents his new enthusiasm would only occupy him part-time – utilised any and all of his record company contacts to try and interest them in his new group.

Today, it is hard to appreciate the distance between Liverpool and London. Half a century on, the 200-mile, pre-motorway drive occupied most of the day. But it was not simply the geographic distance. The country's capital represented success. It was where the BBC and national newspapers were based, where all the record and film companies were. London was where all the key political, gastronomic, fashion and entertainment decisions were made.

True, there were regional outposts, *The Manchester Guardian*, BBC regional offices, independent TV companies, but to succeed, you had to make it in London, otherwise you remained … provincial. It was a point Charlie Gillett emphasised in his landmark book, *The Sound of the City*: "Until the Beatles made their first record … it had been very difficult for any group based outside London to gain access to the record companies. It had almost always been necessary for ambitious musicians, singers and groups to move to London and hope to attract the attention of somebody who mattered.

"Without the reputation that came through records, groups outside London had to depend on the support of people who knew them through direct hearing, which meant that a group famous in Newcastle could be unknown thirty miles away on Teesside, and that groups in south Lancashire had little demand in Yorkshire".

In an early piece while trying to fathom the UK Beatle obsession, in December 1963 in *The New York Times* magazine, Frederic Lewis identified "The significance of the [Liverpool] sound is that it is a raspberry blown in the direction of London".

So, during the dog days of 1961 as it lurched over dispiritingly on into 1962, as the first artists in his management stable, Brian applied himself on their behalf. One of his first acts was to discard the leathers and smarten the group up so they could appear alongside pop idols of the day, not looking like a menacing gang of bikers. As they plied their trade in the clubs and caverns of darkest Merseyside, Brian literally made them get their act together: no more larking about and ad-libbing. Tighter, disciplined performances were now the order of the day as their new manager energetically shepherded his charges into the new year.

What was necessary, what Brian needed to convince the group of his belief, was a record contract. That is what would elevate them above their peers. Again and again, Brian made the long journey from Lime Street to London. Emerging under the lovely old

Euston Arch, soon-to-be-demolished in the shock of the new, hailing a cab to Manchester Square or Albert Embankment, headquarters of the country's record labels. As an unknown quantity, all Brian had going for him was his reputation as a record store manager, and his zealous championing of an unknown group from a faraway city.

Again, it is difficult today to appreciate the challenges facing the fledgling manager. Aside from the geographic distance, there was a certain mindset within the record companies. Yes of course there were pop *groups*, but aside from a brief spell in the spotlight, their job was to back the name above the title, the featured singer: Cliff Richard *and* the Shadows; Johnny Kidd *and* the Pirates; Adam Faith *and* the Roulettes; Wayne Fontana *and* the Mindbenders; Bern Elliot *and* the Fenmen; Peter Jay *and* the Jaywalkers; Shane Fenton *and* the Fentones; Rory Storm *and* the Hurricanes; Brian Poole *and* the Tremeloes… This was a further obstacle Epstein had to face, to persuade the executives that his group had no featured frontman, in his eyes, they were all equal.

It was a hard sell, made all the more difficult by what Brian had on offer. All the jaded A&R men could hear was a record, 'My Bonnie'. But Brian had to persuade them to go against their natural instinct, and *not* to listen to the singer, but rather focus their attention on his clients, the backing group. Epstein's inexperience was manifest, what opened doors for him was his standing as manager of one of the North West's biggest record retailers. So, Mr Epstein would be granted a few precious moments to try and convince the jaundiced executives that his group would be "bigger than Elvis". Polite rejections led to a dejected Brian catching the train back to Lime Street, where he would be met by eager Beatles, whose faces soon fell as he relayed the latest rejection to the youngsters. It grew to be a depressingly long list – EMI subsidiaries HMV and Columbia, as well as Oriole, Piccadilly, Phillips and Pye…

A typical letter to gain an appointment was to EMI's General Marketing Manager, Ron White, a month after Brian had seen the group for the first time. It ran, enthusiastically, "These four boys, who are superb instrumentalists, also produce some exciting and pulsating vocals. They play mostly their own compositions and one of the boys has written a song which I really believe to be the hottest material since 'Living Doll'…"

It's all there, written in the record magazine prose of the time, that nervous confidence, the fact that they come as a self-contained unit, the comparison with reigning monarch Cliff. Stilted, yet sincere, the sort of 'grown-up', typed letter you would expect from an enthusiastic manager keen to push his bunch of unknowns onto one of, realistically, only two major UK labels – EMI or Decca.

To keep the group's flagging spirits up, and to build up his status as a manager, Brian was sly. He used to encourage his childhood friend and companion, Joe Flannery, to interrupt pub conflabs with the Beatles with urgent messages – "They believed it", Joe told Philip Norman. "They *really* believed that [Elvis' manager] Colonel Parker had been trying to ring up Brian Epstein in Birkenhead".

Rejection after rejection; lonely and dispiriting train journeys to and from London, then, a new year, a new hope…

The persistent rejections only intensified the North–South divide, highlighting the cultural and geographic distance Brian Epstein had to travel. A stroke of luck came when Epstein made contact with an ex-Scouser Tony Barrow, who was scratching a living at

Decca's London office and gave Brian a foothold. Again, armed only with a copy of the 'My Bonnie' single, Brian's problems were amplified, as he advised anyone who would listen to forget the singer and concentrate on the backing group.

But Brian was persevering on their behalf, and yet again, kismet played its part... A reorganisation of Decca's A&R department coincided with the Epstein pitch. That, coupled with the record company's appreciation of the purchasing power of NEMS, ensured that, finally, someone from London was taking an interest.

The A&R man who agreed to make the journey up to Liverpool and see Mr Epstein's group perform was Mike Smith. Impressed by a lunchtime blast of the Beatles at the Cavern, enriched by a few pints in The Grapes soon after, engaged by the lads' personalities, emboldened by further drink taken with the manager... By the time he tottered back to his hotel, Mike Smith had invited the Beatles to come down to make a demo recording in Decca's London studios. Barely a month after signing with Brian, the group were about to make their first recording in a professional studio. The date was set for 1 January 1962. They were on their way!

It took road manager Neil Aspinall 11 hours to drive down to the Decca audition. With the sort of attention to detail I delight in, the Deep Beatles group reproduced the Booking Card for 31 January 1961, revealing 'Messrs Aspinall and Best' shared their 50/- hotel accommodation. Room 1057 at The Royal Hotel, Russell Square also boasted 'bath' and 'boot cleaning'.

On their arrival, the Liverpudlians took to the London streets. I treasure the image of the anonymous Beatles mixing with the drunken revellers in Trafalgar Square on New Year's Eve 1961 when, within the blink of an eye, they would be the most famous faces in the country.

However hungover, weary, teary or bleary-eyed you were, back then New Year's Day was still a working day in the United Kingdom. So from their hotel, the group were swept up and whisked to Decca's recording studios in leafy West Hampstead, not far from their competitors' Abbey Road location. With Neil Aspinall's assistance, the group lugged their battered amplifiers for the first time into a *professional* recording studio.

It was here in Decca's Broadhurst Gardens that eight years before, at the end of a jazz session, Lonnie Donegan had cut the skiffle songs which would begin the musical revolution that the Beatles were about to continue and develop. Could history repeat itself?

With the sour taste of last night's 'Auld Lang Syne' still lingering, Mike Smith came in to rekindle the interest which the group's appearance at the Cavern only a few weeks before had aroused. With one eye on the clock, and Brian Epstein nervously hovering, the Beatles began their make-or-break audition for one of the only two UK record labels which really mattered. A manic 15 songs were laid down. For years, I attributed the choice of material as being dictated by Brian Epstein who was, after all, rooted in the showbiz tradition which the Beatles would soon blow out of the water. And it was that which explained Epstein's choice of material for that crucial audition – end-of-pier renditions of 'The Sheik of Araby', 'Three Cool Cats', 'Besame Mucho'...

Latterly, Lennon claimed the song selection was down to the group, as a reflection of their stage set. But Buddy Holly was only represented by the ballad 'Crying, Waiting, Hoping' and Chuck Berry's 'Memphis, Tennessee' is mechanical. No Elvis, Gene Vincent,

Eddie Cochran, Fats Domino… The novelty songs sound stilted, while the 'All Round Entertainer' renditions of 'September in the Rain' and 'Besame Mucho' are painful. You could argue that the idea was to demonstrate the group's versatility, but there was little or nothing which conveyed their piledriving mastery of rock & roll.

Of course, Mike Smith and his boss Dick Rowe have gone down in history as the men who failed to appreciate the Beatle potential. And it was only years later, hearing a bootleg of that Decca audition, you appreciate just how right that rejection was. The Beatles sound nervous, the playing is rudimentary, the vocals unengaging, the harmonies, unremarkable; the selection of material, random… George's solos are hesitant, Paul and John's lead vocals flighty and nervous. And really was Pete Best's drumming *that* bad?

Decca's decision to decline the Beatles is legendary, how their detractors must have chuckled. I remember hearing the audition tape when it was bootlegged in the 1980s and appreciating that … Decca were right! There is, understandably, palpable nervousness in the audition; the performances of the Lennon & McCartney originals are muted; the choice of material is undistinguished – their versions of the jokey 'Three Cool Cats', 'Sheik of Araby' and 'Searchin' sound more like what George Martin was producing across town for Bernard Cribbins. There is little, actually *nothing*, to suggest their future greatness. Even Mark Lewisohn politely calls the Decca audition "a lacklustre performance, restrained, subdued, the handbrake on".

Due to his relative lack of experience, Mike Smith had to defer to his boss in deciding which of the two groups he'd auditioned that day that the label would sign. Famously, Decca's decision erred towards Essex rather than Liverpool. Until his death in 1986, Dick Rowe was damned by his choice. It was a decision made all the more ironic when, on 5 May 1963, the Decca executive found himself in Liverpool. He was judging a talent contest at the Philharmonic Hall just as Beatlemania was breaking big. One of his fellow judges, looking for the Next Big Thing, was George Harrison.

Talking to Louis Barfe, Decca executive Hugh Mendl recalled the circumstances: "Dick was a very nice bloke and said to George, 'I'm sorry. I feel so embarrassed'. George said, 'We were terrible, weren't we?… We hadn't had any sleep… we'd driven down overnight. We were awful. I don't blame you'. Then he leant over and said, 'I'm sorry you had all this trouble in the press about it. Do you want to do yourself a bit of good? There's a band called the Rolling Stones and they appear at the Station Hotel, Richmond'."

George Harrison remembered it when we met in 1992. "The problem is there's too many bands… In the old days it was like you were lucky to get in a studio to make a record, nowadays they automatically go round the clubs sucking up every new band and putting them on record… It isn't the spotty kids' faults, it's the record company's fault.

"In films there's a trend and one person signs somebody up and makes a huge hit movie… It works on paranoia, or fear… When *Easy Rider* was a hit, they went out and signed everybody up who had a motor bike!

"When the Beatles hit, they had the auditions at the Philharmonic Hall in Liverpool and I went up there, and every A&R man in England was there – everybody who *didn't* sign the Beatles up, they were there signing everybody else in case there was another one!"

As esteemed Beatle chronicler Bill Harry later wrote: "Frankly, instead of being known as the man who turned down The Beatles, which is inaccurate, [Dick Rowe] should have been lauded as the man who signed up the Rolling Stones". Once Beatlemania exploded, the search was on in every UK metropolis for their equivalent. As early as June 1963, Columbia Records' producer Norrie Paramor was holding auditions at Birmingham's Moathouse Club eager to find the Celestial City's answer to the Beatles.

The Beatles themselves didn't hang around after their first trip to London, and by lunchtime on 3 January 1962, they were back onstage at the Cavern, waiting and hoping. With Brian Epstein smoothly running things behind the scenes, the Beatles kept up a regular round of live work and, at Brian's insistence, widened their fanbase: a 2 February 1962 date was at Manchester's Oasis Club, maybe not a great show, but an event which three decades later would give the city's biggest band their name.

Due to his diligence and business acumen, the group were happy to fall in with their manager's requests – by all accounts Brian rarely *ordered*; he would make a suggestion to John, who would then convey his decision to the remaining three. Thus, at the beginning of 1962, the onstage leathers had gone, as had the smoking and swearing in public.

As Brian's sympathetic biographer Ray Coleman noted, once Brian had persuaded the group into £40 Beno Dorn suits, "The changes were palpable. They had an assertive manager pushing for better fees, and a new mode of presentation. The key difference between their pre-Epstein years and what followed was that he honed a raw, rugged group of rock'n'rollers into a mature, palatable and commercial entity".

A copy of the revised contract between Brian and the Beatles, signed 1 October 1962, later came up for auction, and it was noted that in his managerial role, Brian should advise "on all matters concerning clothes, make-up and the presentation and construction of the Artists' acts also on *all music performed in the course of or in connection with such acts*" [my italics].

They were happy enough to fall in line. After all, it was Brian who was getting them better engagements; it was Brian who got them to London and to a major record label audition. And, on 7 March 1962, it was Brian who secured them their first BBC radio broadcast. Again, it is hard to recall these times when the BBC literally did rule the airwaves. Due to the pressure applied by the Musicians' Union, to hear the original pop releases on 'Auntie Beeb', was strictly rationed. You could pick up the weaving and bobbing signal of Radio Luxembourg with its far wider-ranging playlists, but for the UK, commercial radio was ten years in the future, and the 'pop-tastic' Radio 1 was not launched until 1967.

It was an enthusiastic letter from the teenage David John Smith who wrote to the BBC's Light Entertainment department early in 1962 which led to the group's radio debut. It was after having seen them perform in Preston, he enthused, "These boys combine their schoolboy looks with a thick sound which produces one of the most exciting atmospheres ever to come from white artists".

So, to land a BBC radio spot was quite an achievement, a sign that you had arrived. Before they could hear themselves on the airwaves though, the Beatles had to pass an audition. It was standard practice at the time, everyone, from the Rolling Stones to Nick Drake; Paul Simon to David Bowie had to undergo the process. The Beatles passed, and for that historic debut, appeared on the Light Programme *Teenagers' Turn*, performing Roy Orbison's 'Dream Baby', 'Memphis, Tennessee' and Motown's 'Please Mr Postman'.

It was a pyrrhic victory though. The broadcast was intended as a showcase for the group on the back of their recording contract with Decca. Except that when the news came, it was disastrous: Decca had declined their services.

Over the years, accounts vary about the scale and nature of Decca's rebuttal of the Beatles. But it is believed that over lunch on 6 February 1962 at Decca's Albert Embankment HQ, among the comments that Brian heard were, "Not to mince words, Mr Epstein, we don't like your boys... Groups are out; four piece groups, with guitars particularly are finished... You've got a good business in Liverpool, Mr Epstein, stick to that..." The final decision was taken by Mike Smith's boss, Dick Rowe but, at crunch time, Smith had to decide between two groups he had auditioned on New Year's Day 1962. And his decision was as much geographical as musical.

Brian Poole and the Tremeloes were from Barking in Essex, within the London orbit, not a B-road, back-of-beyond destination like Liverpool. History has not been kind to the group which Decca preferred over the Beatles. Professionally, Poole's group had already proved themselves since their formation in 1959: they had broadcast on the BBC's *Saturday Club* and a 21-week season at Butlin's in Ayr had sharpened them. Once signed to Decca, they took a year or so to hit their stride. Their first hit (UK No.4, July 1963) came, ironically, with 'Twist & Shout', famously included on the Beatles' debut LP.

The Essex group's breakthrough came in September 1963, when they broke the Liverpudlian stranglehold of the Beatles, Searchers, Gerry & the Pacemakers and Billy J. Kramer, with a Motown cover, 'Do You Love Me', a UK No.1. But they could never make that crucial Transatlantic crossover. Poole & the Tremeloes soldiered on with a further two Top 10 hits and a 1965 No.25 'I Want Candy' (later a hit for Bow Wow Wow) before calling it a day in 1966. Without their lead singer, the Tremeloes carried on with a run of successful UK chart hits well into the 1970s. So, in terms of chart success, the Decca decision was not a complete disaster. In the wake of the Beatles' global success, however, it was calamitous, and left egg all over the faces of Decca executives for years to come.

Rejected and dispirited, Brian Epstein knew that the record company executives he pitched his "bigger than Elvis" spiel to did not have the patience to sit while Brian threaded the spools of the 35-minute Decca audition onto a tape machine. So, he called in a remaining few of his favours. Visiting the HMV flagship store on Oxford Street, he played the reel-to-reel Decca tapes to Bob Boast, the store manager he knew, who recommended that Epstein translate the bulky tapes onto an acetate. A service that the store could provide for £1/10/- (£1.50).

And here is another of those fantastic Fab What Ifs... If Brian Epstein had not recalled the name of the EMI store manager from an earlier promotion trip and if the cutting engineer had not liked what he heard and recommended the material to higher-ups at EMI ... Brian Epstein could well have taken the train home from Euston and once again faced the never-to-be Fab Four waiting for him with a further rejection.

For years I had Ted Huntley as the engineer cutting the acetate, but it was cutting engineer Jim Foy who was impressed by what he heard. "Epstein added, proudly, that three of the songs had actually been written by members of the group, uncommon in those days," wrote Lewisohn. "Foy asked if they had been published and Epstein replied that they hadn't".

Here, it is worth pausing to consider the moment. I always pictured that EMI engineer Jim Foy as a boffin in a white coat, or possibly a lower-down-the-pecking-order brown coat, probably smoking, possibly on the verge of retirement. Imagine if he had *not* been impressed by what he heard, then he would not have recommended Epstein seek out a representative of EMI's music publishing arm. So, Brian would have bundled his precious acetate into his briefcase and ventured out onto Oxford Street. Bracing himself he would once again prepare to revisit the record labels which had already, periodically, rejected him and his group.

However, such is the hinge of history, that Jim Foy *was* impressed, and asked Ardmore & Beechwood's Sid Colman to listen. Always on the lookout for new talent, and impressed that this group wrote some original material, Colman encouraged Brian. Once again, it is worth pausing to consider the significance of that decision: few Shadows, Tremeloes, Pirates or Roulettes wrote material worthy of A-side attention.

It was on Colman's recommendation that Brian Epstein first met George Martin in his office in Manchester Square. That meeting with Martin had weighed heavily on Brian's mind. He went round to his aunt and uncle's in Hampstead the night before the Manchester Square meeting. Ray Coleman quoted Brian asking: "What shall I do? Shall I give it all up? I've got one more appointment in the morning. Or should I go back home? I really don't know what to do for the best". In another of those crucial moments in Beatle history, Brian's Uncle Berrel advised against the boy returning to Liverpool, tail between his legs. "Oh, just keep that appointment".

Once again, here is an opportunity to pause and reflect: along with Sid Colman, it had been Kim Bennett, a hustling EMI song plugger who liked what he heard on that acetate. And it was his enthusiasm which began the long, and winding road, which led the Beatles to Abbey. 'Like Dreamers Do' was eventually farmed out to the Applejacks for a UK Top 20 hit on the back of Beatlemania in 1964. It was never considered good enough for the Beatles to be released in their lifetime. So, a song the teenage Paul McCartney had written in Forthlin Road could be said to have begun it all. On the strength of that one song, their future could be said to have lain. Ironic doesn't really begin to describe it…

Brian Epstein was growing increasingly frustrated. The trust 'the boys' had invested in him was not being repaid. He was getting them more money for gigs, but that record contract was eluding him. At one point he used his retail muscle to inform EMI he would cease to stock releases by all the company's labels – HMV, Parlophone, Columbia and EMI. As NEMS was a big player on the North West music scene, his threat was taken seriously. But there was a chasm between retail and A&R to be bridged.

With the Decca rejection still burning resentfully, the Beatles resumed their slog around the clubs and cellars of the North West. A respite came in the shape of a seven-week booking back in Hamburg, but on their arrival, the news hit them of the death of 21-year-old Stuart Sutcliffe. He had died of a brain haemorrhage in Astrid's arms. Despite not having been a Beatle for a long time, Stuart's death hit his bandmates hard. At that age, you think you are immortal – why bother *not* smoking, you've got years ahead of you? Illness is for old people, not those barely out of their teens.

None of the Beatles attended the funeral. They consoled Astrid and Klaus as best they could, then returned to what they were being paid for. The Beatles' residency at the Star

Club was a definite improvement on their original Hamburg venues. Plush, and with a slightly more upmarket clientele, it was still long nights of sex and drugs and rock & roll though. The one bright spot came in a telegram from their manager; Brian had met with Parlophone Records' A&R man George Martin, who wanted to audition them for his label.

*

The crucial Beatle EMI session took place at the company's studio on Abbey Road, NW8, the studio which would become inextricably linked with the group, and with every group which aspired to be the Beatles. The EMI recording studio had opened after the label spent £16,500 to purchase a nine-bedroom, 1830 property in 1929. Two years later it opened as a recording facility. Even prior to the Beatles, the studios had their own lustre – popular musicians such as Glenn Miller, Paul Robeson and Fred Astaire had recorded there. Visitors included Winston Churchill and George Bernard Shaw.

The Beatles' first visit to EMI's Abbey Road Studios took place on 6 June 1962. It was to be Pete Best's only EMI session. That session at Abbey Road was 18 years to the day since another momentous 20th-century event, D-Day. For Beatles Day, in the early evening of 6 June 1962, Neil Aspinall helped the group ('bands' came in the 1970s) unload their equipment. He was as battered and road-weary as the group itself after half a decade hammering round Hamburg and Liverpool.

They taped 'Besame Mucho', 'Love Me Do', 'PS I Love You' and 'Ask Me Why' under the watchful eyes of engineers and the grown-up producer, George Martin. He was not unduly impressed, either with the cheesy Coasters cover, or the self-written originals. But there was an elusive, appealing *something*. It was as much their personalities which attracted him. After criticising the drumming and choice of material, Martin asked the group if there was anything *they* didn't like, prompting George's widely reported criticism of the producer's choice of ties.

The fact that it was that session which led the Beatles to EMI, and George Martin, and that timeless, unrepeatable, unbeatable recording arc, is reason enough for the day to go down in history. But, from what one gathers, an offhand remark from Martin led to the dismissal of Pete Best

and ushered in another significant moment in the group's history.

"It was one of those terrible things you go through as kids. Can we betray him? No". Paul in *Anthology*. "But our career was on the line... as far as we were concerned it was a strictly professional decision... It was one of the most difficult things we ever had to do".

Like the Jack the Ripper murders, the sacking of Pete Best has been sifted through and endlessly analysed. The reasons accumulate: not Liverpool's best drummer; a withdrawn, introverted character, at odds with his three bandmates; heels dug in about that new hairstyle... His fate was sealed that day at Abbey Road, and he has lived with it ever since.

Poor old Pete... History has not even dignified him with being a *fifth* Beatle. He was, for two years, *a* Beatle, but by a cruel caprice and merest whisper, missed out on being a part of their future glory. Like Stalin's opponents during the purges, Pete was airbrushed out of history, and condemned to a life on the margins. Even as *The Beatles Monthly* was telling its readers about the group's history as early as 1963, McCartney was sniffily dismissive: "In those days we had a succession of drummers. None of them were very good and it's hard to remember their names".

The Pete Best Band *did* sign to Decca, and released a rollicking good single, 'I'm Gonna Knock on Your Door', but they were dropped, and Pete became a footnote. It was too much to bear. When I met him at the launch party for the first volume of his autobiography in the mid-80s, I couldn't help but ask what he was up to. "Still in the Civil Service," he said, and you couldn't help but think, "You poor, unlucky sod".

During the eight years of the Beatles' recorded career, for Pete, every waking moment of every single day must have been purgatory… the money, the hysteria, the money, the films, the medals, the money… And he lingered in the shadow, forever speculating on the road not taken. There was a suicide attempt in 1965. He joined the Civil Service in 1968, working in the department which, ironically, helped people find work: "Pete Best will see you now," he remembered. "I think it helped them. Whatever they'd been through, they knew I'd been through it as well. I'd lost the biggest job in show business, millions of pounds and everything that went with it, and here I was giving advice on how to secure employment".

Happily, with the burgeoning Beatle Conventions and renewal of interest in the band following John's murder, things looked up for Pete Best. And with the release of *Anthology* in 1995, finally, after three decades, some Beatle cash came his way.

His band played at a musical opening in London I attended in 2011, *The Million $ Quartet*, and onstage playing loud, good rock & roll was Pete Best and his band. I went for a drink with a colleague afterwards, sitting outside a bar off the Charing Cross Road, and there was Pete and his brother having a drink at a table further down. Had it been any one of the three survivors, they would have been surrounded within seconds, but not Pete… The man who could have been King sat anonymous and unnoticed, his part in that fabulous story all played out. But still with us…

*

Ringo Starr had returned from Hamburg. He too had wallowed in the delights of Sin City, and had remained true to Rory & the Hurricanes. With rings on his fingers, Butlin's again enticed the band. And it was in the incongruous location of the holiday camp at Skegness that John Lennon and Paul McCartney bit the bullet and asked Ringo Starr to join the Beatles.

Ringo stayed to finish the Butlin's residency, then returned to Liverpool, where he locked in with the remaining three to become… the Fab Four. George wrote to 'Jenny' from Hamburg in August 1962, "Ringo is a much better drummer, and he can smile, which is a bit more than Pete could do…"

The first engagement featuring the four who would be Fab was at the Port Sunlight Horticultural Society's annual dance on 18 August 1962. The opening act were the Four Jays, who later changed their name to the Fourmost and were managed by Brian Epstein. The historic venue was Hulme Hall, tickets were 6/- (30p), which gained admission for the dance (7.45–11.30 p.m.) "starring the North's No.1 rock combo, the fabulous Beatles, now recording for Parlophone."

A fortnight before, the first reference to the Beatles appeared in the weekly music press. In *Record Mirror* Norman Jopling asked, "Is the Liverpool area the rockingest part of the great British Isles? A publication *Mersey Beat* just arrived, makes me think this is the case... Names that intrigue are The Beatles (who were billed as big as Bruce Channel in Liverpool)..."

In a sense, Port Sunlight was a perfect location for the first time that John, Paul, George and Ringo, who would later come to epitomise so much of the peace and love the 60s offered, officially played together. Founded by the Victorian industrialist William Lever, it was a model village influenced by the Arts & Craft Movement, which endeavoured, in the words of its founder, "to get back to that close family brotherhood that existed in the good old days of hard labour."

Only four days after that first gig in front of a paying audience, Ringo could be seen with the Beatles, making their television debut. One is struck again by how fate played a hand; you suspect, it could have been one of half a dozen groups that Granada TV chose to highlight at the Cavern that lunchtime. Instead it was "the North's top group The Beatles". Then it was the usual round of shows at the Cavern and in and around Liverpool. Typical was the 'Rock & Beat Spectacular', with 'Top HMV Star Mike Berry' and 'Merseyside's Top Combo, The Beatles'. And, lest we forget, 'The North's Top Big Band, The Syd Munson Orchestra'...

But the big event was a trip to London, barely a fortnight after Ringo had settled on the drum stool, to make their first recordings for a record released under the name 'The Beatles'. Supervising the session would be the man who had been underwhelmed by that June audition, but who perhaps intuited that this lot could be the group to put him on an equal footing with his contemporaries.

For all his success, aged 36, the name of George Martin (1926–2016) was linked to novelty recordings – comedy LPs; one-off releases from comedians or TV stars. He was irked to have missed out on Cliff, Adam and Billy. He had enjoyed his first UK No.1 single in March 1961, the Temperance Seven's 'You're Driving Me Crazy', but the group's success was on the back of the Trad Jazz nostalgia bubble, and by the time the Beatles arrived at Abbey Road, it had long since burst.

Probably the one recording which George Martin produced prior to the Beatles that came anywhere close to matching their seismic impact was the cast recording of *Beyond the Fringe*. The coming together of Peter Cook, Dudley Moore, Jonathan Miller and Alan Bennett for an Edinburgh Fringe performance in 1960 was as random and fortuitous as the formation of the Fab Four. Like the music of the Beatles, it is hard to convey the impact of *Beyond the Fringe* on contemporary audiences. Today, with sacred cows slaughtered as a matter of casual fact, profane language filling the airwaves, institutions and deference dismissed daily, the routines these four young(ish) men came up with sound respectful and un-controversial.

But at the time, the walls of the city shook and the end of Western civilisation was on the horizon. None of the four revolutionaries planned it thus, yet by invoking the Royal family in one sketch, parodying Second World War heroics in another and mocking a serving Prime Minister, the *Fringe* quartet went beyond the pale. They took pot shots at the hitherto inviolate: organised religion, homosexuality, the atom bomb, colour prejudice, anti-semitism, capital punishment… And incidentally, it was very funny. Part of the long-running success of *Beyond the Fringe*, outside the packed houses at the Fortune Theatre, was the LP souvenir, reproduced on disc by George Martin.

The UK's respect for 'The Establishment', the hierarchy of monarchy, the judiciary, Parliament and the upper classes had been hitherto unchallenged. Wartime heroes such as Churchill, Mountbatten, Bader and Montgomery were venerated. Pre-Beatlemania, cricket-playing Bishop David Sheppard; top-scoring soccer star Jimmy Greaves; mountaineer Sir Edmund Hillary were boyhood heroes. While not explicitly anti-establishment, I feel the Beatles played a part in subverting their betters – Lennon's cheeky "rattle your jewellery" was taken in good part by the audience it was directed towards.

Without that fortuitous Beatle meeting, as an EMI staffer, George Martin would have likely lingered in a creative limbo. In his mid-30s, Martin had been unsuccessful in finding his own Shadows, or Cliff. His commercial ear was proven when in 1954 he alerted Parlophone to 'The Happy Wanderer' by the Obernkirchen Children's Choir, a UK No.2 and the first record John Peel told me he remembered buying. I only recently discovered that George Martin had already cemented himself into his country's culture long before the arrival of the Beatles. In 1951 he was the engineer on Sidney Torch's 'Barwick Green'. It is better known as the theme to BBC Radio's *The Archers*, now safely established as the world's longest-running soap opera.

For most of his time though, Martin would have been the on-call man for comedy records by Spike Milligan and Flanders & Swann. He would have stepped outside the pop orbit for occasional film projects, like the score he contributed to the lacklustre comedy *Crooks Anonymous*.

Professionally, he had the desire to succeed and break out of his backwater at Parlophone. He wanted his own Cliff Richard. Indeed during those first sessions, Martin was casting a dividing eye over the Beatles – was it to have been John Lennon *and* the Beatles? Paul McCartney *and* the Beatles? Until he came to realise there was no need to divide and conquer, and appreciate that in their unity lay their strength.

But crucially, he also had the sonic ambition to match that of Brian Epstein's boys. You can hear it on his early work, his production matching the outlandish imagination of *The Goon Show*'s Spike Milligan. These were challenges which helped Martin, in his own words, get "between the cracks" when it came to production. It is no secret that it was Martin's work with Lennon's heroes Peter Sellers and, particularly, Milligan, which helped cement the bond between the prickly Beatle and the patrician producer.

Lennon's sole piece of print criticism was his 1972 review of *The Goon Show Scripts* for *The New York Times* in which he cited the Beatle debt to the Goons and how the show influenced his own 'newspaper', *The Daily Howl*. "I could go on all day about the Goons and their influence on a generation (at least one)". Lennon relished that subversive BBC radio programme as a "coup d'etat of the mind" (he must have enjoyed the 'Drums Along the Mersey' episode). The show was powered by Spike Milligan's inspired scripts and Peter Sellers' uncanny ability at mimicking everyone and everything. And those plots ('The First Albert Memorial on the Moon'; 'The Siege of Fort Night'; '10,000 Fathoms Down in a Wardrobe'), Milligan's perfectionism tested the imagination of the BBC Sound Effects departments to the limit. Those sound pictures then had to be replicated on LP by producer George Martin.

Peter Sellers had made his recording debut at Abbey Road under the watchful eye of George Martin in 1953 on the largely forgotten *Jakka & the Flying Saucers*. The pair worked consistently together throughout Sellers' recording career – even enjoying a UK No.4 in the company of Sophia Loren in 1960 with 'Goodness Gracious Me'. Sellers' Richard III interpretation of 'A Hard Day's Night' was a 1965 Top 20 hit. Less well-known are Sellers' chinless wonder, Irish and cockney versions of 'She Loves You' which were issued posthumously.

According to Mark Cousins on the booklet accompanying the 1993 Sellers box set, it was during the recording of *Songs for Swingin' Sellers* in 1959 that George Martin roped in Matt Monro to sing the Sinatra-pastiche 'You Keep Me Swingin'. He was credited as 'Fred Flange', "the surname of which Martin turned to some years later", Cousins wrote, "in answer to a question by John Lennon. The Beatle had inquired about the strange swirling sound produced when double-tracking of tapes was created electronically, but then run at different speeds. Martin dubbed it 'flanging'. A name this technique, which is similar to phasing, has retained".

From the same Sellers LP, 'So Little Time' remains a very funny look at British rock & roll of the Larry Parnes era, with a roster of aspiring teenage idols ('Twit Conway', 'Clint Thigh', 'Matt Lust', etc.) managed by a Major Bloodnok-type manager. ("It must be very different, training race-horses and rock & roll stars?" the Major is asked. "Of course," he snaps, "horses have got a much better ear for music!") The Dennis Norden & Frank Muir sketch is an astringent comment on the period's youth cult (Twit's ambition is, obviously, to become 'an all-round entertainer'). While Billy Fury, Vince Eager and Duffy Power must have winced when the Major is asked how one of his boys is coping with sudden fame, Sellers replies: "He's just as normal and well-balanced as any other 17-year-old ex-plasterer's mate suddenly earning a thousand quid a week!"

It had been working with the demanding Spike Milligan that helped signpost some of the imaginative soundscapes George Martin would create with the Beatles. The two got on well together, with George Martin acting as best man at Milligan's second wedding in 1962. He also went on to produce Spike's off-kilter but affectionate tribute to the Fabs 'Purple Aeroplane' in 1966.

Despite his rather straight-laced appearance and demeanour, there was a side of George Martin keen to flex his creative muscles. It was the Beatles which gave him that opportunity to test himself to the limit. But Martin had proven himself as a technical challenger just prior to that fortuitous collaboration. Just listen to the 1962 single 'Time Beat' / 'Waltz in Orbit'. Perhaps because the electronic recording was so eerily unlike anything released on Parlophone up to that point, Martin chose to hide behind the pseudonym 'Ray Cathode'. Recorded in conjunction with the BBC Radiophonic Workshop, it recalled the work of Martin's near contemporary, Joe Meek. Indeed, ask most people to name two British record producers and the names of George Martin and Joe Meek are likely to feature highly.

Although coming across, especially to his new northern signings, as being in a class above, George Martin's origins were actually a lot lower down the social ladder. Elocution lessons had led to him coming across as 'posh', and, like Brian Epstein, Martin's dapper appearance made him appear more mature. His wartime service added years – as a Fleet Air Arm pilot, he was to have taken part in the invasion of Japan in 1945, when heavy casualties were to be expected. Fortuitously, for Martin, the atom bombs kept him out of harm's way. On the occasions I met him, he was always endearingly modest about his recording achievements. Charming and urbane, George Martin always reminded me of the Duke of Edinburgh.

I interviewed him in 1983 at Air Studios, alas in London, not sunny Montserrat – "I've always held that the role of the producer is the person who can look back on the picture and not just at the detail… It's like, when you have your picture taken in the school form, the first thing you look for is where am I? You don't look at the picture, you look at yourself, and this is true of … most people who make records, they tend to listen to the bit they were doing… So I think the main role of the producer is to be an impartial critic… I don't see the producer as a Svengali mastermind… I think that the role of the producer has become slightly inflated, and it's strange for me to say that, because maybe I've had something to do with that".

There is just something so timeless, so magical about the Beatle story, and however many times you hear it and however many nuggets are eked out about that spectacular career, a number of facts are set in stone: the Lennon & McCartney combination was breathtaking, unique and unrepeatable; Brian Epstein was not the world's greatest manager, but he got them out of Liverpool and on the road to London. Once there, the Beatles had the unimaginable luck of working with George Martin, who saw in them an opportunity to shape new sonic landscapes. Imagine if they had come under the well-meaning wing of Norrie Paramor, Norman Newell or Ron Richards. Good men all, no doubt, and slickly professional in the bustling pop scene of the early 60s, but none blessed with the prescient Third Ear of George Martin.

Nick Hornby wrote respectfully of the producer: "The Beatles were interested in him partly because he'd spent much of the 1950s producing comedy records… Less than ten years later he was putting vocals on 'Tomorrow Never Knows'… The classical music and the shirt and tie, then the novelty records, then The Beatles, the Dalai Lama, and the t-shirt; that's not just George Martin's biography. It's a potted cultural history of post-war England too".

Thanks to George Martin, there is a muscularity to even those early Beatle recordings, a testament to the producer skills, but also his astuteness in appreciating the greatness so early on. Play CD1 of the *Red* Album and listen to the depth Martin captured. Compare that with the tinny sound of the group's contemporaries during 1963 and 1964 and, yes I mean you, Rolling Stones. But also Freddie & the Dreamers, Brian Poole, the Hollies… good as the songs are, all the recordings are pasty-faced and skeletal compared to the red-blooded beefiness of the Beatles.

George Martin gave the Beatles 100% commitment. His taste was impeccable – he would surely never have sanctioned the cheesy piano break on Peter & Gordon's 'World Without Love' (produced by rival Norman Newell)? He was willing to take risks, to challenge convention. Inspired by what he heard coming off the studio floor, George Martin was allowed to stretch and flex his creative muscles.

Philip Norman put his finger not only on George Martin's abilities, but also his decency: "Other producers with far less input into the music would have claimed a share of … songwriting credit and thus a third of the royalties, or sneaked B-sides written by himself onto the reverse of each chart-busting A-side…" Astonishingly in 1963, 37 weeks of the UK No.1 singles throughout the year had been produced by George Martin. Well worth his EMI salary of £3,000.

I love those documentaries of the period which turn up periodically on YouTube or BBC4: earnest boffins, all wearing ties, while all those nicotine-stained fingers twiddle with faders and other fantastic, futuristic technology. And frequently there, head tilted, is Mr Martin, crisply commanding from above.

By the time the Beatles returned to Abbey Road on 4 September 1962, to start work on their debut single, they had a new drummer – Ringo Starr. As is known, George Martin still wasn't happy with the drum sound, and when the Beatles came, on 11 September, to actually record 'Love Me Do', Martin had employed Andy White for the session. All Ringo could do was shake a tambourine.

Paul remembered those early sessions: making their way into the tradesman's entrance of the studio, an hour for lunch at the Alma round the corner (ciggy, half a bitter, cheese roll) then, "If we'd done a particularly good take they might say, 'Would you like to listen to it in the control room?' We'd think "What, us? Up those stairs in heaven'."

For Eddie Cochran, there were only three steps to heaven. There are eight steps up to the entrance of what was, of course, lest we forget, still known as the 'EMI Recording Studios'. They only became known as 'Abbey Road' seven years later. Eight steps which took the Beatles through reception, down the corridor and stairs, and on into a brave new world…

Then it was out on the promotional haul, which meant the road. Though they could be advertised as 'recording artists', their record would not be in the shops for another month. So Brian concentrated them on their heartland, Cheshire and Lancashire. A gig at Stroud in Gloucestershire drew demonstrably fewer punters than when they played the Subscription Rooms five months before (238 to 468).

Barely a month later, their first record was in the shops. Hardly into their 20s, the songwriters could not believe that their names were there, under the title, on an actual 45 rpm single, released via one of the two leading record labels in the UK. 'Love Me Do' (McCartney/Lennon). Yes, that *is* the credit, and all the original titles on their debut LP are credited in that unfamiliar non-alphabetical style.

It had been a struggle, but the debut single by the Beatles was a Beatle composition – once again, respect to George Martin. Mitch Murray's chirpy 'How Do You Do It' had 'Hit' stamped all over it. The song was intended for either Brian Poole or Adam Faith, it later launched the career of the Beatles' Liverpool rivals Gerry & the Pacemakers. Coincidentally, the songwriter's original demo of the song had backing from future London rivals, the Dave Clark Five. To his eternal credit, Martin deferred to their rejection of the Murray cover, thus paving the way for pop music's greatest professional songwriting partnership to begin…

Friday 5 October 1962 saw the release of Parlophone single R4949, 'Love Me Do' / 'PS I Love You', that historic first release by the Beatles. The label's other releases that week were: The King Brothers' 'Nicola', Johnny Angel's 'Better Luck Next Time', Nicky Hilton's 'Your Nose Is Gonna Grow', Shane Fenton & the Fentones' 'Too Young for Sad

Memories', James Brown & the Famous Flames' 'Shout and Shimmy', the Temperance Seven's 'The Shake', Matt Monro's 'My Love and Devotion', Ken Jones & His Orchestra's 'Dodgy Waltz' and Jill Graham's 'Blow Joe'.

Parlophone had been in existence for over 40 years by the time it played host to the Beatles. Based in Holland, for much of the 1920s it was owned by the German Carl Lindstrom Company – the label's familiar '£' is actually a stylised 'L' for Lindstrom, not the currency the Liverpool group would later generate for the label. Inexorably linked to the Beatles for five years, Parlophone was one of the lesser jewels in the EMI crown, lagging behind Columbia and HMV. George Martin himself admitted Parlophone was "rock bottom".

I believe so much of the Beatles' story needs to be placed in context, for example just how stultified the UK record industry was before they took it by the scruff of its neck and gave it its greatest-ever shaking. On the slow-moving UK LP Charts that week, there were no less than three albums by the Black & White Minstrels in the Top 10. The soundtrack for the film of *South Pacific* had taken up permanent residency. On the *NME* LP charts, *West Side Story* held sway at No.1 and also featured two titles by Joe Brown, a pair from easy-listening maestro Ray Conniff; a Lonnie Donegan *Best of…* and at No.2 *The Best Of Ball, Barber & Bilk,* a reminder of just how established the Trad. Jazz boom had become.

The UK Single Charts were full of familiar names:

1. She's Not You, Elvis Presley
2. Telstar, The Tornados
3. It'll Be Me, Cliff Richard
4. Roses Are Red, Ronnie Carroll
5. Sheila, Tommy Roe
6. I Remember You, Frank Ifield
7. Things, Bobby Darin
8. The Locomotion, Little Eva
9. Breaking Up Is Hard to Do, Neil Sedaka
10. Don't That Beat All, Adam Faith

There was nothing *wrong* with that chart, it made for perfectly pleasant easy listening, in the best non-pejorative sense. There was little there you couldn't imagine sitting down and enjoying with your parents listening to *Pick of the Pops*: the grown-ups skimming the *News of the World*, smoking; the youngsters sipping tea, fighting over the final custard cream, fretting over homework. All listening to the radio. Together.

That Christmas of 1962, the youngers would be cuddling up to Purnell's *Top Pop Stars* annual. There were the usual adulatory, dewy-eyed appreciations of Eden Kane, Billy Fury, Craig Douglas and Mark Wynter. The only group featured were the Shadows. Television was safe in the hands of the Billy Cotton Band Show and the ubiquitous Black & White Minstrels.

'Love Me Do' was released the same day as another icon of the decade made his debut. United Artists appear to have had about as much faith in James Bond 007 as EMI did in the Beatles at the beginning of their career. Ian Fleming had been writing 007 adventures

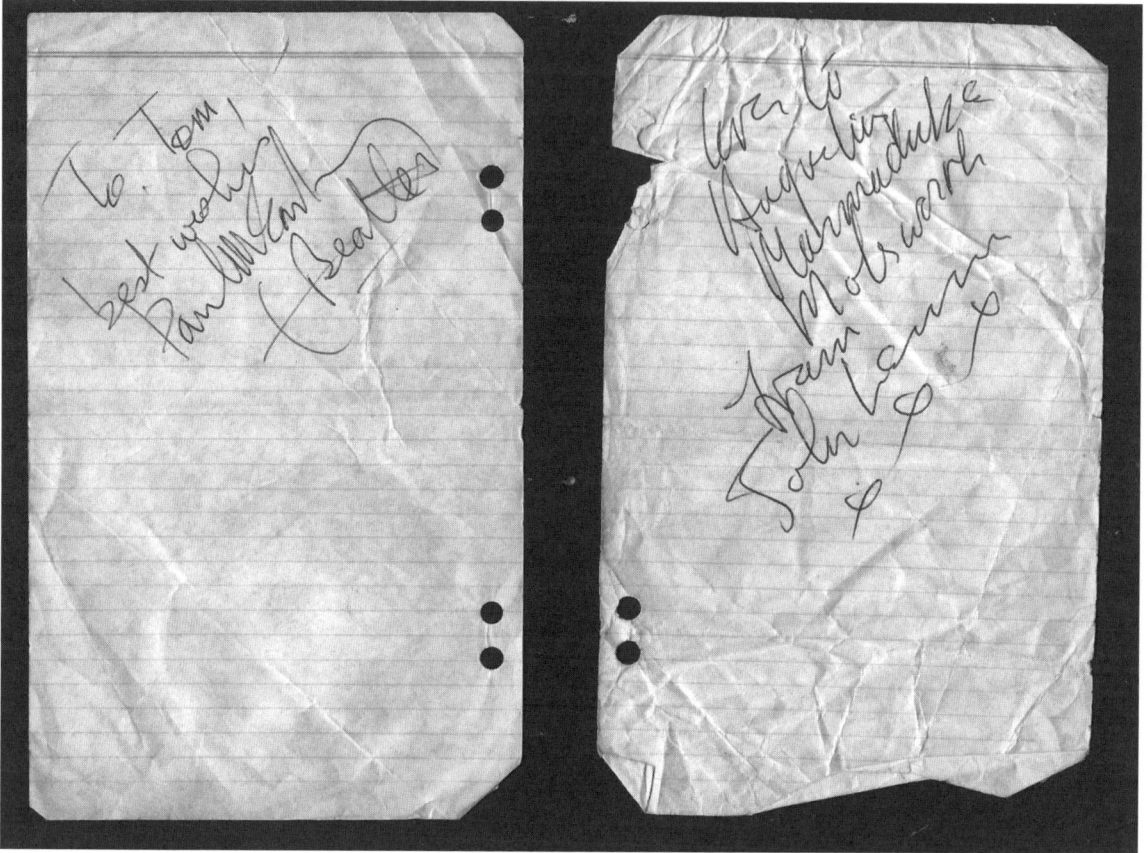

The late Margaret Morton snapped a delighted John and Paul signing autographs in 1963 (though apparently she'd rather have met Peter Jay, with or without his Jaywalkers).

for nearly ten years before Bond made it to cinema screens. The spy's adventures sold steadily, but hopes for *Dr No* were limited.

The James Bond phenomenon began on Friday 5 October 1962, with a Gala Premiere, to which the public were admitted. The film ran at the London Pavilion, United Artists' West End showcase, where, 18 months later, *A Hard Day's Night* would open. But reviewers were equally unimpressed with the screen's 007 as record reviewers were about 'Love Me Do'. *The Times* sniffed, "Perhaps Mr. Sean Connery will, with practice, get the 'feel' of the part a little more surely than he does here". Fleming himself was equally disenchanted, emerging from a screening muttering, "Dreadful. Simply dreadful"

What *was* a success was John Barry's version of Monty Norman's 'The James Bond Theme', which reached No.13 a month after the release of 'Love Me Do'. The prowling, menacing guitar of Vic Flick (crazy name, crazy guy) had a lot to do with the single's success. Vic was the first call guitarist of the early 60s session scene, and went on to play on George Martin's instrumental score for *A Hard Day's Night*. In fact, that legendary 007 Theme had begun life in an earlier Monty Norman musical, *A House for Mr Biswas*, when it was called 'Bad Sign, Good Sign', and was played on a sitar.[4]

In another of those eerie coincidences which percolate the band's history, the weekly *New Society* magazine was launched the same week as they made their recording debut. While the 'white heat' of a Labour government lay a few years ahead, the magazine was sensing a societal change. Its inaugural editorial ran in part: "We live in a climate of uncertainty. Our jobs and incomes may be relatively secure, but few of us are not assailed by doubts about our – and our country's – position in the world, about what moral or ethical standards we should follow, about the nature of human personality and about the whole structure of society. Darwin, Marx, Freud and the pattern of scientific, economic and demographic development have ensured that no traditional idea remains unchallenged. Self-questioning and self-criticism have become characteristic of modern society, even though in many respects much more is necessary."

As for the Beatles and their first hit: Lennon's harmonica, modelled on Delbert McClinton, who he met in Liverpool playing with Bruce Channel promoting his 'Hey Baby' hit, sounds unusual for a British pop release of the period. But frankly, there is little on 'Love Me Do' which suggests the beginning of a phenomenon; its plodding beat, metronomic rhythm and pleading lyrics are fondly remembered because of what followed. But even by the repetitive standards of the time, 'Love Me Do' offered little new.

In his autobiography, Bruce Welch recalls his surprise at the push EMI was giving to the debut from a new group: "Syd Gillingham, who was head of press at EMI, told me that his department had received a directive to promote the Beatles single extensively, not because it was a good record, or because the group had a promising future, but simply because their manager, Brian Epstein, was also a very important record dealer in Merseyside. They didn't want to upset him in case he cancelled his orders with the company".

In an idle moment, I looked at Beatle horoscopes on the 60th anniversary release of

---

4   The group and the spy remained linked. In the dire 1967 *Casino Royale*, the only 'unofficial' 007 film of the era, the very first image is 'Les Beatles' written on a Parisian pissoir.

'Love Me Do'. Patrick Arundell found Libra (John) had "Positive aspects [which] can bring out the best in you and could coincide with a meeting that leaves you ready for zesty adventures. Romance is possible with someone who loves to seize new opportunities and their can-do attitude might be what attracts you to them"... Gemini (Paul) "Excited to explore new interests or to take a step into the unknown... This is a great time to join a group that could help you ease into new interests"... George (Pisces) "Thinking of starting a business from home? From small beginnings something might develop"... Ringo (Cancer) "Dynamic energies might act as a catalyst giving you a powerful push in the right direction. Success is very reliant on your belief in yourself..."

The response to 'Love Me Do' was unremarkable ("they have got a deceptively simple beater which could grow on you", *Disc*... "it tends to drag about mid-way... Not a bad song though...", *New Record Mirror*).

To me, the B-side 'PS I Love You' has more merit; the pleading tone of its lyrics are enhanced by the composer's (Paul) earnest delivery. It acts as the link between the poppy, if trite, ballads of Cliff, Adam and Billy, and the maturity of 'Here, There & Everywhere'. But 'Return to Sender' it ain't, although the novelty of a love expressed through the courtesy of the GPO's Royal Mail next-day-delivery to my mind still rings down the years, and acts as a reminder of those distant times.

Over the years, rumours persisted that it was Brian's clout as the North West's most prominent record retailer had helped hype the disc into the charts by ordering 10,000 copies of 'Love Me Do'. In his exhaustive book on rock managers, *Starmakers & Svengalis*, Brian's brother Clive was emphatic, telling author Johnny Rogan: "I am able to confirm with confidence that this is untrue... It's absolute rubbish! Invoices and statements went through the office and every cheque was either signed by my father or myself. Something like that would obviously have been noticed. Even then, 10,000 records would have cost £3,000".

As 1962 wound down, the Beatles were in a far stronger place than 12 months before. A manager working hard on their behalf; a recording contract and a debut single within the unimaginable precincts of the Top 20. They were not alone in being incapable of imagining where they would be 12 months on. In hindsight of course, *they* were what the world was waiting for. The country seemed to be in stasis – 1962 was indubitably better than 1952. There were no fogs engulfing the capital and killing thousands; everything was off ration; HP allowed household luxuries. The Conservative government was ruling with a steady hand. It was as if the mantra of Tory grandee and 19th-century Prime Minister, Lord Salisbury, still applied: "Whatever happens will be for the worse, and therefore it is in our interest that as little should happen as possible".

In a sense though, the UK was like a pressure cooker waiting to burst as it entered the new decade. In 1962, the foundations were being laid for the transformation which was to explode from London... Art dealer Robert Fraser ('Groovy Bob') opened his first gallery... Peter Blake was profiled in the first newspaper colour magazine, as a 'Pioneer Of Pop Art'. Pop Art itself was described as "a fairground world of juke-boxes and pin-tables, of pop singers and pin-ups, professional wrestling and science fiction". The cracks were appearing: Harold MacMillan's Conservative government was reeling from a 20% drop in support... BBC television launched *That Was the Week That Was*, a programme which did the unthinkable and pricked the bubble of 'The Establishment'... For the first time, the Telstar satellite offered TV audiences in the UK the opportunity to see live broadcasts from the USA... The London Hilton would be the tallest building built in the capital since St Paul's Cathedral... Though in a happy return, disgraced fascist Oswald Mosley was given a good kicking when he visited the East End.

In its December 1962 look ahead to the forthcoming year, *Photoplay* magazine cited, "The Shadows, Britain's most successful instrumental group. There doesn't seem to be any group that can challenge them". Within a year, those challengers would be grinning from the magazine's front cover.

Before the leap into the unknown, there was the return to familiar turf. Reluctantly, the Beatles went back to Hamburg to play out their final contractual obligations at the Star Club. For a group who prided themselves on forging forward, this really was a step back. By now, they had a manager, a record contract; they had made radio and television appearances. Why did they need to trot out the same old stale rock & roll to Kraut punters and drunken squaddies?

Historically of course, what made those final Hamburg appearances so fascinating is that they provide the only audible proof of the Beatles as a bar band, as they sounded, before the world exploded around them. To hear how the groups sounded onstage, Kingsize Taylor put his state-of-the-art Philips RK14 tape recorder on the Star Club stage. During the autumn of 1962, three hours of music were captured, including 120 minutes featuring the Beatles. Once they broke big during 1963, Taylor offered the tapes to Brian Epstein, but was rejected ("As there does not appear to be any commercial value to the recording I can only offer you £20 for your time and effort in producing the tape recording").

With his day job in Liverpool on hold a few years later, Taylor got the tapes cleaned up, and in conjunction with *The Man Who Gave The Beatles Away* (Allan Williams) invited record company executives up to his butcher's shop to listen to the results. Legal battles ensued and it wasn't until 1977 that *The Beatles Live! At The Star Club Hamburg, Germany, 1962* was made available. It was the era of the safety-pin, so the 2LP set was advertised as "when your Granny wouldn't have liked them".

The low-quality but undeniably atmospheric recordings then became available on CD, but a four-day court case in 1998, which even produced George Harrison as a witness, effectively saw them officially withdrawn. George's testimony was fascinating. "Even if John had given Taylor his permission to tape the Beatles performance, then that does not make it legal for the tape to be turned into an album. One drunken person recording another bunch of drunks does not constitute a business deal... We had a record contract and we were on a roll. The last thing we needed was one little bedroom recording to come out. The Star Club recording was the crummiest recording ever made in our name". Apple won the case and all Star Club releases were officially withdrawn.

Even the might of EMI and Abbey Road technology meant that none of the Star Club recordings made their way onto *Anthology 1*. (Dr Hans Olof Gottfridsson's 2015 features for *Record Collector* provides an invaluable source for details of these Hamburg recordings.) Looking half a century ahead, one wonders if in far-away New Zealand, Peter Jackson is applying his audio sleight-of-hand to those historic tapes.

The new year began with a storm, the long, cold winter of 1962/63 has gone down as the Big Chill, and it *was*. I remember trudging to school in wellington boots, through snow drifts that showed no signs of ever appearing to drift away. It lasted until spring. The blizzards raged, the winds howled, our newly-installed central heating was struggling to cope. Wrapped in scarves and sweaters, the early part of 1963 had adults fondly conjuring up the indomitable Blitz Spirit, the whole country once again united against a common foe, except this time it was the hostile and interminable British winter.

Over that bitter winter, the Beatles managed to play nearly 90 gigs. The snow was as deep as 20 feet in some places. Icebergs appeared in the River Mersey. The sea itself froze. Entire communities were cut off.

It felt like it never would end, indeed the snow was still making news by April, but it did end and, as 1963 entered its bright, sunlit uplands, the calendar months unrolled to make it one of the most eventful years in 20th-century peacetime history. Even as a child, I could not help but reel as the events unfolded: the sexual shenanigans of the Profumo affair (kept from me, but impossible to avoid); the Great Train Robbery; Martin Luther King's "I have a dream…" speech; the assassination of John F. Kennedy… And those were just the things which registered on my 11-year-old consciousness.

Other grown-up stuff during those extraordinary 12 months included Harold Wilson being elected Labour party leader; De Gaulle vetoing Great Britain's entry into the Common Market; Beeching's axe falling on rural railways (beautifully captured by Beatle labelmates Flanders & Swann's 'Slow Train')… And, of course, Beatlemania… As Juliet Nicolson wrote, "By the end of [that] winter to admit your ignorance of the Beatles was like saying you had never heard of Henry VIII or cornflakes or God".

And through it all, literally providing a soundtrack to these historic events, was the music of the Beatles. During 1963, the UK benefitted from four singles and two LPs of original Beatle music. 'She Loves You' was the first single to sell a million in the UK. It remained on the charts for 36 weeks! One estimate for Beatles UK singles sales, compiled at the end of the 1980s, had 'She Loves You' as their best seller, with sales over 1,883,000 copies followed by 'I Want to Hold Your Hand' and 'Can't Buy Me Love'. And, of course, 'She Loves You' remained as the nation's favourite until it was overtaken by 'Mull of Kintyre' 14 years later.

All of that lay ahead though. Much rested on the success of the second Beatle single, 'Please Please Me', which fans had to really slog to get hold of with all that snow around. Knowing what we know now, it is strange and rather dislocating to hear Bing Crosby's original 1940 recording of 'Please'. A florid guitar introduction leads Bing ("a gloomy Romeo") into pleading, as his love lends an ear to his pleas. Lennon remembered the song being a favourite of his late mother's.

It took 18 takes to nail 'Please Please Me', after which George Martin found himself satisfied, congratulating the boys on "their first Number One". It wasn't of course and, for half a century since, critics have argued about the absence of 'Please Please Me' from the top slot. Excluded from the *1* CD compilation of 2000, biographers, historians and statisticians have disputed its exclusion. The assiduous Johnny Rogan argued convincingly

I read the news today… Leeds, 1963

(Jack Hickes / Alamy Stock Photo)

that 'Please Please Me' *was* their first No.1. Both *New Musical Express* and *Melody Maker* had the record at the top. But the trade paper, *Record Retailer* disagreed. Rogan wrote that by switching the UK chart statistics from that of *New Musical Express* to those of *Record Retailer* was "nothing less than an Orwellian rewriting of history on a grand scale".

Of the song itself, the repetition on 'Please Please Me' ("Come on, come on, come on…") still works so well… There is an orgiastic element to the song, with Lennon encouraging, provoking, tantalising the listener. Cutting through the crackle of your transistor radio that unfamiliar sound of the harmonica; those girlish harmonies; Paul's thumping bass; Ringo covering his kit; George's little twist before the chorus and climaxing with the drummer's much-mimicked rolls. Even hearing it in 2023 it sounds so much *harder* than what else was around 60 years ago.

Unhappy with EMI's in-house music publishing, around the time of the release of 'Please Please Me', Brian met up with music publisher Dick James. Indelibly linked to the songwriting histories of the Beatles – and Elton John – for many, Dick James was the singer who went riding through the glen on his hit single 'Robin Hood'. With one phone call, James landed Epstein's group an appearance on the popular TV show *Thank Your Lucky Stars*. It was enough to impress Epstein, and lead to a lucrative six-year association for James. "Publishers … worked hard in those days", songwriter Mitch Murray recalled, "and that was worth 50%. Every songwriter in those days signed a contract like that. Dick wasn't unfair – it was just normal practice, like it used to be normal to send small boys up chimneys!"

With a record label, a sympathetic producer and music publisher in place, Brian fitted the final piece in the jigsaw. He got the Beatles, still effectively unknown outside Merseyside, on a bill with the country's top pop singer, Frank Ifield. That December 1962 Peterborough show did not light the flame of Beatlemania. However, in the long term, it allied them to the UK's top pop tour promoter Arthur Howes, Brian Epstein now had all the bricks in place to make his group "bigger than Elvis".

To promote their second single, the Beatles made a breathless round of radio, TV and live appearances, the latter all too often thwarted by the ubiquitous Big Freeze. There they are, in their tiny, tinny transit, manfully steered by Neil Aspinall, up and down and in and out of the pre-motorway landscape of the United Kingdom during the freezing, snowbound early months of 1963. Huddled together, the smoke from their cigarettes mingling with the icy breath, the condensation preventing any real views. But what could they see from their van through the steam? Just acres of white, snowbound fields, slush-filled streets… Breathless halts to sample the tantalising smells from fish and chip shops, and all the while they chugged along, their banter only interrupted by intense efforts to hear their record on the radio. Like maquisards in wartime, the group pressed their ears to the distant, fluttering signal, the airwaves polluted by static, only occasionally broken by their own thrilling harmonies and distinctive harmonica.

In his introduction to *Meet the Beat Groups*, published to coincide with the 1963 phenomenon, Cyrus Andrews carbon-dated "the precise time when Beat Groups began to come into their own… January 19th 1963 [was] an important date. It was then that a number called 'Please Please Me' recorded by a then little-known group called the Beatles crept into the Top 50 Charts at the modest placing of 45th. No special significance was placed on this, yet it was to mark the beginning of a new era – the first faint thud of a new sound destined to change the face of the record charts completely".

Chart progress was largely dictated by one radio show. It is hard today to convey the corrosive, stultifying, overpowering *dullness* of a 1960s Sunday. For adults, the pubs were shut between 2 p.m. and 7 p.m., for kids, the television and radio broadcasts were banal. No wonder that the BBC Light Programme's *Pick of the Pops*, hosted since time immemorial by Alan ('not 'arf') Freeman, between 5 p.m. and 7 p.m. on a Sunday evening was the oasis. Mind you, that was followed by the deathless *Sing Something Simple*, signifying the end of the weekend, time for homework and school in barely 12 hours.

Pick of the Pops really picked up in 1963 with the Beatle Blitzkrieg, and the bombardment of beat groups which came in their wake. With the winter snow finally evaporated, throughout the remaining months of the year the sun shone, the air buzzed and 1963 really did come alive. For much of the year, the programme boasted Beatle music, but also other fabulous British contributions – Gerry & the Pacemakers, Billy J. Kramer, Johnny Kidd & the Pirates, and, yes, Brian Poole & the Tremeloes. There were also swansongs from Phil Spector (the Crystals' 'Then He Kissed Me') and Chuck Berry ('Memphis, Tennessee').

And what of the second-best band to come out of Liverpool… The Searchers? The quartet went through the same one-nighter grind in Hamburg and Liverpool as the Beatles. Their set lists were remarkably similar (the Searchers included 'Some Other Guy' on their second LP; the Beatles didn't record 'Money' until a year after the Searchers). But what I believe made the Searchers special was in their embracing and enhancing of folk music. In recording Malvina Reynolds' 'What Have They Done to the Rain'; the Kingston Trio's 'All My Sorrows' and Pete Seeger's 'Where Have All the Flowers Gone', the Searchers laid the foundations for folk-rock. The Searchers' shadow can be seen to be cast over everyone from the Byrds to REM.

The group's reluctance to sign with Brian Epstein (they didn't want to play second fiddle to the Beatles) was significant – for Brian they were "my group that got away". But a crucial divide which separated the two groups, was that the Searchers didn't write their own material. And once the pool of cover versions had been drained dry, they were forced to rely upon outside writers to supply them. That gave the Beatles (with their own "inbuilt tunesmith team") a head start…

I had actually forgotten just how many familiar songs the John and Paul duo had written which the group deemed not worthy of keeping to themselves – Billy J. Kramer benefitted from 'I'll Be On My Way', 'Bad to Me', 'I'll Keep You Satisfied' and 'From a Window'. Gerry & the Pacemakers were underwhelmed with 'Hello Little Girl', the Fourmost were not. They also got 'I'm in Love' to round off 1963. Peter & Gordon unsurprisingly got something to their advantage; Peter Asher's housemate let them have 'A World Without Love', 'Nobody I Know' and 'I Don't Want to See You Again'. While his friend Bernard Webb tried his hand with 'Woman' for the duo to record. From Rhodesia (now Zimbabwe) Mike Shannon & the Strangers released 'One and One Is Two'; nearer to home, Solihull's the Applejacks had a crack at 'Like Dreamers Do'. Former Cavern hat-check girl Priscilla White followed 'Love of the Loved' with 'It's for You'.

To my mind, *that* is what elevated the Beatles. They didn't need anyone else to supply their material. Once successful, their contemporaries were scrabbling for the best of the cover versions. The Beatles had no need to pester the songwriting chambers of Denmark Street. They didn't have to queue up for material rejected by Cliff, Billy Fury, Adam Faith, Mike Berry, John Leyton, Ronnie Carroll, Craig Douglas, Frankie Vaughan or Eden Kane.

It was that internal dynamic of Lennon & McCartney which gave the group not only their impetus, but the ability to stay ahead of and outside the pack. There was the novelty of a group providing their own material. But under the watchful eyes of Epstein and Martin, that is what turned them into a uniquely self-contained unit. The estimate is that they had pounded through 10,000 hours onstage before they even *entered* a recording studio, so they were instrumentally and vocally tight. Their trump card though was that songwriting partnership – the Beatles didn't *need* to rely on anyone outside their tightly-knit orbit.

The Searchers' hit big with their debut single, 'Sweets for My Sweet', was a UK No.1 in the summer of 1963 during that first bracing burst of Merseybeat. But it was a Drifters song. Likewise, the Swinging Blue Jeans and Gerry & the Pacemakers had to fall back on Tin Pan Alley songwriters or US covers.

"In those days publishing companies did everything", songwriter Mitch Murray recalled. "They had the premises, they had the staff, they'd take your song, pay for the demo, find a singer, finance the recording, fix the record deal and then once it was out there, they would go and promote it. The Beatles changed all that". The group's first mention in a *New Musical Express* feature (26 October 1962) was headlined 'Liverpool's Beatles Wrote Their Own Hit'.

If you were lucky enough to shelter under the Epstein umbrella (Cilla Black; Billy J. Kramer; the Fourmost) you got first crack at a Lennon & McCartney original. Naturally, the Beatles kept the pick of the crop to record themselves, but nonetheless 'Love of the Loved', 'I'll Be on My Way' and 'Hello Little Girl' retain their breezy period charm. They were also confident enough to relegate strong songs such as 'Thank You Girl', 'I'll Get You' and 'This Boy' to B-sides (I do like to be beside the B-side).

Over the years, and particularly while writing this book, I always asked, hand on heart, in those early days, were they *really* that much further ahead than their peers? Were they really quantifiably *better* than the 400 other Merseybeat groups? Talking to Geoff Speed in Liverpool once, I asked him, as a Cavern regular, if he would have singled them out from the Searchers, Gerry & the Pacemakers, the Reno Four, Rory Storm, et al? "Of course, what people don't realise is that seeing The Beatles wasn't that big a deal. They were a local band, you saw them around town, you could see them down at the Cavern whenever you wanted. Back then, the smart money was on the Big Three". Many testified that, live at the Cavern, *the* group were the Big Three. Drummer Johnny Hutchinson was an upholsterer by day, but by night, reversed his drum sticks to pound with reinforced strength – "It was", one Cavern veteran told me, "like the fucking *1812 Overture!*"

The club regulars were impressed that, on occasion, the Beatles would introduce a number as a song they had written. That separated them from the rest of the herd. Indeed on one historic night the future came to the cellar. The last time the Beatles played the Cavern was 3 August 1963. By then they were a nationwide phenomenon, their third release, 'From Me to You' had unarguably given them a No.1 single. Brian Epstein was always very decent when it came to honouring original bookings, made long before. Hundreds squeezed into the cellar for what they knew must be the last time. Tickets were 9/6d, and were only available to Cavern Club members on production of a membership card. You'd think the Beatles would have been enough to draw a crowd, but the bill also boasted support from the Mersey Beats, the Escorts, Road Runners and the fabulously-named Johnny Ringo & the Colts.

Symbolically, there was a power cut when the Beatles played the Cavern. They stood mute as they bid their farewell to the venue to which had given them house room for two years. While the group waited for the electricity to be restored, Paul sat at the piano – which was always onstage – and vamped out a song which later came to be known as 'When I'm 64'. Power restored, the group powered on, leaving behind the best-known venue in all of rock history.

Paul did return to the Cavern for a private visit in October 1968. He joined the group, the Curiosity Shop, onstage and ran through 'Hey Jude' on the club piano. In 1999 he returned and performed at the rebuilt club to launch *Run Devil Run*. He also went back for a 2018 BBC special.

During its ten-year existence, the Cavern really did merit its place as the most important rock venue of all. That, of course, is largely due to the platform it gave to the Beatles: they used the club almost as a rehearsal space, they built up a rapport with their audience; it was the location of their first-ever television appearance… For singer-songwriter John Stewart, the Cavern was "Holy ground". It was the lustre of the Beatles that drew the celebrities to that dark, dank cellar – the VIP book boasted visits from, among others, Huyton-born Rex Harrison, Marlene Dietrich, Chet Atkins, Anna Neagle and Lionel Bart.

It is of course with the Beatles that the Cavern is inextricably linked. With the benefit of hindsight everyone who saw them there achieved an epiphany, like playwright Willy Russell (*John, Paul, George, Ringo… and Bert*) who witnessed them at the Cavern in 1962: "The Beatles kicked into 'Some Other Guy' and a whole new life began from that very moment".

It was only by a whisker that the first Beatles LP was not recorded live at the Cavern. George Martin had witnessed the Messianic reaction the group got at their hometown venue. Perhaps that vibrant atmosphere could be captured on disc? It was not to be, the producer found the Cavern "sonically unsuitable and hygienically unbearable". He was not alone; a London journalist dispatched to investigate the birthplace of the Mersey Sound found the venue a "foetid ill-ventilated hole".

In the footsteps of the Beatles, even the London-centric media sensed there was something surfacing along the banks of the Mersey. Ian Whitcomb later managed to nail that appeal: "Merseybeat was hard and fast and relentless. Filling in the chords was a chunk-chunk-clog made possible by two or even three harmony guitars. One, of course, took the lead lines but the others provided the essential rhythm sound, thick and starchy and solid as a North Country dumpling. Providing a rudimentary base was a bass guitar, usually plodding along on root notes. The whump and thud [of drums] was like work boots on city cobblestones, were faster and heavier than the American style".

So many groups. So much music. And towering over the best and the brightest, 'the Nemperor'. There's that lovely photo from the early summer of 1963: of Brian Epstein, for once centre stage, surrounded by his charges – the Beatles seated alongside Gerry & the Pacemakers and Billy J. Kramer & the Dakotas. Taken in the car park of the Fiveways pub, just down the road from the Epstein family home in Queens Drive. All of them, so young, so dapper… The future lying just round the corner, so full of promise.

*

With the snow disappearing, the Beatles began their first nationwide tour on 2 February 1963. It was a long slog coinciding with the release of their second single, 'Please Please Me'. Billed below headliner Helen Shapiro, the 'dynamic' Beatles appeared halfway through the first half between the Honeys and Danny Williams. Brian Epstein had contacted Arthur Howes to get 'the boys' on a bill, *any* bill.

Package tours were an important opportunity to be seen and heard. Two shows a night across the UK, with bills bulging with one or two headliners, to ensure value for money and a number of up-and-coming acts. Tickets prices were not exorbitant, and the nationwide tour dates (Brighton and Huddersfield; Taunton and York…) ensured that audiences were never too far from their idols.

It was on that gruelling Helen Shapiro tour that the Beatles extended their reach. The first act ever to cover a John Lennon and Paul McCartney composition was tour companion Kenny Lynch, who released 'Misery' on 22 March 1963 – competing with the Beatles' debut album, which also featured the song. Headliner Helen Shapiro had been offered the song originally. Not much wonder she declined 'Misery', the teenager's biggest hit to date had been 'Walking Back to Happiness'.

Kenny Lynch told Spencer Leigh: "We were all swapping songs on the coach, and The Beatles gave Helen 'Misery'. She didn't like the title, which was fair enough, 'cos she was only young. I said 'Oh I like that song, I'll do it'. They said 'Great', but Lennon gave me the greatest rucking in the world because I had Bert Weedon on it… I played the record to John in Dick James' office and he said 'Who's on guitar? It's crap'. I said 'It's Bert Weedon'. He said 'Why didn't you tell me? I'd have done it for you'." Ten years later, Kenny Lynch was one of the celebrities pictured on the sleeve of Paul McCartney's *Band on the Run* album.

Martin Creasy's 2010 *Beatlemania!* gives the most comprehensive account of those wearying UK package tours, 1963–65. I still mourn missing seeing the Beatles live. I think my mum was concerned about the safety of her only child amidst all that hysteria. And I suppose Latin homework took priority.

Round they went on the circuit, two shows a night, every night, in the cold, from venue to venue, from their dispiritingly low billing, while people were still filing in. Gradually, their half-a-dozen song set grew, as did the reception. A prescient review by Reginald Brace in *The Yorkshire Post* predicted that the "four young men from Liverpool … will go from strength to strength this year". By tour's end, at the end of March, they were closing the first half. They were on the way to becoming the most successful group in the country.

One early Sheffield date had been booked by Peter Stringfellow, amidst all the local acts with fabulous names like Dean Marshall & the Deputies, Johnny Silver & the Thunderbirds… Finding the group's manager from the *New Musical Express*, Stringfellow

'The Eppy Centre', Brian alongside Beatles, Pacemakers and Dakotas
just down the road from the Epstein family home, Liverpool June 1963

(Trinity Mirror / Mirrorpix / Alamy Stock Photo)

"called him from a phone box outside the church hall. 'How much for the Beatles mate?' 'I'm afraid they're not free until February and it'll cost you £50' 'Fifty? I can get Screaming Lord Sutch for £50'."

One of the oddest engagements came in April 1963. Following a request from a pupil, Brian agreed for them to perform at the public school, Stowe. The show was taped and was aired in 2023. It makes for fascinating listening. Each song was greeted with polite applause, as one would expect from a public-school crowd. So you can actually *hear* the Beatles perform, on the cusp of Beatlemania. There are nine songs from their just-released debut LP, plus Cavern and Hamburg favourites. All heard and not buried beneath waves of screams.

It was all … building. *Beat Monthly* magazine was launched in May 1963, and its initial editorial enthused about how the Beatles were giving "the music business a kick in the pants… As far as I'm concerned the Beatles were just what the musical doctor ordered. Too many managers didn't look further than the London area to find new talent". Editor Johnny Dean didn't hang around, he launched the 1/6d *The Beatles Monthly* that August.

It's lovely looking through that inaugural issue – we learn that that 'Love Me Do' sold 100,000 copies (!)… John is the heaviest Beatle (11 stone 5 lbs) and Ringo the shortest (5'8"); that George likes "girls, and listening to records with girls" but that "I put driving as my big hobby"… Paul's "main memory of childhood is writing back to front". There's the photo of the group mobbed by fans inside the gates of Abbey Road as they make their way to record 'She Loves You'.

In his memoir, Geoff Emerick recalls the excitement of that 'She Loves You' session and George Martin's restrained but, for him, fulsome praise, "nice job, lads". A *Beat Magazine* editorial ran, "What's this? No single by the Beatles, that fantastic record-breaking quartet in the August chart? Well, first of all their *Twist & Shout* EP is third in the list and is selling like a single. And their follow-up single has an August 23 release date. So though it's a for-sure chart-topper with an enormous advance order it can't be included as yet".

That "for-sure chart-topper" was, of course, 'She Loves You' and was about to tilt the entertainment world on its axis. (In his *Beat Magazine* review, David Gell called it a "gold-plated and diamond-studded hit of the month".) That same week's releases saw Randy & the Rainbows' 'Denise', which was revived many years later by Blondie, and future hits from the Hollies ('Searchin'), Freddie & the Dreamers ('I'm Tellin' You Now'), Little Stevie Wonder ('Fingertips'). But whither Rockin' Henri & the Hay Seeds? David & the Embers?

Earlier in February, between dates in Sunderland and Sheffield, the Beatles were allowed a precious day at Abbey Road to record their first LP. Four of the 14 tracks were already in the can, as A- and B-sides of their first two singles (which is why the subtitle to *Please Please Me* is "with Love Me Do and 12 other songs"). That was a tradition which soon went by the board; as was common with UK LPs, singles were generally not included. It was a tradition the Beatles adhered to, save for film soundtracks and *Revolver*.

There is something heartwarming and eerily prescient about that debut LP. From the cover itself, the Beatles are inviting you into their world. Angus McBean (1904–90) was an established artistic photographer. For him that photo session was just another job which

The Beatles Monthly No. 1

took him away from snapping Vivien Leigh, Audrey Hepburn, Margot Fonteyn or Ivor Novello. He remembered his 1963 commission encountering "a gangling group of four young men in mole-coloured velveteen performing suits of a terrible cut". During the shoot, the photographer asked Lennon how long he thought the group would last? "Oh, about six years I suppose, whoever heard of a bald Beatle?"

It was not the first time the photographer had taken a similar shot in the same location. In October 1961, McBean photographed bandleader Joe Loss, who was seen smiling over that soon-to-be historic bannister.

There remains something strikingly modern about the *Please Please Me* cover photo, the four grinning faces leaning over the balcony of a very 60s skyscraper. Only Ringo looks like he's slipped in from a different era, his Teddy Boy quiff at odds with the exi haircuts of his bandmates. Endlessly parodied, that iconic cover photo merits its place in the all-time greatest LP sleeves. And, while EMI still occupied their Manchester Square HQ, it was expected for every visitor to stick their heads over *that* balcony. And when the record company finally vacated its Central London premises in 1996 and went out west (Hammersmith), they made sure they took that staircase with them. It moved again, in 2003, when EMI moved to Kensington.

As with so much related to the Beatles, that debut LP cover took on an iconic status and, in their brief tenure at EMI, the Sex Pistols were photographed sneering over the balcony, as were Blur. Angus McBean was called back in 1969 to snap the Fab Four, barely recognisable only six years on. Talking to Paul Du Noyer about the break-up, McCartney felt "the most final we got was going back to EMI in Manchester Square and taking that photo. And we all felt spooky, 'This is pretty final. This is full circle. We've started and ended'."

In 2007 there was another lawsuit, this time over that LP cover. An estimated £700,000 of Beatle photographs, including the only surviving proof copy of that *Please Please Me* cover, were binned by a cleaner at EMI's office. Apple and EMI then sued the cleaner's employer, who had taken the priceless photographs to their waste compactor.

One other favoured photographer of the period was Dezo Hoffmann (1912–86). He mourned his mother in the brutal anonymity of the Holocaust. Rumours abounded that his relationships with the glamorous Hedy Lamarr and Marlene Dietrich were more than professional. During the Spanish Civil War, Dezo had forged firm friendships with Robert Capa and Ernest Hemingway. And yet, it was his freewheeling years with the Beatles which continued to enthrall until his death.

On disc, their debut LP was swiftly accomplished. Ten songs cut and completed in a long, working day, then London to Oldham for another gig. I don't know how many copies EMI pressed of that debut LP. But by year's end everyone you knew (or their sister) had a copy. Once the stylus dropped onto the vinyl disc, you were greeted by a welcoming count-in, a "1, 2, 3, 4…" which introduced you to a whole wide world, and all it took was 32 and a half electrifying minutes.

Please Please Me is flawed, which is fair enough, given the time restrictions it was recorded under. But for all its faults (Ringo's pedestrian drumming; George's tepid soloing; the flimsiness of the fledgling McCartney–Lennon compositions…), there remains the suggestion of future greatness. Whether it is the confident opening track or the raw-throated finale of 'Twist & Shout' (the "linen-ripping" vocal George Martin wanted), the LP transcends nostalgia. The sound of Lennon's harmonica was a novelty, suggesting a vulnerability, perhaps based on folk memories of the solitary mouth organ heard wailing across Flanders fields half a century before. But of course, at the time of its release (22 March), no one knew what lay ahead in the remaining months of 1963. What the LP sleeve boasted were the group's first two singles, but by the time it was in the shops and on fans' Dansettes by the middle of April both it, and the third Beatles single 'From Me to You', had hit No.1 on *all* the UK charts.

The *Please Please Me* LP was the template for much of what followed. Room was always found for a Ringo vocal; George was also allowed to step up to the microphone (I still love his tentative vocal on 'Do You Want to Know a Secret', the Liverpudlian twang in that voice – "how much I really cur..."). The cover versions were painstakingly drawn from their enormous repertoire, until the point when the group's own "inbuilt tunesmith team" felt confident enough to fill an entire half an hour with their own material.

As a writer, I am always keen to tie events together, the domino theory wherein one topples against the next and produces a chain reaction. And there are indeed manifold coincidences in the working life of the Beatles. I struggle, however, to adhere to two events which cultural historians link on 11 February 1963 within a short London taxi ride: the Beatles record their debut LP and the poet Sylvia Plath commits suicide.

Just prior to its release, *Melody Maker* gave the group its first cover ("It's happening big for The Beatles"). Despite a quirky photo of the group occupying 75% of the front page, the rest of the cover was a reminder of the weekly paper's roots: 'Paris Jazz Weekend £12'... and a sidebar of tour dates for Sarah (Vaughan), Dizzy (Gillespie) and Stan Kenton. The influential *Melody Maker* LP review ran, "The Liverpool group is one up on the batch of pop groups in the country for their combination of top-class twang and exciting all-stops-out vocal work which links into a formidably commercial sound". Equally enthusiastic were *ABC Film Review* who called the LP "a programme of red-blooded 'beat' music".

Four months after its release, George proudly wrote to his sister Louise, "Our long-playing record has been (and still is) No.1 on the LP charts. Incidentally, it has sold more copies in Gt Britain than anything else since *South Pacific* soundtrack (How about that!)".

Funnily enough, for me, one track from the LP which still resonates is their cover of 'A Taste of Honey'. The first vocal version was by R&B singer Lenny Welch, and it was that 1962 release the Beatles modelled their cover on. It is too often dismissed because it is not a McCartney–Lennon original, and critics see its inclusion as confirmation of Paul's proneness to soft-soaped balladry. But I find it as poignant and atmospheric as a serrated-edged Kodak snapshot. Listening to 'A Taste of Honey' today I am struck by the pictures it conjures up, of smoke-filled cellars, with striped-sweatered beatniks nodding their berets to the beguiling melody, stroking their first defiant attempts at goatee beards. Of leggy, aspiring Juliette Grecos, arms curled around boyfriends' shoulders.

It offers Ringo a rare opportunity to drum with brushes, offering up a jazzy element, reinforced by George's Django-fills. But Paul's double-tracked vocal and his colleagues' wistful harmonies to my mind make this one of the most atmospheric of all Beatle recordings. Interestingly, it was the only track *The Observer* singled out in its review of the LP ("in such a song as 'A Taste of Honey', something fresh and rather touching comes across"). The song was written for Shelagh Delaney's play, and Acker Bilk enjoyed an instrumental hit with 'A Taste of Honey' in January 1963. But the version Paul sings was written for the play's 1960 Broadway production (starring Angela Lansbury).

Shelagh Delaney was only 19 when she wrote her first play – *A Taste of Honey*. In a beguilingly naive letter, she sent it to the Theatre Royal's creative director Joan Littlewood ("Dear Miss Littlewood, along with this letter comes a play…"). The play was a triumph on its initial production in London, and later New York. It was filmed in 1961, with a brassy performance from Dora Bryan, who would later make a further connection with the Fab Four when she enjoyed a Christmas 1963 Top 20 hit with 'All I Want for Christmas Is a Beatle'. Shelagh Delaney's place in pop culture was cemented over 20 years later when she featured as the cover star of a single and album by the Smiths. And Dora Bryan was never known to miss a passing bandwagon, her Christmas 1964 effort was an homage to that other cultural phenomenon, James Bond, 'Oh Oh Oh Oh Seven'.

As well as the songs made familiar as singles, I would also single out 'There's a Place', a gentler, more reflective side of Lennon's songwriting, prior to the climactic 'Twist & Shout'. Of the other covers, Goffin & King's 'Chains' just about passes muster, while Arthur Alexander's 'Anna' also registers.

In 2010, I visited the Fame (Florence Alabama Music Enterprises) Studios, in Florence, Alabama. This is where Wilson Pickett & Duane Allman cut 'Hey Jude' in 1968, the day Martin Luther King was assassinated. Prior to the news breaking, there's a great photo of the wicked Pickett and the hippie Duane roaring with laughter together. As a footnote, Florence, Alabama merits a place in music history, birthplace not only of W.C. Handy, "the father of the blues", but also Sun Records' founder Sam Phillips.

The other Beatle connection is that this was also where Arthur Alexander recorded. As well as 'Anna', the Beatles also covered Arthur's song 'Soldier of Love'. Arthur was unique in having songs recorded not only by the Beatles, but also the Rolling Stones, Bob Dylan and Elvis Presley. Arthur was a bell hop who loved Country & Western music (like Otis Redding and Percy Sledge, he spent a lot of time listening to Nashville's Grand Ole Opry). He cut the first version of 'Burning Love' and died in 1993 of a heart attack in his publisher's office.

*

There was little time for the Beatles to savour their initial early success of 1963… The year was spent in a grinding round of personal appearances, tour supports, headlining appearances, radio and television broadcasts. Their brief forays to EMI's recording studios offered a welcome respite. You can hear the turmoil on *Anthology 1*, as Paul berates Neil Aspinall for losing his plectrum, mislaid somewhere in a provincial B&B or regional theatre.

To keep pace with the pace, the chilly coaches were soon banished, and internal flights were required. In *Anthology*, Ringo recalled, "We were flying from London to Glasgow and there were only three seats left on the plane, and in my naivety I said 'I'll stand'…"

The full certification of Beatlemania came when 'From Me to You' became the group's first official No.1 single. The cover of the 10 April 1963 issue of *Melody Maker* says it all: the jazz-friendly weekly headlined 'Nat Cole-Ted Heath to Tour', also boasting interviews with crooner Ronnie Carroll and jazzman Gerry Mulligan. Then occupying the bottom left-hand quarter, a smiling Lennon nestles next to 'Beatles Back with a Bang'.

In a sense, 'From Me to You' is often overshadowed by the wealth of material which followed. But those head-shaking "Ooh…" harmonies, the effortlessly engaging melody, resonate still. I have an inordinate fondness for 'From Me to You'. It was the single I missed; never made it onto LP until 1966 (I never bothered with that *Greatest Hits*) and only got to love it again in 1973.

By now, they were on that rollercoaster ride. That momentum was further propelled by the release of the single which today still testifies to that first hysterical flush… 'She Loves You'. For their third single of the year, there were already half a million advance orders. 500,000 willing to buy a song they'd never heard. But then it was the Beatles, and they had not disappointed throughout the year.

My 1963 summer holiday was spent at the now-demolished Bracklesham Bay Hotel in West Sussex. It was a time when families always holidayed at home – over the horizon was that mysterious place called 'the Continent'. Without the need to rely on packaged nostalgia, or reflect on lost youth, the soundtrack to that summer was undeniably, without question, the Beatles. My memory was at fault, as I recalled it was 'She Loves You' which was the background to that holiday. Though we'd have been back at home by the time 'She Loves You' was released late in August 1963.

That song was, however, the sea change; it was when the boys as well as the girls became fascinated by the haircuts, collarless suits and Beatle boots. Until then, it was the girls who were spellbound by Cliff, Adam, Eden, Billy… By September 1963 it was the young boys who were mesmerised by the strange-shaped guitars they played; the aggressive stance of the one called John; the enthusiastic hammering of the drummer known by the almost Disney-esque name of 'Ringo'. The way the other two shook their heads and the defiantly long hair shook in tandem.

It is strangely unsettling going through the *Record Retailer & Music Industry News* issue of 15 August 1963, which for some reason I still have. Get past the grinning photo of Mark Wynter and the inserted poster promoting his 'Running to You' (did not chart). There's a double spread of new releases on EMI – alongside familiar names (Lesley Gore … the Four Seasons … Link Wray … Eddie Cochran … Fats Domino) were the old guard (Peggy Lee … Al Martino … Oscar Peterson). Then there were those that never even troubled Where Are They Now enquiries: the Innocents … Alan Drew … Beverley Jones … the Oldham Youth Choir. And there, top of page three, 'She Loves You' (Parlophone R5055), "It's fabulous!!!"

And spread over other magazine titles of the period are all the names *so* familiar from the light entertainment programmes of my youth… Miki & Griff; Alma Cogan; Joe Loss; Susan Maughan; the Springfields; Nina & Frederick; the Black & White Minstrels; Kenny Ball; Kenneth McKellar; Robin Hall & Jimmie MacGregor; Karl Denver; Acker Bilk… All about to be superseded by something so stupendous, on a scale so unimaginable, that even now it gives pause for thought.

It was such a dictatorial world. The BBC policy, to keep Musicians' Union members employed, was to ration original recordings, so that MU members could be then employed to play cover versions for broadcast. The Musicians' Union were determined to keep their members in work, which was why the BBC's pop station, the Light Programme, was only allowed to broadcast a meagre five hours of recorded music every day.

It was like the food rationing which had only been lifted a decade before. Youngsters tuned into *Saturday Club*, *Children's Favourites* and *Pick of the Pops*, and on occasion audiences for these shows touched 20,000,000. So the BBC was crucial. One of the few places to hear the records *you* liked was on the long-running *Two-Way Family Favourites*. This was a Light Programme hosted by Cliff Michelmore and Jean Metcalfe.

It was intended to reunite families with service personnel serving abroad – the Army still had a presence in, among other territories, Aden, Borneo, Cyprus and Germany. I can still remember the messages going out to the likes of "Private Terry Collier at BFPO Monchengladbach…". In *Whatever Happened to the Likely Lads*, Bob tells Terry, "Me and the lads … spent two months and 50 plain postcards trying to get you a request on *Family Favourites*… It was Doris Day singing 'Que Sera Sera'". "I can't stand Doris Day!" "How could I know what your musical tastes were?… You might have been anywhere from Pink Floyd to the Fodon Motor Works Band".

From the buoyant summer of 1963, long into the chill autumn, the ubiquity of 'She Loves You' was the provider of exuberant joy. Loaded with hormonal anticipation, the head-shaking chorus drilled into your head like trepanning. It really was everywhere that song – seek out the YouTube clip of the exultant Liverpool FC fans belting out 'She Loves You' from the terraces of the Kop. They had good ears that crowd, it was the Kop who took 'You'll Never Walk Alone' and transformed it into the footballing singalong. They took their football seriously up there; Liverpool manager Bill Shankly famously commented, "Football's not a matter of life and death, it's more important than that".

I vividly remember the excitement, the ubiquity of that first fusillade. It was as if a switch had been flicked: sisters, cousins and neighbours lost interest in Cliff, show jumping and ice skating and turned their full teenage attention to the Beatles. Even boys just entering their teens were transfixed: no more drawings on schoolbooks of Bren gun carriers or Tiger tanks; pencil-pushing Picassos switched their devotion to sketching electric guitars and drum kits. Gone were the traditional boyhood hobbies of stamp-collecting and trainspotting. Weekly bursts of *The Victor* comic and *War Picture Library* were replaced by titles which detailed the burgeoning Beat Boom.

Cliff-style quiffs were forgotten, and juvenile hair immediately combed forward to cover the forehead. Unable to afford stylish Cuban-heeled 'Beatle boots' (courtesy of Anello & Davide), wellington boots were hauled into service. Oh, and t-shirts, the Beatles favoured t-shirts instead of those unsexy string vests we all had to don. Just look at the horrid fishing-net style vest Cliff sported on the cover of *Summer Holiday*.

It was an epidemic, from the late summer of 1963, right up to the delivery of that first Beatle Christmas Record, the kingdom was united. It really, honestly *did* signal the shock of the new. So much has been written about the all-encompassing, sweeping success of the Beatles at the beginning. But it was all true… It *really* did happen.

They occupied the No.1 slot of single, EP and LP charts. The September *Melody Maker* Pop Poll had them at No.1 Vocal Group with twice as many votes as their nearest rivals, the Springfields. They also landed No.1 and 2 for Vocal Disc 'From Me to You' and 'Please Please Me'. Too early to take into account 'She Loves You', which surely would have topped the poppermost. John Lennon was even singled out as the tenth best 'Male Singer'.

New Musical Express chart historians wrote that at the height of their success the Fab Four "were selling almost as many records in Britain as the whole of the rest of the music industry put together". Christmas stockings bulged with Beatle 'product' – the *NME* Top 30 *singles* chart of 21 December 1963 had them occupying the top two places, as well as two Beatles EPs and – unheard of – *With the Beatles* LP at No.17. There were also two Lennon & McCartney songs in others' hands. Plus, of course, Dora Bryan's plea which found an echo in every UK household – 'All I Want for Christmas Is a Beatle'.

The fan club was receiving 60 sacks of fan mail every week. Fifteen million people tuned in to watch them on *Sunday Night at the London Palladium*. As an indication, only a few years before, the first televised wedding of a royal (Princess Margaret) drew a record audience of 20,000,000. The *Radio Times* printed 10,000 2/- Beatle portraits and were overwhelmed with a quarter of a million fans' requests. Saturday 7 December 1963, an audience of 22,000,000 watched them on *Juke Box Jury*. A breathless, snatched tea break for *Dixon of Dock Green* and *Wells Fargo*, then back to BBC TV for *It's The Beatles*. They topped the bill on the Light Programme for a Boxing Day *Saturday Club*. One BBC executive was heard to grouse, "I don't know why they don't just call it the Beatles Broadcasting Corporation".

Newspapers were full of 'Beatlemania', as they slogged round the B-roads and fledgling motorways of the UK. Queues outside venues in Lewisham, Rhyl, Kirkcaldy, Croydon… Then airborne – Dublin, Belfast, Sweden. To try and combat the incessant screaming, the group upped their Vox amplifiers from 30 to 60 watts.

Just *reading* about those eventful days of 1963 is exhausting. Fleet Street delighted in the fusillades of jelly babies. The deafening audiences. There were photos of overnight queues, teenage girls sleeping on the pavement, overwhelmed St John's Ambulance crews carrying fainting teenagers from theatres. Local police chiefs relished planning 'Operation Beatle', the group's entry and exit on their beat, like a military campaign. Teachers were concerned that pupils were devoting more time to the group than their homework; employers were suspending workers for their Beatle haircuts. Parents were worried at the fanatical commitment their children were displaying.

It was overwhelming, and it wasn't just *them*. As well as dominating the print media, pop charts and airwaves, their songs were being taken up by other acts – in 1963 alone, Lennon & McCartney songs were recorded by Cilla Black, Billy J. Kramer, the Fourmost, Russ Conway and the Rolling Stones. Del Shannon entered the history books as the first American act to cover a Beatle song. In France, Petula Clark did the chanson with 'Tu Perds Tu Temps' ('Please Please Me').

That period of British history has been endlessly analysed, just *why* they captivated the nation. There was the music, of course, their brand of muscular pop was inimitable. The summer of 1963 was, for Fleet Street, 'the silly season'. With its sex in high places, drug-taking orgies, the ongoing hi-jinks of the Profumo Affair could hardly be detailed outside of the Sunday scandal sheets.

So, four ostensibly working-class entertainers, talking in voices manifestly at odds with those which dominated the BBC-controlled airwaves was a novelty. As was their eyebrow-touching hairstyle – cartoonists could gain a novelty smile putting Beatle haircuts on public figures.

Tuesday Rendezvous, 9 April 1963, back from primary school, just in time to settle down with Muriel Young, Ollie Beak, Pussy Cat Willum and Wally Whyton. No need for homework, tucking into probably a jam sandwich, tea and Battenburg cake, glued to one of the two black and white channels available, and there they were… Did the screaming really drown out Muriel's introduction after "John, Paul…"?

There is something unstoppable about the sequence of those names, alphabetically it should have been George, John, Paul and Ringo; by age, Ringo, John, Paul, George. Or was it dictated by the order which of them joined the group (John, Paul, George, Ringo)? It was almost uncannily predictable that when Pope John died in June 1963 he was succeeded by Pope Paul. No wonder that for their 1964 survey, the Office of National Statistics found that the most popular boys' names were Paul (2) and John (5).

Even now, a blast of Beatle music from the summer of 1963, up to and including the Christmas of 1964, immediately evokes a lost world of postal orders, untipped cigarettes, petrol-pump assistants, winkle-pickers, Wimpy bars, triangular milk cartons, the AA Man's salute, Vespas, Izal toilet paper, the *Black & White Minstrel Show*, cartoon cinemas at railway stations, hush puppies, maps with cities called Bombay and countries called Burma and the Congo…

The way they spoke sounded … unnatural. For many years, it was the BBC style of Received Pronunciation which filled the nation's airwaves. Regional accents were not necessarily discouraged, but frowned upon. The avuncular Wilfred Pickles was tolerated. Otherwise, the sepulchral tones of Alvar Liddell emphasised the BBC's 'style'. Hearing Liverpool accents only further demonstrated the novelty of the Beatles as they began their sustained assault.

The *look* of the Beatles was different too during that Merseybeat tidal wave of 1963. Those much-derided circular-necked jackets, the smart Duggie Millings suits. And that hair – the majority of the other groups looked like brickies or panel-beaters. Not John, Paul, George or Ringo.

On 18 April 1963, the Beatles appeared at the Royal Albert Hall for a *Swinging Sound '63* event. Every teenager in London must have made their way there, as *What's on in London* magazine listed the only other musical competition that night – organ recitals from Gordon Reynolds and Gordon Phillips; a performance from soprano Jean Carpenter and the London Philharmonic Orchestra at the Royal Festival Hall.

As Paul told Paul Du Noyer, "I remember this one golden morning. A Sunday morning, I think, by the steps at the back of the Albert Hall. At the top of the steps we all gathered. A summer's sunny morning and it was Mick, Keith, all the Beatles, Yardbirds, Gerry & the Pacemakers – a moment in time. And we were absolutely at our youthful peak…"

In a radio interview, Frank Ifield remembered the Beatles visiting him in the star dressing room while he was headlining at the London Palladium and having to throw them out. They told him it was likely to be the only time they'd get to be in there. Actually, in that long-ago time, prior to the internet, I remember becoming faintly obsessed with

Jolly What Ho!, the LP Frank Ifield recorded *with* the Beatles. Except of course it wasn't, it was an early example of America cashing in on the Fabs' fame. Vee-Jay licensed early Beatle releases with little success, but when Beatlemania broke, they used one of their other signings, poor old Frank Ifield was simply used as padding.

Lest we forget, Frank Ifield landed three consecutive UK No.1 singles while the Beatles were busy establishing themselves. Throughout late 1962 and early 1963, while the Beatles were still to find their feet in the charts, Ifield was leading from the front. Although born in the UK, his career began in Australia, and he found himself sharing chart placings at the end of 1962 with antipodean Rolf Harris, another George Martin novelty act. It is not too fanciful to imagine the pop critics as seeing this double-whammy as the beginning of a new era in Australian pop, with the untested sound of Liverpool condemned to the margins.

And Frank Ifield's country-style yodelling was proving popular – could this be the Next Big Thing in the same way that only a few years before, calypso had been seen as a rival to rock & roll? Pre-skiffle, the Davy Crockett craze was rampant, while Mambo was the thing, with literally hundreds of titles to cash-in ('Marilyn Monroe Mambo', 'Irish Mambo', 'Short Hair Mambo', among others). Pete Frame assiduously chronicled 45 'mambo' singles released in 1955 alone.

No one knew just what the Next Big Thing would be. John Peel told me: "The music business was desperate to find an antidote to rock & roll. They did not like rock & roll. They tried calypso, with Harry Belafonte. When that was a hit they said ah, rock & roll is over… And when 'Tom Hark' was a hit, South African music… Trad Jazz…"

In the early 1960s, Trad Jazz was *huge*, and Bruce Welch pointed out that the success of the Shadows also led to a surge in the popularity of instrumental releases. He singled out the Tornadoes, Duane Eddy, the Ventures, Johnny & the Hurricanes, as well as the Fireballs, Chantays, Safaris, the Spotniks and Wout Steenhuis.

At the eye of the hurricane, it must all have passed by in a blur. Obediently accepting their manager's every dictate, the locations took on a noisy similarity. Smuggled into cinemas for two shows, facing a cacophony of unalloyed hysteria just beyond the stage lights. With hundreds of screaming fans picketing the regional theatres, between shows, the group's recreational activities were over their Scotch & Cokes and Peter Stuyvesants. Other backstage bacchanalia included endless circuits of Scalextric and hours of Monopoly.

The Beatles' seaside sojourn of that eventful summer of 1963 must have provided welcome relief: Margate (6 nights), Rhyl (2 nights), Llandudno (6 nights), Bournemouth (6 nights), Weston-super-Mare (6 nights)… It was a pop-heavy bill – Billy J. Kramer, Tommy Quickly… But as Spencer Leigh pointed out, the 'Exciting Vibes Duo, Tommy Wallis & Beryl' also featured. These were roller-skaters who played the xylophone while whizzing round the stage. The last knockings of variety until it succumbed to the all-powerful pop package tours.

Those summer seasons were one of the last times the group came close to anything resembling a normal life. No need for Neil to load up the van during those residencies. See them tucking into ice creams on the pier, larking on the beach, enjoying uninterrupted sunbathing and go-karting. "After hundreds of one-nighters", they enthused to *The Beatles Monthly*, "it's just wonderful to sleep in the same bed for six nights running".

The fact that they could enjoy the luxury of such residencies suggested there might be a future for them. Not much wonder, when questioned at the time, that few of the groups ever envisaged a career to see them into maturity. With luck, like Cliff, they might be able to switch their success to cinema screens. Or, like Lonnie Donegan, pantomime and cabaret.

On 15 September 1963, there was an historic pairing: one of only a handful of occasions that the Beatles shared a bill with the Rolling Stones. It was at the *Great Pop Prom* at the Royal Albert Hall, in aid of the Printers' Pension Association. Staff at the venerable Victorian auditorium were stunned by the unleashing of Beatlemania and promptly banned them from appearing at the venue ever again.

Much has been made of *The Times* chief music critic William Mann's feature 'What Songs the Beatles Sang' on 27 December 1963. Mocked at the time for his findings of "pandiatonic clusters… the Aeolian cadence… submediant switches C major into A flat major" (observations which left the Beatles themselves baffled) it is perhaps forgotten now the prestige attached to such an article. *The Times* was the paper of national record. So much so that it still carried small ads on its front page, suggesting that *real* news lay inside. That such an august pillar of the Establishment devoted substantial space to a mere 'pop group' was in itself an achievement. Fleet Street's obsession with the Beatles concentrated on their riotous receptions.

Even more extraordinarily Mann singled out Lennon and McCartney as "the outstanding English composers of 1963". Not merely "outstanding" popular music composers. Mann's accolade meant that those still active in the classical pantheon – Benjamin Britten, Peter Maxwell-Davies, Michael Tippett, William Walton – had been overshadowed by composers from the tradition of Tin Pan Alley

Mann did not concern himself with "the social phenomenon of Beatlemania" nor "the hysterical screaming of young girls". Rather he astutely noted "for several decades, since the decline of music hall, England has taken her popular songs from the United States, either directly or by mimicry. But the songs of Lennon and McCartney are distinctly indigenous in character…. And there is a nice, rather flattering irony in the news that the Beatles have now become prime favourites in America, too".

The wartime leaders, Churchill and De Gaulle, were still active. Victorian and Edwardian grandees Harold Macmillan and Anthony Eden had distinguished themselves during the Great War, but that had been half a century before. Respected and deferred to, there was an indefinable sense that something was in the air, a change, and that change was made tactile by the sound of the Beatles during that year. Coming at year's end, a year of unparalleled commercial success, Royal patronage, approbation from *The Times* set the seal on an extraordinary year. Surely with so much accomplished, even for the group's determined manager, there was nowhere else to go.

Not long before his death in 1967, the great Bert Berns (author of 'Twist & Shout', as well as – respect! – 'Here Comes the Night', 'Tell Him' and 'Piece of My Heart') sat in a dingy cafe near the Decca Studios talking to pop's first chronicler, Nik Cohn. Looking at a picture of the Beatles, he shook his head, "Those boys have genius… They may be the ruin of us all".

First published in 1969, Cohn said of the 1996 reprint of *Awopbopaloobop*

Alopbamboom, "If anyone had suggested to me then that the Stones or the Who might still be wearily treading the boards in their fifties, I'd have called for the men in white jackets… All I was doing was trying to get a jump on the mortician". At the time he was writing (1968) even Cohn admitted of the Beatles: "I mean, what is there possibly left to say on them?"

*

In September 1963 the group had taken a much-needed break. While John and his wife Cynthia, Paul and Ringo vacationed in Europe, George and his brother Peter made a little bit of Beatle history. Five months before that epochal appearance on *The Ed Sullivan Show*, the "Quiet Beatle" became the first member of the group to visit America. George's new passport photo shows the quiff replaced by 'the Beatle cut', and the Profession changed from 'Student' to 'Musician'.

It had been on 25 February 1963 that WLS Chicago took a punt and played the Vee-Jay release 'From Me to You', laying strong claim to be the first Beatle record heard in the USA. The station's Dick Biondi was the only DJ to pay the record on any of the nation's 7,000 stations. The label's advertising of the period emphasised 'Big Hits from Abroad', with the Beatles listed alongside releases from Australia, Holland and Sweden.

Louise Caldwell and her husband Robert lived in Benton, Illinois. Keen to promote her younger brother George's work, Louise bombarded local radio stations with Beatle records telling everyone how popular they were at home. Dick James had written to Louise in July 1963 posting a batch of Beatle singles to her and concluding, "Perhaps if you are not too busy you may drop me a line giving me an idea of the reaction that The Beatles are receiving in the States. I feel sure that they will breakthrough in a big way as they are certainly proving to be 'world-beaters'."

Louise had previously been sent a copy of 'From Me to You' by her mother, which she took to the WFRX-AM radio station in West Frankfort, IL. The song was played by teenage DJ Marcia Raubach, who became the first person to interview a Beatle while George was on that holiday. For George, the appeal of the USA was "small blondes… driving, sleeping… Eartha Kitt, eggs and chips, and Alfred Hitchcock movies."

Before leaving home, for his 21st birthday George had received over 30,000 cards. Everywhere he went in his homeland was greeted with the now-familiar hysteria. That Illinois break was one of the last times anything approaching a normal life was possible for George during the next three years.

George savoured a drive-in movie, Cliff Richard's *The Young Ones* (*Wonderful to Be Young* in USA) but conceded, "The concept wouldn't work in England. All you would see of the movie would be the windshield wipers going back and forth." He was spellbound by roller-skating waitresses serving his burger and coveted a black 1958 Oldsmobile. While on his American holiday, George picked up a Rickenbacker 425 and a copy of James Ray's 'Got My Mind Set on You'. On 28 September 1963 he sat in with local group the Four Vests. The 40-minute set had the audience of 75 listening to George run through live favourites including 'Matchbox' and 'Roll Over Beethoven'. As a tip of the Stetson to his enduring fondness for Country & Western, George also performed Hank Williams'

'Your Cheating Heart'. According to Louise, her younger brother had his back slapped by an impressed viewer and was informed, "with the right kind of backing, you could go places".

Prior to departure, George and his brother took time to take in New York. While there they did the usual tourist things, viewing the city from the Empire State Building. George would have cut an incongruous figure amidst the crew-cut Americans. It's a rather engaging vignette, following six months of adhesive adoration wherever he went at home, George could wander untroubled in a city which, within six months, would be the first to add another level to that hysteria.

Then it was back home, to the daily grind of touring, TV and radio promotion, press interviews and, when they had a moment, nipping into Abbey Road to cut *another* breakthrough single, 'I Want to Hold Your Hand'. A million excited British fans placed an order without knowing what it was going to sound like. One thing was certain, it wouldn't disappoint.

By August 1963, Brian Epstein had put his foot down, from then on specifying theatre appearances, the days of clubs and ballrooms were no more. The Beatles were moving further away from their audience. To greet 3,000 fans at the Wimbledon Palais just before Christmas 1963, a steel cage had to be erected before they were allowed to perform. The year had been an hysterical roundabout, riots had greeted appearances in Birmingham, Hull, Leicester, Carlisle... One sensed that the police chiefs quite relished a provincial Beatle appearance. It gave them an opportunity to muster their troops, prepare elaborate entry and exit strategies while keeping 'the enemy' at bay. As an example, for that Wimbledon appearance, all police leave in the borough had been cancelled, as well as all that in the neighbouring Tooting and Mitcham. The police relished the cut and thrust, ex-Army officers executing military style getaways made a change from fingering the collars of battling Mods and Rockers.

It was following the group's appearance on the nation's top variety show, *Sunday Night at the London Palladium* on 13 October 1963 that 'Beatlemania' entered the lexicon. (Mark Lewisohn disputes this, citing the headline over a Vincent Mulchrone article in the *Daily Mail* of 21 October 1963.) Reports vary about just how many howling fans clogged Argyll Street, but the damage was done. The *Daily Mirror* used it the next day and veteran showbiz reporter Don Short gleefully told Bob Spitz: "It was *exactly* the story we'd been waiting for. Up until then I'd merely go round to Claridge's or the Savoy and interview Sammy Davis Jr. one week, Andy Williams the next, but the Beatles had all this drama swirling around them – and they were sexy, a very sexy story".

We know now, and Michael Braun's book later confirmed it, of the drinking, the cigarette smoking, the swearing. The sex was never hinted at; at this early stage of the hysteria, there was a real sense of innocence. It was reflected by the group themselves – Paul, particularly, comes across in filmed interviews with a 'pinch me, I can't believe this is happening to us' look. That innocence was reflected in the songs of the period, like 'Then He Kissed Me' ("he took me home to meet his Mom and Dad..."), or a song the Beatles used to cover, the Crickets' 'Don't Ever Change' ("you're always wearing jeans, 'cept on Sunday"). The group always appeared neatly attired. The Family Doctor of the *Daily Mail* concluded that the Beatles were "young and unspoilt... there is nothing aggressively masculine about them to suggest sex".

While looking at the phenomenon, the conservative *Daily Telegraph* conceded that "some form of energetic self-expression is needed by young people". It polled its readers. "Long live the Beatles", wrote Mrs Lord, "but may we out live the need for them – not by decreasing vitality but by finding something better". Mrs Jones took a stronger line: "Any form of mass hysteria is harmful. Controlled and reasoned action differentiates between humans and the rest of the animal kingdom, between the sane and the mentally afflicted".

Later historians disagreed: "In one important sense, the experience of the Allied soldiers in liberated countries in the summer of 1945 might be compared to what happened about twenty years later, when The Beatles arrived. Then, too, liberation was expressed as a form of mania, which was above all erotic", wrote Ian Buruma in *Year Zero: A History of 1945*.

On 7 December 1963, to testify to their standing, for the first time ever an episode of *Juke Box Jury* was devoted to a single group. The Beatles passed judgement on a pretty mediocre selection of ten singles, only three of which (Elvis Presley, the Swinging Blue Jeans and the Merseybeats) became the Hits of the six the Fabs had selected. A viewing figure of 22,000,000 was reported. "The boys' voices and that of host David Jacobs", Simon Elmes wrote, "could hardly be heard above the constant roar of young fans wailing like a tropical forest full of cicadas at dusk".

Early on in their career, Brian Epstein appreciated that one way for the boys to keep in touch with the fans was through a well-run fan club. From the early days in Liverpool, a fan club was run out of the back room of the NEMS store. It soon became apparent that something more professional was needed as, at its peak, the fan club was running at 80,000 members. Membership was a 5/- postal order, plus a 3d SAE. There were soon fan clubs in Canada, Finland and South Africa.

Back then, bypassing the music press, the only way that a fan could display band (brand) loyalty was through a fan club. Brian Epstein grew frustrated at the piles of unopened correspondence cluttering his London office. He instructed Tony Barrow to find a quick, efficient and cheap method of keeping the fans happy. Barrow remembered a disposable record pioneered by *Reader's Digest*. Thus, the Beatles Christmas flexi-disc was born, another inspired way of communicating.

That first 'Beatle Christmas' included the fun of their first Fan Club flexi-disc ("this is John speaking with his voice"… "somebody asked us if we still like jelly babies"… "the thing we like best is hearing one of the songs John and I have written taking shape in the recording studio…"). A lovely treat, a real novelty and strangely affecting to listen to after all these years.

By their 1964 Christmas disc they had broadened their horizons. Familiar UK locations had been superseded in a bleary zoom of jet travel. They sounded jet-lagged and baffled as to where they'd been. "England, Australia, America, New Zealand", said Ringo, "and Australia … and New Zealand".

The real 1963 Christmas present, of course, came with the LP release of *With the Beatles*. The only way most of their fans could guarantee getting a long-playing record was as either a birthday or Christmas present. You'd have to save an awful lot of pennies, 3d, 6d, half crowns and ten bob notes for that 12" treat. The 300,000 advance orders were unheard-of for a long-player. It *sold* half a million copies on its first day of release. Inevitably, on the back of that overwhelming year, it became the first LP in the UK *ever* to sell more than a million copies.

Again, it is worth pausing to reflect upon that statistic. LP releases by their peers had sold steadily, but an LP was largely the realm of the parent. With the introduction of an LP chart in 1956, its first years reflected the adult purchasers – soundtrack LPs from films dominated –*Carousel, Oklahoma!, The King & I, Pal Joey, West Side Story* and – particularly – *South Pacific*. That Rodgers & Hammerstein musical ran at the same West End cinema for over four *years*, and the album was on the charts for 115 weeks. The London-cast LP of *My Fair Lady* was another hit, alongside three LPs from George Mitchell's *Black & White Minstrel Show*. There were only occasional interruptions from rockers like Elvis and Cliff.

However, as a sign of the times, and just how shifting the sands were, only two LPs were No.1 throughout the entire year of 1963 – *Please Please Me* and *With the Beatles*. From here on there was no going back:22 November 1963, *With the Beatles* in the shops; 22 November 1968, *The White Album*. Five years and a lifetime apart.

Understandably, with the pressure of touring (200 concerts, including dates in Sweden), promotion, broadcasts, writing and recording, *With the Beatles* was an undeniably weaker second shot. Unwittingly released on the day President Kennedy was assassinated, few Beatle fans would have been affected in making their purchase, with Dallas six hours ahead that Friday, the shops would have been shut by the time the news reached the UK.

The Beatles would have heard the news of the Kennedy assassination while waiting to go onstage at the Globe Cinema in Stockton-on-Tees. On their way to Newcastle, they might have read of the deaths of C.S. Lewis and Aldous Huxley, or looked forward to watching the BBC's new children's drama, *Doctor Who* (postponed until the following day as TV tried to grasp the enormity of the Presidential assassination).

To my mind, demonstrably less powerful than their debut LP, *With the Beatles* has its own charms. The stand-out tracks are the breezy opener 'It Won't Be Long' (providing a "yeah" every 2.4 seconds as Rob Sheffield pointed out) and, particularly, the majestic 'All My Loving'. "The innocence of early Sixties British pop is perfectly distilled in the eloquent simplicity of this number", wrote Ian MacDonald. "The Beatles' rivals looked on amazed as songs of this commercial appeal were casually thrown away on LPs".

Early on, theirs was a genuine partnership – each chipping away at the others' suggestions. Those 'nose to nose' collaborations in Forthlin Road, dingy B&Bs and touring coaches continued long after the royalties flooded in. Paul would motor down in his Aston Martin to Weybridge; John would make his way to Cavendish Avenue.

And they were partners for much of their career ("If John had met Gerry Marsden it wouldn't have been the same, would it?" Paul asked Ray Connolly). Other partnerships operated independently – Bernie Taupin would pass over lyrics to Elton John for him to set music ("On Monday morning, October 17, 1969, Sheila fried up a couple of eggs slotted in some toast and brewed three cups of tea while I wrote… 'Your Song'"). Ditto Keith Reid submitting his lyrics to Gary Brooker for Procol Harum. As did early Lennon & McCartney influences, Goffin & King. I love hearing how before she went to play mah-jongg, Carole King left a melody and a note on the piano that lyrics were needed for the Shirelles by the following day. Returning from a bowling match, Gerry Goffin set about the task, and that's how one of the great pre-Beatle classics, 'Will You Love Me Tomorrow' came about.

Jagger & Richards had to be locked in a kitchen to force them to write together. Holland, Dozier & Holland worked in committee (on struggling to find a follow-up to the Four Tops' 'I Can't Help Myself', one commented, "Hell, it's the same old song", and bingo…!). And for all the hosannas heaped on Burt Bacharach, it was Hal David who took the melodies to Tulsa and San Jose, who provided the words for Dionne and Aretha to sing. I was reminded of Mrs Oscar Hammerstein being approached at a party and being told that Jerome Kern wrote 'Ol' Man River' only to respond: "No, Jerome Kern wrote 'dum, dum, dum, dum…'. My *husband* wrote 'ol' man river'".

*

With the Beatles is a necessarily rushed attempt to replicate *Please Please Me*: the frenetic opening 'It Won't Be Long' instead of 'I Saw Her Standing There'; 'Money' in lieu of the earlier, closing 'Twist & Shout'. Is there anyone who has a particular lasting fondness for 'All I've Got to Do', 'Little Child' or 'Hold Me Tight'? Even George dismissed his fledgling 'Don't Bother Me' as "a not particularly good song".

One thing which does survive of that second LP is its striking cover, beautifully shot by Robert Freeman (1936–2019). He had first met the group in Bournemouth in August 1963. They, and Brian Epstein, were impressed by the photographer's atmospheric shots of musicians Dizzy Gillespie, Coleman Hawkins and John Coltrane. That iconic Beatle cover was shot by Freeman in the dining room of Bournemouth's Palace Court Hotel.[5]

The sleeve showed a bottomless black background, the four unsmiling faces staring intently into the lens. Despite the wave of such unimagined success, there was no pause for glee, it was hard to imagine Cliff or Frank Ifield presenting such a stern image on an LP sleeve. Fascinating out-takes from the Freeman sessions later emerged, with the group showing healthy white teeth in engaging smiles, the cover which EMI actually preferred. But the group insisted on the sterner shot. Of course, it also became iconic to new fans when it became the sleeve of their American debut, *Meet the Beatles!*

While it was what was inside the sleeve that really mattered, *With the Beatles* saw Robert Freeman enter a fecund period with the group. For that shot Freeman received £75, an increase on EMI's notoriously parsimonious standard fee of £25 [See also Klaus Voormann and Peter Blake for later LP sleeve payments]. Not spending it all at once, Freeman went on to shoot four more Beatle LP covers. In fact looking at those Robert Freeman covers 1963–65 (*Hard Day's Night*, *Beatles for Sale*,[6] *Help!*, *Rubber Soul*) it is surprising how sombre the group appear. A favourite feature of the colour pop magazines

---

5   This was also the location where future *Year of the Cat* man Al Stewart inveigled his way into the group's presence, by claiming to be the man from Rickenbacker.

6   A good trivia question: on which Beatles LP sleeve do Tommy Steele and Albert Finney appear?

of the period was always 'How Do You Like [Insert Pop Idol Name Here]?' Brian Jones, smiling or serious? Billy J. Kramer, happy or sad?

As that triumphant year of 1963 drew to a close, drenched, battered, exhausted, triumphant, even *they* must have wondered, is that it?

Surfing on the wave of Beatlemania, they really had been everywhere that year. As the shutters drew down on 1963, the reflections began. The most dignified was William Mann's appreciation in *The Times*. At the other end of Fleet Street, the *Daily Mirror* enthused, "You have to be a real sour square not the love the nutty, noisy, happy, handsome Beatles… Beatle people are everywhere: From Wapping to Windsor. Aged 7 to 70…" In the *NME*, Derek Johnson nailed it: "When our descendants study their history books, they will see one word imprinted against the year… Beatles! For just as convincingly as 1066 marked the Battle of Hastings, or 1215 the Magna Carta, so will this present year be remembered by posterity for the achievements of four lads from Liverpool". The *Evening Standard* summed it up simply on their front page: '1963 – The Year Of The Beatles'.

For me, there is a year's end moment: I remember coming back from Christmas lunch at my Aunt Madeline's in Beckenham with my present of the *Please Please Me* LP (how we laughed when my Victorian grandmother asked if we all had to scream as it was unwrapped). And, as my dad took his beloved old blue Jaguar along Wickham Road, I remember looking up to the bedrooms in one of the new Wates houses. And there, their sleeves facing outwards for all to see, was my LP and *With the Beatles*. And I still recall that very envious sensation…

And here's the thing: in May 2022, I am reading an account of how teenage Beatle fan Margaret Ashworth helped Apple and EMI. She had tape-recorded 11 of the 15 *Pop Go the Beatles* shows the BBC Light Programme had broadcast during that heady Beatle summer. The Beeb had long lost the tapes, and Margaret was only too delighted to plug the gap for the 1994 release of *The Beatles at the BBC* with recordings made at her Beckenham home. So, was it *her* bedroom window I drove past on that long-gone Christmas Day?

When 'She Loves You' returned to the top for a record-breaking second time, it was evident there was something unrepeatable and remarkable occurring. Their success was assured, and when it was announced that – for the first time ever – the follow-up to 'She Loves You', 'I Want to Hold Your Hand', had garnered *advance* orders of more than a million copies, it really seemed there was no stopping them. It was apparent that the world of yodelling Frank Ifield, Trad Jazz and twisting novelties was receding into the mists of showbiz history.

Beatlemania... My Limited Experience

My mum wouldn't let me see the Beatles live. I was too precious to be let loose among those screaming fans. And the idea that she could persuade my father to accompany me was unthinkable. The Beatles did come close ... but I never got *that* close. I somehow did get to see the Searchers, in faraway Tooting in March 1964. They were greeted with screams. Dusty Springfield was just entering her solo career. I vividly remember her shocking pink dress and beautiful blonde beehive. I also can still vividly recall the intensity of my unrealistic feelings towards her; age 12, I wanted to marry Dusty Springfield. According to the ticket, Bobby Vee was the headline act. Fond as I am of his songs now, I remember absolutely nothing of his performance.

Everywhere at the time was reporting the madness and hysteria the Beatles prompted with their every appearance. In Barcelona in May 1991, however, I did just get a brief flavour of that madness... I had done some work for Paul's MPL company and at the time was working on IPC's *Vox* magazine. They needed someone to cover a McCartney Spanish club date. I was that man. Checking into the hotel, I showered, dumped my clothes on the bed, changed and made my way to the club. Once on site, I met with the band and Linda recognised me, which led to my gaining backstage access. She was always very nice to me, Linda, and asked what I was doing after the show. I murmured the usual – probably going to some low dive to get hammered on local Rioja. She asked if I would like to come back with her and Paul on their private jet? A moment's hesitation led me to point out that my clothes were still back at my hotel. Not a worry, some poor minion from EMI Barcelona was dispatched to gather my dirty laundry and bring it to me at the club. Phew, the glamour of rock & roll, he must have thought.

Paul and band played a blinder. The capacity can have been barely a thousand, he was hot on the back of the *Flowers in the Dirt* tour where he had premiered Beatle material. Located by the mixing desk, it was, with a little imagination, like being at the Cavern...

Whisked by Trevor, the McCartneys' right-hand man, I was ushered to the backstage exit: there was a stretch of pavement about 12 feet wide from the door to the tour van. Paul was next to me as we exited. He asked what I'd thought, and I burbled about what a great show it was while he bobbed and nodded. Either side of the walkway were fans behind barriers. Devoted fans, keen to reach out and touch the legend, and if they couldn't grab a slice of him, the fat, grey-haired bloke with glasses and a beard chatting to Paul McCartney would do! I was jostled and pummelled and gratefully sought sanctuary in the people carrier. For a few minutes I had experienced what Paul McCartney had been going through since Winston Churchill last spoke in Parliament.

In passing, the only way to travel by air is by private jet. None of this tedious queueing, a car takes you to the aircraft steps, one boards, is settled in comfortable swivel chairs, asked by the awfully well-spoken stewardess if anyone "wants anything before take orf", and away we went, later to gorge on delicious – if memory serves – Indian vegetarian cuisine prior to landing at Lydd.

*

Before they took on the world, the UK clasped the group close to their chest. And I believe that their Englishness and the English culture which produced them too often gets overlooked in any appreciation of their greatness.

Whole books have been written about the Beatles and their package tours. It is fascinating to look at those itineraries and the bills they shared. It takes little imagination to recall those distant days, when 12/6d (72½p) could have allowed you access to those long-gone cinemas like the ABC Carlisle, the Granada East Ham, the Odeon Cheltenham, and witness the Beatles, live, for a heart-stopping 25 minutes.

A fascinating tape emerged, having been made by the Rank Organisation as evidence in a case made by leading UK tour promoters against the PRS (Performing Rights Society). The PRS were asking for increased payments when pop music was played at these venues. The 15-minute tape captured the Beatles live, at the Odeon Leeds on 3 November 1963. It was a rare recording at the height of full-fledged Beatlemania. *The Times* reported when the case came to court, "It would be an overstatement to say that the sound heard [on the tape] was The Beatles. It was much more the sound of 2000 shrieking teenagers with a rhythmic, pulsating thud somewhere in the background". In the end, despite the tape, the PRS won their case.

And it takes little imagination to feel just what it was like to have the BEATLES coming to your local cinema. There really wasn't much to do if you were a teenager during 1963. Saturday you might be dragged along the high street accompanying your mum shopping or help your dad mow the lawn. The cinema offered up big-screen, stereo entertainment in glorious Technicolor. But even on release, there were only so many times you wanted to see *The Great Escape*, *From Russia with Love* or *Cleopatra*.

A copy of *ABC Film Review* of the period had an interview and a colour photo of the group clutching a copy of the magazine. The film magazine regularly featured the group during those touring days, as many of the venues were on the ABC cinema circuit. There was a whole page of Beatle cartoons (sample: "Dad, when are you going to tell me about the birds and the Beatles?"). "Everywhere the Beatles went on the ABC circuit", wrote Norman Taylor, "the fans were sure to follow – in droves, swarms, shoals, flocks. It was our taste of what is called Beatlemania… To adapt the words of their own song, 'With fans like that they know they should be glad'." As a foretaste of the Rutles, Ringo admits he "fancied being a hairdresser and sees himself as owner of a chain of such establishments when too old to be a Beatle. 'Can you imagine a 40-year-old Beatle?' he asks."

The drummer was not alone. Photographer Terry O'Neill was one of the key players in that burgeoning scene. "We all used to go to the Ad-Lib", he told Dylan Jones, "and there'd be the Beatles, the Stones, Jean Shrimpton, Twiggy. You'd be sitting there in rows talking about jobs we'd have to do when we reached 20 or 30 … because none of us thought it was going to last". Dave Clark was equally convinced there was a limit, talking to Nick Dalton years later, "we thought the bubble would burst at any moment". John Entwistle gave the Who a year, tops. It was a sentiment echoed across the Atlantic too, a Brill Building songwriter told Ken Emerson, "We never, *ever* – any of us – thought that this music would be on the radio 35 years later. We thought it would be like calypso, in and out!"

In his engaging autobiography, *What's It All About?*, Michael Caine (who should know) captured the excitement of that zeitgeist: "At the Ad-Lib you were dancing alongside the people who made the music... anybody who was anybody was there and so was everybody who was nobody but going to be somebody tomorrow. There was a buzz every night of dreams coming true and the charge of fresh dreams that would come true some time soon, and the shock as a record was played for the first time and you knew you were listening to a pop classic being born, and the new young genius who wrote it said 'Sorry' as he stepped on your toe as we all whirled like dervishes round the dance floor and into the history of our own chosen field of endeavour".

Showtime ('The new film monthly') featured a guitar-playing George on a 1964 cover and an interview with Alun Owen on rumours of their forthcoming film. "A good sub-title for the film would be *The Travelling Men*, they are *always* on the move... They live in a series of boxes all the time – hotel rooms, cars, dressing rooms. They cannot move from these boxes in case they are recognised and mobbed".

As well as the cinema chains which hosted them, the ballrooms offered a sanctuary for live performance. Offering up ersatz glamour in sooty, industrial cities, places like the Rivoli and the Regal; the Ritz and the Roxy; the Palais, the Rialto; the Locarno... Those fun palaces exercised a strong hold on those who whiled away their youth in them. A decade later, looking for a group name, Bryan Ferry reflected, "I made a list of names of cinemas: Odeon, Gaumont, Essoldo – all those names had a nice ring to them, but they didn't really mean anything except that they were a place you went to escape everyday life". Thus, *Roxy* Music.

While their 25-minute sets were light relief in contrast to their gruelling Hamburg stints of mere months before, they were obligated to perform two shows a night. And, even before Beatlemania was officially sanctioned, they were finding it hard to get in and out of the cinemas before and after their appearances. I remember those old cinemas ... fading from the peak of their 1940s and 1950s grandeur and, in the face of the overwhelming competition from television, having to play host to these ghastly pop groups to keep them open.

The cinema chains' switch to package tours was a determined move to get away from the variety circuit of theatres controlled by Stoll Moss and the like. The rock & roll generation of the 1950s were used to being on variety bills – the music as much a novelty as the jugglers, ventriloquists and comedians who padded out the bill. The cinema chains could offer up non-stop music shows.

In the August 1964 *ABC Film Review*, Frank Batchelor reported breathlessly on the group's appearance at their Edinburgh cinema: "Happily seated before the formidable array of scribes with their favourite whisky and cokes within easy reach and cigarettes lit, the boys good-humouredly answered questions..." His report gives a sense of the madness which they faced on a regular basis: "All the shopkeepers within the vicinity of the theatre had wisely boarded up their windows, all traffic had been diverted and every available policeman had been drafted into the area to control the 6,000 fans who blocked Lothian Road in the vain hope of catching a glimpse of THEM.

"Very soon the theatre foyers began to resemble casualty clearing stations as hysteria-overcome fans were carried out to be revived by a small army of first aid personnel. I even saw a boy faint – twice! Not content with one blackout he went back so the whole thing could happen again".

I once asked Lonnie Donegan why so many of the hits at the peak of his popularity were live recordings. He looked at me as though I'd asked a rather stupid question and said simply: "No time to go into the studio, son."

"Back then, it was all variety bills," he continued. "I did that for six years solid. From 1956 until 1962: two 12-week tours per year, spring and autumn. Winter, you'd do a 12-week pantomime; and there'd be a 14-week summer season. That's why the records were done live – the record company had to follow me round with a van! One number we even did in the toilet at Plymouth, because they couldn't bring an echo chamber with them!"

The cinema queues for the pop shows were controlled by stern-faced, ex-service commissionaires, decked out in quasi-military uniforms, chests bulging with medal ribbons, upper lips adorned by trim moustaches. As was the case with the live shows, the end of every performance was marked with a broadcast of the National Anthem, for which the audience was dutifully expected to stand. As a (not really) rebellious teenager, like so many I was embarrassed by my father's insistence at showing his devotion to his monarch by standing erect as her signature tune was relayed over the tinny house PA at the end of the evening's entertainment. The only way to stop Teddy Boys rioting in Anthony Newley's *Idol on Parade* is having Cyril Stapleton play the National Anthem.

In another one of those Proustian moments which brought that period back so effortlessly, was when the 1966 concert by Bob Dylan & the Band was released as Volume 4 of *The Bootleg Series* in 1998. Finally, after years of fourth-generation bootleg tapes and scratched vinyl, the legendary 'Albert Hall' show (actually, Manchester Free Trade Hall) was available in its entirety in pristine quality. And there it is … following the most incendiary and confrontational rock & roll show of all time, after a scorched-earth 'Like a Rolling Stone', preceded by the infamous "Judas" shout (and Dylan's "I don't believe you… Play it fucking *louder*…" response), there it goes, as the dazed audience departed, preserved on the audio document – the National Anthem.

It must have had the same hollow impact on audiences at those Beatle shows. Sitting unmoved by the Terry Young Six, but worked up into a knicker-wetting frenzy by the Fabs, especially when George and Paul did their trademark head-shaking 'Oohs' round the same microphone… How did you come down from that? By standing for the National Anthem, then supporting or being supported by equally shattered and drained friends onto the yellow-lit streets of Mansfield, Leicester, York or Romford.

It was the ubiquity of Beatlemania which was so overwhelming in the UK during 1963. Michael Braun's *Love Me Do* is undeniably the best; a vital first-hand account of those incredible 12 months. It offers a penetrating fly-on-the-wall chronicle of the period, and has been endlessly pilfered from and alluded to in virtually every Beatle book since. (It was also the first book I ever saw with the word 'fuck' in it.)

Michael Braun (1936–97) was an intriguing character: he worked with Stanley Kubrick, was a confidante of Roman Polanski and planned to turn Stevie Wonder's 1979 *The Secret Life of Plants* into a film. However, it is for his Beatles book he remains best known. In the 1995 reprint, Braun wrote: "In the early autumn of 1963 I travelled to Sunderland… This was the England of the dark, Satanic mills – I felt I had journeyed into the past. The night I arrived I met the Beatles and sensed that I had glimpsed the future". (That was written from the benefit of 30 years' hindsight; Braun concluded his original edition by comparing the Beatles to H.G. Wells' Eloi, "like children, they would soon stop examining me and wander away after some other toy". As if to say, how long would they last before being overtaken by the Searchers, the Dave Clark Five or the High Numbers?)

Talking to Jim Irvin in 1996, Braun said probably one reason he got on so well with them was that he'd interviewed Elvis for a book on music, then came to the UK to track down Tommy Steele and Cliff Richard. "The Beatles were … totally refreshing. There was no face constructed by PR people. They were bright, articulate and funny". With precious few books taking pop music seriously, fortuitously it was the editor who had earlier commissioned *Catch-22* who was a pop fan and gave Braun the go-ahead.

It was true, that everyone from pop fans to pensioners, Prime Ministers to reigning monarchs, classical music critics to DJs, schoolboys to Savile Row tailors, was swept along on that incredible ride. The *Daily Express* sought out to increase its 4,000,000 daily sales in January 1964 by employing George Harrison as a columnist. The Beatles also provided fertile territory for the paper's popular cartoonist Giles.

The look, the voices, the wit, the wisdom, the music which poured out of your transistor radio was everywhere that year. Once the country had recovered from the Big Freeze from every side, the whole nation acknowledged the all-encompassing tidal wave washing down from Liverpool.

The "world's longest-running drama", BBC radio's *The Archers*, got in on the act. Ambridge's answer to the Beatles were 'the Swingalongs'. Despite being set in Manchester, television's *Coronation Street* had Kenneth Cope's character Jed Stone releasing a 1963 single 'Hands Off, Stop Muckin' About' in the Merseybeat vein. The comedy series *The Larkins* (starring David Kossoff, father of Free guitarist Paul) broadcast 'Beatle Drive' in December 1963. A lippy teenage relative comes to teach the family's teenagers Scouse, so the group form the Bobbins, London's answer to the Beatles.

Mods & Rockers was a filmed ballet which opened in time for Christmas 1963. Its principal selling point was that the poster prominently boasted, it was "based on music by The Beatles". Intriguingly the Associate Producer was Larry Parnes, licking his wounds after dismissing the group only a few years before. A sub-*West Side Story* effort ("Groovy young hipsters get down at a coffee bar before tensions erupt at the Vicar's crypt-kicking dance party…") Mick Fleetwood, labouring under an uncomfortable looking Beatle fringe, was the drummer with the house band, the Cheynes. "The Beatles are, of course, interesting as a social phenomenon, but perhaps only because they provoke a greater degree of teenage hysteria and identification than any previous pop music" sniffed Clive Barnes in his review for *The Spectator*.

Admirers came from every quarter. Philip Larkin later famously referenced the Beatles in his poem 'Annus Mirabilis', squeezing sexual awakening in between Lady Chatterley and *Please Please Me*. The mordant Larkin was a Beatle fan. The Hull University Librarian – and post-war Britain's foremost poet – described their work as "an enchanting and intoxicating hybrid of Negro rock & roll with their own adolescent romanticism… the first advance in popular music since the war".

Within a 12-month period, 'They' (no need to ask who 'they' were) had conquered not only the pop charts but had made inroads into children's television and grown-up family entertainment. Any comedian looking for a quick laugh donned a Beatle wig. Politicians used them as an electioneering tool. Trade Unionists too, reminding members of the high unemployment and poor housing conditions in Liverpool.

That 4 November 1963 appearance on the *Royal Variety Show* set the seal on the family appeal. This cemented the 'everyone from eight to 80' span. It was quite a show… Also on the bill was the legendary Marlene Dietrich, George Martin clients, the excellent Flanders & Swann, as well as Tommy Steele and Max Bygraves. Hindsight reveals that the singer with the Joe Loss Orchestra was their regular, Ross McManus, father of Elvis Costello.

It was here, at the home of British Light Entertainment, that it all kicked in. Suddenly they were not just of interest to record-buying teenagers, but also brought to the attention of their parents. The formally dressed audience laughed at John's cheeky "rattle your jewellery" remark; not exactly anarchy in the UK, but not reverential either. The comedian Dickie Henderson had the unenviable task of following the group and joked to the predominantly middle-aged crowd that they were "Young… talented… frightening". It was, undeniably, a watershed moment for British Light Entertainment.

Conservative MP William Deedes (later the inspiration for *Private Eye*'s 'Dear Bill…' letters) wrote fulsomely in the *Daily Express* of that eventful period: "The Beatles herald a cultural movement which may become part of the history of our time… their aim is to be first class in their work… To be top in the beat business demands work, skill, sweat. There is no place at all for the lazy, the incompetent, the slipshod".

In hindsight, the team that controlled the mayhem was surprisingly compact. At its head was the urbane Brian Epstein, with a swirl of secretaries and PAs around him. Publicity was handled by a trio (Brian Sommerville,[7] Tony Barrow and Derek Taylor). While close by and hands on, were erstwhile Liverpool comrades, Neil Aspinall and Mal Evans. Chauffeur and minder Alf Bicknell loomed large.

Covering the *Magical Mystery Tour* shoot for *Melody Maker* in 1967, Miranda Ward marvelled, "It was astonishing how light The Beatles travelled… in terms of their own personal staff they just had Mal Evans and Neil Aspinall with them. Given how huge they were, it was astonishing to think that nobody even seemed to think about security".

Neil and Mal were the trusted insiders, fifth Beatles who had watched them climb from the depths of the Cavern to the very summit that Brian Epstein had promised. In ancient Rome, when a returning general was received in triumph, the whole city turned out to praise him to the skies. Women threw themselves at his passing chariot; emperors made obeisance. He was hailed, elevated to a God-like status. But to ensure that the acclaim did not go to his head, a slave stood alongside whispering as the rose petals fell and the hysteria increased, "You are only mortal…"

As Neil and Mal brought them their fish and chips, supplied them with ciggies, lugged the equipment into battered vans, searched for lost plectrums, tried to keep the rubber-necked local dignitaries at bay, kept the girls at bay – or not – they were the down-to-earth reminders of the group's mortality.

---

7   Sommerville enjoyed a tempestuous relationship with Brian Epstein, and only served as the group's PR for ten months (1963/64), but they were arguably the most turbulent of months. Rather sweetly he let a pair of Ringo's drumsticks go to a sea cadet charity ("we do not normally do this sort of thing because demand could easily get out of hand… [but] as an ex-Sea Cadet I have made an exception").

Unable to venture out from their dressing rooms, the group was sequestered with Neil and Mal, and frequently George's childhood chum Tony Bramwell, who was now in the NEMS' payroll. To while away the time, while the group relaxed, those three of the inner circle waded through the mountains of autograph books which were a feature of every gig.

As they trudged around cinemas, concert halls, television studios and dreary B&Bs, America exuded a powerful pull on the group. The Musicians Hall of Fame in Nashville has a wonderful reproduction of a letter. Written to one of their favourite American groups, on NEMS notepaper, Whitechapel, Liverpool 1 (ROYal 7895) and dated 24 January 1963: "Dear Crickets, When we were rehearsing a TV show the other day we met someone who had known you during your recent trip to England and they told us how you had complimented us. We also heard from EMI that you had a copy of our record. Well we'd just like to say that we take this as a great compliment and appreciate it very much. Yours Sincerely The Beatles."

Famously, America didn't get the Beatles until early 1964. But an influential American artist did. Del Shannon was the first US act to cover a Lennon/McCartney composition. Del was one of the few singers at the time who wrote their own material, but whose records of the period have also stood the test of time. Del Shannon released 'From Me to You' on 3 June 1963 – a good eight months before the group first visited America. Shannon first heard the song when he shared a bill (*Swinging Sound '63*) with the Beatles at the Royal Albert Hall. On its American release, *Cashbox* wrote: "It's an infectious thump-a-twist version of the tune that's currently riding the number one slot in England…"

Del Shannon merits more than a footnote – his records brimmed with innovative instrumentation and imaginative lyrics. However, as with so many, he was swept away by that Beatle earthquake. Rumours of homosexuality and the struggle to maintain a career saw him take his own life in 1990. Further rumours had Shannon approached to replace Roy Orbison in the Traveling Wilburys.

For all the triumphs of 1963, Liverpudlian rivals Gerry & the Pacemakers gave the Beatles a run for their money with their historic first three consecutive UK No.1 singles, which earned them a place in the record books. The run began with 'How Do You Do It', the song the Beatles rejected. Paul always saw Gerry & the Pacemakers as the Beatles' only rivals ("they were a good group musically, we were always worried about them when we were in Liverpool", he told Ray Connolly). Ever fretful, Paul was later concerned by the continued success of the Dave Clark Five.

While the Beatles were undergoing a six-night residency at the local Odeon, and sampling the delights of Llandudno in the middle of August 1963, a film opened in London which equally marked the changes they would soon be applying to British society. On 15 August 1963, John Schlesinger's *Billy Liar* premiered. It is the key Swinging 60s film; the only one to appreciate the power of television; the only one which understands just how potent radio was to otherwise empty lives. It is the only film which depicts the architectural vandalism which was sweeping all aside as the Swinging Sixties drew breath. And, crucially, it remains the only film of the kitchen sink period to pay any cognizance to pop music.

To get a flavour of venues the Beatles would have been familiar with, both as punters and performers, watch the rockers in the film roar up to the Locarno, proudly boasting

'Mecca Dancing'. Follow Billy in and negotiating his way through the hundreds and hundreds of twisting couples: the girls all beehives and stilettos, the preening boys, failed and faded Teds. A brazen show of young adulthood, with everyone smoking, beneath the revolving glitter ball. And marvel again as Rodney Bewes' 'Twisteralla' is performed to the twisting teens, a tune surely ripe for re-appraisal?

Located in an anonymous northern town, (actually Bradford, in the process of having its Victorian heritage gutted), Tom Courtenay is the dreamy eponymous hero. Courtenay, along with Albert Finney and Alan Bates, came to represent a Northern English breakthrough in cinema, in the same way and at the same time as the Beatles and their Merseyside musical peers. But it was Julie Christie who symbolised the breath of fresh air in British cinema which the first Beatles film was soon to tap into.

Julie Christie was caught in a photo opportunity with the Beatles; she was in rep in Coventry in November 1963 while they were appearing in town. Looking rather underwhelmed, the actress was photographed strumming a guitar surrounded by the grinning group. Her appearance in her third film *Billy Liar*, though, (following a debut in the dreary George Martin-scored *Crooks Anonymous*) is lustrous. To Alexander Walker, Christie was "a new type of girl swinging confidently and joyously ... into a future that is part and parcel of an affluent generation's lifestyle centered on youth, dreams and metropolitan delights. With Julie Christie, the British cinema caught the train south". At the end, Billy Fisher never gets to leave, he remains in the fictional Stradhoughton, a prisoner of his dreams. Just a few miles to the south-west, others had been luckier, and had managed that escape...

William J. Mann wrote in his biography of the film's director, John Schlesinger: "The long-neglected working classes and provincial towns were pushing their way to the forefront of music and film and, indeed, all of popular culture; a revolution of style and attitude was underway". It was a point the writer Jan Morris picked up on: "The Beatles ... demonstrated the emergence of a new kind of Briton, fresh from the North, emancipated at once from the triumphs and the doubts of the past, and even from the stale traditions of London".

One of the few 'new wave' British dramas of the era which matches *Billy Liar* is the early Michael Winner vehicle, *The System* (1964). Set in the sort of quintessentially British seaside resort with which the Beatles would have been familiar during the summer of 1963, it is gloriously politically incorrect. Oliver Reed leads his predatory gang out to pick up as many birds as they can during the brief summer season – in America the X-certificate film was unambiguously retitled *The Girl-Getters*. Julie Christie was actually cast but became unavailable and her role is filled by the equally striking Jane Merrow.

The System boasts a thumping theme song from the Searchers, and acknowledges the growing popularity of beat music when it was filmed in Paignton during the summer of 1963. Almost every time teenagers are pictured, they are seen madly jiving and twisting. Strongly influenced by the French new wave cinema of the period, *The System* would have appeared shocking on release with its concentration on casual sex, and without the usual moralising which usually accompanied such hedonistic films.

Yet already by the time of its release, the milk train had left the station...

It was evident just what a shot in the arm the Beatles gave the UK entertainment industry. No longer tied to age, class or tradition, a wind of change was blowing. The UK freeview channel Talking Pictures TV regularly repeats episodes of *Sunday Night at the London Palladium*. Watching them during 2020 reminded me just how grim 'light entertainment' and 'all-round entertainers' really were – crooners like Ronnie Carroll, Matt Monro and Mark Wynter. Comedians Arthur Haynes, Dickie Henderson and the ubiquitous Mike & Bernie Winters (Eric Morecambe was once asked what they'd have done if he and Ernie Wise hadn't been comedians. After a reflective pause, Morecambe answered: "Mike & Bernie Winters!").

Seeing the Beatles on the *Morecambe & Wise Show* early in 1964 (Paul's own favourite TV appearance) reminded you just how they were broadening their appeal. Though in re-viewing, you can see how irked the 38-year-old Morecambe gets at Lennon's cheeky gibe about being famous "not like in your day". In his Morecambe & Wise biography, Louis Barfe reveals that Paul McCartney contacted the producer to appear on their 1977 Christmas special. He was rebuffed as Elton John had already been booked. So Paul had to promote his current single 'Mull of Kintyre' on *The Mike Yarwood Show*.

Another close encounter with the old world of showbusiness came when fellow Liverpudlian Ken Dodd met up with the group on a TV show and asked their advice on how to get "with it" by adopting a new "down to earth" name. Without missing a beat, Beatle George deadpanned, suggesting "Sod". The joke works on two levels... (A) as a "vague term of abuse", a put-down of the patronising, old style entertainment values which the Beatles repeatedly came across as they were making their name; and (B) taking Doddy at his word by putting forward the name of an "upper layer of grass land..." I always loved George's dry, laconic humour; he first introduced himself to lawyer Martin Polden with a phone call, "Hello, this is George Harrison of the famous Beatles".

But for all the hormonal enthusiasm with which they approached recording, there was still the numbing circuit of twice-nightly personal appearances. *The Observer* photographer Jane Bown remembered shooting them backstage in East Ham in November 1963: "They were pretty much imprisoned in this crummy little room, an awful room with terrible wallpaper and gas heaters and ghastly radiators painted with gloss paint... Ringo played Patience; George was very reclusive... Paul was terribly quiet... John was incredibly busy doing nothing".

"Getting decent meals is still the most difficult thing about being on tour," John moaned to Tony Barrow. "In the early days on the road in Britain when most of our concerts took place in cinemas, we just got Neil to buy us hot dogs from the front foyer of the cinema. Then we got round to sending out to caffs for proper hot meals, but by the time they reached us they were greasy, soggy and lukewarm..."

Photographer Robert Freeman also witnessed the backstage tedium – John tuning his guitar, Paul signing autographs and reading fan mail; Neil supplying cups of tea, throat lozenges, fish and chips, guitar strings. "The average band room was about twelve feet by eight," Freeman wrote. "And there was the usual stream of visitors – a charity organiser, a fan magazine editor, a press agent, the lord mayor's wife, the theatre manager's daughter, their tailor, music publisher, manager, a priest, a cripple in a wheelchair…"

We use the term 'disabled' now. And as their fame increased, this was one of the banes of the Beatles' experience. They were held in such esteem that regular visitors included disabled children. Many polio victims would clunk in, legs held rigid in those dreadful metal calipers. I'm not sure their parents bought the idea that being touched by a Beatle would result in a miracle cure. It was the 1960s equivalent of the 11th-century 'Royal Touch'. Perhaps the parents felt there was just something comforting and consoling in being that close to a celebrity. And none were more celebrated than the Beatles.

They were young, but despite the frenzy, the future was uncertain. Lionel Bart was one of the rare 'old school' the group related to, and perhaps was where they saw their future lie. In 2003, with our interview concluded, Paul McCartney turned wistful: "I remember in 1963, someone asking me what I thought I'd be doing when I was 30. I said I thought I'd be wearing a corduroy jacket with leather elbow patches, smoking a pipe and writing musicals with John".

Maybe because it was 40 years after the question which turned Paul to reflect. I love that detail: I bet the jacket, patches and pipe came from a grown-up appreciation, based on his old English master. And having just turned 21, for the boy Paul, 30 must have seemed a lifetime away. And did he really think then that there was a career in 'pop'?

It is disarming to read him talking to Francis Wyndham on the eve of the release of *Rubber Soul*: "Writing songs and performing are equally rewarding – that is when it goes well. But the songwriting looks like being the only thing you could do at 60. I wouldn't mind being a white-haired old man writing songs, but I'd hate to be a white-haired old Beatle at the Empress Stadium playing for people".

So, there they were within 12 months, having achieved everything they could possibly have imagined during those long, fruitless hours spent waiting for Brian Epstein at Lime Street station. Such success, however, also saw them trapped, confined in crummy little rooms, fuelled by fish and chips, distracted by chasing model electric cars around the floor.

The first issue of *Fabulous* naturally had them on the cover in January 1964 and hoping for "more super music to give us as much pleasure in 1964 as they did in 1963". The magazine bulged with Fabness – colour pin-ups, a profile of Brian Epstein. Paul Fry got to visit them in the only flat they ever shared together in Green Street, W1.[8] "Everything is so natural with the Beatles. They're the matiest of mates and make any visitor feel the same way. They'll share anything, offer 'ciggies' round … every time". That day held several photo sessions, a couple of interviews, a visit to their fan club, a trip to confer with George Martin and culminating in two evening shows in Southend".

Readers professed their adoration (Gillian Hickling: "Wow man get in the groove / Come and see the BEATLES move / They're the greatest, they're the most / If only I could get them thro' the post…"). Designed to fit into a school satchel, the 2/6d 'Pixerama Foldbook of The Beatles' was typical: "The fans can tell them apart, but as John has said, 'We're beginning to look like each other… the way people begin to look like their

---

8   In 2018 the property was on the market for £9,000,000.

dogs'"… "John has the leather voice and dry wit"… "George wants to be a businessman one of these days"… "Paul was an English Literature specialist at Liverpool Institute"… "Ringo went to technical college, but says he was educated at Butlin's".

After years of hairdressers being requested for a 'Tony Curtis' or 'DA' (Ducks Arse) haircut, now all the boys were surging forward. At school, the fringes were cultivated and brushed so the cut hovered just above the eyebrows, until it was swept back by disapproving teachers. Pity the curly-headed tykes, wiry hair only became fashionable when Bob Dylan and Jimi Hendrix made it so. In the UK, throughout 1963/64, a moptop was the condition all boys aspired to. I didn't know anyone who splashed out 19/11d on a "Mersey Beat Wig ("Now you can don a Beatle cut quick as a flash")". By April 1964, the president of the National Federation of Hairdressers offered free haircuts to the next group to reach No.1 on the UK charts.

A random trawl through the pop magazines of the period, before they conquered America, reveal a multitude of riches, but they were for *girls*: the Official Beatle sweater… Beatle bracelets for only 7/-… Beatle stockings… an official fan club badge for only 2/3d and two Rice Krispies packet tops (an unopened box was later sold at auction for £2,500)… the 7/11d Beatles Head Square in "washable non-iron acetate rayon"… A&BC chewing gum… Rozita candlewick bedspreads… a Marcasite Beatle brooch watch… autographed Beatle dresses… Maidenform Sweet Music brassieres… Rhona Roy dresses ("as worn by much publicized model Pattie Boyd").

Teenage boys coveted six-guinea Beatle jackets (with the intriguing "Ringo cuff")… Somewhere I'm sure I still have my 11/6d, 2½-inch-high Subbuteo Beatle moulded figures, in their midnight blue suits, complete with detachable guitars. Ringo's drum kit was only a cardboard frontage. I played with them for hours. I used to move them round like I had my Airfix model soldiers only a few months before. They were "No.1 in a series of pop stars in realistic miniature"… I wonder if there was ever a No.2?

Their homeland had succumbed, Sweden had not been far behind, although the group's three-week residency at the Paris Olympia during the first two months of 1964 was not an unalloyed triumph. Homegrown chanteuse Sylvie Vartan was well received, as were Trini Lopez's singalong favourites. "Les Beatles" suffered amplifier problems and audience indifference. It was small beer though, because it was during their Parisian residency that they received news that 'I Want to Hold Your Hand' had reached No.1 in America. Suddenly, inconceivably, the world was within their grasp.

All that Brian Epstein had worked for, all the group had accomplished in England, a year littered with triumph, was behind them. Would they be able to consolidate success in the heartland of the entertainment industry? Or would they, like Vera Lynn, the Springfields, Cliff, Acker and the Tornadoes, fail to *sustain* success in the American market? For all their brash confidence, for all their manager's belief, for all they had achieved… Ahead, lay the unknown…

*"Take care of the sense, and
the sounds will take care of themselves"*

Lewis Carroll, *Alice in Wonderland*

PART II : Show Me That I'm Everywhere

America didn't *need* the Beatles. They already had 'a lot of what they call the most' – Elvis, Hollywood, drive-in movies, sizzling 8oz hamburgers, Cadillacs, Jayne Mansfield, Batman, surfing, air conditioning, Fender Stratocasters, drive-thru burger joints, Coca-Cola, deep freezes, Disneyland, FM radio, Superman, skyscrapers, hot rods, 'two girls for every guy', car washes and Bob Dylan. They could change the many channels on their colour televisions without getting off the sofa. They had more than one radio station to broadcast popular music. No aerial bombardment had scarred their streets during the Second World War. No serious food or clothes rationing had impinged on their citizens.

Their films were screened around the world, their entertainers topped the bills across the globe, their records filled the charts of every nation outside the Iron Curtain. Their armies stood on the borders of Europe and Asia, guarding the world from the Communist threat. Their aircraft filled the skies, ready at a moment's notice to unleash an atomic Armageddon. America was the superpower. Since the searing, blinding flash over Nagasaki, politically, militarily, culturally … America was *it*. Civil Rights legislation was on the books. President Johnson promised a 'Great Society'. For many prior to the mire of Vietnam and the morass of Watergate, America stood, in Lincoln's words, as "the last, best hope of all mankind".

While the first fusillade of rock & roll had faltered, with Jerry Lee Lewis hounded out of the UK, Little Richard turning to religion, and Buddy Holly and Eddie Cochran dead, there was still a throbbing pulse on the American musical scene. Too often, the years between Elvis' discharge from Army service in 1960, and the breakthrough of the Beatles in 1964, is seen as a low point. But just a quick scan of releases of the period reveals a good compilation's worth of classic pop – 'Sea Cruise', 'A Teenager in Love', 'El Paso', 'Tell Laura I Love Her', 'Cathy's Clown', 'Only the Lonely', Save the Last Dance for Me', 'I Fought the Law', 'Boys Cry', 'Will You Love Me Tomorrow', 'Runaway', 'Hello Mary Lou', 'Quarter to Three', 'Johnny Remember Me', 'Crazy', 'The Wanderer', 'Puff the Magic Dragon'… And that's without any Dylan, Elvis, Motown, Stax or Spector.

If Liverpool appeared a remote outpost to the inhabitants of the London entertainment industry, America was the cherished, *Promised* Land. Success in the UK was its own reward, but proof of having arrived meant making it in America, and making that success last.

A survey of 1961/62 showed that less than 10% of the UK population holidayed abroad. From the vantage point of the 21st century, with cheap Transatlantic access, it is hard to appreciate just how remote America seemed to the Beatles and the British Invasion acts which came in their wake. Colin Blunstone remembered how, on the Zombies' first US visit, his mother made him a packed lunch for the flight… and the Dave Clark Five's Mike Smith recalled quitting work on Friday and arriving in the USA on the Monday: not only his first visit to the States, but his first flight *and* first night in a hotel.

John Peel told me: "I went to America in 1960 and, apart from an uncle who was slightly the black sheep of the family and who'd been to the States for a few months, you didn't meet *anybody* who'd been there. It really was an extraordinarily remote place. So the only image you had of it was derived from cowboy books and *True Romance*".

That image was forged by the big screen Technicolor films which filled local Odeons, and presented the States as a luxurious location. It was further enhanced by the popular television series which aired in the UK – shows such as *I Love Lucy*, *My Three Sons* and *The Dick Van Dyke Show* that portrayed the country as a consumer paradise. *Highway Patrol* suggested the spaciousness of the States, their policemen so much cooler than *Dixon of Dock Green*. Though not as cool as the gumshoes who occupied *77 Sunset Strip*. All the while, youngsters could wallow in the TV Westerns like *Cheyenne*, *Gunsmoke*, *Bronco*, *Maverick*, *Wagon Train*, *Bonanza*…

John Cooper Clarke was equally enchanted, and baffled. "What is our ZIP code? What is a pizza? Is garbage the same as rubbish?…" Only George Harrison could speak from first-hand experience following his brief Stateside visit to see his sister Louise the year before he arrived with the Beatles. For all their built-in confidence and sense of achievement, and despite having the nation's No.1 record, the group were uncertain about how things would develop.

Author Michael Braun caught the group's nervousness on that inaugural flight over to the entertainment centre of the world. "Since America has always had everything, why should we be over there making money?" Paul asked Phil Spector who had somehow wangled his way onto the plane. "They've got their own groups. What are we going to give them that they don't already have?"

Certainly, Sweden had succumbed on the back of the Beatles' homeland success, but France had displayed resistance. Their three-week run at the Paris Olympia proved to be the first spell in a manic 12 months where every onstage note was not drowned out by screaming girls. Reviews of that first night were muted. Was this the moment that the bandwagon stopped rolling? As it happened, returning to their hotel after that first desultory performance, any doubts were dispelled: a telegram informing the Beatles that their record 'I Want to Hold Your Hand' had reached the No.1 slot on the American charts. Asked what the Beatles learned in Paris, photographer Harry Benson who accompanied them said, "They learned how to order room service". It would soon stand them in good stead.

The group were ecstatic on learning of the triumph. George Martin (in town to produce German-language versions of two songs) was pictured beaming at a celebratory dinner. Also pictured was their svelte Svengali, Brian Epstein, sporting a broad grin – beneath an uncharacteristic chamber pot perched on his head.

For all their exuberant delight, the group and their manager were mindful of how hard it would be to *maintain* that initial success. The geographical distance meant ignoring the UK and Europe if a sustained career in America was to be achieved. It proved to be a perennial problem – both Slade and T. Rex watched their homegrown success dwindle while they devoted time to cracking the American market. The birth of the promo video proved a godsend.

At the time the Beatles celebrated their achievement in Paris, the transatlantic technology was basic. Telstar had achieved live television transmission between the UK and USA in 1962. But the thought of a beat group performing live in a performance to be seen on both sides of the Atlantic was unthinkable. Film clips were feasible, but in early 1964, the way to succeed in America was with live performance, buoyed by radio and television appearances.

The Beatles were only too aware how 'the UK's answer to Elvis', Cliff Richard, had failed to sustain an American career. In his autobiography, the Shadows' Bruce Welch recalled their first American tour backing Cliff, way down a bill headlined by Frankie Avalon. As "An Added Attraction from Britain", the Shadows had to compete with Bobby Rydell, Freddy Cannon, Clyde McPhatter, Sammy Turner, the Clovers *and* Johnny & the Hurricanes. It was true of other UK favourites – Billy Fury, Joe Brown, Adam Faith, Mark Wynter, Eden Kane, John Leyton, Helen Shapiro, Laurie London, Johnny Kidd, the Tornadoes… All had faltered in their efforts; none had established a permanent foothold on the lucrative American market.

Sure, the Beatles had the nation's No.1 record, but it was their first, and *only*, American hit. Even today, critics insist that hysterical reception was a marketing ploy, funded by their label. In fact, Capitol Records *had* allocated a budget of $40,000. It was spent on 'The Beatles Are Coming' bumper stickers, press kits, adverts in the trade papers such as *Billboard* and *Cash Box* and 'We Want The Beatles' t-shirts.

So, yes, promotional muscle was employed. But that was the job of the American record label which had finally got behind the Beatles. Yet that financial investment does not explain the sheer, unmitigated hysteria which greeted the group on their arrival. Newsreel footage of the time shows the crowd evenly balanced between boys, to a man sporting crew-cuts, and screaming girls modelling Jacqueline Kennedy hairstyles. Even if the fans *had* been paid, could such manifest enthusiasm really be purchased?

An estimated 3,000 screaming fans were there, fighting for space on the terminal roof to catch a glimpse of the group. There had been similar eruptions before – in the 1940s, Frank Sinatra shows were interrupted by adoring screams; whenever Elvis broke cover in the 1950s, his performances were greeted with similar enthusiasm. Looking at the newsreels of those early Beatles visits to the USA, however, I was struck by how equally their audiences were divided. Yes, it was the tearful, screaming teenage girls who were the cynosure for the cameras, but teenage boys appear equally as enthusiastic. And I believe that was one reason for the Beatles' early – and sustained – American success. A group suggested a gang, and gang culture was an important element of American cultural history, be it the popular screen outlaws like Jesse James and Billy the Kid, or the teenage gangs in *The Blackboard Jungle*, *West Side Story* and *The Wild One*.

The American author Elijah Wald later commented on the group's overall appeal: "The fanzines quickly adopted the 'fab four' as ideal boyfriends, with the advantage that readers didn't have to choose between buying records by Elvis, Ricky, Frankie, or one of the various Brylcreemed Bobbys, because all tastes could be accommodated in one group".

In his estimable autobiography *I Wanna Be Yours*, John Cooper Clarke nailed it: "The Beatles looked fabulous… like the characters of some new kind of board. The corporate set-up absolved each member from the onerous responsibility of individual personal fabulousness. The alienated romanticism of the solitary heart-throb (see 'Teenage Idol' by Ricky Nelson) was replaced by this cheeky good-time gang you longed to be a part of".

Coming in on the back of 'I Want to Hold Your Hand' at No.1, much of the label's promotional material concentrated on their haircuts. Rob Finnis found an internal Capitol memo to its sales reps from late 1963: "shortly after the first of the year you'll have bulk quantities of a Beatles hair-do wig… you and your staff are to wear the wig during the business day! Get those Beatle wigs around properly and you'll find you're helping to start the Beatle Hair-Do Craze that should be sweeping the country soon". Creedence Clearwater Revival's Doug Clifford remembered: "We bought Beatle wigs. We went to the drama store, and I guess they were Three Stooges wigs at that time!'

You cannot overestimate the importance of those haircuts – immediately prior to the success of 'I Want to Hold Your Hand', the charts were full of Marine-style barnets (Barnet Fair = hair) courtesy of Bobby Rydell Bobby Vinton, Nino Tempo and Dale (of Dale & Grace, only one of the native acts swept aside in that Beatle hurricane). The sleeve note to *Meet The Beatles!* mentioned that "they wear 'pudding basin' haircuts that date back to ancient England".

On arrival at New York's newly-christened John F. Kennedy airport on 7 February 1964, the Beatles' first thought as they gazed out onto the wintry tarmac was that the rhapsodic fans were for JFK's successor, President Lyndon Johnson. The English visitors were plainly delighted as they descended the aircraft steps. Yet you sense their dazed, dazzled incomprehension. All this? For *us*? Not just the Beatles themselves, but a bemused Brian Epstein and Cossack-hatted Cavern-owner Ray McFall. This was unprecedented. This was a dream come true. Not just to *be* in America, but to be greeted as conquering heroes.

"I remember…", Paul delighted in recalling, "the great moment of getting into the limo and putting on the radio and hearing a running commentary on *us*… 'They have just left the airport and are coming towards New York City'… It was like a dream. The greatest fantasy ever" (*Anthology*).

That first press conference cemented their appeal. Pushed and prodded by stewardesses and cops; drained following their longest-ever flight, they handled themselves with aplomb. The American media were obsessed by their look, so manifestly at odds with their crew-cut US contemporaries. They were spontaneously witty, cheeky, irreverent and confident… everything Elvis and the tongue-tied 'Bobbys' were not. ("Will you sing for us?" "We need money first"… "Are you part of a social rebellion against the older generation?" "It's a dirty lie"… "Are you going to get haircuts?" "I had one yesterday"… "What about the movement in Detroit to stamp out Beatles?" "We have our own campaign to stamp out Detroit".)

It wasn't manufactured or scripted, they were genuinely funny in their spontaneous irreverence. After years of dreary responses from fabricated idols, following spoon-fed PR puff, the Beatles really did provide a breath of fresh air for the jaded American media. "They are absolutely too cute for words", one female journalist gushed.

They were as aware as anyone of the mountain they had to scale. Even if at one remove from his peak, Elvis still packed a commercial punch. Bob Dylan had given pop music a voice on the back of a folk revival which saw Peter, Paul & Mary and Joan Baez regularly riding high on the charts. Motown was hitting its stride as 'the sound of young America', while Phil Spector's Wagnerian pop masterpieces and the Beach Boys' hot rod and surfing romps were proving irresistible to the youth of America.

Perhaps coincidentally, they were surfing a wave: immediately prior to the Beatles' arrival, New York was going through a British phase – *Beyond the Fringe*, Anthony Newley's *Stop the World…* and Lionel Bart's *Oliver!* were all running on Broadway. The British films *Tom Jones*, *From Russia with Love* and *Lawrence of Arabia* were drawing in American audiences. On television, NBC were running a US version of *That Was the Week That Was*, hosted by David Frost.

After initial reluctance (even after deciding to release 'I Want to Hold Your Hand' only 5,000 copies were scheduled to be pressed up) the group's new record label – Capitol – was finally ready to give them a real push. Not only was America ready for the Beatles; the Beatles were ready for America. 'I Want to Hold Your Hand' had been launched on the American market on Boxing Day, 26 December 1963. Barely five weeks later, that hysterical JFK airport greeting still rang in their ears. With a headline appearance on the country's most popular entertainment show, their immediate future was assured.

Looking back, writing in his *Billboard Book of Number One Hits*, Fred Bronson singled out Bobby Vinton's 'There! I've Said It Again' as "one of the most significant number one singles of the rock era. Not because of anything inherent in the song or the artist, but because it signified the end of an era. Following it would be a dividing line as thick and impenetrable as Bill Haley's … 'Rock Around the Clock'. Music would never be the same again". It was Vinton's single which was deposed by 'I Want to Hold Your Hand'."

The first that America had seen of the Beatles was not their legendary appearance on the *Ed Sullivan Show* on the night of Sunday, 9 February 1964, but some time before. On 18 November 1963, Edwin Newman reported on *The Hunter-Brinkley Report* on the phenomenon which was sweeping staid, old-fashioned Great Britain. Commenting on the Beatle hysteria, Newman noted that the group came from the tough "Merseyside section of Liverpool".

A few days later, on 21 November 1963, CBS News' London correspondent Alexander Kendrick screened footage of the hysteria which greeted them when they performed 'She Loves You' in the UK. It was screened by Sullivan's sworn rival Jack Paar, who disparagingly explained to his mainly adult studio audience, "we've never in my seven years at NBC … ever had a rock & roll act. But I'm interested in the Beatles as a psychological, er, sociological phenomenon… The girls go out of their minds. Does it bother you to realise that in five years these girls will vote, raise children and drive cars?"

However, it was that head-turning, life-changing epiphany on the *Ed Sullivan Show* that did it. That was the one that United the States. That was the one that flicked the switch, which moved a generation up a gear. It was 15 minutes, a quarter of an hour, which, for one heart-stopping appearance, gave Elvis, Stax, Dylan, the Rat Pack, the Brill Building and Motown pause. Following that breakthrough television appearance, Frankie Avalon, Bobby Rydell, Fabian, Ricky Nelson, James Darren, Bobby Vinton, Jan & Dean and the Singing Nun were blown out of the holy water.

Ever astute, Sullivan could spot popularity. It was while returning from a talent-spotting trip to Europe that he was waiting at London Airport when the Beatles returned from their Swedish tour. The sight (and sound) of a thousand screaming fans suggested to Sullivan that there might be a slot for the group on his weekly show. It was confirmed by his London agent, Peter Pritchard, who told his boss that the group were the first "long-haired boys" to perform at the Royal Variety Show.

Sullivan's meeting with Brian Epstein in New York on 11 November 1963 confirmed the appearance. It was once Capitol knew the Beatles were scheduled for the nation's biggest entertainment programme, that the label upped their game, and the relentless promotion behind 'I Want to Hold Your Hand' began.

Just *getting* the Beatles to America had been a struggle; in 1935 the UK Musicians' Union had demanded a reciprocal arrangement – for every American group performing in the UK, the Yanks had to take a British combo. Problem was, the Brits wanted Louis Armstrong and Duke Ellington, the Americans weren't interested in George Webb's Dixielanders or the Crane River Jazz Band. The deadlock wasn't broken until 1956, when Louis Armstrong came to play Earl's Court (and bless him, the venerable Max Jones of *Melody Maker* was at Heathrow to literally kiss Satchmo's feet as he touched down on British soil).

The Beatles' work permits were only valid "if unemployed American citizens capable of performing the work cannot be found". So, who did we get while Ed Sullivan got the Beatles? I believe it is not widely known just what that reciprocal arrangement was, but thanks to jazz authority Jon Newey, who wrote in 2008: "According to Charles Lloyd, the 1964 UK tour with the Cannonball Adderley Sextet came about through the Musicians' Union exchange scheme of the time, where they were the exchange group for The Beatles' first visit to the USA in 1964". No doubt the group were well received, but there are no reports of UK Cannonballmania.

So the Beatles *were* allowed to go to the USA. But the troubles did not end there. At a May 1964 meeting of the Musicians' Union, there was a lengthy debate over Ronnie Scott's wish to increase the number of visiting "foreign musicians", thus questioning the reciprocal arrangement. The MU reported a meeting with the Ministry of Labour regarding their policy of the "Transatlantic exchange of 'beat' groups".

The reported continued that "the Ministry argued that 'beat groups' were not bands but were in the most part vocalists who accompanied themselves". The matter had arisen sharply recently when the Beatles had appeared in the United States. The American Federation of Musicians had protested about the appearance of the Beatles, rather bafflingly claiming "that the information provided about the group's form of entertainment had been misleading".

Which rather begged the question of quite what the American Federation of Musicians (AFM) had been expecting? But, boy, did they dig in their heels. Herbert Kenin, AFM President, was there quite properly to protect the interests of his members. However, he stoked the fires with comments such as: "It was the task of the staff … to determine whether or not musicians coming to perform in the States were 'uniquely talented'." Kenin continued: "We don't consider [The Beatles] unique. They are musicians and only sing incidentally. We can go to Yonkers or Tennessee and pick up four kids who can do this kind of stuff". Not comments that found favour with the group's young fans.

The controversy broadened following an article in *Variety* magazine soon after the group's arrival in America. Had it remained in the trade paper, things might have remained muted. But Victor Riesel's article 'Keeping Out the Beatles', was reproduced in newspapers across the country, and it was this article that indignant teenagers responded to in their outraged thousands. Riesel's piece began: "Let each stand in his place. At my side is a man of awesome courage. . . this fellow is Herman Kenin [who] just doesn't believe the Beatles are culture. He is not much impressed by "Yeah, Yeah, Yeah…'."

Outraged Beatle fans took up their pens to write to the AFM President (Kenin), and *the* President (Johnson). Typical was one from a trio of Beatles fans:

Dear Mr Kenin…

In the article it indicated that you intend to keep the Beatles out of America, unless there is a reciprocal exchange for the performance of American musicians in Britain… In our opinion, we feel that if U.S. musicians… were any good, they would not need the government to help them… In addition, we do not think adults have a right to stop the younger generation from enjoying what it loves and wants: the BEATLES!!!! Please give us a chance to enjoy something we love! Please don't ask us to Hold Your Hand in this action… Sir, you have a big fight ahead of you: for we who have stood amongst the screamers, the twisters and the jumpers know what a fight it will be. Hell hath no fury like a Beatle-nik spurned!

Respectfully,

Cindy Westendorf and Linda Hausfeld and Carol Herbert Beatle fans, and – PROUD OF IT!!!!!!

The Musicians' Union report on the matter concluded rather nostalgically, "although exchanges formerly involved jazz musicians, nearly all those now visiting the United States from Britain constituted 'beat' or 'pop' groups".

(Details of the above controversy were drawn from Michael Roberts' fascinating article on the MU/AFM dispute for the Cambridge University Press, 2010. Incidentally, while the victory appeared to be on the Brits' side, Roberts points out that the words "Rock & Roll" did not appear in the AFM newspaper until 1969).

The AFM were not the only unit fighting a rearguard action; in May 1965, *Time* magazine stated, "There are dozens of rock & roll groups in the USA who can play better than the Beatles". To illustrate their point, for the cover, they chose the Beach Boys, Righteous Brothers, Peter Noone and Trini Lopez.

*

For the Beatles' American TV debut, there had been 50,000 ticket applications for the CBS-TV Studio's 728 seats in New York. *TV Guide* alerted audiences what to expect that night: "England's Rock and Rolling Beatles make their American television debut and 30 policemen will be on hand in case a 'Beatle-Mania' reaches the riot pitch as it has in England".

It was a phone call from Granada TV to a pair of documentary-making brothers only hours before the Beatles landed that fortuitously gave us a compelling fly-on-the-wall account. The Maysles brothers had got to the airport to chronicle the madness and accompany the group into their awestruck arrival in Manhattan. The Maysles' up-close documentaries on Bible salesmen, Marlon Brando and the 1960 Presidential election had been critics' favourites. The brothers went on to shoot *Gimme Shelter*, the film of the infamous Altamont Rolling Stones concert.

Through the Maysles brothers' lens, you capture the sheer delight of seeing the Beatles being… *there*. They are enchanted by the novelty of it all – armed policeman, commercial radio, the variety of TV channels, the food on offer. The cabs, the limousines, the drinks. They were used to Beatlemania at home, but this was going up a rung, and they revel in every mad minute of it. There's a great moment when Paul is asked a ponderous question about the cultural significance of it all? "It's not culture, it's a good laugh".

The ubiquitous Murray the K is seen clinging limpet-like to the group. Prior to 7 February 1964, Murray Kaufman was on the slide; his WINS show was losing out to other New York stations like WABC and WIMA. But Murray inveigled his way into the press conference at JFK, literally at the feet of the Beatles, bombarding them with questions and impressing George with his hat. As Tom Wolfe wrote of the DJ soon after: "Cuba, de Gaulle, unilateral disarmament, Lyndon B. Johnson, South Viet Nam it wasn't the sweep of history, but in the league of disc jockeys covering the first moments the Beatles set foot on the earth of America, it was a historic scoop".

Murray's initial appeal ("What's happening baby?… You're what's happening baby"… his jaunty use of the word "baby" regardless of gender) soon palled. Other DJs grew jealous of his access. The Beatles didn't care one way or the other. Murray the K meant nothing to them. They were unprepared for his bluster or tenacity, Murray was far more of a loose cannon than Brian Matthew. But in the flood that followed, Murray was soon dispatched, his role as 'the fifth Beatle' soon forgotten. Though not by Murray.

America overwhelmed the group on that historic first visit. But they were not intimidated by their reception. Neither were they threatened by Ed Sullivan, they didn't have to bend the knee to the king of US TV talent. *The Ed Sullivan Show* was never screened in the UK. They had already seen off Morecambe & Wise, Keith Fordyce, Bruce Forsyth, Ken Dodd and Pussy Cat Willum.

The question I kept finding myself asking, looking at the contemporary footage: was *why* did the Beatles arouse such hysteria? And all, effectively, on the strength of just *one* song, 'I Want to Hold Your Hand'. As far as 'I Want to Hold Your Hand', the composers themselves were not so sure. On the original manuscript of that game-changing song, Paul had written a schoolmasterly "3/10… See me". America had ignored their previous single releases. True, their new label had more muscle, and even if Capitol had paid for that airport reception, they could not have afforded to have carried on paying for that *persistent* hysteria which marked that first US visit.

Of course, 'I Want to Hold Your Hand' was a great song, a breath of fresh air which nonetheless built on earlier efforts. Elijah Wald effectively analysed the elements which led to the song's US success: "[it] had the hand claps of the girl groups, the melodic sophistication of the best Brill building compositions, a rhythm perfectly suited to the new dances and the loose energy of the surf bands".

To their eternal credit, the Beatles were always good at acknowledging just how much of an influence American music had had on them. It wasn't just the obvious names above the title (Elvis, Buddy, Chuck), but in early interviews, namechecking Chuck Jackson, Ben E. King, the Shirelles, Smokey Robinson… In 1964, they sent a telegram to Tamla-Motown which smacked of coming from the heart: "Very many thanks for your cable. We mean every word we said about you in the States and are very sorry we did not meet in Detroit. Hope this will be rectified later this year. You will be most welcome here at any

"Is Tessie O'Shea on the way…?", with Ed Sullivan, 9 February 1964

time. Regards to Mary Wells, The Temptations, the Contours, the Marvelettes and Martha and the Vandellas. Very sincerely John Lennon Paul McCartney George Harrison Ringo Starr".

They reminded America what they had been in danger of losing. No wonder Bob Dylan called his breakthrough 1965 electric LP *Bringing It All Back Home* in recognition of what the British Invasion groups brought back to the States. "America should put statues up to the Beatles", Dylan said in 1997. "They helped give this country's pride back to it".

When the 'Fab Four' did appear, America was immediately captivated. Looking at them objectively, in action that February night, the front line were not conventionally handsome, the novelty was in their faces framed by *that* hair. The group were not what one earlier fan sighed of Elvis, "a delicious hunk of forbidden fruit". The smiling drummer at the back had the engaging appeal of a Harpo Marx or even *Mad* magazine's Alfred E. Neuman. They looked so at odds with earlier teen idols – when he opened his mouth the guitarist displayed undeniably English teeth[9]; the other guitarist squinted, rather menacingly.

The songs they sang were certainly different to what young America heard on their transistor radios. There was the novelty of the Beatles being a group, four individuals, so when George took a solo he was allowed more space than Scotty Moore behind Elvis. And the two mop-tops doing the head-shaking, harmonising, 'ooh' thing is still enchanting. They were cute, bubbly, and not threatening.

Was that an integral part of the appeal? For the girls certainly, but was there a homoerotic element, the swivelling heads full of hair; the falsetto harmonies; Paul and George within kissing distance round a microphone as they harmonised? Academic Steven Stark found that "The Beatles' androgyny can be located in an English tradition from Elizabethan cross-dressing ("mumming") to J. M. Barrie's *Peter Pan*, whose forever-a-boy title character is still traditionally played by a female actress onstage".

And the way John stood, legs akimbo, with that thousand-yard stare. As if the 'Sorry girls, he's married…' caption mattered. In later years, it was a running joke in *Q* magazine, using the photo caption to accompany some particularly unattractive new pop idol. Mind you, for John it was all fairly academic what he saw – without his glasses he was blind as a bat. Offstage he would fashion thick black spectacles in the style of his hero, Buddy Holly. One of the great favours Lennon did for the youth of the United Kingdom from 1966 onwards was in making the wearing of those awful cheap National Health spectacles fashionable.

Re-viewing footage of those early American tours, it was apparent this was more than mere hysteria, this was *madness*. The enthusiasm never waned, the excitement never palled, the fury never abated… Bemused reporters and journalists came away baffled from interviewing besotted fans. It was sheer, incomprehensible adoration they encountered. The fans' weeping, adoring incoherence was something new. It certainly was not manufactured and, equally, it could not be articulated. Such fervour transcended mere enthusiasm. It was an enthusiasm teetering on insanity.

---

9 Apparently, following their desultory meeting with Elvis Presley, after the group had left, Elvis asked his friend Larry Geller why, with all that money, they didn't do something about their teeth.

There is much fun to be had looking at that footage from 1964, if you can tear yourself away from the Fab Four. At times the girls do play up to the cameras while the boys look like they are desperately trying to grow their hair on camera. Those audiences make for compelling viewing: the women look like they are auditioning for *The Stepford Wives* while, by and large, the guys all resemble astronauts.

For all the joy at that reception, it soon becomes apparent that they are prisoners of their fame – "Aren't we going out?" a Beatle is heard plaintively asking in the Maysles film. Photographers are literally in their face at every opportunity. All the while, a suave and slightly baffled Brian Epstein hovers. This was his dream come true too. No need to pester disinterested record company executives, TV producers or radio programmers. From now on, they would have to come to him.

Photographer Harry Benson remembered Brian's mantra: "'Don't worry, it'll all work out'. And he'd say it so calmly while all the madness was swirling around him".

There is a delightful naivety to that first trip. Brown ale, fish and chips and the Light Programme are now a memory. Scotch and coke, 8oz burgers and fries and Paul marvels as he flicks the dial of his transistor radio at the sheer wealth and variety of the music on offer. They endorse radio stations they've never heard of. They listen to America going mad over them.

I still marvel that it was all on the back of 15 minutes of TV and one song. An estimated 73,000,000 tuned in to watch the Beatles' American TV debut that February night. Showbusiness personalities, curious evangelists breaking their Sabbath pledge; chart rivals, mesmerised teenagers. Whole families watched together. The New York crime rate dwindled as gangs forswore stealing hubcaps to tune in.

Over the years we have all seen the clips of their performance. What is fascinating now is seeing the entire show when it became available on DVD. Having to sit through all that terrible primeval, antediluvian 'entertainment'. Comedians Charlie Brill & Mitzi McCall… a hapless Dutch magician… impressionist Frank Gorshin (getting big laughs out of the riff that film stars may one day become President!)… 'Two Ton' Tessie O'Shea… The cast of *Oliver!* featuring a young Davy Jones – watching the show at home that night was one Micky Dolenz: "I distinctly remember saying 'God, I'd like to be one of the Beatles!' You have to be careful what you wish for".

Then, cute as puppies, brimming over with confidence, John, Paul, George and Ringo tear into 'All My Loving'. They gather round a microphone for the familiar 'Oohs' and a nation succumbs. They are given name captions, so similar under all that hair y'understand. They smile, they appear to almost pinch themselves for real. They are manifestly wallowing in the moment.

They are not intimidated by their host. Sullivan himself remains a uniquely American phenomenon, he meant diddly-squat in the UK, aside from that shifty persona and his eerie resemblance to Richard M. Nixon. In truth, Sullivan himself appeared more excited about the upcoming appearance of Mitzi Gaynor than 'The Beedles'. Those outside the USA were not aware of the Sunday night phenomenon which was the Sullivan show. It was required Sunday night viewing, and its impact could not be underestimated: for example, following the Clancy Brothers' 1961 appearance, sales of their trademark Aran sweaters leapt by 700%.

After all that old-school showbiz flotsam that February night in 1964, even now, all these years on, the impact of the Beatles when they finally *do* appear remains seismic. With one flick of the hair ('her') they launch the 1960s in the United States. And of course it is, rather bafflingly, with the great Beatles single that never was, the LP track 'All My Loving'.

Too often cliché runs riot, but what cannot be denied is that when the Beatles appeared on *The Ed Sullivan Show* that Sunday night, an entire generation of musicians took it as a cue to begin their own careers. In New Jersey, the teenage Bruce Springsteen sat waiting for the *moment*: "Jolting my system with ten thousand watts of high-voltage anticipation... heart pounding waiting for the first pealing of the Rickenbacker, Hofner and Gibson guitars... The Beatles... In 1964 there were no more magical words in the English language".

Tom Petty: "I saw The Beatles on TV and I thought I could either be a farmer, or I could do that". Billy Joel was equally smitten: "I thought, those guys they don't look like Fabian. They were quite obviously not Hollywood glamour boys. The Beatles were working class guys, like me, playing their own instruments, writing their own songs, proving that people like me had a chance to make it in music".

In Canada Neil Young concurred: "Oh yeah, we got the Beatles right away. They were a group. Up to that point we'd only really seen guys in front of a band like Roy Orbison... But this was a group that played and wrote their own songs and were self-contained".

With their No.1 single and their stunning TV debut, the Beatles immediately became an all-pervasive influence... Like the rest of young America, Jimmy Morrison interrupted his Film Studies at UCLA to watch *The Ed Sullivan Show* that night... In Oakland, California, John Fogerty was disenchanted with the Singing Nun, then went and bought every record with the word 'Beatles' on it and thought, "Man, this is the coolest"... Brooklyn-born Tony Visconti fashioned a Scouse accent... The Doors producer Paul Rothchild stated, "The first week The Beatles were on the radio, the possibilities changed – the world changed". The men who would be Byrds watched.

George Thorogood pinpointed the moment: "After the Ed Sullivan Show, Feb. 9, 1964, at approx. 8:04pm, after that moment every album, every guitar, every set of drums that was ever sold ... 10% should have gone right into their pocket!" "The Beatles changed the world, literally overnight", Steve Van Zandt enthused. "There were no bands in America on February 8 1964. There was one in every garage on February 10 1964".

Tom Petty's drummer Stan Lynch: "I got to meet Ringo... He just gave me a big hug and went 'I know, I know'. Because every drummer just craps their pants when they meet fucking Ringo. What would I be without that first Ed Sullivan show? A plumber?"

Who else do we know tuned in and sensed that shift?... David Crosby, Art Garfunkel, Steve Earle, Jerry Garcia, Jimi Hendrix, Chrissie Hynde, Rickie Lee Jones, Billy Joel, Lenny Kaye, Nils Lofgren, Roger McGuinn, Steve Miller, Gram Parsons, Bonnie Raitt, Todd Rundgren, John Sebastian, Steven Tyler, Loudon Wainwright III, Steve Van Zandt,[10]

---

10 The future E. Street Band guitarist later realised a lifetime's ambition, when McCartney joined him onstage for 'I Saw Her Standing There', and performed with his band at the recreated Cavern in 2017. An event captured on the Macca to Mecca DVD – thanks to Mike Saunders for the groovy title.

Joe Walsh, Don Was, Brian Wilson, Warren Zevon… Other enthusiastic viewers include the Fonda family (Henry, Peter and Jane), Meryl Streep, Whoopi Goldberg, Billy Bob Thornton, Jeff Bridges and Sigourney Weaver.

Not everyone was convinced though. In 2008 Eric Summe told me that in Northern Kentucky the nuns actually banned his entire school from watching the Sullivan show that epochal night. News reporter Larry Kane was taken aside by his father prior to him joining the group on their first American tour and was warned, "these men are a menace to society". Featured on the cover of the influential *Newsweek* magazine a fortnight after that television debut, the magazine commented, "Visually, they are a nightmare; tight, dandified, Edwardian-Beatnik suits and great pudding bowls of hair. Musically they are a new disaster; guitars and drums slamming out a merciless beat that does away with secondary rhythms, harmony and melody… Their lyrics (punctuated by nutty shouts of 'yeah, yeah, yeah') are a catastrophe, a preposterous farrago of Valentine-card romantic sentiments".

Reporting on the first American tour, in August 1964, the headline for *The Cincinnati Enquirer* ran, 'Young Fans Drop Veneer Of Civilization For Beatles'. America had seen its youth run wild over Sinatra and Elvis, but they were native born. There appeared to be a real suspicion of these alien invaders. *Hootenanny* magazine came on the back of the folk revival, spearheaded by Dylan, Baez and Peter, Paul & Mary, raged an editorial in late 1964: "Beatlemania is the shrieking of hysterical girls; it is fans lined up for hours for a glimpse of a quartet of shaggy Teddy Boys… Tom Dooley was a time-steeped ballad of an actual episode, while I Want to Hold Your Hand is a souped-up, over-engineered love song. The difference between them speaks volumes about the merits of folk song and the Merseybeat. The Kingston Trio started something very constructive in American music. If the Beatles end it we'll all be the losers".

Dean Noebel of the Christian Crusade warned of Communists who had "contrived an elaborate, calculating and scientific technique directed at rendering a generation of American youth useless through nerve-jamming mental deterioration and retardation… The destructive music of … The Beatles … reinforces … mental breakdown". A 1965 publication by the Christian Crusade, *Communism, Hypnotism & The Beatles*, warned of the Pavlovian response to their music and suggested their music exercised an hypnotic effect on listeners. The book revealed that Nicholas Topping, promoter of an early Beatle concert, was found to have folk song books by known Communists Pete Seeger and Paul Robeson.

The irony, of course, is that at the same time, as the Cold War remained frozen, those Communists back in the USSR were warning *their* youth of the destructive power and pernicious influence of that self-same group of bourgeois capitalists. As late as 1978, a member of the Polish Politburo was promising that "the trumpets of the Beatles are not the trumpets of Jericho which will cause the walls of socialism to come tumbling down".

But in America, suddenly, over one February night, the chart-hugging singalong world of Mitch Miller was as old-fashioned as the balladeers Elvis had deposed a decade before. For the teenage audience, the Broadway cast LPs which their parents played and re-played were automatically discarded. Folk music was largely relegated to a campus phenomenon. Soul hits were sporadic. Crew-cutted crooners were history. The ambition was to be in a group, particularly one with an English connection. The Beatles were the tsunami which swept over the American music scene, and in a few short months, laid it to waste.

Before what was soon to be christened 'The British Invasion', during 1963 only three British singles had cracked the US Top 40. In 1964, the number was up to 65. Indeed, Spencer Leigh researched the US singles charts, 1955 to December 1963, and found only 1% of entries were by British acts.

The single and LP charts revealed the innate conservatism of the American music industry in that pre-British Invasion period. Film soundtracks (*Breakfast at Tiffany's*, *West Side Story*, *The Singing Nun*) dominated, alongside easy listening stalwarts like Andy Williams. As in the UK, the long-playing record was seen as a 'grown-up' purchase. In July 1963 the influential trade magazine *Billboard* concurred, "The general public identifies the 33 as 'good music', while it classified the 45 with the black leather jacket and motorcycle set".

As a snapshot, the month the Beatles arrived in the USA, Bob Dylan was still perceived as a solo, protesting folk singer. Joan Baez the reigning folk Queen. Peter, Paul & Mary had three LPs simultaneously in the Top 10. The folk revival was in full swing, spearheaded by the Kingston Trio. Long forgotten today, the clean-cut trio kickstarted America's interest in its musical heritage with their 1958 No.1 'Tom Dooley'. Also on the Capitol label, where they landed seven gold records for LP sales, the Trio went on to enjoy *fourteen* Top 10 LPs, including five No.1s. By the Christmas of 1959, the Kingston Trio had four LPs in the country's Top 10, a feat which would not be repeated until 1964 by the Trio's labelmates.

Capitol were quick off the mark, the label's second Beatles single 'Can't Buy Me Love' was released barely a month after the Sullivan appearance. Its seven-week run as the country's No.1 only interrupted by Swan Records' re-release of 'She Loves You' which enjoyed a fortnight's run at the top.

Today, in an era of streaming and downloading, with physical record sales sliding inexorably downward, the statistics of Beatle releases of that manic period remain eye-watering: 'I Want to Hold Your Hand' alone shifted 2,500,000 copies. A survey had 60% of *all* singles sold in the USA during 1964 as Beatle records... *The Wall Street Journal* reported American teenagers spending $50,000,000 on Beatle products by the end of 1964. In 1964, they became the first act after Elvis to have an LP, single and film at No.1 in the USA simultaneously. By August 1965, the reliable showbiz bible *Variety* reported worldwide Beatle sales of 150,000,000.

The greatest criticism levelled at Brian Epstein as manager was the millions he lost on the lucrative merchandising which came in the wake of the Beatles' conquest of America. One account had Epstein selling American rights for Beatle t-shirts for a paltry $48,000. Three days after their arrival, the company had sold three million. Poor Brian, 18 months before his creative ceiling was window displays in the family store. Film of him during that initial visit show him fielding innumerable phone calls, juggling meetings, trying to keep a lid on the madness.

It was when America succumbed that the floodgates opened... Beatle talcum powder, wallpaper, lunch boxes, chewing gum, bubble gum, airbeds, wigs, hair brushes, inflatable models, jigsaws, nodding dolls, cake decorations, wigs, 'magnetic hair games', pomade, colouring sets, brooches, the 'Flip Your Wig' board game…[11]

Then there were all those 'Beetle' items which bypassed the copyright – the Beetle style jacket… Beetle stockings… Beetle badges. Brian's deal with the American company Seltaeb signed away an unbelievable 90% of the profits – eventually a better deal was negotiated, an estimated 46% coming in the Beatles' direction. Following their American triumph, a Blackpool company received an order for 10 *million* sticks of liquorice rock with the Beatle name stamped in the centre.

The merchandising opportunities Brian signed away – one estimate was as high as $200,000,000 – were catastrophic. In mitigation, with his reluctance to delegate, he was effectively flying solo into unknown territories. As early as March 1966, Llew Gardiner wrote: "The merchandising exploitation of the Beatles has not been an entirely happy story for them and manager Brian Epstein.

"Beatles merchandising has been beset by legal action (the biggest legal battle of all is going on in the United States now) and the Epstein organisation spoke to me through their solicitors. How much is merchandising worth to the Beatles? 'I can't tell you for two reasons', said the lawyer. 'Firstly I have been instructed not to and secondly I don't know'. He was however quite sure that the Beatles have suffered at the hands of the pirates. 'The trouble is that Epstein had too much to think about at the beginning… Everything was happening at once'."

"If you take the attitude that the buck stops here, it's Brian's fault", Nat Weiss, Brian's American business partner told Debbie Geller. "He never denied that he didn't know much about merchandising, no one did. But since he took the credit for so much he had to acknowledge his mistakes".

In the same *Arena* profile, Paul McCartney was quoted, "I don't think the Beatles would have been the same without him… now that I'm more aware of the way business works, I can see one or two things we really should have done better… I think he looked to his dad for business advice and his dad really knew how to run a furniture store in Liverpool. This was a little bigger than that".

Those tumultuous early weeks of 1964 left their mark, they ring down the decades. In the immediate aftermath of their arrival, the Beatles' subjugation of America was game-changing and life-altering. Many years later, after cracking the US Hot 100, the media were asking, 'Are Duran Duran / One Direction / Coldplay the New Beatles?' And you had to reply, emphatically "No!" When any one group occupies 14 places out of the American Hot 100, including the top five singles in one *week*… then let those Beatle comparisons begin.

Just let's look at those figures again: during that week of 4 April 1964, cigars fell from the lips of American record executives as they looked at their *Billboard* charts. The entire Top 5 was occupied by the Liverpool quartet, as were positions 7, 9, 14, 38, 48, 50, 52, 61, 74, 78 and bringing up the rear, the record that began it all less than two years before, 'Love Me Do' at No. 81.

Looking back over more than half a century, comparisons really are pointless. The

---

11 In their *Beatles Memorabilia Guide* (Wallace-Homestead Book Co., 1993), Jeff Augsburger, Marty Eck & Rick Rann list over '1000 Fab Four Collectibles'.

reason why that week in April 1964 remains so remarkable is that all those records in the charts were qualified by actual sales. Money changed hands in malls, marts and record stores. Purchasers had to make a physical effort and financial commitment for those precious vinyl 45s. By the end of that Beatle-tastic year of 1964, the group had opened the gates for the remaining British acts.

In July 2019, Drake landed 27 simultaneous entries on the *Billboard* Hot 100; 25 were from his *Scorpion* album plus two non-album tracks. But the majority were streamed. Few, if any, of those purchasers would have queued to buy the product instore. And the Beatles *still* hold the record as the only act to occupy the entire American Top 5 in one week.

Even prior to that all-encompassing chart conquest, for proof that the Sullivan TV show was not a flash-in-the-pan, just look at the reception accorded the Beatles at their first American concert in Washington on 11 February 1964. It is so strange to look back on it. "It was", as David Fricke wrote on the 2016 sleeve of *Eight Days a Week*, "the Cavern writ large: the group in crudely exuberant form under war-time conditions, performing in the round but without a revolving stage. The Beatles, including Starr and his drum kit, turned after every third song to face another section of the audience".

In an age of laser-lit, FX-heavy rock spectacle, it is so engaging to see publicist Brian Sommerville leaping onstage to help turn that drum platform. And boy does Ringo *pound* those drums. And witnessing the hysteria that performance aroused, I maintain that even with any Capitol financial muscle, you could not *manufacture* that sustained enthusiasm. Just look at the devotion in the eyes of those girls, reflecting a desire not quite understood. And the boys, long before the creation of a 'wannabe', those boys would also certainly sacrifice a finger or toe to *be* them.

In its attempt to try and get beneath the hysteria, *Newsweek* grudgingly conceded of that Washington performance that the group were "something more than a no-talent singing quartet inflated by the hot air of press-agentry. They are a band of evangelists … and their audiences respond in a way that makes an old-fashioned revival meeting seem like a wake".

*

The American entertainment industry was left reeling. Surely even Capitol Records were unprepared for what followed. For years in the record business, the Brill Building brand of pop had held sway on American airwaves. Then, virtually overnight, the triumphant teams of Goffin & King, Barry & Greenwich, Sedaka & Greenfield, Mann & Weil had to re-calibrate. That really had been a songwriting factory – Neil Sedaka once told me that at 1619 Broadway, they gave you a room with a piano, a piano stool and a chair for the lyricist. When the hits started coming in, they upgraded you to a room with a window.

Along with Broadway and film LP soundtracks, comedians were popular too. The neurotic, one-way phone calls of Bob Newhart had landed him two No.1 LPs in 1960. And prior to Dallas, November 1963, comedian Vaughan Meader impersonating President Kennedy on the LP *The First Family* was No.1 for three months. Allan Sherman, who remains best known for his 'Hello Mudduh, Hello Fadduh' single, enjoyed three No.1

"Where's Mal…?" Ringo turns roadie, US concert debut, Washington Coliseum, 11 February 1964

(Glasshouse Images / Alamy Stock Photo)

LPs in eight months during 1962/63. The comedian quickly cashed in with 'Pop Hates the Beatles'; set to the tune of 'Pop Goes the Weasel'. He ruefully observed of all the Beatle product available that landslide year of 1964, "To buy my daughter all of those things, I had to sell her brother…!"

Of the hundreds of Beatle tributes that year, a random sample included bluegrass performer and Carter Family enthusiast Bill Clifton, who in 1964 released 'Beatle Crazy' (actually written by Geoff 'Winchester Cathedral' Stephens and recorded in London's Denmark Street). It didn't chart, but it does make for diverting listening: a gentle, spoken country ballad, Clifton routinely cites Beatle achievements in a lilting, mocking voice, and delights at having obtained tickets to see the group perform… in *1989*! On his rip-roaring 1964 *Live at the Whisky A-Go-Go*, Johnny Rivers' cover of 'It Wouldn't Happen to Me' included a nod to the Beatles. Scott Belmer estimated there were 1,000 Beatle comedy, novelty and cash-in records, and over the years, 300 parody LP sleeves.

It was soon an entire country obsessed by the Liverpool quartet. In 2006, the UK's imaginative Ace Records released *Beatlemaniacs!!! The World of Beatle Novelty Records*. It included 'My Beatle Haircut' (the Twitters); 'My Boyfriend Got a Beatle Haircut' (Donna Lynn); and 'I Dreamed I Was a Beatle' (Murray Kellum). In the UK, the 1964 cash-in 'We Love You Beatles' was by the Carefrees. Their singer Lynn Cornell was then married to session drummer Andy White, who'd played on 'Love Me Do'. Other American releases at the time included MOR favourites Arthur Fiedler's Boston Pops Orchestra, Stu Phillips' Hollyridge Strings and Mantovani. All these orchestras released LPs which revealed the haunting melodies, too often obscured by the fans' screams.

A 1964 LP by the Crickets' Sonny Curtis was *Beatles Hits Flamenco Style*. A dozen Beatle songs were arranged by Joshua Rifkin (later to find fame adapting Scott Joplin rags for his soundtrack to *The Sting*). Elektra Records' Jac Holzman was nervous how the LP, *The Baroque Beatles Book*, would be received by the group, but Lennon was delighted "anyone who records Koerner, Ray & Glover is OK with me". The other end of the spectrum was *The Chipmunks Sing the Beatles Hits*.

America really took Ringo to its heart. There was something vulnerable about the mournful-looking drummer at the back. Early on, US teen mags were asking, 'Ringo And Hayley Mills, Is It Love?' A 1964 single, 'Ringo, I Love You' came from Bonnie Jo Mason, soon to find fame as Cher. Hannah Vettese found ten other songs devoted to Ringo alone, including Ella Fitzgerald's 'Ringo Beat'. On the back of his success in the *Bonanza* TV series, Lorne Greene's gunfighter ballad was a US No.1. The fact that it was called 'Ringo' must have helped. There were an estimated 200 Beatle-inspired releases in America during 1964 alone, of which four managed to crack the Hot 100.

One of the cultist Ringo-related singles I discovered was 'Go, Go With Ringo', a 1964 release by the all-girl Whippets. They numbered Bibbe Hansen (Beck's mother) and Jan Kerouac (Jack's daughter) in their ranks. The Beatle connection was furthered, as it was written by Murray the K's mother, Jean Kauffman.

Before they got the bit between their teeth, Lennon & McCartney cited Goffin & King as their favourite songwriters, and the Beatles included three Brill Building songs on their debut LP. The Beatles duly acknowledged their American musical heritage – Elvis, Buddy, Eddie, Fats, Jerry Lee et al. But Country & Western didn't figure much in their repertoire. Ringo's 1965 cover of Buck Owens' 'Act Naturally' was a suitable cover for a film soundtrack, especially when the other three group songwriters were exhausted. George occasionally did add the odd guitar flourish, borrowed from his idol Chet Atkins. George also provided the sleeve notes to the LP *Chet Atkins Picks on the Beatles*.

It was in 1994 that leading C&W artists paid tribute to the group in *Come Together... America Salutes the Beatles*. Willie Nelson turned in a delightful 'One After 909'. The title track came courtesy of Delbert McClinton the harmonica player who had inspired John only a few years before with his playing on Bruce Channel's 'Hey Baby'. Kris Kristofferson concluded the tribute album with a wry 'Paperback Writer'. This from the man who once so accurately sang: "each new thing the Beatles do is better than their last / but if you don't like Hank Williams, you can kiss my ass!"

In his 2000 book *Are You Ready... for the Country*, Peter Doggett discerned a C&W influence seeping into 'I'll Cry Instead' and 'I Don't Want to Spoil the Party', after the Beatles returned from their American tours with a bunch of country LPs. And in 1970, of course, Ringo's second solo album was the engaging *Beaucoups of Blues* cut in and with Nashville's finest. (Opening its review, *Rolling Stone* indicated how Ringo was regarded at this point: "Correct me if I'm wrong, but I would venture to guess that not many people … could say that they look to Ringo Starr for New Horizons in Pop Music…")

*

During that extraordinary year of 1964 America succumbed on a scale unseen since Elvis swivelled his way into notoriety eight years before. There had been successful pop stars since then, but none from Great Britain, and certainly nothing remotely on this scale. The persistent releases on various US labels maintained the momentum. It soon became apparent that 'I Want to Hold Your Hand' would be more than a single hit.

In terms of pre-Beatle press coverage for Middle America, it was Sinatra's 'Rat Pack' who exercised a perennial fascination. The swaggering, chain-smoking, Martini-style machismo of Frank, Dino and pals held the public spellbound. "For some reason that perhaps only a social historian of the future will be able to explain", wrote Richard Gehman at the time, "no group of male human beings … excites, fascinates and dazzles … the American public quite as much as Frank Sinatra and his friends". That was all about to change.

The impact on the American entertainment industry as 1964 progressed was truly seismic. It caught *everyone* off-balance. In his engaging account of the glory days of the old-style showbiz monarchs, Shawn Levy's *Rat Pack Confidential* captured some of the impact that change had on Frank Sinatra and his cronies: "What the hell had happened? In November, Jack was President, and they were making their little *Robin Hood* movie… In August, the movie came out: Jack was dead, and this bunch of kids from England with funny suits and haircuts had grabbed up five number one singles – more than Frank, Dean and Sammy had ever had in their lives combined".

Sinatra's antipathy to rock & roll was well known ("cretinous music for goons"), but the Chairman of the Board had survived the original onslaught in the 50s (even having Elvis make his immediate post-Army comeback on a Sinatra TV special) so surely he could outlast and outwit these … haircuts? On the sleeve of a 1965 album, Frank acknowledged "DJs brave enough to give me equal time in Beatleland". Sinatra's long-serving, and long-suffering, valet George Jacobs was there to witness his boss's hostility: "The Beatles were just emerging from England and big change was in the air, but Mr S thought the moptops were a stupid fad, like hula hoops and Davy Crockett coonskin caps… He didn't give them long… He wishes that Sgt Barry Sadler ('Ballad Of The Green Berets') would come and blow Sergeant Pepper into oblivion".

Sinatra did eventually succumb, and when it came to plundering the Beatle catalogue settled, natch, on 'Yesterday'. He was graceful in concert, calling 'Something' "the greatest love song of the past 50 years", though the effect was somewhat marred by attributing the song to Lennon & McCartney! And George, the song's composer, was less than keen on Sinatra's middle-eight ad-lib, "You stick around, Jack…" (though in impish mood, George did sing the ad-lib on his 1991 Japanese tour).

*

The problems Brian Epstein had faced trying to land his group a record deal in his homeland had been a draining experience; America had proved equally resistant. More so because the business had to be conducted by expensive, pre-booked telephone calls or transatlantic telegrams. For all the posthumous faults found in Epstein's management, what no one would deny was his persistence. He genuinely did believe the Beatles would be bigger than Elvis. And once they had conquered their homeland, America was next in his sights, but on his terms.

Of course, even the scattergun standards of Capitol, the Beatles' 'official' American label, could not account for such chart domination. During that hysterical year of 1964, Beatle names could be found on chart hits released by the following labels – Swan, MGM, Tollie, Vee-Jay and Atco, as well as the 'official' big-hitters on Capitol.

Capitol had been bought out by EMI in 1955, and were the first label to be offered product from its UK equivalent. The label had flourished with homegrown releases by Frank Sinatra, the Kingston Trio and Nat 'King' Cole in the 1950s; the early 60s had seen them successfully surf with the Beach Boys. But otherwise Capitol did not unduly find accord with the teenage market. There was an arrangement that every fortnight, packages of EMI releases crossed the Atlantic. But they were met by their American subsidiary with a wall of indifference. To the increasing frustration of George Martin, Capitol bracketed the Beatles along with EMIs Bernard Cribbins, the Temperance Seven and Kenneth McKellar as being unsuitable for their market.

Capitol's Dave Dexter was a dyed-in-the-wool jazz guy, and it was he who blocked US Beatles releases during 1963. His distaste for rock & roll also saw Dexter decline the services of the Hollies, Gerry & the Pacemakers, Billy J. Kramer and, most unwisely given their subsequent American success, the Dave Clark Five, for the label. This allowed early Beatle titles to be put out on the open market. Bob Spitz, in his exhaustive 2005 biography, has copies of 'Love Me Do' and 'Please Please Me' going out to "Atlantic, Columbia, RCA, London, Mercury, United Artists, all the major New York labels". The songs were met with the now-familiar indifference, which was how a small independent label was at the spearhead of the Beatles' plans to conquer the New World.

Vee-Jay was a label run out of Chicago. It was the most successful black-run, pre-Motown label. Founded in 1953, early signings included bluesmen John Lee Hooker and Jimmy Reed. They released records by Betty Everett, Dee Clark and the Impressions aimed at the African-American audience. Vee-Jay hit big with Gene Chandler's catchy crossover 'Duke of Earl', a No.1 in early 1962. By 1962 though, 30% of the label acts were white.

Vee-Jay's Ewart Abner remembered a call from a New York lawyer who alerted him to a group "who were going to be bigger than bubblegum".

The Chicago label could have altered the face of popular music if they'd honoured their contract to the letter, but a dispute over delayed royalty payments saw them lose out. That original contract bound the Beatles to the label on a five-*year* contract, which would have taken them into the *Sgt Pepper* era. One can only speculate how a tiny Chicago label could have coped with the ensuing hysteria. Indeed, would there have *been* any hysteria? Did it need the muscle of one of the American majors to propel that incredible story? In the end it was when Capitol exercised muscle, and a legal battle saw Vee-Jay lose "the Beattles" (sic). In the end, Vee-Jay did okay out of the group they had initially championed: as Beatlemania raged across the continent, the label spun their 14 Beatles songs onto four LPs, ten singles and one EP!

The label's next big act were the phenomenally successful, Italian-American Four Seasons. That explains another album which kept me baffled for years. In October 1964 an LP was released, and billed as 'The International Battle Of The Century', *The Beatles Vs The Four Seasons*. In that pre-internet era, was this a priceless collaboration? Rather, it turned out that one side was culled from Vee-Jay's *Please Please Me* LP, the other gathering Frankie Valli's group's hits.

Another label that dropped the Beatle ball was Swan records, run out of Philadelphia. It was part-owned by Dick Clark, host of *American Bandstand*, the TV show which had given house room to all 'the Bobbys'. But even the label's release of 'She Loves You' didn't make any impact on its first American release in September 1963, nearly four months before 'I Want to Hold Your Hand'. Dick Clark remembered that the song "sounded old-fashioned, real mid-50s, kind of hollow". His interest waned further when he was shown a photo of the group. Played on his 'Record Revue' slot, 'She Loves You' met with a muted but quite perceptive response from his teenage panel: "all right, sort of like the Everly Brothers and Chuck Berry mixed together".

Such was the talismanic power of 'The Beatles', that in the three months between 'I Want to Hold Your Hand' and 'Can't Buy Me Love' – Capitol's official releases – five further Beatle singles registered in the US Top. One of which – that "kind of hollow" 'She Loves You' – landed Swan a two-week run at No.1.

Much has been written about just *why* it was the Beatles who accomplished that American breakthrough. There was the music, obviously, the look, the wit and charm, but there had to be something more. There was undeniably something different about them. Teenage American fans "liked their laughter…"; "The Beatles are just so funny and nice and, well, cool…"; "Jimmy Dean was in the same class as The Beatles because he was tough".

Their every move was dutifully chronicled in the youth magazine market, among them *Confidential Teen Romances*, *Teen Times*, *Teen World*, *Hollywood Teenager*, *Teen Seventeen*, *Teen Parade*, *Modern Teen*… Their allegiance pledged to the newcomers, and promising details of "The Beatles Magic Moonlight Contest"… "The Beatles Our 'Naughty' Nights" and breath-taking revelations of how "I Kissed All Four Beatles".

The Beatles also received the accolade of appearing in DC Comics. A 1964 issue of *Jimmy Olsen* featured 'The Red-Headed Beatle of 1000 BC', with Superman himself expressing concern: "Great Krypton! Jimmy has started a **Beatle** craze here in the ancient past. He's as popular as **Ringo**". A March 1965 Marvel comic boasted 'The Human Torch and The Ever-Lovin' Blue-Eyed Thing Meet The Beatles'. Hollywood stars familiar from teenage movie outings in Liverpool now danced attendance. At a charity event in August 1965, the likes of Edward G. Robinson, Burt Lancaster, Groucho Marx, Dean Martin, James Stewart and Rock Hudson all queued up to be photographed alongside the new phenomenon.

The notoriously hard to please Jerry Lee Lewis also acknowledged them: "Thank God for the Beatles… They got rid of all the Bobbys, swept them aside like wheat before the chaff." He was referring to the bland, clean-cut US teen idols such as Bobby Vee, Bobby Vinton, Bobby Rydell, Bobby Darin… The eminent American historian William Manchester cast a caustic eye on the pop market of the period, painting a grim picture of those pre-Beatle idols: "To a striking degree, they were all alike – short youths, running to fat, who were prepared for public consumption by strenuous dieting, nose surgery, contact lenses and luxurious hair styles. And they couldn't sing… When they played in public, they would mouth the words while the records were being played over the loudspeakers".

Paul Anka had a successful career even *before* he wrote the English lyrics to 'My Way'. As well as his own teenage hits, Buddy Holly covered Anka's 'It Doesn't Matter Anymore', a landmark recording for its use of strings. Like Bobby Darin, and still only 22, Anka was one of the clean-cut kids who were blown out of the water by Beatlemania. But when I interviewed him, between jaw-dropping stories of Elvis, Sinatra, Marilyn and President Kennedy, Anka was sanguine about it all: "When I looked at my future, I was always quite… *European*. I'd go back to the States and tell them about bidets! The croissant! About four guys I saw at the Olympia in Paris called the Beatles.

"I remember [Bobby] Darin saying I don't know how we're going to survive this. All we had to look up to was the Rat Pack. What did we need to survive? We needed to put on tuxedos. We needed to become performers. And I needed to write, because I didn't believe that when my voice changed I'd be a singer – I was a writer. So, I started writing 'It Doesn't Matter Anymore'; 'The Longest Day Theme'; the *Tonight* show theme… That side of my life made me secure, that I would always have.

"As I began working Las Vegas, got to know Sinatra and those guys, I felt I was basically a student. They taught me. I said I can do this. I can stay for five years and do this. I know what I'm doing. I may not have a hit record but I can make my way. I just knew that as soon as the Beatles hit, we were wiped out."

Paul Evans had written hits for Bobby Vinton, Elvis and the Kalin Twins, and acknowledged he "saw the writing on the wall. The safe and solid world of the Brill Building and Tin Pan Alley, where I was so comfortable, was collapsing. I would continue to write and record, but I was not at the center of the pop music world anymore... I waited for the English artists to go away..."

The scale and sustained success of that overwhelming Beatle conquest of America still continues to fascinate even today. One element that I maintain played a crucial part was that their arrival came in the aftermath of the assassination of President Kennedy. A nation was in mourning, sobbing for its fallen leader but, within three months, something fresh, invigorating and positive came to shine some light into that darkness. Over the years this theory has see-sawed, with critics over-emphasising or underestimating its significance.

To my mind, it began with a fan letter from Sharon Flood quoted in Michael Braun's brilliant, fly-on-the-wall account of the Beatle rise ("you are the first happy thing that has happened to us since the tragedy on November 22. You are the first spot of joy to come to a nation that is still very much in mourning...").

Emmylou Harris was equally convinced, looking back many years later: "I fell in love with the Beatles along with everyone else, shortly after the assassination of JFK. In America, it was like the end of innocence, a terrible, horrifying thing. There was a blackness, a cloud over everyone. So when the Beatles came along with their great haircuts and joyful music, it was like the clouds parted, the sun came out and it was all right to be happy and feel innocence again".

Paul Gambaccini concurred: "The country had been in deep mourning over the assassination of John F. Kennedy", he told Spencer Leigh, "deep, deep mourning and it had really needed an up. It was such mourning that the Singing Nun was No.1 – this was like penance. Everyone wanted to be happy again and the Beatles with 'I Want to Hold Your Hand' were the first positive thing to come along".

"In America, the state of shock which followed the death of Kennedy lasted longer than in Britain", wrote historian Christopher Booker a few years later. "As the hysteria died down, a deep gloom fell over America, which was to last over two months. And then, in the first week in February, the trance was broken..."

It was just coincidence, but only five weeks before their arrival, New York's Idlewild Airport had been renamed The John F. Kennedy Airport. It would be the first piece of American land the Beatles set foot upon.

Sadly today, used to reading accounts of tragic school shootings, massacres at country music festivals and an awful rise in gun crime, you cannot appreciate the visceral shock of the Kennedy assassination in Dallas that bright afternoon of November 1963. The murder went to the heart of America, but it also cut a swathe through Europe and the UK. Kennedy's recent visits to England, France, Ireland and West Germany had been greeted with pop star rapture.

At the time of his death Kennedy *was* the future, with a second 1964 term guaranteed. Following the shooting in Dallas, his nation needed to lick its wounds and heal. Part of that healing process I do believe came with that undeniably catchy song about holding hands. It was performed by the head-shaking, cheeky and too-cute-for-words quartet from a place few Americans had ever heard of, a port city in a distant country of which they knew little.

The news filtered across the Atlantic of the Beatles' American triumph. And, like Liverpool must have felt a year before, the UK sensed we were going to have to share them with the world. The newspapers carried breathless reports of just how America was succumbing, so their return to their native soil was significant.

At the time, the only Saturday afternoon television available in the British Isles was on two black and white channels. On 22 February 1964, they were, as usual sport-heavy – ITV always seemed to be showing wrestling matches with Jackie Pallo and Mick McManus, which even to my youthful eyes never looked entirely … *authentic*. The BBC flagship was *Grandstand*, hosted by David Coleman. The afternoon-long programme covered horse racing, in-season cricket and rugby with the avuncular Eddie Waring ("'e's off for an early bath"). The afternoon highlight came with the eagerly awaited football results ("Hamilton Academicals, 1" [pause] "Celtic… 2"). However, that Saturday afternoon, such was the significance, *Grandstand* interrupted its sport to cover the Beatles' triumphant return to home turf.

There is a great Dezo Hoffmann shot, taken standing behind a grinning Ringo as the group descend the aircraft steps to be greeted by a tarmac full of photographers and fans; though Hoffman later recalled how concerned the Heathrow authorities were that so many people got onto the tarmac. The Beatles' homecoming concentrated on the estimated 10,000 screaming fans with their 'Welcome Home' banners. On home soil, no record company incentive was necessary, no financial inducement required to fabricate the return.

There is a lovely 15-minute clip in the BBC archive as a sheepskin-jacketed David Coleman respectfully greets the group as conquering heroes. Fans slept overnight in sub-zero temperatures to be present for "one of the most remarkable sights in Britain today". Coleman pointed out that these were "never before seen scenes at London Airport – apart from a Royal homecoming". But I'll bet even Her Majesty never witnessed such a welcome. Polly Elwes braved the crowd who were delighted to have them back, "they can keep Elvis if we get to keep The Beatles". Then there they are, on the aircraft steps, baffled and delighted by the sights and sounds. All descend, all clutching precious armfuls of American LPs.

Coleman's interview, conducted in a haze of cigarette smoke has its moments, of their three days off water-skiing and fishing. Of visiting Cassius Clay (later Muhammad Ali) in his training camp, prior to his bout with 7–1 favourite Sonny Liston. Lennon manages a deft, "Liston, do you want to know a secret…" plug. What I found fascinating was Ringo's reaction when asked about the incident at the British Embassy in Washington. The drummer had been savaged by someone who should have known better, snipping a priceless lock of Beatle hair. He laughs it off, before facing the camera with the timeless comment, "tomorrow never knows".

An astonishing story about that historic return surfaced in 2000. The group had been presented with ten American gold discs. These were withheld from the Beatles, Brian Epstein, EMI and NEMS. Her Majesty's Customs & Excise impounded them at the time as no one was willing to pay the import duty (perhaps £11 per disc). The reason was that customs officials ruled that the discs could not be allowed into Britain duty-free because they "quite definitely" did not meet the exemption for items "awarded abroad to any person for distinction in art, literature or sport". They lingered in the vaults until 1994 when they went on display in the Customs & Excise Museum, appropriately located in Liverpool.

Job done! Returning home from USA in triumph, 22 February 1964 –
a year before they'd been playing the Oasis club, Manchester

(Photo 12 / Alamy Stock Photo)

The *Daily Mirror* had championed the group throughout the year. Perhaps because it was established as the 'workers' paper', the *Mirror* saw them as a healthy antidote to the middle-class showbiz elite. Their return from the USA had the paper trumpeting on its front page, "Yeah Yeah USA".

Others were not so welcoming. The philosopher Bryan Magee inquired, "Does anyone seriously believe that Beatles music will be an unthinkingly accepted part of daily life all over the world in the 2000s?" Writing in the left-wing *New Statesman*, Paul Johnson warned of "The Menace Of Beatleism". Incandescent with rage at the way the group were being received by every strata of society, Johnson railed: "The growing public approval of anti-culture is itself … a reflection of youth… What were we doing at 16? I was reading the whole of Shakespeare and Marlowe". His rant was as much directed at their audience ("huge faces bloated with cheap confectionery and smeared with chain store makeup") as the group themselves. In fact, Johnson's vituperative article received the most complaints of any in the magazine's then-half-century history.

The Beatles' return from the USA marked another sea change; until then, the UK music press had a close relationship with the acts, "chummy, not cutthroat", veteran journalist Keith Altham told Paul Gorman. "When the Beatles cracked America it all began to change, as the realization hit that there was huge money involved. It became more serious: more accountants, lawyers, press agents…" For those, in the eye of the hurricane, they were, like their hero Buddy Holly, 'Changing All Those Changes'.

While 'I Want to Hold Your Hand' had been the breakthrough Beatles single in America perhaps, even more remarkably, the follow-up 'Can't Buy Me Love' notched up advance orders of an unbelievable 1,700,000…! That's nearly two *million* people buying a record they had never heard. Paul McCartney told me when he was working on a film score: "Chevy Chase told me he remembered queuing at the record shop for a new Beatle record. You had to have a chit you put in weeks ahead, and you'd be in line, like rationing!"

The plethora of product during the years of that Beatle broadside was overwhelming, and for UK listeners, it remains disconcerting listening to the American versions of the group's LPs. The juxtaposition of tracks baffled the band too – on the existing live recordings, in the between-songs chat, you can hear the group trying to work out which LP the song was from. Capitol knew that anything they released with the word 'Beatle' on guaranteed sales. It hurled them past the rivals: RCA still had Elvis, who by then was relying on the increasingly insubstantial soundtrack LPs. Columbia relied on Broadway cast albums and the Mitch Miller Singalongs while their new signings Bob Dylan and Barbra Streisand were just beginning to make an impact.

All were swept aside by Capitol's flagship signing. The label's other big signing, the Beach Boys, landed a No.1 with their *In Concert* LP. But *The Beatles Story* was the label's Christmas present. This was a double LP consisting of predominantly the spoken Beatle word, but it nonetheless managed to shift a million copies.

In hindsight, it is surprising how slow off the mark Capitol were in the wake of the Beatles' overwhelming success. They signed Quicksilver Messenger Service, the Band and Steve Miller, all whose releases received respectable reviews, but sales were relatively modest. Capitol's other big hitter was the inexplicable, and almost entirely American, success of Grand Funk Railroad. The power trio became only the second band to play

Shea Stadium after the Beatles. In 2008, Billy Joel became the final act to play Shea prior to its demolition. Paul appeared as the piano man's special guest for 'I Saw Her Standing There' and 'Let It Be'.

If such a thing were possible, the Beatles paved the way across the Atlantic, and opened the floodgates for all that followed. Suddenly tanned surfers, beefy football jocks and pomaded pop stars were old hat. America was hungry for pale, hairy Brits willing to provide a big beat. The Dave Clark Five were the first group to make an impact on the US charts immediately after the Beatles – 'Glad All Over' hit the American charts in March 1964, barely a month after the Beatles' arrival. The astute Clark soon appreciated that America was where the group's real success lay. Astonishingly for all their popularity at home, the DC5 only ever undertook one UK tour. They did make more appearances on *The Ed Sullivan Show* than any other UK group.

Such was the ubiquity of the Beatles' American success that any UK group was painted with the same brush – it made little difference where the Kinks, Yardbirds or Animals (initially promoted as 'the Beatles' buddies') came from, so long as it was the British Isles. That led to the manifestly London Dave Clark Five being touted by a trade paper advertisement as "the Mersey sound with the Liverpool beat", while Chad & Jeremy were marketed as "the Oxford sound".

Pop commentator Ian Whitcomb recalled being in a leading London record store at the time and overhearing a customer "ask for Louis Armstrong's Hot Five, only to be told 'All groups are divided into cities'". On the back of the Beatle conquest of America, John Lennon's favourite newspaper the *Daily Mail* returned to Liverpool in February 1964 and reported that the city now boasted over a thousand beat groups.[12]

America soon went not just Beatle but Anglo crazy. In Florida alone, the American Beetles, Limeys with London Sounds and the Buckingham Palace Guards flourished. One of Sam Phillips' last hurrahs at Sun Studios was to follow his son Knox's advice and jump on the bandwagon. Randy & the Radiants was the Memphis rearguard to the British Invasion. They were Searchers-soundalikes, who began recording at Sun in 1964, a decade after Elvis and at the location which went on to inspire the Beatles.

During those early American tours, while revelling in the frenzy, the four Beatles were still capable of acting as open-eyed fans when it came to meeting their idols. An encounter with Fats Domino on their first American tour in September 1964 left them dazed. They fell at his feet and serenaded the Fat Man with 'I'm in Love Again'. Carl Perkins became an intimate. Elvis' bass player Bill Black opened for them on their 1964 Tour. Chuck Berry they met in St Louis on the last tour in 1966.

The 1965 meeting with 'The King', Elvis himself, was desultory: despite their Messianic status, the Liverpudlians were nervous – Paul told me John was literally shaking at the prospect. According to the Memphis Mafia, Elvis too was nervous. He had seen off all opposition since 1956, and still not yet 30, Elvis was facing his first serious competition. He was locked into a seemingly endless series of "crappy beach and bikini movies".

---

12 Despite its impressive 21st-century sales, today the newspaper is disliked for its right-of-centre stance. Yet it remained required reading for Lennon and McCartney and is the only newspaper mentioned in a Beatles song.

He was curious about this new phenomenon, screened their two films, and agreed to a meeting. On the way out, Paul extended a cordial invitation to Elvis to visit them. It was not to be. "I'm not going up there", Elvis told his acolyte Marty Lacker, "I did my duty. I met them, and that's it".

I caught Paul once in reminiscing mood and asked him for his memories of that epochal meeting. He remembered Epstein and 'Colonel' Parker went off into a business huddle; George tried to score some dope and Ringo played pool. John and Paul tried to engage Elvis in (a little less) conversation: "I do remember we walked in and there were these girls on a sofa with Elvis, one of whom – who I think was Priscilla – scuttled off and Elvis stood up and turned the TV off with a remote control". I waited for more: the only-ever summit between the King of rock & roll and the world's most influential and widely-imitated band. "That was *it*?" I asked incredulously. "He turned the TV off with a remote control?" "Well it was pretty fucking cool for 1965," Paul laughed.

While 1963 is remembered as the high watermark of British Beatlemania, 1964 was when they became a global phenomenon. With *A Hard Day's Night* in the can, it could be screened in territories Epstein felt not fit for personal appearances, as well as saturating territories which had already succumbed.

In a sense, they had become themselves, they were the Beatles, even if they were only the Threetles 30 years too early. Tonsilitis saw Ringo having to miss Danish, Dutch and early Australian dates, so Jimmy Nicol was drafted in to the drum stool. Brian was adamant that the dates should proceed and recognised the problem: "The difficulty was finding someone who looked like a Beatle and not an outcast".

Once again, it is worth reflecting on the *scale* of the Beatles' success during that head-turning, hair-shaking period: on their 1964 Australian tour, half the population of Adelaide – 300,000 – turned out to see them as they proceeded royally in a nine-mile motorcade. It was estimated as the largest-ever gathering on the Continent. At the Liverpool premiere of *A Hard Day's Night*, 250,000 Merseysiders lined the streets to welcome them back…

The world outside Abbey Road and away from the music weeklies were keen to be seen courting the Fab Four. The politicians were hurrying to curry favour; Prime Minister, the 64-year-old Conservative Alec Douglas-Home, called the group his "secret weapon. If any country is in deficit with us I only have to say The Beatles are coming". Labour leader Harold Wilson was keen to be seen with them at a showbiz awards ceremony. Even the Duke of Edinburgh had to enter the debate. The Queen's consort was quoted as saying, "The Beatles were on the wane". A courtier responded to Brian Epstein: "Should read 'I think The Beatles are away at the moment'… Prince Philip sends his best wishes for continued success".

In 1964, just a few years before Britain was officially declared 'swinging', the British economy had been in dire straits. The Beatles undeniably helped the export trade. But even they were not enough. Within hours of gaining office, Labour Prime Minister Harold Wilson's Chancellor, James Callaghan was at his desk staring at the nation's balance of payments deficit, an eye-watering £800,000,000. His predecessor, the Conservative Reginald Maudling stuck his head round the door with a jaunty: "Good luck, old cock. Sorry to leave it in such a mess".

To help them escape the madness in May 1964, student Graham Rowe found himself a job translating for a 'Mr Leslie' (John) and 'Mr Hargreaves' (George) on a Polynesian holiday. Just getting them to the South Seas with Pattie ('Miss Bond') and Cynthia ('Mrs Hargreaves') required the sort of covert operation 007 himself would have approved of: Luton – Amsterdam – Vancouver – Honolulu. Brian Epstein devoted over a page to the operation in his autobiography. Three weeks cruising round Tabu, Tahiti and Bora Bora relieved some of the pressures of Beatlemania. Their American fans were unimpressed though. Writing to *Teen* ('Young America's Beauty, Fashion & Entertainment Magazine') 15-year-old Anne Hungerford was outraged: "They go traveling round the world with girls… How can you be loyal to boys who do things like that even if they are the Beatles".

Their work rate during those phenomenal years of Beatlemania was phenomenal. The relentless grind, the pressure not to slip, the endless creative demands, their goldfish-bowl existence. There were recording, radio and TV appearances to be slotted in. UK, US, European and Far Eastern tour dates had to be accommodated. Not even a day off was allocated on their return from that first American trip. The first film was squeezed into a hectic six weeks. The day after filming was completed, the Beatles were rehearsing a TV special. A decade later the pressure was off, looking back over a calendar year, Led Zeppelin's Jimmy Page was able to blithely inquire of a journalist: "1974 didn't really happen, did it?"

*

DJ Larry Kane travelled with the group on their first two American tours and has provided a fascinating, breathless account of American Beatlemania and its subsequent hysteria. In his book, written years later, he reflected that despite Presidential elections, wars, riots and the birth of celebrity culture… all anyone ever wanted to know was: What were *they* like? But even the seasoned Kane was surprised when the 39th President of the United States, Jimmy Carter, asked the same question.

The hysteria they aroused in their American audiences has been well documented, Larry Kane's observations catch some of that fervour. He claims that, early on, the Beatles were attracting obsessives, the fans with the thousand-yard stare which meant that *they* were the ones who Paul *really* wanted to see; that they were the ones John *needed*; that they were the only ones who could comfort George and Ringo…

The Beatles' sexual exploits are an avenue which still today is rarely visited. We can only imagine at the shenanigans. Anyone close to them was fair game from the female fans. With what was on offer, fidelity to wives and girlfriends must have been an afterthought. After years of grappling with Scouse suspender belts and Hamburg knee-tremblers, America was a guilt-free sexual paradise.

One eyewitness who spoke candidly was photographer Harry Benson, when he told Mark Beaumont in 2021: "The road crew used to pick up girls and make sure the band weren't in a room with 15-year-olds. That was very important. I remember, one night George wanted a bottle of whiskey in the hotel, so he went to the room where the road crew were – and they were all there with loads of beautiful girls. He brought the other three down to see, because the roadies had sifted out all the pretty girls! There was hell to pay…"

Outside it's America, Indianapolis, 3 September 1964
("The best view of the country is over the
blue shoulder of a policeman" John Lennon)

In his iconoclastic 1970 *Rolling Stone* interview, John compared those touring years with *Satyricon*, Fellini's ribald take on the debauchery of Ancient Rome. "John was a dedicated womanizer", journalist Chris Hutchins confirmed. "The sexual traffic flowing in and out of his hotel bedrooms exceeded that of any of the others in the group". This was just before the term groupies was applied, but looking at *Eye of the Storm*, the 2023 exhibition of Paul's photos, I was struck by how many captions featured "unknown woman backstage".

It was true, *anyone* associated with the group proved to be an irresistible magnet. John Peel was hacking out a living in Dallas in Texas. He missed out on homegrown Beatlemania, but by dint of his accent and a blatantly false "I'm never out of the Cavern, me" routine he soon became station KLIF's 'Official Beatle Correspondent'. When it was announced that "our man from Liverpool" would be making a personal appearance at a Dallas department store, Peel was mobbed. He later wrote, "It wasn't long before girls anxious for a Beatles surrogate started arriving outside my modest home… If they were anxious to sacrifice their virginity to a Man From Liverpool, it was churlish even unpatriotic of me to refuse to cooperate".

It was hard not to see how the group could *not* be tempted: young men in their early 20s, their hormones raging, libido at an all-time high, the object of national veneration. It was not just teenage girls, mature women too were literally hurling themselves at the four men. In the same way as meeting their musical idols was exciting, so was encountering screen stars: one can only imagine the throb the 21-year-old George Harrison experienced when he was courted by Jayne Mansfield. This was the girl who couldn't help it, the girl he had drooled over in Liverpool cinemas.

Soon, however, even the lure of America had palled. The accommodation was luxurious ("The group occupied a £50 a night suite overlooking Central Park", the *Daily Mail* dutifully reported). The food was quantifiably preferable to what was on offer in the old country. The sophisticated Peter Stuyvesant cigarettes were a cut above the untipped Woodbines; the Scotch & Cokes a country mile ahead of the mild & bitters found in The Grapes.

Yes, they could travel by plane instead of being squeezed into a rusty transit van, but they couldn't *see* anything of the Promised Land. Their impressions of America were from aircraft flights or through limousine windows. Any public outing was a security nightmare. Photographer Henry Grossman remembered asking Ringo whether he liked what he'd seen of America. "He took me to the window of his hotel room, pointed to a brick wall across the parking lot and said, 'That's what we've seen'. They were trapped".

They used to come alive onstage, but now, their every performance was drowned by hysterical screaming on an unparalleled scale. To cope with the insatiable demand, promoters persuaded Brian Epstein to put the group into ever-larger venues. For all the residual fame, money, sex and on-tap hedonism, the group still prided themselves as performers. But once America had succumbed, each show became a 30-minute farce. Every note, shaking head and onstage movement was greeted with a fervour which rendered every song unheard beneath a barrage of screams.

For their second *Ed Sullivan Show*, recorded in Miami, they were under the watchful eye of policeman Buddy Dresner. Visiting his family gave them a brief stab at normality:

Dresner introduced them to grilled cheese sandwiches; he took them waterskiing and to their first drive-in movie (the Elvis vehicle *Fun in Acapulco*). Looking at photos of them larking around swimming pools, I was struck by just how *pale* they were, but typical of pallid Brits abroad.

Barry Miles was at the heart of the British scene of the 1960s, and was particularly close to McCartney. He remembers Paul asking his housemate Peter Asher to rifle through the Beatle's sock drawer for something. Peter found thousands of dollars wrapped in rubber bands which the Beatle had obviously forgotten about.

As well as the almost limitless merchandising on offer in America, the look was something eager to be copied. As well as the Beatle wigs, a magazine *Beatle Haircuts* was on sale. This would allow American girls to alter their hairstyle. Until then, they largely copied from Jackie Kennedy. By 1964 teenagers were offered "Beatle Bangs, Bouffants, Bubbles Bobs and Baby-Dolls".

By the end of 1964, they really were *everywhere* – from *Mad* magazine to *I Love Lucy*; from *Dr Kildare* to the British Ambassador's residence in Washington. The December 1964 issue of *Esquire* had a cover feature by none other than Gloria Steinem – 'John Lennon: Beatle With A Future?'

On the home front, Fleet Street still couldn't get enough – with its 4,000,000+ circulation, the *Daily Express* granted them five front page covers … While in *The Beano*, Teacher serenades the Bash Street Kids in a Beatle wig, "Let me hear your two times table / That is if you are all able / Yeah! Yeah! Yeah!" The weekly comic's rival, *The Dandy* also jumped on the bandwagon: the 1 February 1964 edition cover had Korky the Cat observing 'The Fabulous Beatle Mice' and their hit "She Loves Cheese, Yeah! Yeah! Yeah!" In 1963 Paul revealed his ambition "To have my picture in *The Dandy*". It was realised in that comic's final edition in 2012.

You can access the past with such ease now, but it was odd chancing upon the 1964 edition of *Girl Television & Film Annual*. Their Top Pops were cover star Bobby Vee, Kenny Lynch, Jo Anne Campbell, Frank Ifield, Patti Lynn and Frank Kelly. Okay, so it was printed in 1963, but surely even then the impact of the Beatles must have registered in the office of Odhams Press. But yes, just sneaking in on the 'In Harmony' section on page 108 a moody picture telling readers that "this group have attained their success, not only as instrumentalists, but also singers… John, the leader of the group … likes black, steak and chips and jelly…"

Even their television appearances were different… *Around the Beatles* had them clowning around, Shakespeare-style. They performed in the round, watched over by enthusiastic fans. A ticket for the show was very strict: "No admission without a birth certificate". The Jack Good-produced programme was a ratings hit – 7,610,000 UK TV viewers tuned in, placing it comfortably in the most-watched show of the year, even beating Miss World 1964.

The group's Christmas present for 1964 was their 6th UK No.1, 'I Feel Fine', which found few favours in, of all places, *The Observer*: "A good, robust tune, but it's a bit spineless and snug compared with their earlier efforts. The best thing about it is the fascinating, far-out guitar intro. Paul McCartney's bluesy vocal on the flip, 'She's a Woman', carries rather more bite".

The Beano jumps on the bandwagon…

Such was their tidal wave of popularity, that suddenly 'pop' music was reaching out far and wide. Fleet Street was fascinated, as were the television networks. I have vivid memories of huddling round the black and white TV we owned, encased in its mahogany cabinet. For a couple of years (1964/65), ITV used to broadcast highlights of the *NME Pollwinners' Concert*, recorded at the Empire Pool, Wembley, a few weeks beforehand. Flickering black and white images of your pop favourites, unless you were lucky enough to get along to a performance, this was the only opportunity to see them *move*. There they all were, liberated from the printed page – the Beatles and Rolling Stones; Freddie & the Dreamers and the Bachelors.

Throughout the remainder of 1964 the Beatles' musical triumphs and popular success continued unabated. As the hysteria showed no sign of diminishing, their only competition was themselves. One has only to look at the comprehensive diaries of the Beatle years to marvel at their workload. Every day is chronicled, you can marvel at how hard they worked. The years between 1963 and 1966 McCartney admitted to me were "a blur". Epstein had them on the necessary treadmill of tour–single–radio session–EP–gig–TV appearance–promotion–interview–LP– single–tour date …

Then, barely a year into their rise, a feature film had to be slotted into that already bulging schedule. What was fortuitous was the timing and managing to get the film made in such a short space of time. What was even more miraculous was how well it turned out. *A Hard Day's Night* was an international phenomenon. It is forgotten that, now the film is routinely celebrated as one of the great rock & roll movies, it was originally intended as a vehicle for an LP. The American studio's prime interest was a soundtrack album. The film, envisaged as little more than a swift cash-in on a group who, the studio hoped, would still be remembered by the time of its release. In the event, United Artists soon appreciated what a goldmine they had on their hands – the *Hard Day's Night* soundtrack LP sold 1,500,000 copies in America within a fortnight, even if it was padded out with non-Beatle instrumental performances.

As with so many elements of the Beatles' success, timing was of the essence. By the time they had signed the Beatles for their 1964 film debut, the Los Angeles-based studio United Artists had tapped into a rich vein with the James Bond 007 franchise. *Dr No* had been followed by *From Russia with Love* (it opened on 10 October 1963), both of which had become global box office gold.

Bond producers Saltzman & Broccoli missed out on *both* bites of the cherry: as well as the 007 films, their Eon Productions were contracted for one non-Bond title for United Artists. Journalist Donald Zec suggested the producers might look to the Beatles for a film? Saltzman asked Broccoli, "Would you rather make a film with four long-haired schnooks from Liverpool who nobody's ever heard of when we've got Bob Hope?" The subsequent Hope vehicle *Call Me Bwana* did not unduly trouble cinematic audiences.

The immediate success of *Dr No* had made the United Artists executives look to Europe, which until then they had considered little more than a cinematic backwater. Their decision was justified by the unexpected, runaway success of the studio's 1963 *Tom Jones*. Former "angry young man" John Osborne transformed Henry Fielding's bawdy 18th-century novel into a Swinging 60s-style romp which swept that year's Oscars.

The prime Interest from the film studio in a Beatle movie was the soundtrack LP that a film would generate. United Artists Records had been launched in 1957. The label had enjoyed success with music from movies such as *The Magnificent Seven*, *Exodus*, *Never on a Sunday*, *The Pink Panther* and, particularly, the third 007 film, 1964's *Goldfinger*. So, it made perfect sense to back a low budget, black and white film about a pop group who had begun enjoying success outside their native Great Britain. But it had to be done cheaply – and quickly – to cash-in. The American youth market was notoriously fickle.

United Artists had established its own London office, and fortuitously, London was on the verge of 'Swinging'. John Boorman, who went on to helm the Dave Clark Five's own (and only) cinematic outing, *Catch Us If You Can*, recalled that buoyant period in British cinema to Peter Cowie: "During the early and mid-sixties, all these American producers were camping out in London, trying to make pictures, because there was this feeling that somehow the younger European directors held the secret of how to attract an audience. There was a huge loss of confidence in the States, in the studios". The director of the Beatles' debut film, Richard Lester, laughed, "You [could] walk down Wardour Street and Paramount will offer you a three-picture deal!"

This was confirmed by United Artists' Vice President David V. Picker: "Looking to expand United Artists' publishing and film soundtrack albums for our music subsidiary, I asked our teams of film executives in New York and London to make some recommendations for potential groups with whom we might develop a programme of low-budget features with the hope that we might strike gold.

"Our London office suggested a then-unknown group: The Beatles. We negotiated a deal with … Brian Epstein, and to say we got lucky would be an understatement".

Anticipating a hard bargain, and after witnessing the unparalleled success the Beatles were achieving around the world, United Artists' executives would have settled for the group and manager receiving 75% of the profits. They were surprised when Brian Epstein opened the bargaining saying he wouldn't settle for anything less than … 7.5%!

Typical of the pressure the group was under, the day they returned from their inaugural American tour on Saturday 22 February 1964 … jet lag, phah! The next day found them recording a TV special. The following Tuesday had them locked into Abbey Road to complete their sixth single and work on tracks for an EP. They then had to prepare songs for the soundtrack album of the film which would begin shooting barely a week after their return from the USA. But they were young and full of pep. Buoyed by their American triumph… Film stars? Sure, why not?

Time was of the essence, as was the budget. Producer Walter Shenson had moved to the UK, where he had overseen low-budget, but successful comedies, *The Mouse That Roared* (1959) and *The Mouse on the Moon* (1963). The latter directed by Richard Lester. Shenson eventually brought *A Hard Day's Night* in for a paltry £189,000. The group were lucky that director Richard Lester was behind the camera, his closeness to Peter Sellers and fellow Goon Spike Milligan – like that of their record producer George Martin – was shorthand for similar sensibilities, and cemented his standing with the Beatles.

Another good call was Liverpudlian scriptwriter, Alun Owen (1925–94). His ear caught the authentic Beatle voice, amplifying the documentary feel of their first feature. Lennon sneered that Owen was nothing more than a "professional Scouser". Owen retorted, "it was better than being an amateur one". *A Hard Day's Night* is also credited as the location for the first use of the word "grotty". Owen's script was actually nominated for an Oscar but lost out to a minor Cary Grant vehicle, *Father Goose*. Owen's *was* a good script. While the group felt it typecast their characters, it is full of memorable exchanges, such as when Robin Ray's floor manager fingers Ringo's skins, George laconically, alliteratively warns him, "He's very touchy about those drums, they loom large in his legend".

It was Owen who also presciently supplied the film's most enduring exchange. As they are crammed into a train compartment, the Beatles are confronted by a stuffy, middle-aged, middle-class passenger Richard Vernon.[13] "We'll have that thing off as well…" he snaps as Ringo starts listening to his transistor radio.[14] Paul remonstrates: "We're a community. Up the workers and all that stuff…" before being pummelled by Vernon's "elementary knowledge of the railway act". John acknowledges, "You can't win with his sort", to be met with Vernon's dismissive, "I fought the war for your sort", to be silenced by Ringo's killer, "I bet you're sorry you won."

It is a key scene from *A Hard Day's Night*. It is a pivotal moment of British cinema of the 1960s. Any parent reluctantly dragged along to see the Beatle film will have silently appreciated the exchange; the war, after all, had been over for less than 20 years. As schoolboys, the group would have been familiar with UK cinema fare of the 50s – *The Dam Busters*, *The Cruel Sea*, *Reach for the Sky*, *The Colditz Story*, *Angels One-Five*, *Ice Cold in Alex* … and dozens more. The sands were shifting though.

Cinema biographer William J. Mann wrote about the British cinema of the period. He noted that between 1960 and 1965 there were dramatic cinema closures – from 3,034, down to 1,971. Yet box office receipts held steady: "This … was not a surge of the general populace leaving their television sets… Rather, this was a movement of *young* people who … had come of age after the war, for whom the old traditions held little relevance and who were looking for new ways, new ideas, new paradigms".

I remember seeing *A Hard Day's Night* at the long-gone East Dulwich Odeon. And I mean *seeing* it, I could not hear a word issuing from the screen. From that call-to-arms opening chord (G 11th, suspended 4th), the normally staid suburban cinema exploded in a barrage of screams. I had never heard anything like it, I couldn't even spell hysteria let alone witness it. The gruff, ex-service commissionaires were equally unprepared: I remember them prowling the back of the stalls, their shouts of "Shurrup" occasionally breaking through the wall of wails, as the teenage girls screamed at their favourite Beatle.

So, with a memorable script and a sympathetic director, *A Hard Day's Night* already stands as a remarkably good film. With the added ingredient of the Beatles it races into a class of its own. For so many reasons it stands as the perfect pop movie: the group's irrepressible personalities; chock-full of cracking songs, supported by a stalwart cast of British character actors shot by a director who had the good sense to capture just what was

---

13   This was Vernon pausing briefly on his way to play the manager of the Bank of England in another top 1964 earner, *Goldfinger*. I found it funny to think that on that train, Vernon was cast to epitomise all those stuffy, ossified Great British character attitudes before the Beatles. Yet at 39, he was only the same age as Lennon when he began recording *Double Fantasy*.

14   It was what we pressed to our ears prior to the Walkman, before the iPod, before the smartphone…

unfolding before his very eyes… But primarily, of course, it is because it is … the Beatles. *A Hard Day's Night* is the champagne bottle which launched rock & roll cinema.

Seeing it again on its 40th anniversary cinema release was an experience: the opening scene of Norman Rossington opening a triangular cardboard carton of milk was positively Proustian. As was Ringo's visit to the dingy pub, with its mousy cheese sandwich, darts, shove ha'penny and skittles. Lester had to snatch location shots wherever and whenever he could, the fan network was incredibly well informed, he remains convinced there was "a mole in the production department… as suddenly 2,000 kids would appear from nowhere, like mushrooms". Everywhere *they* went was sacred ground. Choreographer Lionel Blair remembers a fan throwing herself in the car pleading, "We want to breathe the same air as they are".

Now of course, with Lester's frenzied, choppy directorial style, I appreciate the fast-cutting, frenzied debt the film owed to French new wave film, like *Breathless* and *Jules & Jim*. Too young to see such saucy X-certificate films, I was also ignorant of the black and white, Northern neo-realism influence of *Saturday Night and Sunday Morning*, *A Taste of Honey* and *Billy Liar*.

Given the exigencies of the shoot and the pressure to deliver on a manic six-week schedule, it remains a remarkable document. Prior to filming, Lester managed to spend time with the group, coming away impressed with their natural wit and camaraderie, but also overwhelmed by their claustrophobic existence. He told Peter Cowie that this impacted on the film's style: "They were told what to do and put upon, in low corridors, low rooms, low ceilings – they were hemmed in and oppressed by people telling them what to do. And at a certain point they break out and say 'Sod this'."

It was a feeling Lester amplified when he spoke at the film's 50th anniversary screening at the BFI Southbank in conversation with Mark Mawston[15]: "I saw John when they'd just come back from a trip to Sweden and I said 'Did you enjoy Stockholm? And he said 'It was a car and a room and a room and a car and a cheese sandwich'. And I thought, well that's probably half the film right there".

What came across watching the 50th anniversary DVD was how effective it was at capturing the frenzy, how the group were constantly steered, prodded and manipulated. There is a naturalism to *A Hard Day's Night*; while the group may have carped at Alun Owen's 'typecasting', there is a real spontaneity which was missing from Cliff and Elvis vehicles. And remarkably, given the studio's desire to cash-in on a quickie, pop music flash-in-the-pan, I was struck by how little music there was in the film. Sure, there are the songs which occupy the first side of the soundtrack LP, and chunks of *With the Beatles* in the disco sequence… But the music enhances and enriches the film, unlike with their clunky cinematic contemporaries. The Beatles are allowed room to roam.

Again, I was struck by how the group bond and rally against the pressure: aside from

---

15 In another of those pointless but nonetheless fascinating Beatle coincidences, Mawston spoke to *Cinema Retro* magazine, telling them that it was his grandfather's helmet Lennon borrowed when the group were disguised as policemen to gain entry to Newcastle's City Hall. His vigilant grandfather had "watched Lennon and McCartney scribbling away, sitting facing each other in the canteen… I asked if they might have been writing a song together. My granddad said 'I'm sure it was, as one of them would write a line, then turn it round and show it to the other, who would then either change a few words or write a line'". It turned out to be 'She Loves You'.

the Beatles themselves, there are few sympathetic characters in the film. On re-viewing it was surprising at just how iconoclastic a film it was. Given their fame and public image, one would have expected a jaunty, colourful extravaganza, celebrating their astonishing success. Instead what was delivered was a rather bleak, black and white account of a group struggling to get through a day in the life.

I was surprised at how much Lennon dominates the film – as the bane of Norman Rossington's life, he is allowed more time to himself, and manages to include a plug for *In His Own Write*. Poor old Paul's solo scene was cut. As well as the confrontation with the stuffy Richard Vernon, it is Lennon who subverts the screen musical tradition by interrupting Lionel Blair's well-practised routine with a sarcastic "why don't we do the show right here?" A cheeky nod to the beloved tradition of earlier, cliched Mickey Rooney and Judy Garland efforts.

For UK audiences, the casting of *A Hard Day's Night* was another element in the film's success – Wilfred Brambell was particularly astute; a familiar face from TV's *Steptoe & Son* (which began the day after the first Beatles' Abbey Road session in 1962), he was the rag and bone merchant, known to millions via his son's scornful "you dirty old man". Playing Paul's grandad, he was repeatedly introduced as "very clean". And that supporting cast… the film is filled with familiar faces from British television: washboard maestro Deryck Guyler; ubiquitous dancer Lionel Blair; irritating polymath Robin Ray; silly asses Derek Nimmo and Jeremy Lloyd; the bloke who went on to be Lord Bellamy in *Upstairs Downstairs*; the unflappable Michael Trubshawe as the casino manager; dolly birds Susan Hampshire and Charlotte Rampling pirouette in the disco…

But the most intriguing cameo is that of Kenneth Haigh, as the insufferable advertising executive who beards George about teen fashion. Less than a decade earlier, Haigh had electrified theatre audiences as Jimmy Porter, the original 'angry young man' in John Osbourne's *Look Back in Anger*. As rebellious and iconic as the group he now starred alongside, Haigh was replaced for the 1959 film by Richard Burton.

You will look in vain for Haigh's name on the credits; he insisted as being uncredited. Producer Walter Shenson recalled: "He's a Shakespearean actor and, like a lot of established people back then, he didn't want to be associated with The Beatles".

While undeniably a landmark in the history of British theatre, as influential in its own way as the Beatles were on music, *Look Back in Anger* remains a nasty, misogynistic play; Jimmy's rants may have struck a chord with audiences in the mid-50s, but the character has not worn well. Reading John Osborne's description of Jimmy in the opening stage direction, I was struck by the similarities with another Angry Young Man, John Winston Lennon: "He is a disconcerting mixture of sincerity and cheerful malice, of tenderness and freebooting cruelty, restless, importunate, full of pride, a combination which alienates the sensitive and insensitive alike… To many he may seem sensitive to the point of vulgarity. To others, he is simply a loudmouth. To be as vehement as he is to be almost noncommittal".

Road manager Norm was played by Liverpudlian Norman Rossington (1928–99), who had starred alongside Albert Finney in one of the most acclaimed of the British 'kitchen sink' films, *Saturday Night and Sunday Morning*. Rossington went on to cinema immortality by being the only actor to appear in movies with the Beatles and Elvis – the dire 'Swinging London' *Double Trouble*, which was filmed on a Hollywood backlot.

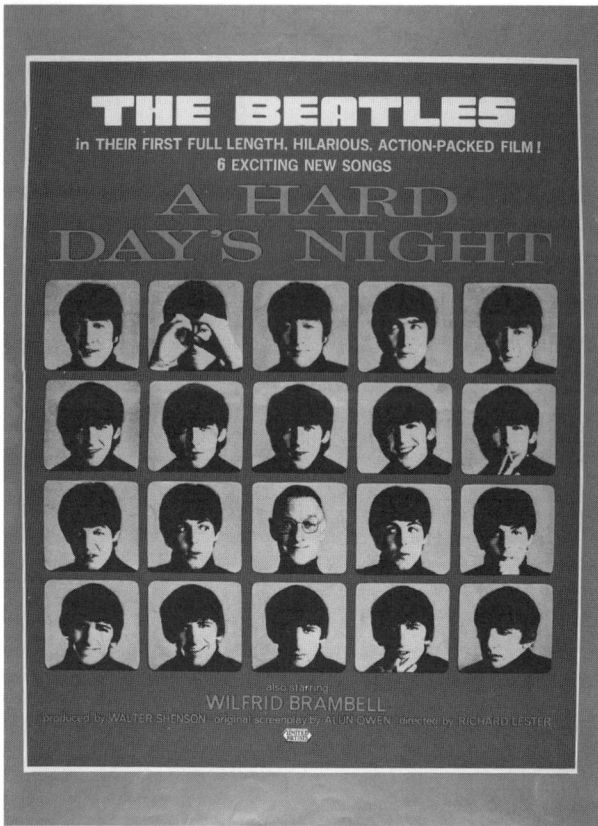

Rare campaign book which every cinema manager screening
A Hard Day's Night would have received

It was only pointed out to me recently (thanks Mr Sugar) that the soundtrack to *A Hard Day's Night* was not just the first Beatle LP to feature nothing but Lennon & McCartney compositions, but the *only* Beatle LP to feature nothing *but* Lennon & McCartney compositions (another good pub quiz question, that). The duo went into overdrive, providing seven songs for the film, and a further six for the UK soundtrack LP. Given the pressure they were under, the album contained some of the best-loved Beatle material of the era – the title track, the jaunty 'I Should Have Known Better', the poignant 'And I Love Her', perhaps the first fully realised Beatle ballad; the uplifting 'Tell Me Why' and 'You Can't Do That' and the florid folk of 'Things We Said Today'…

Cliff's previous hit *The Young Ones* (1961) was little more than a "hey, let's do the show here" version of those earlier Hollywood musicals – will Cliff and pals be able to stop demolition of their youth club? (Spoiler alert: they do). With some expense spared, the title song sequence was shot at the Ruislip Lido. *Summer Holiday* was set against more glamorous locations: a grim black and white opening sequence of rainy British seaside, explodes into colour as Cliff and the gang board their double-decker bus. Then it's off to France, Yugoslavia and Greece on a breezy journey. I have to say, it does retain its period charm on DVD, but, gor blimey, it don't half go on!

Intriguing how the Beatles' musical influence at the time, just reflect how soon it had wormed its way into the work of peers… Was it more than coincidence that Roy Orbison's 1964 No.1 'Oh Pretty Woman' incorporated a 'Yeah, Yeah, Yeah' refrain? And was the refrain of Bob Dylan's 'It Ain't Me Babe' ("No, no, no…") a reaction to 'Yeah, Yeah, Yeah'? Or Cliff Richard's jaunty 'On the Beach' from summer 1964's *Wonderful Life* was notable for the Brit Pop King's inclusion of a snatch of 'Twist & Shout'?

People forget just how successful Cliff Richard was in his pre-Beatle heyday, not just in the charts, but also at the box office. His were the films by which *A Hard Day's Night* would be judged. After James Bond, *Summer Holiday* (1963) was the second most successful film release of the year at the UK box office. Such were the crowds in Leicester Square, poor old Cliff had to miss his own premiere.

It is worth reflecting that, along with Cliff, the group's only other cinematic competitor was Elvis. Presley was then stuck on the Hollywood treadmill, live performance and rock & roll a long way back in his past. The same year that *A Hard Day's Night* arrived in cinemas saw the release of no less than *three* Presley movies – *Kissin' Cousins*, *Viva Las Vegas* and *Roustabout*. Each undistinguished accompanying soundtrack offered little in the way of value (the *Roustabout* LP weighed in at a paltry 20 minutes), or song quality.

On film, as with so many other areas of culture, the Beatles reinvented the cultural landscape. A random trawl of UK pop films prior to *A Hard Day's Night* revealed just how bad things were. *The Extra Day* (1956) has Dennis Lotis as the object of teen desire (his character's fan club run by Beryl Reid). Hearing him sing, the ubiquitous character actor Colin Gordon remarks, "modern music reminds me of a walrus sucking on a lollipop" (had he heard it, Lennon could surely have got some lyrical mileage out of that line).

Beat Girl (1960) is a dire example of just how the British film industry treated 'youth culture'. The great David Farrar, a long way removed from *Black Narcissus*, has trouble with his teenage daughter, who insists on hanging out with a group of rebellious friends in deepest, darkest Soho. The fact that Soho is represented by just one tatty film set undermines any potential atmosphere. Adam Faith is a guitar-toting, sneering Elvis wannabe while a twirling Oliver Reed is listed only as "plaid shirt". It was British Lion's attempt to draw in the *Rebel Without a Cause* crowd, but *Beat Girl* was five years too late, dramatically limp and shot in dingy black and white. A couple of years away from 007 triumphs, John Barry provided a listless soundtrack. There is, however, a great scene as Farrar returns to his Kensington home to find it taken over by Jennifer's gang – "Get out of here," Farrar roars, "you jiving, beatnik scum".

Released on the cusp of Beatlemania, 1963's *It's All Happening* faces stiff opposition as the worst of the lot… Oh no, it looks as though Tommy Steele's orphanage may have to close, unless the toothy singer can get celebrity friends like Marion Ryan, Russ Conway and Shane Fenton to help out. And, phew, in the nick of time, catastrophe *is* averted.

In case there remain any doubts about just how good *A Hard Day's Night* was – and is – thanks to the UK Freeview channel Talking Pictures TV, you get to check out the opposition. Here are the predictable cash-in vehicles for poor old Billy Fury – *Play It Cool* and *I've Gotta Horse*. John Leyton, Freddie & the Dreamers and Mike Sarne's *Every Day's a Holiday* (aka, *Seaside Swingers* in the USA, "When the dreamers meet the screamers, it's the swingin'est hit that ever swung").

Just about keeping its head above water was 1963's *What a Crazy World*. Beatle favourite Joe Brown makes a decent fist of Cockney layabout Alf Hitchens, while Susan Maughan flounders. The film also boasts a halfway decent score by Alan Klein. *What a Crazy World* has a harder edge than its contemporaries and, while Marty Wilde's bunch of teenage layabouts don't exactly match the menace of Marlon Brando's motorcycle gang in *The Wild One*, there is a grittiness on display. Light relief is provided by Freddie & the Dreamers at the local British Legion dance. Was there ever a less fashionable 60s group than this? It's not that 'the Dreamers' or 'the Dakotas' or 'the Fenmen' were … ungainly, they were just *ordinary*. Again, contrast those posed photos with those of the Beatles, and the Fabs just exude confidence and charisma. They don't look like panel beaters, postmen or dustbin men.

It is further intriguing to speculate that, had Brian Epstein been offered the opportunity for 'the boys' to appear in *What a Crazy World*, he would no doubt have seized it. There are pictures of the Beatles larking about with the film's co-star Susan Maughan and, during the early part of 1963, Epstein was desperate to get the group to as wide an audience as possible. You could just about picture the Beatles running through 'I Saw Her Standing There' or 'Love Me Do', eager to be seen on the cinema screen.

The same thought occurred when I was watching the 1964 oddball, *Saturday Night Out*. Set in and around London's Docklands 20 years before its redevelopment, the characters make their way to a chirpy Cockney pub. And who should be playing there? Why, it's the Searchers.

In the UK, *A Hard Day's Night* was the second most successful film of the year, preceded by the third 007 outing *Goldfinger*. However, it did beat *Zulu*, Norman Wisdom and Cliff in *Wonderful Life*. America too took the film to its heart. On its release, showbiz Bible *Variety* hailed its strengths as "a wacky, offbeat piece of filming, charged with vitality and inventiveness by director Dick Lester… No attempt has been paid to build the Beatles up as Oliviers… [offering] the Beatles a chance to display their sense of humor and approach to life".

Following the body blows delivered by 'She Loves You' in Britain and 'I Want to Hold Your Hand' in America, *A Hard Day's Night* consolidated the Beatles' knock-out success. Their triumphs on disc and in performance were assured, but their conquering of the world of cinema meant that they really had climbed to the top. *A Hard Day's Night* is where the Swinging 60s began, brimming with all its 'Fab' and 'Gear' energy; its sexy models and its kick against the pricks. It is the bridge between a world of pin-striped chauvinism and kipper-tied optimism. In it lies all the frenzy of the soon-to-be Sixties. In it lies the hope. They *are* the future.

*

Of course, it wasn't *just* the Beatles. For all that has been written, filmed and postulated about the 1960s, there was undeniably something in the air. The music provided the soundtrack but, in fashion new names such as Mary Quant, John Stephen and Barbara Hulanicki, models like Celia Hammond, Jean Shrimpton and Twiggy were in evidence. Those chippy photographers Bailey, Duffy and Donovan were snapping like there was no tomorrow (for them, they believed there probably wasn't).

Equally unsettling to the theatrical Establishment was the ascendancy of working-class actors led by Michael Caine, Tom Courtenay and Albert Finney. Like kids being given a Scalextric set to play with, advertising rakes Hugh Hudson, Ridley Scott and Alan Parker were sharpening their skills before moving on to bigger cinematic projects. Even hairdressers like Vidal Sassoon were given the pop star treatment.

In 1965, David Bailey boxed up the movers and shakers of the era – his *Box of Pin-Ups* contained lustrous black and white prints of, among others, Lennon & McCartney, Terence Stamp, Jean Shrimpton, Michael Caine, David Hockney and, disturbingly, the three Kray brothers. It is, in a sense, a Polaroid of a moment.

Newly arrived from Australia, Clive James later wrote: "If you believed the glossy magazines, Swinging London was a place where you could run along the King's Road and meet Julie Christie running the other way. People you knew, or anyway people known by people you knew, were working as extra in Antonioni's *Blow-Up*... The barriers were down, the hunt was up, the fame was afoot. Actually, it wasn't quite like that. The youth scene consisted, as it always had, of awkward parties with alcohol still the strongest stimulant... The music really *was* good. Every new Beatles LP moved things on to a new plane of rhythmic sensuality as if we were all ascending from floor to floor in a transparent building that swayed more as you climbed higher".

Yet, somehow, still, it is *A Hard Day's Night* that remains emblematic of those changes. The look, the pace, the irreverence, the *energy* that fuelled that most dissected of decades are all contained in those exuberant 90 minutes. In 1979, Walter Shenson was approached by United Artists regarding *A Hard Day's Night*. "It was in the contract that with these low budget pictures that the producer got the rights back after 15 years", he told Gillian G. Gaar. "I received a letter from United Artists asking me what to do with the negative and the prints... I said 'Keep 'em. Why don't you just keep distributing the picture?' And their attitude was 'Oh no, they're all finished by now...'"

And yet, for all that Beatle lurch forwards, I still find it fascinating how linked to the past they were… It is extraordinary to find in the pages of *Record Collector* pictures of Beatle singles as 78 rpm releases! In the UK, EMI and Decca had deleted 78 rpm recordings from their catalogues in June 1962, coincidentally the month the Beatles auditioned at Abbey Road. Those breakable 78s were what you heard Bing Crosby, Winifred Atwell and Alma Cogan on, not the *Beatles*. Not geared for production of 7", 45 rpm vinyl, as late as 1965 Argentina, Colombia and the Philippines were also producing the old-fashioned discs. India alone released 20 Beatle 78 rpm releases between 1963 and 1965. Their popularity ensured by the fact that they could be played on wind-up gramophones in the country's predominantly rural areas. Rock On's Ted Carroll remembers selling ten Beatles 78s to Elton John, who had a jukebox specifically to play the shellacs.

In cinemas, for a while, 007 and the Fabs were joined at the hip – *Dr No*, lest we forget, had been premiered the same week as 'Love Me Do'. *Goldfinger*, the third Bond adventure, opened a couple of months after *Hard Day's Night*. But, this time, the secret agent had lost his fondness for the Fabs, remarking on drinking unchilled champagne, "That would be like listening to the Beatles without earmuffs". Incidentally, Ian Fleming's wife Ann, who was notoriously snobbish and extremely sniffy about her husband's success with his 007 books, nicknamed her husband 'Thunderbeatle'. The link between the spy and the group was evident on the cover of the first issue of the popular UK *Rave* magazine in 1964. The Beatles – natch – were the cover stars, all sporting 007 badges as the magazine boasted a new "power-packed Ian Fleming story" featuring James Bond.

The studio had been concerned that the lucrative American audience would not comprehend the Beatles' Liverpudlian accents on screen. Paul later told Roy Carr: "We said look, if we can understand a fuckin' cowboy talking Texan they can understand us talking Liverpool." I was reminded, years later at a screening in London of *Slade in Flame* – a film which many critics (well, alright, Mark Kermode) regard is as good as *A Hard Day's Night* – Noddy Holder introduced the film, laughing that on its American release, the distributors were concerned about the group's Brummie accents. We sophisticated metropolitan critics chuckled, then found ourselves scratching our heads at the almost incomprehensible Black Country dialogue.

A Hard Day's Night at least gave the Beatles breathing space. It could be screened in territories yet to be conquered, or shown in those which had already succumbed. Alongside the publication of Lennon's first book, *A Hard Day's Night* added another string to an already bulging bow. But more, and still *more* was required during the hectic frenzy of 1964.

*

In Britain, it could be controlled – signed to Parlophone, under the watch of Brian Epstein, only three Beatles single releases during 1964 were sanctioned. Ironically, during that all-conquering, world-beating year, for the first time ever, on 7 March 1964, the official UK Top 10 singles chart was occupied entirely by UK acts – and remarkably (amidst the Bachelors, Stones and Tremeloes) the Beatles weren't among them.

They were, of course, still on that tour–TV–radio treadmill, with any downtime devoted to recording under the watchful eye of George Martin. Astonishingly, the producer

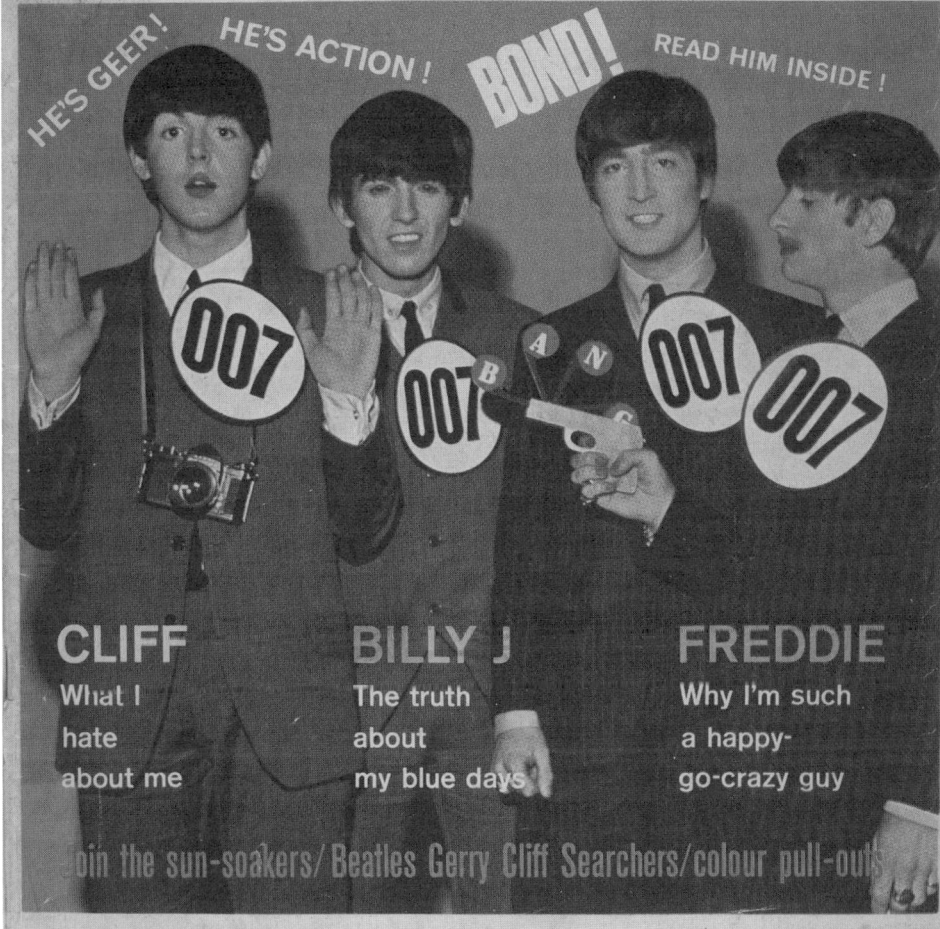

Rave 1964, author's copy, George's eyes inexplicably blacked

remembered his only "real row" with the Beatles was when they refused to record German language versions of their hits in Paris early in 1964.

In fairness, Martin himself was under a lot of pressure too. He was also producing records by Gerry & the Pacemakers, Ella Fitzgerald, Alma Cogan, Billy J. Kramer and Cilla Black, as well as getting those German-language Beatle versions in the can. A magazine profile of him at the time revealed he was supervising Matt Monro's six *Eurovision Song Contest* entries before flying to New York where he was intending to make "live-concert recordings at Carnegie Hall with both Shirley Bassey and The Beatles".

In America, the stampede ran unchecked – *Billboard* recorded an incredible 19 Beatle singles in their charts during those tumultuous 12 months, including four No.1s. Then of course there were those LPs which for years baffled fans on both sides of the Atlantic – bits of *Please Please Me* and *With the Beatles* were grafted together to produce hybrids such as *The Beatles Second Album* or *Something New*.

As a taste of the truly dire state of American pop, while the Beatles were making their initial impact on the marketplace, you are directed towards the Serendipity Singers. A close-harmony group, their jovial singing style was dictated by the Glee Club and prolonged exposure to the breezy singalong efforts of Mitch Miller & the Gang. 1964's 'Beans in My Ears' was their second hit, a trite antidote to the melancholic protest of Bob Dylan; the sublime greatness of Motown and seismic pop of Phil Spector.

Eventually, of course, the homeland of rock & roll was determined to find 'the American Beatles'. Record labels grew desperate as they steeled themselves against the British Invasion. In hindsight, there were few real rivals: the Byrds went ahead with their jingle-jangle brand of folk-rock, which actually owed a heavy debt to the Beatles' Liverpool contemporaries, the Searchers. But with their compelling harmonies, and unrivalled access to the songs of Bob Dylan, the Byrds were strong contenders.

Like so many of his generation, Greenwich Village stalwart John Sebastian was spellbound by what the Beatles brought back home. So much so that he formed his own quartet. Much of the success of the Lovin' Spoonful (aside from Sebastian's own engaging 'Daydream' and 'Summer in the City') was the group's 'own Ringo'. Zal Yanovsky was recruited as much for his resemblance to the English drummer as his own guitar-playing abilities.

And, of course, there were the Beach Boys. In his memoir, Tony Barrow intriguingly recalled that prior to their American breakthrough, and uncertain of how the American marketplace would initially respond to the British group, Capitol suggested the Beatles as the opening live attraction for the label's other group, the Beach Boys.

While I would happily testify to the genius of Brian Wilson, the Californians suffered from a worrying lack of quality control. It's a mystery as to why some of their early affecting, and effective, albums were marred by such juvenilia as '"Cassius" Love Vs "Sonny" Wilson', 'Our Favourite Recording Sessions' and 'I'm Bugged at My Ol' Man'. On LPs, it is inconceivable to think of the Beatles of the period sanctioning songs such as 'Be True to Your School' or 'All Dressed Up for School'.

And sublime as the music on *Pet Sounds* is… that *cover*…!

I suppose as principal songwriter, it was the enormous pressure on Brian Wilson, with often as many as five LPs being prepared, recorded or released every year. Not much wonder that, on 23 December 1964, Brian suffered the inflight breakdown which led to his taking a writing and production backseat rather than a performing role. He had acknowledged that "the Beatles had eclipsed a lot of what we'd worked for". So, it was in his new offstage role that he prepared what many regard as the first 'grown-up' album from the Californians, *Beach Boys Today!* (containing the flawless 'When I Grow Up', 'Help Me, Rhonda' and the Fab-influenced 'Dance Dance Dance'). It was, however, marred, inexplicably ending with the pointless fly-on-the-wall 'Bull Session with Big Daddy', which found the group reminiscing about their recent European tour.

Even with the strain removed from performing, the pressure remained on Brian to supply product – the Beatles now had three in-house songwriters. November 1965's *Beach Boys Party!* allowed Brian to briefly take his foot off the pedal – among the album's cover versions, and as a testament to their ubiquity, three Beatle songs were included. But, by the time of its release, Brian was planning the album which would see the Beach Boys overtake their Liverpudlian rivals…

Despite the scale of their popularity in America, the Beatles were poorly served by the music industry establishment, notably the conservative National Academy of Recording Arts & Sciences (the Grammys). The 1964 awards gave precedence to 'Girl from Ipanema' over 'I Want to Hold Your Hand' for 'Record of the Year'; *Getz/Gilberto* over *A Hard Day's Night* or *Meet the Beatles!* for 'Album of the Year'; 'Hello Dolly' over 'A Hard Day's Night' as 'Song of the Year'.

The Beatles *did* see off Petula Clark, Astrud Gilberto, Antonio Carlos Jobim and Morgana King as 'Best New Artist'. They also triumphed in the 'Best Performance by a Vocal Group' category. What must have really stuck in the collective craw was to find Petula Clark's 'Downtown' winning 'Best Rock & Roll Recording'. Discovering that the Academy awarded 'Best Engineered Recording – Special or Novelty Effects' to *The Chipmunks Sing the Beatles* probably didn't cause many champagne corks to be popped either. But then, in his comprehensive book on the Grammys, Thomas O'Neil pointed out: "The bottom line is that … the 5th Dimension have won more awards than the Beatles". In 1968, *Sgt Pepper* became the first rock – indeed *only* Beatles LP – to win 'Album of the Year'.

As if they cared; the group had other priorities. Nineteen sixty-four found them taking on the world, with their first American tour, as well as an extensive trawl round the UK. There were also dates in Canada, Denmark, Holland, Hong Kong, Australia, New Zealand and Sweden. It was there that the group made a lasting impact on another impressionable teenager. Bjorn Ulvaeus remembered meeting his future Abba songwriting partner Benny Andersson: fuelled on 'the Beatle drink', whiskey and Coke, they "got out our guitars… went into a park and sat under some big oak trees singing Beatles songs together until the sun came up".

What of course remains remarkable is not only the quantity of Beatle material produced during that hectic period, but the *quality*. The *Hard Day's Night* soundtrack alone should have been deemed sufficient, but the demand was always for more. The machine demanded its sacrifice, and, besides, no one was sure how long this would all last. So pump 'em out… 'Can't Buy Me Love', the *Long Tall Sally* EP … 'I Feel Fine'.

Then, to satisfy the Christmas market of 1964, *Beatles for Sale* was handed to UK fans.

At the time, of course, it was a Fab new album from the Fabs, and indeed, does include some of their most beguiling work, like 'Baby's in Black' and 'I'll Follow the Sun'. Indeed, Derek Taylor was not wide of the mark when he suggested in the sleeve notes that 'Eight Days a Week', 'No Reply' and 'I'm a Loser' were "seriously considered" as 1964 Christmas singles. But in hindsight, from the weary faces pictured on the cover, to the Chuck Berry, Little Richard, Buddy Holly and Carl Perkins' cover versions, it was obvious that the strain was beginning to take its toll on the treadmill.

But such was the wave of enthusiasm for anything Beatle-related, the contemporary reviews were unreservedly enthusiastic ("The latest package from the Beatles is worth every penny asked… overflowing with absorbing and distinctive Beatle trademarks", *NME*… "the boys don't limit their tempos to the medium kind like they did for most of *A Hard Day's Night*", *Disc*… "This is an album that will probably go down in pop posterity", *Record Mirror*).

Then there was the Christmas residency at Hammersmith Odeon. No slack was allowed, and even before they finished their theatrical run, the new year of 1965 had begun with the usual frenzy of recording.

The pace was unremitting. I remember a press officer in the 1990s telling me his charges rebelled at being told they had to undertake a photo shoot *and* an interview on the same day. Just look at Barry Miles' or Mark Lewisohn's chronicles of what was expected of the Beatles during those turbulent times. But they were young, full of pep, bursting with vim and vigour, only too happy to have swapped Allan Williams' overloaded transit for state-of-the-art limos.

What is too often overlooked once you scrape away all the pressure is how they were expected to flourish artistically in that hermetic bubble. It has been said many times that every new Beatles release at the time was greeted with amazement at the time – "How are they going to top *that*?" But, dutifully, blessed with the harmonious Lennon & McCartney partnership, they did. Early on, Tony Barrow had assured fans that "their own built-in tunesmith team … has already tucked away enough self-penned numbers to maintain a steady output of all-original singles until 1975!" That, coupled with the emergence of George as a songwriting force and the creative wisdom of George Martin ensured that the well need not run dry.

Of the group's two principal songwriters, I like to think of them as rooms… John's would be cluttered, magazines, books, overflowing ashtrays, tape recorders sprawled across every available surface, cigarette burns scarring every desktop. He would spend many fruitless hours sifting and sorting until he found what he wanted. Paul's would be a more orderly space: books on shelves, cigarettes extinguished in ashtrays, newspapers folded, lyric ideas in ringed notebooks. Paul could find what *he* was looking for within minutes, chaos and creation never sat well with McCartney. But of course, it was that fruitful *collaboration*, that collision which led to the Beatles' canon as we know it. Those 'eyeball to eyeball' collaborations in Forthlin Road which had been replaced by hotel rooms during those long hauls up and down the UK. Then time devoted to actual 'songwriting sessions' as John and Paul edged up the property ladder.

In later, better days, Paul would swoop down to Weybridge in his Aston Martin for writing days, each one chipping in words, phrases, chords until there was something they

Please Please Me

THE BEATLES

■ GEORGE HARRISON (lead guitar) **■ JOHN LENNON** (rhythm guitar)
■ PAUL McCARTNEY (bass guitar) **■ RINGO STARR** (drums)

SIDE ONE

1. **I SAW HER STANDING THERE**
   (McCartney-Lennon)
2. **MISERY**
   (McCartney-Lennon)
3. **ANNA (GO TO HIM)**
   (Alexander)
4. **CHAINS**
   (Goffin-King)
5. **BOYS**
   (Dixon-Farrell)
6. **ASK ME WHY**
   (McCartney-Lennon)
7. **PLEASE PLEASE ME**
   (McCartney-Lennon)

SIDE TWO

1. **LOVE ME DO**
   (McCartney-Lennon)
2. **P.S. I LOVE YOU**
   (McCartney-Lennon)
3. **BABY IT'S YOU**
   (David-Williams-Bacharach)
4. **DO YOU WANT TO KNOW A SECRET**
   (McCartney-Lennon)
5. **A TASTE OF HONEY**
   (Scott-Marlow)
6. **THERE'S A PLACE**
   (McCartney-Lennon)
7. **TWIST AND SHOUT**
   (Medley-Russell)

Recording first published 1963

Pop picking is a fast 'n' furious business these days whether you are on the recording studio side listening out, or on the disc-counter side listening in. As a record reviewer I find myself installed halfway in-between with an ear cocked in either direction. So far as Britain's record collecting public is concerned, The Beatles broke into earshot in October, 1962. My natural hometown interest in the group prevented me taking a totally unbiased view of their early success. Eighteen months before their first visit to the EMI studios in London, The Beatles had been voted Merseyside's favourite outfit and it was inevitable that their first Parlophone record, LOVE ME DO, would go straight into the top of Liverpool's local hit parade. The group's chances of national chart entry seemed much more remote. No other team had joined the best-sellers via a début disc. But The Beatles were history-makers from the start and LOVE ME DO sold enough copies during its first 48 hours in the shops to send it soaring into the national charts. In all the busy years since pop singles first shrank from ten to seven inches I have never seen a British group leap to the forefront of the scene with such speed and energy. Within the six months which followed the Top Twenty appearance of LOVE ME DO, almost every leading deejay and musical journalist in the country began to shout the praises of The Beatles. Readers of the New Musical Express voted the boys into a surprisingly high place via the 1962/63 popularity poll . . . on the strength of just one record release. Pictures of the group spread themselves across the front pages of three national music papers. People inside and outside the record industry expressed tremendous interest in the new vocal and instrumental sounds which The Beatles had introduced. Brian Matthew (who has since roped in The Beatles to many millions of viewers and listeners in his "Thank Your Lucky Stars", "Saturday Club" and "Easy Beat" programmes) describes the quartet as *visually and musically the most exciting and accomplished group to emerge since The Shadows*. Disc reviewing, like disc producing, teaches one to be wary about making long-term predictions. The hit parade isn't always dominated by the most worthy performances of the day so it is no good assuming that versatility counts for everything. It was during the recording of a Radio Luxembourg programme in the *EMI Friday Spectacular* series that I was finally convinced that The Beatles were about to enjoy the type of top-flight national fame which I had always believed that they deserved. The teen-audience didn't know the evening's line-up of artists and groups in advance, and before Muriel Young brought on The Beatles she began to read out their Christian names. She got as far as John . . . Paul . . . and the rest of her introduction was buried in a mighty barrage of very genuine applause. I cannot think of more than one other group — British or American — which would be so readily identified and welcomed by the announcement of two Christian names. To me, this was the ultimate proof that The Beatles (and not just one or two of their hit records) had arrived at the uncommon peak-popularity point reserved for discdom's privileged few. Shortly afterwards The Beatles proved their pop power when they by-passed the lower segments of the hit parade to scuttle straight into the nation's Top Ten with their second single, PLEASE PLEASE ME.

This brisk-selling disc went on to overtake all rivals when it bounced into the coveted Number One slot towards the end of February. Just over four months after the release of their very first record The Beatles had become triumphant chart-toppers!

Producer George Martin has never had any headaches over choice of songs for The Beatles. Their own built-in tunesmith team of John Lennon and Paul McCartney has already tucked away enough self-penned numbers to maintain a steady output of all-original singles from now until 1975! Between them The Beatles adopt a do-it-yourself approach from the very beginning. They write their own lyrics, design and eventually build their own instrumental backdrops and work out their own vocal arrangements. Their music is wild, pungent, hard-hitting, uninhibited . . . and personal. The do-it-yourself angle ensures complete originality at all stages of the process. Although so many people suggest (without closer definition) that The Beatles have a trans-Atlantic style, their only real influence has been from the unique brand of Rhythm and Blues folk music which abounds on Merseyside and which The Beatles themselves have helped to pioneer since their formation in 1960. This record comprises eight Lennon-McCartney compositions in addition to six other numbers which have become firm live-performance favourites in The Beatles' varied repertoire. The group's admiration for the work of The Shirelles is demonstrated by the inclusion of BABY IT'S YOU (John taking the lead vocal with George and Paul supplying the harmony), and BOYS (a fast rocker which allows drummer Ringo to make his first recorded appearance as a vocalist). ANNA, ASK ME WHY, and TWIST AND SHOUT also feature stand-out solo performances from John, whilst DO YOU WANT TO KNOW A SECRET hands the audio spotlight to George. MISERY may sound as though it is a self-duet created by the multi-recording of a single voice . . . but the effect is produced by the fine matching of two voices belonging to John and Paul. There is only one 'trick duet' and that is on A TASTE OF HONEY featuring a dual-voiced Paul. John and Paul get together on THERE'S A PLACE and I SAW HER STANDING THERE: George joins them for CHAINS, LOVE ME DO and PLEASE PLEASE ME.

TONY BARROW

USE EMITEX CLEANING MATERIAL
The use of "EMITEX" cleaning material (available from Record Dealers) will preserve this record and keep it free from dust.

TRADE MARK OF THE PARLOPHONE Co., LM.

LONG PLAY 33⅓ R.P.M • **E.M.I. RECORDS LIMITED**
(Controlled by Electric & Musical Industries Ltd.)
HAYES · MIDDLESEX · ENGLAND
Made and Printed in Great Britain

Printed and Made by Ernest J. Day & Co. Ltd. London PMC 1202 PCS 3○

Author's copy, *Please Please Me*, underlined
'all-original singles from now until 1975!'

were satisfied with, which they would then lay on George, Ringo and George Martin. Paul told Miles he and John allowed themselves a three-hour limit during those visits, and if nothing came, on to the next. He said that they never took drugs when writing, though when pleased with the results, would reward themselves with a joint.

To Paul Du Noyer, he admitted, "writing music in the beginning was just a way to avoid covers because all the other bands knew all the other songs, and we wanted something individual. That's what started Lennon and McCartney… It wasn't some hugely artistic motive. Pretty mundane motives really, just to have songs the other bands couldn't sing before we went on, and then to get a swimming pool, get a car. Very shallow motives. Then you started to realise there was more to it…"

Much of the process Paul went on to reveal in his *Lyrics* book. In all our conversations, I was always careful not to invoke 'The Beatles'. I was there to hear him talk about his latest project. But I always had the sense to remain silent if he did open up. At one of our meetings, I remember Paul delighted at dissecting the mechanics of his craft: "The basic thing you have to have is a tune that hasn't been heard before, words that haven't been said before. If you've been doing it for a few years, all those things are automatic. But then you try and make it something more than that. There's another area then. To try and make it special for yourself. The rules in that area are not so well defined. What can bring that little speck of fairy dust is very diverse, there are millions of ways of reworking it, leaving it, changing one line, changing it all. I'm never really satisfied, that's the other slight problem, unless it jumps up at you and says 'I'm finished'."

He became very animated, leaning across the table, eyes widening as the years peeled away: "I remember John bringing in 'Girl' that we'd just written the week before. I remember coming into Abbey Road, Number Two, sort of summer-ish… I'd just come back from a holiday in Greece so I was all bazouki-ed out, hence the guitar sound on the record, that's my Greek holiday creeping in there.

"John and I arrived at the studio, midday sometime, with George Martin and Geoff Emerick, George and Ringo, and all of them saying, 'OK, what are we going to do?' And the great thing I realised, shit, the producer didn't have an idea what we were throwing in… the other two guys in the band didn't know… It was like you'd written it on the spot for them, and you can't get any fresher than that".

*

For the Beatles, 1965 was *another* of those watershed years. In no small part because of them, the outside world was altering as strikingly as the music the group was making. It's the year when Kenneth Tynan calculatedly became the first person to say "fuck" on British television… Jean Shrimpton shocked in her miniskirt… Boutiques proliferated along the King's Road and down Carnaby Street… *Poets of the World* sold out the Albert Hall… Bob Dylan went electric… The end of an imperial era was marked by the death of Sir Winston Churchill… More countries peeled away from the British Empire and into Commonwealth… "'Beatle' Hair Is Danger In Factories", reported the *Daily Telegraph*… And for the first time ever, Liverpool FC won the FA Cup.

Under intense pressure to tour, to record, to film, to broadcast… inevitably the demand took its toll. Three of the four *Long Tall Sally* EP tracks were covers, as was nearly half of *Beatles for Sale*. Of the original material, and given the pressure, I'm afraid I do regard their late 1964 to mid-1965 output as below-par. While 'I Feel Fine' is revered for its innovative use of feedback, it lacks the spontaneous joy of earlier releases, it sounds contrived. 'Ticket to Ride' always struck me as one of their more leaden efforts, just lumbering along. 'Day Tripper' sounded like it was knocked off to meet a deadline. Only 'We Can Work It Out' carved a fresh furrow; a waltz-like half-ballad which was defiantly at odds with anything else coming out of your transistor radio that Christmas of 1965.

At this stage, while there were tours, film projects and business decisions to be made, Brian Epstein was very much involved on a day to day basis.

Such was his status, Brian even found himself edging into the limelight as a TV host. During 1965 he was filmed in London introducing UK acts (Wayne Fontana, the Moody Blues, the Band of Angels) to American audiences on the weekly *Hullaballoo* show.

In April 1965, Brian also hosted an event at London's Talk of the Town, the bastion of the country's traditional showbusiness establishment. It was to celebrate the third anniversary of NEMS. It was another string to his bow when Brian had wrestled Beatles' UK tour promotions away from Arthur Howes and Tito Burns. The tours too soon came under the NEMS umbrella. So as well as "their own built-in tunesmith team", music publishing and a handle on UK live appearances, North Eastern Music Stores had made remarkable progress.

"This is a young company", the lavish programme thrilled, "staffed by young men and women whose experience has grown alongside that of their organization". Funny to think that only three years later, when the Beatles launched their own organisation, Apple, they likened it to "Western Communism".

For all their global celebrity and status, while they were regarded – long before the dread phrase came into currency – as 'National Treasures', even Brian must have been surprised at the next hurdle the group overcame. In June 1965, it was announced that – Shock! Horror! – a pop group would become Members of the Most Excellent Order of the British Empire. It was, admittedly, the lowest of the three honours, ranking below a CBE and OBE. It was undeniably a ploy by the newly-elected, 48-year-old Harold Wilson to court the youth vote (though back then, only those over 21 were eligible to vote).

Wilson's decision predictably sparked outrage, his thorn-in-the-side colleague Tony Benn MP confided in his diaries: "no doubt Harold did this to be popular… I think Harold Wilson makes the most appalling mistake if he thinks that is the way to buy popularity".

The bitterest reactions came from those who had been ennobled for wartime service. These were not necessarily crusty old Colonel Blimps. Many who complained would 'only' be in their mid-40s. One estimate has letters two-to-one against the award to the Beatles. There were reports that medal holders protested outside Buckingham Palace, throwing their medals over the railings. Others appreciated it was in recognition of the group's contribution to British industry; the lucrative export field and their own contributions to the country's economy – the level of income tax the Beatles' paid was eye-watering. The MBE was not an empty gesture. Unlike, many felt, King Charles III's award to TikTok sensation Blackpink in 2023.

Their manager's exclusion was noted, but as ever it was the wry George who observed

A slightly bemused Mr Brian Epstein, Saville Theatre, 26 October 1965

that the letters equally stood for 'Mr Brian Epstein'. Supporters of the award appreciated the group's raising "'pop' music to a degree of sophistication… never before attained". The group themselves took it all in their stride. The final decision I am sure would have been taken to please their parents. The recognition would have repaid the years of concern the fathers, mothers and aunts had endured while the group struggled in dingy cellars.

If the group were baffled by their rise, their parents were shell-shocked at the scale of their success. John's Aunt Mimi remained sceptical, while Jim McCartney had actively encouraged Paul's musical ambitions. The Harrisons and Starkeys had long championed their children. Like all dutiful pop stars of the era, the Beatles saw that their parents were looked after. They bought them up-market properties away from the Liverpool grime. Hunter Davies dutifully visited the Harrisons, Jim McCartney and the Starkeys, and found "The fame of their sons' fame had taken them completely by surprise… Ringo's mother, Elsie, and his stepfather Harry were the most stunned by it, almost frightened, caught like rabbits in the searchlight of fame".

Of those medals, much fun was had in 2023 when Beatle autographs were auctioned by Joy Goodman. Her dad George was getting his MBE on the same day and dutifully asked for Beatle signatures. His opinion no doubt shared by many, "though I don't know what she sees in you". George Goodman got his medal for his dutiful career as a Birmingham fire prevention officer, though as press reports chortled there was no evidence that he liked to keep his fire engine clean.

In America, a different type of distinction was bestowed. At the conclusion of the 1964 World's Fair in New York, in October 1965 a time capsule was buried. When opened in 6965AD, it was intended to give the inhabitants of Planet Earth a flavour of where Mankind had got to midway through the 20th century. Among the contents were tranquilisers, cigarettes, credit cards, the Bible, a bikini and … a copy of 'A Hard Day's Night'. Not everyone was convinced. Columnist Walter Johnson felt that the group's contribution "could be that they will be remembered for their rags-to-riches type success story… if this generation is lucky, the people that find the capsule will have no means which to listen to the Beatles of 1964".

Nineteen sixty-five was the year they took on Europe, with gigs in France, Italy and Spain. Even the novelty of playing a bullring couldn't mask the monotony of the same 12-song set. But it was also the year when the Beatles upped their musical ante, and that was largely due to Bob Dylan. The group had been aware of the singer-songwriter while in Paris at the beginning of 1964, and had followed his career closely. And enviously. They were struck that Dylan patently didn't give a fuck – storming off *The Ed Sullivan Show* when the producers questioned his choice of material. Rarely did the Beatles rile the press; Dylan defiantly refused to play the interview game with journalists ("I don't have to explain my feelings, I'm not on trial here"… "I'm just trying to answer your questions as good as you can ask them").

Virtually singlehandedly, Dylan had also been busy elevating the pop lyric since 1963. Few would tackle the scope of his compositions. The dystopian sweep of 'A Hard Rain's A-Gonna Fall' or challenging scope of 'Chimes of Freedom'. Then again, no one had written love songs as coruscating as Dylan's.

Dylan had been keeping a weather eye on the English group too. His closest biographer

Robert Shelton recalled Dylan spellbound by the Beatle harmonies and the "I get high" boast of 'I Want to Hold Your Hand' (typically, he misheard the line). Such was the Beatle power by association that American advertising for Dylan's records boasted, "Dylan: Bigger Than The Beatles In England!... Has Been named The Strongest Influence On The 'Mersey' Sound" (It also rather bafflingly claimed that the singer had broken "All Attendance Records in the British Empire").

In 2010, *Uncut* reader Stephen Conn remembered his mother telling him about seeing the Beatles at their second US performance at Carnegie Hall in 1964. She recalled a boy with curly hair and nondescript green jacket politely getting up to let her pass. She later recognised him as Bob Dylan. The singer-songwriter had appeared at Carnegie Hall in October 1963, but the Beatles were the first 'pop' act to play the prestigious venue, an accolade denied even to Elvis Presley.

Pointedly, it was Dylan who loved to turn them on. At an encounter of 28 August 1964, engineered by journalist Al Aronowitz, Dylan rolled a joint and passed it round. Rather than lose the hip high ground, later the group claimed to have smoked dope before then. For Aronowitz, a long-time Dylan supporter, "I was as proud and happy as a Jewish matchmaker... This was a marriage made in Heaven. I knew I was stage managing a major event, certainly in the history of pop and maybe even in the overall history of culture".

In the style of a medieval monarch, John passed the joint to Ringo for first blast before succumbing. Even the subdued Brian Epstein couldn't contain his glee after his first joint. Laughing uproariously, "I'm on the ceiling..." High as kites, giggling explosively, they were convinced that they had seen the Seven Wonders. Of that moment, Paul instructed Mal Evans to commit his wisdom to paper. On reading it back later though, the McCartney philosophy left much to be desired... "There are seven levels". The Beatles soon came to rely on the hipper marijuana to help them unwind rather than the stodgier whiskey & Coke.

Lennon, particularly, was wary, but envious of Dylan's freewheeling wordplay. It was undeniably Dylan who got the group punching above their weight. The non-specific Beatle love songs of the period appear under the Dylan influence. He jauntily repaid the debt (1966's 'Fourth Time Around' left few in doubt the debt as to how much the melody owed to 'Norwegian Wood'). Whenever he appeared in London, the Beatles were there. One intriguing encounter took place in May 1966 when Dylan was controversially touring with his electric band. Paul and John went to link up with him at the London Hilton. Together, the trio began collaborating under the influence. Dylan expert Michael Gray found evidence of a tantalising (if ultimately unremarkable) Dylan/ Lennon/McCartney collaboration 'Pneumonia Ceilings' ("I'm sick and tired of your applesauce tears... Thermometers donat [sic] tell time no more...").

It was on that tour that a visibly strung-out Dylan undertook a limousine ride with the clearly nervous Lennon. Like the earlier summit with Elvis, it was not a memorable encounter. A clearly stoned Dylan telling the chauffeur, "I'm gonna turn you into Ronald Colman..." and Lennon playing second fiddle while trying to salvage something from the encounter ("come, come boy... pull yourself together").

While he was in exile in Woodstock during 1967, Dylan played *Sgt Pepper* and found it "A very indulgent album... I didn't think all that production was necessary". There is

He'd love to turn you on… Bob Dylan ushered past Neil Aspinall,
Del Monico Hotel, New York, 28 August 1964

(Trinity Mirror / Mirrorpix / Alamy Stock Photo)

still speculation that when you turn the sleeve upside down on Dylan's 1967 comeback LP *John Wesley Harding*, an image of the four Beatles can be discerned. Jury still out on that one.

Three of the Beatles (John, George and Ringo) trooped down to the Isle of Wight in August 1969 to see Dylan play his first UK show in three years. Paul was waiting alongside Linda in hospital, awaiting the birth of their first child, Mary. George played some energetic tennis with Dylan, but the 'superstar jam' the music press were speculating on (Dylan plus sundry Beatles and Stones) never took place.

Another missed opportunity came when Ray Foulk, who had beguiled Dylan to the island in 1969, wrote to George Harrison: "The greatest achievement that could be attained in the music festival sphere would be for the Beatles to perform at the next IW Festival. We are not professional promoters but we are ambitious and want to make a distinct mark on society on behalf of the young people of the world." But the letter arrived while the Beatles were in the process of breaking up, and the 1970 headliner was Jimi Hendrix.

Aside from Dion, Bob Dylan was the only singer to appear on the *Sgt Pepper* cover. Lennon cited him in 'Yer Blues'. In 2013, Dylan paid a poignant tribute in 'Roll On John' from his *Tempest* album (his last of original material for eight years). The song mentions Liverpool, Hamburg and the Quarrymen. Cites 'A Day in the Life' and 'Come Together'. I find it is a strangely affecting song.

Who knew what went through the mind of 79-year-old Bob Dylan during Lockdown, but one of the few good things to come out of the pandemic was Dylan's first album of original material in eight years. *Rough & Rowdy Ways* ranged far and wide – from Walt Whitman to Indiana Jones; Anne Frank to Field Marshal Montgomery – and on the extraordinary 17-minute 'Murder Most Foul', Bob mentions the Beatles' impact in the aftermath of the JFK assassination.

Intriguingly, as part of HMV's 'My Inspiration' series of adverts, when asked in 2008, Paul selected lines from Dylan's 'She Belongs to Me'.

(Dylan chose Robert Burns' 'My Love Is Like a Red, Red Rose'.)

The Dylan influence was clearly evident on the songs from the Beatles' *Help!* LP, notably 'You've Got to Hide Your Love Away'. There was also an edgier, more knowing element to much of that soundtrack material which suggested a Dylan hand. But the album also boasted some true Beatle belters – 'The Night Before', 'I've Just Seen a Face', 'It's Only Love'. As ever, crisply produced, elegantly played and once again demonstrating an almost casual brilliance. ("This album could easily be titled 'The Many Moods Of The Beatles'. Showcased in 14 tracks are ballads, rock'n'roll, folk, country and western and a helping of straight pop", *Record Mirror*… "This LP is the ideal cure for the depressions! It's a gay, infectious romp which doesn't let up in pace or sparkle from start to finish…", *NME*).

The LP also provided another striking cover image. The plan, of course, was to have the group signalling the film's title in Morse. They were struggling to come up with a theme song, 'Eight Arms to Hold You', so 'Help!' came easier. But in the end, photographer Robert Freeman was unhappy with the way that title looked. So the record you're holding, according to the front cover, is actually NUJV!

1965's *Help!* was budgeted at $560,000, four times the cost of their first film, and was in colour. Too often disregarded (not least by the group) as inferior to *A Hard Day's Night*, at the time, *Help!* offered a colourful distraction with added exotic locations. One of the English settings held a resonance – standing in for the film's Buckingham Palace was Lord Astor's Berkshire mansion, Cliveden. It had been there in the summer of 1961 that the Secretary of State for Defence, John Profumo MP, met an attractive teenage model Christine Keeler. It was a liaison which effectively helped topple the Conservative government in 1964. Six months after filming at Cliveden the group would find themselves at the real Buckingham Palace when they received their MBEs.

Help! had a genuinely witty script, actually better than you might remember. Enthusiastic performances from the four principals and a fabulous supporting cast (Alfie Bass, Patrick Cargill, Warren Mitchell, Dandy Nichols, Jeremy Lloyd – again – and a pre-*Rumpole* Leo McKern).

The orthodontic gardener was one Bruce Lacey, a British eccentric. Early "rubbish" recordings with his group, the Alberts, were produced by the ubiquitous George Martin. A near-neighbour of Fairport Convention, he was commemorated on the band's second album with 'Mr Lacey'.

And, of course *Help!* came with a soundtrack bulging with timeless Beatle classics.

My mum took me along to see *Help!* on release in summer 1965. We went to the London Pavilion and I remember loving it. The songs, of course, but also the sense of liberation the film offered. It is a cliché that we only had two clunky black and white television channels, and that 'youth culture' lay a long way ahead. But to watch the Beatles capering on skis – a sport then associated with the well-off – and larking in sunny, turquoise waters … *Help!* seemed like the last blast of colour before a dismal autumn, and the loathsome rugby posts went up on the muddy school playing fields.

Re-viewing the film of *Help!* is … fun. From their suburban lifestyle, each having their own front door ("Lovely lads, so natural… not spoilt…"). Except, like 10 and 11 Downing Street, it all merges into one big house behind closed doors. It was a trick that convinced their audience that they were "still the same as they was, before they was".

The star appeal of sultry co-star Eleanor Bron undeniably helped. She was the sister of future Bonzo Dog Band producer Gerry; her seductive charms were forged in the Cambridge Footlights, and soon allied to the post-*That Was the Week That Was* satire boom. Some of John Lennon's few solo activities within the Beatles included appearing in episodes of Peter Cook and Dudley Moore's *Not Only, But Also* – the first promoting *In His Own Write* (alongside *Hard Day's Night* co-star Norman Rossington) in 1965. In 1966, he played an up-market toilet attendant for the same show, marking the first time a wider public had seen his NHS granny glasses.

Help! (aka *Eight Arms to Hold You… Who's Been Sleeping in My Porridge?… Where Did the Ringo?*) had begun life as a Peter Sellers vehicle, but had been put on hold following his near-fatal 1964 heart attack. Playwright Charles Wood (later to adapt *How I Won the War*) took a turn on the original story by Marc Behm, who was the writer of *Charade*, the best Hitchcock film Alfred Hitchcock never got round to making.

Help! is undeniably flawed – George in particular is given little to do; the 'Goodness Gracious Me' accents of the Indian characters jar; the songs are grafted on rather than integrated. Plus, many of the scenes show how clearly uncomfortable the group were at 'acting'. They were happily settled as their characters in their first film. But I do love that iconoclastic opening – the best-known, most envied, widely emulated group in the world first appear having darts thrown sticking in their familiar faces. It is a nicely incongruous beginning, and there are other strong moments – Patrick Cargill's police inspector not a million miles from his supercilious doctor to Tony Hancock's *The Blood Donor*... There's Lennon smirking, losing himself in multiple copies of his second book... The nicely shot song sequences, on Alp, Bahamian beach or at Stonehenge give the film an extra dimension.

And if seen as the second-best Beatle film, *Help!* was still light years ahead of the competition. Enthusiastically reviewing the Beatle film early in 1966, David Quinlan marvelled, "How incredibly naïve the Americans still are when it comes to making pop musicals. Herman's Hermits, second only in popularity to the Beatles in America, get incredibly flabby, directionless treatment in *Hold On!*"

On its release, every cinema manager showing *Help!* would have been sent an Exhibitors' Campaign Book. It makes for fascinating reading today: They could purchase a 30" x 40" quad crown poster for display for only 3/6d... a Beatles colouring block was free to newspapers... "Traders could also link-up with the film title with the obvious slogan: Let us 'Help!' you – removals, furnishings, estate agents etc"... "Have the title song record played in your theatre and in factories well prior to the play date. Get local dance bands to play the music and give a plug to the picture. Try to get the record played wherever there is a P.A. system installed"...

Other schemes included loudspeaker vans touring busy districts and housing estates, carnival floats ("have a local jazz group on the float plugging the song hits"), coffee bars and travel agencies. Most intriguing of all and, mindful of the film's Salisbury Plain sequence, cinemas are offered the opportunity to give peace a chance – "Link up with local Army information offices... You could be lucky and find that one of the servicemen in the picture, from the Royal Tank Regiment, Royal Scots or Royal Ulster Rifles has a local connection".

The reviews were encouraging, even from traditionally staid titles ("These boys are the closest thing to the Marx Brothers since the Marx Brothers...", *Daily Express*... "*Help!* is almost consistently funny, sometimes almost confusingly fast, and above all a contrast to its predecessor. Its social satire is directed inwards as much as out...", *The Spectator*... "A crazy succession of verbal and visual gags whipped across with great speed and gimmicky humour", *What's On In London*... "a good, nimble romp with both giggles and belly laughs...", *Variety*).

July 29th 1965... another day, another Royal Film Premiere, this time with proceeds going to the Variety Club Heart Fund and the Dockland Settlements School of Adventure. The usual hysteria greeted the tuxedo-clad group when they appeared at the London Pavilion. In the end, *Help!* had, er, helped United Artists out of a jam: the studio's expectations had been high for that year's Biblical epic *The Greatest Story Ever Told*. George Stevens' film was the most expensive film ever shot on American soil, but its box office returns amounted to a meagre one third of the final budget.

So, compared in print to Schubert, on film to the Marx Brothers... and on disc they were untouchable. The relentless momentum carried them along. This was, after all, what

Help! campaign book

Opening of *Help!*, before the darts went in

(Everett Collection Inc / Alamy Stock Photo)

they had dreamed of in grimy cellars and on British Rail platforms. But like the man said they were the stuff "as dreams are made on…"

Just chronicling the Beatle activities of 1965 is exhausting, let alone living through them. You can follow it all in the books – the MBEs, the second film, the final UK tour, a North American tour (including Shea Stadium), the two LPs, meeting Elvis… Yet to me, overshadowing that eventful year, is one song… 'Yesterday'.

Take a quiet moment, and just listen to it now. Hear it afresh: an astonishingly mature piece of work. It stands as the one song which … elevated the Beatles. Poignant and reflective, the creation of a world-weary Paul, impossible to credit he was only 23 years old. Hard to believe that his belief is in yesterday, the time gone by, rather than tomorrow, and what lies ahead… It is a song made too familiar from elevator performances; from ghastly James Last-style easy listening; from saccharine ballad covers.

What is manifest on that original version by the composer is its depth and maturity. The shimmering, incandescent quality of that melody, not hauled from a classical recording or plundered from a TV advertisement, but drawn from the genius of a boy wonder, in an attic room, as the world reeled around him. All the while bombarded by fans, plagued by concert appearances, dogged by recording sessions, nagged by filming commitments…

Yet from that chaos came the sublime majesty of the world's most recorded popular song. Take time, slot in the CD, or drop the needle on the second side of *Help!* or pluck it from cyberspace. But do it when you have time to listen and luxuriate in the sheer quality of Paul McCartney's original recording of 'Yesterday'.

As ever, George Martin struck the right note, persuading Paul that a string quartet would be perfect to enhance the song's mood. Once again, Martin's years of experience led him to the right quartet – two violins, cello and viola. Session musician Ken Essex achieved his place in musical immortality and earned his five-guinea fee for his viola contribution. His place further ensured as he went on to be one of the string quartet who played the theme tune to the BBC's best-ever sitcom, *Fawlty Towers*.

I suppose it was that song which helped cement the image of McCartney as 'the soft Beatle', but as he said in *Anthology*, "When I used to talk to John about his childhood, I realised that mine was so much warmer. I think that's why I grew to be so open about sentimentality in particular. I don't really mind being sentimental. I know a lot of people look on it as uncool. I see it as a pretty valuable asset".

He could never believe that what he had written *was* original. Years later he told me he was convinced it was a classical melody he would have heard on the BBC's Third Programme, which would have echoed round the Ashers' Wimpole Street home, where he was based. Or a classical piece used on a television advert which had lodged in his brain. Famously not familiar with written music, Paul kept the melody by egging it on with the refrain "Scrambled eggs, ooh baby how I love your legs…" It was written while the Beatles were filming *Help!* and I remember Dick Lester telling me that a piano was permanently installed on the set to capture any songwriting sparks. And how, between takes at Twickenham, Paul would play the song to anyone and everyone, asking if they recognised the melody. He remained still unconvinced that this was his original tune. Eventually Lester snapped: "Look, no one knows it, but you *have* to come up with some better lyrics!"

No one of course can cite the precise moment of inspiration, or what inspires creation. You never do *Hamlet* every time out of the traps. You craft it. Songwriter Don Black once congratulated McCartney on 'Yesterday', and recognised his response as "a good day at the office". Prosaically, Ian Dury reflected: "A good song will get off the table and go out in the street and get a minicab down to Tin Pan Alley. It'll look after you".

Certainly, of the rock & roll era, 'Yesterday' maintains its place as the most covered song in the history of recorded music. I still find it incredible to think that 'Yesterday', that most beguiling of all ballads, was cut in the same session as McCartney's bouncy 'I've Just Seen a Face' and his raucous 'I'm Down'. The *total* cost for the 'Yesterday' session came to £69, taking in the session musician, producer and performers' fees (as it was a Beatle session, as well as McCartney, Lennon, Harrison and Starr each also received their £7 performance fee).

In England, the song was effectively buried on the second side of the soundtrack to the Beatles' second film. But it did not take long to take on a life of its own. The world took 'Yesterday' to its heart, and the composer found himself overtaking Gershwin, Porter, Berlin et al. in terms of song popularity. Fond as he is of the song which arguably cemented his reputation as a composer, McCartney views it almost objectively.

In one of our off-the-record chats, I asked him his own favourite Fab song, expecting 'Yesterday', or any one of a dozen other classics. He immediately cited 'You Know My Name (Look Up the Number)', because he reasoned, everyone *knew* all the well-known ones, 'Here There & Everywhere', 'Long and Winding Road', 'Hey Jude', they were the ones which occupied the airwaves. No one played the B-side of 'Let It Be', and he always had fond memories of the innumerable sessions that lightweight little song took up. ("Silly little song, took years to record, piecing it together, finally thinking we'd better finish it up. Didn't it come out on the B-side of 'Let It Be'? Great, what a place for it".)

For years, despite the fact that there were an estimated six million 'Let It Be' singles in circulation, it was the hardest-to-find Beatle song. Much of it had to do with the less than revered state that Beatle single purchasers looked after their 45s. It was only when it appeared on the 1978 *Rarities* LP and subsequent *Anthology* CD that it was able to be re-appraised. And then not too fondly. But like the rocking knight, I have a soft spot for its silliness, with John (manifestly insincere MC) and Paul (schmaltzy MOR crooner) having a pop at that golf-playing, superficial showbiz meritocracy they did so much to destroy.

'Help!' was John Lennon. 'Yesterday' was Paul McCartney. Much later, the world was riven by Paul's suggestion that the songwriting credits for songs in which neither partner had a hand in, could be reversed. "This has got blown up out of all proportion", Paul told me. "The songs that I'm talking about are the ones that John, in his interviews, said weren't his. I'm not wiping John out, just putting it in the order we did it. But by then of course, John had died, so it was no good me saying I don't think John would have wanted to be on 'Yesterday' or 'Blackbird' – same as I didn't need to be on 'Give Peace a Chance'".

McCartney laughed when he told me that one of the last conversations he had with John was along the lines of every time Lennon walked into a hotel lobby, the pianist started playing 'Yesterday'. McCartney said he was used to it; for him it was 'Imagine' that the well-meant pianist struck up.

It was during 1965 that the caustic Lennon found time to illustrate his own softer side, perhaps pushed by the acclaim accorded 'Yesterday'. The Beatles' Christmas present to their English fans that year was the *Rubber Soul* LP. It marked the first time that, amidst the chaos of touring, filming and the promotional helter-skelter, that the group conceived of the 14 tracks as a cohesive whole, paving the way for their albums for the next two years.

'In My Life' caught Lennon in a strangely reflective mood. The original autobiographical version included references to Liverpool landmarks Penny Lane, Church Street, the Dutch, the overhead railway ('The Dockers Umbrella'), the tram shed and St Columbus. It had been prompted by the journalist and author Kenneth Allsop, who was a good journalist in print and on TV. He wrote a very good history of the American hobo. He wrote me a very nice letter advising against it when I expressed interest in becoming a journalist. He died in 1973, he was 53 years old. Allsop asked John why his songs weren't more autobiographical. That desire percolated into 'Norwegian Wood' and 'Nowhere Man' as well as the elegiac 'In My Life'.

So, in cosy Weybridge, at Allsop's prompt, Lennon recalled bus journeys of actually not that long ago, but in reality, a lifetime away. Soon, though, he rejected those lyrics as "the most boring 'What I Did On My Holidays Bus Trip' song and it wasn't working at all". The final better-known, less personal lyrics were recorded in October 1965, and again could be found, almost buried on the second side of a UK Beatles LP.

In 2000, a millennial panel of songwriters – including Paul McCartney, Carole King, Jim Webb and Brian Wilson – rated 'In My Life' as No.1 in 'The 100 Greatest Songs Of All Time', beating, among others, 'Yesterday', 'Hey Jude' and 'Let It Be'. Its theme obviously resonated and the song went on to endure an exhaustive life of cover versions, including those by Johnny Cash, Bette Midler, Keb' Mo', Ozzy Osborne and Sean Connery.

I find it more than coincidence that the same year as John's most reflective ballad was released, his absentee father moved in a similar direction. Freddie Lennon (1912–76) had a brief reconciliation with his son, and in December 1965 released a single 'That's My Life'. I think I am alone in finding it a strangely affecting song. Just a few months shy of joining the Jimi Hendrix Experience, among the musicians involved were Noel Redding and Mitch Mitchell. Such was the power of the 'Lennon' brand at the time that Freddie even recorded a Dutch-language version of the song.

At the single's launch party Freddie was joined by labelmate, a young David Bowie. In one of those intriguing, but probably pointless coincidences, Freddie Lennon once worked as a barman at the Toby Jug in Tolworth. The pub, demolished in 2000, was where distinguished Bowie biographer Nicholas Pegg cites as the location for "the first date proper of the Ziggy Stardust tour". So rock's most influential alien made his first contact with the planet earth where the father of one of rock's leading avatar's was potman.

I would argue that *Rubber Soul* stands as the group's greatest pure pop LP. George's writing ('Think for Yourself'; 'If I Needed Someone') was coming along nicely. Paul wasn't exactly slouching – 'Drive My Car' acts as a piledriving album opener, with a nice lyrical sting in the tail; 'Michelle', a ballad as heartfelt as any in his catalogue while the jaunty 'I'm Looking Through You' stands midway between slow and fast, old and new Beatles. It's a song which verges on the cynical, as Paul details love's "nasty habits". My contention is that what elevated the LP is because *Rubber Soul* is the album which Lennon really *bothered*. Looking back, he was notoriously dismissive of his fledgling songwriting efforts ("garbage"... "rubbish"), and in later years, spellbound by Yoko, exercised little real quality control. By 1965, ironically during his self-loathing "fat Elvis" period, it nonetheless inspired some of his best-ever work: one LP containing 'Norwegian Wood'; 'Nowhere Man'; 'Girl'; 'The Word' and 'In My Life'. Songs of substance and maturity, inspired by real life encounters, drawn from experience.

For UK fans, for the third Christmas running, December 1965 delivered the traditional, wonderful Beatle LP of all new songs. From its distorted cover, *Rubber Soul* offered a treasure trove of wonder – what was that weird sound on 'Norwegian Wood'? Who was the 'Nowhere Man'? How many French O-levels did it take to comprehend 'Michelle'?

Actually, contemporary reviews were largely negative ("not their best on first hearing... Without a doubt the Beatles sound has matured but unfortunately it also seems to have become a little subdued. You Won't See Me' and 'Nowhere Man' almost get monotonous", *Melody Maker*. "Previous LPs have been well above average, but *Rubber Soul* is nowhere near as good", *Disc*). However, Allen Evans in *New Musical Express* enthused, "The Beatles are still finding different ways to make us enjoy listening to them... Altogether a good album, with plenty of tracks you'll want to hear again and again, liking them better each time".

While Beatle LP sleeves such as *Sgt Pepper* and *Abbey Road* are hailed for their impact and influence, *A Hard Day's Night* and *Rubber Soul* are equally captivating. For the film soundtrack, those multiplying portraits are compelling, while the distorted faces on *Rubber Soul* somehow suggest the music progressing inside its sleeve.

Profiling Dick James' Northern Songs as 1965 wound down, the *Investor Review* noted its current net assets of £459,000, its financial position as "strong at present" and duly noted that the Beatles and their music were "likely to last for some time". Even the financial correspondent of the up-market *Queen* magazine was impressed, noting that John and Paul's initial shares of £20 were now valued at £450,000 each. "The London Stock Exchange, pin-striped and bowler-hatted, was little short of affronted at the appearance of Northern Songs. They're now cautiously prepared to discuss it. 'Still risky, because it's tied to two particular persons'". Later on, the article notes that all those two "particular persons" really want from Northern Songs is "a recording studio and an office".

A 1965 UK TV special further cemented their homeland standing. *The Music of Lennon & McCartney* was an old-fashioned variety show, this time built around the group's music. Previously, such television tributes would have been in the hands of 'all-round entertainers': a familiar face (Dickie Henderson, Bruce Forsyth, Max Bygraves) would sing, dance and introduce special guests. That 60 minutes of prime-time television would have been devoted to the music of a pop group, who only three years before had released their debut single, indicated the esteem in which they were now held. John and Paul were plainly ill-at-ease in their role as hosts, but the calibre of their guests was testament to the Beatles.

Their status as 'national treasures' was confirmed when it was announced that Harrods would open their doors so the group could undertake their Christmas shopping in private. Hitherto that privilege had been reserved for the Royal Family.

For all their fan loyalty and ubiquity, even with the approbation of *The Times*' William Mann, there was still a certain amount of … resentment. The author Hanif Kureishi remembered his music teacher informing his class that, "Lennon and McCartney could not possibly have written the songs ascribed to them; it was a con – we should not be taken in by the Beatles, they were only front-men… 'Who did write the Beatles' songs, then, sir?' someone asked bravely. Mr Hogg told us that Brian Epstein and George Martin wrote the Lennon/McCartney songs. 'Real musicians were playing on those records', he said".

Alan Johnson MP recalled: "I remember, the Beatles had broken through, sitting on the number 11 bus, going to school, listening to this conductor having a conversation with an elderly passenger and they were saying, 'Oh, of course, those kids couldn't have written those songs themselves. How could they? It's been done in Tin Pan Alley. The music industry is doing it for them'. And, this was a big thing, that the Beatles didn't really write their songs, because no one could *believe* that two teenagers from Liverpool, two working class lads, could write songs like 'Yesterday', and 'Can't Buy Me Love'. I remember sitting there, burning with resentment, to intervene in this argument, because I was on the other side of the generation gap".

*

With *Rubber Soul* the Beatles were once again pushing the envelope. For homegrown competition, there were those snapping on the Beatles' Cuban heels – the Animals, the Who, the Dave Clark Five, the Yardbirds, the Kinks. But of them all, only the Rolling Stones came close to matching their popularity, if not their achievements. It was the Stones' manager Andrew Oldham (who had begun working as a Beatle PR) who convinced Jagger and Richards to write their own material. The Stones' well of covers (Lennon & McCartney, Buddy Holly, Howlin' Wolf) was running dry and, to sustain their momentum, Mick and Keith had to become the Stones' "own built-in tunesmith team".

"Andrew convinced Mick and Keith they could write", Charlie Watts acutely testified in *According to the Rolling Stones*. "Thank God he did, because without those songs we would have been another Freddie & the Dreamers, remembered for playing 'Going to New York' at Ken Colyer's Club on a Sunday afternoon".

It took the Stones time to catch up. They could never match the production depth of the Beatles and lyrically were one step behind. On disc, it was not until 1968's *Beggars Banquet* that the Stones came close to matching their rivals in the long-playing field. With producer Jimmy Miller, the Stones proceeded through their imperial phase – *Let It Bleed*, *Sticky Fingers* and the one which still divides opinion, the sprawling *Exile on Main Street*. As a working unit, the Beatles never made it into the next decade, and the Stones' louche swagger held sway. Still does as it happens.

For four years though, the American market suffered from a rag-bag of albums, with Beatle songs sliced and diced like ham on a David Greig's counter. During 1965 alone, *Beatles VI* cobbled together B-sides and material from *Beatles for Sale* and *Help!* The US *Help!* soundtrack contained six non-Beatle instrumentals. The sublime *Rubber Soul* had its coherence undermined by the inclusion of tracks from *Help!* It was only by 1967 that the UK and USA achieved parity.

By the beginning of 1966, even the four principals plus their harassed and increasingly nervy manager were wondering just where they could go. What else was there to achieve? Unlike their pop predecessors, they had conquered and built on their success in the all-important US market. They had triumphed in their cinema outings. A grateful monarch had ennobled them. Financially, sexually, creatively they were at the 'toppermost of the poppermost'.

For their New York date of August 1965, I doubt if anyone, not Freddie & the Dreamers, the Animals, nor even the Dave Clark Five or Rolling Stones could have filled Shea Stadium. I once asked Paul what his memory was of that show. "Seagulls", he smiled, "it was like listening to thousands and thousands of squealing seagulls". Among those "seagulls" were Whoopi Goldberg, Barbara Bach, Meryl Streep and Linda Eastman. Keeping a watchful eye were Mick Jagger and Keith Richards.

As if sensing the momentous scale of the event, the concert was filmed. The BBC broadcast the show in March 1966. Tom Sloan, the Head of Light Entertainment commented: "You will see scenes of unrestrained joy and agony which have no parallel in the entertainment business". There is evident delight at the event, if not the onstage sound. They seem to be enjoying themselves, John hamming it up on the organ, and as confused as any UK fan as to which US Beatle LP certain songs appeared.

"I remember we met the Lovin' Spoonful backstage… the first time that people had come in our dressing room, which was the sacred area…" Paul told me. "We went through the baseball PA… Four little hand mikes and they ran everything through the PA. It all had to be re-voiced, people don't know that. I'm giving the secret away. I remember going into Wembley and they're going 'there's no sound… just white noise, screaming'. So we had to go in and re-voice the whole show for the picture".

For many years, Shea Stadium was the condition every major act aspired to. In 2001, just days before 9/11, after interviewing Art Garfunkel, he graciously asked if I'd accompany him to see a baseball game. "Where?" "At Shea Stadium." "What, where The *Beatles* played…?" I inquired breathlessly. "Well, yes," smiled Art, "but *we* played there too, Patrick…!"

Just look at the primitive equipment provided to fuel that historic 1965 Beatle performance, at the time, the largest paying crowd a rock group had ever played to. There were no monitors, they couldn't hear themselves. They couldn't hear a note they played. Neither could the crowd. The Who's bassist John Entwistle remembered the band opening for the Beatles in Blackpool: "The old theatre dressing rooms always had a speaker feed direct from the stage mics. The noise of the little girls screaming was so deafening… The direct feed allowed us to hear their words loud and clear… 'It's been a hard day's cock'… 'I wanna hold your cunt'…"

Touring with his All-Starr Band in later years, Ringo was asked where he wanted his monitor placed. "What's a monitor?" Legend has the drummer bouncing offstage after one of those ear-splitting 60s shows and telling John, "I thought 'Hard Day's Night' sounded good." "I wasn't playing 'Hard Day's Night'." "Well I was…!"

One of the few occasions Brian let his neatly combed hair down had been at one of

What us, worry? On their way into the history books – again!
Shea Stadium, 15 August 1965

(Keystone Press / Alamy Stock Photo)

those mad American shows. Fellow manager Simon Napier-Bell told Debbie Geller: "He went into the crowd of girls and he just screamed like one of the girls, which is what he said he'd always wanted to do from the first minute he'd ever seen them. He had spent his whole life being restrained and wearing suits and suddenly he just screamed and became the mad fan he wanted to be".

By his own admission, Shea Stadium was the zenith of Brian Epstein's achievements on behalf of the group. He can be seen in the documentary, scanning the crowd. Brian looks rather baffled. As if to say: are these really the same four, leather-clad scruffs I had first witnessed in the cellar of a Northern port less than four years before? Was it at Shea that Brian reflected on that journey – British Beatlemania and cinema triumphs; the conquest of America, MBEs, unimagined riches…? Post-Shea, did he wonder, was there anywhere else to go? Did he, I fancifully imagine, like Alexander the Great weep as there were no more worlds left to conquer?

There were other acts who briefly held his attention – the Circle (renamed after Lennon's inability to let a word alone, the Cyrkle). With a jaunty cover of Paul Simon's 'Red Rubber Ball' they were denied a US No.1 by the Beatles. Brian dropped the ball when Tony Bramwell got him along to the basement of Les Cousins to witness a folk singer who'd impressed him. Epstein came away unconvinced by Paul Simon: "a bit small and Jewish-looking".

One of Brian's few interests outside the music business was bullfighting. Was it this which in 1963 saw George Harrison testifying in a jeans advert, "The smartest men in Spain gave LYBRO the 'Flamenco' idea"? Brian was fascinated by El Cordobes, who, thanks to his combed-forward style, was, naturally, 'The Spanish Beatle'. Prior to his involvement with the pop world, Brian had made solitary trips to Madrid, Valencia and Seville. On the back of his Beatle success, for a while he even managed an English matador, Henry Higgins (named after the elocution expert in *Pygmalion*). But Brian's management expertise did not extend to the corrida.

Perhaps it was in the ring that he could worship from the stands the athletic, balletic matadors; revel in the crowd's appreciation of a deft manoeuvre. Here was all the skill, the artistry, which the artist in Brian would appreciate. But also, the excitement of real danger; of dancing on the edge.

*

Just looking on YouTube, or DVDs of *Anthology* and *Eight Days a Week*, you can see the weariness etched on those still young faces. The resentment of trudging out to some baseball stadium to play songs they were bored with, which they couldn't hear, to an audience who didn't want to listen. What was being achieved under the matchless eye of George Martin at Abbey Road could never be replicated onstage in Arkansas, Tennessee or Wyoming. Beatlemania was just that: hysteria. The appearance of those four men on a concert platform flicked a switch in their predominantly teenage audience, and tipped them over the screaming edge. It was the continued enthusiasm which the Beatles generated that took their fan base to another level. The boys styled themselves on the group, they wanted to emulate the Beatles by forming their own groups. It was the girls who screamed loudest, and filled their bedrooms with Beatle souvenirs.

Madcap as their lives were, hemmed-in and full of havoc, the one thing the Beatles could not tolerate was boredom. And the due process of live performance was plain boring. As the recording of what was to become *Revolver* began in the spring of 1966, the prospect of live dates held little appeal. They would be performing material they had wearied of, or songs which would be impossible to replicate through the primitive 1960s PA systems.

There is a marvellous clip of the Beatles making their way to the stage in some anonymous American cow hall. Looking chippy and thoroughly Fab, in their state-of-the-art suits, all with their groovy sunglasses. They are more than just physically removed from the cops who are there to protect them; they move in a different universe. The police are all armed and tubby, looking just like the redneck Rod Steiger in *In the Heat of the Night*. And moving smoothly, effortlessly, sublimely by them are the Beatles.

It was proving to be too much of an effort; creatively they felt that they had so much more to offer than belting out old-hat hits to berserk audiences who were there for the experience of being in the same room or stadium as their idols. Financially, touring made sense, in their manager's eyes, the performance fees perhaps going some way to balance those lucrative, lost merchandising opportunities.

And those desultory press conferences of the period. Long gone were the irreverent and chirpy responses, the eager cat and mouse fencing with journalists of only a few years before. ("Any treasury of their public wit", wrote Jonathan Gould, "would be heavily weighted toward the first year of their success".) Here were men wearied by the same old same old, visibly frustrated and bored by the repetitive scenarios. But to break the tedium, wasn't Lennon talking out of his arse when asked if they would write a song protesting about Vietnam? "All our songs are anti-war?" What, 'Hello Little Girl'? 'Not a Second Time'? 'I Don't Want to Spoil the Party'…?

The staleness was setting in; the repetition of touring, the puppet-like second film, the repetition… Outside the inner circle, they were inviolate – in print and on film. On disc, they were smashing records. Albeit quite literally.

The crunch came with John's "Bigger than Jesus" claim, made to Maureen Cleave (1934–2021) in April 1966. It went largely unremarked in his homeland. The Church Information Office did officially respond at the time: "It was recognised that John Lennon's views were based on ignorance of the subject and were not worthy of comment". Trendy vicar, the Rev. William Shergold of St Mary's Paddington wondered if the Beatle comment was in the light of their earlier rival recently coming and testifying his Christian beliefs at a Billy Graham Crusade: "I think it may have been a reaction to Cliff Richard coming out on the side of the angels".

London Life reader Eric Swayne wrote in support: "It's high time that somebody came out in support of John Lennon… Millions of kids wait in the pouring rain for hours for a glimpse of the Beatles, but how many bother to walk the few hundred yards to their church on Sunday?"

It was America that took objection to the comparison. Likely as not it was the spark which ignited a larger fire. Perhaps after years of making obeisance to these alien invaders, America felt it was time to fight back.

The comments went unremarked when published in several American magazines, but it was the July edition of the teenage *Datebook* which stoked the controversy. For all the changing attitudes, the Bible Belt of the Deep South still clung to the traditional values of white picket-fence conservatism. Even if Christ's call to "love thy neighbour" found little resonance in the racist enclaves of Alabama and Mississippi.

As an indication of the American mindset, that same issue of *Datebook* had Len ('1,2,3') Barry on its cover insisting that 'English groups won't last. There is no longevity in dirt'. *Datebook* also listed its ten most admired adults, a list heavy on astronauts, evangelists and Presidents – living and dead.

Once the "bigger than Jesus" story broke, there was the chilling sight of bonfires of Beatle records blazing. Disc jockeys suddenly became evangelists, encouraging listeners to bring their discs along to 'Beatle bonfires'. It all drew uncomfortable parallels with Nazi book burnings 30 years before. Prior to their final American tour in 1966 there was the equally unsettling sight of the 'ghost-robed' Ku Klux Klan and their warped members denouncing the group and picketing their concerts.

To their credit, and like Elvis before them, the group always testified to the influence of black music on their own. It was a point emphasised in Ron Howard's *Eight Days a Week* documentary, the Beatles always refused to play to segregated audiences. They turned down a tour of South Africa and were shocked at the evident racism south of the Mason-Dixon Line. They threatened to pull a concert at the Gator Bowl, Florida in September 1964 on learning it would be before a segregated audience. This was at a time in the 'land of the free' that black and white were not only seated separately, but drank from different water fountains.

In the wake of Martin Luther King's pacifist Civil Rights movement, the Student Nonviolent Coordinating Committee was an African-American organisation, aimed at attracting younger members. Julian Bond of the SNCC told Brian Ward how he and other young black Americans responded to the Beatles: "They were so fresh and irreverent. So close to a little bit of what we imagined ourselves to be – contemptuous of adult forms and not willing to conform to the standard way of dressing or thinking… They were irreverent and we were irreverent and I think there was a kind of identification there".

Hot on the heels of that religious controversy came the sleeve for the American release of the 1966 *Yesterday and Today* LP. The album was again cobbled together, this time from *Help!*, *Rubber Soul* and *Revolver*, but that wasn't the cause for controversy. The group were seen holding severed heads of dolls and raw meat while grinning in butchers' coats. The record label felt it too extreme for the youth market, so one weekend in June, an anodyne shot of the group was glued over the original cover.

A memo from Capitol Records' press office explained the group's intention, and pointed the finger as to where the blame lay: "The original cover, created in England, was intended as 'pop art' satire". Photographer Robert Freeman called his cover 'A Somnambulant Adventure'. Capitol executives thought otherwise, and an estimated 60,000 copies had to be withdrawn. Today, an original of 'the butcher cover' could go north of £16,000. Just today, as I write, an autographed 'butcher sleeve', also signed by the photographer Robert Freeman, was on eBay for a snip less than £120,000.

Away from the controversy, for creativity and seclusion, the Beatles could sequester themselves behind the walls of Abbey Road. Their hectic schedule meant that Beatle recording sessions often continued into the small hours. That left the older EMI staff unhappy, so younger engineers like Ken Scott, Geoff Emerick and Chris Thomas were only too happy to pitch in.

For a different trip, on a different level, LSD opened the doors of perception. It was George's dentist John Riley who turned John, George, Pattie and Cynthia onto the drug in the spring of 1965. Unknowingly, the Beatles and their wives' drinks were spiked – colours became exaggerated, sizes distorted... Riley's girlfriend Cyndy Bury told Steve Turner that she apparently ran around shouting, "The Bismarck is sinking! The Bismarck is sinking...!"

Lennon and Harrison were not the first to succumb to the mind-altering power of the drug. Swiss chemist Albert Hoffman ingested lysergic acid diethylamide on 19 April 1943, and recorded the experience in his journal: "Beginning dizziness, feeling of anxiety, difficulty in concentration, visual disturbances, desire to laugh..."

A decade before Lennon began the first of his "thousands" of trips, the urbane superstar Cary Grant had become an equally enthusiastic proselytiser. "All my life I've been searching for peace of mind", Grant told a journalist at the time when the drug was still legal. "Nothing really seemed to give me what I wanted until this treatment..." Then, sounding like Lennon during his later primal scream period, Grant admitted: "I took LSD with the hope it would make me feel better about myself. I wanted to rid myself of all my hypocrisies. I wanted to work through the events of my childhood, my relationship with my parents..." Over a hundred sessions, the star ("the best and most important actor in the history of cinema", according to the critic David Thomson) endeavoured to connect with his inner Archie Leach.

The Beatle intake of drugs from 1964 onwards was often compared to the macho culture of Liverpool that bred them. Back then, it was how many pints the dockers could throw back which separated the men from the boys. The prellies they took to fuel them on those long Hamburg nights were equalled, indeed exceeded, by the strong lager they used for lubrication. Such peer pressure was later translated into reefers and acid.

Much time had been spent on that difficult third Beatles film... One project United Artists pitched to further the Fabs' film career was the group as *The Four Musketeers*, with childhood pin-up Brigitte Bardot as Lady DeWinter. As with a number of other projects, it remained unrealised, though Dick Lester *did* later make that film, with Faye Dunaway, and the Beatle Musketeers replaced by Richard Chamberlain, Frank Finlay, Oliver Reed and Michael York.

Richard Lester diligently turned up for every anniversary of those first two Beatle films. A talented director beyond *A Hard Day's Night* and *Help!*, Lester was stunned by the death of his friend Roy Kinnear on location for the *Musketeers*, and effectively retired from film-making. He came back for the compelling *Get Back*, the 11-minute film which was shown before Paul took to the stage for his 1989 *Flowers in the Dirt* tour. They tried to pin the promo video thing on him but Lester wryly distanced himself from the compliment: "MTV have said I was their putative father, but I insisted on a blood test!"

Post-*Help!*, the top candidate for the film to get them out of their United Artists contract was *A Talent for Loving*. It was a comedy-western, based on a book by Richard Condon, who also wrote the novels *The Manchurian Candidate*, and later *Prizzi's Honor*. Producer Walter Shenson admitted that the idea was "problematic", but said the novel had the right anarchic spirit. Ringo particularly would have enjoyed pretending to be a cowboy. The Beatles declined. Shenson did later produce 1969's *A Talent for Loving*, starring Richard Widmark and Topol, subbing for two of the Fab Four. Marketed as "A professional gambler trapped into marrying within a Mexican family under an Aztec curse". Widmark admitted that it was his "worst-ever film".

At one point, the Beatles wanted Stanley Kubrick to direct them in *The Lord of the Rings*. John, Paul, George and Ringo would respectively play Gollum, Frodo, Gandalf and Sam. The trilogy was required cult reading (though debate rages just how many of the film's future stars ever bothered to read it). The main stumbling block was that Middle Earth creator J.R.R. Tolkien turned them down. It's not clear whether Tolkien appreciated how unsuited the four would be to a fantasy epic, or whether he had a more personal objection. In a letter, he once wrote: "In a house three doors away dwells a member of a group of young men who are evidently aiming to turn themselves into a Beatle Group. On days when it falls to his turn to have a practice session the noise is indescribable."

Frankly, *The Lord of the Rings* was never going to happen anyway as, by 1966, Kubrick was wholly immersed into his three-year struggle to bring *2001: A Space Odyssey* to the screen. Later, grappling with music for the finished *2001*, an associate on the film remembers the director confessing: "I just had to fire my fourth composer. I'm starting from scratch… I'm even thinking, should I contact The Beatles?" In the end, of course, Kubrick memorably stuck with the classical soundtrack he had originally used as a stopgap score.

When I contacted the Stanley Kubrick Archive in London, they had no record of any correspondence between the director and the Beatles concerning the Tolkien project.

There was one Kubrick connection with the group: the director used excerpts from Gyorgy Ligeti's electronic works for the *2001* soundtrack. My musician colleague Neil McArthur remembers nervously escorting the Hungarian to Studio 2 at Abbey Road for a session. He was unprepared for the classical composer's delight. "Here!" he said, throwing his arms wide. "Here, is where *Sgt Pepper* was born!"

It took Peter Jackson nearly half a century to fully realise *The Lord of the Rings* as a cinematic epic. It was the success of the film trilogy which allowed the director liberty to pursue a number of heartfelt projects, including in 2021, a 'reimagined' *Let It Be*.

That third Beatle film remained a Damoclesian sword hanging over them. In 1968, Neil Aspinall flew in a panic to India. "I visited them in Rishikesh, but only to stop them making a movie, really. There was a suggestion they should make a movie with the Maharishi. I'm not quite sure what it was supposed to consist of, but they did have a three picture deal with United Artists…" (*Anthology*).

One film which came under serious consideration was *Up Against It*. Playwright Joe Orton was on the same wavelength as the group, and only seven years older than Lennon. He arrived with a bang in the West End with his black comedies *Entertaining Mr Sloane* and *Loot* in the mid-60s (Paul was 'an angel' on *Loot*, investing £1,000 in the production).

Orton did have meetings with Brian Epstein and a lunch with Paul during the summer of 1967, but in truth, there was little likelihood that the film would have gone ahead. In his diary, Orton confided, "the boys in my script have been caught in flagrante, dressed in drag, blown up a war memorial, become involved in dubious political activity, dressed as women, committed murder, been put in prison and committed adultery". It was certainly a long way from the communal house of *Help!*

Brian Epstein declined. Orton was killed by his jealous lover. At his funeral in 1967, the newspapers got great mileage that it was not a hymn the playwright requested, but rather 'A Day in the Life'. One alternative title Orton had impishly suggested for his Beatle film had been *Prick Up Your Ears*, which later was used as the title of the first Orton biography.

In the end, *Up Against It* was made – as a BBC Radio 3 play, broadcast in 1997. It starred Blur's Damon Albarn, then at the zenith of Brit Pop, and Joseph Fiennes. Also, in a nice piece of casting, it featured Leo McKern, 30 years on from terrorising the Beatles in their second film.

A further film subject which, briefly, intrigued a Beatle has, I believe, never been written about before. In 2009, I made a BBC Radio 4 profile of the author Len Deighton. An early adaptor, Deighton was one of the first people in London to have a car phone, on which he refused to return two calls which claimed to be from the eminent philosopher Bertrand Russell. Deighton did return the third call, and when the two men did eventually meet, Russell revealed an earlier encounter.

In the summer of 1966, Paul McCartney had met with the 94-year-old philosopher and anti-war activist. Details of the meeting are vague, but as the only Beatle living in Central London, Paul's network of contacts was impressive. Soon afterwards, McCartney also made contact with Len Deighton to discuss a film project.

Deighton had burst on the scene the same year as the Beatles in 1962, when his first novel, *The Ipcress File* was published. Deighton's laconic spy (he was only named "Harry Palmer" when Michael Caine played him in the 1965 film of *Ipcress*) was light years away from the suave urbanity of Sean Connery's 007. In 1966 Deighton had become determined to get a film version of Joan Littlewood's stage play *Oh! What a Lovely War* onto the screen. Deighton had flown from Portugal to see the play. It was a virulent revue, which had premiered at the Theatre Royal, Stratford East in 1964. A caustic production, utilising familiar songs from the Great War, it was a virulent assault on the 'donkey' generals who had caused nearly a million British troops to die in the charnel house of the First World War.

Following his meeting with Lord Russell, just prior to leaving for their final American tour, McCartney was invited by Deighton for dinner at his home in Borough, SE1 on 8 August 1966. Paul had obviously been impressed by what the peer had had to say. Russell's pacifist principles dated back to the Great War and would have chimed with McCartney's anti-war feelings. From what Len Deighton remembered, when we met and spoke in 2009, Russell had tried to convince Paul to *do* something positive with the power the Beatles had by then accrued. Perhaps the group could be convinced to appear in an anti-war film?

Talking to his biographer Edward Milward-Oliver, Len Deighton remembered: "The Beatles had been on to Bertrand Russell about wanting to make an antiwar film. Russell suggested they speak with me. I said I had no time to write and/or set up another movie; I was deeply committed to getting *Oh! What a Lovely War* to the screen. But Paul McCartney came to dinner with us at the Elephant and Castle, where I cooked a big curry meal for him.

"I said that the Beatles could be the Smith family that I'd invented for the *Oh! What a Lovely War* screenplay but Paul didn't like the idea of it being a First World War story because he felt it wouldn't send a message of the sort he wanted about Vietnam."

It remains a tantalising What If…? The Beatle parts would have prefigured the Victorian slash Edwardian phase of the *Sgt Pepper* era. However, finding themselves surrounded by screen titans such as Laurence Olivier, Michael Redgrave, John Gielgud, John Mills and Ralph Richardson would surely have undermined their faltering belief in their own acting abilities.

It took a further three years for *Oh! What a Lovely War* to reach the cinema screen, and Deighton was bitterly unhappy with director Richard Attenborough's approach to the subject, which he regarded as soft- soaping. In mitigation, I and many others, found the 1969 film of *Oh! What a Lovely War* to be, and to remain, profoundly moving, and a worthy testament to the youth who were sacrificed in their thousands in the bloody quagmire of the Western front.

One of the most engaging passages in Craig Brown's *One Two Three Four* was his 'Six Degrees of Separation', but of course with the Beatles that number is often reduced. Following Paul's meeting with Bertrand Russell, Brown made the connection: "Russell remembered childhood meetings with William Gladstone. Gladstone himself used to breakfast with the elderly William Wordsworth (b.1770). So, it's 'Blackbird' to 'Daffodils' in three meetings… the Beatles concertina time in the most extraordinary way".

*

Brian Epstein had blocked off the first three months of 1966 to accommodate the shooting of the group's third film. With it remaining unrealised, for the first time in three years, they found themselves with time on their hands. Holidays were taken; George got married and recording resumed. The Beatles' first single of the new year was a signpost to the road which read 'Been There, Done That' and 'The Future'. Paul's 'Paperback Writer' was a workmanlike A-side, driven by his funky bass and some trilling Lennon & Harrison harmonies, though how much substance they attached to the song can be discerned by their singing the nursery rhyme 'Frere Jaques' on the chorus.

The single marked one of the few occasions the group had not sung about love in all its forms, but McCartney appears confused about an author's true trajectory: if you are lucky, the paperback edition of your book follows the hardback publication, destined to reach a wider readership. It is not 'based upon' another novel (Edward Lear or whoever), it is the second edition of an original work.

The Future was where John's 'Rain' took you. It is largely due to the shifting tectonic plates of Ringo's drumming, which elevate the song from Lennon looking at the rain in his English garden. No surprise that it was Ringo's own favourite Beatle performance. And the song's drone style foreshadowed the Fabs' fascination with all things Indian the following year. 'Rain' also consisted, as many have laughed, of "the entire Oasis catalogue right there".

It was while filming *Help!* that a swami had fortuitously given George a birthday present. *The Illustrated Yoga* came on George's 22nd birthday. While filming the Indian restaurant scene at Twickenham, bored between takes, George became intrigued by the sounds the musicians were producing from the sitar. It led to 'Norwegian Wood', and beyond... (In its *Rubber Soul* review, *NME* were puzzled by the "Arabic-sounding guitar chords in between"...)

There was something so ... timely about 'Norwegian Wood'. I remember the vogue for the sleek, modern lines of all things Scandinavian in the mid-60s. It was a way of showing off; of neighbours stating, 'Hey, we're so... modern'. Sideboards, flooring all fashioned from Scandinavian wood was a statement that we'd finally moved on from post-war utility furniture. And that those old, inherited lumpy brown furnishings so emblematic of the 19th century were good and gone.

While 'Paperback Writer' may not have been the strongest Beatle single, the accompanying promo video for the 1966 single had the group looking inestimably cool in all manner of shades. It is worth remembering how the visuals marked another step forward for them. And that is another reason as to why they remain so intriguing, their shifting image. Paolo Hewitt told Helena Barrett of those stylistic shifts: "They were trying to move away from tough, working-class macho Liverpool. One of the great things about the Beatles was their wide-ranging music, and they did the same in clothes. That same jumbling up of all kinds of styles". From those snappy Beatle boots and on to those circular collar suits... the snappy Duggie Millings' threads... the military-style Shea Stadium jackets... the colourful *Sgt Pepper* outfits... the retro Fair Isle sweater vogue... the knee-length coats when everything else was mini... So synonymous with changing fashions, always a step ahead. How we laughed when the *Pepper*-era Beatles donned those dated circular collar 'Beatle' suits, four years on, for a promotional photo.

A desultory nine dates towards the end of 1965 saw the last-ever Beatles UK tour. Provincial theatres held as little appeal as American stadia. It was all a step backward, and the one direction the Beatles always took was forward. One of the supporting acts on that final tour were the Paramounts, soon to metamorphose into Procol Harum. The group's Gary Brooker told me he used to stand in the wings and watch the showers of jelly babies, still hitting the stage, "like arrows at Agincourt".

No one quitting Cardiff's Capitol cinema in the late evening of 12 December 1965 would have realised they were witnessing the end of an era. A nice pre-Christmas treat, bobbing along to the Beatles as they ran through a selection of songs from recent LPs and a couple of singles. And if you weren't one of the lucky few, not to worry, they'd be back in Wales as they had been every year since 1962.

Taking time off from the *Revolver* sessions, 1 May 1966 saw the Beatles' last-ever UK public appearance, topping the bill at the Empire Pool, Wembley for an *NME Poll Winners* concert. Creatively, their hearts were in the LP they were fashioning, a quantum leap forward from *Rubber Soul*. Presenting themselves to squealing admirers was a regression. They felt their fans could be better served by a progression in the music they were making, rather than the regressive farce of personal appearances.

You can tell how little they looked forward to the show – on arrival, Lennon threw a strop about them preceding the Rolling Stones in what the *NME* called "the line-up of the century". Well, up to a point, yes, alongside the country's two leading groups were also the Who, Dusty Springfield and the Yardbirds. Oh, and Dave Dee, Dozy, Beaky, Mick & Tich.

The Beatles did grudgingly appear to receive awards, presented by the looming Clint (*Cheyenne*) Walker, in London to film *The Dirty Dozen*. Black-clad they disinterestedly toy with their trophies as the World's Top Vocal Group ("which they are likely to be for a long time", the *NME* editor enthuses from the stage).

Dutifully the group then went off on tour, to Germany, the Philippines Japan and America. Again, we sense the palpable lack of interest in the global trawl. If any one event confirmed the group's antipathy to touring it was their experience during their time in the Philippines. Snubbing a dictator and his wife, however innocently, is never recommended. For one of the few occasions in their professional career, the Beatles faced hostile fans. They were jostled, shoved and threatened. These Filipinos wanted to harm them, not snatch a souvenir or lucky touch. The delay of their departure from the country was nervously extended, as a real sense of threat percolated the group and their entourage as the aircraft waited for take-off. When they finally did leave, one senses it was the straw that broke the camel's back. Whatever lustre there once had been in live performance, had been rubbed off by the Philippine experience.

In June 1966 the Beatles played the Budokan in Japan. For once, the courtesy the Japanese extended to visitors transferred to a Beatle concert, and for the first time in an age, they could actually hear what they were playing onstage. It is strange to see footage of that final 1966 tour, particularly when the group get behind Paul for 'Yesterday'. Even audiences then must have sensed that this was not the same group which had inspired such head-turning hysteria only two years before. These were grown men, in their stylish new outfits.

The Tokyo charge d'affaires Dudley Cheke reported back that Carnaby Street could cash-in on the gear worn by the "Agreeable, talented and quick-witted young musicians". He was also able to secure two guinea tickets for the shows for Japanese dignitaries to further cement relations.

Thirty years later, the capital boasted its own Cavern Club, a Tudor-style pub, one of three franchises in Japan, filled by Beatle tribute bands seven nights a week.

A stopover in India from the Philippines had allowed George his first sight and smell of the country which would play such a formative influence on his life. "The biggest disappointment I had was a realization of the extent of the fame of the Beatles – because there were so many dark faces in the night behind a wire mesh fence, all shouting 'Beatles! Beatles!' and following us… I thought 'Oh no! Foxes have holes. Birds have nests, but Beatles have nowhere to lay their heads" (*Anthology*).

The captivation soon followed, when he returned with Pattie that September. Newly-shorn, this was the trip which found George at the feet of Ravi Shankar, savouring the music, culture and philosophy of the sub-continent which was to pre-occupy him for the remainder of his life.

Some light relief had been provided by a return to the Beatles' German stamping grounds. What thoughts must have meandered through the minds of Lennon and McCartney as they took a late-night stroll down the Reeperbahn. How far they had travelled since

Final UK performance before paying audience,
NME Poll Winners, 1 May 1966

(PictureLux / The Hollywood Archive / Alamy Stock Photo)

arriving there only a few years before as teenage waifs and strays. Now, as self-contained millionaires, imprisoned by the very popularity they had so eagerly sought back then, they could only revisit in quiet desperation.

Of that German re-visit, George recalled in *Anthology*: "The good side was that we were coming back to play after all our fame and fortune, and when we'd been there before we'd been playing dirty nightclubs to work our way up. The bad bit was that a lot of ghosts materialized out of the woodwork – people you didn't necessarily want to see again, who'd been your best friend one drunken Preludin night back in 1960. It's 1966, you've been through a million changes, and suddenly one of those ghosts jumps out at you".

By then, dispirited and manifestly fed-up, the high-watermark of that first full hysterical outbreak of 'Beatlemania' may well have peaked. Following the Far East and Europe, it was time to be, in George's phrase, "beaten up by the Americans again". A second Shea Stadium show in 1966 witnessed unthinkable empty seats. Other dates on that final US tour were also not sold out. That last-ever tour was a desultory experience – Lennon's Jesus comparison hung like a cloud over them... The group were manifestly bored with their slapdash 30-minute performances... To leave behind the complexity of what they were accomplishing at Abbey Road knowing that it could never be replicated onstage would have jarred... Roadie Ed Freeman was amazed at the organisation to get the world's most popular entertainers onstage, "So amateurish". Not that the audiences cared about what was coming out of the paltry 100-watt amplifiers or stadium PA sound systems. They were happy to be in the same space, however vast and remote, as ... the Beatles.

One July day in 1966, Kenny Everett, a DJ on pirate Radio London, was sitting "twiddling my thumbs" when he received a call from the station boss saying, "We'd like you to follow the Beatles around, 32 cities in 40 days". It was, Everett later recalled, "The Greatest Day Of My Life". It was prompted by an offer from Bassett's, the manufacturer of the jelly babies which had made the Beatles' life hell on early tours. The company was keen to commemorate its link with the group. As the contemporary adverts ran, "We name no names, but a certain pop group is believed to rate Jelly Babies top of the sweet parade. Yeah, Yeah, Yeah..."

By then, the group had outgrown the sweet barrage. In America though the bombardment was the heavier jelly *beans*. Bassetts felt it was time to remind the world of their saccharine association. Thus they were willing to sponsor a 'Big L' DJ to accompany the group on tour. It was a good choice, Everett (1944–95) was a fellow Scouser, and a fervent Fab fan.

His interviewing technique was, by his own admission, "the pits". He was too overawed in 'the presence' to fashion questions and even when he got an answer getting it broadcast was a primitive, technological nightmare. Everett would telephone London from America where a Radio London staffer would hold the telephone earpiece and record Everett's breathless reports onto tape and then broadcast the scratchy results. Too often static and hysterical Beatle fans made the shows all but inaudible. "It was Armageddon mixed with a bit of Gotterdammerung", Everett later recalled.

For all their flaws, those reports did capture some of that madness, as Everett found himself in the eye of the hurricane: witnessing the contrite Lennon at press conferences, saying he could have chosen 'television' as a comparison instead of the Son of God; the

Another day, another press conference – Munich, 23 June 1966

Ku Klux Klan gleefully burning crosses, and Beatle records; the Cincinnati show which saw the bulky Mal Evans electrocuted; the exploding firework which George thought was a gunshot…

The tour was a duty call. You sense they were itching to get back to Abbey Road and fashion the follow-up to *Revolver*, not stand, be pelted by sweeties and run through songs which they had, by and large, lost interest in. But back then, the tour was how the fans got to see you; dates were undertaken to interest your audience in your latest 'product'.

One thing that might have made that final American sortie enjoyable was a plan to record at the legendary Stax studios in Memphis. Keen to soak up some of that juicy Southern soul, Mal Evans was sent on a reconnaissance mission. But he returned with the view that the studios in the predominantly black neighbourhood of downtown Memphis would pose a logistical nightmare, and the group's safety could not be guaranteed.

Label historian Tim Sampson kindly directed me towards a letter George wrote to Atlanta DJ Paul Drew in May 1966 which introduced another element. Written from 'Kinfauns' during the recording of *Revolver*, George asked, "Did you hear that we nearly recorded in Memphis with Jim Stuart (sic)? We would all like it a lot, but too many people get insane with money ideas at the mention of the word 'Beatles', so it fell through".

The Stax label, home to Otis Redding, Isaac Hayes, the Staple Swingers and Sam & Dave, were flattered that the world's most famous group wanted some of their magic to rub off. In 1970, the Stax 'house band' – Booker T & the MGs paid homage with the LP *McLemore Avenue*, an album which drew heavily on the newly-released *Abbey Road*, and pictured the group crossing the road outside the Stax studio in homage to the Beatle LP cover.

Even at their peak, they were used to keeping their ears open: "I used to get 45s sent from America", Paul told me, "I'd get ten records a week, soul stuff, what was charting in America sent over. George had a good Chess collection, he had a lot of Stax and Chess". Indeed a 1965 feature on George's jukebox found it surprisingly full of Booker T, Lee Dorsey, Edwin Starr, Otis Redding, Joe Tex, Marvin Gaye, Don Covay, Wilson Pickett. And nostalgically, Ritchie Barrett's 'Some Other Guy'.

And Kenny Everett was there on 29 August 1966, in San Francisco, when the Beatles played their last-ever concert to a paying audience. There was something in the air, aside from jelly beans. Following the Philippines, and four long years of live performance in clubs, theatres and stadia, it was time to take stock, and a step back. Lennon took a selfie on that stage. Paul asked Tony Barrow to tape what they all sensed would at best be a hiatus, at worst, the end of life on the road. But the 30-minute cassette ran out before the end of the 33-minute concert.

Many years later, home movie footage shot by teenager Barry Hood emerged. Grainy and bleached it may be, but it provides compelling evidence of that final show. There are the group, isolated on a stage in the middle of a baseball stadium. It reminded me of the equally stilted footage shot by Abraham Zapruder one morning in Dallas, Texas in November 1963.

Symbolically, that Candlestick Park performance ended where it had all begun less than a decade before. Paul let rip on Little Richard's 'Long Tall Sally' before the plugs were pulled and the Beatles quit the concert stage. Paul's fondness for the flamboyant

Mr Penniman was well-known, he included Richard's material with the Beatles as well as his own rock & roll testimonials *Choba B CCCP* and *Run Devil Run*. Odd then, as an afterthought, that he never found space for Little Richard's 'Poor Boy Paul'.

How excited were the group to be hunkered down in a baseball stadium bunker feasting off a pre-show meal of roast beef and Yorkshire pudding? Boredom kept at arm's length by visits from Joan Baez and Ralph J. Gleason, hatching plans for *Rolling Stone* magazine. Whiling away time, the group and Baez doodled on a tablecloth which the caterers supplied. It was proudly displayed in their shop window, offers of $300 were even declined. Stolen a week later, it was auctioned in 2022 for $88,000.

Were the omens there? Exhilarated by what they had achieved on their new LP, released three weeks before the show, the tedium of running through songs which meant as little as old postcards held little appeal. Was the prospect of a real autumn break more exciting to them than the Pavlovian experience of a Beatle 'concert'? Was it John's 'Jesus' comments which accounted for the unsold seats? Exactly a month before that final show, Bob Dylan had taken a tumble from his motorcycle. Hindsight reveals that it was probably a minor accident, but it gave Dylan breathing space. It got him out of a TV special, another American tour, a break from the looming deadline for his first novel, recording a follow-up to *Blonde on Blonde*… But at the time, and during his 18-month exile, the rumours persisted: the CIA had got him; he was in a drug rehabilitation unit… hideously scarred, he would never appear in public again…

Four weeks later the Beatles quit the stage of Candlestick Park and entered their own exile. It was not as mysterious as Bob's, but in retrospect, rock's greatest poet and the world's most influential band both disappearing did seem to mark a further end to an era.

After that windswept and desultory San Francisco finale, harried into a van, bumped to the airport, before escaping on their plane, George famously declared: "That's it, I don't have to be a Beatle anymore". He was not to know that as a performing unit, *that* really was it.

Or, as the White Queen told Alice as she ventured through the Looking Glass, "I've done all the screaming already… what would be the good of having it all over again?"

*

In America particularly, as they wound down that final tour, their teenage fans were growing increasingly baffled by their idols. Kenny Everett's biographers caught that dichotomy: "Singing about knowing what it's like to be dead while pre-pubescent girls wet their pants with excitement and pelt you with jelly babies. It doesn't make sense".

Following the Beatles cartoon series, which built upon their *Hard Day's Night* personae, young America was soon beguiled by another Fab Four. By more than coincidence, the first episode of *The Monkees* was screened within a fortnight of the Beatles' last-ever concert appearance. Here were four readily identifiable individuals, larking about in a 'zany' fashion and finding room for a couple of the best Brill Building efforts on each show.

The Beatles held the high ground though, and then, just as the summer holidays were coming to an end, came *Revolver*, the brightest star in the Beatle orbit to date. The album balanced buoyant with affecting, other-worldly music with football anthems. The LP found McCartney in a melancholic phase, containing not only Paul's threnody for "all the lonely people", but also the heart-broken lament 'For No One', a bitter reflection of a love that never was. The wistful 'Here, There & Everywhere'. ("Even at the time, people would ask me, 'Are you conceited?'" McCartney told me once. "I'd say no, not really, but if you ask me do I like Lennon and McCartney songs, then I say I have to be conceited! In my view, you'd have to be stupid to say they're not *good*...")

Lennon sensed the competition this time around, with *Revolver* containing some of his best-ever contributions to the canon – the dreamlike 'I'm Only Sleeping'; the cosmic 'She Said She Said'; the world-weary 'And Your Bird Can Sing'. And most bands could have built a career out of the middle eight of 'Doctor Robert'... If you were old enough, you might discern a drug vibe to those songs. Less innocent minds caught something not quite quantifiable, wisps just out of reach, but containing an element that was somehow... unsettling. And that's before you got to the LP's closing track.

Revolver also marked George's development as a songwriter, scoring three tracks, including the piledriving opener, 'Taxman' – a Beatle first, incidentally, as the first composition to mention real people (Prime Minister Harold Wilson and Conservative opposition leader, "Mr Heath"). As someone whose spirituality was unquestioned, George also took a particular interest in the *secular* side of things. The song came from the heart, at the time Harold Wilson's Labour government's rate of super tax was 98%, which barely left the Beatle with the price of a pint and a packet of fags out of every one of his hard-earned 240 old pennies.

George wasn't the only pop star concerned with pecuniary matters; the Kinks' contemporaneous 'Sunny Afternoon' found Ray Davies bemoaning the avaricious taxman.

It had been while confined to a hotel bed in the Palace Court Hotel in Bournemouth in August 1963 that George wrote his first song, 'Don't Bother Me'. The motive appeared financial as well as creative; George poured his heart out to Astrid Kirchherr, expressing concern about his future income: "You know that John and Paul are going to be very rich when they collect the money by writing all those songs..." while George envisaged himself as "poor and hungry".

In 1963, fashioning those legendary Beatle suits, Duggie Millings was charging £31 per suit. On an invoice, George noticed the new ones were £32 each. A put-out Millings pointed out to the cost-conscious Beatle the rising cost of cloth. By 1964 George emphasised, "I'd like to build up a really big business... have the shares quoted on the Stock Exchange". As photographer Robert Freeman remembered that in *Help!*, George "wore a pink shirt to match the pink copy of the *Financial Times* he carried under his arm". Talking to Alan Freeman in 1965 George had remarked: "I suppose I ask more questions about what happens to our money than any of the others. When I meet the accountant I try to find out what our money is being invested in. But I don't always get answers!" Freeman wrote that of "one of his less endearing qualities ... he keeps an extremely watchful eye on his money".

In fairness, as Dominic Sandbrook later observed, "Who can blame him? He had grown up in a council house, the son of a bus conductor and a shop assistant... It would have been bizarre if he had *not* shared the material ambitions of other working-class youngsters who had grown up in the 1950s".

On *Revolver*, George's 'Love to You' was a more fully realised effort than his earlier sitar tinkering; Jonathan Gould lovingly, colourfully described, "its first cascading arabesque of shimmery, bejeweled notes, the track unfolds like a musicological expedition East of Suez, as the first in a series of quixotic attempts to translate the formal elements of Indian raga into the format of Western pop".

There was not the reverence for pop music back then. While we eagerly followed the Beatles, Stones, Kinks and Who, in the unlikely event that none of their latest work came up to snuff, not to worry, there was always something else as exciting coming down the pike next week.

I mean, I know now, but appreciated even then, that *Revolver* was a magnificent piece of work, with its 14 tracks better even than *Rubber Soul*. Without articulating it, you just sense the LP marked a … progression. From that frenetic one-day burst to nail *Please Please Me*, *Rubber Soul* had occupied 80 hours of studio time. By the time of *Revolver*, nearly a month of working days (220 hours) had gone into its creation.

God alone knows where my 14th birthday present copy of the original *Revolver* LP is. It was replaced on vinyl. Then CD (thinking about it, my very *first* compact disc). Then the 2009 remastered CD. Treating myself to the 2022 box set. New technology allowed proper instrumental separation… studio out-takes provided the usual hairs-on-the-back-of-the-neck glee… In his *Record Collector* review, Jamie Atkins nailed it: "For many, *Revolver* was the album that turned a healthy interest in the Beatles into a lifelong love affair. It's the sweet spot where effortless pop exuberance collides with razor-sharp minds expanding with the possibilities of what music can do".

It is worth pausing to consider just what the Beatles managed to condense into those extraordinary 35 minutes of vinyl: the sweep from up-tempo Stax influences to inspired balladry; from jaunty singalong to the sound of tomorrow. While we now appreciate just how much *Revolver* pushed the envelope and paved the way for *Pepper*, it is worth playing it alongside their rivals' companion work.

The Rolling Stones' *Aftermath* was released four months before *Revolver*, and the Stones album has frequently been cited as their breakthrough LP. Listen again though, only five of the 14 tracks have any substance; the lengthy 'Goin' Home' has been cited as a landmark track, but even Stones expert James Hector concedes, "Frankly, it doesn't achieve much during its 11 minute duration…" And for every 'Lady Jane', the album contained fillers such as 'Think', 'Take It or Leave It', 'What to Do'… even Jagger's reading of the mighty 'Out of Time' palls next to Chris Farlowe's far punchier version.

So, try pitching *Aftermath* against *Revolver*, and there's simply no competition. Any album which includes – random selection – 'Eleanor Rigby', 'Here, There & Everywhere', 'And Your Bird Can Sing', 'Good Day Sunshine' and 'Tomorrow Never Knows', immaculately overseen by George Martin, ineffably demonstrates just why there remains such an enduring and timeless fascination with the recorded work of the Beatles.

For 'Eleanor Rigby' alone the album would be memorable… The name from where…? Eleanor Bron? Wine merchants Rigby & Evans? The Eleanor Rigby buried in Woolton graveyard? A Victorian Liverpool City Hospital scullery maid? It took the – and I do not use the word lightly – genius of Paul McCartney to fashion those elements into an anthem for "all the lonely people". Typically, Lennon later claimed a large percentage of the lyric, though claims also come from George, Ringo and Pete Shotton who did contribute ideas during the song's genesis at Lennon's Weybridge home. Following on from 'Yesterday', it marked the 24-year-old McCartney as being touched by the hand of a songwriting deity.

Whoever and however the song flowered, one thing remains: 'Eleanor Rigby' endures. In Nashville in 2013 I talked to songwriter Billy Montana. Like the old days of the Brill Building, Music City USA has a whole street devoted to songwriters clocking in for a 10–6 stint. Billy had written hits for Sara Evans, Tim McGraw and Garth Brooks. He told me one of his songs had been streamed 24,000,000 times. He had seen $600 out of it. I asked him, in his opinion, as a professional songwriter, which one song he wished he had written. Immediately without hesitation and enthusiastically he responded 'Eleanor Rigby': "So much out of so little… just *listen* to it: the melody, the lyrics, the production, and all in, what, just over two minutes!"

In a sense, 'Eleanor Rigby' was the song which allowed the Beatles to sit at the grown-ups table. It was the song that led Hunter Davies on the path to that only-ever authorised Beatles biography. While it was the Beatles who had helped curtail George Melly's career as a jazz vocalist, when he turned to journalism, casting a caustic eye on the pop scene, he still remembered the "delighted awe" when he heard 'Eleanor Rigby' for the first time: "It seemed to me that pop had come of age".

If Paul's brilliant song was a highlight, *Revolver* wasn't short of others. The upbeat McCartney magic was spread over 'Good Day Sunshine' and 'Got to Get You into My Life'. The pub singalong 'Yellow Submarine' can still be heard today on football terraces (delighted to learn it was Yoko's favourite Beatle song). John's 'She Said She Said' and 'Doctor Robert' were other eerie forerunners of a sonic tomorrow.

'Tomorrow Never Knows' was the signpost to … 'Beyond'. In its review *NME* wondered how you could turn off your mind and relax "with the electronic, outer space noises, often sounding like seagulls?" It was on this track you can see just how agreeably George Martin morphed with the Beatles. Lennon wanted his voice to sound like "the Dalai Lama on a hilltop". Not a request the avuncular producer would have received from Matt Monro. But, as ever, you can just picture Martin rubbing his freshly-shaved chin, puffing pensively on a cigarette, straightening his tie and asking John for a few minutes while he considered how such an effect might be achieved. Engineer Geoff Emerick marvelled at Martin's patience as the group's production requests became increasingly 'far out'. He remembered that the producer's "stock express of disapproval whenever he thought one of them was talking nonsense" was the headmasterly, "Oh, honestly!"

It took more than drugs to create what was heard on *Revolver*; this was the sound of the Beatles' musical imaginations expanding. Up to then only EMI had been able to offer the facilities to realise those sounds inside their minds. Now, they were just as able to tinker with the new technology at home. It was 'Tomorrow Never Knows' that got the group interested in tape loops and led to *Sgt Pepper*. I love George Martin's reflection: "They would bring me in these loops, like cats bringing in sparrows…"

Of that technology, David Hepworth commented on the head-on clashes which took place regularly at Abbey Road as the Beatles began flexing their sonic muscles: "[The] combination of hallucinogenic drugs on the one hand and Heath Robinson practicality on the other… This was the place where *The Tibetan Book of the Dead* met *The Handbook of Practical Electronics*".

Klaus Voormann later revealed he got just £50 for his *Revolver* cover. He remembered showing them the rough proof at Abbey Road and emphasising, "Everyone else does colour, you do black and white". And there they were, Beatles of all ages struggling to get out of each other's hair. Robert Freeman's draft cover was equally striking, a photomontage of Beatle faces that can be seen in the 2022 *Revolver* box set.

That package came replete with innumerable aural delights – the usual fly-on-the-wall opportunities to hear the group probe for the perfect version as various versions were discarded on the way. The one track which attracted the most attention was 'Part 1, songwriting work tape' of 'Yellow Submarine'. For over half a century, everyone has assumed it was nigh-on a 100% McCartney creation. However, *this* time round there is the opportunity to hear Lennon pitch in with a jaundiced, almost folk-style lyric which could have appeared on 'In My Life'.

McCartney remembered playing the album to Bob Dylan. "Oh I get it," Bob sagely responded, "you don't want to be cute anymore". On its release, *Revolver* left a number of critics baffled. It was savaged in *Melody Maker* by Ray Davies ('Tomorrow Never Knows': "I can imagine they had George Martin tied to a totem pole when they did this"). One fan wrote to *Beatles Monthly* after listening to the LP convinced the group had gone "stark, raving mad".

They were in the minority. To their credit, contemporary reviewers appreciated just what a giant step the Beatles had taken on their seventh LP. ("There are still more ideas buzzing around in the Beatles' heads than in most of the pop world put together... the result is a veritable goldmine of ideas...", *Melody Maker*... "It isn't easy to describe what's here, since much of it involves things which are either new to pop music or which are being properly applied for the first time, and which can't be helpfully compared with anything", *The Gramophone*.)

It had been in its 15 April 1966 issue that *Time* magazine christened London 'The Swinging City'. The article began pointing out how London had seized the baton from Vienna, Paris and New York as the epicentre of "what's happening". It revelled in the "uninhibited and kinky" capital, with an arc that swept from Princess Margaret to Cathy McGowan. Youth was emphasised (Harold Wilson was the youngest Prime Minister of the century) and how 30% of the UK was aged between 15 and 34. This was the territory of 'the new elite', with the switch from aristocracy and the City of London to discotheques, hairdressing salons and boutiques. Also singled out were the young, "sporting their distinctive regional accents like badges". Few could have had any doubt of whom *Time* had in mind.

It *was* an extraordinary flashpoint in our nation's history. The class divide crumbled, aristos came down from their ivory towers to mingle with the oiks who had made their way up from below the salt. Old Etonian, gallery owner Robert Fraser, grandees Tara Browne, Christopher Gibbs and Jane Ormsby-Gore were all happy to cultivate the new pop aristocracy. The hoi-poloi cheek by jowl with the highfalutin. It was a time of re-invention, thus Twiggy's manager Nigel Davies was reborn as 'Justin de Villeneuve'.

This was a London where a pint of beer cost 10p, the average house price was £3,620 and a ticket to the World Cup Final on 30 July would have set you back 50p. The English team's 4–2 triumph over *West* Germany (emphasising the Cold War division), set the seal on that year of years.

London became a magnet: wide-eyed provincials flocked to the capital. Film-makers like Antonioni came to put their finger on the zeitgeist. From abroad, children persuaded their parents to alter their holiday destinations. I love the scene at the conclusion of the *Dirty Dancing* movie, set in the summer of 1963, and written with the benefit of hindsight, but nonetheless touching, poignantly addressing the end of the old:

"Lots of changes, though, Max."

"It's not the changes so much this time. It's that it all seems to be *ending*. You think kids want to come with their parents and take fox-trot lessons? Trips to Europe, that's what the kids want… It feels like it's all… slipping away."

*

By their exhausting standards, 1966 proved to be a relatively quiet year for the Beatles. There had been that lull at year's onset when plans for the third film remained unrealised. But, following the summer '66 tour dates, the group had real time on their hands. Paul hung around the London avant-garde scene and went on safari. Ringo hunkered down in the Surrey countryside. John went to Spain on location. George went to India to study the sitar – aside from LPs of Indian music, the only 'pop' album he took was Dylan's *Blonde on Blonde*.

With the touring on hold, Brian Epstein's importance inevitably diminished. Time was hanging heavy. A gap was widening. In the bunker at Abbey Road, 'the boys' had George Martin to work with. Brian would advise, but never interfere with their music. As the group reconvened at the EMI studios, sporting unexpected facial hair that autumn of 1966, Brian appreciated that for the first time in three years, it would be too late for a new Christmas Beatle LP. He must have hoped though, that a single could be squeezed out, perhaps along the lines of their previous success: the coupling of the jaunty, singalong 'Yellow Submarine' with the poignant, reflective 'Eleanor Rigby' had proved globally successful.

Both were largely McCartney efforts, and while the popular image of the group is tough, rebellious John versus crowd-pleasing Paul, the fact is that it was far from the truth. As far back as 1965, McCartney had contacted Delia Derbyshire, who ran the experimental BBC Radiophonic Workshop (and famously worked up the *Dr Who* theme) to provide electronic backing for 'Yesterday'. With an ear close to the London underground scene, it was McCartney who sailed close to the wind attending avant-garde concerts by Luciano Berio and Cornelius Cardew.

Ian Peel's exhaustive book, *The Unknown Paul McCartney: McCartney & The Avant Garde* tells you all you need to know about the extent of Paul's experimentations. Throughout his careers, these odysseys took him far away from his image as 'the soft Beatle'.

It was Lennon who dismissed "the avant garde" as "French for bullshit", while he remained in suburban Weybridge, sitting in his nowhere land. Little did he know what lay ahead when he met his second wife. That autumn 1966 break proved hardest for the group's founder. On 5 September, barely a week after the end of their US tour, John Lennon flew to Germany to begin filming *How I Won the War*. He was terrified at the prospect of enforced idleness, and admitted he only took the role "because it was Dick Lester who asked me; because it was anti-war and because I didn't know what to do because the Beatles had stopped touring."

While Dick Lester went on to make a number of rewarding films – *The Bed Sitting Room*, *Juggernaut*, *Royal Flash*, *Robin & Marian* – it was *How I Won the War* which took on a life of its own. The reason of course is not the star, Michael Crawford, nor Charles Wood's script, nor the director. It is an opportunity to see John Lennon undertake a rare solo activity while still a Beatle. Lennon's haircut for the film was front-page news. (Less-publicised was the trim George took during his visit to India to study with Ravi Shankar at the same time.) Equally arresting were John's NHS 'granny glasses' he wore for the role of Private Gripweed, which were to become his trademark look.

Incredibly, the film was originally planned as a vehicle for Norman Wisdom. But with its satire bordering on farce – Crawford's platoon are ordered to build a cricket pitch behind enemy lines during the 1942 North Africa campaign – Lester's *How I Won the War* is very much locked in the late-60s, anti-establishment, anti-war mood. Michael Hordern gives his usual reliable performance; solid support comes from Roy Kinnear and Lee Montague, and Lennon is *good* as the grovelling Private Gripweed, relishing the Goon-influenced dialogue: "Are you married?" "No, I play the harmonica".

Lester's intention was to mock the heroics of war films, which flourished in the UK throughout the 1950s. But, when it opened in 1967, critics pounced on the film's mockery and traducing of British valour. Churchill, who had only died a few years before and was enshrined as the nation's saviour, is seen as a ventriloquist's dummy, demanding more battles. It's not a *bad* film, but it is a film of its time, and one which time has not been kind to.

How I Won the War attracted headlines at the time such as: "The Next Row Looms Over Lennon…"; "No Children At Beatle's Film" and "Outrage!" Editorials castigated Lester for his mocking of Our Finest Hour, but a more considered opinion came from *The Sunday Times*' eminent film critic Dilys Powell when she reflected on the film's mocking tone: "They … remind me what the world might have been like, what might have happened to many of my friends, if it had not been for people ready to fight and even to undertake apparently lunatic missions in the Western Desert. I can't help thinking Mr. Lester with these passages undoes what he has done in undermining the war-glory boys".

Historically, however, it was what occurred off-screen that has endured. On a windswept Spanish location, there was little to do but play knockabout cricket. The longueurs of film production left Lennon isolated and bored. The gates of the Spanish villa he shared with Michael Crawford sparked a memory. So, during the lengthy spells of down time, Lennon cast his mind back to the view from his garden at Menlove Avenue. Hard to believe, it had only been ten years before.

Once he finished filming, Lennon returned home to pick up on his day job. In November 1966, the sands were shifting once again: he met Yoko Ono for the first time and, later that month, the Beatles returned to Abbey Road to begin recording their follow-up to *Revolver*. The first song they cut was the only one John had begun while filming *How I Won the War*… 'Strawberry Fields Forever'.

Once recording began, with its dislocating structure and state-of-the-art effects,

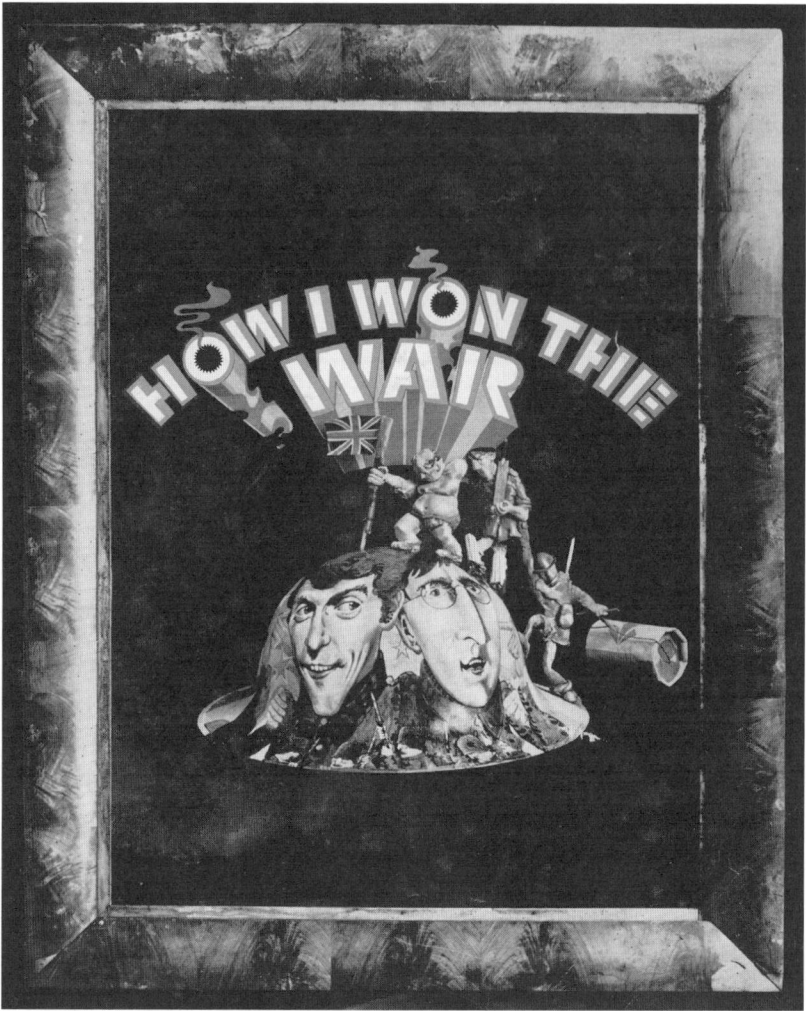

How I Won the War campaign book

innumerable versions were recorded, with nobody able to decide which was the best. It led to Lennon blithely asking George Martin: "Why don't we join them together? You could start with Take 7 and move to Take 20 halfway through to get the grandstand finish?" Long used to Lennon's demands, even Martin professed to be stumped. "There are only two things wrong with that, John", the long-suffering producer replied, "the Takes are in completely different keys, a whole tone apart and they have wildly different tempos". "Well," smiled John, "I'm sure you can fix it, can't you?" (He did. The edit can be clearly heard on CD, exactly one minute into the song.)

If people thought 'Tomorrow Never Knows' had been a detour, 'Strawberry Fields Forever' was emphatically, undeniably, a wholly new direction. This was uncharted territory for pop, a place where 'nothing was real', where the listener was invited to 'tune in', a phrase which was just beginning to have clear drug connotations. These fields were where everything was a dream and, indeed, there was a dream-like quality to the song: the ethereal shapes conjured up by what we know now as a Mellotron, before Ringo's familiar drums crash in. But even his percussive underpinning was strangely unnerving; jarring and dislocated. There was nothing to hang onto in the song. All those hesitations you know, er, I mean… no visible chorus, just a reference to a fruit always associated with tennis at Wimbledon. And it never seemed to *end*… weird, discordant noises and some remote voice mentioning a favourite condiment to accompany the Christmas turkey.

The vocal was jerky, hesitant; uncertain and unsure. Talking to Ken Sharp in 1998, George Martin remembered a dinner he'd had with John many years later. Lennon hated the sound of his voice on record, and wanted to re-record everything he'd done with the Beatles. "But I realised John was a dreamer. In John's mind everything was so beautiful and much better than it was in real life. He was never a person of nuts and bolts. The bitter truth is music *is* nuts and bolts, you've got to bring it down to horse hair going over a bit of wood, people blowing into brass tubes. You've got to get down to practicalities".

Just before the end of 1966, Paul too had got back down to work. 'Penny Lane' is a McCartney triumph, a vignette "part nostalgia for a place… blue suburban skies as we remember it". The composer had fond memories of Mr Biolletti's barber shop,[16] the bus shelter in the middle of the roundabout, the two banks, the fire station on Allerton Road. 'Penny Lane' came sprinkled with sufficient psychedelic garnish, but the rest of the characters came to linger in the popular imagination: the banker sheltering from the rain, the poppy-selling pretty nurse, the barber with the tonsorial photos in the window, the fireman with his very clean machine, the fish and finger pies… all, undeniably, very strange.

In tandem, and on release, the songs were soon linked to their native Liverpool. While the lyrical references may have been nostalgic, the music that accompanied them was radically forward looking.

Outside Abbey Road, it was also time to take stock. On New Year's Eve 1966, Hunter Davies, a young *Sunday Times* journalist, wrote to Brian Epstein. On Paul's advice he was

---

16 I was inexplicably delighted when talking to Saira Quli to find out that her first boyfriend was Justin Bioletti, son of the legendary barber.

pitching a book ("not a fan book"). Not knowing his letter would arrive at such a pivotal moment, Davies was confident that "I'm sure the boys and you yourself might forget in the years to come exactly what happened… I'm sure there's need for a full anatomy of the Beatle phenomenon".

So 1966 drew to a close, and with no new album on the horizon for the lucrative 1966 Christmas market, Brian Epstein had sanctioned *A Collection of Beatles Oldies… But Goldies*. It was a workmanlike Greatest Hits (and one of the very few official Beatle releases never made available on CD). All the hits were there, as well as the US-only 'Bad Boy', another Larry Williams cover. Of passing interest was the colourful cover, cleverly tapping into the recent 'Swinging London' phenomenon. Interestingly, it only made No.7 on the UK chart.

Defectors switched their allegiance to the Monkees, who promised a weekly burst of japes and capers, though quite what the 'something' this 'young generation' actually had to *say* remains unclear. Like those who live through any historical epoch, hindsight is a wonderful thing. But of course, be it a world war or a change in musical direction, few knew what the future held. Save for perhaps a handful of people working in an otherwise anonymous recording studio in north-west London.

As with so many elements of the music machine, it was the Beatles who introduced UK record buyers to the novelty of the double-A-sided single: radio favoured the more listener-friendly 'Penny Lane', while 'heads' latched onto the other-worldly 'Strawberry Fields Forever'. Yet another record-breaking achievement of that remarkable 45 came with the fact that it was the first rock & roll single in the UK to be released in a picture sleeve.

Perhaps it was the unfamiliar, other-worldliness of 'Strawberry Fields' which denied it the UK No.1 spot. No 'She Loves You' this. After ten straight chart-toppers, their 1967 release broke the run. More likely though, it was due to the last-minute substitute on *Sunday Night at the London Palladium* of Engelbert Humperdinck for Dickie Valentine. Engelbert sang 'Release Me' and the show's vast Sunday-night, predominantly MOR audience kept the 21-year-old country song at No.1 for six weeks. In recompense, Engelbert's 2001 *I Want to Wake Up with You* album included his version of 'Penny Lane', which he had kept off the top in 1967.

Sunday Night at the London Palladium was the country's equivalent of *The Ed Sullivan Show* and, such was the UK's fascination for all things Scouse at the time, I'm convinced the reason Jimmy Tarbuck took over from Bruce Forsyth as compere of the popular Sunday night variety show was as much to do with his birthplace and Beatle haircut as his comic skills. His second appearance as host in 1965 had cockney comedian Arthur Haynes berating him at the way you'll never succeed in 'the business' unless you come from Liverpool.

Thanks to the Beatles, Liverpool almost ran parallel to London in terms of impact. In 1966 the paperback *The Penguin John Lennon* gathered together his two books in one volume. Penguin were not slow off the mark the next year to publish *The Mersey Sound*. A poetry anthology gathering Adrien Henri, Brian Patten and Roger McGough, it went on to become one of the country's most successful ever poetry titles, with sales in excess of half a million.

The 'Penny Lane' and 'Strawberry Fields Forever' single was cut just before the end of 1966. Engineer Geoff Emerick was not only one who marvelled at the progress since 'Yellow Submarine', calling the new songs "one vast, giant step toward something that was better than we'd ever heard… into a new generation and a new time".

With no new single to end the year, it was a time to reflect. In *Pop Teenbeat Annual*, Albert Hand wrote sagely that, "1966 was a year of problems and questions… To many fans, the idea that The Beatles … might wish to stop being The Beatles … seems ludicrous. They cannot estimate or even begin to understand what started out as a great adventure years before, when you had no money and there was all the world to gain, can become not only a bore but a physical strain when you have enough money to provide you with a rich man's income for the rest of your life, and yet the public still requires you to perform, expecting each of your offerings to be better than the last, and yet still forcing you to lead a life that is constantly circumscribed by the necessity of securing you from the over-eager admiration of your fans".

For Hand, who also ran the UK Elvis Presley Fan Club, he felt the answer to the dilemma facing the group was to follow Presley's route into films as 'the new Marx Brothers'. In fact, they chose to go entirely in the opposite direction…

As 'The Summer of Love' dawned, the Beatles were avatars of that capering, colourful era. They never made it to the first rock festival at Monterey, but a signed poster from them did. The Beatles never played a rock festival, but their songs and collective mantra hovered over these huge events. The Beatles were seen as totemic by influencers like Timothy Leary: "I declare that The Beatles are mutants. Prototypes of evolutionary agents sent by God, endowed with a mysterious power to create a new human species, a young race of laughing freemen". Ringo had been more prosaic: "I'd like to end up sort of unforgettable".

In America, the most arresting new music was coming out of San Francisco. Like many, the Beatles were fascinated by the intriguingly-named outfits – the Grateful Dead, Quicksilver Messenger Surface, Love, Jefferson Airplane, Big Brother & the Holding Company… After mercifully quitting the city in summer 1966, George famously returned to San Francisco during August 1967 to check out the hippie capital. "It was horrible", George's wife Pattie remembered, "full of ghastly drop-outs, bums and spotty youths, all out of their brains… They looked at us expectantly – as if George was some kind of Messiah".

In *Melody Maker*, Harry Pules (a name, I'm afraid, that sounds like a character from *The Goon Show*) accompanied him during his disillusioning stroll. "You are our leader, George." "No, you don't want to be following leaders, me or anyone else". One persistent fan kept trying to lay STP on him. "Hey, George, I tried to give you a gift that would turn you on, man, and you put me down, man, I don't like that, man, that was wrong, man". Handed a guitar and asked to play, George acquiesced. "Here's a G. And an E and so on, up and down the scale". The implication being, man, that anyone can do it, not just a Beatle.

Sequestered in the studio, no one knew what *they* were attempting, but they could be seen on their way in and out of the EMI studios, and their image had altered demonstrably. Doorstepped by an ITV news crew on their way in to recording in late 1966, all sported facial hair. The way the Beatles looked was a sign of the times. The way they *sounded* confirmed that any new Fab music was going to be more akin to 'Tomorrow Never Knows' than 'Yellow Submarine' – though, typically, both those songs had been found on one LP. Their first single of 1967 was the signpost to where they were going. The question was, were we prepared to follow?

Kenny Everett had got first dibs on 'Strawberry Fields Forever'. As well as his closeness to the group, he also had a year-long association with Brian Epstein's PA, Peter Brown. This led to further Beatle endorsements ("This is James Paul McCartney, Upper 5B, saying that Kenny Everett is just about one of the finest disc jockeys in the world..."). He oversaw the 1968 and 1969 Beatles Christmas records and remained a devoted admirer to the end.

Everett's much-loved spell at London's Capital Radio during the 1970s included his quest for the world's worst record. It was won by Jimmy Cross, with his 1964 necrophiliac ode 'I Want My Baby Back'. Was it just coincidence that the tasteless winner began with Cross driving his 'baby' back from a Beatles concert? At Everett's funeral, 'Strawberry Fields Forever' echoed round the church.

The first Beatle single in four years *not* to reach No.1 was enough to prompt a healthy mailbag to the pop weeklies; *Record Mirror* devoted half a page to the controversy – "They may be outrunning public taste and losing fans by their intellectual releases" (Alicia Fortinberry); "Could it be that beneath our mini-mocking, freakout-flashing, pop-painting exterior we harbour such old-fashioned things as 'love, girls, emotion'. How many really understood 'Strawberry Fields'?" (Concetta Verga); Michael Puttick spoke for many 1967 fans: "Six months is too long for a single; ten months much too long for an 'original' album".

In *Melody Maker*, on the eve of the LP's release ("reported to be revolutionary, carrying the cryptic title *Sergeant Pepper's Lonely Hearts Club Band*"), Alan Walsh wrote, "As far as the trappings of pop are concerned – TV, tours, interviews etc – The Beatles are incommunicado. No contact with their fans, no appearances. And, it seems little likelihood in the near future of a start to their long-awaited third feature film. The unworldly, almost god-like existence of Beatles 1967 does give rise to the question: is pop becoming too clever, too complex, too hip?"

It was the pirate station Radio London, thanks to Kenny Everett's Fab inside track, which got the world exclusive on 'the new Beatles LP'. On 12 May 1967, three weeks before release, the *Sgt Pepper* LP was broadcast. It is one of those disorientating experiences hearing the broadcast now. Amidst the missing person announcements, DJ John Peel, later the personification of everything hip and alternative, is heard telling listeners of a "Big L party night" at the Carlton Ballroom, Slough. Or enticing them to attend stock car racing in Wimbledon, or tag wrestling in Eastbourne. Peel, sounding a lot less Scouse than when he emerged on Radio 1, does however confidently confirm that the Beatles "are two years ahead of everybody else" with their latest release.

Disc & Music Echo too went into overdrive. "Another masterpiece of musical genius... Digested it matures like a good wine, becomes exceedingly heady, and will inevitably knock the rest of pop for six with its sheer beauty and potency". A month later the paper exulted at finding the "real Sgt Pepper". Sgt Graham Pepper was serving with the USAF at Mildenhall, and was flattered, but admitted was more of an Ernest Tubb fan.

On its release, opinion on *Sgt Pepper* was divided, the *Melody Maker* letters page was filled week after week: "It's practically a new art form"; "What the Hell are the Beatles trying to do to pop music?" There was concern about that switch in musical direction. Reporting in the trendy *London Look* magazine, John McLeod cautioned: "they have veered so far from the accepted pop 'blueprint' that one might almost think they were bent on discarding a few hundred thousand of their fans…"

At the *Sgt Pepper* playback in May 1967, Jack Hutton from *Melody Maker* was equally impressed by "Brian Epstein's luxurious town house", as well as "a long genuine antique table [groaning]… under huge dishes of cold meats and vegetables served by white-jacketed waiters. To drink there was a choice of gazpacho, a cold soup, or champers. The champers won handsomely".

I remember everyone thinking at the time, how could even the Beatles come up with a tune to match such a cumbersome title? And there was talk at the time of it being 'a concept album'. That was an entirely new … concept. In reality, on listening, there was little to link the songs to any narrative. The idea that the LP was a concert by Sgt Pepper's band pretty much disappears after the second track until they remember it as a reprise for the album's penultimate track.

The 'concept' theory grew in favour when you *looked* at the LP; until then, if you wanted to select a track, you consulted the LP sleeve, and dropped the needle on the appropriate track. *Sgt Pepper* did not allow you that choice. There was no indication in the vinyl grooves as to where 'Fixing a Hole' or 'Lovely Rita' actually began, or ended.

The LP which was at one time *perhaps* intended to be an autobiographical Liverpool mini-opera, featuring both of John and Paul's memories, might have given it the idea of a concept album a coherence. But, by early 1967, Brian Epstein was concerned at the lack of what the industry now calls 'product'. He pressured George Martin to release 'Strawberry Fields' and 'Penny Lane' as a single. He could then get back to finishing the album recording, which was stretching on and on. It was a decision Martin always regretted.

In the prestigious *Melody Maker* Poll of 1967, the Beatles' 45 was beaten as Single of the Year by Lennon's favourites, Procol Harum's 'Whiter Shade of Pale'. However, the Beatles held the top slot as British and International Group, with *Sgt Pepper* the No.1 LP Disc in both sections.

From the cover in, *Sgt Pepper* felt like Alice tripping, and falling down the rabbit hole. It took years to identify everyone on that iconic cover. As if to acknowledge the journey from 'She Loves You' to 'A Day in the Life', standing next to the real-life Beatles were the grinning waxworks of four years before. Four years! These days, that's about the time it takes a band to get the drum sound right.

We now know that the original plan for the sleeve was for them to be dressed up in Salvation Army-style costumes, perhaps posing around a flower clock familiar from municipal gardens of their youth. But then the colourful feel of the period took over. Sometimes, as previously indicated, the *look* of the Beatles was as important as what they sounded like. Rarely more so than during that transitional 1966/67 period.

Doctor in Clover (stay with me) was the last of the phenomenally successful film series based on the books of Richard Gordon. Dirk Bogarde had jumped ship, and Leslie ("Hel-lo") Phillips came on board. It was released in 1966; in life, Phillips was 42, on film he's admitting to 35, but his love interest declares him too old and his moustache

as "old fashioned". Moustache duly shaved off, a Beatle fringe combed forward and a trip to Carnaby Street finds him hitting the groove. The film contained a reference to "a hard day's night" and to cash-in on the capital's trendy image, was renamed *Carnaby Street* on its American release.

When the Beatles emerged with moustaches during the autumn of 1966 they made facial hair fashionable. The very idea of a Beatle with beard or moustache was unthinkable, indeed both *Hard Day's Night* and *Help!* got comic mileage out of their fresh faces adorned by goatees, moustaches and beards.

It was also when Lennon broke cover in the NHS glasses he had adopted for *How I Won the War*. The look suggested a harkening back to the very unfashionable Victorian era. By the time of the release of *Sgt Pepper* during the middle of 1967, Victoriana was in full swing. One of the most popular boutiques was *I Was Lord Kitchener's Valet*, the hero of the Victorian militarism, its logo based on the iconic First World War recruitment poster. Jimi Hendrix's favoured jacket of the time was that of a veterinary surgeon from the Crimean war.

One of the most anticipated films of 1967 was John Schlesinger's *Far From the Madding Crowd*, relocating Swinging London's most glamorous couple, Terence Stamp and Julie Christie (the "Terry and Julie" of 'Waterloo Sunset'), from contemporary London to 19th-century Wessex. Stamp's dashing Sergeant Troy, with his sexy sabre wielding and blood-red uniform jacket could well have stepped off the *Pepper* cover.

Soon after came Tony Richardson's iconoclastic *Charge of the Light Brigade*, reuniting David Hemmings and Vanessa Redgrave immediately after their archetypal Swinging 60s outing in *Blow-Up*. But this time the trendy couple were fashionably attired in costumes which would have passed muster at the Great Exhibition.

Coinciding with that Victorian revival, the TV event of 1967 was BBC2's *The Forsyte Saga*, John Galsworthy's novel rendered into 26 episodes about the rise and fall of a Victorian dynasty. On its repeat on the mainstream BBC1 in 1968, it was garnering an incredible 18 million viewers an episode, one third of the entire country. I only learned recently that George Martin was always quick to curtail Sunday Beatle sessions so he could get home in time for *The Forsyte Saga*.

While the Beatles held sway during the six months of recording *Sgt Pepper*, the EMI Studios at Abbey Road were still a working studio. Among other acts recording there while the Beatles fashioned rock's most influential LP were Ambrose Slade, Pink Floyd, the Zombies, the Pretty Things as well as classical artists and many on the EMI roster. But it was the Beatles who kept the lights burning late into the night.

George told me about breaking into the studio's fridge in search of milk for their endless supply of tea. He wryly recalled "the boffins" patrolling in their knee-length white coats, and the lesser-ranking staff in brown.

On its release, *Sgt Pepper* was everywhere. Within days it was evident that this was more than just 'the new Beatles LP', exciting and enticing as that was. This was, in the words of one of their early heroes, and one sadly missing from the cover, Eddie Cochran,

'Something Else'. It was watching *Anthology* on the album's creation that I envied those glimpsed to be there at the recording of 'A Day in the Life' – Mick Jagger, Donovan, Mike Nesmith, the Fool… I liken it to being by Melville's side as the last full stop was added to *Moby Dick*… Picasso brushing off *Guernica*… Welles calling 'cut' on the final frame of *Citizen Kane*.

Seventeen-year-old Peter Frampton picked up a pre-release copy in Petticoat Lane ("I didn't come out of my room for about three days. I just played it nonstop"). Robert Stigwood played it to his latest signings; "nobody could believe it," Barry Gibb recalled. "It frightened us to death".

Playwright Tennessee Williams called *Sgt Pepper* "the most original, the most beautifully poetic album of songs" that he had ever heard. Abbie Hoffman, a Marxist of the Groucho rather than Karl persuasion, felt that it expressed "our view of the world". Paul McCartney told me he remembered receiving a telegram from the actor James Fox: "*Sgt Pepper* rules!" In fondly retrospective mood, the album's architect confirmed that one of the highlights of his professional career was tripping along to the Brian Epstein-owned Saville Theatre within hours of the album's release to witness Jimi Hendrix deliver a blistering performance of the album's title track.

In a year-end reprisal, the hard-to-please Norman Jopling of *Record Mirror* found flaws: "the uninspiring reds on the inner sleeve, and … lack of clarity in the centre photograph…" but sagely concluded, "This album points the way for the development of long-playing pop. Pop artistes with enough ability to sustain long-playing pop. Pop artistes with enough ability to sustain 40 minutes or so can think in terms of telling lengthy musical stories… and to make LPs… as artistic productions in their own right rather than as reproductions of concert performances".

Not everyone was on the same side of the generation gap: the ultra-right-wing John Birch Society was convinced that the album displayed a fluency in brainwashing techniques, culled from Communism. Maryland Governor Spiro Agnew (soon to be Vice President under Richard Nixon) tried to ban the LP from the airwaves because of its determination to encourage listeners to get high.

At the time, everyone associated the going upstairs for a smoke to be drug related. And Paul did admit there was a knowing smirk about the lyric. But what got overlooked was that in Britain, smoking cigarettes was only permitted upstairs on a bus. The most obvious drug connotation came with the giddy weirdness of 'Lucy in the Sky with Diamonds' (LSD – geddit?). But to his dying day Lennon – always keen to take credit for any pioneering element in the group – strenuously denied that was in his head when he wrote it.

The cover alone was intriguing enough, pre-*Mojo*, before the internet, it took ages to identify everybody on that crowded cover. Some faces were easy: Dylan (Bob and Thomas), Lewis Carroll, Brando… But bald bloke top left? Chap in cowboy hat? Man waving behind Paul's head? It hadn't been just the Fab Four who pitched in names, designer Peter Blake earned his £200 with some of his suggestions. If they thought it would be pored over as scrupulously as any annotated Shakespeare manuscript, the Beatles might have spent a little longer on deciding just who should occupy that valuable space. As it was, the *Sgt Pepper* cover has gone on to become one of the iconic images of the era.

The pink and white inner sleeve was a nice surprise; the cardboard cut-outs raised a smile. Another rumour surrounding the LP was, according to *International Times,* that "the moustache in the cut-out given with the record gives highly interesting results when eaten..." The soldier pictured on the cut-out was more than a mere sergeant. Somehow the true identity of this professional soldier, who served with distinction in the Boer and Great Wars, was revealed as Major-General James Melville Babington (1854–1936). Peter Blake amended a picture which had been found in the book of *Celebrities of the Army.*

Many years later I attended a preview at the Imperial War Museum of an exhibition about Lawrence of Arabia. Talking to the curator I found one error: I had forgotten that T.E. Lawrence was peeking out from behind Lewis Carroll on the LP cover, which was represented in the exhibition. But they had the *Pepper* release date as 1987, I pointed out that was the CD release date, which sent an anxious curator tearing back with the Tipp-Ex.

Of more significance on that historic cover was the decision to include the lyrics on the back sleeve, another first for the Fabs. They knew that *Sgt Pepper* was more than the sum of its parts. This was a record on which they had something to say, and they wanted the world to read it as well as hear it.

Its emblematic cover, proudly displayed in teenage bedrooms, carried under students' arms; the music percolating from every tranny and hi-fi... One indication of an album's influence is the way it is adapted and soon parodied. Soon after *Sgt Pepper*, Frank Zappa and his Mothers of Invention parodied the sleeve with their *We're Only in It for the Money.* The Beatles had their idols as inspirations, Zappa went the polar opposite: Lee Harvey Oswald at his moment of death... President Johnson... Guy Fawkes... the Phantom of the Opera... nightmare visions, and all the while Zappa was warning the youth of America to be wary of entering 'Camp Reagan', the "final solution for the non-conformist hippy problem".

With the UK pirate radio stations soon to be sunk by Postmaster General Tony Benn, the strictly-controlled BBC airwaves were wary of the LP's contents. Internal correspondence reveals the Corporation's concerns over 'A Day in the Life'. Correspondence between the BBC's Frank Gillard and EMI's Sir Joseph Lockwood began with a weary, "I never thought the day would come when we would have to put a ban on an EMI record, but sadly this is what has happened over this track... we cannot avoid coming to the conclusion that the words 'I'd love to turn you on' followed by that mounting montage of sound could have a rather sinister meaning".

Sgt Pepper was very much a Paul construct: he mapped out the concept while returning from his Kenyan safari ("We were fed up with being the Beatles," he told Barry Miles. "We really hated that fucking four little mop-top boys approach. We were not boys, we were men..."). From that, he built the idea of the Beatles disappearing behind a facade, conjured up by the oddly-named ensembles which seemed to be pouring out of San Francisco every week.

Lennon's growing fascination with Yoko and his crumbling marriage found him largely on shore leave ("I've got nothing to say", he sang on 'Good Morning'). The lyrics of 'Being for the Benefit of Mr Kite' were copied almost verbatim from a circus poster. Converted to the power of LSD, the true side of Lennon was apparent, and imagine the loyal Cynthia's reaction when she heard her husband singing about beating his woman and keeping her apart from the things she loves?

THE BEATLES (circa 1967)

PARLOPHONE

In and out of style, Parlophone press photo

The 50th anniversary release revealed a plethora of alternate takes. They were intriguing and offered the usual tantalising fascination of being a fly on the wall at Abbey Road during those momentous sessions.

All those Lego bricks of takes, plus little bits of studio banter and rudimentary backing tracks were fascinating. What you get with the Beatles are snippets, works in progress; nonetheless, lovely, these are join-the-dots fragments which go into making the picture whole.

For all the album's majesty, it's funny how much filler made it onto what is still venerated as rock's most influential album. I doubt if 'Getting Better', 'Fixing a Hole', 'Lovely Rita' or 'Mr Kite' make it onto many 'Best of the Beatles' lists. Any two of those could have been dumped in favour of 'Penny Lane' and 'Strawberry Fields'. Indeed it is fascinating, if fruitless, to speculate just how that original concept of a Liverpool childhood could have sounded: John could have dusted down the original lyrics to 'In My Life'; George's 'Only a Northern Song' was primed… As Hunter Davies revealed, John and Paul were writing *together* at that stage, so there surely could have been a genuine collaboration between Lennon and McCartney about just what they did remember from those long-gone Liverpool days?

For his 1966 holiday, Paul had contributed the soundtrack to *The Family Way*, and 'When I'm 64' was certainly cut from that same Wilfred Pickles, grim-up-North, cotton weave. The tune had been in Paul's head for years and it proved a nice antidote to the earnestness of the rest of the LP. Ian MacDonald summed up the song's appeal nicely: "His father Jim had turned sixty-four… and [it] was placed like a comic brass fob-watch suspended from a floral waistcoat, amid the multi-layered psychedelic textures of *Sgt Pepper*, providing a down-to-earth interlude after Harrison's complex and serious 'Within You Without You'."

Building on 'Eleanor Rigby', 'She's Leaving Home' is cut from the same sad cloth. Paul's song has a genuine, heartfelt poignancy, a timely reminder of the divisions which divided the generations at the time of the album's release. In another of those almost supernatural coincidences, the song's subject (based on a newspaper account Paul had read while recording the album) was Melanie Coe; the same teenager who had once won a Brenda Lee miming prize on *Ready! Steady! Go!*, her prize had been presented by none other than Paul McCartney.

It is astonishing to think that – what I still maintain is – rock's most influential LP, was put together on 4-track. Just think, no synthesisers, no auto-tuning, no sampling. By the time of the album's 20th anniversary, 48-tracks and more were possible. "We had to invent our own tools," George Martin told Kurt Loder, "rather like cave men". A comment from the producer on the *Anthology* DVD stood out for me, how he was struck by the group's "eternal curiosity" about what could be accomplished in the recording studio.

As well as fashioning the album with its cut-ups, tape loops and other- worldly sounds, George Martin dipped back into his own past to introduce the "lovely audience" you hear at the album start. Martin was keen to capture that "wonderful hush" of an audience just immediately prior to the performance commencing; before curtain-up. So he went back six years to the Fortune Theatre, and borrowed that 'hush' from a performance of *Beyond the Fringe* which he had recorded for disc.

Through his contacts and over the years, Martin had built up a strong relationship with session musicians, especially in the classical world. One estimate has over 100 musicians playing on the album, many taking time off from their day jobs. For his 2007 World Service documentary, *It Was 40 Years Ago*, producer John Sugar assembled some of them. The general consensus was that, if it was a call for an 11 p.m. session, it was the Beatles. David Mason (1926–2011), who supplied the distinctive trumpet on 'Penny Lane', was typical: "I played with Von Karajan, I played with Malcolm Sargent, I played with the Royal Philharmonic Orchestra, but all I *ever* get asked about is two takes in a one-hour session at Abbey Road in November 1966…!"

It was a cri-de-coeur echoed by many of the classical musicians who came into the Beatle orbit. Sheila Bromberg (1928–2021) was the harpist who supplied the flowery opening to 'She's Leaving Home'. For her £9 session fee she supplied various versions, but with a bit of studio flummery, they used the first. She confessed she did find it "a little bizarre", that of all the music she'd performed during a long professional career, "I am noted for four bars".

To begin at the beginning, and to end at the end. Remember, the record players on which *Sgt Pepper* first rotated, never really ended, the arm and needle kept going, bouncing against the record's centre to the last syllable of recorded time. So, to keep listeners rapt, gobbledygook ran as long as the needle stayed in place. As late as September 1967, three months after the album's release, the letters page of *Melody Maker* was still exploring the hidden track. This was another Fab first, not listed on the sleeve, not a track as such, but hidden when you thought it was all over. "Revolve the record in an anti-clockwise direction with the stylus in the stop groove. All will be revealed," advised Richard Mutt. Others discerned "Everybody there is superman"… "never needed any other way"… "I never could see any other – ba, ba, ba, ba"… "I never could see any of them"… "I never could be happy… I never could be happy…"… "Lucy's got his underpants"… "A happy man is Superman…"

One of the highlights of the 2017 anniversary release was the album's alternate ending, the group humming the last chord, the ubiquitous "Om", the call to the soul within, as frequently heard during the 1960s as the 'Hare Krishna' mantra. It would have made a particularly apt conclusion, "Om, the Hindu symbol for the nature of Brahman", Martin Gardner wrote, "the Absolute, the god behind the lesser gods whose tasks are to create, preserve and destroy all that is".

Immediately after the album's release, as if to emphasise just how far they'd travelled, in *Melody Maker* Alan Walsh wrote about cover versions: "Six songs covered from their last album, only three from their new 'Sergeant Pepper' best-seller. All of which indicates that the Beatles are progressing more and more away from the idea of conventional commerciality".

In keeping with the mood of the times, and a hallmark of the UK record industry, no singles were released from the album. In 2007, however, Pete Nash undertook a fascinating survey of *Sgt Pepper* single releases from around the globe – Italy, Japan, France, Venezuela, Spain and Sweden were only some territories that extracted LP tracks and pressed them as 45s. Oddest couplings came from the Philippines ('This Boy' / 'She's Leaving Home') and South Africa ('Please Mr Postman' / 'Lucy in the Sky with Diamonds').

Hindsight has not been all kind to this landmark LP. Too much tied in to the prevailing psychedelia… just what exactly *was* the concept?… too varied for its own good. However, I maintain *Sgt Pepper*'s place as rock's most *influential* LP. Even without the benefit of hindsight, *Sgt Pepper* marked a dividing line between what pop music had accomplished, and what it could achieve.

It may not be the best Beatles album, and it undeniably has weak spots, but its impact at the time basically just upped the game. *Sgt Pepper* was a world of its own, a stained-glass window of 20th-century culture, with its lyrics there for all to read; with its colourful inner sleeve and cut-out gifts and, ultimately with its extraordinary sonic audacity, that one LP altered the aural landscape. With *Sgt Pepper's Lonely Hearts Club Band*, the Beatles altered the shifting tectonic plates of what 'pop music' was capable of.

Of all the millions of words written about the impact of that landmark LP, amidst all the speculation, analysis and dissection, I liked Mark Ellen's wry comment that it marked "an organic shift, rather than strategic design, Stockhausen, the Beach Boys and Lewis Carroll were being ushered in the front door while Elvis, Buddy Holly and Carl Perkins were shuffled out the back".

Immediately post-Pepper, the psychedelic revels continued – at Abbey Road alone, the Hollies ('King Midas in Reverse); the Pretty Things (*S.F. Sorrow*); Pink Floyd's *Piper at the Gates of Dawn*; Tomorrow ('My White Bicycle'); Simon Dupree ('Kites'); the Moles ('We Are the Moles') were all sculpted from the *Pepper* model.

I believe the impact of *Sgt Pepper* and its influence had much to do with the full-page review that appeared in *The Times* on 29 May 1967. That the paper of national record would devote an entire page to a long-playing record by a pop group was unheard of. It was William Mann who had famously written in 1963 of "the flat submedian key switches, so natural in the Aeolian cadence at the end of 'Not A Second Time' (the chord progression which ends Mahler's 'Song Of The Earth')".

Four years later he was equally captivated. Much of the article monitors the progress made by "the young teenagers of 1963" (Bee Gees, Cat Stevens, Kinks, New Vaudeville Band) before zeroing in on the Beatle accomplishment: "Any of these songs is more genuinely creative than anything currently to be heard … in relationship to what other groups have been doing lately. *Sergeant Pepper* is chiefly significant as constructive criticism, a sort of pop music master class examining trends and correcting or tidying up inconsistencies and undisciplined work…"

In an extraordinarily extravagant piece for *Queen* magazine in December 1967, over three pages, the cultural commentator Frederic V. Grunfeld poured praise on their achievements while name-checking Caruso, John Cage, Bea Lillie, Schubert, Villa-Lobos, Stravinsky, Freud, Brecht, Wagner, Kafka, Brahms and Fred & Adele Astaire. Reflecting that, post-*Pepper*, "their recent oeuvre … is a great eclectic circus of Indian raga, Salvation Army, Benjamin Britt-ish, tailgate, gutbucket and aleatoric chance-music, all handled without hang-ups or uptightness".

Given that he was writing about a mere pop group, Grunfeld sagely and quite presciently concludes: "In years to come, when we look back on this epoch … we shall find that their four faces tower above the scene like the American presidents carved from Mount Rushmore. And it shall henceforth be known to posterity as The Age Of Beatles".

In America, Langdon Winner's hyperbolic reflection in *Rolling Stone* called the release of *Sgt Pepper* "the closest Western Civilisation has come in unity since the Congress of Vienna in 1815…" The LP undeniably caught the mood of the times, but I would posit the 1918 and 1945 Armistices as equally unifying.

In its review of the LP, *The Times of India* naturally singled out George Harrison's 'Within You And Without You'. "It sounds quite Indian with sitar and table (sic) accompanying his philosophic thought". The paper also commented on how, "The Beatles have changed their dress, their music. They now sport droopy French moustaches and colourful costumes, practice mysticism and their sounds have begun to explore farther reaches in the musical firmament".

In *The Observer*, George Melly was less impressed by *Sgt Pepper*: "The record is not perfect, even on pop's terms. On the musical side there is a tendency to overdo the curry powder… while on the literary front the straight psychedelic excursions seem to confuse poetry with woolly nursery surrealism".

The Beatles' old Cavern compadre Gerry Marsden agreed: "By the time the Beatles began with [drugs] in the mid-1960s I knew it was useless having conversations with them about it. I said to myself 'Idiots' – and I was proved right, because their weakest songs were written while they were indulging".

They were in the minority.

Listening again afresh, as with so many Beatle projects, so many of the pieces *fitted*: Ringo's contribution should not be underestimated – the mournful vocal which is so suited to 'With a Little Help'. But it is the thunderous drums which power 'A Day in the Life' which still cause the windows to rattle. Too often, Ringo's percussive powers were a cause for mockery (notably Lennon's apocryphal, "he's not even the best drummer in the Beatles"). The group were fascinated by drums which could *power* and provide a strong foundation for their ambitious material.

Gerri Hershey recounted an encounter as the Beatles had begun recording *Pepper* during the autumn of 1966. At a press reception to mark the Four Tops' appearance at Brian Epstein's Saville Theatre, Lennon was heard inquiring of the Tops' Laurence Payton, "Tell me something, man, when you cats go into the studio, what does the drummer beat on to get that backbeat? You use a bloody *tree* or something?"

And don't forget George… Ringo dutifully played along, John allied himself to Paul's concept, but *Pepper* was never an album George Harrison felt comfortable with. George Martin later admitted the reason he placed 'Within You Without You', the sole Harrison contribution, at the beginning of the original Side II, was so people could skip it! That was indeed the course most of the times when I played the LP, those languorous, languid lyrics spread over five lengthy minutes. That weird drone, that other-worldly music, literally music from another world, well, another continent at least…

Beatle George was less than enchanted with *Sgt Pepper* ("not as enjoyable as *Rubber Soul* or *Revolver*"). Bitter from the desultory world tour, his mind was elsewhere: "I'd just got back from India, and my heart was still out there. After what happened in 1966, everything else seemed like hard work. It was a job… and I was losing interest in being 'fab' at that point" (*Anthology*).

There is no doubt though that 'Within You Without You' was the five minutes that fuelled the West's fascination with the mystic East for the remainder of the decade. My parents had met and married in India by the end of the war, and spoke fondly of the country. There was the odd curry house in London; Peter Sellers made us all laugh on 'Goodness, Gracious Me'. And that, frankly, was about the bulk of the Jewel in the Crown's impact on the Mother Country.

While it may be one of the tracks frequently skipped on its LP release, George's 'Within You Without You' really did open ears to world music. After doodling with the sitar a couple of years before, George immersed himself in the culture and music of India, which manifested itself with his only contribution to the album. To his credit, it was George himself who insisted on the laughter at the track's close to undermine its earnestness.

Everyone appeared to immediately succumb to All Things Indian – every bedsit was perfumed by joss sticks; you couldn't move round Soho without bumping into the Hare Krishna mob. EMI were quick off the mark with the cash-in LP *Lord Sitar*. Island signed Quintessence ("the first rock group to attempt to blend blues, jazz and rock with Indian ragas and Hindu chants and mantras…") Following George's toe in the water on 'Norwegian Wood', we witnessed Brian Jones' cross-legged performances on the Stones' 'Paint It Black'; Traffic's 'Paper Sun'. But in all honesty, most of us were on Kevin Costner's side in 1989's *Field of Dreams*, reminiscing about "majoring in the 60s". And wryly confessing "I *tried* to like sitar music…" Like the audience at Madison Square Garden in 1971 for the Bangla Desh concert, applauding Ravi Shankar's tuning up.

'Within You Without You' kickstarted what came to be known as 'Karma Cola', the drift Eastwards. It seemed like everyone knew someone who was opposing Horace Greeley's advice and heading East. Within months, joss sticks, budget sitar LPs, tangerine-coloured Hare Krishna adepts, vegetarian curries, gurus, kaftans, sheepskin coats … all seemed to appear in the wake of that one song. The Road to Katmandu replaced Route 66. The protagonist of Al Stewart's 1974 'Modern Times' sets off for Nepal with a canvas sack containing only paperbacks of *Lord of the Rings* and *On the Road*.

The subcontinent too had fallen under the Fabs' spell. The 1965 Bollywood film *Janwar* had pop group Ted Lyon & the Cubs shaking their Beatle haircuts to 'Dekho ab toh kisi ko nahin hai khabar'. The tune was more familiar as 'I Want to Hold Your Hand'.

'A Day in the Life' was the album's majestic conclusion, a weary Lennon reflection, touching on a *Daily Mail* report about the parlous state of Blackburn's roads… his *How I Won the War* experience… the death of Tara Browne,[17] and pepped up by Paul's chirpy middle eight. I *still* remain convinced the "turn you on" line was about smoking upstairs on the top of the Huyton bus, that was the only place you *could* smoke.

Despite all the bile contained in Albert Goldman's near 700-page hatchet-job Lennon biography, I felt his writing about the song captured its spectral magnificence: "Then, out of nowhere, comes sailing in, like a ghost ship with an ice-encrusted bowsprit the bleak, despairing, yet resigned voice… sounding like the eternal note of sadness and offering a view of ordinary life, culled from that day's *Morning* (sic) *Mail* that totally annihilates

---

17   Marianne Faithfull was only one who found the Guinness heir's death so shocking: 'We were young, and most of us had never known anyone our age who had died".

and eventually blows up Paul's jolly Toby Jugg vision". I interviewed Goldman for the BBC World Service and was barely able to contain my hostility, particularly when he smugly announced that Antonio Carlos Jobim was a far more influential musician than John Lennon.

Among the 40-odd classical musicians in fancy dress who George Martin had assembled on the session for that epic conclusion was classical violinist David McCallum. Father of the actor, and, as a session musician, the man who suggested Jimmy Page might try using a violin bow on his electric guitar.

One of the very few outsiders admitted to the inner Beatle circle was Hunter Davies, fashioning his Beatle biography. That in itself was quite an achievement. In 1967 his publishers – Heinemann – were unconvinced that there would be a market for a biography about a 'pop group' by the time it was published. And even Hunter's £3,000 advance had to be split between his agent, and the Beatles, who received £1,000.

Hunter's account of the writing sessions of *Sgt Pepper* at Paul's house at Cavendish Avenue is one of the few fly-on-the-wall accounts of pop's greatest songwriting partnership in action. I did a radio programme with him many years later and remember him marvelling about those sessions, how the lyrics were written on scraps of paper, often decorated with florid psychedelic doodles, which Hunter picked up and took home to amuse his young children. He used the scraps from the studio floor for papering the walls, until "I woke up one morning to find that the stuff on my walls was more valuable than the house!"

To his credit, Hunter Davies did donate some original handwritten Beatle *Pepper*-era lyrics to the British Library. You can see them still, in their dimly-lit room of treasures. There they sit, next to illuminated medieval manuscripts, the Magna Carta and a Shakespeare first folio.

Then you keep coming back to that cover… Up to *Pepper* it was the label's in-house photographer, given ten minutes to snap a shot of the smiling group in question to put on cover. Then a music journalist or PR would be slipped a tenner to write some fulsome notes on the back.

One of the few new things I learned for the 50th anniversary was the fact that it signalled Pete Best's return to the fold: Lennon apparently remembered that Pete's dad had been awarded medals for valour during wartime service, and asked Mona Best if he could borrow them for the cover shoot. If that is true, that would mark the first contact in five years.

Then there are the cover out-takes – Lennon's wilfully controversial inclusion of Hitler… Gandhi removed by a nervous Sir Joseph Lockwood for fear of offending the Indian market. If anyone involved had thought the cover would be perused as closely as the Turin Shroud, more imagination would probably have been given to those included in that stellar montage. Ringo was happy to go along with everyone else's suggestions; George wanted nothing but gurus; Peter Blake probably had as much input as any of the group. For it to be truly reflective, *Sgt Pepper* really *should* have found space for Richmal Crompton, Buddy Holly, James Dean, Dennis the Menace (UK version), Geoffrey Chaucer, Rupert the Bear, Eddie Cochran, Bill Haley, Chet Atkins, Spike Milligan, Delia Derbyshire, Lonnie Donegan, Lightning Hopkins, Margaret Rutherford, sweet Gene Vincent and Pete Best…

Over the years, *Sgt Pepper* was routinely voted Greatest Album Ever Made, until it was superseded by *Revolver*, then *Rubber Soul*, then *Pet Sounds*… The debate rages: even Paul didn't call it the *best* Beatle album (*Mojo* June 2017). But it remains a landmark: the first album to have lyrics on its sleeve, the first 'concept' LP, the first hidden track, the first to take you on a trip…

While hindsight may find *Pepper* marooned in 60s psychedelia, it stands as pop's most *important* LP by dint of all those landmarks. And the fact that the group spent six months fashioning just 13 tracks. *Pepper* was the sound of a gauntlet being hurled down… the sight of a bar being raised… the evidence of a line drawn in the sand. *Sgt Pepper's Lonely Hearts Club Band* upped the ante. From mid-1967 on, in popular music, there was pre- and post-*Sgt Pepper*.

It cannot be blamed for what followed in its wake – *Sgt Pepper* paved the way for the Stones' lifeless attempt to replicate it on *Their Satanic Majesties Request*, ("Save me from my disciples", moaned Oscar Wilde).

In fact, like the majority, I have long since felt that the Stones' *Satanic Majesties* was a dismal, pale copy of *Sgt Pepper*. On its release, only *Record Mirror* was truly, favorably disposed to the album ("This LP should do for them what *Sgt Pepper's* did for the Beatles. That is, show them as a group capable of appealing as much to the more discriminating and aware record buyer as to the younger fan element"). Mind you, the music weekly was part-owned by the Stones' own record label, Decca!

Caught in the psychedelic tsunami which followed, every band (by then, they were 'bands') were happy to call their next LP "our *Sgt Pepper*".

With the Beatles, and their eighth LP, such was its bravura and audacity from the cover in, that you really did feel you had entered a whole brave new world, once again, courtesy of the act you've known for all these years…

For years, the only real rival to *Sgt Pepper* was rumoured to have been the Beach Boys' lost and legendary album, *Smile*. Prior to 1967, it had been a quid pro quo arrangement: Brian Wilson had been knocked out by *Rubber Soul*. Stoned in Los Angeles, the LP "flipped me out so much. I said 'I'm gonna try that, where a whole album becomes a *gas*'." The gauntlet had been thrown down, with the resultant *Pet Sounds* in the shops a few days before *Revolver*.

The Beatles were equally impressed by what the Beach Boys had achieved (to this day, Paul still cites 'God Only Knows' as "the perfect song"). Brian was subsequently blown away by *Revolver*, which found him endeavouring to equal it. He informed his wife: "I'm going to make the greatest rock & roll album ever made".

With the schism between Brian and Mike Love; the gap between Brian and the other Beach Boys; Brian's increasing drug use and paranoia… *Smile* was always going to be a problematic production. It did produce two undeniable masterpieces ('Good Vibrations' and 'Heroes & Villains'). 'Surf's Up' was in with a chance. But the lengthy genesis saw it tumble and fall, and *Smile* became legend rather than LP. When the 'finished' version of the Beach Boys album finally appeared in the 21st century, it was apparent that it had offered no real competition to *Pepper*.

Even the weaker moments on *Pepper* towered over 'Vega-Tables', 'Wind Chimes' and 'Do You Like Worms'. As the sessions continued, Brian became less and less convinced that he could top, let alone equal, the Beatles. So he kept tinkering, the sessions stretched on and on, and the album lurched into limbo. That fanaticism took its toll not just on Brian as creative savant, but the group themselves. For a radio documentary, talking to Al Jardine years later, I asked him for his memories of those *Smile* sessions: "God", he laughed after a long pause, "it was like … *Groundhog Day!*"

On hearing the finished *Sgt Pepper*, Brian almost burst into tears. "Oh my God, the Beach Boys are going to go down the tubes". A further decline in the American group's standing came when they refused to appear at the Monterey Pop Festival. The subsequent *Smiley Smile* and *Friends* LPs did them few favours, while their short-lived 1968 tour with the Maharishi was a catastrophe. It took the Californians years to regain their critical and commercial heights.

There is not space to list the calumnies committed in the name of *Sgt Pepper*, though I would single out the tracks of many of the Moody Blues albums, whereby the drummer felt determined to commit his poetry to vinyl. And most Yes LPs after *The Yes Album*. And most King Crimson LPs following *Lizard*. And *The Lamb Lies Down on Broadway*. And… well you get the picture.

For all its far-outness and retrospective appreciation of "the summer of Love" and "1967, the year it all changed…", *Sgt Pepper*'s run as the UK's No.1 LP was preceded by the soundtrack to *The Sound of Music*, and succeeded by *Val Doonican Rocks… But Gently*. It was the sound of Middle England's stalwart rearguard action. The headline on the front page of the final 1967 issue of *Melody Maker*, the year of *Pepper* (and 'Strawberry Fields' and *Our World* and *Magical Mystery Tour* EPs and 'Hello Goodbye'*)* plus debut LPs from Pink Floyd, Procol Harum, the Velvet Underground, the Jimi Hendrix Experience … was 'The Year of Engelbert!'

Philip Larkin was an enthusiastic champion of the Beatles, but he wrote ruefully in a letter of his impressions of *Sgt Pepper*: "Their fans stayed with them, and the nuttier intelligentsia, but they lost the typists at the Cavern".

In America, the Monkees ('the pre-Fab Four') were manufactured to tap into the lucrative US teen market which, by 1967, the Beatles had long lost interest in addressing. In fairness, the Monkees were playing at being pop stars, but I would contend that with the help of Goffin & King, Boyce & Hart, Neil Diamond etc., their debut album was as good a slice of contemporary pop as anything else on the market.

The Monkees themselves were not under any doubt as to where their allegiance lay – Mickey Dolenz was pictured in the *NME* delightedly grinning, sitting cross-legged next to Paul McCartney. And Dolenz's quirky 1967 'Alternate Title' single paid homage to "the four Kings of EMI". Mike Nesmith was admitted to the *Sgt Pepper* sessions, and years later marvelled at the music the Beatles produced. "I can listen to it in wonder and just say to myself 'This is celestial. This is coming from the stars'".

The Beatles' American teenage audience were clearly baffled with the direction that they were taking; it wasn't just the moustaches, it was them ingesting platefuls of weird. Reporting from a *Pepper* recording session, Judy Sims of *Teen Beat* noted, "Nowadays distortion can be incorporated successfully into a complete instrumental sound effect. And who would have thought that playing a backing track BACKWARDS would be not only acceptable but well worth experimenting with!"

The problem was of course with the Beatles leading from the front. By then every pop group – the Stones, the Who, the Kinks – was expected to be self-contained, and not to have to rely on outside sources, however high their quality. In the end, the Monkees chafed at the restrictions placed upon them, and *their* audience grew up and drifted away. Small wonder that for Don Kirshner, the Monkees' founding father, his next project was the Archies, a cartoon group over whom he could exercise what the Clash would later call 'Complete Control'.

A March 1967 UK Poll comparing the Beatles and the Monkees had 61% in favour of the Fabs, with only 38% supporting the arrivistes. Comments included, "I'd rather have an aged Beatle than a childish Monkee"… "Can you imagine any of the Monkees writing a song like 'Yesterday'?"… Although one comment rang true for the Liverpudlians' fans: "We don't see much of the Beatles but the Monkees have their own weekly series".

Enshrined as 'the Summer of Love', the soundtrack to the year was *Sgt Pepper*. It was in the air, for all those that succumbed to the patchouli-soused, kaftan-clad, whimsical, psychedelic pleasures of the period. For a full picture of the hippie stand against Val and Engelbert, *Pepper* could be heard, in close harmony, with those key sounds of that summer – 'A Whiter Shade of Pale', 'San Francisco (Be Sure to Wear Some Flowers in Your Hair)' and 'All You Need Is Love'.

However, the Stones' 1967 Summer of Love anthem, 'We Love You', was actually a stronger record than many of their rivals. From the pounding introduction of Nicky Hopkins' piano, Charlie's driving drums and Jagger's engaging distortion of grammar… all combined to deliver a memorable statement. Even the prison doors and authority footsteps are a timely reminder, a flavour of the time. When Mick and Keith were busted at the infamous Redlands party, it really did look like the battle lines were being drawn: Us versus Them. Made all the more striking by Keith's defiant statement from the dock: "We are not old men, we are not concerned with petty morals…"

It was where the societal shifts coincided with the artistic flowering that make those 12 months of 1967 so significant. Harold Wilson's Home Secretary Roy Jenkins oversaw the legalisation of abortion in the UK, while the Sexual Offences Act decriminalised consensual homosexual behaviour between men over the age of 21 in England. In a tragic irony, the law legalising homosexual acts between consenting adults, only came into force in July 1967, a month before Brian Epstein's untimely death.

His contract with the Beatles had expired in February 1967. Travelling to renew it in a chauffeur-driven limousine to the company's Manchester Square HQ, Brian allowed himself a rare moment of self-satisfaction. He revelled in being welcomed into the boardroom, when only a few years before he had been "crawling round the record companies trying … to get the tapes played".

Brian was satisfied with the increased royalty rate he secured (10% of the retail price, double that of any other artist on the label) and the creative lever he had insisted on (70 songs spread over a nine-year period). It was a remarkable deal for the time. Mind you, Brian was dealing from a position of power: while the manic phase of Beatlemania may have passed, every single release by the group was greeted by pre-release orders running into the hundreds of thousands.

Tony Barrow recalled Epstein snapping at him early in 1967 as his five-year contract with the group was expiring. "Tony, for God's sake realise that I've done all I can. There are many ways in which the Beatles are no longer co-operating with me… There's a limit to the grovelling and pleading I can do". Had he lived, there is no doubt that Brian Epstein's role in managing 'the boys' would have lessened. It is fascinating to speculate though that, had he lived beyond his meagre 32 years, the whole Apple quagmire and subsequent financial catastrophe *might* have been avoided.

In his last television interview (28 July 1967) on the newly-launched *News at Ten*, Epstein loyally defended his and Paul's decision to take LSD: "I think if the Beatles put out a bad record, the public wouldn't buy it… This is another misunderstanding… they won't accept it readily just as I don't think people will readily accept LSD, simply because Paul McCartney and myself and others have said they take it".

His last contact with the group he had steered to unimaginable fame came when they were recording in August 1967. Tie-less but apparently tense, Epstein had been concerned about the controversy the *Sgt Pepper* cover might alight. It had passed. He would have been equally worried about the pressure of the Beatles' appearance on the television special *Our World* a few months before. But even appearing before an estimated audience of 400,000,000 caused his group little concern.

"It might seem unbelievable", Geoff Emerick later wrote, "but it's the truth, the only things that were repeated on 'All You Need Is Love' for the record release were the snare roll at the beginning and two lines of the lead vocal". Everything else had been recorded live in front of the world's largest-ever television audience.

That European television link had been explored since 1956 on a yearly basis with the, even then, much maligned *Eurovision Song Contest*. Since Beatlemania, critics had asked why, if their songs could conquer the world, Lennon and McCartney would not submit an entry that would surely bring home the Eurovision bacon? Neither man felt they should waste their talent on such an outmoded concept. Only two months before *Our World*, Sandie Shaw had landed the UK its first Eurovision winner in Luxembourg, with 'Puppet on a String', the template for many subsequent Eurovision winners.

Millions customarily watched the *Song Contest* all over Europe. With the Beatles in self-imposed exile, with no new LP or concert appearances in almost a year, the opportunity to see them perform live, even on television, was too good for their worldwide audience to miss.

The event was sponsored by the European Broadcasting Union, utilising three satellites, a million miles of cable and 6,500 technicians bringing live pictures from 26 countries. Given that one of the group selected to represent Great Britain had admitted taking the illegal drug LSD only weeks before the broadcast, it is testament to the Beatles' status that they were allowed to go ahead.

Only a few years before, one would have imagined Peter Pears or Benjamin Britten, Sir Malcolm Sargent (who was keen to meet the group at Abbey Road in 1964), Yehudi Menuhin, Margot Fonteyn, Graham Greene, Laurence Olivier, Jacqueline Du Pre or Sir Donald Wolfit (who Paul had fond memories of meeting on the Abbey Road steps) as Her Majesty's official cultural representatives.

In this era of mind-bending technology all squashed onto your mobile phone, the impact of *Our World* over half a century ago may be diminished. Only five years since the first live transatlantic television broadcast via Telstar, the very thought was mind-expanding. The idea that you could sit in the comfort of your home, a Senior Service smouldering in the ashtray as you popped another can of Double Diamond, watching events from all four corners of the world *as they happened*…! So it was on 25 June 1967, with a little help from their friends (Mick and Marianne, Eric Clapton, Keith Moon, Graham Nash etc.) at Abbey Road that the Beatles brought their world to *Our World*.

The BBC's sole instruction had been to "keep it simple". On 17 May the programme's producer, Derek Burrell-Davies had sent an enthusiastic telegram to BBC executive Aubrey Singer: "*Our World* beat group… aware challenge… responsive to world stage… writing new number with words such as Hello Love Me Us Them We Together. Intend indicate Swinging London".

It was that "keep it simple" instruction, so that viewers of all nationalities would understand the contribution, which probably explains the Common Market-friendly opening of 'La Marseillaise'. When John demoed 'All You Need Is Love', George remarked to Paul, "Well, it's certainly repetitive". Steve Race was presenting the London segment for the BBC and remembered "George Harrison seemed detached, in a world of his own. 'Boring isn't it?' I remarked. He smiled, and nodded in agreement. Making history can be a tedious business". The throwaway snatch of 'She Loves You' at the song's conclusion is a nice example of early Beatle sampling.

"Because of the mood of the time", George Harrison later reflected, "it seemed to be a great idea to perform *that* song while everybody else was showing knitting in Canada or Irish clog dances in Venezuela!" When it came to be seen in *Anthology*, the song was colourised to great effect.

Also on TV, 'All You Need Is Love' reached a smaller but equally committed audience when in February 1968, it was heard in the final episode of Patrick McGoohan's bafflingly cultish *The Prisoner*. I remember the letters page of *Melody Maker* at the time full of correspondence along the lines of, "Well, it's all very well for The Beatles to sing 'All You Need Is Love', but what about O-Levels?" "Apprenticeships are important too…"

To their manager's delight, the *Our World* broadcast went ahead without a hitch (Brian must have been dreading a John "rattle your fucking beads" ad-lib). On a day-to-day basis, Brian Epstein's dealings with 'the boys' were long gone. Like errant children, they had outgrown their manager. Epstein loyally tried LSD to keep up. But his business capability had lost its Midas touch. Of all the NEMS acts only Cilla Black and the Beatles occupied his time, and manifestly his grasp was slipping. At the time of his death, negotiations were in hand with Robert Stigwood, manager of the Bee Gees ('the new Beatles') to take over.

The plan was that Stigwood, who had proved his managerial muscle with the Bee Gees and Cream, would handle all NEMS' clients aside from Cilla and the Beatles, who would remain on Brian's watch. Even with that proviso, the group steadfastly refused – Paul told Brian, "We will record 'God Save The Queen' for every single record we make from now on and we'll sing it out of tune".

It is fascinating to speculate what would have happened if Stigwood *had* got involved. Following his rejection, he went on to successfully manage groups at both ends of the rock spectrum – the 'underground' phenomenon Cream and the chart-friendly Bee Gees. Later,

Ready to reach the whole wide world, 24 June 1967

of course, Stigwood managed a rich fusion of film and soundtrack with the 70s triumphs of *Saturday Night Fever* and *Grease*. Ironically, the spectacular failure of Stigwood's 1978 film of *Sgt Pepper* was what marked his departure from the entertainment field.

As to the question of managing the Beatles following Brian's death, family loyalty resumed, with his younger brother Clive (1936–88) briefly involved. With Stigwood out of the picture, in reality there were few other contenders. Colonel Tom Parker, even if he had been allowed free admittance to the UK, was happy with Elvis, his only client. The days of Larry Parnes' pop empire were long past. The Who's flamboyant Kit Lambert was too freewheeling. Simon Napier-Bell was too young, the Small Faces' Don Arden, too terrifying.

As 1967 proceeded, Brian lost the ties and suits, but also lost interest. He did help negotiate a deal for – of all things – the Monkees' inaugural UK shows in 1967, as well as enjoying Sunday shows at his Saville Theatre. Ultimately though, Brian remained terrified that when his contract with the Beatles expired, they would abandon him. One of his last negotiations on the Beatles' behalf was squeezing that improved royalty rate out of EMI. As it was retrospective, it meant a large lump sum, which Brian suggested should be invested for tax purposes into a Beatle-owned business, thus laying the foundations for Apple.

A 1966 Epstein profile by John Viner was headlined 'Tough yet easily hurt, smooth, dignified, artistic, brilliant, socially charming... these are some of the qualities to which Brian Epstein's friends attribute his success. But what of the future?' Brian spoke of envying John and Paul's ability to write songs ("because that is basically a creative talent"); his unflappable nature ("When I'm worried I chew my nails"); his fondness for "a Spanish cold soup called gazpacho". The feature concluded, "Mr Epstein has a look of extreme permanence about him". Less than a year later, he was dead.

On the surface, Brian had everything going for him. But a corrosive guilt ate away at him. It was something his personal assistant Wendy Hanson recognised when she told Ray Coleman, "The isolation, withdrawal from the world and his feelings of guilt were terrible. Jewish guilt, homosexual guilt and drugs guilt were all there".

In the last interview he gave to *Melody Maker* just three weeks before his death, Epstein was asked what he feared most: "Loneliness. I hope I'll never be lonely". In that paper's obituary, Mike Hennessey perceptively noted of a man he counted as a friend, "the impression I formed of Brian Epstein was of a man desperately wanting to be creative, to express himself artistically, but knowing in his heart that he was destined for second-hand fame – the reflected glory of the Beatles for whom his devotion and admiration were absolute".

For all the conspiracy theories which came later, it appears Epstein's death *was* an accidental overdose of sleeping pills, mixed with alcohol. One of the first on the scene was Brian's personal assistant Joanne Petersen, who told Peter Robinson: "He looked very peaceful, with a book open beside him and correspondence spread over the bed. It just looked like he was asleep".

Brian Epstein's death left all those who knew him shaken. Brian was only 32 when he died. With his RP speech and well-cut suits wardrobe, he always somehow seemed older. For the Beatles, in hindsight it was the beginning of the end. They relied on Brian for the boring stuff; the stuffy boardroom negotiations; the overview of song publishing; those *meetings*… One senses, had he lived, with his hand steady on the managerial tiller, Brian would have avoided a lot of the later excesses and rash decisions which came to sour the group's last years.

Hindsight has revealed Epstein's many managerial flaws – the millions lost in poor merchandising deals; the fumbled royalties with EMI; the myriad unsuccessful musical clients… Posthumously, Brian's reputation has suffered. Ray Coleman's authoritative biography was aware of the manager's other business failings, such as Brian's woeful lack of musical perception. He had undeniably taken the Beatles to the pinnacle of pop stardom, but his dealings with the Big Three and the Fourmost were flawed. His King Midas in Reverse touch was also apparent with the flop acts he signed – Tommy Quickly, Michael Haslam, the Ruskies and the Rustiks.

But I maintain Brian Epstein deserves more credit than for being the man who lost the Beatles their millions. It was Brian who spotted that elusive *something* in that group in that cellar. It was Brian who persevered when everyone else was willing to wash their hands of them. It was Brian who detected the marketable chemistry. It was Brian who championed the Beatles to disinterested record company AR executives. If for nothing else, it was Brian Epstein who got them out of Liverpool and down to London. It was Brian who took them from the stage of the Knotty Ash Village Hall to the Royal Albert Hall. It was – crucially – Brian who secured them a recording contract. It was Brian who got them to the world. For those achievements alone he merits eternal credit.

Taking them all into consideration – Sam Leach, Allan Williams, Bob Wooler – Brian's assistant Tony Bramwell summed up his achievements nicely: "Brian was the only one who could see over the Mersey".

It was on his watch that Brian took a provincial UK pop group, competed with, and then overtook their American rivals. It was in tandem with Brian Epstein that the Beatles broke the US stranglehold. It was Brian who engineered the TV, radio and film deals which cemented his group's reputation.

In his thorough book on UK pop management, *Starmakers & Svengalis*, Johnny Rogan found fault with Epstein's "naivete and provincial-mindedness… [but] judged in the context of his time, however, he was no worse than most of the other British pop managers and subject to the same lousy deals offered by the powers of the day… but it is not easy to put a price tag on the public respect and artistic reputation that Brian helped his protégés achieve. What scale can measure the dreams of a generation?"

Rex Makin was the Epstein family solicitor, and knew Brian well. Asked by Spencer Leigh in 1999, would they have made it without Brian? "Indisputably, they would *never* have made it. They would have been another group from Liverpool… There were a lot of groups at that time who perhaps did not have the tuneship of Lennon and McCartney or the authorship of Lennon and McCartney, but without Brian they would never have been projected into the big time and ordered the worldwide, perennial reputation they enjoy today".

With their decision to quit touring, Brian's hold on the group had lessened. His homosexuality made Brian even more isolated. He struggled to sustain any relationship.

As with any celebrity, in any relationship, he questioned: do they like me for who I am or for what I represent? As far as we know, Brian's relationships were largely unhappy. In his memoir Tony Barrow remembered, immediately following his death, a man who called himself one of Brian's closest friends rifling through the Epstein collection of hand-made silk shirts, then inquiring, "without a trace of grief 'Do you think I'll be able to unpick these initials?'"

In the end his brother Clive delivered a nice epitaph: "Brian Epstein changed the world but didn't do it any harm. Isn't that reason enough to remember him?"

In 2000, a sweet McCartney letter to Brian was auctioned, written just months before their manager's death. Paul chivied, "Your biggest trouble is you take it all too seriously". Also included was a newspaper cutting, 'Who Cares' to which Paul added, "Some people do, friends, and the time has come to listen to them".

Touchingly, the last words of Brian's ghost-written 1964 autobiography, *A Cellarful of Noise*, were, "I think the sun will shine tomorrow". It had been for Brian, a bright blaze for six incredible years, it had shone, brightly, brilliantly, in a journey from a Liverpool basement to a Mayfair penthouse. His tragedy was an untimely death – reflect again, aged only 32. And even worse, that which he dreaded... a solitary death.

*

As the year wound down, they had to proceed without Brian's guidance. It was from here on that the Beatles ceased being 'John's group'. For the remainder of their career as a working band, it was the steady hand of J.P. McCartney MBE who was steering. Looking back at 1967, it was an *eventful* year: three non-album singles – one frequently regarded as the greatest in rock history; one casually performed live in front of television's largest ever audience. Oh, and the most acclaimed album *ever*. And now the Beatles still had one final shot in their locker: a TV special accompanied by a double-EP of all-new songs.

To say that *Magical Mystery Tour* was keenly anticipated was like saying *Sgt Pepper* was a quite good LP. BBC1 Controller Paul Fox couldn't believe his luck when he was offered a TV show produced, directed and featuring all new music by the Beatles.

In the UK, Boxing Day falls on 26 December. It's a day when the hangovers kick in, the dreaded turkey curry surfaces and whole families slump in front of undemanding television entertainment. It is a day to recover from excess. A day when nothing too demanding is required.

Magical Mystery Tour was squeezed on BBC1 between a Petula Clark Variety special and Norman Wisdom's 1958 film *The Square Peg* – all good, solid, post-Christmas family viewing. Then the nation settled down for some no doubt zany nonsense from the group the nation had taken to its heart.

Hindsight has been kinder to *Magical Mystery Tour* than it deserved. Ill-conceived in a vacuum following Brian Epstein's death, it was the first of Paul's plans to try and keep the group together. Self-indulgent, sprawling, plotless... what damned *Magical Mystery Tour* on its premiere was that this freewheeling psychedelic caper was only ever seen in black and white! Later 'heads', who witnessed underground screenings in *colour* came back raving. The quarter of the UK population who tuned in that Boxing Day night came away complaining.

The absence of a story you could live with, if the episodes themselves had been engaging or entertaining. You didn't necessarily need a plot, but you needed something to keep you watching. And it was hard to reconcile the chirpy Fabs of only two years before with these TV wizards pointlessly cavorting. You can understand why they felt the need not to call upon Dick Lester but, really, *Magical Mystery Tour* needed a steadying directorial hand... Perhaps following his trippy take on *Alice in Wonderland* in 1966, Jonathan Miller might have been a good fit. Or Lindsay Anderson or John Schlesinger.

A few months after the television's premiere, Roger Eldridge wrote: "John Lennon was hoping that an artistic fantasy would emerge from the anarchic and haphazard travels of a bus full of cinematic amateurs. But what he failed to realise … was that if he aimed a camera at a gang of extroverts rushing wildly about a disused airfield, the effect which came across on the screen would be a gang of extroverts rushing wildly about a disused airfield … and nothing more".

The group themselves had no real idea what to do with the sprawling footage they had shot that summer. They blithely informed editor Roy Benson a fortnight should be enough to hack it into shape. The weeks turned into months. For example, there was no sequence to illustrate the instrumental 'Flying'. Benson had worked with Stanley Kubrick on *Dr Strangelove*, and remembered the hours of aerial sequences the director had shot. He simply lifted some to go with the song. Even though it was screened on Boxing Day, the notoriously pernickety Kubrick – locked into the third year of his *2001* shoot – was on to the hapless editor railing at the inclusion of *his* footage.

And yes, it must have been a lark flicking through *Spotlight*, picking out half-remembered faces of thespians from telly afternoons to include in the cast. But letting Ivor Cutler, who blighted innumerable John Peel sessions, have his own way was just *tedious*. There were undeniably moments in its 60-odd minutes – Victor Spinetti's ranting recruiting sergeant; Lennon's oleaginous waiter shovelling spaghetti… And how lovely to see the vintage Bonzo Dog Doo-Dah Band (featuring the world's best-named bassist: Vernon Dudley Bohay-Nowell). An example of how *Magical Mystery Tour* could have turned out came with the 'Your Mother Should Know' sequence: the incongruity of *Pepper*-era Beatles soft-shoeing their way through Busby Berkeley-style choreography is matchless.

The lack of narrative only highlighted the brilliance of the music… And it was the music that mattered, and to which you returned. When the music matched the visuals ('I Am the Walrus'; 'Fool on the Hill') you could forgive them almost anything. The mention of 'knickers' landed 'I Am the Walrus' a BBC radio ban. The song was another rooted in Lennon's Liverpool adolescence, with its policemen, English gardens, Corporation t-shirts, Lewis Carroll, a revolting child's rhyme… But then it enters the weird world of 1967, with its Hare Krishna, Lucy in the sky and we are all together vibe. For good measure there's even a random bit of Shakespeare thrown in.

The handwritten lyrics for 'I Am the Walrus', Lennon's self-described piece of nonsense, sold for £810,000 in 2010. Lennon later admitted he chose the wrong figure from the Lewis Carroll poem. Lennon's fondness for the creator of the *Alice* books was well-known. He can be seen on the *Sgt Pepper* sleeve just behind Marlene Dietrich. Carroll also gave Humpty Dumpty advice Lennon took to heart: "When I use a word, it means just what I choose it to mean, nothing more nor less".

Lennon never took his lyrics too seriously. On 'Glass Onion' he played fast and loose with those who interpreted Beatle lyrics. DJ John Peel recalled an encounter when Lennon was reading a weekly music paper's review of a new Beatle record: "Why?" "I like to find out what my songs are about".

After years of filleting their UK LPs the only real improvement their American label Capitol made for the group was to enhance the UK's *Magical Mystery Tour* set. The American market had never taken the EP format to its heart. But by bolstering the two Extended Plays into an album with that year's stand-alone singles and B-sides ('Hello Goodbye', 'Strawberry Fields Forever', 'Penny Lane', 'Baby You're a Rich Man', 'All You Need Is Love') the American *Magical Mystery Tour* merited its place in the official Beatle discography.

Beneath its haphazard surface, half a century on, there was something diverting, and mildly engaging about *Magical Mystery Tour* on re-viewing it, in colour. What made it real fun were the out-takes, like a pie-eyed Paul crooning 'You Made Me Love You'. And that Fair Isle sweater he favoured…! Fond memories of charabanc outings, all fuelled by brown ale and fish and chips, viewed through the hallucinogenic prism of the Summer of Love.

Rob Young wrote affectionately of the DVD anniversary release: "It could be The Beatles' love/hate letter to GB, in all its pettifogging absurdity and geographical littleness. In the film's faded Kodak visual ambience, you sense the September light beginning to fall towards winter. The bus is a music hall full of nostalgic baggage for vanishing communities…"

Try as they might with anniversary reissues (McCartney citing Bunuel; Martin Scorsese chirping about them "breaking all the forms…") *Magical Mystery Tour* was a desultory detour. As the first major project following Brian's death, it did not bode well. Goo Goo G'Joob indeed…

In his diaries, Python's Michael Palin recalled a 1975 meeting at Apple; George was keen to have *Magical Mystery Tour* put out as the support film for the Pythons' *Holy Grail* film. Viewing it for the first time in eight years, Palin was with the general perception of the 1967 film: "Unfortunately, it was not an unjustly underrated work".

The public were baffled by the 1967 variety Beatles. Those moustaches… that discordant song about a field of strawberries… the admission that they had taken *drugs*… that dreary TV special… And that was without all that bewildering stuff about Transcendental Meditation? Something to do with toothpaste…?

So few years separated those changes, it was hard for many to reconcile the apple-cheeked ingénues with their shaking heads and love songs and their verse, chorus, verse, chorus, middle-eight, verse, chorus to fade… with the mustachioed weirdies and their lonely hearts club band. It was hard to believe they were all still in their 20s.

It had been the year which signalled the end of the steadying hand of Brian Epstein. Brian wouldn't have stopped them doing *Magical Mystery Tour*, but he might have given it more purpose. In a sense and, in hindsight, it was the beginning of the long, slow decline. Without Brian, it was McCartney who took on the paternal role. It was Paul who loved the *idea* of the Beatles, and wanted to do everything he could to keep them functioning. On the horizon, John was soon to become besotted by Yoko; George was subsumed by all things Indian; and Ringo was looking to pursue an acting career. But cohesion was necessary, they were still bound as a band. They were *still* the Beatles.

From mid-67 on, until the end of their career, it was McCartney who held the reins. It was Paul who had propelled *Sgt Pepper* and who, for better or worse, convinced them to undertake a *Magical Mystery Tour*. During the remaining three years of their career as a functioning band, it was Paul's songs that took priority as A-sides.

At the time in America, the Fab fanbase had drifted to the clean-cut Monkees. A *Life* magazine cover of July 1967 said it all: the Beatles were almost unrecognisable from the Fab Four of barely a year before. The magazine headline said it all: 'The New Far-Out Beatles'; the accompanying photo coincidentally sharing a cover with another feature: 'Marijuana's Turned-On Millions'.

Symptomatic of America's turning away from the turned-on Beatles was the song which deposed the wonderful 'Hello Goodbye' in the American charts in January 1968, 'Judy in Disguise (with Glasses)'. John Fred Gourrier misheard the third track on *Sgt Pepper*, and by combining a 'Lucy in disguise' type lyric with a TV advert about a living bra, had come up with a substantial slice of bubblegum. The song's success suggested that the teen audience was going for the simpler pop elements than those that the Beatles were offering.

What took them further beyond their teenage fans' comprehension was their falling under the thrall of a guru. The Sanskrit word 'guru' meaning 'weighty' was not in wide circulation. The Beatles' infatuation with the Maharishi was greeted with the sound of heads being loudly scratched. The UK at the time was still largely a Church of England, 'All Things Bright and Beautiful', church on Sunday, *Pilgrim's Progress*, Sunday school, *Songs of Praise* nation. What were the cuddly Beatles doing cosying up to a little Indian man? Following Brian's death, the poorly received *Magical Mystery Tour*, the pressure to 'top' *Sgt Pepper*… Paul admitted "we were ripe for saving".

They were not the first rock stars to succumb – "When Maharishi came through Los Angeles in 1965", the Doors' Robby Krieger wrote, "he held a meeting within walking distance of my parents' house. Only about a dozen people attended. Three of them would go on to form the Doors". To the Beatles, a few years later, Maharishi offered an oasis of calm. Of their initiation, George revealed the pecking order: "Mick Jagger was also there. He was always lurking around in the background, trying to find out what was happening. Mick never wanted to miss out on what the Fabs were doing" (*Anthology*).

Another 1967 detour took them to the Mediterranean. Plans to buy a Greek island in the wake of the fascist generals' coup displays just how little they were interested in politics. After the overthrow of the democratic government, the Greek generals instigated bans on long hair on males, miniskirts and the music of the Beatles. Kostas Gavras' sadly under-rated film *Z* chronicles that brutal period.

In 2023 Helena Smith found out more about that trip, including John's response to a Greek journalist: "Unfortunately the social inequalities in England are so big it wounds me psychologically. Greece is a wonderful country, fantastic climate, great people … and that's why we are seriously thinking of buying a small Greek island and setting up our own hippy commune where we could live undisturbed for half of the year."

It would have escaped Lennon's notice that one of the Colonels' first was a crackdown

Didn't we have a lovely time…?
With Maharishi on their way to Bangor, August 1967.
Authorised biographer Hunter Davies bottom left

(Trinity Mirror / Mirrorpix / Alamy Stock Photo)

and hippies branding them "drug addicts, sex maniacs and thieves". In mitigation, with *Sgt Pepper* in the shops, *Our World* aired and *Magical Mystery Tour* gestating, the group were entitled to some down time. Not long before he died, Brian wrote to his business partner Nat Weiss in the tone of a loving parent keeping an eye on his wayward children: "The boys have gone to Greece to buy an island. I think it's a dotty idea but they're no longer children and must have their own sweet way".

In 2020, the guitar-shaped Ethereal Island was on sale for £9,000,000.

Denied their own island as a sanctuary, Transcendental Meditation offered up an inner calm. But their involvement with the Maharishi during the turbulent summer of 1967 put further distance between the group and their fans. For while they were regarded as the benevolent rulers of the underground, the hippie sub-culture, many of the Beatles' fans who bought their records were, by and large, small 'c' conservative.

That tumultuous year had begun with what many still think of as the greatest *ever* pop single… then *Sgt Pepper*… 'All You Need Is Love'… the Maharishi… *Our World*… Brian's death… TV special… double *Magical Mystery Tour* EP (only 19/6d). It ended with their traditional hold on the Christmas No.1. With advance orders of 300,000, 'Hello Goodbye' is too often overlooked, its lovely Ying and Yang lyrics, the driving rhythm, the catchy 'Hey-la' fade, it remains one of my favourite singles. Though *Record Mirror* opined, "deliberately repetitive, medium-pace item. It sounds like a send-up, the lyrics (what there are) mean nothing…". Hey-la…

It was also the only time the Beatles sported their *Sgt Pepper* costumes outside the photographic studio, when they wore them for a promotional video, filmed at Brian's Saville Theatre, to promote 'Hello Goodbye'. I remember viewing it years later, and being spellbound by the Beatles *moving* in their colourful costumes away from the static LP sleeve. Some of the footage was also utilised for Peter Jackson's 'Now & Then' video.

They were restless, rootless, looking for a direction. Before, Brian might have tried to interest them in a business deal or a film project. With him gone, their frailty was revealed. Live performance was out: none were interested in nodding-dog performances in echoing stadia. Besides, there was no way the technology that fuelled *Sgt Pepper* could be replicated onstage. The prospect of them goofing around in a film Marx Brothers-style held no appeal.

Then, the fruit that tempted Eve, the fruit that provided the concept of Original Sin began to occupy the Beatles. In January 1968, 'The Beatles Ltd' became 'Apple Corps'. Their first solo business outing, the Apple boutique lasted barely six months. Today it is probably best remembered for the towering psychedelic mural looming over Baker Street. Apple the company, however, is still going strong, over half a century on, largely fuelled by anniversary Beatle releases.

It was after the wife of the 3rd Earl of Burlington, Lady Dorothy Savile, that the street which remains the second best-loved London location associated with the Beatles was named. In London, if you wanted to catch a glimpse of a Beatle, you split your time between Abbey Road and Savile Row. Prior to its Beatle connections, the street already had a distinguished history: running parallel to Regent Street, hard by is the Albany, "the most exclusive bachelor apartments in London". Nearby is Heddon Street where, only four years later, David Bowie would take rock & roll on its most seismic journey since the break-up of the Beatles when he posed for the cover of 1972's *Ziggy Stardust*… LP.

Sgt Pepper teaches the band to play… Saville Theatre,
'Hello Goodbye' shoot, 10 November 1967

Savile Row enjoyed a long association with tailoring. Henry Poole & Co. occupy No.15, the tailors who fashioned the first tuxedo for Edward VII when Prince of Wales. No.1 Savile Row was originally home to the Royal Geographical Society and where Doctor Livingstone's body had lain in state.

However, it is No.3 Savile Row that continues to exert such a strong pull. From here the Beatles tried to be businessmen, and from where Apple spread its seeds. After Apple left it became the HQ of the Building Societies Association and until recently, a branch of Abercrombie & Fitch. The clothes giant had to pay £16,000 after "inappropriate redecoration" had taken place in the Grade II listed building. Robert Davis of Westminster City Council crowed, "It has certainly been a long and winding road to get this judgment…" It was only in 2019 that a plaque was finally, belatedly, erected marking the location as that of the last ever Beatle performance before an audience. It was hard not to be saddened today by the sight of 3 Savile Row. It was the address from which so much had been promised and so much expected.

For all the organisational flaws and idealism that enveloped Apple (Zapple, Apple Films, Apple Electronics, the Apple school), Apple Records flourished. Mind you, it didn't hurt that its launch single was one of the best-loved and best-selling Beatle songs ever, 'Hey Jude'.

Neil Innes remembered McCartney in the studio overseeing production on the Bonzo Dog Band's 'Urban Spaceman'. Ever the professional, Paul was hands-on, and quick. Between takes he played something he'd just written and asked his opinion. The Innes thumbs went up and Paul smiled: "Good, I'll play it to John". Again, there was an echo of that Northern one-upmanship.

He's said it since, but when we spoke, McCartney reflected: "It's always the line you *didn't* think fitted that seems to work. 'The movement you need is on your shoulder', which just fitted and I was always gonna fix it, it was always a line down to be re-worked. I played it to John and he said that's the best line in it! I said don't be silly, it's … like a bloody parrot on your shoulder. But he said, 'Well *I* understand it'."

Although the song remained on the UK charts longer than any Beatle single since 'She Loves You', and although it was their longest-running US No.1 (nine weeks), on its release the knives were out. *Melody Maker* devoted a whole page to its readers after Radio 1's Tony Blackburn asked his listeners for their verdict after admitting, "Frankly, I think 'Hey Jude' goes on a bit at the end". G. Pearson of Hull agreed: "I wish they wouldn't spoil their songs by prolonging the endings till they reach monotony"; Gary Merrin "quite liked it, but it could be a bit shorter". While Frank Sweeney preferred "their older recordings, the *Sergeant Pepper* album for instance… it goes on too long. That's the trouble with so many of the modern pop records – there's too much repetition".

One unforeseen controversy in the single's promotion came when Paul thought it would be fun for a guerrilla campaign of spray-painting the title around London. However, the sight of the word 'Jude' brought back many unhappy memories to Jews who had fled Hitler's Germany 30 years before. Back then, the word was painted to deter 'good' Germans from entering Jewish-owned shops.

One benefit of the single's 1968 release was that it got the band back playing in front of an audience. Elaborate plans for what we now call a 'promo video' were dropped and so it was back to basics: the Beatles performing their new single in front of an invited audience. That way it could be screened worldwide without the group leaving home. Called in for service was the dependable Michael Lindsay-Hogg, who had shot the 'Paperback Writer' and 'Rain' promos beforehand.

He recalled the 'Hey Jude' shoot to Graeme Thomson in 2020: "After every take we had to reload the reels, which took about 10 minutes… the band just stood on the rostrum and talked amongst themselves, had a cigarette. Then in the second break, they realised that there were 100 or so people just standing around. They hadn't played to any kind of public audience since they'd stopped touring in 1966. Slowly, they began to strum and play, Ringo came in with a beat… They started with Tamla Motown songs, which was always the place they went if they couldn't think of anything else to do… 'You Really Got a Hold on Me', so during every break they would sort of play for the audience, and everybody had a good time".

Given what we know now of what was going on behind the Beatles scenes at the time, there is a sense of joy and liberation in the act of performing 'Hey Jude' before an appreciative crowd. Indeed, looking at that audience in retrospect, what is surprising is that how very *un*-Beatle like the crowd are.

Recently a letter came to light from Apple at their Wigmore Street address requesting audience members to see a performance by the Beatles on 4 September 1968. "If you are able to come in the uniform of your profession", the letter stated, "would you be kind enough to bring with you a change of clothing… generally speaking we want to see people as they are when they are working". Taking part in an historic TV moment required bringing the letter outside the Grosvenor Hotel, hard by Buckingham Palace, at 4.45 p.m. on the day.

In the UK, the ubiquitous David Frost introduced the band, twitching nervously as they vamped his show theme and 'It's Now or Never' before settling into an accomplished 'Hey Jude' in front of a delighted audience. As the band 'Na-na-na…' to their hearts' content, the crowd flood the stage – skinheads, rude boys, pensioners, mini-skirted boppers, Sikhs, 'straights', bee-hived girls, dapper mods… Barely a long-haired hippie in sight.

If any record can be said to typify the distance that John and Paul had travelled, their final single of 1968 was it: Paul's engaging, marathon singalong 'Hey Jude' got the airplay, while the underground press singled out the B-side, John's (non) call to arms, 'Revolution'. Lennon clearly couldn't make up his mind if he was In or Out or which side of the barricades he was on during that turbulent year.

By then, Yoko Ono was beginning to take priority over his commitment to the Beatles. Other distractions were to hand too. Seven years on from those iconic Hamburg shots, Astrid Kirchherr (under her married name of Astrid Kemp) reappeared on the Beatle scene. Hers is the head shot of George that appeared on his soundtrack to the 1968 film *Wonderwall*. While the film is largely forgotten, it merits a footnote in Beatle history: as the first solo album to be released by a Beatle, while still in the group. George's soundtrack to *Wonderwall* was released on 1 November 1968, beating John Lennon's *Two Virgins* to the racks by three weeks.

The film, which premiered at the Cannes film festival on 17 May 1968, cost £60,000 and was shot in four weeks. Jack McGowan and Jane Birkin starred – the latter in place of Marianne Faithfull, whom the producers were convinced would end up being "carried out on a stretcher." In 1995, of course, 'Wonderwall' was also the No.2 hit with which Beatle-obsessives Oasis ended the year.

The goose that laid the golden egg for their Apple label was obviously the Beatles. But Apple releases also included memorable releases from Mary Hopkin, Billy Preston, Badfinger, James Taylor and the Radha Krishna Temple. As Andy Davis wrote on the sleeve of the excellent 2010 CD compilation *Come and Get It: The Best of Apple Records*, "Let it be remembered that around a quarter of its singles charted in the UK or the US – that's a hits-to-release ratio that few other labels have ever achieved".

Practicality and pragmatism triumphed over idealism. An advertisement in the UK music press requested unsigned acts to submit their material to an address in Baker Street. The word 'Beatle' was not mentioned, but those in the know made the 'Apple' connection. The Beatles themselves had little interest in the avalanche of tapes which poured in. One which did bring out the schoolboy in George and John was Brute Force's 'The King of Fuh'. Much sniggering was undertaken at the prospect of Radio 1 playing a song with the chorus of 'fuh-king'. George's personal assistant Terry Doran later said that the most used piece of Apple's office equipment was a stamp with 'Fuck Off' on it.

But they should have known better... among those whose services the label were to decline included Crosby, Stills & Nash, Fleetwood Mac, Yes, Queen, Gilbert O'Sullivan, David Bowie and, allegedly, the Band, which I find hard to believe as George was particularly enamoured of their work. As a working label, Apple carried on into the 1970s, Stefan Granados reckons the last group to ever record at the Apple Studios was a pre-fame Ian Dury with his pub rock outfit Kilburn & the High Roads.

Typical of the label's luck was their fourth album release, the eponymous debut of a lanky American singer/songwriter, James Taylor. On his debut album, he refers to the Beatles as "a holy host of others" on 'Carolina in My Mind' (the same album's 'Something in the Way She Moves' also played a hand in a later George Harrison composition). Taylor was signed to Apple by Peter Asher, the label's head of A&R, and was inevitably "a huge Beatles fan". The album was recorded in London and, as Taylor told Pete Zollo: "Just the fact that I was in this pantheon, really being present where they were recording *The White Album*. It was just amazing".

Disappointed and disillusioned by the way Apple handled the LP, Taylor and his now-manager Asher quit the label. His next album 1970's *Sweet Baby James* was a landmark release, defining the singer/songwriter genre and one of the decade's best-selling LPs. But it was released on Warner Bros.

*

New Musical Express editor Andy Gray breathed a sigh of relief as 1968 dawned: "Last year... I was writing in gloomy mood, saying that I thought the Beatles were fast leaving their fans behind with bearded faces and ultra-sophisticated music and lyrics. I pleaded for them to become more neat and tidy in their appearance, and more simple in some of their musical outlook..." *Teen Set* magazine in America concurred: "Readers will take delight and note that John and Paul have shaved off their blechy and ugghy mustaches and beards, leaving only beautiful, gorgeous, sensitive, happy, honest faces to be seen..."

It wasn't just musically that the Beatles were changing, evolving; in 1968, for the fifth time in only four years, Madame Tussaud's had to remodel to keep up with their changing look. Aptly, the Beatles were the only pop waxworks on display in their Marylebone Road museum.

In August 1968, *Melody Maker*'s Alan Walsh was asking 'Why Does Nobody Love The Beatles?' He cited John & Yoko's activities (and records), the Maharishi, LSD, the flop of the Apple boutique, Paul's split with Jane Asher. For all the bright, psychedelic mayhem of *Sgt Pepper* and the hiding behind masks of *Magical Mystery Tour*, the next Beatle album would, as usual, offer something completely different.

Even the look would cause no comparison with *Pepper,* or even the equally flamboyant *Magic Mystery Tour* covers. For Christmas 1968, the forecast was white. All white. Pure as the driven snow. For the Romans, a white stone marked a "joyful day"; to Native Americans, the white wampum was "the deepest pledge of honour. And lest we forget white Knights … white magic… In *Brewer's Dictionary of Phrase & Fable* white "denotes purity, virginity, simplicity, innocence, truth and hope".

In his magnificent, cathedral of a novel *Moby Dick*, Herman Melville wrote: "Therefore… symbolize whatever grand or gracious thing he will by whiteness, no man can deny that in its profoundest idealized significance it calls up a peculiar apparition to the soul". Thus, *The Beatles* and *The White Album*.

Talking to Michael Bracewell, Richard Hamilton recalled his role in the *White Album* cover. The painter was cross at being kept waiting in the Apple outer office: "I hadn't come in with the intention of doing a white album cover. It was just provoked by this irritation I had of seeing all this nonsense going on". He recalled Paul had a very hands-on approach once the concept was agreed. Then it came to the numbering: "I said 'I'll have Number One' and Paul said 'Not on your nelly… we'll have the first four'. So I made mine Zero!"

That *White Album* numbering still continues to fascinate over half a century on. One assumes No.1s 1 to 4 went to the creators; would George Martin have been eligible for No.5? Or Yoko? Graham Thom found an Australian release of No.00038. ("It has small, round promo-only stickers on each album – maybe lower numbers were given to record executives?") How then did *Record Collector* reader Steve Taylor's mum pick up 0000005 from a local Rumbelows? The debate still rages: how many copies were printed of each number? If, as rumour has it, the Beatles themselves received either ten or a dozen copies each to hand out to family, friends and employees, how were *they* numbered? How many copies were printed with the same number?

Richie Unterberger spoke to Mark Haverkos, "the world's most dedicated *White Album* collector, owning the UK No.4 and US numbers 7, 10, 11". Apple's Tony Bramwell recalled "there were four sets of the first 20, because they realised early on that the low numbers would be highly collectable". If there *were* duplicates, then all four Beatles would presumably have got 1-4. Then came the numbering for separate mono and stereo versions. Then there were the differences between US and UK pressings. *Then* there were the differences between the US and UK mono *and* stereo pressings…! It all makes cracking the Enigma code look like *The Oldie*'s 'Moron Crossword'.

Mind you that confusion makes for profit – a *White Album* autographed by all four

Beatles was auctioned for £136,800 in 2013. Ringo's 0000001 US mono copy was sold in 2015 for a staggering $790,000, at the time the most ever paid for a record. A copy of John Lennon's 0000006 was auctioned in 2024 for 'only' $162,500.

One intriguing alternative cover caught my attention in 2009. John Byrne (best remembered for writing BBC's *Tutti Frutti*) was also a talented artist – he designed sleeves for his mate Gerry Rafferty's group Stealer's Wheel. He was commissioned to come up with a sleeve for the Beatles' 1968 album, which was duly delivered, then rejected. It did, however, grace the cover of the 1980 compilation *The Beatles Ballads*.

You cannot but admire the tenacity of American artist Rutherford Chang, with his collection of two *thousand* copies of *The White Album*. He explained in a 2013 interview, "The serial numbers made collecting them seem natural, and the more I got, the more interesting it became. As you see, many of them are written on, and each has a story". I inherited mine from a family friend, missing the inner poster, the LPs were scratched and a tantalising telephone number in biro on the sleeve.

Then there were all those lovely little differences between the Mono and Stereo versions. In Mono, 'Blackbird' has different bird sounds… 'Helter Skelter' is 52 seconds shorter… 'Yer Blues' ten seconds longer… On 'Back in the USSR' Paul's final drumbeat can be heard… 'Piggies' offers different porcine sounds… Oh, and the clever sequencing that found all the 'animal' songs gathered together on Side II…

In 2022, an internet debate raged: the colour photos in the original LP release in America measured 7 ¾" x 10 ¾", whereas the UK snaps were 8" x 11 ½"… This sort of demented trivia is a reason why *they* still exercise such a potent hold. The internet is fecund territory for this sort of debate, and makes for diverting reading, though you sense an evening spent in the company of those who post could be a little… demanding.

*

The year 1968 had begun with a head-clearing exercise as, still under the spell of the Maharishi Mahesh Yogi (1917–2008), all four group members plus consorts flew to meditate at the Maharishi's ashram ('Place of the Wise One') in Rishikesh. For all the later criticism, scorn and cynicism, the break gave them a breathing space. It also proved to be an incredibly fertile period creatively, with much of the groundwork for *The White Album* and *Abbey Road* laid there while not silently meditating. (The secret password each was issued with included Lennon's 'Be Here Now', later the title of Oasis' third album).

All those who entered the Maharishi's ashram had to forsake drugs, and donate a week's salary – a news report at the time estimated every Beatle sacrificing £11,000 each. Ajoy Rose's 2021 documentary *The Beatles and India* showed intriguing archive footage demonstrating just how relaxed the group were during their break.

It was George who stayed longest and meditated hardest. His state of mind was encapsulated when he celebrated his 25th birthday at the ashram. The Maharishi gave him a present: "George, the globe I am giving you symbolizes the world today. I hope you will help us all in the task of putting it right". George allegedly turned it upside down with the observation, "I've done it".

The riots and assassinations which were to characterise 1968 lay just over the horizon as the Beatles decamped to Rishikesh to unwind. Here they could regroup, reflect on the previous four years of madness, mourn their manager, find tranquility and solace in music. No one, not even a Beatle, could see what turbulence lay in the future, but their Indian sojourn provided a break, a holiday from the madness. They cleared their heads, forsook drugs and wrote an estimated 48 songs while at the ashram, virtually a song a day.

After a much-needed and spiritually refreshing break, the Beatles withdrew their love from their guru. Ringo quit early, then rumours of the Maharishi's less than spiritual interest in female converts caused the remaining three to flee. The Maharishi's interests were not wholly pure in the world of harsh commercialism either. It soon became evident he was planning a TV special on the back of the group's involvement, and on an LP sleeve he boasted himself as "the Beatles' spiritual advisor" as well as touring with the Beach Boys. Despite John's scathing 'Sexy Sadie', neither Paul nor George completely distanced themselves from the Maharishi in later years.

Soon after their return from India, it became apparent that the world needed more than the love and peace that had been proffered during 1967… Patchouli, beads and kaftans gave way to tear gas, napalm and riot shields. Calming music drowned out by invading tanks. Nineteen sixty-eight was a year when what was happening in the real world did intrude into Abbey Road and onto the music they were making. Most notable was John's 'Revolution', while Paul claimed 'Blackbird' was inspired by the Black Power issues of the period.

The world was riven by unrest. It truly was a chaotic, troubling and concerning year: Robert Kennedy and Martin Luther King fell victim to assassins' bullets. Russian tanks rolled into Czechoslovakia to crush their easing of the hardline Communist rule. There were big anti-Vietnam protests in "sleepy London town" while Enoch Powell's "rivers of blood" speech raked up racial tension in the UK. In Chicago the full, brutal force of Mayor Daley's police force was unleashed against protestors at the Democratic Convention. Martin Luther King's non-violent, Civil Rights protests were being edged out by the gun-toting militancy of the Black Panthers – the black power salute of victorious US athletes at the 1968 Mexico Olympics was an image which was soon carried around the world.

Another enduring image of the year was the South Vietnamese police chief blowing the brains out of a Viet Cong prisoner. It was taken during the Tet Offensive of January 1968, at a time when America was convincing itself that they were gaining the upper hand. In fact, Tet was proof that America could not win the war. Viet Cong guerrillas almost overran the American Embassy in the capital of Saigon. They also nearly captured the South Vietnamese radio HQ, but a loyal technician defied them – by broadcasting Beatle tunes to prove the government was still in control.

It wasn't just the widely reported clashes in London, Paris and Chicago, militant student activism and sit-ins took place across the USA, while there were similar disturbances in Germany, Egypt, Brazil, Mexico, Italy and Japan. Even Spain, creaking under Franco's dictatorship, witnessed student protest. It was on the cobbled streets of Paris though that the real revolution looked like it might take place. Groaning under an archaic educational system, French students took to the streets to battle riot police. This was the climate into which Lennon couldn't decide whether to be included, or not.

The spell with the Maharishi at Rishikesh had proved a diversion, provided a calming influence, and the group returned with a suitcase full of songs, many of which proved to be among the most enduring of their career.

Steve Turner speculates that on their return from Rishikesh, "their familiarity with mantras led to an increased use of repetition… 'You Know My Name…' "repeated 28 times"), 'All Together Now' ("title repeated 29 times"). It reached its high point in 'Hey Jude' (with over four minutes of the sound 'la' repeated 220 times). But there was something soothing, mantra-like in that hypnotic repetition.

Prior to their return to recording, the group assembled at George's house to routine the material they'd roughed out in India. They were spoilt for choice, some material was held over for *Abbey Road*, even *Imagine*. The choices were whittled down for what became *The White Album*. However, the smoothly the Esher sessions went, there was a friction, which seeped into Abbey Road. By then there was evident tension within the group. The ubiquity of Yoko Ono and her limpet-like adhesion to John meant that, for the first time in their career, the quartet came close to becoming a quintet. Prior to Yoko, girlfriends and wives had graciously been invited to sessions, on occasion even provide anonymous backing vocals. But their opinions had never been sought, and their suggestions never encouraged. To have a partner actually *sing* on a Beatle record was unthinkable. Until 8 October 1968, when Yoko sang a line on John's 'Continuing Story of Bungalow Bill'.

The majority of Beatle fans were baffled by the relationship. A 1968 American single, 'John You Went Too Far' by Rainbo would probably have sunk without trace, had 'Rainbo' not later to be revealed as Oscar-winning actress Sissy Spacek. Tom Paxton gave us 'Crazy John'. Even irritating squeaky-voiced jazz pianist Blossom Dearie weighed in with 'Hey John'.

While George had felt on the margins during the recording of *Sgt Pepper*, the sessions for the recording of its follow up saw further fissures. It wasn't *all* tense during the recording of *The Beatles* (aka, of course, *The White Album*), but it was far from smooth sailing. The 2018 box set highlights that there were enough tensions to reveal the disparate elements: George Martin felt he no longer held the reins; Ringo walked out; group members found Yoko's constant presence unnerving; many of the tracks were solo efforts…

Long-time recording engineer Geoff Emerick quit, unable to take the tension. In his memoir, Emerick recalls McCartney carping at a George Martin suggestion for his vocal on 'Ob La Di…' until the producer snapped, "'Then bloody sing it again… I give up. I just don't know any better how to help you'. It was the first time I had *ever* heard George Martin raise his voice in a session".

Engineer Ken Scott told Ken Sharp, "we had a blast and they were great to work with… I don't think I ever worked on a project … where at some point someone hasn't lost their temper. It's short lived, it's just an outburst. If you consider that *The White Album* took six months, that's gonna happen several times. It was just the odd outburst and everything else was fine".

As ever, it was in the words of Bob Dylan, "the pettiness that plays so rough". Geoff Emerick remembers George Harrison seething that Yoko had helped herself to one of his McVitie's digestive biscuits: "It almost didn't matter what the argument was about. By this stage whenever the four of them were together it was like a tinderbox, and anything could set them off… even something as dumb as a digestive biscuit". Even today, Beatle scholars are unsure if they were the plain or milk chocolate variety digestive.

George Martin was quoted on the 2018 box set: "It's rather like the students revolting in France. Youth is realising its power. I was very much the boss and they were the pupils. This naturally changed with their success and power. They want more say about what goes on". In the same book, Giles Martin wrote: "Whenever anyone mentioned to my dad that *The White Album* was their favourite Beatles record, he would grimace. Not because he disliked the album, it was more to the fact that the recording sessions for it had been so different to previous Beatles albums. In 1968, he lost the classroom". Engineer Ken Scott came up with a similar comparison: "They were like the kids who had left home".

During the frequently tense recording of *The White Album*, there were a couple of reminders of the way they were: famously the Fab Four bunked off from Abbey Road to Paul's house to watch the TV premiere of *The Girl Can't Help It*. It was a rare opportunity to revisit childhood memories as the 1956 film trumpeted its rock & roll glories and once again displayed Little Richard's pithy observation of Jayne Mansfield's attributes: "she got a lot of what they call the most". "We hadn't seen that in a while, and the thing I loved about it", Paul told me much later, "was that they *honoured* rock & roll with that film. It wasn't crappy black and white, cheap – it was Hollywood!" Further 50s nostalgia occurred while recording 'Revolution #1'; one of the brass players was Don Lang, who the band recognised as a regular on the must-see 50s BBC TV rock show *Six-Five Special*.

Back in the studio though, there was undeniably … a tautness. And that was largely due to the incursion of Lennon's paramour. Hunter Davies remembers being at Abbey Road one day during 1968 to find Yoko umbilically attached to John: "I was as amazed as the other three Beatles… and see her sitting there… 'Who the fuck is this?' they were mouthing at each other".

Engineer Geoff Emerick was a bitter observer of the period from when Yoko made her entry into the tight-knit Beatle camp: "No one other than Neil and Mal had ever infiltrated Beatles sessions to that degree, and you could tell from the icy chill and the looks on the faces of Paul, George and Ringo that they didn't like it one bit… Once Yoko had left the control room, George Martin turned to me. Shaking his head sadly he said 'What on earth is John thinking?'"

Talking in 1998, George Martin confirmed: "It was uncomfortable because she was the first one to break the stranglehold. Here you had a castle of four corners. Even I wasn't part of that. And they were impregnable, the four of them together were bigger than any individual parts. Then Yoko comes in and one corner is exposed".

McCartney seethed at Barry Miles: "She'd say 'Beatles should do this and Beatles should do that'. And we'd be like 'Excuse me, love, it's THE Beatles'. She even took that away from us". Tony Bramwell remembered John whingeing, "She just wants to be one of us. It's hateful that someone can be treated with so much hostility just because she loves someone", causing even Ringo to snap, "Well she's not a Beatle, John, and she never will be".

Looking back for *Anthology* Ringo reflected: "Yoko being in the studio was a new thing. It was all new. We're very Northern: the wives stayed at home and we went to work – we dug coal mines and they cooked dinner. It was one of those flat-cap attitudes… I think Maureen came to the studio five or six times… Pattie came several times at the most. I don't remember Cynthia coming much… And suddenly we had Yoko in bed in the studio".

Revolution Canine, Paul and Martha, St Johns Wood, 1968

Tony Bramwell confirmed to me: "Yoko was just *awful*. George couldn't stand to be in the same room as her. She treated minions, secretaries, assistants, like shit". In mitigation, it wasn't Yoko who 'broke up the Beatles'. For John, she was 'The One'. Muse, mother, mistress, mentor… *This* was now his most important partnership. Yoko provided solace, support and what he felt was artistic motivation. For John Lennon, inspiration was undeniable. Separation was unthinkable.

For all the tension, disputes and edginess, on release, the double LP was a treasure trove. I would contend that here is the last time Lennon really got out of Yoko limbo while still a member of the Beatles. If you look at the singles on the 2000 *1* CD, the bulk of the material from 'Yesterday' on comprises Paul songs. *The White Album*, however, is the sound of John Lennon *bothering* – the roaring 'Happiness Is a Warm Gun'… the cheeky 'Glass Onion'… the thumping 'Bungalow Bill'… the reflective 'Dear Prudence'… the scabrous 'Sexy Sadie' (I'm sure Lennon would have relished knowing it later became the name of a popular inflatable sex toy)… the poignant 'Julia'… the musically dynamic 'Revolution'… the melancholic 'Cry Baby Cry' which always suggests a strong Lewis Carroll influence to me ("Alice fancy dress party on lawn", John wrote on a provisional track listing)… the engaging 'I'm So Tired' (still love that crazy 'cigarette' and 'stupid get' rhyme)… and that middle eight on 'Everybody's Got Something to Hide Except Me and My Monkey'… "I always preferred it to the other albums", John said later. "The *Pepper* myth is bigger, but the music on *The White Album* is far superior. I wrote a lot of good shit on that".

Paul was no slouch either, from the emphatic opening of 'Back in the USSR' – complete with some imaginative, tongue-in-cheek Soviet

references – via 'Blackbird', the reflective 'Mother Nature's Son' and 'I Will'; the pounding 'Helter Skelter' and 'Birthday'. Here was Paul shucking the 'soft Beatle' tag. I am probably in the minority having a soft spot for Ringo's jaunty C&W 'Don't Pass Me By'. George too excelled with the harmonious 'While My Guitar Gently Weeps' and wry 'Piggies'.

It was the Orwellian fable of the pigs becoming porcine masters in *Animal Farm* which inspired the song. But this was one of the songs so tragically misinterpreted by Charles Manson. In 1969, the Manson gang went on an orgy of killing in Hollywood. The charismatic Charlie was tragically convinced that the Beatles were sending him secret messages on *The White Album*. Interviewed for a *Rolling Stone* feature, Manson cited 'Revolution #9' as "the battle of Armageddon, the end of the world". 'Rocky Racoon' ("Coon… it means the black man is going to come into power again") and 'Piggies' were the other titles Manson was convinced were for his ears alone. "It's an unconscious thing… The music is bringing on the revolution, the unorganized overthrow of the Establishment. The Beatles know in the sense that the subconscious knows".

Manson locked on to 'Helter Skelter' soon after the album's release. To his deranged mind, it foretold the Apocalypse. The tragedy, of course, is that there is no way Manson would have associated his own Armageddon with the sort of childhood fairground treats the Beatles referenced on the song. The Sharon Tate murders, carried out by what the media called a gang of 'hippies', was a signpost to the end of 60s idealism.

In 2020, *Kerrang!* magazine polled the Most Evil 50 Songs, and there, amidst Cradle of Filth, Cannibal Corpse and Marilyn Manson, at No.45 was 1968's 'Helter Skelter'. It was of course the tragic Manson misinterpretation which led to its inclusion.

While regarded as a minor addition to *The White Album*, at the time 'Ob-La-Di, Ob La Da' carried quite a punch. The shuffling unfamiliar rhythm would not have found a place on any serious rock music fan's turntable at the time. It recalled calypso, which in the 50s threatened to overtake rock & roll as *the* musical novelty fad. It came back into fashion with Bernard Cribbins' 'Gossip Calypso', under the watchful eye of George Martin. Lance Percival's topical calypsos were also in vogue during the early 60s. But 'Ob La Di...' was, to the casual listener, ska or bluebeat. To the later aficionado it was reggae.

By 1968, reggae was skinhead music, boot-stomping, working-class stuff, nowhere near as thought-provoking as *A Saucerful of Secrets*. Reggae wasn't taken seriously by 'heads' until Bob Marley's *Catch a Fire* five years in the future. But, as ever, the Fabs got there first. And there was that saucy fun with gender they were having, Desmond doing up his pretty face; the very idea of a man being called 'pretty' would not register in the hurly-burly world of rock & roll until Ziggy Stardust teetered into the new decade.

Then there was 'Revolution #9', ironic that the longest track the Beatles ever released was also the most unlistenable. The great advantage when the Beatle catalogue was made available on CD meant that you could programme and skip 'Revolution #9'. This is where I detect the cold, dead, arty grip of Yoko. Here, I believe, she pressured John into misguided 'musique concrete' territory, allowing space for her haiku interpolations. George, bored with being a Beatle, had a hand in the collage, seeing it as a nice iconoclastic kiss-off. There are those who venerate the song (Ian MacDonald devotes four pages to it).

To his eternal credit in 1996, with his ear pressed to the hi-fi, Colin Harper sat and transcribed 'Revolution #9' and unearthed all the mumbled messages ("taking our sides"... "impervious in London"...?) and the song publishers charged him £100 for the privilege.

I wondered if Lennon had re-read 'William at the Garden Party', where Richmal Crompton's anarchic hero is mistaken for musical phenomenon 'Frankie Randall': "William's familiar spirit of devilry came to his aid. He crashed both his hands upon the keys in a sudden ear-splitting discord. He ran his fingers up and down the keys. He crossed one hand over the other, he hurled himself wildly at the bass and then at the treble. His audience listened in amazed silence. He kept up a Bacchanalian riot of inharmonious sounds for nearly ten minutes, then he stopped and turned his sphinx-like expressionless face towards his audience".

In his incisive Beatle biography, *Can't Buy Me Love*, Jonathan Gould calls the track, "Shapeless, formless, gormless, 'Revolution #9' is an embarrassment that stands like a black hole at the end of *The White Album*, sucking up whatever energy and interest remain after the preceding 90 minutes of music".

Indeed, I would contend that for most listeners, then as now, 'Revolution #9' stands as the King's New Clothes: no one having the guts to stand up and say to Lennon: "This is absolute bollocks. It has no place on a Beatle LP. If it has to have a home, save it for *Unfinished Music No.3*".

Geoff Emerick recalled Lennon playing the finished track to bemused Beatles. "Not bad" was Paul's diplomatic comment. "Not bad?" Lennon exploded: "You have no idea what you're talking about. In fact, this should be our next bloody single! This is the direction the Beatles should be going in from now on". Indeed, even the wayward 'What's the New Mary Jane', cut from the same 'Revolution #9' cloth, would have been an improvement.

Despite the set's penultimate track ("utter mayhem… maddening") *Record Mirror* still granted the release a 5-star review, reflecting a popular view of the period: "*Sgt Pepper* was the ultimate, or so it was unquestionably voted. The most popular question since then has been 'What else can they do – what else is left?' When the distinguished four release an LP or single it forever remains in a class of its own and is never considered comparable to the ordinary charts…" The review sagely concluded, "The only comparison is with their own past releases. They are essentially a chart in themselves".

In his review in *The Observer*, Tony Palmer blithely began by stating Lennon and McCartney were "the greatest songwriters since Schubert". He concluded, "At the end all you can do is stand and applaud. Whatever your taste in popular music, you will be satisfied here… if you think that pop is just rock & toll, then the Beatles have done it better… if you think that pop is mind-blowing noise, then the Beatles have done it better – on distant shores of the imagination that others have not yet even sighted". (The entire *White Album* review was, inexplicably, included on the sleeve of the *Yellow Submarine* soundtrack LP.)

The *Melody Maker* review was surprisingly short, suggesting the weekly only got it right on deadline ("with over 30 songs it takes an awful lot of digesting") but the paper also wondered how many Beatle fans could afford the £3/14/10d for the double set, though did note there were already 300,000 advance orders. Interesting to see other releases that week in November 1968 (blues heavy Otis Spann, John Lee Hooker, Jimmy Reed) plus old favourites (Bing Crosby, Connie Francis, Astrud Gilberto). You could also see the industry gearing up for Christmas, with Best Ofs… the Beach Boys, Cilla Black, the Seekers, Frank Sinatra, Peggy Lee and Nat King Cole heading for the high street stores.

The *White Album* debate continued to rage in the pop weeklies' letters pages. In *Melody Maker* dated 14 December 1968, a correspondent could not "agree with the criticism of 'intellectual pop critics' in general simply because some of them have raved blindly over a Beatles album which is slightly below standard". That week's lucky LP winner from Kensington, SW7 was Andrew Lloyd Webber.

Spread over 93 minutes, you did get a lot of music for your bucks. Even today, opinion is still divided; George Martin maintained it would have made a brilliant single album, while its defenders argue that the inclusion of maverick material like 'Wild Honey Pie' and 'Why Don't We Do It in the Road' demonstrate the group's willingness to experiment. Personally, I think you could have ditched 'Sexy Sadie', 'Savoy Truffle' and 'Yer Blues' as not being up to par. The penultimate track obviously should *never* have been included. But for all its wayward wilfulness, even today, *The White Album* still continues to delight, and surprise.

The 2018 box set really came alive on Disc 3, *The Esher Demos*, with all three songwriters setting up their stalls and pitching their wares. The engaging studio banter on the studio floor suggests it wasn't all as tense as previously reported. These out-takes are the intriguing building blocks as they ascend to the familiar final version.

While the cover was deliberately blank, the interior was visually rich, from the four posed portraits, to the fold-out collage. There was fun to be had in scouring the poster – Yoko, of course, nice smiling snap of Brian Epstein, Mal and Neil, Paul's excised 'naughty bits'…

With their image altering as swiftly as dew in the morning sun, some new publicity photographs of the group were required. Whole books have been written about the band's 'Mad Day Out' in July 1968, when they trolled round London with photographer Don McCullin on a photo shoot to produce those new images. One of the most intriguing locations was St Pancras Old Church, a building steeped in literary connections – a rendezvous for Mary and Percy Bysshe Shelley, while Dickens and Thomas Hardy were regular visitors. Famously, the church grounds provided the location for the shot which had the Beatles standing by railings, surrounded by curious onlookers which went on to grace the sleeves of the *Red* and *Blue* albums five years later.

Although they went on to become some of the most iconoclastic and widely-seen images of the band, in his autobiography, McCullin barely devotes half a page to that Day Out. In 2019, he was more forthcoming: "The group were good guys, but it wasn't my cup of tea. It was all a bit inconsequential… Yoko Ono was a nasty little bully, telling me I was standing in the wrong place. I'd recently seen soldiers killed and maimed in front of me in Vietnam. Her opinions meant as much to me as treading on a cigarette".

Even with John's caprices, Paul's broken engagement to Jane Asher, the Maharishi detour, the low points of *The White Album*, as 1968 wound down … the world was still at their feet. Whims and caprices could be accommodated by the fact they were the *Beatles*. Victor Spinetti remembered working with John on a theatre project around the time: "He said, 'Hey Vic, let's go somewhere warm'. I thought he meant the next room but we ended up in … Marrakesh".

Also lined up as a treat for fans leading up to Christmas 1968 was the hardback publication (30/-) of Hunter Davies' biography. David Hughes in *Disc & Music Echo* was underwhelmed: "The Beatles were the last real stars and now they are desperately trying to make themselves appear as ordinary and nasty as possible. For what? … the whole aura surrounding the book is one of finality and leaves the reader with the feeling that it's now all over for the Beatles. The excitements of Liverpool, Hamburg and America are all in the past, and the unwritten future seems unimportant – as if the Beatles are now finished".

The blood, toil, sweat and tears that went into the recording of *The White Album* paid off. Even without much change from four quid, it was the UK No.1 LP of Christmas 1968. It *was* a nice package, with the portraits and poster. A package that was amplified half a century later with the lavish box set. As Jamie Atkins wrote in *Record Collector* on its 2018 release: "If you had told them that the material which they left off *The White Album* would have been on sale for £100 you'd have been laughed out of Abbey Road".

*

By 1969 it has to be said, in certain sniffy circles, that the Beatles and Rolling Stones and Bob Dylan (after the low-key *Nashville Skyline*) were seen, in some quarters, as, perhaps, dare it be whispered, in an age of *Tommy*, *In the Court of the Crimson King*, *Santana*, *Blood Sweat & Tears*, *Led Zeppelin II* and *Ummagumma* … a little 'old-fashioned'?

As the year progressed, the counter-culture emerged from the underground. *Hair* was running on Broadway and in London. Over 50 festivals were held in Europe and North America. Of them all, of course, the best known was Woodstock, largely due to its 3LP souvenir and three-hour documentary. In a major 12-page feature looking back at the August festival, *Rolling Stone* marvelled, "Out of the mud and hunger and thirst, despite the rain and end-of-the-world traffic jams, beyond the bad dope trips and the garish confusion, a new nation had emerged…"

While not at Woodstock, the Beatles were represented: with performers stuck in the endless traffic jams, Richie Havens was persuaded to fill in on the Friday afternoon with 'Strawberry Fields Forever' and a lengthy 'Hey Jude'. The highlight of Joe Cocker's set was, of course, 'With a Little Help from My Friends' and Crosby, Stills, Nash & Young contributed 'Blackbird' during their set.

For the two premier groups, the Beatles and the Stones, they had been hard at it for six long years. They had begun as pop stars, falling in line with the prevalent, moribund showbiz dictats of the period, which they had then helped overturn. As the 60s edged towards its end, newer groups were felt to be pushing the boundaries of what was now thought of as 'rock', a music performed by 'bands'. Publications like *Rolling Stone*, *Crawdaddy* and *ZigZag* took musicians' opinions seriously. Gone were the Favourite Colour? and Ideal Girl? questions from the weekly inkies or US teen magazines. New bands drew on blues, built on psychedelia, incorporated classical influences, boasted of 'rock operas', devoted entire LP sides to one suite. As the 60s began winding down, eyes were on the 70s prize. Family's Roger Chapman was only one of the new breed who felt, "The Beatles have been a major influence on the whole music scene but I don't see them being an influence anymore".

While the internal dissent became public, the idols were equally capable of responding as fans. I remember Ray Connolly telling me about the way things were… He was one of the very few UK journalists who witnessed Elvis on his return to the concert stage in Las Vegas in 1969. Ray then flew up to New York to interview Bob Dylan prior to his return to live performance at the Isle of Wight after a three-year absence. But all Dylan wanted to talk about was Elvis: who was in the band? What material was he playing? On returning to London, Connolly went to Apple to hang out, bumping into John Lennon; and all *he* wanted to hear about was Elvis… Who was in the band? What material was he playing?…

Following their desultory meeting in 1965, Elvis took against the Beatles in a big way. He despised their drug taking – Elvis' prodigious medication, after all, was for *prescribed* drugs, so in his eyes that was legal. In his surreal meeting with President Nixon in 1970, Elvis, travelling under a favourite pseudonym ('John Carpenter') was buoyant when he arrived in Washington. Coercing the President, Elvis received a Bureau of Narcotics & Dangerous Drugs badge. Even Elvis couldn't engineer a meeting with FBI Chief J. Edgar Hoover, though one of Hoover's agents reported a conversation he had had with the singer: "Presley indicated that he is of the opinion that the Beatles laid the groundwork for many of the problems we are having with young people by their filthy unkempt appearances and suggestive music while entertaining in this country during the early and middle 1960s".

Ringo was upset. "That's very sad to me that he felt so threatened… This is Mr Hips, *the man*. And he felt we were a danger. I think that the danger was mainly to him and his career" (*Anthology*).

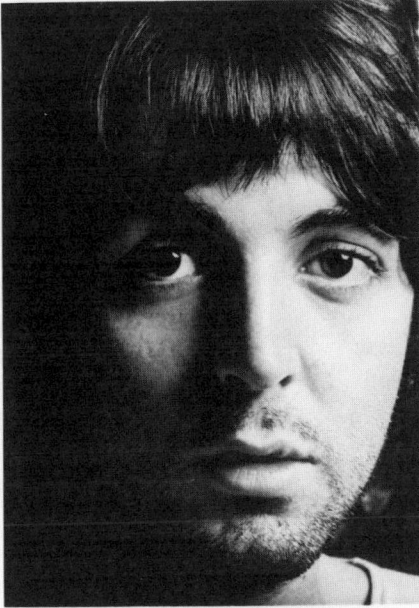

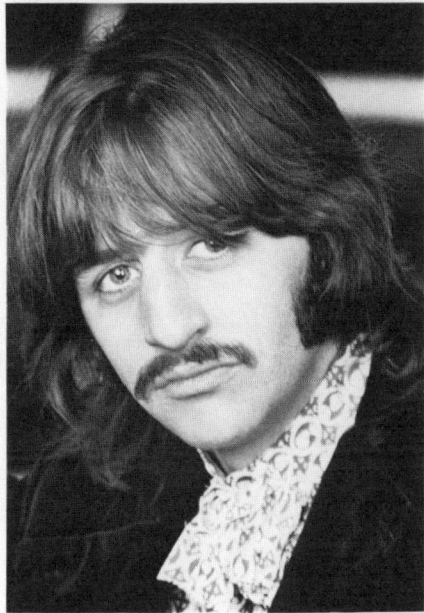

THE BEATLES

PARLOPHONE

1968 press shot

By 1969, the Beatles' main rivals, the Rolling Stones had pioneered a particular type of R&B, still strong on the blues, but had begun their 'imperial' phase with *Beggars Banquet* and *Let It Bleed*. The UK 'Blues Boom' was also in full swing, led by Fleetwood Mac (in its original Peter Green incarnation), Cream, Ten Years After, Taste, Savoy Brown, the Aynsley Dunbar Retaliation, Blodwyn Pig, the Keef Hartley Band, the Groundhogs, Chicken Shack, Led Zeppelin and Jethro Tull… All of whom relied on a blues-based, powerhouse, steamroller style of playing. All of whom were receiving respectful coverage in the music press of the period.

The other side of the coin was progressive rock, pioneered by Pink Floyd, King Crimson, the Nice, Yes, Moody Blues, Genesis, Emerson, Lake & Palmer, Santana, Quicksilver Messenger Service, the Steve Miller Band, Procol Harum … all of whom seemed to be taking pop music out to the further reaches of the galaxy. The Who's *Tommy* was hailed as "the first rock opera". In America, Chicago Transit Authority and Blood, Sweat & Tears were imaginatively fusing jazz and rock, while Miles Davis' *In a Silent Way* was bringing jazz into the rock auditorium.

There was still a perception though that the Beatles had the Midas touch, anything associated with them turned base metal into gold, which can be the only explanation for why, in 1969, Mercury Records released an LP by the Fool… They would be the Dutch clothes and sleeve designers then, not exactly known for their musical expertise.

The dedicated 'Apple Scruffs' were still there in all weathers ("We see at least one Beatle a day. Mostly it's John and Ringo, Paul and George don't come in so often"). In November 1969, 19-year-old American Cathy told *Record Mirror*'s Robert Partridge, "I came over here on holiday and really loved it… It's like a story book land, you read about kings and queens, but over here you've got them for real". "Lizzie", Partridge wrote, "is really big in Beatle fan terms. She was one of the two fans who were on that record 'Across the Universe'… And that's really big".

The tensions arising from Yoko's ubiquity, thus taking John's eye off the Beatle ball, were tied in with the decline of the Apple empire and the battle for the Beatle millions. A troublesome shoot for the group's third film as 1969 began… all could mark where the rot set in.

Then there were all the technological breakthroughs Alex Mardas (1942–2017) promised to deliver. In a way, 'Magic Alex' has come to symbolise all the promise and folly which was behind the original Apple. Alex's reach certainly exceeded his grasp – plans for a 72-track recording studio… an ultrasonic curtain… a magic telephone… a robotic butler… a spaceship…! Of the 100 odd patents applied for, *none* were accepted. All came to naught; Beatle insider Tony Bramwell estimates Alex's schemes cost the Beatles somewhere in the region of £300,000.

For all their offhand rebuttal of capitalism, the group were dumbfounded at the money which had slipped through their fingers. They needed a manager to handle that side, and leave them free to make the music which was still capable of generating those millions.

One estimate had Apple losing £20,000 a week. "If it carries on like this", John told Ray Coleman, "all of us will be broke in six months". In typical offhand fashion, John and Yoko decided to get a businessman, a *proper* businessman to look at the Apple accounts. A man in a suit. The only suit they could think of was Lord Beeching, the man who had earlier scythed through the UK railway system just as Beatlemania was breaking out.

At the meeting with Lennon and Yoko, Beeching sat and sifted through the chaotic accounts, before making eye contact with the shaggy-haired Beatle and his muse, offering the priceless advice, which could have acted as the company's epitaph: "Go back to music".

"I had very little to do with Apple", George recalled, "I think it was basically John and Paul's madness, their egos running away with themselves or with each other. There were lots of ideas, but when it came down to it, the only thing we could do successfully was write songs, make records and be Beatles" (*Anthology*).

Another figure emerged to drive a further nail in the Beatle coffin. For many, this was the snake who entered the garden, and exiled the group to the east of Eden. More blame accorded to him than even Yoko as the figure who broke up the Beatles.

As the British Invasion had crossed the Atlantic, canny accountant Allen Klein (1931 - 2009) soon found himself dealing with acts like the Dave Clark Five and Herman's Hermits. Both outfits had achieved considerable American success. All the while though, the native New Yorker had kept his eye firmly fixed on the two acts who swam on a sea of dollars: the Beatles and the Rolling Stones.

Klein used the prohibitive British tax system as the carrot, coming up with elaborate tax investments in which he encouraged his clients to invest. The money was only taxable once it was paid out. As the payments could stretch over years, sometimes decades, the tax demands were a lot more lenient. It also meant that interest accrued nicely on the accounts.

The Rolling Stones had, initially, undeniably benefitted from Klein's schemes. But as the 60s drew to a close, the Stones were keen to lose the American. In her autobiography, Marianne Faithfull cited Mick Jagger's "fairly diabolical" plan: "He would fob Klein off on the Beatles… John, who was susceptible to utopian joint projects such as alliances between the Beatles and the Stones said 'Yeah, what a fucking brilliant idea'. It was a bit of a dirty trick, but once Mick had distracted Klein's attention by giving him bigger fish to fry, Mick could begin unravelling the Stones' ties to him".

Phil Kaufman, who worked with the Stones, remembers Klein in action in 1969: "He was a little guy with a cigar. He was marching up and down, talking about the Stones and Apple. He delivered a great line. They were arguing about the decision-making process. He said: 'You know, Mick, there were four Beatles and there are only two Rolling Stones'!"

With a canny ear to the ground, Klein discerned the chaos at the heart of Apple empire and turned his attention to the Beatles. It was during the dog days of the group, and as they swam rudderless Klein offered himself as their saviour – a *Disc* headline of February 1969 read, 'Stones £sd boss joins Beatles'.

There was obviously *something* about Allen Klein that went beyond the caricature of a praying mantis, who "entered the Beatles' story as a villain from central casting and never escaped that role", wrote Peter Doggett. "Yet we are asked to believe that three of the four Beatles found this 'beady-eyed', 'grossly overweight' 'scorpion' such an attractive figure that they were prepared to trust him with their futures. Clearly the Demon King didn't always exude the stench of sulphur".

Knowing what we know now, there's an intriguing picture in the 27 September 1969 issue of *NME*, the one advertising *Abbey Road* on the cover (and Nick Logan's review of *Astral Weeks* – 'Van's Gone a Long Way from Them'). "Happy scene at Apple Records… after the signing of the contract giving the Beatles increased royalties from Capitol Records… and other benefits". A smiling Yoko, John, business manager Allan Klein and a *smiling* Paul McCartney… Rarely seen photos from the same session have Paul, learning how Klein had increased the group's US record royalties, can be seen bending the knee and kissing the Klein hand.

When sides were drawn, it was, sadly, John persuading George and Ringo to side with him and back Klein which drove a wedge in the group. Paul found himself isolated, favouring his in-laws, the Eastmans, as the preferred legal way out. It was that great divide that effectively, tragically, sealed the fate of the Beatles.

There undeniably *were* riches to be had: in his book about *The Lost Story of 1970*, David Browne claims, "EMI received a check for $10,738,198 representing royalties for American sales of Beatle records between September 1, 1969 and June 3, 1970". Six-month sales, for just one territory.

What is so sad in reading (or writing) about these last days of the Beatles as a functioning band is the despair, the fissures, the bitterness. For the first time since their formation, it was three against one. Until the Klein versus Eastman divide, all Beatle decisions had been unanimous. Perhaps this was just the boil that needed to be lanced. Hindsight, of course, is a wonderful thing. I do believe, however, that if the group had taken time out after the rewarding *Abbey Road*, a six-month break or year off could have helped the healing. Put the *Let It Be / Get Back* film project on hold, get the solo projects off the stocks and into the shops, appoint an independent financial consultant. Then, maybe, even go out on the road. With secret gigs as 'Ricky & the Red Streaks', as Paul wished, they may well have stuck it out. As it happened, it was not to be. Back then, bands didn't do gap years.

Klein steamrollered round Savile Row, his stern financial acumen brazenly at odds with the building's airy-fairy 'Western Communism'. Looking at the books, Klein charmed John and Yoko, decimated Apple, and terrified EMI. One occupant remembered a game of Happy Families, but with Klein applying the same terrifying tenacity to the card game as he did to the business deals.

Whole books have been written about the Apple experience and the complex financing which led to the group's split. What was in no doubt was that the company built on the best principles was foundering and floundering. The Beatles had soon tired of the day-to-day business, the staff they had running the company took advantage of their absence, the company was haemorrhaging cash. In the wake of Brian Epstein's death, *someone* was certainly needed to put the house in order. Tony Bramwell got the elbow. Only the loyal Neil Aspinall was spared the chop. By appointing Allen Klein to lead them out of the quagmire, John, George and Ringo effectively drove the wedge which isolated Paul, who favoured his in-laws over the man he saw as an outlaw.

The tragedy was that the group themselves were bored witless: they had no interest in the growing mound of demo tapes and were baffled by the business side of things and the men in suits. But their future was being decided in boardrooms by those self-same businessmen.

It was around this dislocating period that Dick James sold his share of Northern Songs to UK showbiz mogul, Lew Grade, whose ATV Corporation now owned a healthy 35% of the Beatles' publishing. Allen Klein found a City consortium with a 14% holding, which, coupled with the Beatles' own shares, could have tipped the balance firmly in the group's favour. However, in true confrontational form, it was the peace-loving Lennon who snapped. At a meeting with his putative partners, he roared that he was "sick of being fucked around by men in suits, sitting on their fat arses in the City". Said fat arses duly withdrew their offer, and the apple fell into Lord Grade's lap.

Boardroom battles, starting companies from scratch, emptying a flop boutique, coping with the intrusion of John's paramour… still the Beatles found time to function. 'Lady Madonna' was aimed at the fans who had been left baffled by the diversions of 1967 and 1968. This was the group 'as nature intended'. A rambunctious rocker which duly acknowledged the influence of Fats Domino. Music fan Ray Connolly called Paul out on its origins – Humphrey Lyttelton's 'Bad Penny Blues'. "You're not supposed to say that", the composer replied sheepishly.

On top of Apple crumbling, Klein versus Paul, and Paul versus John and Yoko and Ringo *and* George, there was the thorny problem of that third Beatles film which was necessary to release the group from their contract. The animated 1969 feature *Yellow Submarine* did not, on the film company's part, meet the stipulation which United Artists held over the follow-up to *Help!*

That cartoon still resonates, with the 1999 re-release reconfiguring the soundtrack, and the 2019 reissue happily made available in cinemas. One of the *Yellow Submarine* writers was Erich Segal, an American professor of Greek and Latin at Yale University. For $16,000 he delivered an early version of the script, though uncertain of what he was really doing: "The producer told me this film would be a big deal because *Sgt Pepper* had already sold three million albums", Segal recalled. "I was so hermetically sealed in my academic world that I said, 'Er, Mrs Pepper must be very happy!'"

Segal was soon to break even further from academia's hermetic world. The film of his 1970 novel *Love Story*, on its release on Valentine's Day 1971, went on to become the most successful film release of that year. One of the film's taglines was, "What can you say about a 25-year-old girl who died… That she loved Mozart and Bach? The Beatles? And me?"

While flawed, there is much to enjoy in the *Yellow Submarine* film – the 'Eleanor Rigby' sequence; the increasing interest in all things Victorian; the tip of the hat to pop artists Bridget Riley, Alan Aldridge, Andy Warhol and David Hockney… The film has its fans and detractors, though on its release, the hard-to-please film critic Alexander Walker was strangely enchanted, calling it "the key film of the Beatles era. It's a trip through the contemporary mythology that the quartet from Merseyside have helped create. It's a pop voyage – a 'mododyssey' is the word I suppose – that sails under the psychedelic colours of Carnaby Street to the turned-on music of *Sgt Pepper's Lonely Hearts Club Band.* It combines sensory stimulation with the art of the now in a way that will appeal to teenage ravers and Tate Gallery-goers alike".

In a further animated diversion, I was unaware until researching this book that Walt Disney was keen to incorporate the group into his 1967 *The Jungle Book*. The four vultures who taunt Mowgli do have English accents, of the Dick Van Dyke *Mary Poppins* variety. There is one Scouser who diehards maintain was 'George'.

As the group switched between Savile Row and Abbey Road, as the suits pulled the strings, another Beatles LP came hot on the heels of *The White Album*. Christmas record tokens would have been lavished on the expensive double LP. The January 1969 release of the *Yellow Submarine* soundtrack saw it reach No.3 on the UK LP charts. But otherwise this curio is the skeleton in the Beatle recording closet. Predominantly because half of it was George Martin instrumentals, plus two already available back catalogue songs.

Contracted to supply material for the *Yellow Submarine* film, Lennon pitched in with a thrown-together 'Hey Bulldog',[18] while George contributed the jaundiced but amiable 'Only a Northern Song', which would have sat happily on *Sgt Pepper*. Paul's contribution, I would contend, is a song of its time and one which deserves more attention: 'All Together Now' fits in perfectly with the 'All You Need Is Love' vibe of the era. Like a lot of the Beatle material, some of the influence can be discerned in remembered nursery rhymes. 'All Together Now' is the song the group contribute in their lovely little cameo at the cartoon's conclusion.

For one song alone, the *Yellow Submarine* soundtrack merits serious consideration: George's majestic' It's All Too Much' stands as the high watermark of English psychedelia. With classical trumpet and a snatch of the Merseys' 'Sorrow' (a David Bowie favourite), Harrison taps into the zeitgeist. A letter to his mother of the period tells her not to worry about the Indian experience and meditation, which adds extra resonance to the line about being "everywhere", but ensuring the writer will be home in time for tea. There's silver suns and birthday cake. A variation on the classic English lines of Rupert Brooke "and is there honey still for tea"? For years I've wondered what John shouts at the beginning of the song. ("To your muff?") Dedicated Beatle fan Elizabeth McFarlane says it's "To your mother".

When we met, George smiled when I mentioned the song: "Someone said to Bob [Dylan] that song, 'Man in the Long Black Coat', about that line 'people just float', What does that mean? He said it doesn't mean anything, it's just a rhyme with 'coat'! Then they think he's putting me on, he's hiding the real symbolic meaning. But having written with him, that's what it is. You just need a word that rhymes.

"It was kind of like that in the psychedelic, hippie period – if you were stuck for some deep meaning, you'd just say anything, and people would think it had a deep meaning… omnipresent, very English. No matter how good it is, I'd still like a cup of tea, thank you very much".

George's interest in India, meditation and Krishna continued throughout his life. Musically though, by the time of his engaging 'Old Brown Shoe', his music was no longer wholly infused with tablas and sitars. His contributions to *The White Album* and *Abbey Road* marked the apogee of his composing during the Beatle years. Marking his 26th birthday, 25 February 1969 and on completing 'Old Brown Shoe', George sat down in

---

18   Apple's Tony Bramwell had been required to shoot a promo for the *current* Beatles single, 'Lady Madonna'. But with the Beatles in Rishikesh, he fell back on the band, filmed while recording the Lennon song. While a minor addition to the Beatle canon, Tony told John Harris he retains a fondness for the song, that 'Hey Bulldog' "was when everything was still happy and swinging. It was probably the last time they were optimistically Beatles, without bits of bickering and separate activities… It was the final time they were four happy moptops, together in the studio, doing a track the old-fashioned way".

Fixing holes in Pepperland

Threetles on their way to Pepperland, 1968

Abbey Road and demoed 'All Things Must Pass' and 'Something', not a bad birthday present.

If Brian had lived he surely would have found the energy to do battle with 'the suits', and been able to come up with a happier compromise to ease the group into a new era. But only two days into the New Year of 1969, barely eight weeks after completing *The White Album*, a grumpy, disaffected group, Yoko in tow, assembled at Twickenham Studios to be filmed recording their new LP. It would give them the opportunity to release what would effectively be their first-ever 'live' LP. It would conclude with their first concert in three years. With a final, triumphant concert performance, finished product could then be translated into a TV show to compete with Andy Williams and Tom Jones, who were enjoying global network success.

The Beatles would not just be recording, but filmed *writing* their new LP. It was evident that as with *Sgt Pepper* and *Magical Mystery Tour*, Paul was the one taking charge. John adhered to Yoko and had little interest in the project. Isolated on his drum riser, Ringo can't wait to get started on *The Magic Christian*. George is chafing at being a Beatle having witnessed the camaraderie of the Band first-hand. One of the more poignant moments of the Peter Jackson documentary is Paul pleadingly asking John if he had any *more* new material...

Removed from the familiar, convivial atmosphere of Abbey Road, relocated to a vast, drafty aircraft hangar, circled by cameramen, bothered by sound engineers, harassed by editors with their clapper boards; they were frustrated at the lack of efficient recording equipment... Any musical momentum could be halted as film reels were laboriously changed. They were alternately freezing in the cavernous studio or sweltering under the arc lights ("like playing table tennis in the middle of a football stadium", Glyn Johns recalled)... It was a *terrible* way to begin the New Year. And a fatally flawed enterprise: trying to create new music, to be filmed together while in the process of effectively disintegrating as a group.

Let It Be director Michael Lindsay-Hogg was the go-to man. He had cut his teeth on *Ready! Steady! Go!*, shot Beatle promos *and* the Rolling Stones' *Rock & Roll Circus*. Michael's artistic precedents were impeccable – his mother, Irish actress Geraldine Fitzgerald, had starred in respected Hollywood films such as *Wuthering Heights* and *Dark Victory*. She was the daughter of a prominent Dublin lawyer, whose firm E&T Fitzgerald is mentioned in James Joyce's *Ulysses*.

There were also strong rumours that Michael was the illegitimate son of none other than Orson Welles. In his engaging autobiography Lindsay-Hogg recalls his first meeting with the Beatles at Abbey Road in 1966. Asked to pitch ideas for a promo video, he must have been disconcerted to be asked by George if he had seen *Citizen Kane*, and be told he should do a video "like Rosebud". Perhaps George had dim memories of Andrew Sarris in *The Village Voice*, citing *A Hard Day's Night* as "The *Citizen Kane* of jukebox movies".

Lindsay-Hogg recalled a conversation with Welles following the release of *Let It Be*: "'Are you happy with the movie?' inquires Welles. 'Some of it.' 'How so?' 'It's hard when your stars are your producers. And there were four of them.' 'I know what that must be like... That level of fame can be hard to deal with.' 'I know.' I said this in a way to show I recognized the connection between the Beatles and the extraordinary youth and fame that had been his. He'd made *Citizen Kane* when he was twenty-five".

Approached by McCartney at the end of 1968, Lindsay-Hogg was told of the plans for a television special. The *Let It Be* director would have his work cut out: "After a while it became clear that though Paul was the driver of the bus, one or two of the others might get off at the next stop".

It could be a poisoned chalice, but one thing Lindsay-Hogg was determined to have was an ending. This would be a triumphant concert by the world's best-loved band, playing to an adoring audience. But these would not be screaming hysterical fans. These would be *admirers*, the sort of respectful crowd who appreciated how the Beatles had altered the arc of popular music in a few short years.

The weekly music press of the period was full of speculation about where and how the next Beatles concert would take place ("It will definitely be free", Paul told *NME* in December 1968, "and we may now do the show in a television studio"). That same month, *Melody Maker* quoted Beatle spokesman Derek Taylor saying how well Paul and George had got on with Andy Williams during a London visit, and that "Andy may appear on the Beatles show".

The letters page of the weekly was full of letters from fans, upset that there would be no more concerts or albums, frustrated at John and Yoko's activities. The *NME* letters page of course was called 'From Us to You' which had inspired the 1963 Beatle hit.

I am grateful to my old friend Alec Cormack for finding the following: The newly-launched *Time Out* magazine excitedly ran with a Live Gigs listing for December 1968. Among the usual suspects (Pete Brown's Battered Ornaments; the Beach Boys at the Finsbury Park Astoria; the Bonzo Dog Band at the London Palladium) was the tantalising listing, "The Beatles, 14–21 December, Three 'live' concerts at the Roundhouse, Chalk Farm Road, NW1".

If the gigs *had* gone ahead at that time, they'd have faced some stiff competition in how to spend their £sd in the capital: folkies could have seen Al Stewart, Jackson C. Frank, Fairport Convention and John Martyn. Blues outfits out and about included Taste, Ten Years After, Chicken Shack and John Mayall. Progressive fans were catered for by the Nice, Van Der Graaf Generator, the 3rd Year (sic) Band and Julie Driscoll with the Brian Auger Trinity. Future Wilbury Jeff Lynne could be found fronting the Idle Race at the London Hospital Medical School. Oh, and the trendy Flamingo Club were proud to announce the Dave Davani Five.

What turned out to be the Beatles' final gig could have been *so* different... Michael Lindsay-Hogg was captivated by a Roman amphitheatre in Tunisia – to get an idea of how spectacular it *could* have been, you can see the location featured in the 1956 film *The Black Tent*. Here, the Beatles would be filmed playing as the sun rose, and gradually, from the desert, tribes of every race, colour and creed would come to fill the seats while the group provided the soundtrack under the blistering African sun. The tribes would gather to pay homage.

Or how about the Beatles as house band on the newly-launched liner the *QE2*? Or playing outside the Houses of Parliament? Or at the still under construction Liverpool Cathedral? Or even returning to be filmed back to the Cavern? The general consensus was that, for the first time playing together in public for three years, it should be somewhere spectacular.

In 2019 our problem with bees (stay with me) saw Paul Bond come to our house. While he was sorting out the bees and chatting over a cup of tea, I asked what he did before he retired. Turned out he was a cameraman on the *Let It Be* film.

He had begun as a teenager in 1963, training in documentaries, and commercials. The year before he hooked up with the Beatles he had worked on the Rolling Stones' *One Plus One* ("the roof caught fire on that one"). In later years, Paul went on as director of photography on *Downton Abbey*. Years later he did a few days on the ill-fated *Give My Regards to Broad Street*. "It was very sweet, on my first day Paul saw me and remembered me and came to give me big hug". What became *Let It Be* was his first feature film.

"Twickenham was the most stupid venue, a vast, enormous stage, and this little band stuck up in one corner, echoing all round and freezing cold. It was enormous, not conducive to anything creative, just keeping warm!

"I remember Paul saying, 'Come on boys we've signed the contract, we've got a fortnight to go, let's get this bloody thing finished'. When George Martin turned up it was like the headmaster had arrived, and they smartened up a bit.

"A typical working day didn't start very early, because *they* never did, and we finished pretty early. They were not long days, but once you started, with two cameras turning over all the time, reloading them and synching up was hard work.

"It was originally shot on 16mm then transferred to 35mm when it was screened as a film. Back then, 16mm was the size of your fingernail. Reloading 16mm is easy; reloading a bigger 35mm meant you would have lost the spontaneity, with two cameras filming *all* the time.

"There was tension, no question. It was very tense. There were times when they were all having a good time and laughing, but when it came to the business…! Lennon was the one who was kicking up full-time, not wanting to come in tomorrow. John never talked to us which was odd as we were together for a month.

"Yoko didn't say much. But anytime possible they were just clinging onto each other and distracting. Always there, which proved quite a distraction, other girlfriends and wives came and went but she was there *all* the time clinging to John.

"Once we got to the Apple basement, things improved, this was their home territory. Paul came in on the bus in his big black coat and with his beard. I got on well with him, he was delightful, very approachable".

Half a century later Paul Bond was invited to a preview of Peter Jackson's *Get Back*. "When I saw that footage, I could not believe what he had done". Even more jaw-dropping was the sight of his 22-year-old self being taught piano by Paul McCartney. "When I mentioned it, my dad bought me a piano on the strength of it. I hadn't played before, and I wasn't very good on it. I was just curious about how Paul wrote songs. It was a bit of conversation. We were together for a month, and there was quite a lot of time on our hands".

Paul Bond's abiding memory of the shoot were all the rumours percolating about the location for the film's finale: the Beatles in concert. "Was it going to be onboard the *QE2*? The Himalayas? The Pyramids? The Arabian desert? In the end, the only trip was five floors up to the rooftop. It was absolutely freezing up there, and hard work as a clapper boy knocking out so much film every day. The director of photography Tony Richmond said we need an extra camera, so I shot all the girls climbing out of windows.

"It has to be said that the Apple roof was a bit of a let-down".

*

A front-page story in the first *Melody Maker* of 1969 had announced, "The Beatles' first live appearance for over two years was scheduled to take place on January 18. The plan was to have a run through, a rehearsal and then a complete show – each with a different audience so as many people as possible could see the group in action again".

It is worth emphasising just how crucial it was for groups to play live back then. That was how acts kept in touch, a three-year absence was unheard of. Stop-gap promotional films of the group performing their current single was not enough. With precious little TV or radio allocated to the burgeoning rock scene; with a reliance for news on the weekly inkies, the way a top group communicated was by the live experience. In September 1968, *Melody Maker* had devoted a half-page feature asking, 'Will We Ever See The Beatles On The Road Again?'

In the end, those grandiose plans came to nothing. They just couldn't be arsed to venture far, so made their way upstairs for what became … Legend. The four gathered on the stairs under the Apple roof, *still* undecided about whether to ascend, when surprisingly, it was John who barked "Let's go". So with a flourish, the group's founder led his Wild Bunch to their finale.

From up there, it wasn't much of a view: no desert panorama, no foaming ocean. The London skyline had barely altered since the aftermath of the Blitz 30 years before. Only the Post Office tower loomed above the office blocks, but no Shard or Gherkin; no red lights of cranes warning low-flying helicopters.

Would that rooftop gig retain its mesmeric power if it had been the first of many? Unlikely. That blustery performance maintains its potency because of what followed. Or rather, what did *not* follow. This is the last time the 'Fab Four' ever performed before an audience. This time there was no screaming. The audience were Apple staff and office employees from surrounding buildings, intrigued by the racket.

Without any effort, they *could* have played in front of a celebrity crowd of mates as they had done on *Our World*. They could have filled any stadia… They could have persevered and found an exotic location as a backdrop (The Taj Mahal… The Grand Canyon… Ayers Rock… The Colosseum). Instead, they grudgingly clambered up to the top of a London office building. Once plugged in and geared up, those final 42 minutes together displayed a sense of joy and unity, Paul and John egging each other on; Billy Preston bopping along. George did look grumpy and Ringo, chilly, but ever professional, they persevered. They went right back ('One After 909') and looked forward (the new single, 'Get Back').

Of equal interest to me in re-viewing is the audience. Those candid camera moments offer a snapshot of the capital at a specific moment in time. It is fascinating to see the young executives, their hair demonstrably longer, and the secretaries, their skirts temptingly shorter than when the Beatles began recording. Did those passers-by and skiving office workers appreciate what they were seeing and hearing? Did those figures precariously making their way across neighbouring rooftops sense they were witnessing history? Of

EXCLUSIVE 100 MIN PREVIEW OF

THE
BEATLES
GET
BACK

AT
CINEWORLD LEICESTER SQUARE
WC2H 7NA
ON
TUESDAY NOVEMBER 23
ARRIVALS: 4:00PM   SEATED BY:4:45PM

ATTENDANCE SUBJECT TO ADHERENCE
TO COVID-19 SAFETY PROTOCOLS

Apple   Disney+   WINGNUT FILMS

Original Docuseries Streaming November 25
#TheBeatlesGetBack @DisneyPlusUK

ADMIT ONE

SEAT NO:	ROW	H	SEAT	29

Paul Bond

Get Back preview

course not. It was a novelty, a diversion. Something to tell the boss why you were late back from lunch. Maybe one day someone will do a forensic *Sgt Pepper*-style examination of just who was there as spectators to the end of an era.

I loved the way the police from Savile Row station, just up the road, responded to the event. Politely inquiring if they might gain entry, the Plod proceed. As a point of interest, the nervous young policeman called to the scene to stop the gig was Ken Wharfe, who later became Princess Diana's bodyguard.

Thanks to Mick Houghton, one person I learned who heard them was a name which would become familiar in the next decade. Mike Batt was a songwriter on contract to Liberty Records. He worked alongside Andrew Lauder (later to sign the Stone Roses) who had a friend… Wayne Bardell worked in the Apple building and, to get to the roof, the Beatles had to make their way via his office. A quick phone call alerted the young Batt in his Albemarle Street office, just a few minutes away from Savile Row.

"I definitely do remember standing in the street," Mike Batt told me, "and hearing the blast of music coming from the roof – 'Get Back' came over loud and clear, albeit swamped in the echo from surrounding buildings. I saw that there were people on the roof, you'd see the odd head pop up, but not recognisable faces.

"It was odd, because it was just a stroll over from the office, hearing it, and 'Ah, that's great. Now let's go back to the office'. No incredibly big deal at the time, just 'Ah, brilliant, what kind of sandwich do you want?'"

So, there it is, that elusive Wombles/Beatle connection.

Although it was only a few steps up from his office, the ever-loyal Neil Aspinall missed the last performance by the band he had shepherded since 1962 – he was in hospital having his tonsils removed. It was Neil who oversaw the Apple empire ('custodian of the graveyard' was his job description) and genuinely merited the honorarium of 'Fifth Beatle'. Paul was by his bedside when he died in 2008.

So memorable has that Beatle rooftop gig become that it has since been emulated by U2, Paul Weller, Blur, James, Echo & the Bunnymen and Paul McCartney… It was the way of saying hello, and goodbye.

The *Daily Mail* of 30 August 2019 had an account by Joan Collins of the event. She was to later marry Apple's Ron Kass, who on 30 January 1969 was still married to his first wife, Anita. But that doesn't daunt Dame Joan and her priceless recollection: "I remember going up to the roof of Abbey Road for [the Beatles'] last concert when they played 'Hey Jude', but leaving before I succumbed to a high from all the marijuana being smoked."

Wrong, on *so* many levels…

*

The filming and recording of what became *Let It Be* was tortuous. The miraculous equipment Magic Alex promised failed to function. The film studio was inhospitable. Tensions which could normally be sorted by a quorum now rose to the surface. The ubiquity of the cameramen, often attempting distracting close-ups, coupled with Paul's headmasterly pushness. In one famous exchange which made it to the finished film,

Passing the audition, 30 January 1969

(Hoberman Publishing / Alamy Stock Photo)

George complains: "All right, I'll play whatever you want me to play, or I won't play at all if you don't want me to play". In *Anthology*, Paul was quoted as saying, "I tended to talk down to him, because he was a year younger. I know now that was a failing I had all the way through the Beatle years. If you've known a guy when he's thirteen and you're fourteen, it's hard to think of him as grown-up".

It was all too much... George's diary entry of 10 January 1969 says it all, economically: "Got up, went to Twickenham, rehearsed till lunch – left the Beatles, went home... had chips later at Kinfauns". He was still three weeks short of his 26th birthday.

George was perhaps the one who was feeling most isolated: Ringo had a burgeoning film career; John had Yoko and plans for a breakaway group; Paul had Linda, and a willingness to keep the band together as a working unit... George had his solo albums (*Wonderwall* and *Electronic Music*) but they were on the margin.

It was not without coincidence that another cultural landmark arrived later in 1969, one which provided George with a future. It was well-known that from the outset that George was a huge Monty Python fan, and that his backing of *Life of Brian* effectively began a second career as a film producer and the creation of Handmade Films. He was particularly close to Python's Eric Idle, who told George of the problems the team were facing with funding for their third film, to which Harrison replied: "Well, when the Beatles were breaking up, Python kept me sane, so I owe you one".

The two men remained close: Idle remembers moaning to the Quiet One about the problems he had writing within Python – he was the only one of the team who wrote alone, and therefore had problems getting material accepted by Cleese and Chapman, Jones and Palin. "Try being in a band with Lennon and McCartney", George dryly responded. Idle's 2018 autobiography (*A Sortabiography*) is at its best when he describes his friendship with George, and the guitarist's quiet asides, such as, "If we'd known we were going to be The Beatles we would have tried harder".

As the Beatles struggled to film and record in the increasingly tense, chill days of January 1969, another ingredient to be added to the mix were the Band. Not any old band, but *the* Band, the group who had backed Bob Dylan on his acrimonious 1966 world tour. I interviewed Robbie Robertson years later, after the outrage had died down, when that gig at the Manchester Free Trade Hall – the 'Judas' show – was recognised as the most scorched earth, incendiary live rock & roll show *ever*... he concurred, "You know, we'd listen to tapes of every show back at the hotel amidst all the booing and jeering, and look at each other, and say well it's not *that* bad".

By 1968, the Band had begun their own stand-alone career. Their debut *Music from Big Pink* was the LP that transfixed everyone who heard it – Eric Clapton, Fairport Convention, Brinsley Schwarz and particularly, George Harrison. Even the curmudgeonly Roger Waters was emphatic: "After *Sgt Pepper*, it's the most influential record in the history of rock & roll". For Elton John, those first two albums (*Music from Big Pink* and *The Band*) "were like somebody switching a torch on and showing us a new path to follow". I remember when I interviewed Elton on one occasion, and was amazed, given his well-publicised bouts of memory-shortening drink and drugs, at his power of recall. One of the reasons he was still working at Soho's Musicland, even after he began his own recording career, was to get first dibs on the new LPs ("That second

Band album, with the mock-leather cover, 59/11d on import…")

"John Lennon told me 'Don't Let Me Down' was a direct attempt to do what The Band was doing", Robbie Robertson told Sid Griffin. "George Harrison told me stories about that too… Starting with *The Basement Tapes* and then into Big Pink and our second album, you can see our recording technique was that we never went into a recording studio, that we brought the atmosphere with us".

A testimonial from George was used in advertising for their second album: "I always dug The Band. I liked *Big Pink* and this album is far superior". And that hunkering down, in a circle, playing live, watching each other, egging each other on, was what the Beatles were *attempting* at those Twickenham sessions. But the medicine that the Band mixed up in the basement was never matched by the Beatles during those cold, unaccommodating days of early January 1969.

The sound of the Band was grown-up music, made by men. Looking like Civil War deserters and sounding like roving minstrels, the Band took music in a totally different direction from the screaming psychedelia of *Sgt Pepper* ("We were rebelling against the rebellion", Roberston told me). Here was a detour to rural Arcadia, music made in harmony.

To get close to that source, George visited and recorded with Dylan. As *Let It Be* began its run in cinemas in May 1970, *Rolling Stone* wryly reported on a Dylan session in New York with "George Harrison, lead guitarist for a reportedly defunct British rock and roll group, the Beatles".

George loved the roots Bob had been digging up with the Band on what was rock's first bootleg LP, *The Basement Tapes*. And even if their joint efforts ('Working on a Guru'; 'I'd Have You Anytime') hardly suggested a triumphant collaboration between rock's most eminent songwriter and one of his most ardent disciples, it gave George an indication of what might be accomplished outside the Beatles.

However, group loyalty, plus pressure to get a finished LP *and* film in the can saw George return to his day job, and the sessions continued. The drummer is unhappy, so Paul suggests they re-recruit Jimmy Nicol to circumvent Ringo's reluctance to travel… George wonders why anyone would be interested in watching them *rehearse*… John wants Eric Clapton in… George walks out… One senses the steadying hand of Brian Epstein was missed (rather sweetly remembered as "Mr Epstein" on film).

In theory, with a paucity of original material, the group fell back on familiar favourites. The Beatles revisiting their musical past was a tantalising prospect. As teenagers during the long, late afternoon of the 1950s, Paul McCartney and John Lennon would play truant from school and sit together at the McCartney home at 20 Forthlin Road, 'one on one, eyeball to eyeball' trying, painstakingly, to piece together their own songs, influenced by the music they heard crackling out of Radio Luxembourg, and the 78s for which John saved up his pocket money.

Uncut magazine ran a fascinating pie-chart of material the Beatles performed at what they call 'The Get Back Sessions': Bob Dylan and the Band (15) come close to tying with 60s Pop (16). But any hope of full-fledged versions of 'The Weight', Like a Rolling Stone', 'Stuck Inside of Mobile…', 'Macarthur Park', 'Let's Dance' or 'Bo Diddley' are quickly undone. I remember the tantalising lists which appeared of the songs tackled during those sessions… the Beatles Sing Bob Dylan – 'I Shall Be Released', 'Mighty Quinn', 'Blowin' in the Wind'… But of course in actuality, they are half-remembered fragments. The bulk of the Twickenham and Apple sessions are pieces of a jigsaw puzzle, but someone's forgotten to include the picture the puzzle is meant to be. So they let it be, with odd lines, works in progress, cover versions, arguments, rehearsals, squabbles…

They also attempted ten Elvis, half a dozen Little Richard and Chuck Berry, but under the lights, with memories faltering, with tension mounting, only snatches were ever attempted. These are scraps, half-remembered lyrics, played with a patent lack of interest. There are few finished versions. The listed songs read better than they sound.

Among the earliest of the original songs attempted was a Lennon song, directly inspired by the then current skiffle craze and its inordinate fondness for train songs. 'One After 909' was firmly in the tradition of Lonnie Donegan's 'Rock Island Line' and 'Cumberland Gap', as well as the skiffle-heavy 'Last Train to San Fernando' and 'Freight Train'. John and Paul retained a great fondness for their skiffle song, and in 1963 – when they broke big with the Beatles – they dusted it down. 'One After 909' was cut at an early Abbey Road session, but discarded due to George Martin's lack of enthusiasm. Later, at the fag end of the Beatles, 'One After 909' was disinterred once again, and this time it did appear – as a jaunty, skiffle singalong on their 1970 valedictory album *Let It Be*.

The album also contained a snatch of that smutty old Liverpool singalong 'Maggie Mae', which all four Beatles would have remembered from the cleaned-up skiffle version released as a single by the Vipers, way back in 1957. The theme was familiar from folk standards such as 'Barrack Street' and 'New York Girls' – sailor on shore leave undone by scheming harlot. It was also a song McCartney returned to in 2017, when under heavy disguise in a cameo, he reprised it in the fifth instalment of the *Pirates of the Caribbean* franchise, the incomprehensible *Salazar's Revenge*.

In 1969 though, the world's most fabled and widely-imitated group was now clearly struggling. But though it was sad to watch the Beatles going through the musical motions, it was also intriguing to see the best-known composers in rock & roll busking through half-remembered songs from their adolescence. All redolent of teenage years. And all from those innocent days before their world went completely mad. By then, they had been tempted in the wilderness, they had been to the mountain top, they had surveyed the seven wonders, and now the only way was down.

'Get Back': amidst all the trouble and strife, involving Billy Preston was a masterstroke. Like having the best man along if you are having a row with the wife, bringing in an old compadre helped to defuse the situation. While Preston's playing is smooth and exemplary, it was more his mediating presence that had the most impact. As the last stand-alone, original single the Beatles released ('The Ballad of John & Yoko' only mustered 50% of the group), 'Get Back' was a suitable swansong. Paul's cheeky lyrics (Loretta Martin getting it while she can recalled the fish and finger pies of a few years before), and Ringo's shuffling, swing beat propelled the song along. It was advertised as, "The Beatles as nature intended… there's no electronic whatchamacallit…"

There was a determination to make the LP as 'natural' as possible. The film was the device to free them from their film contract. The album, one which saw them get back to their roots. Lennon particularly chafed at outside interference – George Martin: "John, your guitar's out of tune". John: "We don't want any of your production shit on this record".

Following a desultory fortnight at Twickenham, the group repaired to their own Apple Studios in Savile Row. This is where the lines get blurred: the plan was for a "new phase", "trousers down" Beatles LP (aka *Get Back* or *Let It Be*) but dipping in and out of the songs which would constitute that 1970 release is material which would surface on the last album they make together, 1969's *Abbey Road*. And there are snatches of songs McCartney and Harrison would later render on their solo albums…

At the time, confusion surrounded what the new Beatle LP would consist of. I don't think I was alone in fully understanding that haphazard Beatle chronology of 1969; it wasn't until 1976's *NME Encyclopedia of Rock* revealed *Abbey Road* as "the last tracks chronologically that the Beatles cut together. Ironically, it showed them still as buoyant as ever".

That whole period at the beginning of 1969 had been swathed in mystery. It led in September 1970, to *Rolling Stone* running an intriguing fiction about the 'The Beatles Album No One Will Ever Hear'… *Hot As Sun*. The LP includes 'Proud As You Are' and 'Zero Is Just Another Number'. Three copies of the master tapes are obtained; Apple and EMI agree to pay the $100,000 ransom, but due to a spate of aircraft hijackings, "has been X-rayed out of existence!"

A beautiful 'official' copy of the aborted 1970 *Get Back (with Let It Be and 11 other songs)* LP sleeve surfaced in 2018, complete with Angus McBean cover shot and chirpy Tony Barrow sleeve notes ("The boys aren't called The Boys any more. The Four Mop Tops and The Fab Four were finished when they sucked their last jelly babies"). The copy appeared courtesy of Laurence Goodman, then working for Trade Platemaking Surfaces, just down the road from me, in Camberwell. The company took the original artwork, photos, typography etc. and created the metal plates which were then printed by names familiar to 1960s LP buyers, such as Garrod & Lofthouse and Ernest J. Day.

Because of the valedictory look of *Let It Be*, and the sound ("Thank you and on behalf of the group… I hope we passed the audition") most people thought that black-lined LP was their epitaph. It came after an eventful year, even by the hectic standards of the Beatles.

Nineteen sixty-nine saw John and Yoko get married, and have their well-publicised haircuts. They masqueraded as the Plastic Ono Band. They stayed in bed in luxury hotels for Peace. They planted acorns for Peace. Lennon returned his MBE (in actuality, an empty gesture, as the medals cannot be returned). They released albums of "Unfinished Music" ("Unlistenable Music" most agreed). They campaigned to get a posthumous pardon for James Hanratty. They colluded with Black Power activist Michael X… In their enthusiastic championing, the Lennons were perhaps too gullible – the Hanratty case was reopened in 2002, and, based on DNA evidence, it was proved "beyond doubt" that Hanratty was guilty of the A6 murder. In 1975, Michael X was hanged in Trinidad, convicted of murder. "Bore, fool or saint?" asked *NME* of John.

Lennon's ego-fuelled odyssey of the period found him – literally – wrapped up in Yoko, their 'appearances' together frequently conducted in bags. Lennon was impervious and immune to criticism. He was an artist. Creating *art*. Not fooling with a pop group he'd started as a teenager. As early as January 1970, George Melly was withering: "John Lennon … has tried to advance beyond pop and in conjunction with Yoko Ono, offers a series of gestures of increasing desperation expressed in the vocabulary of a clapped-out avant-garde".

His ego ran rampant – while a return to rock & roll roots, 'The Ballad of John & Yoko' remains the fly in the Beatle ointment. It was also, as Phil Swern dutifully noted, the only Beatles No.1 not to mention the title anywhere in the song. Writing of the song in 2009, Sean Egan was withering: "One didn't have to feel particularly religious to find repugnant the self-aggrandizement of Lennon comparing himself to a man dying in agony in a crucifixion simply because he'd not been waved through French customs like a potentate and had been mocked in a few newspapers. The song actually marked a period in which Lennon became increasingly pompous and egotistical".

Deftly avoiding accusations of sexism, misogyny and racism, latter day critics have been scathing about the second Mrs Lennon. In 2021 Ian Penman felt that "Ono led Lennon to a place that was, arguably, the worst of both worlds. A baby food version of the avant-garde. Fuzzy political gestures lacking any real slog or engagement. Buzzword slogans that read like Mao Zedong subbed by Patience Strong".

Equally scathing was Ian MacDonald, normally loyal in print to Lennon's excesses but with this "outrageously egocentric" song he found fault with Yoko's "fatuous fugue of legs, bottoms and bags… Under the ostensibly selfless holy foolery they indulged in during 1968–70 was a core of exhibitionistic self-promotion… they jetted round the world in first-class seats selling [peace] at third-rate media-events… Of all the dangerous ideas Ono unloaded on her spouse around this time, the most damaging was her belief that all art is about the artist and no one else…"

Indeed, the case Lennon makes for his stigmata appears to be the media's refusal to take bed-ins, bagism and finding a wedding location seriously.

Incidentally, could you imagine Lennon's withering condemnation if the group's second single release of 1969 had been 'The Ballad of Paul & Linda' ("Standing in our farm up in Scotland / Got away to shear us some sheep")…?

As an indication of just how far apart he'd grown from his earlier, erstwhile partner, Paul was shocked when John suggested they try trepanning. While many found fault with what they saw as McCartney's innate conservatism, with some reason, the idea of having a hole drilled in his skull lacked appeal.

John had become spellbound, hypnotised by his Japanese partner. I sense it was Yoko who convinced John that, somehow, all this 'Beatle' business was beneath him. That his true vocation was as an artist; an artist who needed a new collaborator, to elevate his thoughts, his ideas, his vision, his *art* above three-minute pop songs. It was McCartney's firm hand on the tiller which propelled the group during their final, glorious phase. All those singles – 'Hello Goodbye', 'Lady Madonna', 'Hey Jude', 'Get Back', 'Let It Be' – *all* were Paul compositions. The latter was bafflingly denied the UK No.1 by, of all things, Lee Marvin's 'Wand'rin Star'.

Following the Lennons' marriage, the American Beatle Fan Club issued a plea: "Please try and understand that we should give Yoko the same chance we are going to be giving Linda and that Maureen and Patti got. I know the news is shocking, but I suppose if it will make John happy we should all be enthused too".

Misogyny aside, much of the hostility directed towards John's Japanese wife was, of course, racist. Many Beatle fans would have known fathers and uncles who had suffered in Japanese hands during a war which had barely been over for 20 years by the time Lennon met his muse. But the rank hostility and antipathy towards the Japanese was still widespread, primarily with the Japanese treatment of Allied Prisoners of War on the infamous Burma Railway. A shocking 22% of Allied POWs died while held captive and subjected to unimaginable hardships and torture. Later memoirs such as *The Railway Man* and *To War with the Walkers* revealed the full extent of the horrors to which the Allied prisoners were subject.

At no point did the Japanese government ever apologise for their barbaric behaviour. Emperor Hirohito did not make a state visit to the UK until 1971. And his visit attracted demonstrations and calls again for a public apology for the way the Japanese treated their prisoners. None came. *Private Eye*'s cover "Piss Off Bandy Knees" was typical.

There was also suspicion that Yoko was ruthless in achieving attention; McCartney remembered her approaching him before she met Lennon, badgering him for original song manuscripts. She also has a canny eye for headlines, such as *Number 4*, better known as 'the bottoms film'. Even the heady denizens of the London underground scene were wary of Yoko's artistic motives, sensing more than a whiff of self-publicity.

And as for Yoko's music... At Twickenham in January 1969, Glyn Johns "heard this extraordinary noise that sounded like someone stepping on the cat... it turned out to be Yoko... How anyone could have considered her intrusion to be in any way musical is a complete mystery to me". He was not alone. Just listen to 'Whole Lotta Yoko' on the Stones' *Rock & Roll Circus*, backed by, perhaps, *the* supergroup (Clapton, Lennon, Keith Richards, Mitch Mitchell), Ms Ono squeals and wails thereby distorting any collective enjoyment. And apropos of Yoko's contribution, does anyone actually *listen* to *Live Peace in Toronto* without skipping her contributions? Lennon was besotted and blinded. We suffered for his art...

Apple's Tony Bramwell told David Cavanagh: "John had been Yoko'd... We finished up with a lot of her records on Apple, which were very difficult to promote. I got into trouble with the BBC. They asked me, 'Why are you bringing this crap round?' I said, 'Listen, she's John Lennon's missus'." DJ Andy Peebles was equally scathing, as he told Lesley-Ann Jones: "The bottom line was, to me, that she was just an average Japanese artist who got lucky, and wrecked the greatest band Britain has ever produced".

In tandem with Yoko, John saw his musical future more along the lines of the Plastic Ono Band. This freewheeling ensemble would be looser-limbed than the restrictive Beatles. It would not be necessary to lock heads with Paul. It would give him greater creative control, no longer the need to seek anyone else's approval. "With the Plastic Ono Band", John said, "anything goes".

In what proved to be his last-ever UK gig, on 15 December 1969, Lennon's Plastic Ono Band headlined a charity show at London's Lyceum Ballroom. Ill-rehearsed and under-prepared, few would cite the show as memorable. Introducing 'Cold Turkey' Lennon announced it as "a song about pain". Most listeners that cold night would have concurred.

Marvelling at the all-star line-up (George, Clapton, Keith Moon, Delaney & Bonnie) *NME*'s Alan Smith noted the half-full venue before reeling from Yoko's 40-minute "War...

Peace…" riff, "the physical result… gave me one of the worst headaches I've suffered since don't-know-when…"

The song in question, 'Don't Worry Kyoko', was shortened from its 40 minutes to a more manageable 15 for its inclusion on *Some Time in New York City*. Even with the best will in the world, there is little of any real merit to be heard. A piledriving riff, as Yoko caterwauled, may have been the musical future Lennon was looking forward to. He was in the minority. After years under the baton of George Martin, tiring of the Beatles' studio complexity, Lennon welcomed the spontaneity the Plastic Ono Band offered. But spontaneity isn't *always* a good thing.

The fourth side of *Some Time in New York City* was devoted to the Lennons jamming with Frank Zappa and the Mothers of Invention in 1971 – 'Jamrag' and 'Scumbag' were cut from the same 'freeform' cloth as the Lyceum show. Just prior to his death, in 1992 Zappa remixed the Lennons' tracks and released them as the tellingly-titled 'A Small Eternity with Yoko Ono'.

Even defenders of Yoko's work with the Fluxus group and her performance art likened her singing to "essentially screaming like a pained dolphin"; while her critics had to smile at a 21st-century t-shirt – 'John Lennon Broke Up Fluxus'.

Plastic Ono Band may have given Lennon the freedom he desired, but few would give it priority over the work he undertook with the group he had founded back in 1957. Insiders, outsiders, all sensed the end was nigh. And as the end approached, ironically, for the first time ever, *The International Who's Who 1969/70* listed all four Beatles. They were still ignored by the UK *Who's Who*. They were, after all, just pop musicians. As if they cared, worn down by internal bickering, struggling to keep their business empire together, endeavouring to finish a third film, locked into recording not one but two LPs, they were nominally still the Beatles. But by then it really was too late.

Being the Beatles though, they still had one last shot in the locker…

*

For many, 1969's *Abbey Road* remains the pinnacle of recorded Beatle achievements. That is largely due to the lengthy suite which occupied much of Side II on its original release. There is a sweep and majesty, and while the segue may occasionally jar, if this was the Beatles in the doldrums, they still outdistanced most of their contemporaries by a country mile. Coming in at over 47 minutes, the LP also offered remarkably good value.

With material culled from Rishikesh and Esher, what's not to like? The LP included probably George's best-loved Beatle songs. And a storming, snarling McCartney on 'Oh Darling'. That vinyl second side began with George's ethereal, archetypal summer song, 'Here Comes the Sun' and progressed through snippets and fragments, soaring orchestral sweeps, restrained drum solos, edgy guitars, flawless harmonies and concluding with Paul's observation about the balanced equality of love… I say again: what is not to like?

The world agreed. By 2019 it was estimated worldwide sales of the album exceeded 30,000,000, up there alongside *Sgt Pepper* and *1* as the most successful Beatle album ever. The cover also made an otherwise anonymous London street into a shrine.

Abbey Road is not perfect, and indeed Side I has its weak points – I personally find

'Come Together', 'I Want You' and 'Octopus's Garden' soon outstay their welcome. And Paul's whimsical 'Maxwell's Silver Hammer' has a lot to answer for... Apparently during the recording of *Double Fantasy*, Lennon became very sentimental about the Beatle era. When asked by respectful engineer Lee DeCarlo what had caused the Beatles to break up, Lennon replied immediately: "Maxwell's Silver Hammer!"

On release, the *Abbey Road* LP shocked fans with its hidden track – while the sleeve listed 'The End' as the conclusion, a bit of hiss and Paul bangs in with the shortest track the Beatles ever officially released, 'Her Majesty'. The Beatles had, of course, tried the trick LP ending on *Sgt Pepper*. But, short as it was, 'Her Majesty' was a song, and once again, the group upped the ante. Hidden tracks really took off with the advent of the CD era and the extended time limit available – 'Her Majesty' is now listed on the *Abbey Road* CD sleeve.

Kurt Cobain had been a Beatle fan from the get-go, his first composition ('About a Girl') was written after playing *Meet the Beatles!* to death. Further impressed by the Beatle sleight of hand, Cobain ensured that the breakthrough Nirvana album, 1992's *Nevermind* kept fans on their toes. According to Nirvana chronicler Chuck Crisafulli, Cobain "decided to bring a little vinyl-era playfulness into the digital age with 'Endless, Nameless', and it wasn't long before every self-respecting 'alternative' band was hiding a bonus track at the end of their CDs".

But what really elevates *Abbey Road* is the side II suite, provisionally titled 'The Long One'. It shouldn't really work, these are after all snippets, odds and ends which were never fully realised. And yet... Thanks to George Martin's magisterial editing, scraps like 'Mean Mr Mustard' meld seamlessly into 'Polythene Pam'. Where it *really* sparks is when Paul muscles in coming in through the bathroom window, slumbering in gold and carrying that weight. Even today, one of the highlights of Paul McCartney in concert is hearing that medley come to life in performance.

After the stresses and strains of *The White Album*, the tension of the Twickenham and Savile Row sessions which fed into the – still unreleased – *Let It Be*, *Abbey Road* was a return on so many levels. They were back at the studio that gave the LP its name, with George Martin behind the board, the producer recalled "it was a very happy time".

After the chaos surrounding *Let It Be*, when Paul asked George Martin back to produce he was assured it would be "like the old days". Their erstwhile producer was surprised: "After [*Let It Be*] I thought it was the end of the road for all of us. I didn't really want to work with them anymore because they were becoming unpleasant people – in themselves as well as to other people..." For once Martin laid down conditions: engineer Geoff Emerick came back on board, and the recording would be made at the EMI Studios where it all began.

Like the old days of only a few years before, in the end, at the end, it was a mutually rewarding experience. Of all his groundbreaking work with the group, towards the end of his life, George Martin singled out *Abbey Road*, "because it was the last one we did", he told Jonathan Wingate. "It had a nice feel about it, because I think we all knew it was the last one, so we thought, 'Well, we might as well make it as good as we can'."

Engineer Jeff Jarrett remembers Martin telling him during a session he supervised for the LP, "I can't remember word for word what he said to me", Jarratt told Mark Lewisohn, "but it was something like 'There will be one Beatles there, fine. Two Beatles, great. Three Beatles, fantastic. But the minute the four of them are there is when the inexplicable charismatic thing happens, the special magic no one has been able to explain'."

There are those who would happily settle for everything the group recorded, from Take 1 of 'Love Me Do' to the final mix of 'Teddy Boy'. What made the Beatles so remarkable was their innate instinct about what was the best, there and then. Somehow, the 2019 box of *Abbey Road* lacked the heft of its predecessors. The instrumental backing tracks, scraps of fragments; fractions of snippets. It was nice to hear 'Her Majesty' restored to its right place on 'The Long One', but were *three* demo versions of the song necessary?

I was in Nashville September 2007 and remember seeing a young band do a song from the *Abbey Road* medley and delighting to their manager that it was from the LP's second side. He looked completely blank, because one side of a CD was all they knew. It left me feeling like Caxton explaining his technique to a smartphone owner.

Then there was that cover… The original concept was to call the album *Everest*. Then the world's most fabled and influential band would fly to the tallest place on the planet to be photographed. In the event, they just couldn't be arsed. So, it was six snaps in ten minutes on a North London zebra crossing one summer morning.

Ah, but what *time* on that August day? 10 a.m.? 11.35 a.m.? Astronomer Bill Tarver told Craig Brown, "On August 8 the sun is due south (180 degrees) at 12.06 GMT (13.08 BST). It thus has another 38 degrees of arc to travel before it's local noon. The sun travels through 15 degrees in an hour, so it is two hours, 32 minutes before noon, or 10.34 BST".

It wasn't entirely spontaneous; McCartney had roughed out how he envisaged the procession on the LP cover. The day before, photographer Iain Macmillan (1938–2006) had undertaken a trial run with four EMI employees. But the ensuing black and white shots lacked sufficient gravitas, not enough height. So on the day the four Beatles strolled across, Macmillan shot from a step ladder. Such is the legend associated with the *Abbey Road* cover, that in 2021 the *camera* (Hasselblad 500C) Iain Macmillan used that day was auctioned for over £35,000.

Of the six frames, Paul wasn't wearing shoes in the one chosen for the cover (Number 5). Mmm, oh, and the VW registration pointed out that *if* he hadn't been killed in a car crash, he would have been 28. To confirm his demise, George was the gravedigger; Ringo the undertaker and John the minister. Once, when discussing lyric interpretation and Beatle myth with McCartney, he paused and told me: "*Abbey Road* and the cover. I only had my sandals off because it was hot. Honest! Really! It's normal. Life is pretty okay. It's not weird and crazed, man, it isn't a big voodoo trip".

McCartney and original photographer Iain Macmillan returned to that zebra crossing in 1993 for the cover of his *Paul Is Live* album. And this time, cheekily defying the 'Paul Is dead' rumours, the VW number plate read '51 IS'. The original Volkswagen belonged to Abbey Road resident Paul Benda. He sold it to a 'Marjorie'. It is now in the VW Museum in Germany.

Debate still rages about who was who and what was what on the cover –the *suits* they wore that summer's day (apart from George's denim) all came from their Savile Row neighbour, Tommy Nutter, but designed by Edward Sexton. And just who was the man by the police van? American tourist Paul Cole? Or local resident Tony Graves? The three decorators on a break (Derek Seagrove, Alan Flanagan, Steve Millwood) have been confirmed. Indeed, of all the forensic examination of that cover, the only remaining unidentified figure is the blue mini-skirted girl swishing past *that* road sign. For those with time on their hands (a *lot* of time), I can happily direct you to Roger Stormo's exhaustive article on his *Daily Beatle* website. This is the annotated *Waste Land* of Beatle analysis.

The *Abbey Road* LP was released in September 1969. At the time the cover seemed a bit, pardon the pun, pedestrian. In the event and as time went on, it became not only the most widely celebrated Beatle cover, but one of the most parodied.

The Beatles themselves did not know it, less than a fortnight after the unified cover, 20 August 1969 is a date which deserves to be remembered in rock history. That was the day all four Beatles were together to supervise a mix for the album which was to be named after those EMI Studios in which, for the preceding seven years, they had made history. (On its original release *Disc & Music Echo* sniffed that the title was "uninspired".) Historically the date is significant as it was the last time that John, Paul, George *and* Ringo ever convened together at Abbey Road. From then on, the group members would be more familiar with the insides of boardrooms and law courts.

A few days later the quartet were photographed at the Lennons' new mansion, Tittenhurst Park. Bearded, mustachioed, sullen… they bore little relation to the fresh-faced quartet who had charmed the world only a few years before. Only George's bright red tie provided a splash of colour in the otherwise sombre wardrobe.

Thanks to the assiduous Mark Lewisohn, we now know that the last, the *final* recording session as 'the Beatles' came on 3 January 1970, when Paul, George and Ringo returned to Abbey Road to nail a full version of George's 'I Me Mine'. John was away in Denmark. In his usual laconic way, captured on *Anthology 3*, George explains his absence: "You will all have read that Dave Dee is no longer with us. But Micky and Tich and I would like to carry on the good work that's always gone down in Number Two".

Historically, the last Beatle to record while the group were still together was Ringo. He came to Abbey Road on 1 April 1970 to overdub drum parts on three songs scheduled for *Let It Be*, under Phil Spector's watchful eye. On the same day, Lennon's lithographs of fucking Yoko were branded obscene. The policeman who led the raid (Detective Inspector Frederick Luff) opened the proceedings: "Many toilet walls depict works of art of similar merit. It is perhaps charitable to suggest that they are the work of a sick mind. The only danger to a successful prosecution, as I see it, is the argument that they are so pathetic as to be incapable of influencing anyone and therefore unable to deprave or corrupt".

Less than a fortnight later, Paul's decision to quit was front-page news. By then they had all gone their separate ways. In *New Musical Express* dated 20 December 1969, reporting on a £2,000,000 offer for a 13-show US tour, the paper presciently stated: "It is now evident that no amount of money will tempt John, Paul, George and Ringo into undertaking further live dates as the Beatles – because of the divergence of their individual careers – and that the group will almost certainly never again appear on stage in its present form".

*

The *Abbey Road* reviews were respectful. ("A vast improvement on their last album...", *Melody Maker*; "[it] touches peaks far higher than did their last album", *The Sunday Times*). While others carped, "You will enjoy *Abbey Road*. But it won't move you", *The Guardian*; "The end of side two sounds like a load of unfinished songs dumped together to clear the cupboard", *The Observer*. Crucially, *Rolling Stone* were unimpressed: "It does tread a rather tenuous line between boredom, Beatledom and bubblegum. Side two is a disaster..."

Melody Maker reader J.A. Nunn concurred, "after hearing *Abbey Road*... the Beatles are not an influence on the music scene any more. In fact, in *Abbey Road*, you can hear traces of the Beach Boys, the Who, Fleetwood Mac, the original Animals and Traffic..." Ironically as *Abbey Road* slipped down the LP charts in spring 1970, it was interesting to see the other side of the Progressive coin, with well-placed albums by Nana Mouskouri, Val Doonican, Herb Alpert, Jim Reeves, Andy Williams and Mantovani. Unbelievably five years on, the *Sound of Music* soundtrack was *still* there.

For all its commercial success, we know now that *Abbey Road* was the last *proper* Beatle album. A unified front was needed for the press and public, but behind the scenes and away from the walls of the studio they so identified with, all was far from well. The writing was on the wall... The fissures were evident. Solo Beatle activities (film scores, acting roles etc.) had previously taken place during a hiatus in the group's activities. As the decade wound down, following the comforting release of *Abbey Road*, the world outside assumed all was well on the inside. But internally, there was much chafing at the Beatle bonds.

In September 1969, following on from Plastic Ono Band singles, Lennon ill-advisedly took to the stage of a rock & roll revival festival in Toronto. Unrehearsed, determined to give Yoko her place in the spotlight, the show was little more than a debacle (as can be heard on the subsequent *Live Peace in Toronto* album). Little Richard's authorised biographer Charles White was predictably scathing: "Fame had swollen [Lennon's] ego making him unable to acknowledge that black men like Chuck Berry and Little Richard were the true kings of rock & roll... Under great pressure, as always, from his Svengali Yoko Ono to maintain his top billing by going on after Richard, Lennon nevertheless knew that artistically he was hardly able to tune Richard's piano".

As Richard's producer Bumps Blackwell confirmed: "When Richard finished he laid the audience out so much that when Lennon and Yoko came on, they were washed out... When Yoko started squalling she sounded like a bull moose in mating season... They bombed totally. Jim Morrison and the Doors wouldn't go on until things had calmed down".

The ever-loyal *Beatles Monthly* reported that only half a dozen of the 20,000-crowd actually booed.

While the Beatles were sundering, their great rivals were surging ahead. The Rolling Stones built on the success of *Beggars Banquet* (1968) with what many consider their best-ever LP, *Let It Bleed*, which was released to coincide with the band's triumphant American tour of autumn 1969. Those shows delighted the critics; the audiences grew more enthusiastic. Jagger revelled in the moment. Here, perhaps, was the moment when the see-saw finally tipped in his direction. After years of being one step behind, Jagger could pull ahead. No longer would the Rolling Stones need to play second fiddle to the Beatles.

As they blazed across America during the autumn of 1969, the Stones had the world at their feet. Bob Dylan was holed-up in Woodstock; Led Zeppelin were still testing the waters; Pink Floyd was still perceived as an 'underground' outfit. The Beatles were effectively split. Year's end saw Paul and Ringo were busying themselves for their solo debut LPs; George revelling in the anonymity of playing guitar behind Delaney & Bonnie and John was up to his white-suited neck in the Plastic Ono Band.

George's particular idols, the Band, did not make their UK concert debut *as* the Band until 1971, but he was captivated by the similar, rootsy sound of Delaney & Bonnie. If you'd come along to Croydon's Fairfield Hall sometime before Christmas 1969, the long-haired, bearded rhythm guitarist *might* have seemed familiar. George was always the one who scrupulously tried to maintain his musical high standards, even during the heady touring days. He diligently turned up prior to appearing in front of thousands of screaming fans, knowing that not a note could be heard.

George reflected when we met: "It all shrivelled up. The spotlight caused a lot of damage really, it wasn't all negative really, but the spotlight and what happened to the Beatles... It was a huge success, a wonderful thing, but there were hidden pitfalls, you've got to watch you don't go off the rails and get carried away. Egos can go crazy. Plus, as a musician you find yourself playing the same ten tunes day in, day out, all round the world, the skills of being a musician start disappearing".

If that Stones '69 tour had ended in Boston as intended, it would have cemented their position as the greatest rock & roll band in the world. But the pressure was on for the band to play a free festival, to show their commitment to the underground and counterculture. Only four months after the triumph of Woodstock, here was their opportunity to score. Jagger could crow to Lennon, "Well, the Beatles never played a festival. The Stones did!" Here, also, was the opportunity for that long overdue Rolling Stones film: a documentary of the band at their peak playing to the delighted thousands in the California desert. But it was not to be: the last-minute switch to a desert location was a ghastly wilderness, the rock & roll Golgotha... Altamont.

*

If the Beatles' arrival in America in 1964 had provided a healing balm, the Stones' gruesome Altamont show of December 1969, in the wake of the Manson murders, came to symbolise the end of the dream. The Beatles were in their death throes, they had given their all during the intervening years, there was no likelihood of them arriving like the 7th Cavalry to save the day.

Then on 10 April 1970, much to John's chagrin, 'Paul Quits the Beatles' is front-page news. As the group's founder, it was John who wanted to trumpet their end. Lennon was seething. He had told Ray Connolly in confidence that *he* was the one who was quitting. John railed at having his thunder stolen. The rumour was confirmed in the press release which accompanied Paul's debut solo LP. It was all over, bar the shouting, the lawsuits and reunions.

The signs had been there: In December 1969, the *Beatles Monthly* closed, its circulation down to 26,000 from a high of 330,000. Editor Johnny Dean (born Sean O'Mahoney, 1932–2020) had been a loyal supporter from 1963. But by the end even the editor's support was ebbing and the magazine was fighting a losing battle with the Lennons' extreme posturing. Covering an event, Dean wrote: "John and Yoko were believed to have made an appearance though they were concealed by a huge white bag… so maybe it was someone else!"

Dean cited reasons for closure as drugs, girlfriends, solo projects, lack of group activities, absence of live appearances… written at the time, his weary resignation shone through: "The *Beatles Book* belonged to the Sixties. It can't do the right job for the Seventies". Fundamentally, Dean regretted the lack of humour: "Ever since Apple started, everything seems to be so very, very serious. Nothing is just plain fun anymore".

When it finally appeared, as what turned out to be the last LP released by the Beatles as a functioning band, *Let It Be* had the taint of finality about it. The album was undeniably flawed, even the running time, something the group had always been generous with before. And given the supposed wealth of material there was to draw upon, the results were lacklustre – George's contributions were hardly major; John was plainly disinterested (or uninterested, I can never remember which).

You sense George lacked the commitment anything which didn't sing the praises of an Indian guru, while John had nothing heavier to say than how Fab Yoko was. It was Paul's album – the title track alone was a substantial achievement, while 'Long and Winding Road' was hardly minor.

For me, I could have done with a bit more fly-on-the-wall 'Maggie Mae'. But I treasure the record for its opening; we know now that 'Two of Us' was written for his new wife Linda, but for many, the sight of John and Paul clustered round the same microphone as they sang of shared memories and journeys undertaken together… The years peeled away, like the wallpaper at Gambier Terrace.

The reviews were damning, finding fault with the price, length and song quality: "a disappointing, self-indulgent album"… "uninspired and undistinguished"… "frequently juvenile". The release of the lavish 59/11d *Let It Be* box was slammed by *NME* as "a cheapskate epitaph, a cardboard tombstone, a sad and tatty end to a musical fusion which wiped clean and drew again the face of pop music". The headline over Alan Smith's review ran 'New LP Shows They Couldn't Care Less'. *Disc & Music Echo* carped at the £2/19/11d cost (almost double the price of a standard album at the time) and the "disappointment that the album runs barely 15 minutes each side". It concludes "Does it stand up on its own? Will it be better having seen the film? Is it worth £3?"

In his *Rolling Stone* review, John Mendelsohn put the blame on the producer: "To Phil Spector, stinging slaps on both wrists. He's rendered 'Long and Winding Road' virtually unlistenable… Spectorized it evokes nothing so much as dewy-eyed little Mark Lester warbling his waif's heart out amidst the assembled *Oliver!* orchestra and choir". Perhaps understandably having *his* album mix rejected, Glyn Johns was suitably scathing ("John gave the tapes to Phil Spector who puked all over them, turning the album into the most syrupy load of bullshit I have ever heard").

A detailed letter of 14 April 1970 to Klein, cc'd Phil Spector and John Eastman, made Paul's indignation clear:

"In future no one will be allowed to add to or subtract from a recording of one of my songs without my permission…

1) Strings, horns, voices and all added noises to be reduced in volume.

2) Vocal and Beatle instrumentation to be brought up in volume.

3) Harp to be removed completely at the end of the song and original piano notes to be substituted

4) Don't ever do it again".

It also showed how seriously he took the process. In later years, when McCartney was battling to retain the ownership of his own songs, people snarked, "Why bother? He's got all that money". But they missed the point, they were *his* songs. There had never been, nor would there be, a 'Long and Winding Road' had Paul McCartney not sat down and written it.

And all the while there was that niggling problem of the third and final film to free the Beatles from their contract with United Artists. Once again, the firm hand of Mr Epstein was greatly missed. The origins of *Let It Be* saw it destined for television. But then, somewhere along the line, it was appreciated that 90 hours of film could be turned into a 90-minute feature film. Typically bullish, Allen Klein insisted, "*Let It Be* made more money for them than all the others put together. They wanted it for TV but I told 'em that was stupid".

Already the clouds were gathering over the *Let It Be* film. Even prior to its release *Rolling Stone* said that the "initial word on the *Let it Be* film is negative. Those who have seen it say that the film is embarrassing, but apparently The Beatles don't care about that anymore".

Jann Wenner accompanied John and Yoko to a screening of the film. Lennon left in tears. The critics concurred when it was finally released in May 1970. "I felt I was sitting at the deathbed of one of the greatest group talents to escape from the trivial treadmill of so much pop music", bemoaned veteran film critic Tom Hutchinson. "I regret the passing of an institution; I regret that this film should be judged as a suitable hearse for that institution".

As an example of changing times, when *Let It Be* premiered in May 1970, that week's *Melody Maker* carried details of Leonard Cohen's poetry readings… features on how 'Ten Years After Are Just Starting'… adverts for Manfred Mann's Chapter Three and Van Der Graaf Generator… a Jim Morrison interview… adverts for gigs by Blodwyn Pig, Deep Purple, Fotheringay, Soft Machine, Colosseum, Tyrannosaurus Rex, Humble Pie, Mott the Hoople, Genesis… It was all a long way from 'Octopus's Garden'. The paper's Mailbag had become a familiar battleground for Lennon and McCartney to snipe at each other. That week's page was dominated by a letter from the disgruntled (now) ex-Beatle Paul McCartney answering criticisms of his newly-released solo debut ("Does he really think we'll believe that he played all the instruments? It's obvious George Martin had a lot to do with it…")

With no group members attending the UK premiere of *Let It Be*, with the album's funereal packaging, with all the rumours and gossip, it was evident that the end was nigh. One of the problems that *Let It Be* faced on its theatrical release was its darkness. Literally, the murkiness of Michael Lindsay Hogg's 16mm footage blown up into 35mm.

The grainy film, the sombre tone, the poignant sight of Paul trying to haul his disinterested three amigos into something – anything! – was a truly dispiriting experience. Of course, in hindsight, we know that the Beatles had one last ace in the hole, and return to greatness with *Abbey Road*. But for half a century the *Let It Be* project was to be their swansong. A dispiriting LP and a bleak documentary of break-up...

We were not to know it. They were not to know it. But as the 1960s, the decade they virtually invented, came to wind down, the Beatles ceased to operate as a functioning group. It was hard to take, and the general public reasoned, once John had got that meddlesome Yoko out of his system and they'd all had a good shave, the Fab Four would reconvene. Pop groups like that didn't split up, not forever. It was inconceivable, as Ray Connolly wrote, "the notion that one day soon they might not exist was about as unlikely as the entire Royal Family abdicating".

For years, since their elevation into near-legends, the question of when the four Beatles were finally in a room together for the last time ever has pre-occupied and fascinated fans. Their 'firsts' are tantalising and optimistic, their 'lasts' make for depressing reading: that last, windy rooftop jam; the last time all four were at Abbey Road; the grumpy last photo session; the final time the fractious Fab Four were in a room together... (The general consensus is that following Lennon's return from his Toronto show, business meetings at Apple took place on Wednesday 17 and Thursday 18 September 1969, and one of those dates was *the* last time...)

Intriguingly in a BBC Radio 1 interview as late as March 1970, George had still been talking about working on a new Beatles album: "I'd like to do an album as well, just to get rid of a lot of old songs... And I expect by that time we should be ready to do a new Beatle album. So I think really the next Beatle album should be a very good one..."

As Peter Doggett wrote of that "epochal moment... A saga that had begun in passionate commitment to rock 'n' roll music ended in a life-draining argument about the consequences of that passion". Simon Garfield was equally emphatic: "You can date the death of sixties' idealism, the end of a generation, the time teen died out for good, not just the year or the month, but to the day and perhaps the hour. It was when Paul McCartney sued The Beatles, 31 December 1970".

Although the actual split had been confirmed, with the end of the decade that they had come to define, a chill wind greeted the Christmas of 1970, the first in seven years without a Beatles album to cheer us up. A cobbled together LP of fan club releases was a sad reminder of the journey from youthful exuberance to sombre maturity. Hard to believe half the band were still in their 20s.

Hindsight, of course, has immense benefits; it is likely that, had they been allowed a year off, some sort of future for the group might have ensued. Or, if they had taken advice from John Lennon's beloved Goons: "Which side are you on?" "There are no sides, you fool, we're all in this together".

What we had for Christmas treats that year instead was Paul's fragmentary solo debut; George's majestic, if sprawling arrival with *All Things Must Pass*, Ringo's jaunty *Beaucoups of Blues*. And to put us all in the spirit of good Christmas cheer, John's harrowing *Plastic Ono Band*. Yo, ho, and indeed, ho...

My 1970 Christmas treat LP to myself was none of those: in its lavish package, *Let It*

And in the end… August 1969

Be came in around three quid (ditto George's offering); the reviews for Paul's solo debut didn't sound like it contained much in the vein of 'Eleanor Rigby' or 'Lady Madonna' and Ringo's was a Country & Western album for God's sake... I consoled myself with the third, and second-best, album by King Crimson, *Lizard*. But even then, you could not escape the shadow of the Beatles, one song, 'Happy Family' recorded the Beatle break-up: "Happy family, one hand clap, four went on, but none came back..."

In the press release which accompanied his solo debut, McCartney was emphatic about not writing with John, was he missing the other three or planning a new single or album with the Beatles? "No". Talking to Paul Du Noyer many years later, McCartney knew the odium he faced as 'The Man Who Split the Beatles': "It was a pretty shitty time for me... I had to sue the guys, and as you know, Liverpool, the mates, no matter how much we were arguing, it's the one thing you don't ever want to do... It was the right thing to do but I knew I was walking into that Valley of the Shadow of Death..."

When the end did come, it came with a bitter irony: John keen to quit and immerse himself in Yoko, but beaten in the drama by the release of *McCartney* and the press seizing on the 'Paul Quits the Beatles' angle. On 10 April Derek Taylor issued one of his laconic press releases to confirm the fissure: "Spring is here and Leeds play Chelsea tomorrow and Ringo and John and George and Paul are alive and well and full of hope... The Beatles are alive and well and the beat goes on..."

The coverage in the trade magazine *Billboard* was, as you would expect, more business-like in its announcement: "The Beatles, the symbol of the British influence on the global music industry and the catalyst of what came to be known as 'the British Years' are no longer a group".

The issue of *New Musical Express* the following week bulged with McCartney (mind you it also boasted a cover strapline, 'Presley Says: I Am Coming'). The weekly had the inside track on the group, as Alan Smith's wife worked for Apple. 'Paul Is Still A Beatle' his page 2 feature emphasised ("Paul McCartney has no more 'quit' the Beatles at the present time than did John Lennon by recording with the Plastic Ono Band or Ringo Starr recording his current album of oldies...").

In hindsight, the Beatles recognised the split had been hastened by being pushed into preparing the *Let It Be* film and LP. They needed a break. The time-consuming business at the rotting Apple was taking its toll. John's obsessive fascination with all things Yoko separated him further from his group. George's increasing wish for a simple Band-style music and life outside the group. Ringo's film career was on the up which saw him no longer reliant on group efforts. The three versus one in choice of managers... The negatives were far outweighing the positives.

So, a year or two off, meant George could forge ahead with his own songs, Paul could have made sweet music with Linda, John less so with Yoko and Ringo... well, he'd have managed.

As the Beatles split, they probably, realistically felt, that the group would be remembered. Still youthful, they could forge ahead with solo albums; film projects, but with the weight of the Beatles off their shoulders. It had been a journey, From Blue Suburban Skies to Across The Universe. As the 1970s dawned, that ensemble, that journey was over. To all concerned, that was *it*. The path from schoolboy skiffle to global phenomena had been achieved in 13 years. A professional career of just eight years. So, as John Wayne emphatically expressed in *The Searchers*, "Just put an Amen to it". In fact, to everyone's incredulity, the Beatles' journey was not only *not* over, it remains never ending…

We know that now. Then, with turning 30 still a milestone, they could have taken a deep breath, consolidated forces; they could have reconsidered, regrouped. But instead, they went their separate ways. Rumours percolated but, even at the time, I always felt there was an air of *real* finality in a letter from Paul McCartney to *Melody Maker* on 29 August 1970. Finally putting an end to the "limping dog of a news story which has been dragging itself across your pages for the past year, my answer to the question 'will the Beatles get together again' is… no".

Dear mailbag.

In order to put out of its misery the limping dog of a news story which has been dragging itself across your pages for the past year, my answer to the question; " will the Beatles get together again"....

is no.

Paul McCartney.

Paul's 1970 letter to *Melody Maker*

> "*Alice laughed, 'There's no use trying,' she said. 'One can't believe impossible things.'*
>
> *'I daresay you haven't had much practice,' said the Queen. 'When I was your age, I always did it for half an hour a day. Why, sometimes I've believed as many as six impossible things before breakfast.'*"

Lewis Carroll, *Through the Looking-Glass*

PART III : The Beatles: Carry That Weight

So, that was that then, Paul had said so in print. John emphatically agreed. George's triple solo, transatlantic No.1 album debut seemed to confirm it. Ringo was happy as a name-above-the-title film star. It was all done and dusted. The dream was over. As the 1970s got underway, the Beatles were no more. And that's the way it was to stay. Finally. Forever.

It is tantalising to imagine them not splitting. In more recent times, a band with that many problems would have taken time out, gone off the road, re-grouped, issued some desultory solo albums, then appreciated that it was the *brand* which shifted product. On his split from Pink Floyd, I remember talking to Roger Waters, responsible for the bulk of what we now think of as classic Pink Floyd material. He had been playing to an American 3,000-seater, while "they" (as he sneered) were filling 90,000-seat stadia. In the end Waters returned to those big venues by concentrating on the material (the brand) his audiences wanted to hear from the man who wrote them.

While the new decade began, the world gritted its teeth to prepare for what lay ahead ("can't get no worse"). With the idealism of the 60s already receding, the fairy tales ahead proved to be grimmer in nature – the Kent State shootings, Nixon re-elected, the Vietnam War escalated by the invasion of Cambodia, Israeli athletes massacred in Munich, the Weathermen's bombing campaign. In the UK, IRA explosions, Angry Brigade bombs, aircraft hijackings, England losing to the still-divided *West* Germany in the World Cup, trade union disputes, soaring inflation, oil shortages, the first No.1 of the era – Rolf Harris' 'Two Little Boys'... And all under a Conservative government. We put away childish things and braced ourselves.

Whatever optimism the Beatles had offered during their professional existence was soon dissipated by the sad spectacle of the group and their advisors trudging through the law courts, as ever-more withering denunciations were read out by the men, not only in suits, but wigs. It was dispiriting and protracted. Only a few years on from being told that love was all we needed, newspapers diligently reported bitter accounts of division, rancour and outright hostility.

Looking ahead and coping with the new wretched realities left little opportunity to look back. Beatle nostalgia did occasionally percolate. Five years since the Candlestick Park gig? It can't have been ten *years* since 'Love Me Do'... A 30-year-old Paul McCartney? Each of the four were busy labouring under the Beatle shadow... And with each solo release came the inevitable comparisons – 'My Love'? Mm, well it ain't exactly 'Yesterday'... 'No.9 Dream' in preference to 'In My Life'? The news that George's *Extra Texture* "contained the new single 'You'" hardly set pulses racing... *Mind Games* not cracking the UK Top 10... *Goodnight Vienna* only scraping to No.30... How did they sleep?... 'Ram On'... 'Boogaloo'... 'Aisumasen'... 'Ding Dong'...

Each release carried its own magnetic charm, due to the 'ex-Beatle' tag. But as the decade drew on, every solo LP just seemed to undermine what wonders they had fashioned as 'A Beatle'. In fairness, they'd already squeezed at least two lifetimes in before they slogged the solo route. They were entitled to a break.

Even with the individual foot off the accelerator, there retained some still mystical thread which drew you back to them... Every time an ex-Beatle broke cover to toe the line, to play the game, to promote new product, the inevitable question of a reunion arose, to be batted aside as deftly as a Gary Sobers' off-cut. On they beat throughout the 1970s

– John, Paul, George and Ringo – "boats against the current, borne back ceaselessly into the past".

Dutifully, the new decade introduced fresh idols, some achieving the same level of hysteria as the Fabs – the irony of Ringo Starr filming Marc Bolan at the height of T-Rex's fame was not lost on critics. The Bay City Rollers attracted the same sort of hysteria – 'Rollermania' Vs 'Beatlemania' was a brief competition. Ziggy-era David Bowie scaled that Everest (and remember, at that last-ever Ziggy show, Bowie included 'Love Me Do')… Elton John effortlessly sold out Wembley Stadium… Slade did the three consecutive No.1s shuffle… Then the Jam followed that triage… Glam Rock, Prog Rock, Pub Rock, Punk Rock, Southern Rock, Country Rock, Folk Rock, Disco – all found shelter under the umbrella of the 1970s.

Here was an opportunity to give pause for thought: with *double* LPs on offer from Led Zeppelin, the Rolling Stones, Elton John and the Who, as well as Mike Oldfield's *Tubular Bells* which seemed one giant leap. With *triple* LPs from Emerson, Lake & Palmer and Yes… With gigs moving to ever-larger venues, and Led Zeppelin concerts the equivalent of a Cecil B. DeMille spectacle, just over half an hour of *Please Please Me* didn't seem that substantial.

The music press were getting their jeans all in a tangle with a plethora of 'new Dylans' – Bruce Springsteen, John Prine, Steve Goodman, Loudon Wainwright III … were firing up. Mind you, "there didn't seem much wrong with the old one", Kris Kristofferson, laughed. Then Dylan himself was back in harness, hitting new commercial heights in the mid-70s with his first-ever US No.1 LPs (*Blood on the Tracks; Desire*). With Pink Floyd taking us to the dark side of the moon… With Deep Purple, Caravan and Procol Harum recording entire LPs with symphony orchestras, what need had we of the Beatles? We had all those new releases to look forward to, and little need for looking back.

And yet, and yet… It's true, you always *do* remember, with great clarity, and a sense of disbelief, the first time you met an actual *Beatle*… A brief spell in PR in the mid-1980s had me writing a press release for McCartney Productions Ltd, which handled Buddy Holly Week. An MPL executive, I'm pretty sure it was the late Alan Crowder, liked what I'd written, and I was summoned to Soho Square. It was all done in such a hurry I didn't have time to panic.

Nervously waiting in one of what appeared to be many boardrooms, it was the voice I recognised as he made its way along the corridor. Still strikingly Scouse, he came in talking with Linda. He was worried about the boy one of their daughters was seeing in Sussex, muttering about him being a "real punk". Linda was sticking up for her daughter's choice of boyfriend. And I found myself thinking: "Blimey, Paul McCartney is worried about the company a teenage girl is keeping. You should hear what they said about *you* not that long ago…"

Making conversation, someone asked if they'd seen the Clint Eastwood film on TV over the weekend, and they replied that it was only on in the London area, and they couldn't get that in Sussex. And yet again, I found myself musing, "Crikey, if even he was only half as rich as you read, Paul McCartney could afford to buy the whole bloody *network*…!"

These thoughts stayed silent as I was introduced, the hand (not the fabled left) was shaken, and we settled down to business. Hand on heart, I can't remember the next sequence of events (aside from thinking, heart-pumpingly, approximately every 30 seconds, "Fuck me, I'm talking to Paul *McCartney*"). Two decades of experience ensured that he was very good at involving you – eye contact, ensuring you had the hot drink requested earlier, nodding and giving the impression of listening intently as you, frankly … babbled.

The subject of Buddy Holly was obviously high on the agenda and I do remember telling the assembled group that I just recently bought a "new" Buddy LP. *For the First Time Anywhere* had gathered together a collection of undubbed tracks by Buddy and the Crickets and had only just been released on LP, as the title suggested, for the first time, anywhere. What I *do* remember is that, on learning this, Paul turning to one of his business associates and inquiring: "Is that one of ours?" It was like a despot asking for a list of subjugated territories. It was an offhand, rather imperious inquiry. One which suggested … *power*.

Over the years I did quite a lot of work for MPL on various projects. I used to joke we went back a long way. I mean, I knew Paul McCartney before he was knighted. Many hours were spent with him, on and off duty. He was always punctual, courteous, and even after a long delay, seemingly interested in my activities ("How's the Springsteen book doing?"). Well, of course, the cynics would say, he has people to do that for him, to remind him.

My abiding impression was of someone affable and … nice. "Well", the critics sneer of him again, "he's good at that, isn't he?" As if to say it was John who shot from the hip, and that Paul put the PR sheen on it. But over the years, if it *was* a mask of amiability put on for PR purpose, I never once saw it slip. Of course he was only human, and that affability may not always have been evident at MPL's Soho Square offices if someone dropped a bollock, or didn't come up to snuff at a recording session when Paul was calling all the shots.

He maintained an easygoing charm, putting you at your ease, wilfully aware of your nerves and by a wink or a nudge, implying hey, we're all the same. Except of course we weren't. I wasn't, and never could be, Paul McCartney.

Watching him in action was spellbinding, listening to him reminisce, to hear him speak of sessions, gigs, record releases, tour itineraries, van journeys… you had to remind yourself that he was one of only four who knew of these things. Well, okay seven, if you included Neil and Mal, and Brian. But in the eye of that hurricane, the centre of the global storm, only four of them ever went on stage as the legendary *Beatles*. Only four had the weight of the world on their young shoulders. By the time I first met McCartney, one of them was reluctant to revisit the era, one had all but had it blotted out by booze and drugs and one had been shot dead. Even after John's murder, when it was announced that Paul was rumoured to be getting bullet-proof glass installed at his MPL HQ, the critics *still* pounced.

Over the hours spent in Paul's company, I was eager to wallow in his memories of that seismic Beatle era. But I did sympathise with the way he was inevitably, invariably sucked back to times long gone. During the 1970s and 80s, he was at pains to avoid the subject. By the time of his 'comeback' 1989 *Flowers in the Dirt* tour, however, he'd happily reconciled with that past.

Over the years, I was occasionally asked in by MPL, to sit in and monitor interviews, and report back if any line of questioning piqued the McCartney interest. After quarter of an hour, even I was bored witless, sensing the monotony, the weariness, the inevitable inquiries… What *he* wanted to talk about was the album he'd spent a year working on; the musicians he'd gone head-to-head with in Sussex, Montserrat or Los Angeles. What the journalist wanted to hear about was the group he'd publicly quit on 10 April 1970.

Dexterous and diplomatic, McCartney was used to it. He had after all been fielding the same questions since, approximately, 11 April 1970. Watching him in action, Paul had become adept at switching the conversation ("Yeah, funnily enough, there's a track on this new album that reminded me of the Beatles…" "Mm, there's a little trick on my new album which I used to do with the Beatles").

They all got used to it in the years since the split. They knew that it was as much *brand* as band when it came to the Beatles. The endlessly parodied LP covers… the legions of 'new Beatles'… the anniversaries… the biographies… the memoirs… All around that one group, 1957–1970, 12 LPs, and, what, 227 songs?

Every ex-Beatle album inevitably drew comparisons with that canon. Grinding his teeth, George would read how *Living in the Material World* didn't stack up against *Revolver*; Paul would seethe that *Red Rose Speedway* wasn't compared favourably to *Abbey Road*. John could not comprehend why *Sometime in New York City* was not as respectfully received as *The White Album*. While Ringo, ironically, at the very beginning, basked in reflected glory with a spectacularly successful solo career.

They just would not go away. Was it only coincidence that in legend, "the beetle was supposed to conceal in itself the secret of eternal life?" Or that the beetle was associated with Ra, the Egyptian Sun God, allied to creation, life and resurrection?

Even after John's murder in 1980, all of the three survivors were regularly quizzed when they broke cover… "Yes…" it was true, the Beatles *were* getting back together… All those reunion rumours that surfaced – *Melody Maker* were convinced Klaus Voormann was joining on bass… George would *definitely* be joined onstage at the Bangla Desh concert by Ringo, Paul and John… Wings at the Kampuchea benefit, 1979 at Hammersmith Odeon? *Absolutely*, George and Ringo would join the band onstage… Money was on a 'reunion' at Live Aid 1985, this time with Julian Lennon… In fact, from memory, the only Beatle element on that historic day was when Elvis Costello took part in 'the global jukebox' by performing "an old Northern English folk song", 'All You Need Is Love'… Later, ready money was on George, Paul, Ringo … and Jeff Lynne as the line-up in a Traveling Wilburys offshoot…

George spoke fondly of his "other group" when we met in 1992. The Wilburys gave him the camaraderie he relished along with a degree of playful anonymity. The group only made two highly enjoyable albums before tragedy overtook them. George told me that prior to Roy Orbison's death they had commissioned David Leland (*Personal Services*, *Wish You Were Here*) to come up with a Wilburys movie. He smiled and with his F1 hat on, spoke, tongue in cheek, of "the next generation of Wilburys – Nigel Wilbury, Ayrton Wilbury… Tom Petty says, 'Well, I'm waitin', soon as I see the big "W" in the sky, I'll be there!'"

A familiar name which inevitably cropped up when a Beatle reunion story surfaced was that of Sid Bernstein, and his regular multi-million-dollar offers to reform. In fairness, it was Bernstein who had impressed Brian Epstein by booking the group into Carnegie Hall even *before* their Ed Sullivan appearance. It was Bernstein who had set up the triumphant 1965 Shea Stadium show. A 1979 offer had $500,000,000 on the table, the idea being that a Beatle reunion could benefit the Vietnamese boat people.

The post-split reunion rumours just would not go away as long as the four Beatles were still active. They subsided during John's period of house husbandry, but didn't stop. In May 1976, New York's *Village Voice* ran an advertisement from 'The International Committee To Reunite The Beatles' ("We are the people, let us try not for monetary gain, but for the beauty and deep meaning of their music we all love..."). It was a well-meaning ideal, put together by American businessmen, with Mohammad Ali as its figurehead. The idea was that every fan would contribute $1 each, and thereby help alleviate child poverty.

In 2006, a report appeared in the *New York Post* from a Capitol records executive stating that a clause in Paul McCartney's 1979 contract with CBS had allowed him to record with "John Lennon, Richard Starkey and George Harrison as The Beatles". This, experts allege, is the open door which, somewhere down the line, *could* have led to that historic reunion.

Long after they had ceased working together, there was an almost Messianic faith in 'The Beatles'. It was almost as if those four individuals coming together could solve all the world's problems – that North and South Vietnam would be united; that Palestinians and Israelis would drop their hostility; that the Northern Ireland 'Troubles' could be resolved; that the Berlin Wall would tumble and Nelson Mandela walk free. As it happens, the last two *did* happen, but without any Beatle involvement.

It was in 2004 that a positive link with the Beatles and worldwide goodwill *was* established. An obituary of Sir Godfrey Household noted: "in 1967 EMI was flush with funds from the unanticipated success of The Beatles' recordings, and he was given a free rein to pursue product research..." In development at EMI, Household invented the CT Scanner, which married X-ray and computer images to further probe inside the body. It went on to win him the Nobel Prize. His obituary concluded, "The combination of The Beatles' success with the British system of research subsidies and the genius of one engineer ... changed the face of modern medicine".[19]

"As far as I'm concerned there won't be a Beatles reunion as long as John Lennon remains dead", George said emphatically in 1989, six years before 'Free As a Bird' and the Beatle reunion. Of them all, George was the most reluctant to dwell on his Beatle past – get him on gardening, the Rutles, bookbinding, Formula 1 racing, Monty Python sketches or Dylan lyrics and he was happy as a pig in mud. Once 'the Fabs' (his own favourite name for them) were mentioned, you sensed an inward grimace.

Talking to Klaus Voormann in Munich once, I asked if he remembered all those music weekly front pages about him replacing Paul? "Ach..." he was dismissive. "How could *anyone* replace Paul McCartney?"

Legendary bands getting back together was always a thorny issue; despite unimagined carnal delights, fan worship and a lifetime of financial security, it was the niggling squabbles which persisted. The row in the back of a Bedford A30 van, a snatched

---

19   Thanks to *Word* reader John Foyle for pointing this out.

girlfriend, a songwriting credit, a missed musical cue onstage… these were the itches that could not be scratched. Typical was the rancour which caused Pink Floyd to split, and which resurfaced following their Live 8 reunion. The ill-humour which characterised every Who reunion was not untypical. An Eagles reunion would only happen "when Hell freezes over" (later the title of their 1994 reunion tour!). I would hail the Stone Roses as one of Britain's best bands; their 1989 debut as much a line in the sand as *Sgt Pepper* or *Never Mind the Bollocks…* But a five-year hiatus only saw the desultory *The Second Coming*. A 2012 reunion led to further dates, then a hiatus when the singer allegedly called the drummer "a cunt", before a final split. And if you just want to see group camaraderie go belly up, just watch *The Commitments*.

Prior to *Anthology*, the reunion the world was gagging for did come close to happening. It was in private, away from all that intense media scrutiny. It was a story I heard while researching my Lonnie Donegan biography and provided an astonishing revelation. In May 1979 Lonnie found himself in exalted company, as a guest at Eric Clapton's wedding reception. Clapton – who had married Pattie, George Harrison's ex-wife earlier in the year – hosted the star-studded reception at his Surrey home. Besides Lonnie, there was Mick Jagger, Bill Wyman, Jeff Beck and Jack Bruce; but the real star-turn came when Paul McCartney, Ringo Starr and George Harrison climbed onstage to play together for what would prove to be the first and only time since the Beatles' split.

Jonathan Clyde, who had run George's Dark Horse Records in the UK, and was there as a guest, told me: "It was a stunning, beautiful May day in England… There was a marquee, with food and drink, and I was standing there and Lonnie came up, who I didn't know, and said, 'You've got a camera, will you take a picture for me?'

"So we went outside and he gathered Paul, Ringo and George, and asked me to take a photograph, which I did. It was quite a moment for me actually…

"I do remember thinking this is extraordinary, as Mick Jagger was belting out 'Get Back' with Paul, and George and Ringo! This is as good as it gets, and if John had been living in England, he'd have been at the wedding. It was a great day, a lovely party, and they were the dance band for the party!"

Lonnie was centre-stage when the 'dance band' went on to do a jaunty medley of rock & roll and skiffle hits. In fact, as the Fab guests grew more and more inebriated, a cunning plan was hatched: as Lonnie Donegan was the man who had so inspired the Beatles back in the 1950s, might he not be just the man to bring them back together in the 1970s?

Clapton was a generous host, and the details are hazy, but Paul, George and Ringo were all convinced that Lonnie was the only person who could winkle John Lennon out of his self-imposed seclusion in New York. As a young teenager, John owned more records by Lonnie Donegan than by Elvis; so, reasoned the other three Beatles, Lonnie – the man whose music brought the Beatles together in the first place – would be the perfect emissary. Alas, like so many plans launched on a wave of champagne, Lonnie's transatlantic mission never got further than the Surrey hills.

John and Paul were in sporadic contact throughout the 1970s, while the 'Threetles' were reunited for *Anthology*. Tragically, the final time the three were together was at a Manhattan hotel on 12 November 2001. George's cancer had advanced, and less than three weeks later he was dead.

One of the most intriguing Beatle connections during my journalistic career came in 2004 when I was interviewing Tom Jones. Now *Sir* Tom, and bulging with credibility. But back in the late 60s, when his TV show was on commercial television, the tuxedo-clad, hit-making, hip-shaking singer was anathema to us culture-widening music crowd. But people forget that Tom's TV show gave priceless airtime to Crosby, Stills, Nash & Young, Joni Mitchell, Janis Joplin and the Who. There was one guest who wanted to be on, but whose manager was notoriously … protective.

Tom was one of the few singers that Elvis Presley really admired, and while performing at the same time in Las Vegas, the two men grew to be close friends. One day Elvis called Tom up about appearing on *This Is Tom Jones*: "He told me he'd love to do it. I said great, we'll do the whole show, you and me", Tom told me. "Elvis said fine, but I'll tell you what else I'd like to do. Elvis said, 'Have the Beatles really split up?' I said yeah. This was back in 1970. He said, 'It's a shame that… because what I'd like is we could do a show, we'll have the Beatles playing and we'll do the singing – but we won't let them sing, he said they can just do the oohs and aahs'. Elvis Presley, me *and* the Beatles. Can you imagine that!"

*

The 1970s were bookended with the bitter break-up of the Beatles and the death of Sid Vicious. So enshrined in our culture and history today, it is perhaps hard now to appreciate that with the shifting musical landscape, the flurry of solo LPs and the legal bitterness, back then, the Beatles were not the potent musical or cultural force we think of them as today. It took John's murder, the CD renaissance and the parlous state of pop music which offered an opportunity to reflect on the brilliance of the music they made together… All help remind us of their accomplishments, but 'twas not ever thus.

The music scene had changed beyond recognition in the decade since the innocent trilling of 'Love Me Do'. Midway through the 1970s, Led Zeppelin were shattering box office records thought held previously inviolate by the Beatles. In May 1973, the band played a show in Tampa, Florida, which drew 56,443 paying customers, thus beating the Beatles at Shea Stadium seven years before (55,600).

Zeppelin were a juggernaut, steamrollering across America ('Believe It Or Not' an incredulous *Daily Express* 70s headline ran, 'They're Bigger Than The Beatles'). It was *Led Zeppelin II* which deposed *Abbey Road* in the UK LP charts. In September 1970, after six years at the top, the front page of *Melody Maker* screamed 'Pop Poll Rocked', and there was the reason: 'Zeppelin Topple Beatles'.

Led Zeppelin controlled their career in a manner their peers envied: they never released a UK single and interviews were tightly controlled, that effectively meant that the group's offstage anonymity was preserved. At gigs, the hysteria was evident, but at home, Bonham, Page, Plant and Jones could move largely unbothered. Financially too, manager Peter Grant exerted a power which Brian Epstein could never have conceived of. In concert, promoters saw 90% of the gate go to the band and their notorious manager. But then, even 10% of a Led Zeppelin gate was financially worthwhile.

Rumours of that scale of success hinted at Satanic links. To achieve those heights, souls had to be sold. The band travelled in their own jet. Their tours were notorious for their libidinous behaviour. Their arrogance was only tolerated because of their stature. Their notoriety preceded them. At an industry event, Peter Grant introduced himself: "Hello, I'm Peter Grant, I manage Led Zeppelin". "Hey man," Bob Dylan responded, "don't come to me with *your* problems".

At the conclusion of one of their tumultuous tours of America during 1973, Zeppelin held a party, and one of the guests was George Harrison. Curious about the band's gigs, he asked one of the roadies who goes on first? He was told no one, the band played the entire show. What about an intermission? Nope to that too. "Fuck me," laughed the Quiet One. "When the Beatles toured we were down for twenty-five minutes and could get off in fifteen".

On tour in 2016, the E. Street Band drummer Max Weinberg joked that each of Bruce Springsteen's shows was longer than an entire Beatles *tour*…! Max was a huge Beatle fan, right from the beginning: "I had a school friend who was on a trip to London", he told me. "It was with her parents in November 63 and she brought back *With the Beatles*, so I had a couple of months head start". I asked him for comparison with the Beatles and the E. Street Band. "The Beatles' experience was one big blur, because it happened so fast that they made it so big, and they were young. We were much older. I would always make a point of walking out of the concert hall behind Bruce – so my being recognised was never a problem!… It was actually a lot of fun, I was 34, so it was kind of like playing at being a Beatle".

The sheer *scale* of rock shows in the 21st century I find overwhelming. On her 2023/24 *Eras* tour, Taylor Swift will play to over six million fans. The size of those venues is staggering, just look at her Pittsburgh gig in 2023, it makes Shea Stadium look like the Cavern. In Canada, with its population of 38,000,000, there were 31,000,000 ticket applications. The tour easily eclipses all that has gone before to become the highest-ever in rock history.

Writing in *Variety*, Chris Willman compared Taylor's jaunt to victory runs by Madonna, Springsteen, Jacksons and U2: "Having seen all those tours at least … I can vouch that as much as those moments in touring lore deserved their reputations, there are few direct correlations with the once-in-a-lifetime phenomenon we're seeing today. Really, the only thing it can be compared to is a Beatles tour.

"Something was indisputably lost when the band broke up in 1970 without ever having toured behind the most fruitful period of their career. Imagine what it would have been like if the group had found a way to stay together long enough to do its own version of an *Eras* Tour — something that allowed an explosion of the pent-up energy any fandom has in wanting to hear great music as part of a collective, public experience? They were the originators of bedroom pop, the stuff that changed your life through a set of headphones, but there's an experience of rock 'n' roll that never reaches its complete fulmination until it's shared with an electrically charged audience that feels the same way you do about what you've all been identifying with and devouring in the privacy of your own homes".

Of course, you cannot compare Taylor with them. Back in the day, a UK Beatle tour was announced, you filled in a form for tickets, dispatched your cheque or postal order – or queued at the venue's box office – then got your ticket. Their final UK tour was a modest nine dates in December 1965 – two shows a night to audiences totalling, what, 36,000?

Too much Taylor for a Beatles book? Leaving her music aside, I am simply fascinated, and drawing comparisons to how the live experience has altered over the years. Scientists at her Seattle show measured seismic activity equivalent to a 2.3 magnitude earthquake. One economist estimated, "If Taylor Swift were an economy, she'd be bigger than 50 countries". Jan Moir marvelled, "It is hard to grasp just how big this *Eras* tour has become… with some even claiming that Swift has single-handedly stopped the US from falling to recession".

Oh, and as if *that* wasn't enough: the 2024 Superbowl attracted America's largest TV audience since the 1969 Moon landings. And what drew those 122,000,000 viewers was pop singer T.A. Swift.

*

As the 1970s drew on the Beatles suddenly seemed rather old hat. What had once been challenging, now seemed rather quaint and archaic. Those haircuts, those suits, that abiding *cuteness*. That lack of interest was palpable when the Beatles films were show on UK television – *Hard Day's Night* (1970), *Help!* (1971) and *Yellow Submarine* (1974). According to film and TV historian Sheldon Hall, "viewing figures are not available as they were shown at off-peak times, which does rather suggest a lack of interest".

The battle lines were drawn, and that unassailable stature was under threat from the Floyd and Zeppelin; Caravan and Zappa; Elton and Bowie; Yes and Jethro Tull; Genesis and Roxy Music; the Doors and Queen; Chicago and the Eagles… In the early 1970s, Crosby, Stills, Nash & Young looked like they had the chops to step up to the plate – to use Americanisms. Their second album *Déjà Vu* had advance orders unseen since the landslide 60s. In concert, they conveyed onstage harmony and presented a sense of community. Such was their status that "they could have started their own *religion*", producer Paul Rothchild wryly observed.

Suddenly in the 1970s, three-minute singles were back in the UK charts, singalong contributions courtesy of Slade, the Sweet, Mud, David Essex and T. Rex. In concert there were scenes reminiscent of Beatlemania. For all of John's political posturing, and George's mysticism, the group they had left were, from memory, regarded as anachronistic, at a time when 'Rock Music' was pushing the barriers, expanding the frontiers.

It was a time when a major label could release an album as left-field as John Cale's *Paris 1919*. While other big companies would encourage 'Progressive' labels under their aegis. Of course, hindsight reveals the bankruptcy of the majority of that much vaunted new music. Like the joke about the Grateful Dead fan who goes to see the band for the first time without taking drugs, and midway through 'Dark Star' turns to his fellow Deadhead and asks: "What *is* this shit?"

A 20-minute Ginger Baker, Carl Palmer or John Bonham solo was definitive proof of the way rock had 'progressed' in the 70s. But who listens to those drum solos on disc with pleasure today? To his own great relief, the Beatles wisely limited Ringo to a 13-bar, 15-second fill during their swansong studio sessions. Nor did George emulate guitar gods like Eric Clapton, Jimmy Page or Alvin Lee. The veneration accorded guitar and drum solos was something which the Beatles wisely ignored.

There was so much Beatle bitterness. As the 70s progressed, John publicly sniped at Paul on the letters pages of *Melody Maker*: "(I'll bet you your piece of Apple you'll be living in New York by 1974 (two years is the usual time it takes you -- right?"). Paul's reply was beetles copulating on the sleeve of *Ram*. The album's opening track, 'Too Many People' was a direct pop at John, with Paul tiring of Lennon's public criticism and his preachy politics. It didn't take John long to get back on disc either, the object of Lennon's scorn on 'How Do You Sleep?' from *Imagine* was not hard to discern. An early version was even more direct, "How do you sleep, you cunt…?"

Their own post-Beatle highlights came early on (*Imagine*, 1971 and *Band on the Run*, 1973). George coasted on the success of 1970's *All Things Must Pass*, but revealed feet of clay with subsequent solo releases. Ironically, Ringo's was the most successful solo career immediately following the split. Between 1971 and 1974 the amiable singing drummer landed no less than six US Top 10 hits, including two No.1s.

Following that spell in the sun, of them all, Ringo struggled most with a post-Beatle career. Desultory attempts were made at film-making, film acting, furniture design and photographic books. A 1995 Pizza Hut advert was fun, with the drummer trying to get the band back together, only to be joined by three of the Monkees. He could also be found fronting Skechers' footwear campaign ('Rock Out In Comfort'). But much of the time, with time hanging heavy, Ringo sought refuge in tax exile and alcohol.

Finally, from 1989 on, Ringo's All Starr Band kept him occupied, and he later admitted, gave him a purpose, weaning him off the demon drink. Along with other grizzled survivors (Dave Edmunds, Gary Brooker, Greg Lake, Jack Bruce, Joe Walsh, Ian Hunter) Ringo could fill an evening with *his* Beatle songs and solo hits. It may not have been the Cavern or Shea Stadium, but this *was* a Beatle, singing Beatle songs.

In pursuit of Yoko's daughter Kyoko, the Lennons had left the UK in August 1971. John was never to return. Prior to flying to New York to conduct an interview with him on the release of *Double Fantasy*, *Melody Maker* editor Ray Coleman spoke to John on the phone; Ray was one of the few UK journalists Lennon had any time for. He told Ray he was planning a private visit to his homeland early in 1981, "to see if anyone remembered me", Ray told me. It was of course, never to be.

In one of those ironies nobody would believe if it was written as fiction, John's final departure from the group he had started occurred in that place where dreams and fantasies were realised … Disney World. On one of his rare reunions with his first-born Julian, John and lover May Pang took Julian to the Florida resort. In the hotel next to the fantasy park, on 27 December 1974, John became the last Beatle to sign the papers which officially dissolved the Beatles partnership. As befitting, it was the signature of the group's founder which finally, legally, formally ended the Beatles.

On 9 April 1975, the High Court in London announced: "All matters in the dispute between Mr McCartney and John Lennon, George Harrison and Ringo Starr have been fully settled". It was one day short of five years since Paul announced he was quitting the group. In the end, in the Gothic surroundings of the Royal Courts of Justice, after years of sniping, discontent and bitterness, it was all over. Finally. Forever. For the time being…

It is worth pausing to reflect just how far the Beatles had slipped away from the culture by that point. To celebrate its fifth anniversary in 1978, London's Capital Radio came up with a Hall of Fame to commemorate the best single releases of the past 25 years. This was the era of 'I'm Not in Love', 'Bohemian Rhapsody' and 'Bridge over Troubled Water'. The highest Beatle entry was 'Hey Jude' at No.7. In 1979, Allan Williams' plan for a new Liverpool statue stalled when worldwide contributions stalled at £230.[20]

Over the years, whenever meeting up with colleagues from the *New Musical Express*, one reader's name always came up: 'Samuel K.P. Ampong'. It was his plaintive letter to the paper which was pinned up at the paper's reception desk throughout the 1970s, a question every *NME* contributor remembers – 'Where is Beatle band?'

*

George and Ringo persevered with solo LPs, each successive release generating lower sales, achieving less and less airtime. Any real focus was on the two prime movers in the Beatles; Paul managed an impressive collection of work during the 1970s. While his first two albums of the 1970s were heavily criticised, subsequent reissues have found both *McCartney* and *Ram* happily re-evaluated. Paul's real gift to his American fans back then came on his 1976 tour with Wings, when five Beatle songs were included in the set. A 12-track *Wings Greatest Hits* in 1978 bulged with an impressive selection of his post-Beatle achievements, including a James Bond theme and the UK's biggest-selling single.

Even after a series of lacklustre 1970s albums, the main focus remained on Lennon. Surely the architect of the Beatles had one more ace up his sleeve? There must be more musical muscle than what *Mind Games* offered? Even during his five-year, mid-70s absence, people were convinced John was hatching some magical renaissance. The music press salivated at the rumours that Lennon was recording again. There were tales of record labels offering eye-watering sums for a return to action.

Finally, the silence was broken. I was at *Melody Maker* when '(Just Like) Starting Over' was released, and there was a palpable lack of interest after just one play on the office stereo. Ian Pye's review of the subsequent *Double Fantasy* was headlined 'Silly Love Songs'. *NME*'s Charles Shaar Murray concurred ("It sounds like a great life, but it makes for a lousy record… I wish Lennon had kept his big happy trap shut until he had something to say that was even vaguely related to those of us not married to Yoko"). In 2007, *Word* magazine voted it 'One Of The Worst Comebacks Ever' ("the worst bit of sugar-packed domestic slop to ever come from a Beatle").

What happened in the immediate aftermath of the album's release manifestly overshadowed its content. Even today, it would be a hard heart who can listen to 'Beautiful Boy' and not be moved, knowing what was to follow. Lennon happily allowed *Double Fantasy* to be a 50/50 split, but it would be fair to say that critics and fans tended to concentrate on John's contributions rather than his wife's. Yoko's previous solo LP, 1973's *Feel the Space* had not unduly troubled chart statisticians. A kinder view might be

---

20   Thanks to John Harris' *Mojo* feature for pointing this out.

that John's soft-centred reflections on house-husbandry, fatherhood and devotions to his second wife were balanced by Yoko's harder-edged sandpaper rockers.

It was Radio 1 DJ Andy Peebles, forever to be remembered as 'the man who conducted John Lennon's last-ever interview', who shed light on the collaboration. In a revealing interview with Lesley-Ann Jones for her Lennon biography, Peebles spoke frankly and at length of Yoko's self-serving role around the release of *Double Fantasy*: "'If we are going to do this,' she said, 'I need to make it clear to you that this interview will be fifty per cent about John, and fifty per cent about me'. I felt like saying 'Who on earth are *you*? You're the woman who has done for singing what Wayne Sleep has done for Rugby League'."

The general mood was that, however wrong-footed a comeback *Double Fantasy* was, it was good to have Lennon back in the arena. And surely his next album would have a little more … heft. It would surely have moved away from domestic bliss and reflected wider issues. And if the price of that was a full partnership with Yoko, well 50% of John Lennon was surely better than no John Lennon at all?

The news of John's murder broke in London on the morning of Tuesday 9 December 1980. As the film editor of *Melody Maker* I was at a preview of *Flash Gordon* and only by the time I got to the office (those Stalag Luft III portacabins on Meymott Street) did I hear the tragic news. The bulk of the staff were at the printers in Colchester getting that week's issue done and dusted.

We were too busy for the news to really sink in. There had been nothing like this. Even the death of Elvis three years before did not achieve the seismic impact of Lennon's murder. This was different. This was John. This was one of ours, snatched before his time, a *Beatle* gone. Murdered.

The next four days were spent in a miasma of Beatle music as I punched out thousands of words on his music 1956–70. The grief was subsumed in meeting impossible deadlines. I remember cracking up only once, as 1970's 'My Mummy's Dead' came on; my own mother had died only five months before.

Tragically, the January 1981 issue of *Playboy* with the Lennon interview had gone to press before his murder. The interview concluded with John being asked about his 80s dream? "Well, you make your own dream. That's the Beatles' story isn't it?" Ironically, that issue's cover star was Barbara Bach, just a few months before she married Ringo.

Lennon took over the news agenda. The shock of his senseless murder obviously brought its own wave of nostalgia. The airwaves were full of recent ballads as well as a wave of Beatle memories. One of the few positive aspects came with heartfelt calls for the introduction of gun control. Alas, sadly ignored. The death ensured a re-appraisal of *Double Fantasy* and a subsequent three-month run of Lennon UK No.1s – 'Starting Over', 'Imagine'. 'Woman' and Roxy Music's cover of 'Jealous Guy' were only broken by 'There's No One Quite Like Grandma' and (inexplicably) 'Shaddup You Face'.

One of the oddest professional occasions I ever attended was a lunch at the Grosvenor House Hotel in 2003 following a plaque-unveiling ceremony, commemorating Lennon at the location of the original Apple boutique on Baker Street. My wife and I shared a table with Burt Kwouk (Inspector Clouseau's 'Cato'), Anita Harris and Frankie Vaughan's widow, Stella. I remember her telling us how she laughingly begged her husband to have an affair with his co-star when he made his American film debut in *Let's Make Love*. It was, of course, the headline 'Frankie Goes To Hollywood' (to star alongside Marilyn Monroe) which inspired another bunch of lippy Scousers.

That lunch was made even weirder by two special guests: in what must have been one of his last-ever public appearances, the distinguished figure of Sir John Mills made his solitary way to the podium, where, from memory he told an off-colour joke which had little to do with the late Beatle. Then exited alone. The other guest was Jean-Claude Van Damme; who arrived surrounded by a phalanx of bodyguards; I am still trying to figure his connection with John.

The shock was total, and global, except in Lennon's hometown. Bob Wooler christened the ghoulish flock as "death watch Beatles". Playwright Alan Bleasdale was in a Liverpool pub soon after and overheard a pensioner saying, "If there's all this fuss about John Lennon, imagine when Ken Dodd goes!"

It was John Lennon's murder in December 1980 which finally, of course, marked The End Of The Beatles. After this, there was no going back. Except Lennon's pointless murder did not mark the end of the Beatles. You could argue rather that it signalled a new beginning.

*

Of them all, it had been George who was keenest to shed that ex-Beatle tag, like a rattlesnake sheds its skin. Financially though, his old band were his nest egg. Like a benevolent bank, the Beatles were the account George could always draw upon when the going got tough.

Following his death in 2001, much was made of the contradictions in George Harrison's life: the spiritualist who loved Formula 1 racing; the mystic who famously fought the Inland Revenue over every pre- and post-decimal penny; the deep thinker who bankrolled Monty Python… There was a definite dichotomy: the breadhead Beatle, the one who wanted to find out where the money was going, the one who wrote the songs moaning about the amount of income tax he paid. The air-polluting, carbon-damaging motor-racing fan who was never happier, like George Orwell, than when gardening – George dedicated his *I Me Mine* book "To All Gardeners Everywhere". But equally, this was a man allied to spiritual questing, a seeker of religious truths, who held his heartfelt values to the end of his days.

Recording in 1974, George's old friend Klaus Voormann confirmed those imbalances, as he later told Graeme Thomson: "George would go from good to bad… With *Living in the Material World* you had the feeling that now he is very religious, he's meditating and getting up at five in the morning. Then suddenly he goes out and starts doing a lot of coke".

George always seemed to have a chip on his shoulder, beginning with his schooldays and the time he felt he wasted there. He always mistrusted authority. He would have *loathed* National Service if called upon. I loved his only son Dhani's comment when he joined his school's Combined Cadet Force: "it was the only way I could rebel. Marching round in an air force uniform *really* pissed him off!"

It was George who was keenest to shuck the Beatle mantle, investing more energy and effort into his Friar Park property than he did his music. "I'm not really a career person, I'm a gardener basically". My friend James Morrison bumped into George at a party once, and rather than bore him with Fab questions just asked him "How's the garden?" The two then spent a very pleasant afternoon.

In 2008, George's widow Olivia put together a garden in his memory at the Chelsea Flower Show. Designed by Neil Innes' wife Yvonne, the garden told the story of George's life in four stages. The *Radio Times* feature was headlined 'My Sweet Lawn'. In 2021, to commemorate the, belated, 50th anniversary of *All Things Must Pass*, Ruth Davis created a pop-up garden in Chelsea based on the original album cover, including gnomes.

1974 had not been a great year for ex-Beatles. For one of the very few times, a solo single by a Beatle failed to crack the UK Top 30; George's 'Ding Dong' stalled at a lowly 38, while John's US No.1 'Whatever Gets You Thru the Night' only managed an equally dispiriting 36. (Paul excelled with the two key tracks from *Band on the Run* – the title track and 'Jet', both Top 10.)

It was also in 1974 that George undertook his ill-considered tour of America. The anticipation of the first solo tour of the States by a Beatle was unprecedented. But it was a near-catastrophe: doped-up rock fans sat through the opening act of Ravi Shankar's classical Indian music, which offered little opportunity to boogie. Regularly doing coke and smoking Gitanes meant Harrison's voice was shot. While his decision to include only a few Fab songs (including the flimsy 'For You Blue') further alienated the audience.

During the 1980s, George was better known as a film producer than musician, while gardening took precedence over recording. Though in 1988 he did find solace and a return to skiffle with the cosy alliance of the Traveling Wilburys. George's fondness for George Formby had always been evident, though there were worrying rumours that he passed that on enthusiasm to Bob Dylan when they were Wilburying together.

When I spoke to him in 2003, Paul reminisced about playing 'Something' in memoriam to George. He remembered George talking about the composition of perhaps his most famous song, like McCartney and 'Yesterday', Harrison was convinced that 'Something' must have existed in the ether before he wrote it. In concert, Paul would famously perform 'Something' on the ukulele George had given him, the one he called 'The Gibson'. "I mean, I *liked* George Formby, but George was fanatical about him, he was even in the George Formby Fan Club! Once he got good on the uke, he learned all Formby's songs. George was nice like that – he knew *all* the Dylan songs; he knew all the Monty Python sketches. If George liked something, he *really* liked it, and learned it all".

In the aftermath of the Beatle breakup, it was Paul who persevered. He put up with the derision poured on Wings as he steered them to enviable commercial success. For the remaining three, it was galling that he – by digging his heels in, thereby fomenting the Beatles split – had also been proved right about Allen Klein. By 1973, Harrison, Lennon and Starr chose not to renew their contract with their feisty American manager.

Coupled with his correct intuition concerning Klein, it was Paul who came up with a back catalogue, solo and with Wings, which gave him those fortuitous 'two bites of the cherry'. He assured me when we spoke in 2001 that there hadn't been an elaborate master plan ("I didn't want to do a Blind Faith type of supergroup… Paul and Linda would have been a duo. I don't think that would have been good, a bit too Nina & Frederick – which is not an act I was ever big on"). His decision to include his wife in his new band was widely condemned.

The couple's first 'tour' with Wings was one of ad-hoc guerrilla appearances during February 1972. That was what Paul had envisaged as a way the Beatles could return to their roots. He told me the itinerary was entirely spontaneous – the band stood outside his London home, roadie on bus, coin tossed up to go North or South… so Nottingham it was.

McCartney remains a fascinating figure; in hindsight, his contribution to the Beatles has been overshadowed by the Lennon legacy. And post-Beatles, there is that dichotomy: the composer, keen to sail far, far out on the HMS Avant Garde, who released a cover of the theme from *Crossroads*. A man simultaneously remixing with Nithin Sawney, while working on an album of rock & roll covers; happy to try his hand at classical symphonies while recording songs from the pre-rock & roll era.

When he fell he fell big – few have any fondness for 'Ebony & Ivory', and I stand by my review of the time: "The bland leading the blind".

By 1979, Paul was enshrined as the most successful composer and recording artist of all time. In 2002, for his appearance at the Las Vegas Grand, he was paid $4,000,000, which was estimated as £500 per *second*! He is one of the few who could play *Monopoly* with Bill Gates for real money. His status is assured. His financial future secure. His musical legacy unassailable. Yet he remains restless.

Even a cursory glance at his back catalogue might give him pause for thought at his unparalleled post-1970 success. Yet every year or so, McCartney will grit his teeth and re-enter knowing the marketplace. He *knows* that every review of new 'product' will, inevitably, be unfavourably compared to his work over half a century before. Paul could no more escape the shadow of the Beatles than their most ardent fan. As he nears his end, Paul McCartney became a Beatle fan.

*

By the mid-70s, we had begun to realise that the icons of the 60s were only human. Back then, the likes of Dylan and the Beatles appeared wise beyond their years, we (I) really thought they had all the answers. So much was *invested* in them. J.D. Salinger had discovered it 20 years before, when *Catcher in the Rye* became the handbook for every misunderstood teenager. Tired of the attention, Salinger withdrew from the public eye for the rest of his life. Which of course meant that *he* became the story. Like the fictional cult writer, Terence ("he hung out with The Beatles") Mann, snapping at his followers in *Field of Dreams*: "I want them to stop looking to me for answers, begging me to speak again, write again, be a leader. I want them to start thinking for themselves…"). Or Graham Chapman's advice in *Life of Brian*: "Look, you don't need to follow me. You don't need to follow anybody. You've got to think for yourselves. You're all individuals". "Yes! We're all individuals".

On a similar canvas, we turned to rock stars in interview and on concert platforms. Typical was Greil Marcus: "'This is *it*", my editor Marvin Garson said in the spring of 1969, as he sent me off to cover the Band's national debut in San Francisco. "This is when we find out if there are still open spaces out there". Or Paul Simon, on the 1974 LP of his debut solo tour, after a spellbinding run through S&G and solo work, a voice from the audience pleads, "Say a few words…" As if the author of 'The Boxer' or the calming 'Bridge over Troubled Water' could supply the *answer*. Or Ralph J. Gleason's half page in *Rolling Stone* on Dylan's *New Morning* under the headline 'We've Got Dylan Back Again!' He writes of the anxiety of the Nixon Presidency, Timothy Leary's bust, Kent State, the Middle East conflict… "the most reassuring thing in this year of bombings… It's all there. All that ever was and all we'd hoped for… He's coming out again. Come on Bob! We need you. That's the truth, man we really do. Come out, Bob, come out!"

In fact, they were, like us, groping around for answers to the same baffling questions. They just did it with a higher income, more talent and better clothes.

Incredibly, given the Beatles' phenomenal success in America during the 1960s, and despite an unparalleled run of No.1 LPs, the first album to ever *enter* the American albums chart at No.1 was Elton John's 1975 *Captain Fantastic & The Brown Dirt Cowboy*. Avowed Beatle fan Elton was the biggest solo act of the decade, at one point, 2% of *all* records sold in the world were by Elton John. And of course, it was onstage alongside The Artist Formerly Known As Reginald Dwight that John Lennon made his final stage appearance.

Prior to the birth of his second son, Lennon was curious as to the competition – he worked with David Bowie on 1975's *Young Americans*, the title track of which quoted from 'A Day tn the Life'. Lennon identified Glam Rock simply as "rock & roll with lipstick on". *Young Americans* also included Bowie's take on 'Across the Universe'. Bowie remembered Lennon's songwriting advice at the session: "Look, it's very simple: say what you mean, make it rhyme and put a backbeat to it".

Quite often at the time, the Beatles were frequently remembered in song – on Chicago's debut LP, the band's 'South California Purples' cited 'I Am the Walrus'. Kevin Ayers' 'Song for Insane Times' (on *Joy of a Toy*) "and everyone sang a chorus of I Am the Walrus". The *Hair* soundtrack mentioned "George Harrison of the Beatles" on the wistful 'Frank Mills'. The song was inspired by a 1966 letter in *Rave* magazine's 'Boys & Girls, Lost & Found' section. Rather sweetly, in the days before texting, email and WhatsApp, Helen Dodge of Vancouver was looking for a boy she saw at a Rolling Stones concert who "resembles George Harrison. My friend and I are the girls he waved at".

'Day Tripper' was referenced by Roxy Music on 'Re-Make, Re-Model', and 40 years later by the Stone Roses on 'Fool's Gold'. Other random namechecks or song title references take in the Who ('The Seeker'), Pink Floyd ('Let There Be More Light'), Peter, Paul & Mary ('I Dig Rock & Roll Music), Electric Light Orchestra ('Shangri La'), the Clash ('Julie's Been Working for the Drug Squad'; 'London Calling'), John Fogerty ('I Saw It on TV'), Billy Joel ('We Didn't Start the Fire'), Paul Simon ('The Late, Great Johnny Ace')… Plus Cheap Trick, Merle Haggard, Shania Twain, Dream Academy… Mott the Hoople's breakthrough courtesy of David Bowie on 'All the Young Dudes'. Later there was little doubt who Ian Hunter had in mind when he sang in 'All the Way from Memphis' about the journey from "the Liverpool docks to the Hollywood Bowl". Perhaps the ultimate tribute came with Barclay James Harvest's 1975 'Titles', all lyrics compiled from ten Beatle songs.

One imaginative compression was Nilsson's 1967 'You Can't Do That', which incorporated a handful of Fab song titles, which led to John and Paul naming their favourite

American *group* as Nilsson. Lindisfarne's Alan Hull wrote a touching '100 Miles from Liverpool', while John Tams' eloquent 'Written in the Book' from 2019's *The Reckoning* reasoned "Lennon and McCartney have a lot to answer for".

In theory there was enough exciting new music during the 1970s to stop you getting too nostalgic. But away from the charts, and in other areas, the group bubbled beneath the surface.

The Beatles were soon infiltrating fiction; they provided the only way Peter Miller could afford his Jaguar XK150S in Frederick Forsyth's *The Odessa File* (1974): "Normally he never read the gossip about pop stars… but the three faces rang a bell in his filing cabinet of a memory". The investigative journalist had been researching a feature about the Saint Pauli Gang in 1961 and met a contact in the Star Club. Later, the proceeds from his 'How Hamburg Discovered the Beatles' story bought him his dream motor. And Robert Harris' alt-History *Fatherland* (1992) imagined a Nazi Germany in 1964, If Hitler Had Won. Early on, Harris cites a piece by a Nazi music critic attacking the "pernicious, Negroid wailings of a group of young Englishmen from Liverpool, playing to packed audiences of German youth in Hamburg." R.J. Ellory's *Three Bullets* (2019) was an intriguing 'What If…' Kennedy had survived Dallas and was due to address the 1964 Democratic National Convention at the Boardwalk Hall in Atlantic City. JFK's security detail discuss the venue: "'The week after, we're done, The Beatles will be playing there". "The who?" "The Beatles, it's an English pop group." Sorensen shrugged, none the wiser.'"

Stephen King let slip the number of his books which included Beatle song references (14 since you ask). No prizes for where Haruki Murakami got the title of his 1987 novel *Norwegian Wood* from.

Professionally, I became jealous when I discovered that it is estimated that somewhere in the world, somebody buys a Lee Child novel every nine *seconds*. I thought I'd find out why, and after reading *Killing Floor* (1999) I could see why. What I was unprepared for was Jack Reacher's methodology; knowing the suspect was a Beatles fan, Reacher alights on a 'Paul Lennon', 'Paul Harrison', 'Paul Starr'… And just when you thought there couldn't be any more – Josh Pachter edited a collection in 2023, *Happiness Is a Warm Gun: Crime Fiction Inspired by the Songs of The Beatles*.

Going even further back, 'Lucy' was the name given to the missing link, discovered in Ethiopia in 1974. The fossil skeleton was over three *million* years old. The find revealed that this primate walked on two legs, thus becoming the ancestor "from whom we are all descended". She was thus named because geneticist Donald Johanson who discovered her had 'Lucy in the Sky with Diamonds' playing on his Walkman.

Willy Russell's *John, Paul, George, Ringo and Bert* opened at the Liverpool Everyman in May 1974. The premise was what every visitor to Liverpool finds: that 'Bert' was every cab driver, barman, doorman, retailer and pub drunk who "coulda bin in de Beatles". The play's stellar cast included Bernard Hill, Trevor Eve and Anthony Sher. Rather than attempting to replicate Beatle music, the songs were sung solo by Barbara Dickson.

An American production of *Beatlemania* opened on Broadway in 1977, with sound-alikes playing the Fab Four. It was put together by the managers of Aerosmith and Ted Nugent, with Beatles music playing against "a panorama of changing forces within American society".

It opened in the UK in 1979, which is where the line-up of the Bootleg Beatles[21] first met. Intriguingly, in an injunction from Apple to the show's producers, John Lennon was quoted as saying, "I and the three other Beatles have plans to stage a reunion concert". The suit was settled in Apple's favour in 1986. Not everything 'Beatle' had the Midas Touch – *With a Little Help from My Friends* (1981) featured a troupe singing Beatle songs, but ran for only eight days in London.

In 2016 I went to the Churchill Theatre in Bromley to watch *Let It Be: A Celebration of the Music of The Beatles*. What struck me was how many young, I mean *really* young people, were in the audience. The show was a game of two halves – note-perfect replicas of Beatle songs grew tiresome (and I think their Paul was right-handed). But there was an eerie moment when 'John' came onstage in his *Sgt Pepper* costume and sat down at a piano and began to play 'A Day in the Life'. It was… spine-tingling.

A recent estimate had over a thousand Beatle tribute bands doing business around the globe. In their homeland, there are believed to be 22 Beatle tribute bands – in Northampton alone! While Paisley has to struggle along with only six. Ohio Express, if remembered at all, is for their bubblegum 'Yummy Yummy Yummy' hit. Realising it would not be long before the bubble (gum) burst, in later years they rebranded themselves as tribute band Hard Day's Night.

There they are, in all their Fab grinning glory – the Caverners, the Liverpool 4, Fab Forever, Rain, the Magical Mystery Four, the Beattles, the Beat Tells, Japan's the Mendips, Poland's the Bootels, France's Choking Smokers, Finland's Cellophane Flowers, Norway's Det Betales. South Korea's 'Rutle Seoul' covered both options. And the one I particularly like the sound of – The Fab Faux… They run the gamut from those inimitable Dougie Millings' suits to full psychedelic majesty.

Of them all, the Dutch band the Analogues take the biscuit. Playing the six LPs the Beatles never performed live. I witnessed them in action at a sold-out Philharmonic Hall in Liverpool. They are not the most visually … arresting group. One looks like Graham Nash, others reminded me of the Wagner Group of mercenaries. But close your eyes… You know after reading Mark Lewisohn's *Beatles at Abbey Road* book just what the instrumentation was on those records. But there is something *seeing* those instruments played in order to so successfully replicate that sound. They are particularly effective when the four-man brass section and quartet of string players augment the line-up.

They give a new meaning to 'verisimilitude'. And if there are occasions you think, maybe I should have stayed home with the Blu-Ray and a bottle of Malbec. In the end, boy did they carry that weight a long time.

All over that 2023 Beatle Weekend were … the Beatles. So let me introduce you to… Chile's the Batles… Sweden's the Bertles… Indonesia's G-Pluck… Japan's the Hips (watch out, guys, they're girls!)… Colombia's Nowhere Boys… Brazil's Rubber Soul…

Could you put a cigarette paper between 'tribute' ("act, statement or gift intended to show gratitude, respect or admiration") or 'impersonate' (to intentionally copy another

21 Celebrating their 40th anniversary the tribute band have been together four times longer than the Beatles. They met George Harrison at David Gilmour's 50th birthday party. After hearing them play he joked, "You probably know the chords better than I do".

person's characteristics such as behaviour, speech, appearance...")?

While it is very boring for anyone who did not live through the 1960s to be bored, yet again, about how great it all was, you have to appreciate the very nature of the times. New releases by the Who, the Kinks, Pink Floyd, Jimi Hendrix and the Stones, each seeming to up the ante. The very fabric of society shifting, and every new LP by Dylan, the Beatles, was like the Tablets Moses brought down from Mount Sinai. Little can match that excitement or anticipation today.

Only, perhaps, one thing: talking to my young friend Thomas Dylan Brooke he questioned that opinion. When he and his sister Eleanor were growing up, he argued that the announcement and arrival of the new Harry Potter title could match that anticipation of a new Beatle LP. Indeed, for the launch of the fifth title in the series – *Harry Potter & The Order of the Phoenix* – only the Royal Albert Hall was considered a suitable venue for the event. One June evening in 2003, 5,000 excited HP fans crammed the venue to greet J.K. Rowling at the event which *The Guardian* described as "close to Beatlemania".

Like Tom and Eleanor, their step-sister Laura grew up on the Beatles; her favourite Beatle was Ringo. It was a disillusioning experience, her father remembers every Laura inquiry: "Was *that* a Ringo song?" being batted into the long grass.

As well as their music beaming out across the universe, the world of Beatle podcasts soon grew. I can't write while listening to the spoken word, so it's a closed book to me. But of the ones I did monitor I was intrigued by *Nothing Is Real*. Put together by Steven Cockcroft and Jason Carty, I was struck by Jason's comment, "For people like me who weren't born when it all happened, it's difficult to believe it happened at all".

Of course, the 60s were not all bright clothes and great music. The decade was balanced by tragedy and conflict (Aberfan, thalidomide, the Moors Murders, the Sharpeville massacre, Ronan Point, Biafra, the Czech revolution crushed, My Lai...). But the Polaroid version is of colourful personalities, living their hedonistic lives to the extreme. And there was little doubt who provided the soundtrack to that most tumultuous of decades...

Few should doubt just how grim the early 70s were in the UK compared to the previous 'swinging' decade. The trade unions exerted enormous power, their endless strikes leading to a head-on collision with Edward Heath's government in early 1974, which saw the introduction of the three-day week... We were advised to brush our teeth in the dark. Television broadcasting was rationed and broadcasting ceased at 10.30 p.m. The pubs were lit by Dickensian candles. There were the queues for petrol as the Middle East tightened its stranglehold on oil production. Aircraft hijackings were frequent. The Six Day War further increased the gulf between Israeli and Arab. Home-grown terrorism came in the virulent and violent shape of the IRA, as it intensified its bombing campaign on the mainland: in 1974, IRA bombs ripped apart two pubs in Birmingham, killing 21 civilians. By the mid-70s, the IRA had targeted the Tower of London, the Old Bailey, Euston station, Harrods, Mayfair and Westminster restaurants... During 1974 and 1975, the capital averaged one shooting or IRA bombing every week. Aldershot, Bristol, Coventry, Guildford and Manchester all witnessed IRA bombs. But not Liverpool, never Liverpool, not with England's largest Irish population.

As if to mirror the escapist fodder Hollywood provided to escape the misery of the Great Depression, by the mid-70s, rock & roll had got bloated, self-indulgent, out of touch and escapist. Pink Floyd, Yes, Emerson, Lake & Palmer and Led Zeppelin were playing cavernous halls. Triple albums of unimaginable tedium were filling the shelves. Teenybop acts like T. Rex, Slade and Mud were fun, but not to be taken seriously by serious-minded 'heads'. David Bowie was changing direction as often as his socks. What had once been challenging and confrontational, chippy and rebellious, was now as cosy and threatening as Val Doonican. Disco was despised and dismissed by the head-bobbing, LP-buying fraternity.

There was a clear and snobbish distinction between chart music and underground acts. Neither the Floyd nor Zeppelin would sanction UK single releases. Neither courted popularity with the weekly music press. Radio 1, 'The Nation's Favourite', concentrated on daytime, chart-friendly output. An early evening hour was granted to *Sounds of the 70s* for LP tracks to be heard, while John Peel sailed stalwartly on leading up to midnight. Television audiences divided their loyalty between the Top 30-friendly *Top of the Pops*, while their sniffy peers would stay up later for *The Old Grey Whistle Test*.

New Musical Express ran Mick Farren's infamous 'The Titanic Sails at Dawn' feature in 1976 (the headline was from Dylan's 'Desolation Row'). Farren was bemoaning the current state of music, the aloofness of the acts, the increasing distance between the bands and their audiences.

It was soon followed by its notorious 'Hip Young Gunslingers Wanted' advert, which recruited the game-changing Tony Parsons and Julie Burchill as *NME* staff writers.[22] Pub rock was keeping the breweries happy, fuelled by small-scale acts such as Brinsley Schwarz, Kilburn & the High Roads and Ducks De Luxe. Punk was on the horizon. But in the meantime, nostalgia was the future…

In cinemas, George Lucas' *American Graffiti* ("Where were you in '62?") and Ray Connolly's *That'll Be the Day* (both released in 1973) looked fondly back. Richard O'Brien's *Rocky Horror Show* celebrated 1950s sci-fi with its camp rock & roll retro. David Bowie, Bryan Ferry and John Lennon all released LPs in the mid-70s which lovingly recalled their earlier influences. The Flaming Groovies began a loving look back to the 60s. One of the era's most memorable singles, Don McLean's 'American Pie' was an enigmatic eight-minute wallow in rock & roll nostalgia.

For years, the music press always found plenty of 'new Beatles' to write about – Badfinger were an obvious example. A quartet signed to Apple by longtime Beatle insider Mal Evans, with their biggest hit donated by Paul McCartney. Followed by, oh, other 1970s acolytes such as Pilot, Cockney Rebel, the Knack, Scarlet Party… The nearest to post-*Pepper* Fabs came with the original Jeff Lynne/Roy Wood incarnation of the Electric Light Orchestra. Bless him, Nick Lowe always saw Rockpile as "The Beatles going backwards". They would begin with four solo albums, *then* make a group LP…

With pop in the doldrums; with the big acts only reluctantly breaking cover once a year, the inkies were waiting for The Next Big Thing. When the music weeklies ran out of 'new Beatles' to write about, the Best Album Ever Made polls became a feature. A 1974 *NME* Poll for the All-Time Greatest LP had *Sgt Pepper* comfortably at No.1. By 1993

---

22 At 24 I too became a freelance Hip Young Gunslinger, though concentrating more on Steeleye Span and Lonnie Donegan than the Sniveling Shits or the Members.

the magazine's poll found it lodging at 33, its place at the toppermost of the poppermost usurped by *Pet Sounds*. Small consolation that *Revolver* was No.2.

Throughout the 1970s, *Sgt Pepper* was routinely voted No.1. But things changed during the 1980s and 90s with the launch of monthly magazines like *Q*, *Vox* and *Mojo*, all of which celebrated rock history's movers and shakers, rather than the weeklies' sneering dismissal of them as "dinosaurs". In August 1995, *Mojo* polled its writers, and, gasp, horror shock! – *Sgt Pepper* not greatest album ever made sensation! It wasn't even on the Top 50. This was a poll topped by *Pet Sounds*, *Astral Weeks* and *Revolver*. In September 1998, Colin Larkin's *All Time Top 1000 Albums* again had *Revolver* at the top, with *Sgt Pepper* No.2. Regularly for a while, *Revolver* was edging its successor out of pole (poll) position.

Over the years, there began an abiding obsession in just *how* the Beatles did it. It was a question regularly tackled by the rock monthlies. Their editors appreciated that a Beatle cover would generate higher sales. The CD revolution allowed you the nearest opportunity to being there. With the EMI archives opened up, writers were able, after two decades, to fill in the gaps. This led to the publication, in 1994, of the late Ian MacDonald's *Revolution in the Head*. The author's detailed dissection of the Beatles' entire recording oeuvre was showered with praise, and undeniably helped further enhance their status. When he was good, MacDonald was on the money, describing 'Love Me Do' as "the first faint chime of a revolutionary bell, [it] represented far more than the sum of its simple parts. A new spirit was abroad: artless yet unabashed – and awed by nothing". But 75-odd pages on a Sixties Chronology struck me as redundant. Did it affect the group that, during the recording of *Revolver*, Ian Brady and Myra Hindley were arrested for the Moors Murders? Or that while they were filming *Magical Mystery Tour*, Sweden switched to driving on the right?

I always felt McDonald's book ran a pale second to Mark Lewisohn's *The Complete Beatles Recording Sessions* (1988). This was rock music's DNA, its Double Helix. On the recording of 'I Want to Tell You', for example: "five takes of the rhythm track (piano, drums, guitars) were taped before George chose the third as being best, and went back to overdub his lead vocal. More instruments – tambourine, maracas and more piano – were also added. A tape-to-tape reduction copy was then made… Handclaps were added to this and the song was complete except for a final overdub on 3 June. A quick recording".

The book was, with Apple and EMI's full cooperation, the first ever volume to chronicle and annotate just what they accomplished, and more importantly, *how* they did it. There was no room for speculation (none of that "John's reference to chapatti in 'What's The New Mary Jane' is believed to be…") the diligent Lewisohn simply dealt with "Just the facts, ma'am". Because he was one of the very few to listen to everything, from Take 1 of 'Besame Mucho' to the final mixing session to complete *Abbey Road*, Mark's book remains the firm foundation on which every subsequent Beatles book has been built.

Frustratingly this definitive volume remains out of print.

*

Prior to 1973, there had only been one Beatles *Greatest Hits* package. Panicking at the prospect of a Christmas without a new LP in 1966, Brian Epstein persuaded Parlophone to push out *A Collection of Beatles Oldies ... But Goldies*. It had filled a gap in the market, but it was like leaving *Lawrence of Arabia* after the Intermission. Nothing, obviously, post-*Revolver* could be included. They hadn't sailed those seven seas yet.

However, it was the 1973 *Red* and *Blue* double albums which ticked a lot of boxes. Three years on from their last LP, here was the first opportunity to fully reflect on what the Beatles had achieved, here was their legacy. For those that missed it first time round, this was their introduction to that El Dorado of popular music – familiar singles placed alongside key LP tracks to paint the fullest picture to date.

The releases meant there was no need to seek out favourites from much-loved, battered LPs, EPs and 45s scratched at 60s parties, or mislaid in flat moves. And for newcomers, the *Red* and *Blue* albums were a crucial and eye-opening opportunity to appreciate just what all the fuss had been about. For those too young to appreciate the hysterical 60s, here was their first introduction to the phenomenon.

When the contract with EMI lapsed in 1976, the floodgates opened – the albums *Magical Mystery Tour*, *Hey Jude*, *Rock & Roll Music*, *Love Songs*, *The Beatles Ballads*, a 'Movie Medley' single. For the first time, a Beatles LP – *Rock & Roll* – appeared on EMI's budget label, Music For Pleasure. In 1979, 'Get Back' was licensed to the EMI subsidiary Harvest for the LP *A Monument to British Rock*. It appeared alongside tracks by Procol Harum, Wizard and Them, and for the only time, found the Beatles sharing a label with Syd Barrett, the Third Ear Band and Shirley Collins.

Years later, when the *Red* and the *Blue* collections were released on CD, even the most diehard Beatle fan might have paused before purchasing. CDs offered up to 80 minutes' worth of playing time, so the *Red* album *could* have made it onto a single CD. Beside, inevitably there was duplication: long-suffering partners might have pointed out, this could well be the *eighth* official copy of, say, 'Let It Be' which had been purchased – the original 1970 single and LP, the 1973 *Blue* Album, the 1976 single re-issue, 1980's *The Beatles Ballads*, 1982's *Beatles 20 Greatest Hits* (US edition), *Reel Music*, 1988's *Past Masters* Volume II. It was definitely, unquestionably time for something new...

In 1988, two albums of *Past Masters* had rounded up non-album singles, B-sides and EP tracks. But it took the onset of compact discs to do the job properly, and even then Apple bided their time. And even *then*, it was not until a new century that the definitive Beatles' Greatest Hits was made available. And even *then*, disputes still raged regarding the exclusion of 'Please Please Me'.

1 was released on 13 November 2000, as *Music Week* reported, "backed by a monstrous £1.5m marketing campaign – the biggest in EMI's history – which should get long-lapsed record buyers back into the shops". The release coincided with the Beatles' finally launching their own website. "You'd have to be a Martian not to know about this album", a label spokesman gloated. By year's end *1* was No.1 in 20 countries with global sales of 13,500,000. It went on to become the biggest-selling UK album of the year, with sales of 1,880,101 copies. In time, it went on to sell 30,000,000 worldwide. Thus, 40 years after they broke up, the 21st-century's best-selling album was by ... the Beatles.

Prescient as ever, Beatle PR Derek Taylor on his sleeve notes to 1964's *Beatles for Sale* speculated that, "The kids of AD2000 will draw from the music much the same sense of well-being and warmth as we do today".

In this ever-changing world in which we live, getting accurate figures is a hard task. Pre-the streaming revolution, I read an estimate that in America alone, the Beatles were responsible for a jaw-dropping 183,000,000 album sales. Worldwide sales of their catalogue were estimated at an even more astonishing one *billion*. That would be 1,000,000,000.

When I asked Ringo if he had any insights into the album's spectacular success he was emphatic: "The music! It's only the music. The success of the *1* album proves that, who'd have believed it? We always sell enough records – but 30 *million*! That was incredible. But that was great you see because it's the *music*. There's no shots of us, there's no little video or anything. It was like: here's the record, do what you like. And it still held up. And that's the one thing I'm really proud of, that the music we made, the songs they wrote at that time, still are as modern, and from the success of *1*, as popular as they were all those years ago".

Its success was very much due to the McCartney half of the partnership, the bulk of the No.1 singles came from the pen of Paul – leaving aside say half a dozen 'eyeball to eyeball' John and Paul collaborations, 12 of the 27 tracks were effectively solo McCartney efforts. "It is an unfortunate fact for people who don't like me", he told me in 2001, "that I wrote the majority of it (*1*). It's not something I want to boast about, until people start having a go at me, then I say, 'Well, wait a minute, you can't like that album and have too much of a go at me, because I'm very much in evidence on that album'."

It is always something which gets his goat – he was the 'soft Beatle', John was 'the hard Beatle'. John was the genius who elevated the group. Paul was the smarmy balladeer. McCartney was the one who sucked up to the press, Lennon was the rebel. Lennon was the psychedelic avatar while McCartney skulked in the Asher family's attic. Those critics were, and remain, wrong.

While it was Lennon's group at the beginning, and many of the best-remembered quotes came from John's lips, from about the time he met Yoko, through to the closing bitter business crises, Lennon's interest in being a Beatle diminished. That was the day job, for Lennon, he felt the creative juices only really flowed in partnership with Yoko. It was McCartney who tried to hold the group together, to steer them forward. They had all felt Brian Epstein's death, and missed his curating their career. Without Brian, it was up to McCartney to carry that weight: *Sgt Pepper*, *Magical Mystery Tour*, *Abbey Road*, *Let It Be* … all primarily Paul constructs. Some flawed projects, perhaps, but fired by his desire to keep the group *going*.

The 2000 compilation album's success led Apple to appeal to "the *1* Generation", those who never knew the Beatles as a working group, who weren't even alive when John was murdered. The decisions for releases, remasters, reissues still lie with the Fab Four – Paul, Ringo, George's widow Olivia and Yoko, with a little help from the loyal Neil Aspinall (1941–2008), who was in house right up until his death.

The Aspinall obituaries were fulsome, pointing out not just Neil's loyalty, but his determination to see the Beatle legacy preserved and not frittered away, like that of Elvis in the aftermath of his death. "He was shrewd, constantly creative, always open to new ideas and fiercely loyal", EMI's Tony Wadsworth remembered. "As a result, this outwardly ordinary man made extraordinary things happen". Neil's memoir would have made a fascinating, fly-on-the-wall account by the real 'fifth Beatle', but such was his devotion to the group, it remained unwritten.

Throughout the 70s there were the solo LPs to review; the sporadic reunion rumours, the anniversaries, the cover versions… As the lawsuits snaked through the courts, the letters pages of the music weeklies (*Melody Maker*, *NME*, *Sounds*, *Disc*, *Record Mirror*) were rueful. Almost as if the squabbles sourly mirrored the disillusionment of the new decade. Typical was Paul Collins from Liverpool writing to *Sounds* in January 1971: "It was sad to see the Beatles squabbling in public… I, for one, was disappointed that they should finally find themselves in conflict over money". Those public squabbles did take some of the sheen off the magic, like the curtain parted and revealing the real *Wizard of Oz*.

I sensed that the public *wanted* Lennon and McCartney to remain together. As, earlier, they had wished eternal happiness on Edward VIII and Mrs Simpson, Don and Phil Everly and Simon & Garfunkel. There is something in a public partnership which can be so … reassuring. As if by staying together it outweighs all the strife, hostility and turmoil swirling around the world. There was such a desire for them, the 'Fab Four', to reunite. So much was still invested in the *group*. It had been their unity which had produced that music. If that camaraderie could be restored, that sense of unity rekindled, one sensed they could re-ignite the passion and pacific beauty of the 60s during that desolate decade, as the 1970s unfolded.

However, back then, I maintain there simply wasn't that *intensity* of interest in the group that we know today. Influential? Sure. Fondly remembered? Absolutely. But there was none of that genuflection. The all-encompassing reverence was on hold. They were not credited with rock's Big Bang. Besides, surely they would get back together? For the Beatles to stay apart was … unthinkable. At that time, even George Martin was honestly missing them – in a 1972 ITV documentary sourced by Keith Badman, the esteemed producer admitted, "I think the four of them are greater than the individuals… because they're all very talented people, but I still don't think they're as great as they were when they were Beatles together".

Part of the reason Martin felt so was that "what kept The Beatles head and shoulders above everyone else", as he told Lesley-Ann Jones, "is that they were prepared to change, do different things. No one record was a carbon copy of another. We never fell into the *Star Wars II* syndrome, remaking something under a different title".

I chanced upon a *Record Mirror* from 1972, with a full colour picture of David Cassidy dominating the front page. Above it was a photo of Lennon next to the headline 'Does Anyone Care Now About The Beatles?'

Throughout the decade, there was a kind of half-hearted speculation: "wonder if they'll ever get back together again?" Fans read of the Lennon and McCartney spats in the music press, wearily watched the tortuous legal spats snake through the law courts. That bitter and prolonged end was still fresh in many people's minds.

Let It Be made its UK TV premiere on 26 December 1975; I remember my friend Peter Hogan saying later in the pub: "As if things weren't bad enough, you get to see the Beatles breaking up on Boxing Day". In fairness to director Michael Lindsay-Hogg when he *began* filming, the Beatles were functioning as a working group; by the time his documentary was released, they had very publicly broken up. His finished 90-minute edit was duty bound to reflect the bitterness he had witnessed.

March 1976 saw a canny campaign by EMI, re-releasing all the Beatles' UK singles at a time when UK single-buying was at a record high. In 1976 alone, five acts (Brotherhood of Man, Abba, Showaddywaddy, David Soul and Julie Covington) released singles, *all* of which each sold a million copies in the UK alone. Five Beatles re-releases made the Top 40; 'Yesterday', never a single in its homeland, scaled the highest, peaking at No.8.

By then though, EMI had dropped the ball with its uninspired packages. The contract Brian Epstein had re-negotiated in 1967 had expired in 1976. Those unsatisfactory compilations proliferated. Such albums were doing little to enhance their posthumous reputation. Incredibly EMI turned down Lennon's offer to do the artwork for their 1976 *Beatles Rock & Roll* compilation. Ringo was incensed with the final cover ("It made us look cheap…").

25 April 1976 is a poignant date, as it was the last time that John and Paul were photographed together. At the time Lennon was mired in his Lost Weekend and had dropped off the radar, while Paul was taking Wings back to the top. When 'Mull of Kintyre' became a surprise UK No.1 in 1977, Fleet Street, as was, dusted down their Beatle files, and found it to be the nation's best-selling single since … 'She Loves You', so that stirred the ashes a bit.

Paul's *Tug of War* album was recorded in Montserrat in 1981 and the album included McCartney's heartfelt tribute to Lennon, 'Here Today'. Carl Perkins was called in as a guest for the LP. The two cut the forgettable 'Get It'. But it was during the sessions, as Carl was about to fly home, that he played McCartney a new song of his, 'My Old Friend', and Paul burst into tears. Baffled, Linda explained to Perkins: "Think about me every now and then, old friend", were the last words John had spoken to Paul in the lobby of the Dakota.[23]

As well as the usual Sid Bernstein reunion offers, and the frequent music press speculation on the group getting back together, in the summer of 1976 promoter Bill Sargent offered the quartet a $50,000,000 guarantee for a one-off closed-circuit Beatles TV concert. *Saturday Night Live* producer Lorne Michaels offered a little less – $3,000 for a four-song slot (but if the others wanted "to pay Ringo less" that was up to them). A week later he was back, NBC had upped the offer to $3,200 *plus* free hotel accommodation ("treated like royalty as pitchers of ice water are hand-delivered… and they can drink the water from *glasses*…")

Paul told me it was one of the last times he saw John and they were watching the programme and *were*, for a moment, tempted, but couldn't be arsed to go down and hail a cab, so they stayed watching the show on television.

In idle moments and quiet news days, the media inevitably tried to stoke up 'Beatles To Reform' stories. Once asked by Tom Doyle about a Beatle reunion, Paul responded: "I think we all just decided we'd done it… What would we do? At various times one of us would get hot on the idea and the big offer would come in, but it was like 'Let sleeping dogs lie'."

"There is a body of work which is very complete", Paul told me in 1991, "it goes from A–Z, why start now ruining it and picking away at it?… We packed our suitcases, got on the train and left".

---

23 I learned this from a *Goldmine* interview Carl Perkins did with Tom Frangione and Ken Michaels.

Any opportunity for a Beatle reunion was raw meat thrown to the lions of Fleet Street and the music weeklies. When a get-together *did* occur it was off the beaten track and far from the front page. While I was freelancing for the Ad Lib column on the *Evening Standard* I wrote a squib about Dave Edmunds. His manager was soon on asking if I'd like to come along and see the ever-reliable Edmunds in action for a TV special?

So, one evening in 1985, Peter Hogan and I made our way to the then- unfashionable Limehouse. We were there to see a recording of a show celebrating the career of Carl Perkins; Edmunds was the band leader, and brought along some compadres, including odd Stray Cats and Eric Clapton.

Dave was soon joined by George Harrison and Ringo Starr. Led by Carl, the supergroup ran through all his songs the Beatles recorded – 'Matchbox', 'Honey Don't', 'Everybody's Trying to Be My Baby'. In the pub afterwards we shook our heads, "That was *half* the Beatles!". It was the first time George and Ringo had shared a public stage since the Bangladesh concert 14 years before.

While the future was signposted by Bowie, Led Zeppelin, Pink Floyd, Yes, Jethro Tull et al, no one act dominated the decade as the Beatles had done the 1960s. Elton John came close, but by 1975, with his last US No.1 LP, it looked like he had peaked. With varying degrees of solo success and only five years apart, a Beatles reunion was looking increasingly unlikely. For the carriers of the flame though, they would keep the fire burning. The first Beatles Convention was held in Boston in July 1974. That autumn, the first Beatlefest was held, so successful it went on an American tour.

A UK Beatle Convention took place in the cavernous Alexandra Palace in December 1976. The hall was near-empty and described by one attendee as "a pretty disastrous event". Highlight was Allan Williams signing copies of his book *The Man Who Gave the Beatles Away*. You'd have to have a heart of stone to not feel a degree of sympathy for Williams. Saira Quli was a friend of his daughter, and remembers taking tea at the Williams' household, drinking from "Allan Williams, the mug who gave the Beatles away!"

From humble beginnings in 1977, the International Beatle Week is now a regular fixture of Liverpool's August Bank Holiday weekend, with up to quarter of a million fans flocking to the city.

"I was talking to the guy who organises those Beatle weekends in Liverpool…" ex-Bonzo and lead Rutle Neil Innes told me. "He puts on 147 live bands from all over the world doing Beatle covers. I mean, there's a trio from Argentina who *only* do Sides 3 and 4 of *The White Album*! I said to him there are two types of Beatle fans, those that are into the merchandising and those that love the music. They obviously get off on the mania, what it is like to be worshipped and adored. Typical Liverpudlian, he said I'd rather have a satsuma in my mouth, a polythene bag over me head and a rope round me neck and risk suffocation than wear a *Sgt Pepper* suit!"

While 1977 is frequently perceived as Year Zero with the onset of Punk, with the Clash snarling "No more Elvis, Beatles or the Rolling Stones…", the Beatles were indeed on the margins. Only the most diehard fan would have appreciated where those seminal punks the Ramones had taken their name.

Recorded 12 years earlier, an archive release eerily coincided with that Punk onslaught: for the first time in seven years, a *new* Beatles LP was released. Coming during the blitzkrieg-bopping year of 1977, *The Beatles Live at the Hollywood Bowl* even got mohawks nodding in approbation at how well it stood up – two guitars, bass and drums with only one song clocking in at over three minutes. All *very* punk.

There had been talk of a live Beatles album right back to the early days as the phenomenon exploded in America. Capitol had a track record with in-concert LPs from the Kingston Trio and Judy Garland, so there were plans for a *Beatles Live at Carnegie Hall* as a US-only release as early as April 1964. The American Federation of Musicians, however, had other ideas. They refused to license an English group recording on American soil. They relented by the time the group returned for their first American tour in August 1964, which is where the 1977 release tapes originated, from Beatles performances at the Los Angeles landmark, the Hollywood Bowl in 1964 and 1965.

In an April 1977 *NME* bulging with the Sex Pistols, Clash, Buzzcocks, Jam and Slaughter & the Dogs, Charles Shaar Murray's review was ecstatic, delighting that its release "proved beyond a shadow of a doubt that the Beatles lost none of their rock & roll balls when they got Epsteinised and went pop… performed with exemplary rock & roll muscle, *The Beatles Live At The Hollywood Bowl* is an album that contains great pop music alongside freshness and timelessness, the familiar combined with a fistful of lovely moments and charm plus guts… If you ever got off on The Beatles, then be prepared to get off on them again".

In his original 1977 sleeve notes, George Martin explained how the recording was put together from "the vintage three track tapes to modern multi-track, remixed, filtered, equalised and generally polished". He added wistfully, "In the multiplatinum, sophisticated world we live in today, it is difficult to appreciate the excitement of The Beatles' breakthrough. My youngest daughter Lucy, now nine years old, once asked me about them. 'You used to record them didn't you Daddy? Were they as great as the Bay City Rollers?' 'Probably not,' I replied'. Some day she will find out".

In 2016, Ron Howard's film *Eight Days a Week* made a strong case for the Beatles as a performing outfit. My problem with the documentary was that it was so… *American*. The narrative was along the lines of, "The Beatles were popular in England, Europe, then they went to America…!!!" In fairness, Howard was a fan (and American). He got a Beatle wig for his 1964 birthday, and a few years later, his English teacher was using Beatles lyrics to teach poetry. As a young actor, Howard remembered advice Henry Fonda had given him, which he felt applied to the Beatles: "If you don't take a career risk every 18 months or two years, you're not really trying, and you're gonna start going backwards".

Apple's Jonathan Clyde revealed that planning for a live Beatles concert film had begun in 2003, so it took 13 years to realise. The guardians of the Beatle legacy, like the mills of God, grind slowly.

It had been in 1977 that NASA sent music into outer space, a 90-minute compilation featuring Bach, Blind Willie Johnson, Louis Armstrong and Chuck Berry.[24] Record

---

24 One of the best-remembered sketches from *Saturday Night Live* had Steve Martin as an announcer saying that in the wake of the Voyager odyssey, they had received the first intelligible words from an alien source in outer space: "Send more Chuck Berry".

compiler Ann Druyan worked on the Voyager Golden record, and remembered that 'Here Comes the Sun' was a strong contender: "All four had responded so enthusiastically about letting us use it. [The publisher] demanded an exorbitant fee. The whole record project cost $18,000 and they were asking $50,000…". In February 2008, to mark the agency's 50th birthday, NASA transmitted 'Across the Universe' to Polaris, the North Star, over 430 light years from Earth.

It wasn't just EMI who were traducing the Beatle name during the 1970s, don't forget 1976's *All This and World War II*. In what universe might a 90-minute cinema documentary of black & white World War II footage played out against a soundtrack of Beatle songs be considered marketable? True, there were some engaging covers – Bryan Ferry's 'She's Leaving Home', Elton John's 'Lucy in the Sky with Diamonds', Rod Stewart's 'Get Back', 'Tina Turner's 'Come Together'… but Keith Moon, Status Quo, Lynsey de Paul, Frankie Laine…?

Then there was the 1978 film of *Sgt Pepper's Lonely Hearts Club Band*. On paper, it was one of those films that could *not* fail. But – spoiler ending – it did. Spectacularly. Director Michael Schultz came off the triumph of 1976's *Car Wash*, the modest film containing one of the best-ever put-down lines, the gay Lindy's: "Honey, I'm more man than you'll ever be, and more woman than you'll ever get".

The Bee Gee-heavy soundtrack to 1977's *Saturday Night Fever* had overtaken *My Fair Lady*, *The Graduate* and *South Pacific* as the best-selling soundtrack ever released. What could go possibly wrong, thought Bee Gees' (but never Beatles) manager Robert Stigwood? ("What we're doing", Stigwood said pre-release, "is enhancing and drawing a dream around these songs", proudly boasting of the film's $12,000,000 budget. The Heartland set alone accounted for $1,000,000).

Hot off *Saturday Night Fever*, here were the Bee Gees, the world's biggest group, and an all-star cast performing songs by the world's best-loved band? How could it fail? Even on paper, the story was … flimsy. Billy Shears' grandson (Peter Frampton, the man behind the world's best-selling *live* album) revived grandpa's group in Heartland to fight off the Future Villain Band (Aerosmith). As well as the Gibb brothers, as well as marking Steve Martin's film debut, the vehicle also found room for a bewildering cast – Earth Wind & Fire, Billy Preston, Alice Cooper, Donald Pleasance, and, no, really missus, Frankie Howerd. Somehow George Martin was inveigled in as Musical Director. Martin appreciated the "mythology of the Beatles". He told *Rolling Stone* prior to the film opening: "if the film is a total flop, my name will be mud. And if it's good, my name will be mud".

"We can't lose. *But we lost!*" Peter Frampton told Bob Mehr many years later. "Robert Stigwood had just come off *Grease*… and so the thinking was we absolutely cannot lose here. But there was no script and no director wanted to touch it… [Michel Shultz] was a very nice man but I don't think he'd ever heard the Beatles before the movie… They said I had an accident so I didn't have to go to the premiere".

On its release, the film was savaged – even the kindly Fred Dellar of *NME* was moved to call it "the most star-studded and inevitably disastrous rock film ever… Totally ill-conceived from start to finish". In his comprehensive overview of rock soundtracks, Martin C. Strong called it "the most derided film of all time and certainly the most critically savaged musical of all time". (Mind, you he hadn't seen *Cats…*).

In *The New York Times*, Janet Maslin's *Sgt Pepper* review was scathing, and prescient: "Is it a film? Is it a record album? Is it a poster, or a t-shirt, or a specially embossed Frisbee? [It] is the ultimate multimedia mishmash, so diversified that it doesn't fully exist in any one medium at all. This isn't a movie, it's a business deal set to music".

As fast as *Saturday Night Fever* LPs had leapt out of the stores, the soundtrack to *Sgt Pepper's Lonely Hearts Club Band* flew back in. Eight million copies of the soundtrack to what *Rolling Stone* called "the worst film of the decade" were shipped out to stores. Five million were returned. The film's spectacular failure effectively finished Stigwood's career. A salient reminder that not *everything* with the Beatles name attached guaranteed success.

Finally, on disc, the Beatles' *Rarities* (1980) delivered – the two German language hits… B-sides… Ringo actually drumming on 'Love Me Do'… a different six-bar ending to 'And I Love Her'… the two seconds of gibberish which conclude the UK version of *Sgt Pepper*… six extra drum beats of 'I Am the Walrus'… the delightfully silly, first-time-on-LP 'You Know My Name (Look Up the Number)'…

Beatle discographer Neville Stannard explained: "Many American releases of Beatle songs differ from British versions in the mixing and stereo separation, which came about due to the original method by which the Americans assembled a Beatles record: the original multi-tracked master tapes recorded in England were sent to Capitol who would then transfer them to the two-track stereo master required for the production of a record almost inevitably achieving a different balance and stereo separation from the British release".

A few years later, we had almost got "the Beatles album that millions have been waiting for". EMI employee John Barrett was suffering from cancer (which claimed him in 1984) and was looking for a project to occupy him while he underwent treatment. The label bigwigs felt that a trawl through the complete sessions the Beatles had undertaken during their recording career might be fruitful.

Barrett soon found out that there were few actual 'unreleased' recordings, the Beatles were very good at deciding what should make the final cut. However, Barrett found that "the possibility of adding any number of 'layers' to a tune was used in full by the Beatles, who composed … 'paintings' in sound like a master painter using a palette of infinite richness". In other words, there were plenty of out-takes of familiar songs to happily fill one good, old-fashioned vinyl LP.

At a record fair, like thousands over the world, I picked up a bootleg copy of what became the *Sessions* LP, the forerunner to *Anthology*. *Sessions* was all set to go. EMI executive Brian Southall provided explanatory sleeve notes: "There remains … only a very limited number of tracks of which after all these years a release could be considered. When the time came for the next album or single, there was an abundance of new material and besides, the group's sound and approach had changed, so a number left over from, say, the *Revolver* sessions was unlikely to be included on the *Sgt Pepper* album".

It was a joy to hear legendary lost tracks like 'What's the New Maryjane' (not quite the lost masterpiece we had been led to believe). Or an early and thoroughly Fab, breezy original take of 'One After 909'… the punishing 'Not Guilty' (one of 101 takes, and then left off *The White Album*)… the lacklustre but historically fascinating version of 'How

THE BEATLES
SESSIONS
15A
16A
17
17A

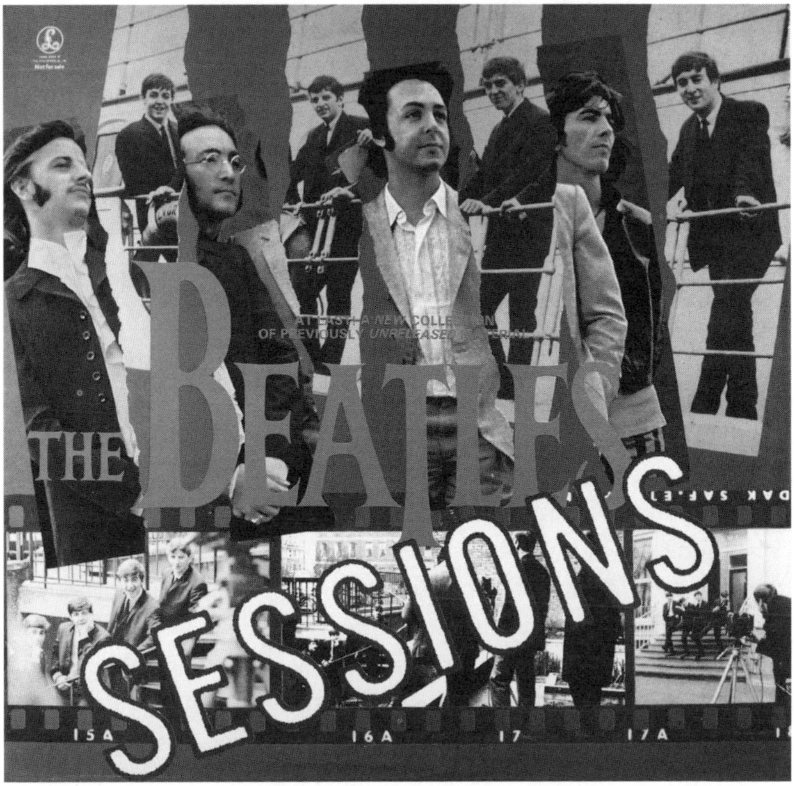

The LP that never was

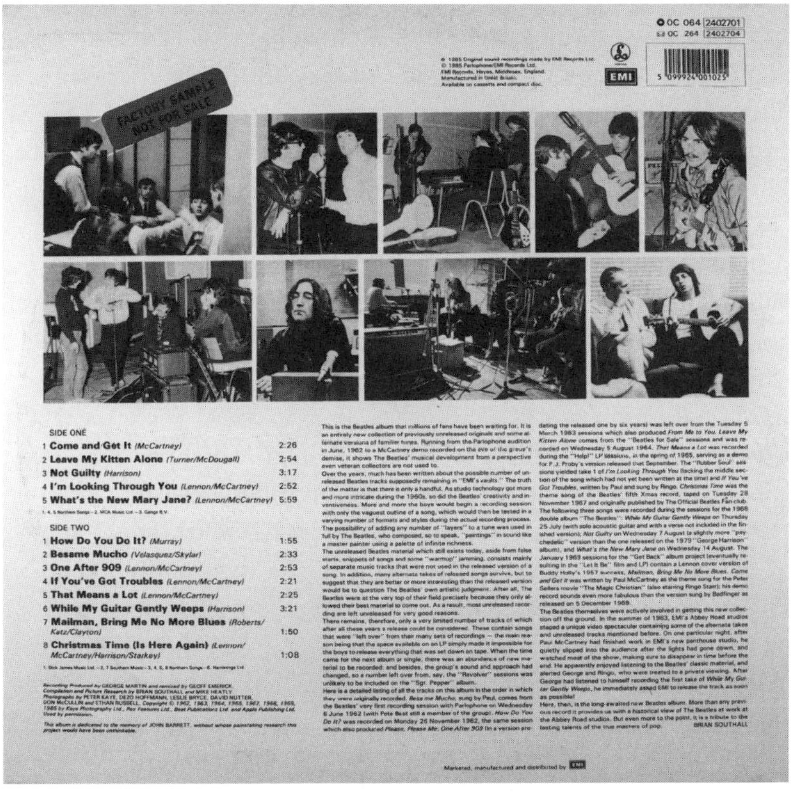

FACTORY SAMPLE
NOT FOR SALE
EMI
SIDE ONE
1 Come and Get It (McCartney) 2:26
2 Leave My Kitten Alone (Turner/McDougall) 2:54
3 Not Guilty (Harrison) 3:17
4 I'm Looking Through You (Lennon/McCartney) 2:52
5 What's the New Mary Jane? (Lennon/McCartney) 5:59
SIDE TWO
1 How Do You Do It? (Murray) 1:55
2 Besame Mucho (Velasquez/Skylar) 2:33
3 One After 909 (Lennon/McCartney) 2:53
4 If You've Got Troubles (Lennon/McCartney) 2:21
5 That Means a Lot (Lennon/McCartney) 2:25
6 While My Guitar Gently Weeps (Harrison) 3:21
7 Mailman, Bring Me No More Blues (Roberts/Katz/Clayton) 1:50
8 Christmas Time (Is Here Again) (Lennon/McCartney/Harrison/Starkey) 1:08
Recording Produced by GEORGE MARTIN and remixed by GEOFF EMERICK.
Compilation and Picture Research by BRIAN SOUTHALL and MIKE HEATLY.
This album is dedicated to the memory of JOHN BARRETT, without whose painstaking research this project would have been unthinkable.
BRIAN SOUTHALL

Do You Do It?'… the alternate 'While My Guitar Gently Weeps'… It was an LP treasure trove, with illuminating recording details and rare photos.

Long before the official archive releases, I spoke to Paul about unreleased Beatle material which might surface: "Outside of 'Three Cool Cats', 'Leave My Kitten Alone', a couple of little things, there is no more. We were quite careful there wasn't much more, we had the spectre of Buddy Holly and the Fireballs, of Jim Reeves" (when posthumous recordings were clumsily overdubbed).

Reasons for the withdrawal of *Sessions* are vague – one theory is that any Beatle release would overwhelm Paul's *Give My Regards to Broad Street* film. So, sadly, *Sessions* just went on to thrive as a bootleg. Having gone through the EMI tapes, the LP did, literally, help open the doors. In 1983 the Abbey Road studios opened up to the public for the first time. *The Beatles at Abbey Road* was a multi-media presentation. It allowed those who'd paid to sit in No.2 studio to hear some of the alternate takes scheduled for *Sessions*. What a joy it was to be *there*; there, where *they* stood and recorded, inside that cavernous hall. With only 135 seats for each show, which ran from July to September 1983, the event nonetheless attracted over 20,000 visitors.

It was a thrill being there. Recording studios are not all cut from the same cloth. Visiting Sun Studios in Memphis, you are struck by its size. It is a tiny shoebox of a place, with 'X' literally marking the spot where Elvis sang and, inadvertently, invented rock & roll. Coincidentally, I had been inside Abbey Road No.2 Studio the week before I visited Sun for a press event. It is a cathedral of a space, intended for orchestra recordings until hijacked by the Beatles. One souvenir remains: the coloured lights the Fabs had installed to give the place a bit more atmosphere. That long staircase to the control room was familiar from photos. Mick Jagger told me his abiding memory of watching the Beatles recording at Abbey Road was sprinting up and down that "bloody staircase".

Recording studios don't have atmosphere. They are factories, they are rooms to record sound, *pristine* sound. So pretty much every studio has the same look: the walls are baffled, a Big Brother window from the control room overlooks your every move, and the room intentionally exudes a dead sound. You are cut off from the outside world. Yet you are in a room where you can create your *own* world.

Of course, Abbey Road has long exercised a mesmeric pull to any band wishing to be 'the new Beatles'. A musician acquaintance pointed out that with all the 21st-century technology available, you didn't *need* the cavernous studios in NW8. So latterly, the huge studio has played host to the large orchestras necessary in fashioning epic film scores – *Alien*, *Raiders of the Lost Ark*, *Lord of the Rings*, among others.

In 2005, the studio hosted the Abbey Road Film Festival, an opportunity to watch the films in the studio where their scores were created. But in his introduction to the festival brochure, Nick Hornby acknowledged what *really* sprang to mind when you mention the recording studio: "Think of Abbey Road and the first thing that comes to mind is… Actually, even the laziest writer in the world could not hope to complete that sentence and get away with it. Just about everyone of a certain age has one – and only one – association with Abbey Road; even the people who live there probably think of two bare feet, a blue sky and a zebra crossing before they think of their own homes, and to try and draw your attention elsewhere is probably a little bit like asking you to discuss the books in the Dallas Book Depository…"

The studio finally got the book it deserved in 2022. David Hepworth's chronology was illuminating, with his trademark wry observations, the fans "come to this particular London pavement, like pilgrims of long ago… to momentarily genuflect and re-enact something which occurred in the same few feet in a few minutes during a lunch hour fifty years earlier… Religions have been based on flimsier foundations". He quotes Noel Gallagher on the magic of Studio 2: "If you're doing strings in that room, it sounds like the Beatles… it stirs the soul like nowhere else. There's something magical about this place. I don't think it's just the canteen".

*

Over the years, the venerable BBC radio had served the Beatles well. Their group appearances had been on the old Light Programme, rebranded as Radio 2 in 1967. It was from those early *Saturday Club* and *Pop Goes the Beatles* shows that millions got to hear the Beatles perform. By the time Radio 1 launched, also in 1967, the group had stopped doing concerts and any performances were shot as promo films for television broadcast. However, with the Beatles nominally still together, interviews with the group were broadcast in 1970 on Radio 1's *Scene & Heard*.

On BBC radio's speech-heavy Home Service (now Radio 4), the creator of *Desert Island Discs*, Roy Plomley had been keen to have all four Beatles marooned, but Brian Epstein declined on their behalf. The group's manager did appear on the programme of 30 November 1964 ('She's a Woman' was his Beatle choice, plus 'All My Loving' by the George Martin Orchestra, his only other 'pop' choice).

I was always baffled by Brian's choice of book, *Elected Time* by Thomas Merton. One critic described it as "the autobiography of a young American Cistercian… [it is] a drama unfolding the working of a divine Providence that makes all things turn to the good of a soul that is being led to its liberty from sin to sanctity, from death to life". Maybe not such an odd choice after all.

Paul McCartney was the guest on the 40th anniversary show of 30 January 1982 (a 50s rock & roll-heavy selection with John's 'Beautiful Boy' as his "if allowed only one choice"). He was followed on 31 July 1982 by George Martin (his Beatle choices were 'Here, There & Everywhere' and 'In My Life').

In 2020, Andrew Gustar, in his research on *Statistics in Historical Musicology*, found that the first Beatles track chosen was 'She Loves You', picked by David Jacobs on 25 May 1964. The most popular non-classical act were, predictably, the Beatles, who had been chosen 296 times on *Desert Island Discs*, with Frank Sinatra (240) and Bing Crosby (166) on their heels. Predictably, 'Yesterday' was the most popular, followed by 'Hey Jude' and, jointly, 'A Day in the Life' and 'Eleanor Rigby'. Unfortunately, the Radio 4 archive does not have a chronicle of more up-to-date figures.

Castaways have washed up some unusual Beatle choices: the venerable, and much-parodied Scots TV reporter Fyfe Robertson chose 'Come Together'… Perhaps in atonement for keeping it off No.1, Engelbert Humperdinck selected 'Penny Lane'… Suave actor Douglas Fairbanks Jr plumped for 'Strawberry Fields Forever'… Director General of the BBC during the 'Day in the Life' crisis, Hugh Greene, chose… 'A Day in the Life'… Incidentally, Dodie Smith, the author of *101 Dalmatians*, was a major Fabs fan. She had been so incensed by the BBC banning 'A Day in the Life', that she kept refusing to appear on *Desert Island Discs*, only relenting in her final years.

Outside of Abbey Road, while in existence as a working band, the one place the group came to life were the sessions they undertook for the all-powerful British Broadcasting Corporation. For music fans, entertainers and performers, the BBC was the main outlet for performing and listening to their favourite music. And for years, those with long memories recalled hearing the Beatles on the network, frequently performing songs which were never recorded elsewhere.

Legend has Ringo being approached by a fan to sign Beatle albums, in the days when he was freer with his signature. Latterly, autographs obtained are by Ringo 'Sotheby's' Starr. One of the titles put forward was a beautiful 9CD release which, when opened up, created a replica of the BBC's Broadcasting House on Portland Place. It was *The Beatles at the BBC*, described as "a visually stunning 12" x 12" package that is aesthetically superior to most box sets you'll find from any major label". "Funny", the drummer is said to have remarked, "I don't remember releasing that one". When it was pointed out it was a bootleg, cue outraged drummer fulminating at Apple, the BBC and EMI… It was that outburst which finally opened the doors for the subsequent 4CDs of official *Beatles at the BBC* releases.

Like the Civil Service, the British Broadcasting Corporation was run on clearly delineated bureaucratic lines, which meant they kept their house in order, thus providing fuel for two *Beatles at the BBC* radio documentaries, which had been broadcast in 1982 and 1988. Together they trawled through the group's 52 sessions for the Corporation. Between March 1962 and June 1965, 88 songs were taped, 36 of which had never been made available on record. These were the songs they were fresh from performing in clubs and cellars, before the roar of the crowd drowned out their voices, and before they had developed real confidence in their own material.

Here, at last, 1994's *The Beatles at the BBC* offered up the missing link between the Cavern and Abbey Road. As you listen it is worth recalling that these performances were recorded in the brief intervals between stints at the recording studio, or in an odd few hours before piling into a van before a gig. They were never intended for posterity, but rather as spontaneous moments snatched from the ether for the immediate delight of their fans, then gone with the wind.

"Perhaps no act can ever again expect such undivided mass attention", Paul Du Noyer wrote later of those sessions. "Media have multiplied and channels proliferated; endless electronic alternatives vie for our time now. But 10 million people would tune in to *Saturday Club*… When everyone was hearing the same thing at the same moment, the situation was uniquely potent".

The group enjoyed their time there, forging a strong bond with former Old Vic actor, presenter Brian Matthew. *Saturday Club* soon established itself as a teenage lifeline when it began broadcasting in October 1958, "Matthew established a special rapport with his audience" wrote Bob Woffinden. "[They] knew that he was providing almost their only opportunity – apart from coffee-bar juke-boxes – to hear contemporary music; to hear it in a refreshing, non-patronising context".

Other familiar engineers and producers were recalled with fondness. Once, being visited in his wilderness years at the Dakota, a friend told John that *Saturday Club* producer Bernie Andrews asked to be remembered. He reported Lennon was genuinely touched: "Oh, does he remember me then?"

Years later, in *Anthology*, Paul was equally nostalgic: "I had a radio by my bed and I would lie there until about eleven. The most delicious lie-ins of your life are those teenage lie-ins: wake up feeling great, turn the radio on and *Saturday Club* is still on for an hour. So we really wanted to be on that, and we knew that it had a huge audience".

The Beatles at the BBC was a mixed bag. Unlike the majority, I have a soft spot for the jaunty 'I'll Be on My Way', the only unreleased Lennon & McCartney original on the set. It fits blissfully into that period of pop innocence of summer 1963, just the right amount of June light and moonlight (although, of course, realistically, every calendar month turns to moonlight)... The release also offered the only official record release of the Beatles performing the unofficial Merseybeat Anthem, the pounding 'Some Other Guy', British Beat in excelsis... For 'The Honeymoon Song', Paul would have been familiar with the film theme after hearing popular Liverpool act Marino Marini & His Quartet performing it. And to the teenage songwriter, rhymes of 'ceiling', 'feelings' and 'reeling' would have seemed the acme of sophistication...

To hear the Beatles tackling Elvis, Buddy and Carl favourites was a joy, offering a tantalising snatch of what audiences in Liverpool and Hamburg would have feasted on... There remained a real charm in hearing the interaction between the group and DJs. 'Crinsk Dee Night', finds the group sanguinely taking the news that they are No.1 in Portugal. For UK listeners, listening again to the group on shows such as *Saturday Club* and specials like *Pop Go the Beatles* was a nostalgic feast. These were the audio equivalent of those serrated-edge, black & white Kodak holiday snaps, just before the world ratcheted up into full-blown colour.

For many *The Beatles at the BBC* was a dream come true, the missing link from their hometown to full-blown global Beatlemania, an opportunity to hear the world's most fabled group hammering through the songs that their Benzedrine beat had kept audiences rocking in Hamburg and Liverpool. Paul Du Noyer made a point of the number of "greasy 12-bar stuff... things they learned to play because it would stop some big bastard lurching on stage to smash a bottle over them".

In truth, once the official excitement wore off, it's not a record you would play in preference to, say, *Rubber Soul*. And in all honesty were their versions of 'I Got a Woman', 'Too Much Monkey Business' or 'To Know Her Is to Love Her' manifestly *better* than versions by their Liverpool contemporaries? What you got was a joyous slab of nostalgia which at best gave you an indication of what you missed on a beery night out at the Star Club or a Cavern lunchtime.

In the UK, demand outstripped supply – "beyond the wildest dreams of EMI", *Music Week* reported – within only four days the set had sold 180,000 copies. Within six months, *The Beatles at the BBC* had sold 5,500,000 worldwide. Thirty-three-year-old Steve Bennett became the first UK purchaser, when he queued for five hours to be the first through the doors of Tower Records' flagship store in Piccadilly Circus at midnight on 1 December 1994. Like the huge Coca Cola sign which used to dominate Piccadilly Circus, or the adjacent London Pavilion, the Beatles too outlasted Tower Records, which closed in 2009.

The release of *On Air: Live at the BBC Volume 2* in 2013 was even less appealing. It was one of the few occasions that Apple dropped the ball. There were fewer rare and unreleased examples. The bulk were reproductions of existing, familiar studio recordings, and only a small handful of genuinely new versions, such as a nice take on Stephen Foster's 'Beautiful Dreamer'. The paucity of 'new' material was reflected in sales – the collection was a UK No.12 and No.7 in America.

*

When it came to the full-on 'Beatle Revival', I believe it was the release of the group's UK LPs on compact disc in 1987 which rebooted interest in the band, and began the renaissance which continues to this day. Following John's murder, fans knew that now nothing actually *new* could be released under the Beatle name! But hearing that familiar music in a new, state-of-the-art format was … tempting.

It offered UK fans the opportunity to relive the glory days – 25 years since 'Love Me Do'; 20 years since *Sgt Pepper*. Then there was the delight in hearing those 12 albums in a bright, new, exciting fashion. Writing in the trade paper *Music Week*, Adam Woods confirmed that, "it took the re-release of the Beatles catalogue to truly christen the compact disc catalogue market".

There was something genuinely exhilarating in hearing those familiar records again. Some critics found fault with the unimaginative packaging and the stereo mixes. These had been mostly undertaken without any Beatle involvement back in the day. For the less demanding there was a real frisson in hearing McCartney's bass thumping out of those shiny silver discs; Ringo's powerhouse drumming, or the little piano fills, and guitar flourishes.

The CD era also saw bootlegging kicked into overdrive. Prior to the *Anthology* releases, Beatle bootlegs were primarily culled from the Decca audition, BBC sessions and the hundreds of hours of *Let It Be* recordings. Instead of the 40 minutes of music which could be accommodated on a vinyl LP, CDs allowed double that space. One anonymous bootlegger came to a Beatlefest with CDs culled from those familiar sources, but pressed on the new-fangled compact disc format. He had apparently approached a US pressing plant saying he worked for EMI and requested 'promo copies'. An observer recalled, "He showed up at a Beatlefest in LA with a rucksack with CDs in it", author Clinton Heylin wrote, "and sold 'em for $100 apiece… To this day I don't know who the kid was. He just walked in and walked out with thousands of dollars".

With the appeal of the Beatles showing no sign of diminishing, the bootleggers too upped their game – take the 5CD + 1 DVD 'Limited Edition' (i.e. bootleg) *Abbey Road* box which could be found at record fairs. Beautifully compiled and illustrated, it was done with a care and attention to detail that the group's official label were forced to take notice of.

Two labels, Swinging Pig and Yellow Dog, hovered up the best of the unreleased material onto 'master tape quality' CDs. The *Ultra Rare Trax* and *Unsurpassed Masters*

SGT. PEPPER ON CD

PARLOPHONE

A new format for a new age

IT WAS 20 YEARS AGO TODAY

S'& PEPPERS
LONELY HEARTS
CLUB BAND

"We're guaranteed to raise a smile"
"Our production will be second to none"

JOIN US IN STUDIO 2
at
ABBEY ROAD
on
1st JUNE 1987 AT 1.00pm

TO CELEBRATE THE WORLD'S MOST FAMOUS ALBUM

SGT. PEPPERS LONELY
HEARTS CLUB BAND

3 ABBEY ROAD, LONDON

R.S.V.P. Terri Anderson
EMI — 20 Manchester Square
01-486 4488

This invitation admits one person
only and that must be the person named
unless otherwise arranged

releases of 1988/89 sent "EMI executives scurrying". By 1992 alone, there were an estimated 1,400 Beatle bootleg ('Beatleg') titles available. *The Hot Wacks* roundup ran to an astonishing 64 pages.

Rolling Stone reported that "The bootleg CD market really began to soar following the 1988 debut of the *Ultra Rare Trax* series, a collection of superb-sounding out-takes and alternate takes by The Beatles". Ringo was quoted later in Jeffrey Ressner's feature: "I always felt that what we put out was what we thought was the best". Diehard fans disagreed, in 2000, a 16CD box appeared culled from the *Let it Be* sessions. In 2006, Nigel Oliver was put on trial following an undercover operation by IFPI in conjunction with Apple. He was arrested in Windsor after trying to sell 504 tapes from the *Let It Be* sessions for £250,000. Even if potential purchasers knew that this was the Beatles below par, there remained something magnetic in anything and everything to do with the group.

The 5CD *Artifacts* bootleg box pushed the envelope further. From sweaty Hamburg cellars to a blissful Indian ashram, from 1958 to 1970, these hundreds of unreleased recordings alerted the surviving Beatles the lengths fans would go to. Bruce Eder wrote in the *All Music Guide*, "One strongly suspects that the existence of this five-CD box … was largely responsible for getting Paul McCartney (and others) to take a serious look at what was in EMI's vaults, resulting in the release of the Beatles' *Anthology* series".

None of the principals were that keen to go back and pick at the Fab scabs: Paul's solo career was progressing nicely, George had Handmade Films and Ringo muddled along. George Martin *did* go back and sniffed, "there were one or two interesting variations, it's all junk. Couldn't possibly release it".

And yet. And yet… The release of the BBC sessions… six *Anthology* CDs, the *Eight Days a Week* live souvenir, plus lavish box sets has undermined the Beatle bootleg market. The bootleg tapes from the live shows were as remarkable for the noise from the audience as the music generated from the stage. Yet there remains a dedicated audience for every crumb scraped from the Fabs' table.

Of course, for the American market, with the 1987 CD releases, here was the opportunity to hear the albums as the group originally recorded them and intended them to be heard. While there were no new tracks, the correct configuration allowed a fresh opportunity to marvel. American writer Rob Sheffield made an interesting point in his engaging memoir: "*Revolver* was one of the 80s most influential releases, up there with *Thriller* and *Legend* and *Straight Outta Compton*, up there with *1999* and *Appetite for Destruction* and the *Big Chill* soundtrack. It might sound strange to call *Revolver* an 80s album, but like *Legend* or the *Big Chill*, it created new ways to access pop history as a living thing. You can trace the whole Britpop explosion in the 90s (see Oasis, Pulp, Blur, Radiohead, the Verve and countless others) to the revisionary experience that went with the 1987 *Revolver* CD".

It is worth pausing and reflecting on that Britpop explosion, which was allied to that Beatle revival. Looking at the period, Dylan Jones found it "remarkable how often you see the word 'Beatlesque'. This could have been referring to anything from 'Penny Lane' style piano clusters, an overuse of cellos, close harmonies, colloquial lyrics, nonsense words, gang-like group photographs, upbeat radio interviews, 1960s-inspired clothes, pop-art graphics, pudding-bowl haircuts, jangly guitars, rudimentary drumming – you could take your pick".

Paul Weller has long testified to the debt he owed to the group, but it took Oasis to pick up the baton. From their original 1994 breakthrough, the lippy Mancs brought a verve and vigour to the flaccid UK music scene. Take That, Right Said Fred and Mr Blobby were hardly setting rock fans' pulses racing. When Oasis swaggered on, bottoms were duly kicked. England swung again – Liam Gallagher and Patsy Kensit were *Vanity Fair* covers stars and Noel Gallagher rocked up to 10 Downing Street. Superlatives were hurled and comparisons made when Oasis played Knebworth in 1996, and an astonishing 4% of the UK population applied for tickets. It was their high watermark, and Oasis imploded following 1997's *Be Here Now*.

For the American market, this was another crucial element of the Beatles releases on compact disc; these were the original LPs reproduced as the group intended. Goodbye *Beatles '65*, *The Early Beatles* and *Yesterday & Today*; hello *Help!*, *Rubber Soul* and *Revolver*. These were the releases that the Beatles sanctioned, not Capitol records.

When the Beatles' American LPs were belatedly released on CD in 2004, it was a disorientating experience for their UK fans. I doubt if few had bothered to buy the original LPs on release, a quick scan would have revealed there were no new tracks. Well, one, a cover of 'Bad Boy, which eventually made its way onto *A Collection of Beatles Oldies*… And reading the track listing was not the same as *listening* to them. So there was that disconcerting element, having 'I Saw Her Standing There' *not* opening the Beatles' debut LP. And the confusing vinyl jambalaya that ensued over the next few years – the cut and paste mish-mash which found their second album diced and sliced on that US debut. And what was 'She Loves You' doing on an LP!! Or, 'I Want to Hold Your Hand' rendered in German!!!

For the American market, the Beatle CDs as nature intended was a point Aaron Milenski picked up on in 2020's *Galactic Ramble* book: "Somewhere in the mid-90s, *Revolver* overtook *Sgt Pepper* as the Beatles (and, thus all of rock'n'roll's) critical favorite. The obvious reason is that when it was finally reissued on CD, American critics listened to it in its full 14-song glory for the first time and its newness excited them in a way the Beatles hadn't in nearly 40 years."

Today, able to stream any recorded music from any era without leaving your at-home computer, you forget just how expensive it was to replace your vinyl LPs with the shiny, indestructible compact discs. My 1988 CD of *Past Masters* purchased from Our Price was 'only' £12.99. The tenth anniversary of the Beatle CD releases in 1997 was marked by an EMI campaign, which saw the CDs reduced from a staggering £16.99 to 'only' £9.99 each. All then proceeded to enter the UK Top 200 charts. *Music Week* Editor Paul Williams wrote: "The Fabs were among the last significant acts to make their recordings available on CD, but when at last they did appear… it was the trigger that persuaded many to ditch the vinyl and tapes and invest in a CD player".

But the real Beatle bonanza lay a few years ahead…

11 February 1994 is another key date in Beatle history – the first time in a quarter of a century that Paul, George and Ringo sat down to record together. When I spoke to Paul around the time of the *Anthology* DVD release, he remembered watching a preview: "We did 'Blue Moon of Kentucky', and there's a very poignant little bit at the end. The three of us after we've done the whole day, just chatting… How do you remember meeting Elvis?

I say, well he was standing up, Ringo says no he never stood up. Nobody could remember anything. But we were sitting by George's lake… and I said, well listen George, thanks very much for having us, it's been a great day. And he said great to have you here – very nice, little family thing. And Ringo says I always love being with you guys! I tell you, it did my head in when I saw it".

With the increasing technical sophistication available, and eastern European factories only too happy to punch out bootleg CDs, EMI and Apple decided to fight back. There was proven to be an insatiable, global audience for Beatle product, and while *Anthology 1* had perhaps failed to capture a wider, younger demographic (those used to digital, 96-track, compact disc technology weren't as excited at hearing a 1958 shellac recording) it left the bulk of Fab fans, like me, in a state of invigorated nostalgic bliss.

On the evening of Monday 20 November 1995, I went out to get a pizza so I could sit down at 8.30 to watch the TV premiere of 'Free As a Bird'. Because it clashed, my wife insisted I record the *Panorama* interview that Martin Bashir had conducted with Princess Diana. I vividly recall grumbling to her as I set the video recorder: "Why? What's the point? She won't be saying anything we haven't heard a million times before…!" Well, close, but no cigar…

The new Beatle single attracted controversy, but with 'Free As a Bird' reuniting the three survivors, I thought Paul had a nice take on it: "We took the attitude that John had gone on holiday saying, 'I finished all the tracks… Sorry I can't make the last session but I leave it to you guys to finish it off'."

The reunion had come about courtesy of the one who had little love of being a Beatle. George had thoroughly enjoyed his spell as a Traveling Wilbury, and he was keen to persevere, even following the death of Roy Orbison. He got permission from the estate of Elvis Presley for the King to 'join' the group, but then dismissed the idea as too gimmicky. Mentioning it to Yoko, she remembered the home demos John had recorded, which led to the first official Beatle single in a quarter of a century.

Frustratingly the reason 'Free As a Bird' denied the Beatles their 18th UK No.1 was that Apple were terrified of bootleggers, so it was only released as a single *after* it appeared on *Anthology 1*. Ironically, it was denied the top slot by Michael Jackson's 'Earth Song', the man who had snatched Northern Songs from Paul McCartney. And in a further irony, the current Oasis single 'Wonderwall' took its title from George's film soundtrack. (The second week of 'Free As a Bird' in the charts saw the song compete with Jimmy Nail's cover of Lennon's 'Love' and the supergroup, Smokin' Mojo Filters' 'Come Together').

Opinion was divided about 'Free As a Bird'. Few would rank it alongside 'Can't Buy Me Love' or 'Penny Lane'. Too many found it more in the style of producer Jeff Lynne's Electric Light Orchestra. It had familiar echoes of the Beatles, it was a good forgery, but when considering the group's history, 'Free As a Bird' merits its footnote more as a curiosity that for its musical merit.

I always felt that to deflect controversy about the reunion which no one dreamed they'd see, or wished had never happened, could it not have been released as a charity single? Proceeds to War Child, Nordoff Robbins or a gun control organisation? Or included as the *last* track on *Anthology* with a note: "Look, we three know that this *isn't* 'The Beatles', but with all the new technology available, we thought you might be interested in how we tackled recording with John again. We like the results. Hope you do too. Love, Paul, George and Ringo"

Fans had a field day sifting for Fab references in that 'Free As a Bird' video. One estimate had director Joe Pytka squeezing in 100 Beatle references (poppy sellers... clean fire engines... 64 on birthday cake... Sir Walter Raleigh... bent back tulips... the clues were there). In fact, there is a case to be made that the video was more memorable than the song it was illustrating.

Anthology itself was denied the UK No.1 by Robson & Jerome, whose eponymous debut shifted 213,000 compared to the Beatles' 125,000 in that crucial first week. Some consolation was that both albums contained a version of 'This Boy' and the Beatle influence was felt elsewhere on the charts that week: *Music Week*'s Alan Jones found cover versions of Lennon & McCartney songs on albums by Michael Jackson, Shirley Bassey, Foster & Allen, Chris De Burgh and James Last.

Critics said that *Anthology* was released because Paul wanted to redress the Beatle balance, to reinforce that he was the driving force behind the band, not the martyred John... Or that George needed an injection of Beatle cash to recoup his losses on Handmade Films... Or with his recording career in the doldrums, Ringo, upset at the booming bootleg industry, wanted to feel some of the financial benefits. Yet, even prior to the *Anthology* release in September 1995, the Beatles – with an estimated income of $130,000,000 – were only behind Oprah Winfrey and Steven Spielberg as showbusiness earners.

Other criticisms were of the tracks selected, but these were largely from hardcore Fab fans, who wanted *everything*, from Take 1 of 'Not Guilty' to Take 101. The majority of the 5,000,000 who bought *Anthology* were delighted to be flies on the wall at Abbey Road. Hearing those oh-so-familiar songs deconstructed and reconstructed. It was enthralling listening to them being taken apart and glued back together. I think Mark Ellen summed up a lot of people's feelings: "There's an awkward period when the out-takes seem disorientating or just plain wrong. It's like coming home and finding the wallpaper's changed or someone's mucked about with the furniture... You know it all, the absent vocals, the missing guitar, the hole where the cymbal crash should be. It's appalling really. What have we done with our lives?"

One tantalising inclusion was that very first Beatle recording, 'In Spite of all the Danger'. It had been long rumoured and unheard since 1958. I asked Paul about it and he told me: "Our first song was modelled on an Elvis song, 'Trying to Get to You', which I heard at scout camp... we went to a place called Phillips – just a little feller with his tape recorder in his back room. It was like the dentist's! You paid £5, and there's your acetate. There were five of us who paid £1 each, and we'd each have it for a week to play to our parents and friends, and John Lowe was the last to have it.

"We went off to get famous, but sometimes I wondered what happened to it. I read in the *Radio Times* recently that the 'proud owner' of the first Beatles single was John Lowe, and I thought hold on a minute we each had a pound of that!" Paul did eventually get the acetate back, although it did cost him a tad more than his original investment of 20/-.

'Real Love', the second 'new' Beatles single was equally unloved outside the diehard fan circle. Controversy raged as BBC Radio 1 refused to play it, but most felt – as someone remarked to me – "it sounds like a track from one of those dodgy Lennon solo albums done by Wings".

As the *Anthology* releases continued, rumours had McCartney unhappy with the sequencing of *Anthology 2*, causing an expensive remake and remodel. George apparently had issues with the second volume too, by all accounts vetoing the inclusion of Paul's avant garde 'Carnival of Light'. Written for an event at the Roundhouse in early 1967, it remains one of the few unreleased Beatle recordings which have yet to be bootlegged. It was not even believed to exist, but McCartney confirmed its existence to Mark Ellen, while Ian MacDonald who heard it wrote of "voices, organ, guitar, tambourine, effects and loops". Mark Lewisohn heard all 13'48" "full of distorted, hypnotic drum and organ sounds… a distorted lead guitar… various indescribable sound effects with heaps of tape echo and tambourine…"

When the 'Threetles' got back together for *Anthology*, I liked the reminiscence found in Judith Durham's autobiography. The Seekers' singer was recording at Abbey Road No.2, and during one of the quieter numbers, drummer Dave Mattacks was convinced he heard 'Lucy in the Sky with Diamonds'. Was the rumour then true? That the studio really *was* haunted by the Beatles? It turned out to be Paul and George working with George Martin on *Anthology*, and the sound from the old echo plates was leaking through the rear wall of the studio.

Watching the *Anthology* DVDs, I always found it rather touching to see the three of them sitting there in the control room with George Martin, like errant pupils hauled up before the beak. Watching silently as the tutor juggled with faders in the control room. Or smiling at George's inability to remember which album 'Carry That Weight' was actually on. There was Martin's sleight of hand, as he delighted in separating the vocal and instrumental tracks, digging down deep. With the four of them able to marvel at what they had achieved there, in that place.

Such unity had not always been evident. Prior to the *Anthology* reunion, it was pernicious business issues which still caused friction. In 1988 when the Beatles were inducted into the Rock & Roll Hall of Fame, Paul did spoil the party. His presence came in a fax: "After 20 years, The Beatles still have some business differences which I had hoped would have been settled by now…" George defused the situation responding, "I'm the quiet Beatle. It's too bad Paul's not here because he's the one who had the speech in his pocket". McCartney's reaction was a callous, uncharacteristic and undiplomatic response from that most diplomatic of men.

The bitterness between Paul and George festered. In 1997, when Paul's authorised biography – Barry Miles' *Many Years from Now* – was published, Paul appeared to take pleasure in minimising George's role in the band. For example, McCartney has his 'Here There & Everywhere' opening *Revolver* – it was actually George's 'Taxman'. He cites only two new songs used in *Yellow Submarine*, ignoring George's two substantial contributions to the soundtrack. He hardly mentions George's songwriting at all; critics speculate it was Paul getting his revenge for being largely omitted from George's 1980 memoir *I Me Mine*.

Certainly when it came to plugging new Beatle product, McCartney was always the first over the top. I asked George when we met if he resented the way Paul had effectively hijacked the Beatle myth? "He's entitled to it. He's just as much the Beatles as anybody else. Personally, I'm not interested in trying to be the Beatles, I don't mind singing a couple of tunes of mine I wrote during the Beatle period".

This is where the Quiet One and I parted company as I pointed out the preponderance of Fab material on his own 1992 *Live in Japan* release. George claimed, I felt disingenuously, "'While My Guitar Gently Weeps', 'Something', 'Here Comes the Sun'? Well, *I* don't think of them as Beatle songs. For instance, if the Beatles had stayed together, some of my solo stuff would have been on Beatle albums. If we'd split up in 1967, then some of them would have been on solo albums. It doesn't really make much difference, except being on a Beatle album guaranteed you would sell more copies".

By 1996 the Beatles were the UK's biggest music earners with an estimated yearly income of £48,000,000 on the back of the *Anthology* releases, easily eclipsing wannabes Oasis. With *Anthology* Volumes I and II in the US Top 50, in 1996, 34 years on since that first seismic impact, the most popular British band in America were … the Beatles.

The Beatles had their own say with the 2000 publication of their *Anthology* book. Here was another treasure trove on the back of the six archive CDs – the Beatles in their own words. It was a familiar tale, but for me, the most fascinating elements were the memories of their Liverpool childhoods, Ringo's almost-Dickensian upbringing and the cosy family feeling of George's youth. Critics found fault with the familiarity of the anecdotes. But then, as I pointed out when I reviewed it on the radio, there is nothing you can ask a Beatle that he hasn't been asked a thousand, ten thousand times before. They have been doing this since the UK's currency was measured in £ s d, when measures were imperial feet and yards, New Year's Day was not a Bank Holiday and *everyone* stood to attention when the National Anthem was played.

After years of others getting their pre-decimal six penny-worth, here was something for the fans to treasure. I always found something magical and rather touching about the devotion the group attracted. On 29 August 1996, for example, 16,000 fans went along to Candlestick Park in San Francisco to see tribute band the Mop Tops. They came to the site of the last-ever full Fab concert to pay homage on the gig's 30th anniversary. Or

Ronnie Dannelley's quest to find the exact location and precise measurements of the Cavern, based on an 1888 insurance map. He promised it was "accurate to about one foot or so"… The humorous *Viz* magazine had President of the Fulchester Beatles Appreciation Society proving his devotion to the group "I have successfully raised four Beatles fanatics – two boys, John and Paul – and two daughters, George and Ringo".

In 2003, Paul told Paul Du Noyer: "The truth is, we, The Beatles, have done with our career. We've been and done it. So our attitude is, you don't really find us getting too involved. Except for the *Anthology*… Well, everyone else has written so much about us we should try and get as near as possible in our own words".

Well, that's all very well about your old band Paul, but what about…

the Rutles? The group were the creation of Monty Python's Eric Idle and the Bonzo Dog Doo-Dah Band's Neil Innes (1944–2019). I was a huge Bonzos fan and once spent a lovely afternoon reminiscing with Neil at the Chelsea Arts Club. The Bonzos went from being a bunch of art students with a fondness for 1920s dance tunes ('I'm going to bring a watermelon to my girl tonight') playing in pubs, but were soon onstage at Brian Epstein's Saville Theatre. That led to the Bonzos' appearance as the only other band in *Magical*

Mystery Tour – who can forget Viv Stanshall's gold-suited Elvis routine on 'Death Cab for Cutie'?

In 1968, under the pseudonym 'Apollo C. Vermouth' it was Paul who produced the Bonzo Dog Band's only hit, 'Urban Spaceman'. "Paul was a real pal doing 'Urban Spaceman', and doing the *Magical Mystery Tour* he said how much he liked my stuff on the first Bonzo album", remembered Neil. I feel you can carbon date the Rutles' beginning with Neil's Beatle homage 'Fresh Wound' on the final Bonzos album, 1972's *Let's Make Up and Be Friendly* (following a listless guitar solo a Liverpudlian voice mutters, "C'mon George, snap out of it…").

"It was George who *really* loved the Bonzos", Neil told me, "and he said what should have happened is that the Beatles and the Bonzos, the Rutles and the Pythons should all have got together and had a really good time! It was that like-minded thing and a delight in the absurd, which wasn't just an act.

"George was the one who was always grinning and coming along to gigs. I remember I used to see him a lot at the Nashville Rooms. I think when George's marriage to Pattie was crumbling, and Eric Idle's marriage was also on the rocks, the two of them had a lot in common.

"George was on Eric's [mid-70s BBC TV show] *Rutland Weekend Television*, and one of my things for the show was to come up with songs and visuals to go with them. Rutland being the smallest county, with the smallest TV station with the lowest budgets, it was a very cheap show, which quite frankly is why BBC2 went for it. So the idea of parodying *A Hard Day's Night* was obvious – black & white film, speeded up, four guys running around a field. Easy! Cheap!!

"Eric thought of the name the Rutles. Such was the interest in the Beatles getting together back in the mid-70s in America that *Saturday Night Live* were running this gag *all* the time. They got George on, and the producer Lorne Michaels is waving $3,000 in cash under George's nose saying all this could be yours, just get the band back together, and George going 'All this for *me*?'

"So the Rutle clip was waiting to be shown, which it was, and such was the mailbag that we thought well why don't we do the whole story? George came on board and helped tell the whole story… He cleared it with the rest of the guys and Apple and whatnot, got us some footage. He was in it, and talked Mick Jagger and Paul Simon into coming on. And of course we had the *Saturday Night Live* guys, an impressive list: John Belushi, Dan Aykroyd, Bill Murray.

"'Rutle' ought to be a verb… to Rutle, verb transitive, to emulate or imitate people you admire. You could say that the Beatles were Rutles in the way that they wanted to be like Eddie Cochran or Gene Vincent".

The full-length 1978 documentary (*All You Need Is Cash*) was a treat – Dirk, Ron, Stig and Barry (the Pre-Fab Four) in an affectionate and accurate nod to Fab history ("It was all a ghastly mistake. Nasty, talking to a slightly deaf journalist, had claimed that the Rutles were bigger than Rod. Rod Stewart would not be big for another eight years…" … "Business meetings were crazy… 134 legal people and accountants filed into a small eight by ten room. Only 37 came out alive… In December 1970, Barry sued Dirk… and Stig accidentally sued himself").

What was equally compelling was Neil's spot-on original Rutle material, but clearly echoing the songs the group on whom the fictional band were based. Some of the similarities were wilfully marked – 'Hold My Hand' ('All My Loving')... 'Ouch!' ('Help!')... 'Piggy in the Middle' ('I Am the Walrus')... 'Good Times' ('Lucy in the Sky with Diamonds') and 'I Must Be in Love' (well, pretty much every Lennon & McCartney song pre-1965). Lennon liked the idea of the Rutles, and advised they remove 'Get Up and Go' because it was the only one which lawyers could find was an actual copy rather than a parody.

Ironically, the career of the fictional Rutles soon began mirroring that of their real-life counterparts, the Beatles. The fissure between Neil and Eric recalling that of John and Paul; the endless legal complications over song copyrights... "ATV Music published Northern Songs, the Beatles music, they wanted to take me to court for Beatle copyright infringement", Neil told me. "My publishers said no way, until they found out that ATV had a million-dollar slush fund for court cases. And they said well we'll win, but we might not get costs, and that's when they left me high and dry.

"So I had to assign copyright of Rutles stuff to ATV, in return for 50% of the royalties. Royalties which I have never received to this day. Although it is beginning to dawn on a few people that this is perhaps what should have happened... George tried to do something about it through Apple. It's not worth going there; it's all negative. But the music business is organised crime... there's never been an accounting error in favour of an artist, but there's been hundreds of thousands in favour of the companies. And that tells you something."

It was with a rueful eye that George Harrison watched the development. After one of the many financial meetings, he confided to Neil, "You're supposed to be sending us up, not emulating us!"

Then, like their predecessors, the Rutles split. But as with the real thing, the pressure was on for a reunion... "In 1994 I was in LA, people were twisting my arm saying the Beatles are bringing out *Anthology*, are the Rutles going to do anything? I said oh no, then I thought, well I'll do some songs. So I told Eric and he said well do what you want, kind of thing. I said we're going to do a video, do you want to come along? Peter Gabriel's coming. Eartha Kitt, Cyndi Lauper, Ben E. King, Gloria Gaynor... Oasis nearly came, but they decided to have a fight instead...! When the Rutles' *Archaeology* came out, I took it down to George and played it to him, and he sat there with a big grin on his face."

In a further complication, and sublime irony, Beatle admirers Oasis nicked Neil Innes' own 'How Sweet to Be an Idiot'. "Funnily enough it was Paul's brother, Mike McCartney, who rang me up to say he'd just heard Nicky Campbell on Radio 1 playing 'How Sweet to Be an Idiot' and 'Whatever' back to back and asking people to spot the similarity! My publishers were on the case, and I bear no animosity to Noel, it's easily done..."

Then there was the group that, frankly, *were* the Beatles. A 1977 LP by Klaatu revived memories of the 'Paul Is Dead' period. The clues were there: the album did sound a bit like circa 1967 Beatles; it was on the Capitol label; Ringo used the Klaatu robot on the cover of his 1974 LP *Goodnight Vienna*; the album's best-known song 'Calling Occupants of Interplanetary Craft' was a hit for the Carpenters (who had also covered 'Ticket to Ride'). An article in an American newspaper saying the group *were* the Beatles was circulated with every review copy of the album. But – spoiler ending – as the astute *NME* reviewer (actually, me) reported, "The Beatles they ain't".

As well as the reunions that never were, as the group's status increased in the latter half of the 20th century, there was much fun to be had imagining a world *without* the Beatles.

Ray Connolly's engaging 2019 novella *Sorry Boys, You Failed the Audition* saw the story through the eyes of fan club secretary Freda Kelly. With George Martin saying 'no', the four returned to Liverpool – Paul to teaching; Ringo enjoying his pools-winning ("You always were the lucky one, Ringo"); and George pottering on his allotment, between spells as guitar-for-hire with the Tremeloes and Moody Blues. John just sulked and put on evenings of British rubbish. Paul Du Noyer ran with the fantasy, and imagined George following his dad's profession as driver of the 311 bus, with Ritchie Starkey his conductor ("life has been a mild disappointment for him since Rory Storm & the Hurricanes played their last Butlin's Summer Season in 1966"). In a bar on West 72nd Street, a drunken Scouse seaman called Johnny Lennon swears contemptuously when the flickering TV shows images of the ever-popular Paul McCartney Dance Orchestra". David Quantick's 2013 Sky Arts' *Snodgrass* was in a similar vein, with a bitter Lennon (Ian Hart) ousted from the group after refusing to record 'How Do You Do It' in 1963. "We could have been bigger than the Hollies", 'John' snarls.

I found myself reflecting on this while looking at one of those Sixties Gold UK line-ups: Gerry & the Pacemakers, the Searchers, P.J. Proby, the Fortunes, Brian Poole *and* Chip Hawkes. It is only with a little imagining and a simple twist of fate, that, had things not worked out, history could have been very different… If Allan Williams had continued as manager, with London and a record deal beyond his reach… If Brian Epstein had gone on to manage the more-malleable Searchers over the truculent Beatles… If the Beatles' version of 'How Do You Do It' had been reluctantly released, and bombed… If they had stayed on the Vee-Jay label until 1968… If Ringo *did* leave to manage a chain of hairdressers… All that and more, and you could have seen the Beatles on that circuit. The itinerary looked just the same as those nationwide tours the group undertook at the beginning – Southsea, Plymouth, Ipswich, Brighton, Llandudno… And America nothing more than a dream.

*

Free of alcohol, happily married to his second wife Barbara, and having seen his daughter survive a near-fatal illness, all was good for Ritchie Starkey. He was also happy knowing his son Zak had inherited his percussive skills, ironically including a stint for Beatle wannabes Oasis. Sell-out shows with his All Starr Band, his childhood home in Madryn Avenue saved from demolition, lucrative performer (and occasional songwriting royalties) from 20th- and 21st-century Beatle releases, all was well on the Ringo front. But in 2008 his *Liverpool 8* album was ill-received, worse still was his "No" to Jonathan Ross when asked if he ever missed Liverpool. Outraged Scousers decapitated Ringo in a Beatle topiary and "Traitor" was spray-canned over his old school in the Dingle.

Liverpudlians remain disappointed that the Beatles never came down on either side of the city's two Association Football clubs – Liverpool or Everton. It is definitely *not* true that the *Red* and *Blue* compilations were thus named after Liverpool FC (the Reds) and Everton (the Blues). Paul *was* pictured attending the 1968 FA Cup Final between Everton and West Bromwich Albion. One Beatle acknowledgement for the beautiful game came when Liverpool FC's Albert Stubbins was pictured on the *Sgt Pepper* sleeve. During the 1998 World Cup, England footballers whiled away time during press conferences squeezing song titles into interviews – England centre-back Tony Adams managed to include 'Get Back', 'Something', 'Let It Be' and 'With a Little Help from My Friends' into one media interrogation.

The band's old label wasn't faring much better than the England team. In 2000, a merger between EMI and Warner Music fell through with an astonishing £12,000,000,000 on the table. Vivendi eventually took over the label a decade later. Then, in 2005, the Beatles sued EMI in a row over unpaid royalties in the region of £30,000,000. The matter was settled on "mutually acceptable terms" for an undisclosed sum in 2007. Worse was to come later in 2007 when Guy Hands' Terra Firma paid £4,200,000,000 for the EMI label for a mere 27-month run. Coming on top of a loss of £260,000,000 for 2005/6, they were only too glad to be thrown a lifeline. It all went horribly wrong with critics saying it was **E**very **M**istake **I**maginable. Universal eventually took over the label in 2011, paying 'only' £1,200,000,000.

Even outside of music, the endless fascination with all things Beatle continued. It was around the time of that historic reunion of those three surviving Beatles that they were once again in the news. The National Trust had been established in Great Britain in 1895 (referenced by John in 'Happiness Is a Warm Gun'). Its brief to safeguard the heritage of the nation. Back then, that meant the castles and properties of the high and the mighty, the great and the good. However, the first National Trust location devoted to a living person was not that of a politician, diplomat, painter, nobleman, explorer or scientist, but rather, a Beatle.

The fact that it was Paul McCartney's childhood home at 20 Forthlin Road was certainly a factor. It was not necessarily selected for its historic pop provenance, that was the cherry on the cake. The Trust insisted that the property also provided a living, historic example of post-war council housing ("we wanted to preserve and show to future generations the style of social housing after the Second World War"). But would the equally well-preserved property of, say, Sid & Doris Bonkers have attracted the National Trust? While not in the same exalted property portfolio, George's childhood home at Upton Green became available as an Airbnb during early 2022.

Two tapes are known to have been recorded at the Forthlin Road property on a borrowed Grundig tape recorder, so Paul could hear what his own songs sounded like. During 1958 and 1960, a pre-fame Paul crooned 'The World Is Waiting for the Sunrise' and a first version of 'I'll Follow the Sun'. It also featured the early McCartney & Lennon compositions 'Hello Little Girl' and 'You'll Be Mine'. 'Fancy My Chances with You' would resurface during the *Let It Be* sessions a decade later. There is speculation that, with the technology developed by Peter Jackson, it could be applied to these home recordings and Hamburg tapes.

Over the years, I believe Apple have served the fans well, sanctioning those other tantalising unreleased recordings. But after two volumes of *Rarities*, six *Anthology* CDs, lavish box sets celebrating *Sgt Pepper*, *The White Album*, *Abbey Road*, *Let It Be*, *Revolver* and *Let It Be Naked*. Following four CDs of *The Beatles at the BBC*; following the live

Eight Days a Week… It begs the question, is there anything unissued left *worth* releasing?

While the novelty of compact discs may be waning after 30 years, I suspect fans of a certain age prefer a tactile item rather than a stream. So there may be a case for another tranche of CD releases – perhaps all of the official 12 LPs as double-packs, containing both official mono and stereo versions. Lest we forget, the group displayed little interest in the mixing process pre-*Revolver*, and certainly those first four albums were meant to be heard in mono. Stereo was a luxury few UK Beatle fans could afford.

Well, certainly live tapes exist, but by then, the group were always competing with the audience to be heard, and do we really need a further souvenir of the group hammering through a cursory live show, over a dodgy PA and without feedback monitors? Historically, a live tape of the group at the Cavern from June 1962 would be fascinating as it contains several numbers otherwise unavailable (among them 'Sharing You', 'Dream Baby'). But Paul bagged it at auction and it remains in his private collection, as do the Forthlin Road recordings. While the complete Candlestick Park 'retirement' show would be of interest, alas the tape Paul gave Tony Barrow only ran to 30 minutes, this cutting short their final 33-minute performance. Ditto for the sake of completeness, the entire 42-minute Apple roof gig.

Of the home or studio recordings, we know Peter Asher proudly owns Paul's demo of 'A World Without Love'. And presumably could lay his hands on his former housemate's 'Nobody I Know' and 'I Don't Want to See You Again'. Peter Jackson and his team sifted through the 56 hours of *Let It Be* on film plus 140 hours of audio, though sadly, we were denied the opportunity to hear the 12-minute 'Dig It'. As well as John tackling Paul's first song 'I Lost My Little Girl'? Ditto the Beatles covering 'Save the Last Dance for Me'.

And there are the odds & ends: George's cover of Joe Brown's 'A Picture of You' was left off the BBC releases… The Decca version of 'Love of the Loved' omitted from *Anthology*… The controversial 1967 'Carnival of Light'… the 12-minute 'Helter Skelter'… John's demo of 'Bad to Me'… A rumoured 'When I'm 64' from Forthlin Road…

A Beatle forum asked fans what they would like to see as the next Apple project. Sam Goldberg's response was typical: "I want every minute of studio tapes released, including every demo, practice session and out-take, as well as every separate track of every song on every album…!"

These are the diehards, those who will sit and sift through every take of the aptly titled 'Long, Long, Long'.

Following the critical and commercial success of his *Get Back* documentary, and with the 21st-century technology available, Peter Jackson obviously had the bit between his teeth: "I'm curious to find out what we could do with the Star Club tapes. Taking primitive one-mic tapes of performances in a raucous German nightclub, never intended for anything more than a souvenir of the residency and before the Beatles elicited much attention beyond 'Love Me Do' would be an absolutely stunning achievement."

Sanctioning these, and any other official releases would be of interest to the diehard Fab fan, but would hardly appeal to a wider audience. Under the stewardship of Neil Aspinall, and later Jeff Jones, Apple have curated the most revered back catalogue in rock with the care and respect it merits. It falls on Apple's Director of Production, Jonathan Clyde to explain company policy. Following the plethora of *Let It Be*-era product at the end of 2021, he was asked about future plans. Sounding like an Edwardian statesman: "Diplomatically, there are discussions going on. But there's nothing decided, and that's all I can say".

As each year passes, the demand may diminish, but the company are still looking at a global audience who appear to purchase anything associated with that enticing 'Beatle' brand. Since the release of the BBC performances in 1994, the first new product in nearly a quarter of a century, the Aladdin's cave grows ever-emptier. Is there really a demand for material that shows "The Beatles with their trousers down"?

Given that his idea of "abject misery" was "being interviewed by an English journalist", I had a surprisingly engaging interview with Lou Reed. It was around the time of the Velvet Underground box set. I asked how he felt about it? The dark glasses came down and he stared at me, then growled: "There's a good reason they're called *out*-takes".

Each Apple release was greeted with enthusiastic media coverage and a re-appraisal of those historic and timeless recordings. Following George's death, the anniversary waltz was undertaken primarily by Paul, with a little help from Ringo. Continuing with a see-sawing solo career, Paul would grit his teeth to revisit Beatle memories. He would do 'the Beatle bit' with every inquisitive journalist. There is undeniable pride when he does reminisce, but that doesn't stop the criticism McCartney always seems to attract.

To his credit he has never quit the UK for a tax haven. He can still be seen on occasion travelling by train from Sussex to London. When in London, a stone's throw from Abbey Road, he can be seen on the streets.

With memories of Mother Mary, he did his bit speaking up for the National Health Service. When he speaks (be it nurses' pay, the unfairness of streaming and musicians' earnings) he will be heard.

You sense that his dream ending would be to croak in front of 80,000 adoring fans during a singalong 'Hey Jude'. He attracts criticism for the alleged deterioration of his singing voice; of his dyed hair; of his veggie proselytising; his 'ordinariness'... Yet he remains front and centre a celebrity with a status of his own. Easily one of the most recognizable people on the planet. "I think of him", Elvis Costello reflected, "like he's Buzz Aldrin... Someone who's been to the fucking moon. None of us can conceive what it must be like to have been through what he's experienced. It's a unique experience, probably in the 20th century, to be him".

Venues for a Paul McCartney can hold up to five-figure numbers. Yet he relishes smaller shows – a return to a Liverpool pub; a pre-Glastonbury pub warm-up. It was only recently I discovered the venue for his smallest-ever gig... The green wooden taxi shelters used to be a familiar sight on London streets, now barely a dozen survive. They were un-licensed, and intended for hansom (then black cab) drivers somewhere to go for a cuppa and a sarnie.

One of the few remaining shelters is in Wellington Place, W8 near the McCartney London home. While out walking with his youngest daughter Beatrice, she became fascinated by the little building that looked like something out of a fairy tale. She and her dad were invited in, and on one occasion Paul is believed to have brought his guitar to serenade the cabbies, slavering over their bacon sandwiches, in a space "no larger than a horse and cart".

Thirty years after he admitted taking LSD, Paul McCartney was knighted in a Scouse-heavy 1997 New Year's Honours List, along with Cilla Black OBE and Roger McGough OBE. His beloved Linda lived long enough to see him ennobled. Cancer took her in 1998. I only met her a handful of times, but she was always very kind. On one occasion a year had elapsed, but she remembered both me and my wife's name, and I thought how many thousands and thousands of people the McCartneys must have met since then. I remember a glimpse of the teenage Linda, as she told me of the time she bunked off from her parents' home in Westchester County to catch a rock & roll show at New York's Paramount Theater: "Buddy Holly, Jerry Lee, Chuck Berry… all on *one* bill…" she laughed, open-mouthed at the memory.

The last project Linda encouraged Paul to pursue was his *Run Devil Run* album of rock & roll covers. I interviewed him at the time of the album's release, in his office at his Soho HQ. He sat happily in front of the gleaming Wurlitzer juke box, crammed full of the records he loved as a teenager all those years ago – Elvis, the Everlys, Fats Domino, Bill Haley…

John too felt that nothing he did was quantifiably better than what those revered idols had accomplished during the golden age of rock & roll in the 1950s. What was nice was the way, even with their founder member gone, the Quarrymen persevered. In 1997, to commemorate the 40th anniversary of that fateful day at the Woolton Village Fete when Lennon first met McCartney, the original line-up (minus John) got back together. It led to a series of shows at fan club conventions and anniversary events. I remember talking to Quarryman Len Garry and asking if he wasn't bitter that he'd left prior to worldwide fame, but he shrugged it off, proud of his two beautiful daughters and their progress. "We were just *kids*…" That original Quarrymen revival led to other gigs – they were just back from Japan, and Len laughed and said he got mobbed, so he got to be a Beatle a couple of times a year.

Inevitably, at century's end, there was Millennium madness in the air… A February 1998 poll conducted by *The Guardian*, HMV and Channel 4 polled 36,000 music fans for The Greatest-Ever Album – *Sgt Pepper* was back at the top (the Stone Roses at No.2 and the Beatles competing with themselves with *Revolver* in third place).

By 2020 it was all change again. The 21st century now had a near 75-year history of rock & roll to reflect upon and following the death of George Floyd, the Black Lives Matter movement and the willingness to reflect a BAME (Black Asian Muslim Ethnic) culture, the plates demonstrably shifted. In September 2020, *Rolling Stone* listed rock's 500 Best Albums. There had been a massive switch from earlier efforts, with hitherto sacrosanct 'classics' relegated: *Forever Changes* (180), *Bringing It All Back Home* (81), *Astral Weeks* (60). *Ziggy Stardust* and *Let It Bleed* were on the reserve bench in the low 40s.

This was a poll very much of its time – the Notorious B.I.G., D'angelo, Beyonce, Jay-Z, Kendrick Lamar and eight Kanye West albums all took precedence over the Band, the Doors, Dylan, Led Zeppelin and the Stones. The Beatles *were* there, but way down the pecking order – ten of their albums registered, the highest ranking being *The White Album* (29), *Sgt Pepper* (24) and *Revolver* (11). *Abbey Road* was the toppermost, at No.5, preceded by Stevie Wonder's *Songs in the Key of Life* (4), Joni Mitchell's *Blue* (3), *Pet Sounds* (2) and Marvin Gaye's *What's Going On* at the top.

As for individual songs… The magazine's 500 Best Songs poll of September 2020 was equally intriguing. The stranglehold of 60s and 70s acts was broken by names such as Public Enemy, Outkast and Missy Elliot. In the Top 20, the Beatles were represented by – for the first time ever – 'Strawberry Fields Forever' (7) and their second-highest entry, 'I Want to Hold Your Hand' (15).

Back in 1999, a poll conducted by BBC Radio 2 based on "a panel of songwriters and sales figures" had found 'Yesterday' its 'Song of the Century'. 'Imagine' was No.6. John's anthemic composition was one of the few (along with 'Give Peace a Chance') that overshadowed his Beatle contributions. When I interviewed the 'Yesterday' composer, it was at the time he was embroiled in an argument about Beatle songwriting credits. He was keen to reverse those on the songs which John Lennon had not had a hand in. Cue furore…! Cue "He's rewriting history…!"

In fairness and in his defence, Paul pointed out that he was equally happy to have his name taken off solo Lennon compositions. "I mean I wasn't on the same *continent* when John did 'Give Peace a Chance'." He was also at pains to point out the credits on the first Beatle LP, which read 'McCartney/Lennon'. The reversal was decided at a meeting he was late for, with Brian Epstein and John, he was outvoted because *they* thought Lennon & McCartney scanned better. "John and Brian were chatting… They said it's like Rodgers & Hammerstein…" he told me. "And I swear to God – but I'm the only living witness to this so it's naturally highly dubious! But I *know* that the guys said yeah… you agree to the Lennon/ McCartney thing now and in the future sometime we can change it".

Over the years, it still rankled. I suppose part of it is that when you are that rich, that talented, in a world used to having things done for you, it is the little things which irritate. It is the itch that, however much you scratch, never quite disappears – onlookers remember at the height of their fame, Robert Plant and John Bonham coming to blows over petrol receipts from their impoverished pre-Zeppelin, Band of Joy days.

"When *Anthology* came out…" Paul continued when I challenged him, "it had 'Yesterday' and above the title there was a picture of John… So I thought to myself, I wonder, after 30 years… wouldn't it be nice to reverse that… get a picture of me for that particular song. A picture of John above 'Help!' a picture of George above 'Something'?

"So I rang Yoko and said I wonder if you wouldn't mind reversing it, just on this one song… And she said, 'Yeah, okay', she actually agreed. Then she rang back about an hour later and said 'Ah, no, I've had a think about this and I don't think it would be a good idea'… And *that* was what started the struggle 'cos I'd got all excited and I think I'd probably had a drink and was going 'Yeeeah, that's really nice, I get to put my name in front'. It's stupid… and I was thinking things like, well Yoko wasn't even *there* when they were written… there was nothing written down. So there's no reason she can tell me we can't do it.

"A couple of years ago I was having a drink in a bar in Venice, and I always gravitate to the piano and I'm flicking through the sheet music – 'Fly Me to the Moon', 'Moon River'… And when I got to 'Hey Jude' it was 'Hey Jude' by John Lennon! Now there isn't room on these new computerised tickets for the full credit so, in a hundred years it's going to be 'Hey Jude' by John Lennon.

"There was a poetry book, an anthology, where they used 'Blackbird' by John Lennon and Paul McCartney. Now John didn't actually have a hand in those words... By then of course John had died so it was no good my saying I don't think John would have wanted to be on it. Same as I don't need to be on 'Give Peace a Chance'.

"So, there's the case for the defence, m'lud. But when it all came out it was: Oh he's trying to change it, the bastard. Dancing on a dead man's grave... which is certainly not true. 'Cos you know, I'm a *major* fan of John's".

Well I for one believe him. Yes, he's a multi-millionaire, possessor of a rare Rhodium disc, and he occupies a unique place in popular culture, opportunity has knocked for James Paul McCartney. But those songs he created mean a lot to him. It is *not* that you never give him your money, rather that without him those songs, those songs which are the building blocks of timeless popular music, would not exist. He feels proprietorial toward them. They are, after all, *his* songs.

*

In 2000 *NME* elected David Bowie as 'The Most Influential Rock & Roll Artist of All Time'. My problem with Bowie was always that while I admired the eclecticism and appreciate every house should have a 2CD *Best Of...* there was always something calculating and calculated about The Artist Formerly Known As David Jones. With Dylan and the Beatles their progress was instinctive. In that same poll, Radiohead were No.2, and the Beatles No.3, with the paper pointing out they remained "the most influential band in history for two reasons: they did so *much* and they did it all *first*... The Beatles are now part of the landscape, cultural and generational icons as potent and enduring as Shakespeare and Churchill".

Talking of "cultural and generational icons", in 2004 I travelled to the picture-postcard heart of Middle England, to Cranleigh in Surrey, to interview Ringo at his Grade II listed Jacobean property, 'Rydinghurst'. You announced yourself at the electronic gate, which swung open and you proceeded up the drive to the listed 19th-century vicarage. Set on a gentle rise, the substantial property overlooked green rolling hills, surrounded by stables, a paddock and – most strikingly – three life-sized cows painted in bright psychedelic colours.

On the wall inside his state-of-the-art studio hangs an Abbey Road street sign; a poster for Bob Dylan's film *Dont Look Back* and assorted song lyrics. There's also an old poster, advertising a gig by Lightning Hopkins, Ringo's favourite bluesman, supported by an up-and-coming band called Jefferson Airplane!

I was there to talk up the release of an All Starr Band DVD. He was happy reminiscing ("a lot of the Beatle songs are universal – and I'm lucky I have two of 'em, 'Little Help' and 'Yellow Sub'"). But the drummer had a disconcerting habit, with his throwaway references to his "other band". It was then that, listening to that curious accent, Scouse mixed with mid-Atlantic twang, here was Ringo Starr talking about ... the Beatles.

Ringo cut a compact figure, bearded, in good shape – sessions with a trainer, Pilates, a vegetarian diet, he proudly boasted of quitting smoking "over 12 years ago: 60 a day to none a day, on a Friday". He accepted it was his time with his "other band" which still fascinated: "I had a great 'back', you know what I mean? I loved The Beatles. I *loved*

Rory Storm. I loved the bands I was in before the Beatles …" I asked, did he ever reflect on odd evenings at home how different his life would have been if Brian Epstein hadn't asked you to join the Beatles?

"No. There's a laugh, because while Brian was asking me to join the Beatles, Gerry Marsden was talking to me about being in his band! You make these decisions. It's your life. You get on with it. I can't sit there saying: if only I'd done this. I may have still been in Liverpool. Who knows?"

He confirmed his own personal Fab favourite was 'Rain'… But was otherwise dismissive of his own percussive abilities: "I always wanted to be a drummer, but I never rehearsed or practised… I tried it once in 1958 and that was it. It was the most boring thing for me". He was very disparaging about his drumming: "People who've seen me play say how small my kit is, but I think four is enough to hit – after that I get confused".

As the first Beatle to hit the magic '64' mark, had he never been tempted to do an autobiography? "I've been asked for many years to do my autobiography. But the thing is they only really want the eight years I was in the Beatles. And I say well, I had a long life before that. You'd have three volumes before I made it to the Beatles if you were doing it my way! So I think the closest thing to it are the little interviews, the little quotes and stories around the *Postcards from the Boys*. Everyone loves that. It made it personal and real. So no, I have no thoughts. So *you're* not getting a job!"

Engineer Geoff Emerick had always been impressed by Ringo: "He drummed and drummed and drummed and drummed…! After the sessions the floor was littered with wood chips from the amount of drum sticks he'd gone through".[25]

A recent study revealed that music tourism associated with the Beatles brought over £100,000,000 to the Liverpool economy each year, and helped generate 2,335 jobs. In 2019, a record 300,000 people visited *The Beatles Story*, 800,000 came along to the Cavern Club and over 100,000 visit the childhood homes of the group. It is estimated that this sector is growing at between 10 and 15 per cent a year. (Obviously the Covid pandemic affected such visits 2019/20.)

It was not always so, their hometown was slow to recognise the group's impact. The city's first Beatle Museum (The Cavern Mecca) opened in January 1981 but closed that summer. No financial help was offered by Liverpool Council nor the English Tourist Board. The idea then that an institution honouring a 'pop group' would have been anathema.

Perhaps prompted by the 20th anniversary of the release of 'Love Me Do', the city did eventually crack. In 1982 John Lennon Drive, Paul McCartney Way, George Harrison Close and Ringo Starr Drive were announced. A 2023 survey showed that properties there averaged 12% more than those on surrounding streets. In 2013, Pete Best Drive was unveiled.

Today, it can all be quite overwhelming visiting their home city. You can arrive either at John Lennon Airport, or via the John Lennon Pullman which runs from Euston to Lime Street. Motor down John Lennon Drive, and after a visit to Beatle City, go to the Cavern.

---

25 By the way, that Beatle drum kit – the one with the famous 'drop-T' logo on the bass drum – came courtesy of saxophone repairer Ivor David Arbiter (1929–2005). A part-time drummer, he designed and manufactured drums for over 40 years. It was to his Shaftesbury Avenue shop, Drum City, that Ringo went in 1963 and came away happy with the resulting kit and bass drum logo. Arbiter was also credited for another cultural landmark: in the 1980s he introduced karaoke to the UK.

After a Beatle-themed lunch at The Grapes, go on the official National Trust tour of Paul and John's homes, a detour to Strawberry Field, before unwinding at the end of the day in your room at the Hard Day's Night hotel… It opened in 2008, all 100+ rooms of it at an estimated cost of £8,000,000. Over breakfast you can have your morning tea out of Apple authorised Beatle mugs on a Beatle coaster, and while away the day listening to Beatles Stream – Beatles Radio.com, Beatles-a-rama, Beatles Day on the internet. Twenty-four hours a day. Every day.

Only now, belatedly, has the city come to appreciate that it is 'The Beatles' that forms a large part of the city's magnetic attraction. And while the Albert Dock area contains more Grade I listed buildings than anywhere else in Britain, I maintain many are attracted rather by the photo opportunity by the statue of John, Paul, George and Ringo.

Academic Liverpool finally sank its talons in. From September 2021, the University of Liverpool was offering a degree course 'The Beatles: Music Industry and Heritage'. "This MA is as much about the wider study of Liverpool's – and Britain's – heritage, tourism and culture sectors as it is about the role the Beatles played in them", explained course organiser Dr Holly Tessler.

Typically, elements of their home city remained sniffy about the band. Michael Braun recounted a return in 1963: "'Aren't you Paul McCartney?" "Yeah" "I'm Fred Hoger. I used to know you when you were a fat little kid at the Institute'. The Beatles were home". While, on the release of *Anthology 1*, Liverpool's independent Probe Records store said "We're not stocking it at all. It's HMV, Virgin world, not our sort of thing".

After the Cavern, Eric's was the most influential of the Liverpool clubs, a meeting place for those who would propel the next generation of the city's bands – Teardrop Explodes, Orchestral Manoeuvres in the Dark and Echo & the Bunnymen. In an interview, the Bunnymen's Will Sergeant raged, "I hate the Beatles". In his 2021 autobiography he recanted. "Of course I didn't hate the Beatles, but we were sick of hearing about them… we were desperate to shake off the shadow of the Beatles that pervades every aspect of Liverpudlian life".

Spencer Leigh fights a valiant battle to preserve as much of the city's Beatles heritage, pointing out that prior to Next taking over the site of Brian Epstein's NEMS store, it was previously occupied by the lingerie chain Ann Summers. In 2021 a plan was launched to erect a statue to Brian Epstein which happily was unveiled in 2022. Finally with that, and the biopic *Midas Man*, Brian's role is finally being acknowledged.

That historical importance of the group and their manager is now being appreciated in their home city. After many years Liverpool has finally come to appreciate the fact that for the bulk of the known world, if they recognise the name 'Liverpool', the knee-jerk reaction is 'Beatles'.

The past came back to dog the city well into the 21st century. In 2006, it was suggested that Penny Lane should be re-named. James Penny was an 18th-century trader who fought *against* the abolition of slavery. The city still struggles with its inextricable links to the slave trade. It has been estimated that 80% of the slaves bound for America left from Liverpool. Karl Marx stated, "Liverpool waxed fat on the slave trade". In 2010, the city was talking of erecting plaques explaining locations linked to slavery, one of which would certainly be Penny Lane.

Within days, the debate had broadened, and not for the first time, there was a demand for Penny Lane to be renamed. Liverpool Mayor Joe Anderson responded: "My understanding … is that there is no evidence that Penny Lane is named after slave trader James Penny, it is debated and said that there was a toll bridge that cost a penny there hence its name. We are working with the BAME community and historians to look at this and what we should do".

On a lighter note, a 'Penny Lane' street sign, stolen by drunken students in 1976, was anonymously returned in 2023 where it is now on display. "The removal of street signs is a criminal offence", Liverpool City Council member Dan Barrington solemnly declared. "However, I think we can all agree to just let it be".

After nearly 40 years away, I returned to Liverpool; I was doing some work with the Memphis Tourist Board, and Elvis Presley Enterprises decided it was a good idea to link Memphis and Liverpool. Aside from the musical symbiosis, both cities had grown prosperous on the cotton trade, which of course was fuelled by the slave trade. In later years, it was the bustling docks and lucrative transatlantic liner trade which also helped give Liverpool its prosperity, it now has 2,500 listed buildings. That is reflected by the many leafy Victorian suburbs, the large houses with their red brick, quarried from Woolton. The streets boast a lot of trees, broad roadways, with flowery islands replacing tram lines. Sefton Park boasts an impressive glasshouse, George paid thousands to help have it restored and there is now a George Harrison Memorial Garden, opened in 2002, which he would have appreciated.

The Liverpool link continued in 2012 when the name Calderstones Park Productions began appearing on Beatles releases. It is the part of the Universal Music Group designated to look after Beatle 'product'. The name is that of a park in Liverpool, situated between Penny Lane and Strawberry Field. It is now the new name for John's old alma mater, Quarry Bank School.

At the last count, Liverpool itself can claim over 90 Beatle sites. Primarily Penny Lane, of course, the roundabout with the Barbers Shop emulates the same dropped 'T' (in their case 'B' as in BarBers) as in the band's logo. The Tramshed was *Sgt Pepper*'s but is now empty. A journey takes you along Queens Drive, past the Epstein family home, a prosperous and double-fronted property. Then to Strawberry Field (singular)… ten years ago, its gate was crumbling, leafy branches from trees draping its eroding seven-foot wall. It was built as a private mansion in 1870, and sold to the Salvation Army in 1934. After years of disrepair, it was demolished, but rebuilt and reopened in September 2019. Under the eye of the Salvation Army, the centre is now a Christian community, offering "spiritual exploration" and help to children with learning difficulties. In 2021, the John Lennon 'Imagine' piano was on display, lent by the Estate of George Michael.

When he climbed to the toppermost of the highest tree at Mendips, John let his imagination run riot. He could view Strawberry Field. In the song, there was John's old world infused by his glimpse of the new, it was the reality viewed through the prism of LSD, and memory. Separated by fame, wealth and geography, try as he might to leave it all behind, from London, Surrey or New York, Lennon could never wholly *forget*.

Phil, our *Magical Mystery Tour* guide, was a sharp and snappy Scouser. He told me they had fans from over the whole word, including *Mongolia*… "I didn't know they had *electricity* there…!" He was a lively guide, and spoke of a new restaurant in Chinatown: "All you can eat for 50p, straight up, 50p – only thing is, they just give you one chopstick".

Matthew Street is the site of the original Cavern, the bright Cavern Walks mall then boasted a branch of Vivienne Westwood. I enjoyed a nice pint of Flying Scotsman in The Grapes, viewing their Beatle memorabilia (a poster from a 1962 gig: "Ladies please bring a change of shoes as stiletto heels are not allowed"). There were also items related to the Cunard liners. The day I was visiting, there were the usual pilgrims viewing the Fab stuff, this time from South Carolina. If revisiting, many of the Cavern regulars would recognise The Grapes, and even after all these years, the pub still retains the authentic smell of whiffy toilets.

*

In 1983 Michael Jackson was the biggest pop star on the planet. The December 1982 release of *Thriller* had put him in the pop pantheon; the LP had taken on a life of its own, quickly on its way to becoming the best-selling album of all time. No one really knows how many copies that one album sold, but is believed to be somewhere north of 65,000,000. To get an idea of just how big it became, if *Thriller* were a country, it would be France. By the same margin, *I* would be somewhere between Yemen and Ghana.

A long-time Beatle fan, Jackson had covered McCartney's 'Girlfriend' on his breakthrough *Off the Wall*. He was delighted to work with Paul McCartney – and it should be remembered that the first single lifted off *Thriller* was the Jackson/McCartney duet on 'The Girl Is Mine'. Jackson was manifestly struggling with the success which greeted *Thriller*. That is perhaps what led him to recording with McCartney on a couple of tracks for what became Paul's 1983 *Pipes of Peace* album. Paul McCartney was one of the few people who had experienced what Michael was going through. It was during the sessions that Paul let slip to Michael that he was intending to buy back the Beatle catalogue from ATV Music.

In 1981, a joint McCartney/Yoko bid had been made to Lord Lew Grade, who owned ATV Music, under whose publishing umbrella came Northern Songs. The Beatle songs were the only item the former bass player and John's widow were interested in purchasing, but Grade wanted to shift the entire catalogue in one fell swoop. My understanding is that Paul and Yoko could not agree financial terms to make a joint bid.

As with all publishing catalogues, it was a mixed bunch. The jewel in the crown was undeniably the Beatles' Northern Songs titles. But ATV also published works by others with Beatle connections – such as Lonnie Donegan, Little Richard (Jackson generously later returned his song catalogue to Little Richard), Klaatu, the Searchers and Hurricane Smith. Income too would have been generated by Max Bygraves, Petula Clark, the Muppets and, perhaps with a following wind, the Fabulous Poodles.

Paul convivially explained to Michael that, with a canny eye, he had snapped up the Buddy Holly catalogue, when he had been advised that song catalogues could be obtained, like any commodity. The Buddy Holly Week, in tribute to that early influence, soon became one of the highlights of the London music calendar. Of course it wasn't entirely philanthropic, it all helped generate interest in the Holly catalogue, which would then be reflected in income. But it was a nice conclusion – when the youngster who heard of Buddy's death at Smokers Corner while at school could now repay the debt, and be repaid.

Prior to Jackson's interest, ATV Music had been sold to Australian businessman Rupert Holmes à Court. Michael was as intrigued as Paul had been that you could *buy* song catalogues. Michael dipped his toe in the water purchasing song catalogues of Sly Stone and Dion. It was while setting up the contentious Jackson brothers' *Victory* tour that Michael's accountant John Branca let slip that Northern Songs were up for grabs. "You don't mean *the* Northern Songs do you?" Michael's biographer J. Randy Taraborrelli reported him querying. "'Yeah Mike'", John said. He couldn't contain his enthusiasm. 'We're talking the Beatles, man. *The Beatles*'". So cashing his postal order, Jackson made a $47,500,000 bid for over 200 Beatles songs, beating McCartney, Coca Cola, EMI and CBS in the deal. Jackson did let Holmes à Court keep 'Penny Lane' as his daughter was called Penny.

Jackson's move rankled with McCartney then, it rankles still. "I gave him a lot of advice", Paul reflected later. "And you know what? A fish gets caught by opening his mouth".

"I still find a magic about writing a new song", McCartney told me in 1985. "Still the same feeling I ever had, which is why I'm sorry I didn't win the ownership of all my old songs which eventually went to Michael Jackson. I would one day like to get hold of them. They are your babies, it's a shame when they come onto the marketplace".

This is one of the many misconceptions about McCartney, that the ownership of the song catalogue is simply just about money, that all you need is cash. This is the issue – these are *his* songs, and they are out of his control. It caused the Macca hackles to rise even further when he had to effectively seek permission to re-record his own songs for *Give My Regards to Broad Street*.

In the years leading up to his death in 2009, Michael Jackson was in freefall – his position as 'The King of Pop' fatally undermined. The criminal charges against him were allied to a financial crisis in meeting his legal fees. In 1995, Sony merged with Jackson's ATV Music to become Sony/ATV. Jackson had requested a $140,000,000 loan from Sony, using the remaining share of Beatle songs as security to guarantee the loan. Jackson's latter years witnessed an unholy fall from grace. Prior to his death, his days were dogged by prohibitively expensive lawsuits, combatting accusations of paedophilia and draining criminal trials. Jackson still kept his half of the Beatle song catalogue. Following his death, Sony paid $750,000,000 for Jackson's 50%. For all his enthusiasm for the catalogue, and of all those Beatle songs, Michael Jackson only ever recorded one – 'Come Together' on his *HIStory* collection.

In the 1970s, it was all very different. In 1973, due to his profligate lifestyle, Elvis Presley was running short of spending money, so his manager, Tom Parker, sold all his only client's royalty rights back to his label RCA for $5,400,000, plus a guarantee of $500,000 per annum.

RCA Executive John Deary remembered: "He probably thought they had gotten all the use [sales] out of those masters they could get. I mean, how many times can you reissue the same songs over and over again?... But looking at it from my perspective, knowing

MPL Buddy Holly Week press pack

about all the unreleased out-takes and live performances – which RCA also bought in that deal – it was easy to see that we had just bought the gold mine".

It was in the 21st century that song catalogues ran parallel to traditional investment portfolios. It was Merck Mercuriadis and his Hipgnosis company who were snapping up songs like hungry predators. Among their 65,000-plus titles (including, he was proud of pointing out, 3,700 No.1s) were songs by Blondie, Neil Young, Chrissie Hynde and Eurythmics. Hoovering up such song catalogues didn't come cheap, the company has to date laid out over $2 *billion*.

A *Mail on Sunday* headline read, "Why I fear the next John and Paul may end up as lawyers – and not the new Beatles". It reminded me of Chuck Berry, when he was asked if he would have done anything different in his career? "First I'd have gone to Business School, *then* I'd have learned to play the guitar".

In a fascinating article for *Forbes* magazine in May 2021, Ariel Shapiro dug into the whole lucrative songwriting catalogue business. She began by singling out Ariana Grande's '7 Rings' and its one *billion* YouTube views… and wondering how many viewers recognised its incorporation of Rodgers & Hammerstein's 'My Favorite Things'. She then went on to consult with industry experts about the value of the catalogue of the composers of *Oklahoma!*, *The Sound of Music* and *South Pacific*. Looks like Richard and Oscar came in a respectable third with an estimated $350,000,000, just behind Michael Jackson ($375,000,000) and at the Toppermost of the Poppermost, Lennon & McCartney ($500,000,000).

Despite the wavering market for song catalogues, one can only speculate at how much the Lennon & McCartney catalogue might fetch if it ever became available.

The value of their catalogue so exceeds that of their competitor because so many of the 200-plus songs are recognised as classics. If you bought, say, the Procol Harum catalogue you are effectively buying just one song. With the Beatles you're getting not just the family silver, but the bank itself.

Another of those intriguing Beatle coincidences emerged when I discovered that the Pincus family owned the songwriting copyrights in the USA and Canada for six Beatle songs. Music publisher Leonard Pincus had witnessed a 1963 UK performance by the group, and persuaded his father to purchase 'Misery', 'She Loves You', 'I Saw Her Standing There', From Me to You', 'There's a Place' and 'I Wanna Be Your Man'. This was a timely acquisition, well before the group had registered in the American marketplace.

Those lucrative titles were then passed on to Round Hill music in 2012, that company's Vice-President was none other than Richard Rowe, son of Dick Rowe, the executive who went down in music history as 'the man who turned down the Beatles'. In 2021, it was announced Rowe had gone on to join the Hipgnosis company on the lookout for further song copyrights.

When you use Beatle music, you'd better have deep pockets – 'Tomorrow Never Knows', for example, cost *Mad Men* a cool $250,000 for use in an episode. One line from 'All You Need Is Love' cost more than the 50 classic soul and R&B songs heard in *The Commitments*. Use of Beatle music in Danny Boyle's 2019 *Yesterday* chewed up an estimated $10,000,000 of the film's budget.

Musically, The Beatles still continued to inhabit the landscape. In November 2003, the

Let It Be Naked album debuted on the UK albums chart with first-week sales of 54,500. "Have they just made the greatest garage rock album of all time?" *NME* asked on its cover. The album which was "The Beatles with their trousers down" had actually been a belt and braces job all along – the original Glyn Johns mixes; the Phil Spector overdubs; the officially released 1970 version. The 2003 *Naked* cut out the chatter and with a little help from Pro Tools each track was cleaned, ancillary noise eliminated and it came with a new running order.

Remade and remodelled, the new version included, for atmospherics, 'Don't Let Me Down', originally the B-side to 'Get Back'... *Naked* was seen as 'McCartney's revenge' as the version of 'The Long & Winding Road' had all of Spector's orchestration and choir removed. This was heresy to Beatle fans, but then as Paul's genial PR Geoff Baker said to me at the time, "purchase not compulsory".

And on it went. Soon after, in February 2004, Sam & Mark (me neither) became the third act (after Joe Cocker and Wet Wet Wet) to reach No.1 on the UK singles chart with their version of 'With a Little Help from My Friends'.

*

In auction rooms, it is the Beatles who continue to dominate. They used to be in competition with Elvis Presley, Jimi Hendrix and Queen. Yet now, anything Fab-related is what makes the headlines.

Since Sotheby's first dipped their uneasy toe in the water in 1981, it is Beatle memorabilia which endures. At that first auction, a Tom Jones jacket went for £12, *five* Tommy Steele paintings only raised £38, while Mitch Mitchell's drum kit from the Jimi Hendrix Experience era was a mere £220.

Sotheby's Hilary Kay (now a familiar face on the BBC's *Antiques Roadshow*) remembered it raised the odd eyebrow at the 200-year-old auction house when she told me: "I joined Sotheby's in 1977 and headed a department which was light on its feet and able to respond quickly to changes and developments in the collecting market.

"The idea of holding a Rock Memorabilia auction at Sotheby's was conceived in December 1980 as I listened to breakfast news on the radio and heard of the murder of one of my heroes, John Lennon. I had a hunch that there were many people who, like me, would want to own something relating to the Beatles. I discussed the general idea with folks in the entertainment industry and the consensus was, 'why not give it a go'.

"I was lucky with the first auction. Using a novel method (and one never used by Sotheby's), classified advertisements were placed in tabloid newspapers asking for entries. These advertisements were spotted by journalists and the idea of an out-of-character Sotheby auction became Page 2 news. Entries flooded in for appraisal.

"The first auction, on 22 December 1981, was greeted with wild enthusiasm; the atmosphere and growing hysteria as the audience gathered and queued to enter the auction room at Sotheby's Belgravia was likened to a Beatle concert in the glory days.

"The hunch played off. The first auction created its own momentum and Sotheby's went on to sell some of the most iconic pieces of Rock Memorabilia ever offered to the public. Now, almost 40 years on, the selling and collecting of Rock and Entertainment

Memorabilia is a well-respected multi-million-dollar, worldwide phenomenon.

"Why do the Beatles still dominate memorabilia auctions? Probably for some of the same reasons behind your decision to write a book on the Beatles… The enduring power and influence of the music, the passion of the original fans – the baby boomers – with funds now allowing them to own a piece of 'their' history.

"International and inter-generational popularity may ensure longevity of the market (a CNBC article states that the Beatles' music was streamed more than 1.7 billion times in 2019; with 30% of that streaming coming from those aged between 18 and 24)".

Was she ever tempted, I asked, to sneak anything home? "The hand-painted bass drumskin featured on the front cover of *Sgt Pepper's Lonely Hearts Club Band*. When the drumskin arrived for appraisal and I opened the packaging, every hair on my head stood on end with excitement. I invited Peter Blake, the artist responsible for designing the *Sgt Pepper* cover art, to come in and look at it with me. We examined the drumskin carefully and we talked about the chaos setting up the shoot in March 1967 when Michael Cooper photographed Peter Blake's cover art design. Subsequently, Peter Blake generously wrote a letter confirming the drumskin's provenance". It was later sold for £541,250.

I was at that first Rock & Roll auction of December 1981, writing it up for *Melody Maker*. Looking back, I kick myself at what I *could* have got at 20th-century prices: an autographed *With the Beatle*s, a snap at £320… a Paul McCartney letter from Hamburg ("I think we'll be making some records soon and we'll get them released in Liverpool as soon as possible…") a mere £2,200… a signed 1963 Royal Variety Performance programme, with not only all four Beatle autographs, but also Pinky & Perky for a paltry £1,050…

A decade later, there was speculation that Rock memorabilia was a busted flush. In a 1990 article for *The Independent*, David Lister wrote, "however the market progresses, it is unlikely that the £1,400,000 for Lennon's psychedelic Rolls Royce will be beaten". (In 2000 George Michael paid £1,450,000 for the piano on which Lennon wrote 'Imagine'.)

In 1997, you could get a set of Beatle autographs for £4,950 – in 2013, a similar set would set you back £24,500, an increase of 395%! In 1975, Hunter Davies was burgled and his LPs autographed by all four Beatles were stolen. In 2013 he ruefully noted, "on the insurance, I claimed £2.00 per LP because at that time, there was no extra value in their autographs".

No wonder after 2008, the group's disenchanted drummer used to sign himself Ringo 'Sotheby's' Starr.

We now know that Neil, Mal, Tony and other Beatles were adept at forging autographs. I pinned Tony Bramwell down on this point as we heard the chimes at midnight… In a flash he fashioned all four – John and George were eerily accurate. How much, I wondered, was a set of authentic *forged* autographs worth?

"What would auction houses do without the Beatles?" asked the *Sunday Times* Business section in 2003. Noting that 100 out of 213 lots due at the next rock auction were Beatle-related, the article concluded with the valuation accorded to the group's memorabilia, referencing the Marlene Dietrich cut-out from the *Pepper* cover, "however 'ground-breaking' this album was, five figures is a lot of money for a photograph mounted on cardboard". "When it comes to rock and pop memorabilia", Alastair McCrea of Ewbank auctioneers was emphatic in 2023, "there are two markets: the Beatles and everyone else".

As an example of the upward spiral, take the Abbey Road street sign. When the Beatles first began recording at the north-west London EMI studios in 1962, it fell under the London Borough of Marylebone. After that, in 1965, it came under Borough of Westminster. In 1967, Sir Misha Black redesigned all London street signs, and these are the ones which populate the auction houses. In 2013, one such was sold for £10,625. In 2021 a similar one went for £37,000 – 237 times its original estimate.

For the real artefacts of Beatle history, the sky's the limit: handwritten lyrics to classic songs top the list – 'All You Need Is Love' (£825,750), 'A Day in the Life' (£810,000), 'Hey Jude' (£731,000) 'Getting Better' (£161,000)… Like in the bad old days, when the disabled were wheeled in to be healed by the Beatle touch, today it is as if by owning the manuscript of one of the building blocks of popular music, some of that mercurial magic might be passed on to the owner. More than likely they are purchased by the dreaded 'men in suits' as an investment.

Katherine Schofield, then Director of Entertainment Memorabilia at Bonhams, spoke to me about the group's enduring appeal in the 21st-century marketplace: "What is so fascinating is that I have been at Bonhams for 18 years, and there is so much *new* material coming onto the market. Provenance is always an issue, but specialist knowledge has moved on so much since the 1980s. We can now verify very quickly and identify signatures by their entourage – and also each other!

"This was harder in the 1990s because not so much had been seen, and now the specialist knowledge has increased demonstrably. The provenance for autographs is easier. Lots come up now, signed to a particular person which they would have kept since they were teenagers. They are now of an age and the question is, to leave it to the family or reap the reward?

"Again, what is extraordinary is the number of items which keep appearing. We have two UK sales each year, of 200 to 300 lots each, and I would estimate between 1/3 to 50% are Beatle-related. There is undeniably a real appetite globally for them; it transcends generations, with new films, archive releases and anniversaries that extend their appeal to younger audiences. It is in our culture.

"The way that they dominate auction house prices … the demand for the Beatles remains very strong. There is a steady growth, a steady interest with an audience more discerning: a clear set of signatures is obviously preferred to scrappy ones. There is now enough on the market for people to pick and choose. A bottomless pit of interest. Autographs obtained while the Beatles were still together as a group command the strongest prices, as opposed to those acquired individually".

Incredibly, the group only ever did *four* official autograph sessions – two at local Widnes stores around the release of 'Love Me Do'; one at NEMS in January 1963; and a final one at the chaotic Wimbledon fan club melee in December 1963. With security a priority, presumably Brian Epstein could not guarantee the group's safety following their American breakthrough.

"Signatures from 1966 are rarer", Katherine continued, "because they had given up touring so the fans had less access and they were less visible. A good set meant you had to be in the inner circle, and they command stronger prices.

"While the Beatles dominate, there is a strong interest in the Rolling Stones, Pink

Floyd, Led Zeppelin… In terms of competition, I would say the Stones, probably because there has always been that rivalry, so the Stones from the 60s when they were at their peak. Jimi Hendrix is a lot rarer, but we find that anything from that moment in music history there is a strong market for. Nobody of course knew what it was worth *then*, if items were kept it was because they loved the era; the music touched them emotionally, and the items are all maintained and looked after because of that love.

"We keep waiting for their appeal to wane but it doesn't seem to happen! There *was* a lull 2005 to 2010, and we sensed that the interest was plateauing. But now the interest sustains; they are not being reinvented, the Beatles are becoming slowly and surely a part of our culture, and the culture of the United States. They are part of our lives, and there are people who want to be part of a historical moment so buying something by the Beatles is buying into a moment of history".

Bonhams' most expensive Beatle-related sale was a 1964 Aston Martin DB5 McCartney (the same model as favoured by 007), bought for £3,800 and sold in 2017 for £1,345,000. Tellingly, in Ian Shirley's round-up for *Record Collector* in 2022 of the 101 'most expensive individual pieces of rock memorabilia', 29 were Beatle-related.

The key to the value of auction house items is provenance, the *proof* that what is coming under the gavel is authentic. As those items poured out from the inner circle there was at least a degree of reliable authenticity. Over the years Pete Best, fan club secretary Freda Kelly, Brian's secretary Joanne Newfield, Magic Alex, John's housekeeper Dot … *Yellow Submarine* animators, stage doormen, technicians, policemen, chauffeurs … have all put up their souvenirs to sell. All those who had a fleeting connection with the four who were, and would remain, Fab.

And of course, concerning those Beatle signatures, we now know that the reliable Mal and Neil could forge away, and that George could 'do' John. When I interviewed Harrison, I took along my mono 1963 *Please Please Me* which Paul had signed and Ringo would sign, and while George was signing I was tempted to ask him to "do John while he was at it". But thought, no, hand on heart, that Christmas present from all those years ago has my provenance.

That same interview, I remarked while setting up the tape, how crazy it was with auction houses, that a piece of his *toast* was up for grabs. "That's total bullshit", George laughed. "I ate all my toast, *including* the crusts". (That Liverpudlian twang "crosts"…)

When He Was Fab, A Detour

The reason I got to George in 1992 was to talk up his *Live in Japan* release when I was writing for *Vox* magazine. One of a number of colleagues, we were allowed half an hour or so, as George sat in an anonymous hotel room in Kensington… At least I was spared the dreaded 'round table' format. Here, 'the talent' moves swiftly from table to table, answering European journalists' questions: the man from Denmark wanting to know when they would next be appearing in Denmark? The woman from Belgium wanting to know what they thought of Belgium…?

Here was an opportunity to talk to a Beatle… George was cordial if reserved, we got into a pissing contest about the preponderance of Beatle tracks on what was nominally a George Harrison release ("Well *I* don't think of them as Beatle tracks". "But George, they *did* appear on a Beatles album…"). But Nelson Wilbury opened up, warmly and positively, when the name of his old chum Lucky Wilbury was mentioned, with George reverentially quoting Dylan lyrics like the Holy Writ.

Inevitably, the subject of his 'other band' came up. George laughed about his memories of those crazy years when we spoke: "The Beatles, at the height of Beatlemania, all we did was stand on a stage, sing a few tunes very quickly, shake our heads and go 'Ooooh'. For years it was 'The Beatles', 'The Beatles'… they're whipped into this frenzy. That was what the mania was – even the police would go 'The Beatles Are Coming', and they'd all hop on their motorbikes and go crashing into each other".

It was that mania which so cheesed him off. He took his music seriously, did George, and the all-encompassing mayhem played havoc with that. In *I Me Mine*, George remembered, "They wanted to do a ticker tape parade and I remember saying 'No, no, no'. That imagery of people being shot, Kennedy, Beatlemania, madness. Talk about pressures".

Ironically, the week I met him in 1992, the highest rising album on the UK charts was *Sgt Pepper*, 25 years after its release. As one of only four who could qualify, did George have any insights into the continued, continuing success of his group?

"I think, first of all, you could compare the Beatles to other great things, things that have caused a great stir in history. I think if you try and isolate 'Why the Beatles?' you get into trouble because you sound like these four people are these special agents or something. But why does anything have a lasting effect – positive or negative? I grew up right at the end of the Second World War. I'm 49 years old… I don't think one week has gone by in my entire life when I haven't seen something about Hitler. I could never understand how he bullshitted everybody, but what is this fascination with Hitler?

"He's always shoved down our throats, you turn on the TV in the afternoon, and there he is!… I think the simplest explanation for it is that we accumulate – just as we do in our bank – we accumulate credit and debit. We do that through our own actions – we're getting into a bit of philosophy here, the reincarnation theory, but that's what I think happens.

"Bob Dylan said it like this 'look out kid, it's something you did, God knows when, but you're doing it again'. In the Bible somebody said, 'Whatsoever a man seweth that shall he reap'. So whatever Hitler was, he was a nasty bastard, and he came back as a nasty bastard. And the Beatles, whoever they were, that was the result of what they'd done before – we sentence you to a life imprisonment, but the prison is actually the Beatles. You'll be famous and rich, but you'll be imprisoned by that concept of Beatlemania".

Anthology director Bob Smeaton touched on that when he spoke to Andy Davis about the making of the documentaries: "The Beatles don't know how interested people are in them. They don't realise how big the Beatles are and they don't realise the affection people feel for them… as John says in the show, they were in the eye of the hurricane".

I'd like to have spent more time just talking, but there's always an agenda, and a reason. George was there to push product. I was there to write a feature, get an autograph and boast about meeting a Beatle. I always felt that if you could have just settled down with him and chat, about, oh… gardening, Monty Python, Handmade Films, 'Arthur', Lonnie Donegan, Terry Gilliam's magnificent *Brazil*, or George's songwriting idol, or even George Formby – it would be far less artificial. I remember David Hepworth interviewing George's old mentor Bob Dylan for the newly-launched *Q* magazine, and hearing the following exchange when a minder inquired, "How's the interview going, Bob?" "Okay... but he keeps asking me *questions*...!"

I have always regarded interviewing as a fairly unnatural act, trying to buddy up to someone whose interest in talking to you ranked probably somewhere just above root canal work. If you were lucky, you might click, and the hovering PR dismissed with a wave from the talent and the request for 'a few minutes longer'. Nine times out of ten it was an ordeal slightly less testing than *Mastermind*. Both parties putting a brave face on the procedure.

However, the nature of the beast is that George had broken cover to sell product, the record company people wanted to get as many hacks through the door as they could. When opportunity demanded, George would dutifully be Fab again, but unlike most of us, he didn't live in the past. Rehearsing for his 1991 Japanese tour, guitarist Mike Campbell told Graeme Thomson: "I'll never forget, we were doing 'Something' and when we got to the solo, George stopped the band and said 'I don't remember how this solo goes'. The entire band, on cue, sang the whole song for him, and he goes 'Oh, OK, now I remember!'"

Rarely venturing far from Friar Park, public sightings of George often had a Dylan connection – he joined him onstage in October 1987 when he was touring the UK with Tom Petty & the Heartbreakers, and in 1992 was a special guest at the CBS Dylan 30th Anniversary show at Madison Square Garden. George contributed a storming 'Absolutely Sweet Marie' which was one of the highlights of the show, along with his purple jacket. It marked one of his last-ever performances.

Never one to wallow in nostalgia, George did occasionally dip in... 'All Those Years Ago', his tribute to John, was released only six months after Lennon's murder. While his tongue was firmly in his cheek when he revisited the Beatle Years on his jaunty 1988 'When We Was Fab'. Like all who come into contact with those they admire, I wish I had been able to spend more time with George. The dream is that we get on *so* well that we adjoin to the pub, you get the beers in, and the Quiet One opens up, intrigued by your insights and perception. It didn't happen. I see from my diary it was "a sweaty day", and that at the interview's conclusion, I dropped a script in at BBC Radio 4 (which was never commissioned) then went home to watch a documentary on the CIA. All things passed.

*

Getting back... I had gone along to a Bonham's auction with the Icicle Works' Ian McNabb in the 90s for a *Vox* feature. He splashed out £120 on lot 549, a £1 note signed by Paul McCartney. At the time his explanation appeared entirely reasonable: "Pound notes don't exist anymore. Paul McCartney is the richest man in pop, so I thought an extinct note signed by the richest man in pop is highly desirable".

Pop auctioneers though had every right to be wary... An 'authentic' Lennon autograph was found on an album not released until four years after his death. A Freddie Mercury postcard sent "from Queen's 1969 American tour" was of interest, as the group weren't formed until 1970... An autographed Jimi Hendrix LP was equally curious, as the album in question wasn't released until after the guitarist's death... Five 'John Lennon Shot

Dead' posters from the *Evening Standard* were on sale, after the newspaper had changed its name… Locks of Beatle hair, with provenance from the person *selling* them (of course she's not going to say, actually they're my husband's)…

Auction house estimates vary, but most speculate that between 70% and 90% of Beatle autographs were fakes. "Neil Aspinall probably signed more Beatles autographs than the boys themselves", Tim Jones wrote in *Record Collector* with the sort of forensic detail of the true believer. "Experts recognise his work very easily… He did George Harrison and Ringo Starr well, but his Paul and John were flawed. Aspinall's McCartney invariably saw the 'r', 't', 'n' and 'e' ill defined…"

Literally everything Beatle-related, has come under the hammer… EMI toilet paper, rejected by the Beatles as being "too hard" (£85) – that would have been the notorious Izal brand, the well-known bane to generations of post-war children… The front door from Apple (£18,000)… The jacket Lennon wore on the *Rubber Soul* sleeve (£180,000). In 2014 someone paid £23,000 for John Lennon's… *tooth*. Literally everything but the kitchen sink was up for grabs, *including* the kitchen sink, which was sold from the McCartney family home before the National Trust took over.

I loved a Paul autograph on a restaurant menu (Dinner Dansant 32/6d) and a Nelson cigarette pack signed by Paul, George and John (£520) – my Mum used to smoke Nelson. A discarded Lennon cigarette stub went for £100… In passing on Beatle cigarettes, Paul told Paul Du Noyer: "Rothmans, Senior Service… Peter Stuyvesant, you'd pop 'em up instead of Players where you had to push it and open it, suave and sophisticated".

By and large it is the Hard Rock Café which keeps the auction prices buoyant; you ain't sellin' if the Hard Rock ain't buyin'. Their 92 restaurants worldwide host around 63,000 items of rock memorabilia. They are also in that rarified league as the prices escalate. The Beatles at auction now are far beyond the pockets of their fans.

Of the recorded Beatle items at auction, the problem right there is copyright. The complicated skein of Apple, EMI and, currently, the Universal Music Group mean that any Beatle music has to be approved by them, but more crucially, given the nod by Paul, Ringo, Olivia and Yoko. In 1998 a fascinating tape of the group emerged, a complete set of their performance at the Gaumont, Bournemouth. Recorded immediately prior to the release of 'She Loves You' and the ensuing hysteria. Top ticket price 8/6d (22½p).

Lucky Irene Mellor went along to every one of the group's six nights at the Gaumont; having her dad Tom as the venue's chief technician helped. It was his job to record all the shows at the venue; its high-domed ceiling offered "acoustics second to none". The reel to reel tape then lodged in a family biscuit tin for 35 years. Such a fascinating audio document was sold for a modest £25,300, because it could never be officially released, or played in public, the assumption is that the purchaser was Apple.

It always amazes me what emerges from the Dark Web when it comes to the Beatles – rare photos, which surely could only have come from private collections, or audio evidence long thought lost down the decade. In early 2022, for example, a clip was posted. It was from 5 April 1963, when the group received their first silver disc at EMI's Manchester Square HQ. They performed two songs ('Please Please Me', 'From Me to You') for the company's executives.

It was the ubiquity of the band, and brand, which still astounds as the years pass by…

Google estimated that there are in excess of 30,000,000 Beatle sites on the web. Today I simply Googled 'The Beatles' and was informed of 159,000,000 results. Academia has not been slow off the mark either; among the many Beatle courses are those taught in Texas, Ohio and Southern California. Enormous, unreadable titles on the group spill regularly from universities around the world – 'Is Affirmational Fandom the Shadow Side of Transformation?' or *The Spiritual Rebellion of Muhammad Ali and George Harrison*.

One estimate has a new Beatles book published every fortnight. That is likely an underestimate; a 2021 survey detailed 140 Beatle books published. Another source cites 5,000 titles. What amazes, and delights, is the forensic detail the authors apply. You might think that Piet Schreuders, Mark Lewisohn and Adam Smith's *The Beatles' London* was of limited appeal. But I found myself going down the rabbit hole for hours as I pored over this rock & roll *A – Z*.

There are biographies of Tony Sheridan, Aunt Mimi and Jimmy Nicol… There are memoirs by Alf Bicknell, Peter Brown, Tony Bramwell and Geoff Emerick. There is a book by Mary Hopkin's sister. There are books before they became famous, then when they were overtaken by fame, and day-by-day chronicles. Books about the LPs they made. Books about the LPs they *should* have made. Then books about their break-up. Books about if they *hadn't* broken up.

Whole books are devoted to a specific gig (Shea Stadium, Candlestick Park, Apple roof), or Beatle locations (Rishikesh, Hamburg, the 18 hours they spent in Barcelona). Whole books on a specific song ('Yesterday', 'Dear Prudence'). There are books on individual albums (*Sgt Pepper*, *The White Album*). In 2014 Ted Montgomery gave us *The Beatles Through Headphones*, offering "the Quirks, Peccadilloes, Nuances and Sonic Delights of the Greatest Popular Music Ever Recorded". There are books by the group's hairdresser; *two* books about Hessy's, the Liverpool store where they purchased their instruments. Pat Kinzer has published two books on the Official George Harrison Fan Club. Although he isn't even mentioned by name in the song, there is a biography of Tara Browne because of his Beatle connection. In 2015 Dominik Doeppert published *Conceptual Metaphor Theory in the Beatles Lyrics. Metaphor as Cognitive Phenomena*. I haven't had time to read Dr Heady Delpak's *The Beatles* book, but am sorely tempted, as two of his other biographies are of Jesus and Julie Andrews.

You can learn how to play their songs on solo mandolin, accordion or ukulele. There are books on their spiritual values, finances, equipment, memorabilia. There are worldwide discographies and chronologies. Whole volumes devoted to their visits to Wales, Scotland, Northern Ireland, Spain and Manila; there's a book about the only time they performed in Bath. At the last count, there are *three* books alone on the 'Paul Is Dead' theory. Ray Zirkle has reached the second volume of his look at the way the Beatles releases were advertised. *The Beatles Worldwide Singles & EPs Encyclopedia, Volume 20* dealt with releases in Mexico and Mozambique… I just can't keep up. It is all too much.

It reminded me of the Shakespeare scholars, leaving aside those who wrote books contesting that the plays of William Shakespeare weren't written *by* William Shakespeare. No, those that dissect the Bard's work with surgical precision. For example, that Shakespeare's works contain 15,785 question marks; that 'ears' are mentioned 401 times, while 'dunghill' less than a dozen. That 'hate' is referenced 183 times, but 'love', is all you need, with 2,259 references.

With the same degree of intensity, Lesley-Ann Jones ploughed a similar furrow as she sifted through the canon of original Beatle compositions. Among her finds were that the word 'you' was mentioned 2,262 times; 'me' 1,060 and 'love' 613.

From being the paradigm of a business 'failure', Apple were kept busy long after the group's 1970 split. For years, plans had been afoot for a full-length documentary about the band (*The Long & Winding Road*) which led to Neil Aspinall sourcing and purchasing rare film footage. Collectors who had been hounded over the years and having their collars felt by the 'men in suits' were surprised to find themselves receiving amiable inquiries for that audio or film footage which had slipped through the Apple net.

Otherwise, the company kept a weather eye on copyright, bootlegs, song licensing, official merchandise, which took on a life of its own. There was a Beatles *Monopoly* ("It's All Too Much – Go To Jail"), there was also a *Yellow Submarine Monopoly* edition, as well as a Beatles *Scrabble* ("Love Me Do – Receive One Tile From Each Player"). To cash-in on the *Trivial Pursuit* hysteria of the mid-80s, there was a Beatles edition. But it was withdrawn when it was found to contain too many errors.

It all came to a head in 1978, when flicking through a magazine, George Harrison noted an advert for Apple computers and felt there could be "a potential for trademark conflict". In 1981, Apple Corps reached an agreement with Apple computers for, by all accounts, a meager $80,000. Beatle fan Steve Jobs could go on with *his* Apple, provided he kept it away from music. "My model for business", Jobs had admitted, "is The Beatles. They were four guys who kept each other's negative tendencies in check. They balanced each other and the total was greater than the sum of the parts".

By 1991 and with an eye to the future, in a lawsuit, Jobs claimed that the Beatles' Apple was no longer a functioning company. That led to a smattering of Apple CDs being released, effectively emphasising that the Beatles' Apple *was* still very much active. The two ran along parallel lines, but in 2003 with the launch of iTunes, the two companies clashed head-on. According to one financial expert, "Apple's iTunes music store is central to Apple's strategy to promote its computers as digital entertainment hubs". Apple in London stated, "complaint is made over the use by Apple computers of the word Apple and apple logos in conjunction with its new application for downloading pre-recorded music from the internet".

The case was eventually settled to everyone's satisfaction in 2007. The details have never been published, but insiders estimate that Jobs' Apple paid Apple Corps $500,000,000, that's half a *billion* dollars. By 2023, the late Steve Jobs' company was valued at two *trillion* dollars. It was not until 2010 that Apple allowed the Beatles' music to be downloaded ("It has been a long and winding road to get here", Jobs commented).

Apple logos, a detour: the Beatles' Apple was inspired by Paul's fondness for a Magritte painting. Jobs' designer Rob Janoff took a familiar bite out of the forbidden fruit. Legend has the bite as a nod to the English scientist, Alan Turing whose wartime work at Bletchley Park helped crack the Nazis' Enigma code. Turing, a homosexual, committed suicide by eating an apple laced with cyanide. "It isn't true", Jobs admitted, "but God, I wish it were".

On 16 December 2011, a record 10,000,000 Beatle tracks had been downloaded since iTunes made them available on 16 November 2010. During that first week, 450,000 albums and 2,000,000 single tracks were snapped up, with 'Here Comes the Sun' the most popular song and *Abbey Road* the most popular album. It was on Christmas Eve 2015 that the Beatles' music finally streamed, and they became the third best-selling act in America. An astonishing 50,000,000 streams were noted in the first 48 hours. Surprisingly, Spotify had 'Come Together' as the most popular (1,840,000 plays), followed by 'Let It Be' (1,550,000) and 'Hey Jude' (1,320,000).

A Spotify poll has the Beatles mixing it as one of the few British acts aside from Ed Sheeran and Harry Styles, remarkable given that the chart is almost totally dominated by contemporary acts streamed by a young demographic – Bad Bunny is No.1, Drake No.2 and J. Balvin No.3.

In May 2023, 'Here Comes the Sun' became the first Beatle stream to hit the magic billion mark. It also became the first song from the 1960s to join that club. "The Beatles have such an incredible catalog, and it's one that continually finds new generations of fans," said Spotify's Tricia Rice. "This may be the (band's) first song to cross into the billions club on Spotify, but their listenership continues to stay steady. With over 30 million monthly listeners on platform, the band's music will continue to make impacts for many more decades."

Even before the *Bohemian Rhapsody* film, Queen were one of the few acts which could match the Beatles in tenacity and market penetration. It wasn't just the back catalogue which continues unabated – surviving members Brian May and Roger Taylor had spells with Paul Rodgers and Adam Lambert as front men, effortlessly filling venues under the Queen brand all around the world. Queen's *Greatest Hits* remains the UKs best-selling album, shifting 7,000,000 copies (Abba are No.2 and *Sgt Pepper*, the only original studio album, is third with sales of 5,300,000).

This would always be the problem with the marketing of 'heritage acts'. Once their original audience had died off, would there be sufficient interest to be found in subsequent generations? It was something Elvis Presley Enterprises were forced to address. The loyalty of the King's original fans was tested by uninspired and plain greedy marketing by his label. His 1950s audience was long gone, and their children had found their own idols. Yet by skipping a generation, with strategic merchandising, and the careful stewardship of box set compiler Ernst Jorgensen, the King has yet to leave the building.

There was surely nothing that could affect the *Beatles*? When the current run of box set releases ends, what else was there in the vaults to tempt longstanding fans? And how to entice *new* audiences, in the world of digital platforms, streaming and short attention span. There is so much choice now – a 2023 estimate had 100,000 new tracks being added every *day* to music platforms.

One act that proved it *could* be done were Abba. Ironically rescued from a slush pile, *Mamma Mia* is running onstage all over the world. The two films based on the play helped keep the Swedish quartet's name alive. In 2013, an Abba Museum was opened in Stockholm. But when they announced their avatar reunion and new album in September 2021, the world went a little crazy. When the quartet last released new music, their competition was A Flock of Seagulls, the Goombay Dance Band and Renee & Renato.

Forty years after they split, and thanks to 65,000,000 pixels and 1,000,000,000 computing hours, *Abba Voyage* were ready themselves for some 2022 gigs. However, Abba never achieved the same success in America as in Europe. So, still ahead of the game, if it needed any further confirmation, in 2021 the *24/7 Wall St* website confirmed the Beatles' place as The Most Popular Rock Band Of All Time. It combined the group's place on Spotify (16,700,000 downloads), Facebook (39,700,000 likes) and *Billboard* album charts (19 No.1s) to give them peak place.

Even following John's murder, those reunion rumours just wouldn't go away. Another one sporadically dusted down was a second-generation Beatles – Sean Lennon, James McCartney, Dhani Harrison and Zak Starkey getting together. In 2023, Zak had the best rejoinder: "If we had spent years sleeping on flea-infested mattresses in the back room of a Hamburg club it might work. But we have been swaddled in silken robes in houses so big that it's too far to go and make some toast".

One of the few moments of comic relief amidst all the endless Beatle lawsuits and court battles came in 2006, when the editor of *News Wireless* was interviewed live on BBC News 24 about the Apple Corps versus Apple court case. Asked if he was surprised by the verdict, Guy Goma replied: "I am very surprised to see … this verdict to come on me, because I was expecting that. When I came they told me something else and I am coming… So a big surprise anyway". No wonder he was surprised, as Mr Goma was actually waiting in BBC reception to be interviewed for a job as a cleaner before he was mistakenly hauled into a live television interview, one which he carried off with professional aplomb. The clip has since been viewed over 5,000,000 times.

It had been in 2010 that the Beatles were forgiven, by perhaps a brand even bigger than them. The Vatican newspaper *L'Osservatore Romano* did concede that the group "lived life to excess and even said they were bigger than Jesus", but lauded the band as a "jewel" whose music remained a "consolation".

One area of controversy which remained was the use of Beatle music outside of and away from 'the canon'. This was effectively those 12 LPs released during the group's lifetime, plus the subsequent compilations that rounded up singles and B-sides. That Beatle music was to be heard officially *only* on Beatle-sanctioned releases. Due to the 60-year law on song copyright, only 'Love Me Do' and 'PS I Love You' have ever appeared on those endless *All Time Greatest 60s Hits* CD compilations. The law has now been extended to 70 years since the original release, so we *might* expect a glut in 2033. Or maybe Apple will take a leaf from the Bob Dylan songbook, and briefly make available limited editions of material, thereby extending the song copyrights even further.

In advertising, it really kicked off when Michael Jackson licensed 'Revolution' for a Nike advert in 1987. The shoe company paid a hefty $500,000. What really rankled was that, for the first-ever use of a Beatles song in a commercial, Yoko Ono had approved, believing it would bring "John's music to a different generation". Paul felt otherwise. Over the years, McCartney contacted Jackson about the dilution of the Beatle brand. "I am not happy with the way that Michael has handled it [the Lennon and McCartney catalogue]…" Paul wrote in 1995. "It cheapens the songs".

Beatle songs have since been heard in UK TV and film commercials. But without sunlight intruding, crucially, not *by* the Beatles. So in 2008 for their Christmas TV advertising campaign, John Lewis were allowed to use 'From Me to You' with a kids choir. In 2009 Budweiser used 'All Together'. 'Here Comes the Sun' was heard on a beer commercial, in Spanish… 'All You Need Is Love', briefly, promoted Nescafe Gold Blend. Distinguished the songs may have been, not necessarily those of the performers… the Hours, Rockin' 1000 and Bob Doran…

Not everyone was besotted. The novelist Anthony Burgess had a particular loathing, his fictional Beatles in his novel *Enderby Outside* were "about as horrible in appearance as any four young men could be" (ironic, coming from the author of *A Clockwork Orange* which celebrated the quartet of Alex and his thuggish Droogs). In their diaries, Noel Coward and Kenneth Williams were equally dismissive. Kingsley Amis too took against the Fabs, no surprises there from English literature's Mr Grumpy. Writing to his friend Philip Larkin, who *did* like the Beatles, Amis ranted during John's 1969 antics: "Oh fuck the Beatles. I'd like to push my bum into John Lennon's face for forty-eight hours or so, as a protest against all the war and violence in the world."

The majority, however, celebrated their music, loved the idea of the Beatles and marvelled at the achievements of the Lennon & McCartney partnership. A new, 21st-century generation was chasing the heels of the previous century's pop phenomenon. Songwriting had entered a new era, with collaborations a necessary part of the process, with each writer tackling an individual element to craft a 'perfect' pop song. As one critic remarked, "songwriting credits now read like a war memorial". In America, one man stood alone, listing the most successful songwriters with most No.1s following McCartney (32) was … Max Martin. At the time of writing the Swedish songwriter had equalled Lennon's 26 US chart-toppers, beginning with Britney Spears, and on through Katy Perry, Pink, Taylor Swift…

This was obviously reflected in chart statistics, and how the Beatles stacked up in this new era. In the age of downloads and streaming, Drake and Ariana Grande's 'people' were all claiming chart phenomena. Certainly, in October 2018 Drake achieved the most hits on the Hot 100 in a calendar year. And in February 2019, Ariana Grande became the first act since the Beatles to simultaneously have the US top three singles – but put a marker down in 2074 to see how many people can sing '7 Rings', 'Thank U, Next' or 'Positions'.

Drake did it again in July 2020, registering his 40th Top 10 single. That beat Madonna's 2001 total of 38 when she became the first to exceed the Beatles' 34. Obviously, the 21st-century marketplace was manifestly different from that in which the Beatles achieved their success. Chart rules in the streaming era made *every track* on an album release *immediately* eligible for the singles chart, provided they were streamed or downloaded enough. So, when an Ariana, a Drake or a Beyonce release an album, multiple chart entries become immediately probable.

Intriguingly, Drake's 2021 'Champagne Poetry' found his own songwriting credit alongside that of Lennon & McCartney. The Canadian rapper had made use of the Beatles' 'Michelle' on his own composition.

On the LP charts, in April 2021, Taylor Swift broke a Beatle record, she notched up three No.1 albums in 259 days. The Beatles had done it during 1965/66 (with *Help!*, *Rubber Soul*, *Revolver*), but it took them 364 days. Swift did it again in October 2022, when she occupied all ten places in the *Billboard* Top 10.

It was a pop landscape which had altered irrevocably and unrecognizably since those days of ordering, sight unseen and ears unheard, the new Beatles single. Indeed, with the bulk of record buying diverted to streaming, the concept of 'the single' all but disappeared. Key releases were now categorised as 'impact tracks'. Tracks were 'dropped'. When artists broke cover to promote a new release, they entered 'The Zone'. Pop had gone from a record store to a computer key.

Bands, too, had gone with the wind. A UK singles chart of April 2022 had only two groups in the Top 40. For reasons of economy, record company uncertainty and an increasing reliance on solo acts from pop, hip hop and rap, this was the era of Adele, Justin Bieber and Billie Eilish.

And, lest we forget, in a league of her own, with the power to affect Presidential elections, Taylor Swift.

The music which reached out across generations, era and continents was now having to fight in a whole new competitive marketplace. No longer did music have a guaranteed audience. A new release from Drake, Harry Styles or Rhianna had to compete with a new launch from Nike; the latest smartphone or a new edition of *Grand Theft Auto*. It was the latter which spectacularly eclipsed all that had gone before: on its 2013 release, *Grand Theft Auto V* took in £650,000,000 on its first *day*. That saw it enter the record books as the fastest-selling entertainment product in history.

Creatively, the days of the Brill Building songwriting factory, the Lennon & McCartney collaboration and Bob Dylan's inspiring solo compositions were long gone. Now, songs were put together like Model-T Fords. A 2021 investigation revealed that the last *Billboard* No.1 album not to feature a single additional songwriting credit was Dylan's 2014 *Tempest* – Beyonce's *Lemonade* featured almost 40! For Kanye West's 2021 album *Donda*, 160 people were credited. In contrast, *The White Album* acknowledged 13 plus "all at number 9".

As an example is an article Paul Sinclair wrote in January 2021. For many who grew up with the Beatles he clarified the shifting sands of the music industry today. In December 2020, much press coverage was devoted to Wham's 'Last Christmas' finally reaching No.1 in the UK.

"The truth of the matter is that while many hundreds of thousands of people actively wanted to buy 'Last Christmas' in late 1984, only 1,555 people wanted to do that at the end of 2020", Sinclair wrote. "How do we know this? It's because that's exactly how many digital downloads of 'Last Christmas' were *bought* last week (yep, people still do that, it seems)… That is the only true, comparable measure. The will of fifteen hundred people have overruled the will of a million people. History is re-written".

Fleet Street had much fun on Christmas Eve 2022: the novelty duo from Nottingham Ladybaby landed their fifth consecutive Christmas No.1, thereby beating the Beatles' record of four. The charity single 'Food Aid' benefitted UK food banks. Ladybaby issued "a massive apology to the Beatles and to all Beatles fans". Their total UK sales for all *five* of their No.1 hits were just over half a million, 500,000 less than the last Beatles Christmas No.1 'Hello Goodbye'.

With the Covid virus denying a lucrative income from touring, every Rich List survey of the 21st century, still showed Sir Paul McCartney remaining effortlessly near the top, largely due to his performance and songwriting royalties from his first group. But then, in any attempt to surpass the Beatles' supremacy, equally extravagant claims were made... Neither Nirvana nor One Direction, neither BTS nor Little Mix are likely to stack up against the Beatles. Not that anyone will really care in the future, the loyalty for pop acts has evaporated as the technology develops with terrifying rapidity.

There will, of course, still be Pop Idols. But these will be fabricated objects. No element of spontaneity or camaraderie shall intrude. Those that buck the system will find their shelf-life shortened by an electronic zeitgeist in which 'pop music' will play only a minor role.

The pop marketplace is obviously, demonstrably different from that which the Beatles entered 60 years ago. If you want a picture of the venal 21st-century pop industry, you could do a lot worse than read John Niven's blackly comic *Kill Your Friends*. Put-together pop groups (One Direction, Little Mix) were sanctioned by programmes like *Pop Idol* or *The X Factor*. The huge viewing figures those shows engendered automatically saw the winner's debut release immediately become the nation's No.1 single.

Brixton Academy founder Simon Parkes wrote witheringly of "tacky Barbie-doll bands croaking out their turgid, anodyne pop trash..." The early 21st century was a period which led to him giving up venue management, and I felt that his feelings confirmed just why the Beatles merit such devotion. It also painted a picture of the pop scene as it was when they broke through in 1963, even if written from a 2014 point of view: "From a label's perspective, it made perfect sense. Those pop groups were docile, easily manipulated, and sang the songs they were told to. They sold thousands of records... There was never any worry about helping artists through 'difficult creative periods' because these weren't creative artists. It was far easier for the label simply to drop the act and dredge up a new gaggle of wide-eyed teenagers to bewitch with promises of pop stardom".

Life before, and after, the Beatles... Move over Larry Parnes and tell Simon Cowell the news.

*

The one after 909... It was December 2009 which saw the launch of the remastered Beatle CDs ("Hear Ringo's squeaking drum pedal on 'Words of Love'...", "John's creaky piano chair on 'A Day in the Life'...", "'Misery' sounds very full, with more than a hint of snot in John Lennon's voice...", "It's like we've been listening to them under glass all these years..."). At a total of £370 for both the mono and stereo box sets, first day sales of the remastered box sets generated £1,500,000 sales in UK alone. They became the most expensive releases to ever chart in the UK. That week, the Top 75 featured a total of 16 Beatles albums.

The same period also saw the launch of *The Beatles Rock Band* video game. Here you get to accompany the band in one of six venues (the Cavern, Apple roof, etc.) or on a chosen song. It was "the digital version of the pub or campfire singalong", Simon Garfield wrote, "the 21st century upgrade of the Victorian family parlour concert. If you play well you get mellifluous music that sounds like your heroes. If you sing out of tune, your friends may walk out on you".

It was extraordinary to see the Beatles again on the cover of *NME* in September 2009.

Inside that issue, the weekly carried that era's big names – Muse, Paramore, MIA, Arctic Monkeys, Florence & the Machine… True, the McCartney interview and reassessment tied in with the launch of the *Rock Band* game. But nonetheless, the issue positively *bulged* with awestruck accounts of every album of a band who had last played together over 40 years before.

Was it more than coincidence then that BBC Radio 2 spread their 'Beatles Weekend' over that Bank Holiday? It was not only the release of *Rock Band*, but those controversial CD releases, "All 13 classic studio albums and *Past Masters* digitally Remastered for the first time ever". Cunningly, that release was scheduled for 09.09.09 (The One *After* 909, geddit?).

The value of their back catalogue is inestimable. It is the jewel in the crown in the competitive world of song publishing. It is the oyster in the shell. It is the… oh you get the picture. In 2020/21, Bob Dylan, Paul Simon and Neil Young sold their songwriting catalogue for astonishing nine-figure sums. One could only salivate at the figure if the Lennon & McCartney catalogue became available. Such is the physical value that the vaults at EMI, where the master tapes are stored, are linked to the local St John's Wood police station. On its release, armed guards in the Netherlands supervised the dispatch of the *Anthology* CDs.

In 2021, like something out of *Dr Strangelove*, somewhere near the Arctic Circle, a crypt was being constructed. Once permission had been granted, it would house, among other things, master tapes of the Beatles recordings to be saved for posterity. They would be there for future generations to marvel at. Come Armageddon, it would "withstand the kind of extreme electromagnetic pulses that could result from a nuclear explosion, which could permanently damage electronic equipment and play havoc with digital files."

However much the music was esteemed, the Gordian knot of Apple and the subsequent rancour sadly continued… The bad feeling was highlighted when Paul re-negotiated his EMI contract to gain higher royalties (rumoured in some cases and for some albums to be five times as much as his bandmates)…

As the first to walk out of the *Let It Be* sessions, George's reluctance to become Fab again was manifest. He dutifully accepted that no interview to promote a new album could avoid 'the Beatle question', but he bit the bullet, and when his dry, laconic humour was evident, even became quite cheerful. However, when his second career foundered, it was time to go "oooh" again, as he was overcome by his film production company losses…

George's friendship with and fondness for the Monty Python team found him financing their second film, *Monty Python's Life of Brian* because he "wanted to see it". His friend Eric Idle said of George's estimated $4,000,000 contribution, as "the most anybody's ever paid for a cinema ticket in history". The film made a profit. So, coinciding with his lessening interest in making music, George Harrison turned film producer. Handmade Films had begun wisely and relatively modestly, concentrating on relatively low-budget films with a British bias. They included *The Long Good Friday*, *Time Bandits*, *Withnail & I*, *A Private Function*, all of which did surprisingly well at the box office. However, it started to go belly up when the company set its sights higher – Madonna's 1986 *Shanghai Surprise*, *How to Get Ahead in Advertising* and *Water* were all spectacular flops.

Having a Beatle in the boardroom helped – for *Withnail & I* the original version of

'While My Guitar Gently Weeps' was heard on the soundtrack. The film acts as a threnody on the idealism of the 60s, with Danny the uber-hippie lamenting, "They're selling hippie wigs in Woolworths, man. The greatest decade in the history of mankind is over…"

George was very hands-on, and publicly promoted every Handmade release, and appeared to relish his new role. But financial woes saw familiar lawsuits flying around, and the company was sold in 1991.

It appeared that the sad truth was, to get the Beatles together, all you needed was … a cheque book. Prior to the 1995 *Anthology* avalanche (6CDs, TV documentary, book, DVD box set…) Apple's 1994 turnover was £10,000,000. The following year it was estimated at £75,000,000, with George taking a healthy slice, presumably much of his Handmade losses could be recouped.

The *Anthology* DVDs provide a fascinating look into Beatle history. Talking to me in 1992, George admitted that *The Long & Winding Road* would be the Beatle history for TV, and video. "We had to come up with a different angle, and the angle is: what was it really like? We were there ["thurr"] at the epicentre, and now we're finding home movies and old footage… It's gonna turn into a [Ken Burns] *Civil War*, a 10-hour job. A couple of weeks ago, the director had 45 minutes of footage – and Pete Best hadn't even joined the group!"

Happily – *finally* – Pete Best did okay out of the Beatles! Pete was never a fifth Beatle. He *was* a Beatle, 25% of the line-up, right up until he fell into the abyss of anonymous misery. But thanks to the 1990s *Anthology* avalanche, Pete benefitted, to the tune of an estimated £8,000,000. For his role on the CD releases, he received a performer's royalty for the Decca auditions and initial EMI sessions. Rumours that his image had, like Trotsky's, been edited out of history proved unfounded, he can be glimpsed outside the Cavern on the sleeve of Volume I.

There was also some sweet revenge to be savoured; during the first commercial break when Episode 1 of *Anthology* was screened on UK TV, the lager manufacturer Carlsberg cheekily adapted its familiar slogan for their advert to, "Probably the Pete Best lager in the world".

Always and everywhere, he was dogged by his days with the group. At a 2023 Norwegian Beatles event, he was questioned on the colour of his tie and the shade of the jackets they wore at the Indra club over 60 years before. "Unfortunately, Pete had no recollection of those details". He could look back and laugh in later years; there was a nice reminder of his role in an internet forum. Early in 2020, one of the many Beatle websites asked, "What got you into the Beatles?" And fans wrote of parents buying them 'She Loves You'… Or shaking their heads at the Odeon Lewisham… Or being in the audience at Shea Stadium… The best came from the man himself. Pete Best posted: "When Paul rang and asked me to join". Papering over the cracks, Pete also "thought about it", and sent his replacement best wishes on Ringo's 80th birthday in 2020.

While the Beatles remained inactive, and while Apple were quietly planning their future, there were always the endless cover versions to remind the world just what an extraordinary arc their music spanned. The acts of today render those fabulous songs in a bewildering array of original remakes, note-for-note covers or off-the-wall interpretations.

In 1988, *NME*'s avuncular Roy Carr put together an imaginative *Sgt Pepper Knew*

My Father release to benefit the Childline charity. The top acts of the era (Wet Wet Wet, the Wedding Present, Michelle Shocked, the Christians) each took a track off the seminal 1967 LP to have a go at. It resulted in socialist singer-songwriter Billy Bragg finding himself at No.1 with 'She's Leaving Home' (mind you, one suspects it was the Wet Wet Wet fanbase who bought the A-side, 'With a Little Help from My Friends', which helped to lever the single to the top of the charts).

And don't forget Big Daddy's breathtaking 1992 cover of the complete *Sgt Pepper* album. The story put out was that the group had been touring South East Asia in the late 1950s, when they were captured by a group of Laotian revolutionaries. On their release in 1983, all their subsequent music was conditioned by styles they had heard prior to their incarceration – thus 'Lucy in the Sky with Diamonds' was done in the style of Jerry Lee Lewis; 'Fixing a Hole' (Dion); "Within You Without You' (Beat poetry); and stunningly, 'A Day in the Life' (Buddy Holly).

"Charles Manson stole this song from the Beatles… we're stealing it back", Bono enthused doing 'Helter Skelter' on *Rattle & Hum*. At Live 8 in July 2005, Paul McCartney joined U2 for a version of the title track of *Sgt Pepper*. It was released within 45 minutes and became the fastest-selling download of all time to that point. It also marked the first time a Beatle took part in an official download.

Indeed, the breadth and scope of Beatle covers is a book in itself: Max Bygraves' 'Hard Day's Night' … William Shatner's 'Lucy in the Sky with Diamonds' … Ella Fitzgerald's 'Can't Buy Me Love' … Petula Clark's 'Rain' … Todd Rundgren's 'Strawberry Fields Forever' … the 1970 England World Cup Squad 'Ob La Di…' … Anita Harris' 'Octopus's Garden' … future *Let It Be* producer Glyn Johns' 'I'll Follow the Sun'. Then the hits, notably Joe Cocker's 'With a Little Help from My Friends', Marmalade's 'Ob La Di…', Elton's 'Lucy…'. Oasis used to hammer the shit out of 'I Am the Walrus' … Johnny Cash's poignant 'In My Life' … immediately prior to his death.

Then there's Jimi Hendrix's 'Sgt Pepper…'; Emmylou Harris cut a breathtaking 'Here, There & Everywhere'; Siouxsie & the Banshees had a hit with 'Dear Prudence'. With the Jam, Paul Weller covered 'Rain' and 'And Your Bird Can Sing'; solo he did 'Sexy Sadie'. In 2002 alone, 'The Long and Winding Road' was covered by Gareth Gates and Will Young, George Michael and S Club 7.

There are whole albums of Beatle covers – *Loungegroove* (the rockin' Cyril Stapleton & His Orchestra); *Glass Onion* – songs from the Warner and Atlantic jazz vaults (Ella Fitzgerald's 'Savoy Truffle'… Carmen McRae's 'Carry That Weight'); Bear Records' *Das War Ein Harter Tag: Beatles Lieder Auf Deutsch*… In 2004, DJ Danger Mouse let loose *The Grey Album*, a mish-mash of Jay-Z's 2003 release *The Black Album*. The Mouse admitted "every kick, snare and chord is taken from The Beatles' *White Album*". Or the plain unexpected, 2023 found the 1968 LP *Little Joe Can Sing*. An album by none other than Joe (*Goodfellas*) Pesci, which included three Beatles songs – 'Got to Get You into My Life', 'Fixing a Hole' and 'Fool on the Hill'.

Of them all, and they don't get played that often, the four volumes of *Exotic Beatle* covers were – what's the opposite of – a treasure trove? Music from around the world, Beatle songs from Malaysia, Argentina, Mexico, Brazil … Madagascar! Thrill to Maurice Chevalier's 'Yellow Submarine' … 'Bungalow Bill' in German … Arthur Mullard's

'Yesterday' … 'I Wanna Hold Your Hand' by Balsara & His Singing Sitars … 'We Can Work It Out' sung by cats, dogs & chickens … 'She Loves You' on Irvin's 89 Key Marenghi Fairground Organ … Johnny Prytko & the Connecticut Hi-Tones tackle 'Ob La Di…' polka style! The strong of heart can find them at (www.exoticarecords.co.uk).

Frankly unheard, but all credit to the Durham Ox Singers for Chutzpah. In 1999 they recorded "the first ever cover version" of *The White Album* singalong 'Revolution #9'. Only those of a strong disposition are directed to 'A Day in the Life' rendered by the Portsmouth Sinfonia. They were all trained musicians, but not on the instruments they were given to play. As they approach the song's climactic breakdown, it is the aural equivalent of fingernails being dragged over a blackboard. Slowly. Very slowly…

*

At the height of their mustachioed psychedelic capering, at a formal function, the Queen remarked to EMI's Sir Joseph Lockwood, "The Beatles are turning awfully *funny* aren't they?" Her Majesty, ("a pretty nice girl") turned out to be quite a fan. "Think what we would have missed if we had never heard the Beatles", the Queen said, celebrating her golden wedding anniversary. Rumour had *Yellow Submarine* as one of her late Majesty's favourite films. In 2004, for the 60th anniversary of the D-Day landings, the then-President of France, Francois Hollande asked if Her Majesty was happy with the music the Republican Guard was playing? Diplomatic as ever, Queen Elizabeth II asked if they could "play something by the Beatles".

The Monarchy and the Beatles was further bonded for the opening ceremony of the 2012 London Olympics. It was an event heavy on the 'B's – Beatles, Blake, Bond and Brunel. Her Majesty was escorted to the Olympic Park by James Bond for its opening. And could there be any other way to close the ceremony by a mass singalong of 'Hey Jude', led by the song's composer? On his first visit to Germany as monarch in 2023, while addressing the Reichstag, King Charles III (still gives pause typing that), cited the Beatles as one of the cultural links binding the nations together (mind you, for balance, he was honour bound to include Kraftwerk).

Paul McCartney was invited to the Party At The Palace in June 2002, and opened with one of the few Beatle songs he had never played live: "I was actually very nervous about that", he told me afterwards. "It wasn't so much singing 'Her Majesty' to her, but just me on acoustic guitar, and all the royal people in the box. And then on top of that, I've got to remember the bugger, it's not a song I *do* very often. There's not a lot of call for that one…!"

In the heady flush of the Queen's grandchildren's union – William, Kate, Harry and Meghan – the tabloids christened them 'the Fab Four'. Alas, like the real thing, the media characterised Meghan as 'the Royals' Yoko Ono', and the couples sundered in 2020. By 2023, I heard Meghan referred to as 'Woko Ono'. It's funny, the way that Yoko has become the recurrent symbol, the shorthand as the wedge which was what broke up the Beatles. It can still catch you unawares. In one of Malcolm Tucker's blistering tirades in *The Thick of It*: "Hey you two remaining Beatles and Yoko Ono, piss off". Or on the BBC's masterly comedy-drama *The Outlaws*, the sinister drug dealing puppet master 'The Dean' threatens the Bristol collective: "You're the Beatles of drug selling and I can't break up the band. Don't make me the Yoko…"

*

Around the turn of the century, I was lucky enough to watch Paul McCartney rehearse at the London Arena for his *Back in the World* tour. He was there routining material before an audience of … 18. It was genuinely awe-inspiring to be so up close and intimate, especially when he strapped on *that* violin bass and hammered into a blistering 'Birthday', 'Lady Madonna', 'Back in the USSR'. Or tugging at the heart strings with 'She's Leaving Home', 'Let It Be' and 'Michelle'.

It was odd watching him pour his not inconsiderable energy and talent into a *rehearsal*. A snatch of 'Purple Haze', and "for Rome", 'O Solo Mio'. And the fun he had relishing in seeking out the more obscure material – 'I've Just Seen a Face', a forgotten gem tucked away on Side II of *Help!* nearly 40 years before. For old times' sake, he also dusted down 'Two of Us', 'Ain't She Sweet', even a snatch of 'Those Were the Days'.

And all the while, the 21st century whirled around the bopping figure onstage – bowed heads screamed into walkie-talkies, boffins laboured over blinking computers; scientific types loomed over soundboards; lighting consoles hovered, like the Mother Ship from *Close Encounters*… Harassed employees rushed round with bulging packages, MPL staff juggled ticket requests. Apple HQ are in touch with last-minute queries about the *Anthology* DVDs. Heads are scratched, cigarettes extinguished at the wait for couriers; tense conversations are held on the still relatively novel mobile phones. In the middle of the madness, Paul's long-serving PR Geoff Baker relied on his old tried and tested Fleet Street tactics, endlessly filling a notebook with shorthand notes, page after page of them… "A week's work there, Geoff?" "Just today's messages, mate…"

The new technology allowed McCartney to play freely with the past, and replicate the studio ingenuity which produced that astonishingly influential back catalogue. Just sitting there that day, it struck me that the Beatles had never performed *anything* from half their recorded catalogue in concert. Nothing from *Revolver*, *Sgt Pepper*, *Magical Mystery Tour*, *The White Album*, *Abbey Road* or *Let It Be* was ever heard live by a paying audience.

All the technology 'Team McCartney' had mustered since his 1989 'comeback' *Flowers in the Dirt* tour demonstrated that it was now possible to replicate that music onstage. Here was the complex density of what the Beatles had conjured up at Abbey Road rendered in concert. It was hearing *him* performing *those* songs from that era live onstage which was so spellbinding. On subsequent outings, you could witness entire audiences going through a range of emotions as the man who wrote *those* songs for *that* group was *there*, performing them.

As snaking microphone cables were untangled, as lighting rigs descended and ascended, Paul told me that some nights those songs which mean so much to everyone were still capable of choking him up. Idly chatting he did say that often there was so much to concentrate on during a live performance, there were so many distractions – complex lighting cues, changing instrumentation, checking set lists – that the emotion could be contained. But that it could become overwhelming, usually when remembering his bandmates as he sang 'All Things Must Pass' or 'Something', 'Helter Skelter', 'Give Peace a Chance', or his John tribute 'Here Today'.

He laughed when he remembered that first Beatles tour – squashed on a tour bus with Helen Shapiro and Kenny Lynch, with Mal and Neil squeezing all the gear into the boot. Today he said the road crew numbered 116, while seven chefs created 320 veggie meals a day. All in all, it takes 40 trucks to "mach shau" somewhere in a world still hungry for a taste of that Beatle magic.

In 2003, over a cuppa, as I had passed the landmark 50, we touched on intimations of mortality, and the 60-year-old Paul laughed: "When we were 17, we thought it would end when you were 24, that was like the cut-off age. It was just… *unseemly* to be 24!"

With our interview concluded, McCartney sat himself next to me, chatting amiably as he watched a run-through of the technical elements. Even at the time, it was a decidedly surreal moment: to be seated alongside Paul McCartney watching with him where *he* will be onstage during a Paul McCartney show.

Not as surreal as later though, when I mentioned I was sorry to have missed him run through the *Sgt Pepper* reprise and heard him say, "We've had a request from a young man (!) for this one…" The pre-show dancers were hopping like hamsters on a griddle as he hammered through the song. The audience of 18, even the road crew joined in to applaud that one. Grinning like the Cheshire Cat, McCartney cheekily gagged, "Thank you on behalf of the group and I hope we passed the audition".

*

Just when you thought the well had run dry, along came another Beatle anniversary; another box set, record-breaking auction sale, newly-found tape or memoir. It looked like everyone from the 'inner circle' (Tony Barrow, Alf Bicknell, Tony Bramwell, Peter Brown, Leslie Cavendish, Geoff Emerick, Freda Kelly, Alastair Taylor, George Martin, Ken Scott, Derek Taylor…) had committed their memories to print. That closeness gained them access to Beatle Conventions worldwide. And every year brought more. Devoted fans shook their heads ("Oooh…") at the errors in the ghost-written autobiographies but nevertheless filleted, the published works to build an even fuller picture of the group that was.

Yet there were those that remain tantalisingly unpublished. Neil Aspinall said he never would, but was happy to talk to Mark Lewisohn on the record. Tragically, cancer robbed us of the opportunity to hear one of the *very* few 'fifth Beatles' tell his story. Mal Evans' memoir was believed to be lost following his death but in 1998, thanks to Leena Kutti, the manuscript made its way to Yoko Ono and was finally published in 2024.

Indeed, as she sailed past 90, the 'peerless' Yoko has found a new fanbase. A massive retrospective at Tate Modern opened in 2024 to glowing reviews, with one hailing her as "the mother of almost every trend in modern art". Earlier, her having the audience trim clothing from the artist, *Cut Piece*, one newspaper headline ran, 'Give Piece a Chance'.

Of them all, it remains Jane Asher's reflections on her romance with Paul McCartney which have yet to appear. Jane was Paul's constant companion during those tumultuous years 1963 to 1968. She was not only at the eye of the hurricane, but also the subject of some of the most affecting love songs of the 20th century. Jane really is rock & roll's 'dark lady'. Yet she has steadfastly refused to go on record. While a guest on *Desert Island Discs* she was granted the unique dispensation *not* to talk about that period in her life. When promoting her cakes or dramatic appearances, journalists are politely reminded that those five years are verboten.

I am not alone in wanting to read her account; not of how Paul measured up as a lover, but rather the mechanics of having one of the most famous men in the world sharing her family home. And of those songs… Did Paul turn to his flame-haired companion on occasion and inquire, "What do you think of this one, luv?" as yet another timeless ballad was premiered? Happily married to Gerald Scarfe for nearly half a century, one can only hope that a memoir *has* been written, perhaps for posthumous publication?

Over the years, and almost at random, I began jotting down notes about the way the Beatles have inculcated themselves into the English psyche. It wasn't a calculated list with a book in mind, I was just amazed at how, still, the Beatles *are* just here, there and everywhere… Aside from the lawsuits, re-remasters, box sets and anniversaries, just relaxing watching a 2009 episode of *Midsomer Murders (The Black Book)* plot hinging on a 19th-century painting's provenance. It is found to be a forgery as the four Beatles are revealed in the distance.

So in June 2021 I started looking for random mentions: Don Letts in *Record Collector* about his "obsession" with the Beatles (his memorabilia collection, the country's second biggest, he swapped for a "metallic blue Plymouth Satellite")… Beatles Magna tiles ("Kids, parents and grandparents can play together to build the Yellow Submarine, Magical Mystery Tour Bus…")… Launching the new Ferrari 330MLB ("the fifth Beatle")… News that Liverpool's Abbey cinema (mentioned in the original lyrics of 'In My Life') had been saved from demolition… The Beatles Legacy Committee in Liverpool… A plaque in Penny Lane's St Barnabas church marking Paul McCartney's years there as a choirboy… McCartney on the cover of *Stamp Collector* and *Gibbons Stamp Monthly* … The dedication of one fan who got 60 autographs of the group's co-stars in *A Hard Day's Night*… Nick Cave's opinion that "the best thing Yoko ever did was break up the Beatles"… On what would have been her 60th birthday in June 2021, the media reflecting that at its height "Dianamania recalled Beatlemania"… The furore surrounding Timothee Chalamet was, predictably, 'Chalamania'… Any reference to Pete Best's actress niece Leanne usually mentioned her uncle's old group… Ringo dropping his lawsuit against the 'Ring O' sex toy… Since 2009, 25 June has been celebrated as 'Global Beatle Day' (the day chosen on the anniversary of their *Our World* appearance)… The £860 "uber de-luxe version" of *All Things Must Pass* (including replica gnomes)… 13 September 2021, following Bromley girl Emma Raducanu's US Open triumph, a *Daily Mail* headline "It's Like Beatlemania…" … A demo of 'Happiness Is a Warm Gun' turning up in a garage, inside the sleeve of a Ken Dodd & the Diddymen LP… *Men in Black* referencing *The White Album*… Prime Minister Boris Johnson was born in New York in June 1964, his blonde fringe was a talking point, with his being nicknamed "the blonde Beatle"… A TV documentary about Tony Blair and Gordon Brown where they were called "the Lennon and McCartney of British politics"… Anyone over ten would have been less than thrilled to learn the group had made their Tik Tok debutzz… Greg McKush opened the "world's first Beatle-themed golf course" in Minnesota, with holes named after locations with Beatle, er, links – Abbey Road, Hollywood Bowl, Savile Row etc.… Chancellor Rishi Sunak announcing in his 2021 Budget £2,000,000 for "an immersive Beatle experience" in Liverpool. Culture Secretary Nadine Dorries managed to squeeze four Beatle song titles into her delighted Twitter response… A new book announced for 2022: *I Saw Them Standing There – The World of Beatle Statues* by Chris Slater… The estate of George Harrison choosing to cooperate with a company selling pre-rolled joints, *All Things Must Grass*… The nod to the third track on *The White Album* with the *Knives Out* sequel, *Glass Onion*… Or the plaintive online inquiry, "I've always wondered what type of gum John is always chewing while singing. I would expect it to be chewing gum verses bubble gum. In the movie *Help*, Wrigley's was used as a prop. I prefer the Doublemint with the green packaging but it could be Spearmint like in the movie when Paul had to cover himself after being shrunk. Thoughts?"

Paul himself was on the stump promoting his *Lyrics* and the double-whammy of the *Get Back* documentary and box set. He was everywhere from *Radio Times* to *Reader's Digest*, and all points in between. The media pounced on the Lennon references and were quizzical, if not sceptical, of the literary comparisons McCartney made. The point was they were talking about a dutiful Grammar schoolboy, who had benefitted from an encouraging English master, and for whom University and a teaching career had been an option, if he had not chosen an alternative career path. If mother Mary had lived, she would almost certainly have insisted that Paul continue on an academic path, by all means keeping music as a hobby.

I just found it was all just getting … overwhelming. And that was before Paul headlined at Glastonbury. I thought the nation was going to be given the day off for his 80th birthday, but the days after 25 June 2022 were extraordinary. Barely drawing breath after his American tour, he celebrated the actual birthday off the Greek islands. His warm-up gig at a local Frome pub grabbed the headlines, but it was nothing to the tsunami of praise which followed his 'life-affirming' Glastonbury gig ("Greatest Glasto set ever?"). It was as if the UK had woken from a deep, post-Diamond Jubilee sleep and appreciated just what a genuine national treasure they had in their midst. After Paddington.

The largest crowd in the Glastonbury festival's half-century history were treated to 20 Beatle songs (plus one pre-Fab effort). A nearly three-hour, 36-song set. And as if *that* wasn't enough, who should join him but our old friends Dave Grohl and Bruce bloody Springsteen. Five-star reviews from the national press, typical was *The Independent*: "McCartney's available canon is the greatest in music by such a vast degree that any couple of hours plucked from it at random would be the best gig of the year". It really made one wonder where they'd been; perhaps it was facing up to the fact that – maybe – Megan Thee Stallion or Lewis Capaldi did not have all the best tunes. As if that wasn't enough, the week after, the Beatles' *1* CD benefitted from a near 40% increase in sales.

My thinking in doing this book my way was to emphasise in Part III just how, almost outside themselves, the Beatles and their brand had continued to have such a long, sustained impact on the 21st century. Sifting through it all there were good and bad elements to emerge: the re-imagined *Let It Be/Get Back* documentary was, in a Sellers & Yeatman (look them up) vein, 'A Good Thing'. Stella McCartney launching a Beatles-related clothing range which coincided with all the late 2021 mayhem was 'A Bad Thing'. The cheapest item was a pair of socks – *socks*! – for £70.

It is the overwhelming, enduring level of interest in that one group, those four individuals, and what they accomplished over, basically, 12 LPs during eight frenetic years. The same commitment is not matched by fans of Freddie & the Dreamers, Herman's Hermits or the Dave Clark Five. And really, that intensity shows no sign of diminishing. It isn't just the ordinary fan, 'the civilians' who are spellbound. The Beatles even exert a strong pull in the world of celebrity itself. Presidents, CEOs, sports idols, politicians, film stars … all are left speechless in the company of a Beatle; Seth Swirsky's engaging 2013 documentary *Beatles Stories* gathered together some of them, including theatrical titan Sir Ben Kingsley, almost shaking at the memory of his 1966 encounter. All of the great and the good are reduced to the level of a slavering fan, like Foo Fighter Dave Grohl who recalled his first close encounter with Paul: "I spent the hour before his arrival hiding the mountains of Beatles stuff I had in the house (you never know how much Beatles memorabilia you have, until a Beatle comes to visit").

The most popular special collection Royal Mail stamps of the 21st century were the 2007 issue featuring Beatles LP covers, beating same day issues including 'The Abolition of the Slave Trade', 'British Army Uniforms' and 'The 40th Anniversary of the Machin Definitive', among others… Philip Robinson of the Royal Philatelic Society pointed out that Abkhazia in the Caucasus got philately confused, their 1994 stamp had a grinning John Lennon next to a smiling Groucho Marx.

So much now a part of the fabric of our culture, it was in 1992 that the British Council hosted a documentary exhibition about the group's history which went on tour and displayed in the Council's offices in 56 countries. A question about the Beatles is now included in the UK Citizenship Test… No wonder Dylan Jones wrote wonderingly "of how Apple Corps has turned The Beatles into the quintessential heritage act". In 1990, they really did go across the universe when four asteroids were named after Harrison, Lennon, McCartney and Starr.

Certainly the most ghoulish attribution since Charles Manson came when the authorities were looking for a way to identify the four 21st-century Isis terrorists who beheaded non-believers. A quick way of identifying the quartet of masked executioners was by giving them Beatle nicknames because of their English accents. Mohammed Emwazi ('Jihadi John') was shown in a video, callously beheading aid workers David Haines and Alan Henning. He was killed in 2015. Alexanda Kotey ('George') is serving eight consecutive life sentences.

The *Butcher* cover of 1966's *Yesterday & Today* was the highlight of a *Beatles on the Balcony* exhibition in 2006 at the National Portrait Gallery. "This is the first time we've done a show on a pop group", sniffed Gallery curator, the aptly named Terence Pepper. Fast forward 17 years and his successor was less dismissive, as Paul's *Eye of the Storm* was the Gallery's flagship exhibition.

Also in that 2006 exhibition were the famous 'jumping Beatle' photos. Photographer Fiona Adams did the shoot for the defunct *Boyfriend* magazine on the corner of Gower Street and Euston Road in April 1963. With the property long, the shot later became better known when it was used on the cover of the *Twist & Shout* EP, and better still

Stamp

Guide 2007

Your guide to forthcoming issues and collectibles

Royal Mail

with us it's personal®

Beatle stamps

THORN EMI

The British Council

EMI

PYRAMID BOOKS

5 October 1992

The Beatles - 30th Anniversary Celebrations

Today, 5 October 1992, is the 30th anniversary of
the release of The Beatles' first single, *Love Me
Do*. To commemorate this milestone in British
music's history EMI is re-releasing *Love Me Do*,
the British Council is launching an international
exhibition and an authoritative book by Mark
Lewisohn has just been published. All three
events are being marked today at a reception at
EMI's Abbey Road Studios.

'Love me Do' - Re-release

First released on EMI's Parlophone label, *Love Me Do* was
the beginning of the Beatles phenomenon. It entered the
charts on 11 October 1962 at Number 49, peaking at Number
17. This was the first week of over 400 that The Beatles
were to spend in the UK charts.

Love Me Do (backed with *PS I Love You*) is being re-
released by EMI on Compact Disc, limited edition digipack
CD, tape and 7" single. The digipack contains sleeve
notes on the history of the single written by leading
Beatles' authority Mark Lewisohn, whose book *The Complete
Beatles Chronicle* has been published this month. The
regular CD features the original Parlophone label

when the outline became the logo for Cirque du Soleil's *Love*.

Talking to Mark Ellen about the mash-up for the *Love* show, Giles Martin did admit, "It's like painting a moustache on the Mona Lisa",[26] but emphasised he and his father "only use material The Beatles recorded and nothing additional", although there were apparently four moments which were added (oh, alright then: faint animal noises on 'Because'... police siren prior to 'I Am the Walrus'... a new George Martin string arrangement on ' My Guitar Gently Weeps' and thunderclap and rain on 'Lady Madonna').

"This is the last time I shall work on any Beatles record", Sir George told Paul Williams, "for Christ's sake, I'm 80". He was quite pleased with the wheel coming full circle, writing a new arrangement to preface one of George's best-loved songs for the show: "It's also rather neat that it's kind of a beginning and ending. 'Yesterday' was the very first score that I did with The Beatles and 'While My Guitar Gently Weeps' will be my last".

The *Love* CD from 2006 was intriguing, what *Q* called "a Da Vinci Code for Beatle fans". Like Paul McCartney, many felt the Martins "could go further out". Once the decision had been made to include 'Transitions', segues and welds to probably the most-familiar and best-loved back catalogue in the history of rock & roll, perhaps they *could* have been more audacious. You could understand Apple wanting to put the project in a safe pair of hands, but imagine the relish with which Fatboy Slim, Mark Ronson or JXL could have approached the project.

Love made its UK chart debut at No.3 on first week sales of 173,517 in December 2006, behind an Oasis *Greatest Hits* and Westlife's *The Love Album*. *Love* was at best an enjoyable diversion and certainly didn't diminish their standing.

But, like another group sang, "whoa, oh, listen to the music". Listen to that Beatle music. Again and again and ... marvel. Melodies and lyrics which are as much part of your DNA as your toenail clippings. But with the new technology, just *listen* to some of those McCartney bass lines, as solid as a three-course lunch... George's florid and fluent guitar lines... Lennon's out-of-body leaps of imagination... And Ringo, you could land a helicopter on that boy's drumming... All enhanced and enriched by George Martin's skills.

Even the throwaway early singles, compositions which were knocked off in provincial backstage dressing rooms, or in lugubrious hotel chambers or tour buses, all retain a power which transcends nostalgia. They live on record, and in performance, the songs which constitute the heartbeat of UK Beatlemania. Then there were the songs which were to be found only on LPs – 'It Won't Be Long', 'All My Loving', 'Baby's in Black', 'You've Got to Hide Your Love Away', 'I've Just Seen a Face', 'I'll Cry Instead', 'You Can't Do That', 'Eight Days a Week'...

Listening to the official canon, 1962–70, I developed an unexpected fondness for what came before Derek Taylor called "the years of dash and daring", those catchy, cheery efforts which are contained in the *Red* album. Then you cannot help but reflect on the career arc which found 'I Want to Hold Your Hand' to 'Eleanor Rigby' undertaken in an incredible two years.

---

26 In 1970, *Rolling Stone* reader Fred H. wrote of *Let It Be*, "Don't give Phil Spector any chalk; he might draw a mustache on the Mona Lisa".

Cirque poster, Las Vegas

The days, weeks, months and – thoroughly enjoyable – *years* I've spent writing about the Beatles led to this book. And what I came away with was a fondness for those early songs. For the rock establishment, it was de-rigueur to prefer the *Blue* Album, when the weirdness took over. Yet it was to the innocent and joyous *Red* Album I returned. Not just for a nostalgic jaunt on the ghost train through Beatle Land, rather for the resonant thrill and fulsome frisson of fun which those songs conveyed.

I think it was that sense of – dare one call it – innocence? The fun and optimism which resounded, that first hearing of a new Beatle song, and somehow, anything seemed possible. A random trawl through 21st-century singles and interviews with chart acts displays a worrying amount of homophobia, anti-semitism and misogyny. The Beatles may well have displayed a staunch, Northern chauvinism when it came to their wives and girlfriends ("Girls don't play guitars", Lennon sniffed). But there was none of that overt, harsh *nastiness* in the music of the Beatles.

If you weren't there, you can understand why people are bored with everyone banging on about how wonderful the 60s were, like war veterans reminiscing about long-ago campaigns. And besides, the 60s only swung for a couple of dozen people in and around the King's Road – photographers, designers, actors and three of the Rolling Stones. Stuck in the London suburbs of Forest Hill, Herne Hill or Penge, or on the outskirts of Bristol, Tiverton or Redditch, there wasn't much swinging. But there was the music, always accessible on record player, and that was sensational. And it remains sensational. And leading from the front for the entire decade were, of course, the Beatles. And they were everyone's link to the Swinging 60s. And forever on…

Then, just when you think you've heard it, and seen it all. Just when you think there can't be anything left in the cupboard; just when you think you're all Beatle-d out, something truly spectacular comes along…

The image looms large over Las Vegas… Four smiling faces, beaming from the roof of the Mirage Hotel, in a photo culled from the 1967 *Sgt Pepper* shoot. Like the eyes which hover over the wasteland in Scott Fitzgerald's *The Great Gatsby*, you feel that there is nowhere you can go in Sin City where those ubiquitous eyes won't follow.

I have been to America quite a few times, not as many as I'd like, but I'd always fantasised about visiting Las Vegas. Largely I think because it was so … American. Here was a gambling Paradise in the middle of an atomic nowhere. The city where you could get a degree in High Living. Vegas, shorthand for the Mob… high rolling gamblers… a decadent playground for the rich and famous who are *so* rich and famous they don't need lifestyles. Vegas, where Sinatra and the Rat Pack partied in red-eyed majesty and where Elvis came to be reborn in 1969.

So here I am, finally, January 2019, and it is none of the above that got me here… It is the music of Merseyside airlifted to the desert scrub of Nevada. It's wonderful to be here, it certainly *is* a thrill, ringside in Las Vegas, as Cirque du Soleil's production *Love*, based on Beatle music, unreels before your very eyes during its 13th year.

So spectacular is the show that the venue had to be built around it. Once the magicians Siegfried & Roy moved out in 2003, the circus was in town. The roof was extended, a basement carved out… Such is the scale and scope, it means that the only way to see this spectacular Apple-authorised production is to visit the Mirage Hotel in Las Vegas. Sadly

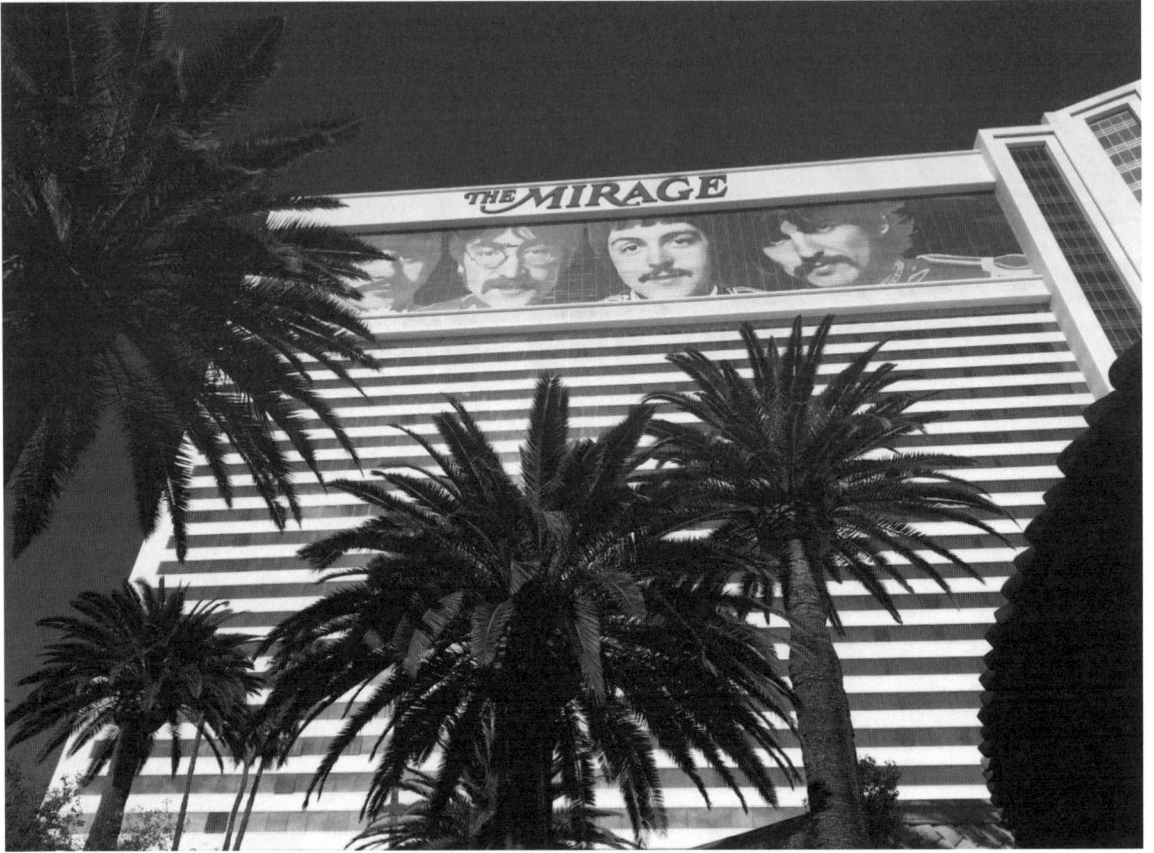

Beatles, *Love*, Las Vegas

for Beatle fans, there is no way this spectacular production is going to turn up at the Hammersmith Odeon.

And 'spectacular' it is. The Cirque acrobatics leave you dizzy, craning your neck as they swerve, swoop, trampoline and bounce all over the place for an exhausting 90 minutes. You literally don't know where to look as the show unfolds. Embraced by familiar Beatle music, in unfamiliar shapes, there is just so much going on… over, under, sideways and down.

It all began with a chance encounter between two Formula 1 racing enthusiats – George Harrison and Cirque founder Guy Laliberte. They met in the pits, clicked and decided to work on a production incorporating Cirque's mind-blowing acrobatics to a soundtrack by George's old band. Sadly, it was one of the last projects George was involved in prior before his untimely death in 2001.

What made the project so tantalising was not just the use of Beatle music, but sourcing it straight from the original master tapes. When the show opened in 2006, and on the subsequent CD release, the feeling was that this was the nearest to hearing the Beatles in action as you were likely to get.

Apple, along with Paul, Ringo, George's widow Olivia and Yoko Ono gave George Martin the freedom to dip into and re-fashion rock's best-loved back catalogue. It proved to be the legendary producer's last Beatle project.

Where that tampering really works is in Las Vegas at the Mirage Theater as *Love* unfolds before your eyes and ears. Listening to Beatle music pouring out of 6,400 speakers offering a 360 degree, 5.1 surround sound is a majestic, all-embracing experience.

Over the course of two years, George and Giles Martin fashioned 120 Beatle songs into the 90-minute show. There were intriguing fusions, imaginative collusions and tantalising overlays – 'Within You, Without You' and 'Tomorrow Never Knows'… 'Drive My Car' and 'The Word'… 'Yesterday' and 'Blackbird'… They were mergers which worked better when witnessed in situ.

There's a nice element in the show where, during 'Being for the Benefit of Mr Kite', you hear studio banter from the Fabs, as well as excerpts from 'Cry Baby Cry'; sound effects from 'Good Morning, Good Morning'; laughter from 'Piggies' and noises from 'I Want You (She's So Heavy)'.

At its best *Love* takes your breath away: the acapella 'Because' ushers in a rocking 'Get Back'. Over your head, by your side and dead ahead, the 26 acrobats and 18 dancers whirl, twist and gyrate. For 'Lucy in the Sky with Diamonds', 'Lucy' herself soars above you on a trapeze, performing incredible feats of acrobatics, all to a background of thousands and thousands of LED lights… indeed, like a sky lit with diamonds.

The 'Revolution/Back in the USSR' sequence has trampolining taken to the limit, as the energetic performers bounce over old VW vans, deftly defying gravity, without ever crashing into each other. It is wholly hypnotic.

Equally impressive is the skateboarding routine which accompanies 'Help'. Tearing up and down 11-foot ramps, they perform at a speed and with a dexterity which is spellbinding. The show concludes with a reprise of *Sgt Pepper* as the entire cast move in a mad fusion before concluding with the affecting ensemble 'All You Need Is Love'.

If there is a criticism, it was quite what all the Cirque acrobatics and aerobatics *really* have to do with the music of the Beatles? The Beatle characters (Doctor Robert; Father

McKenzie; the Eggman…) are fairly arbitrary, and there's no real narrative.

These are minor quibbles though. The entire *Love* and Beatle and Cirque experience is overwhelming, and leaves you reeling. It is a testament to Apple that their handling of the Beatle legacy continues to fascinate and beguile, a long way on from those Beatle Movie Medleys and Beatle *Love Song*s from the 80s.

Love, really, is all you need…[27]

At the show's premiere, you shared Paul McCartney's view, "It's hard to believe that all this came from a few songs we scribbled out on scraps of paper".

On stage, on trapeze, in tribute; in commercials and in new recorded formats; in cyberspace, in galactic black holes, in print and on air; in auction rooms and record charts they live on. On the cinema screen, they took on a life of their own, long after the split… You can Google away for a complete list, but I was struck by the way 'I Saw Her Standing There' was the song which forges the link between Tom Cruise and Dustin Hoffman's characters in *Rain Man*. How *American Beauty* featured Elliott Smith's eloquent 'Because'… The jaunty way 'All You Need Is Love' boomed out of *Love Actually*. The entire soundtrack of *I Am Sam* (2001) had 20 Beatle songs covered by, among others, Nick Cave, Sheryl Crow and Rufus Wainwright. Julie Taymor's *Across the Universe* (2007) squeezed 35 Beatle numbers into it.

The Beatles could still pull 'em in, and many were only too eager to bask in their reflected glory; for the 1994 film *Backbeat*, members of REM, Nirvana and Sonic Youth were on the soundtrack of the film devoted to the group's youth in Hamburg. The pre-Beatle biopic, *Nowhere Boy* (2009) boasted Kristin Scott-Thomas *is* Aunt Mimi. Tom Hanks' only directorial effort, the enjoyable *That Thing You Do* (1996) dealt with the career of the Wonders, an American band inspired by the Fabs – the film is littered with enjoyable little homages.

On film, there were sly cinematic references: the President in Kevin Costner's 1997 *The Postman* was one 'Richard Starkey'. I am sure Ben Kingsley was channelling his inner-Ringo (and nose) in the 2010 *10 Rings*. And it was surely more than coincidence that Kate Hudson played 'Penny Lane' in Cameron Crowe's *Almost Famous*? While Gemma Arterton pitted her wits against Daniel Craig's 007 as 'Strawberry Fields' in *A Quantum of Solace*. No doubt where Natalie Portman's 2019 *Lucy in the Sky*, while light on newspaper taxis, tipped its hat.

The cinematic apogee came with Richard Curtis' 2019 *Yesterday*. Himesh Patel's Jack Malik is the only person in the world who knows that the Beatles ever existed. He can thus claim their catalogue as his own, wisely ignoring Ed Sheeran's advice to alter his song to 'Hey Dude' and putting up with his parents' disinterest in 'Leave Him Be'. Some found the film cloying, I enjoyed its conceit, though felt the Lennon encounter jarred.

In the album sleeve notes, scriptwriter Curtis marvels at the timelessness of those songs, and "got a hint of how eternity happens – it sneaks into every day, the tunes are embedded in children's minds like 'Greensleeves' and national anthems – and it slips from generation to generation". Indeed, watching the film, you marvel at just how much great music, how many styles of music, came out of just *one* band.

---

27 Love closed in July 2024, after having been seen by audiences of 11,500,000.

They have outlived their world. They have outlasted the high street chains their parents took them shopping in (Woolworths, Burton's, Kennedy's, David Greig's)… They have outlasted the boutiques which clothed them (Mr Fish, Hung On You, I Was Lord Kitchener's Valet, Granny Takes a Trip)… The buildings which housed them (the Cavern, Shea Stadium, Candlestick Park) are demolished… The magazines which promoted them (*NME*, *Disc*, *Melody Maker*, *Rave*, *Fabulous!*, *Record Mirror*) are gone… The clubs they partied in (the Ad-Lib, Blaises, Bag O'Nails) are history… the bistros which fed them, all gone…

I return to my fascination with, putting the music to one side, the way that the Beatles' *brand* endures. That familiar dropped 'T' logo seems to be everywhere, on everything. With Apple maintaining a strong hold on that brand, everything is sanctified with a degree of dignity. In a 2014 poll, the Beatles' brand was 16th equal with the National Trust (the current owners of Paul's childhood home). The survey found that the brand "has been well managed and has a range of products that use the heritage of the brand really well and successfully engage new generations of fans. Particularly successful in apparel, the Beatles' is a programme that doesn't seem to age and is kept active by some very proactive licensees".

It is well-known today that the real money in what we used to call rock & roll comes from merchandising. Elvis Presley's manager, 'Colonel' Tom Parker was quick off the mark. In 1956 when Elvis burst onto the world stage, Parker licensed 72 Elvis products (including 'I Hate Elvis' badges to cover the waterfront). Prior to the pandemic, it was the live concert, with its wallet-bursting ticket prices and merchandising opportunities which took priority. At every major gig, the stalls which ringed the venues sold everything from beanie bags to sweatshirts; baseball caps to £20 souvenir programmes. With actual record sales in meltdown, it's the 'merch' which brings in the bucks. For Bruce Springsteen's 1984/85 *Born in the USA* tour, for example, it was estimated that the merchandising alone generated $30,000,000. A recent estimate of the Kiss brand had an estimated 4,000 (four *thousand*) official merchandising items. When interviewed, stars swagger when it comes to talking about the sex and the drugs, but clam up when it comes to cash.

Those opportunities were, of course, unheard-of, unthought-of, while the Beatles were a working band. I'm sure there were Beatle watches back in 1964, but not ones which would have been licensed to the revered Swiss manufacturer Raymond Weil: their limited-edition Beatles Maestro watch went on sale in 2017, while a *Sgt Pepper* one would set you back £1,195 in 2019.

You cannot help but muse. While enjoying a cuppa from my Beatles mug, Christmas 2020 found me occupied by the 1,000-piece, 24" x 24" jigsaw based on the *Sgt Pepper* cover. That was before unlocking my study door with my Beatle key ring and jotting down immediate thoughts with my Beatle City pen, prior to shifting my mouse over my *Abbey Road* mat. Later, a stiff drink (room for development there?) placed on a Beatle coaster while I admired their fridge magnets… Or I could have played with the new range of Corgi toys, with model taxis based on contemporary trade adverts for songs, including 'Hey Jude' and 'Let It Be'. And all, of course, "A Beatles product licensed by Apple Corps

Ltd." That illustrious trademark helped explain how, during 2020, exactly half a century since the last product released while the Beatles were still a working band, one estimate had Apple still earning £137,657 *a day*.

It was that illustrious name which still exercises such a lucrative attraction, and that doesn't even include the music… We are talking t-shirts, polo shirts, mugs, lanyards, teapots, key rings, hoodies, fridge magnets, coasters, towels, bottle openers, condiment sets, Russian dolls, eco bags, tote bags, bum bags… None of which could have been imagined from the stage of the Litherland Town Hall. The Beatle brand had come to represent a hallmark of quality. In a sense, the four constituent quarters were almost irrelevant. It was them united under that unified 'Beatle' umbrella, the brand you've known for all those years.

Of all the "ex-Beatles", it was John Lennon who became the iconic flag-bearer. The one they named airports, locomotives, clothing lines and children after. In the immediate aftermath of his murder, there were snide comments pointed in the McCartney direction that 'they'd shot the wrong Beatle'. John was the edgy rebel; Paul the cosy parents' favourite. John took the Beatles to the edge; Paul was happy to stick to the middle (a chapter in Rob Sheffield's book is wryly headed 'Paul Is a Concept By Which We Measure Our Pain').

I believe much of that criticism was not necessarily aimed *at* McCartney, rather that his songs were those chosen by cosy, easy listening artists – 'Michelle', 'And I Love Her' and 'Here, There & Everywhere' are *easier* to cover, rather than, say, 'Doctor Robert', 'Sexy Sadie' or 'A Day in the Life'.

Through John's death and the mourning that followed, the myth was created of the cool Beatle; the gentle house-husband; the proud father; the advocate of global peace; the man who resisted mortal possessions. Typical was *Mojo* reader Arturo I. Andrade: "John Lennon, a man to whom many (if not most) Beatles fans was, is now, and forever will be THE Beatle". Posthumously, Lennon did actually become, in a way "bigger than Jesus", as he comfortably turned his back on the cities of the world and baked his own loaves.

TRIGGER WARNING…
My Opinions About John Lennon May Upset Some Readers…
However, I would contend that for all the deification following his murder, people often overlook the other side of John Lennon. I felt no need to sift through Albert Goldman's vitriolic, bile-filled biography for evidence. As a teenager in Liverpool, parents would warn their children of hanging around with 'that Lennon'. It was Lennon who mugged a sailor in Hamburg. Lennon the shoplifter. In 1963, a drunken Lennon poured a pint of beer over the sleeping Chris Montez, which prompted further argy-bargy and what were called 'racial jibes' about the Anglo-Mexican singer. Like so many of his generation, Lennon displayed elements of homophobia, misogyny and anti-semitism. But on finding fame, it was Lennon who made little effort to mask his opinions.

At his best, Lennon was sarcastic and irreverent. Quick-witted with a crackerjack imagination, self-belief fuelled him, with an ego to match ("John didn't on the whole tend to enjoy any scenario that wasn't directly about him", Klaus Voormann remembered). At his worst, Lennon could be spiteful, vicious and malicious – on learning of a Judy

Garland suicide attempt he goaded the singer, "show us your wrists". Peeved at Jayne Mansfield, he pissed in her cocktail. He could immediately spot weakness in others, and soon feasted off it. His Liverpool contemporary, the intimidating Big Three drummer Johnny Hutchinson, never liked Lennon: "He only seems a hard case to types like yourself that've never been in a fight", he told Spencer Leigh. "He wasn't a hard case to me. He was a bully who didn't pick on people his own size". Like they say in Liverpool, Lennon "couldn't punch a hole in a wet *Echo*".

Poet Johnny Byrne (1935–2008) lived above Lennon at 3 Gambier Terrace and had an equally low opinion of him. "He treated his wife Cynthia and his kid abysmally", he told Jonathon Green. "Even with all the pain of his background and all that there was a type of total brutality in his attitude to people". Photographer Dezo Hoffmann was one of a small group of privileged insiders during Beatlemania. He later wrote of a picture of Lennon smiling, "but you could never tell – like a dog who has rabies, you never knew when he would jump and bite". ("'Beware the Jabberwock' my son / The jaws that bite, the claws that catch…".)

All too often, it was Beatle manager Brian Epstein who felt the lash of the Lennon tongue. Lennon's snide homophobic and anti-semitic comments read even more uncomfortably today. "If you're not queer and you're not Jewish, what are you doing coming to work for NEMS?" he asked publicist Tony Barrow. Lennon would frequently snipe at their manager's sexuality and Semitic origins, raging within Epstein's earshot that "Hitler should have finished the job". The provisional B-side title of 'Baby You're a Rich Fag Jew'. Even Lennon's most sympathetic biographer, Ray Coleman, reported further jibes: spotting Brian's passport on tour, Lennon's snide, "Oh look, he's a Jew and he's got a British passport"… Greeting a visitor to Brian's house, "Have you come to blackmail him? If not you're the only bugger in London who hasn't". It was Lennon in a letter who warned, "watch your arse in Brighton – loads of queers".

At Paul's 21st birthday party Lennon was at his most objectionable. In attendance was the Fourmost's Billy Hatton, who told Spencer Leigh: "John Lennon wasn't a nice guy when he was pissed… He was vicious when he was drunk… He came staggering down to the marquee where I was, and Billy J. Kramer was there with a good-looking girl … on his knee. Lennon grabbed Rose's tits. Rose gave him a backhander and Lennon punched her".

And lest we forget, it was at that same event, that the first time the name of John Lennon ever appeared in a national newspaper. That would be when the drunken Beatle punched the shit out of the group's longtime and loyal supporter, Bob Wooler.

The Cavern DJ had made a nudge-nudge, wink-wink comment to John about his Spanish holiday with Brian Epstein, which the robustly heterosexual Lennon took offence at. He drunkenly piled into the harmless Wooler. This was not, as some have argued, a playful playground spat; Lennon's assault left Wooler with three broken ribs, a cracked collarbone and broken nose. Dr Gould's later letter to the Epstein family solicitor said that X-rays revealed a "fracture of the nasal bone… the nose will be swollen, sore and tender for several months".

The *Daily Mirror* reported on 21 June 1963 – in an article headlined, "Beatle In Brawl – Sorry I Socked You" – "Guitarist John Lennon, twenty-two-year-old leader of the Beatles pop group said last night 'why did I have to go and punch my best friend? I was so high I didn't realise what I was doing…'"

Wooler remembers it was Billy J. Kramer who pulled Lennon off the helpless DJ, to be dismissed, "You're nothing Kramer. You're fuck-all. We're the top!"

It was typically boorish, brutish Lennon behaviour. But even then, while publicly contrite, Beatles PR Tony Barrow remembered him "muttering that he wasn't sorry at all, that he hadn't really been all that pissed and that Bob deserved it".

Such an event was symptomatic of how quickly and venomously Lennon could turn. His contemporaries remember him as a bully, always picking on someone weaker or smaller, they couldn't imagine him tackling the notorious Garston Teddy Boys. "I was a hitter. I couldn't express myself", Lennon told *Playboy* just prior to his death. "I fought men and I hit women". It wasn't just his tongue he used in anger. Thelma Pickles, an early girlfriend from Art College, remembers spurning John, "When I … got up to leave, he became rough and whacked me one – his fist connected somewhere between my shoulder and my head…" she told Mark Lewisohn.

While in the early days of the Beatles, political correctness, gay rights, the women's movement, disability awareness … all lay in the future, but Lennon was cruel and venomous in his piss-taking impressions of what he called "cripples" and "spastics". Defenders call it his self-defence mechanism, yet onstage footage of him has him aping the permanently disabled. It was done in a manner which was offensive then, and is wholly unacceptable today.

Politically too he was off-centre, even ignoring the clunky agit-prop of *Sometime in New York City*, at one time, Lennon was considering playing a benefit concert for the IRA. Long before the Republicans were legitimised and the Peace Process became a reality, in the UK during 'the Troubles', the IRA were perceived as little more than murdering terrorists. Johnny Rogan quoted the IRA's Gerry O'Hare: "We were up to speed with [Lennon]… He was taken very seriously because he offered to do a concert, one in Dublin and one in Belfast…"

On the London *Evening Standard*, Ray Connolly was a journalist who was close to John, and had witnessed the many Lennon moods and passing bandwagons. Of John, he observed: "He imagined himself as a leftwing revolutionary, but that was just another craze, as, like a cushion, he often wore an imprint of the last person who ineffectually sat on him… If you like to think of him as the peace-loving, martyred saint of Yoko Ono's rewriting of history, you've got him dead wrong".

As a father to his firstborn, Lennon too was, to put it mildly, deficient. You might put it down to the rigours and pressures of recording and touring, "he … was not the kind of father to indulge a child's needs", photographer Robert Freeman remembered. Freeman was a Lennon neighbour, when he was hiding under the pseudonym 'Mr Hadley' prior to moving to Weybridge. John Dunbar too remembers Lennon at home in Surrey snapping at the young Julian: "No I'm *not* going to mend your fucking bicycle".

The way in which Lennon manoeuvred Cynthia into the role of the guilty party when it came to getting a divorce was contemptible. "I was really quite terrified of him for 75% of the time", she wrote later. His all-embracing adoration of Yoko, and the birth of Sean, meant that Julian was pushed further into the shadows. From the age of 11, he estimated he never saw his father more than ten times and was understandably bitter: "I felt he was a hypocrite. Dad would talk about peace and love to the world, but that peace and love never came home to me". Talking to Mary Riddell, Julian was unequivocal: "There was no love at all for me… As a father, I have no respect for him. None whatsoever".

In the 1970s, an extraordinary tape emerged from Aunt Mimi responding to John's request for details of his family history. As ever, she did not hold back: "My dear boy you're not the second Messiah… You are a speck in the ocean… For years I've heard you yelling and shouting about love, but it seemed to me your heart was full of hate".

Lennon's carapace was that rebellious, hard man bluster. For all the new man, bread-baking, house-husband in later years, people forget Lennon was a quintessential male chauvinist pig. And we can only speculate at the epic and systematic scale of his infidelities before the long-suffering Cynthia was cast aside ("I'd always had some sort of affairs going", he admitted when talking about 'Norwegian Wood') . Even at the beginning of their relationship, "he was sullen and moody most of the time", she told Lesley-Ann Jones, "and his rages could get out of control".

I believe there was a vicious side to John Lennon which is too often overlooked. And for all the faults I find with Yoko, there is no denying that on her watch, she did sand off the rough edges of this broody, troubled and tempestuous individual. It could be argued that Yoko redeemed John. Mind you, there was a lot of redeeming needed.

There remains, however, something compelling about this maddening, mercurial, quick-witted, talented man. His early death robbed us of a talent, though on the evidence of his last LP, there were strong signs that talent had diminished. For all his many, *many* faults, the Beatles were Lennon's group. He formed them. He dictated their early repertoire. In early interviews he is regularly introduced as the group's leader. It was Lennon who provided the spark at those early, joyous press conferences. It was Lennon who provided the grit in the oyster which helped fashion the group's greatness.

Following Brian Epstein's death, you sensed Lennon's interest in his group waning, and it was Paul who steered them through their final years. John's partnership with Yoko placed a further wedge between him and his bandmates. Having lived half a dozen lifetimes by the time he hit 40, Lennon was allowed to relax and unwind. It is fascinating, if fruitless, to speculate his future had he lived. Further paeans to Yoko, or a hard-hitting commitment to 'the truth' he claimed he was always searching for? Reunion with his estranged colleagues, or seeking out new musical alliances to be forged?

For all my criticisms of John Lennon, I still find myself smiling at his quips, (asked for "a quick word", he cracked back "Velocity") I can marvel at the musical path he ploughed in conjunction with his buddies, 1963–70. Of his post-Beatle years, they are clouded by the events of 8 December 1980. While I find fault with the man, it has to be said that the world was undeniably enriched by John Lennon's presence, and felt a severe loss when he was so brutally taken from it.

When the Lennons left the UK in September 1971, it was never intended to be a permanent departure. The intention was always to return to Tittenhurst Park, their Georgian mansion near Ascot. It had been there a few years before that the last-ever Beatles photoshoot had taken place in the estate's 72 acres.

Appointed house-sitters for John and Yoko in absentia were Paul Wheeler and his then-wife Diana. Paul had been a university friend of the singer-songwriter Nick Drake. In one of those inconceivable coincidences, as doctor to the British colony in post-war

Burma, my Uncle Wallace Lusk was the GP who attended to the infant Nick Drake. That led to my writing the first-ever biography of Nick.

Brian Wells, a Cambridge contemporary of Nick's told me when he visited Tittenhurst Park to see the Wheelers: "There was all this Beatles memorabilia – the statues from the cover of *Sgt Pepper*; the *Pepper* uniform and in John and Yoko's bedroom there was … John Lennon's Rickenbacker guitar, and some guy said come and see this, there's a whole *wall* of them!"

I always found the image of Nick Drake visiting the Lennon mansion in 1971 strangely touching. This was Nick, a footnote to a footnote during his lifetime. His record sales scarcely registered, a career almost over as soon as it had begun, and the darkness which was to take his life only three years later already on the horizon. Here was this damaged, lost soul wandering around the empty mansion of a millionaire rock icon who would never return.

"John and Yoko had gone", Paul Wheeler told me. "It always struck me as an allegory of the times, this abandoned estate… They hadn't definitely gone for ever, which is why we were still there, they could have come back any day". Of course, they never did. Years of exile saw the Lennons finally settle permanently in New York in the 1970s, where recording became an afterthought as the couple raised their only child, Sean.

In the ten years between the Beatle split and his untimely murder, Lennon was frequently scathing about his years in that band. In interviews he would dismiss much-loved songs as "rubbish" or "garbage". His contentious interview with Jann Wenner, originally published in *Rolling Stone* (then later as *Lennon Remembers*) further helped demolish the Beatle myth. In the wake of the scaled-down *Plastic Ono Band* LP and his Primal Scream therapy, Lennon was at his most egotistical ("People like me are aware of their so-called genius at ten, eight, nine… In school why didn't they see that I'm cleverer than anybody in this school… I never forgave [Aunt Mimi] for not treating me like a fuckin' genius or whatever… Nobody says it, so you scream it: look at me, a genius for fuck's sake".

It was that "fuckin' genius" angle National Lampoon parodied on their 1972 *Radio Dinner* LP ("I could have been a fisherman, but I can't because I'm a fuckin' genius"). The actor playing John turned out to be Tony Hendra (1941–2021), later better known as Spinal Tap's long-suffering manager Ian Faith.

A devout reader of the music press, Lennon would often fire off letters – too often lambasting McCartney in *Melody Maker*. But in 2015 a fascinating letter surfaced: in a 1971 interview with *ZigZag*, folk singer Steve Tilston reflected that becoming rich and famous might dilute the quality of his own songs. Lennon wrote to him c/o the magazine: "Being rich doesn't change your experience in the way you <u>think</u>. The only difference basically is that you don't have to worry about <u>money</u> – <u>food</u> – <u>roof</u> etc…" John even included a phone number (Ascot 23022) for the folkie to ring for further advice.

Poor old Steve Tilston was even more surprised when he only learned of the letter's existence in 2015, when it was sold at auction. It never reached him at the time. The dispiriting experience led to the Al Pacino film *Danny Collins*. Talking to Alan Franks at the time of the film's release, Tilston said his one regret was that he never got a chance to take his guitar down to Ascot and jam with Lennon: "I suppose what's painful is that it's a road not taken. All of us in our lives are faced with choices of ways to go. What I resented, but don't anymore, is that with this one I didn't get the choice".

Lennon's standing diminished throughout the 70s. The harrowing *Plastic Ono Band* was followed by the sugar-coated but esteemed *Imagine*. It was downhill from there. Even long-time Lennon champions *Rolling Stone* called 1972's *Sometime in New York City* "incipient artistic suicide… embarrassingly puerile… Only a monomaniacal smugness could allow the Lennons to think that this witless doggerel wouldn't insult the intelligence and feelings of *any* audience". A De-Luxe 50th anniversary edition of the double LP was shelved, "due to lack of commercial potential".

Few were really impressed by *Mind Games* ("mediocre… After four solo albums, each lousier than the last…" were only some of the reviews).

Walls & Bridges scored better by its association with the globally conquering Elton John. Neither LP, however, demonstrated that Lennon was flexing any real creative muscle.

I draw comparisons with Arthur Conan Doyle. For him, those Sherlock Holmes stories were "the day job", written for profit. He always believed he would be remembered as a writer of historical fiction – but who recalls Brigadier Gerard today? Whereas the casebooks emanating from 221B Baker Street endure. Lennon I felt always thought of the Beatles as his adolescence, and that his music from 1970 onwards marked his maturity. Realistically, only a handful of songs from that period emerge with any real merit. A retrospective return to form came on 1975's *Rock & Roll*. The rest was then silence… Disco, Glam, Prog, Punk, all passed the reclusive Lennon by.

It was the Dakota Building, that gloomy Gothic landmark, which provided Lennon a sanctuary during his retirement. A landmark for native New Yorkers who named it, as it seemed as far out of town as the 39th state. Prior to the Lennons, it was only familiar to UK residents as the creepy residence which gave the Devil house room in Roman Polanski's 1968 shocker *Rosemary's Baby*. Over the years, the sombre building played host to Rudolf Nureyev, Lauren Bacall and Leonard Bernstein. John and Yoko bought the apartment (after being approved by the building's board) from the actor Robert Ryan. It had been to that apartment Bob Dylan repaired for a party celebrating his return to the concert stage at the *Woody Guthrie Memorial Concert* in January 1968.

Five years away from the public eye gave rise to innumerable rumours about John Lennon. The scrupulous Johnny Rogan wrote of the "wildly varying accounts" of Lennon's Dakota days, "tales of fad diets, nicotine and caffeine addiction, drug consumption, temper tantrums, sexual frustrations, erotic fantasies, spiritual unrest, religious conversions, magic rituals, neurotic behavior, wild mood swings, extreme fasts and vows of silence, spending sprees, excessive indolence, elongated periods in front of a television, horoscope readings, secret vacations and much else has been mentioned…"

I do believe that it was during those five years away that Lennon became a more rounded human being. The birth of his second son seemed to be a sort of salvation. The pressure was off. There was no one to lash out at. There was no need. Now he had a purpose. His infamous 'Lost Weekend' looks like the last flourish of the old belligerent Lennon. Reunited with a pregnant Yoko gave him the stability that he had for so long been searching. For all my criticisms of the second Mrs Lennon, I do believe Yoko exorcised the demons which had contributed to Lennon being such a prickly, confrontational adult.

And, from being a sailor on the far reaches of the avant garde, Yoko developed an unerring sense of business. Happy to lock horns with the dreaded 'men in suits', she undertook the minutiae of handling the couple's financial business. She did so spectacularly well. Elton John once sent the Lennons a card, "Imagine six apartments / It isn't hard to do / One is full of fur coats / The other full of shoes". As John Higgs commented, "It takes some doing to be such an excessive consumer that Elton John feels moved to comment on it".

With Yoko adapting the role of a man in a suit, it left John plenty of time to dream, and reflect on that "long, strange trip" his rollercoaster life had been. From sullen schoolboy staring from Pier Head to the far horizon, to rebellious rocker, a path which even his fertile imagination could never have imagined. Scaling sexual Everests, riches beyond his wildest dreams; bathing in critical acclaim, benefitting from global adoration. To the multi-millionaire in his New York apartment, sporting his old school tie and finally able to look back fondly on what he had achieved, John Lennon had earned the apparent tranquility of those final years.

For all his flaws, faults and imperfections, John Lennon deserved a better end than that which found him on a cold December night in 1980. Answering a fan's request, he turned, and the five bullets slammed into his wiry frame. As the news broke, the tears fell, the tributes paid, the sense of loss was an almost psychical ache. The cuttings files were ransacked, the obituaries were polished. It was a time when the world genuinely was united in mourning.

As a macabre point of interest, the assassin's unfired sixth bullet now resides in Scotland Yard's Black Museum. It is kept alongside ghoulish memorabilia commemorating Jack the Ripper, Dr Crippen and Ruth Ellis. The bullet was the one used for forensic analysis in America, but because John was a UK citizen, it was handed over to Scotland Yard.

On what would have been – incredibly – his 80th birthday in October 2020, once again the airwaves were full of those songs and that man. Invariably all of the tributes emphasised the positive side of Lennon's life. That emphasis was not unique, because of ownership and the licensing of the songs and film copyrights, none of the film-makers would be allowed to undertake a truly objective portrait. All of John and Yoko's activities are taken at face value; any suggestion that staying in bed in a Hilton hotel, or answering questions from inside a bag, were a farcical and futile waste of time, would be met with short shrift. Plus, the crucial audio material which Yoko controlled would be refused.

As she passed her 90th birthday in 2023, much was made of Yoko's financial acuity and her canny accumulation of her estimated $500,000,000 fortune. Cynics suggested that this was more to do with her husbanding of her second husband's copyrights and the royalties from the group he founded in 1957 rather than, say, sales of her 2016 album *Yes, I'm a Witch Too*.

Somewhere down the line, it would be a fascinating exercise to see or read a fully-rounded portrait of this frustrating, talented and complex man. It was Lennon who corralled a bunch of Scouse teenagers into a group and steered them to unimagined greatness. But that journey was undertaken in tandem – with his songwriting partner, with the development and ready wit of the guitarist and the undeniable charm of the drummer. Lennon alone would never have had the patience of Brian Epstein to chair business meetings, or the patience of George Martin to steer each song to its sonic summit.

As the shock subsided, the world appreciated that in terms of getting back, that really was *it*. Lennon's death closed the door on any possible Beatle reunion. The group would carry on, however, in fans' hearts, in print, on vinyl, compact, disc and film; in technology yet to be invented, in space, underground. In legend…

*

As many have marvelled, the coterie around the Beatles was miniscule. Brian had secretaries and staff to run NEMS. The public relations side was effectively saying 'No' to the world's press. It was two old friends who were closest to the group, and the pressures on Mal Evans and Neil Aspinall, particularly during those hysterical touring years, were unimaginable. Those two confederates were loyal and steadfast, observing the Sicilian code of 'omerta'.

It was under their only real manager Brian Epstein's watchful eye, that the group prospered and flourished. Epstein kept a wary watch on the outgoings, but his bubble around the group was built on trust. The forging ahead, I believe, was due to the building blocks of the McCartney & Lennon partnership. Being able to draw on their own reservoir of self-written material helped put them ahead of the game. However astute other managers were, however competent other record producers, where the Beatles scored was that with John and Paul on board, in-house, they were a self-contained unit. And that is why, I maintain, from early on, they raced ahead. What elevated the Beatles was their own "built-in tunesmith team".

Compared to, say, the Searchers, I think there is an interesting point to be made about just *how* good the Beatles were at the beginning. On a Friday lunchtime at the Cavern, or a Saturday night out in Litherland? Aim of evening: Get pissed. Pull bird. Dance. Shag… And the group you were dancing to … at the time, fairly incidental.

Harder-edged by Hamburg; a wider repertoire than their peers, in all honesty, hand on heart, were the Beatles *better* than the Searchers? Or the Big Three? Or Faron's Flamingoes? Or the Remo Four? Or any one of half a hundred groups treading the same circuit at the same time? In his autobiography, future Beatle producer Glyn Johns remarked, "The one thing that struck me about The Beatles in those early days was how relatively ordinary they sounded without the vocals. They could have been any competent group of the day, but as soon as the vocals were added the magic was there".

On record, of course, they improved; the world witnessed that. And that is something which George Martin can take eternal credit for. Their only immediate rivals, the Rolling Stones, were supervised by their hustling manager as producer. On disc, the Stones had to rely on Andrew Loog Oldham, who by his own admission could barely produce his way out of a paper bag. "He's an idiot", the Small Faces' Ian McLagan confirmed to Shawn Levy. "He has no idea about sound. He couldn't produce a burp after a glass of beer".

Herman's Hermits, the Honeycombs, Freddie & the Dreamers, Wayne Fontana & the Mindbenders, the Applejacks … all had to rely on in-house, largely disinterested staff producers. Their contemporary releases sound so … threadbare. It is worth contrasting and comparing: a random example, 'From Me to You' with Herman's Hermits 'I'm Into Something Good'. The latter sounds incredibly limp, and with a totally inappropriate piano interlude, remarkably *thin*. The record has no depth. It survives solely on cosy nostalgic memory.

The mechanics of the pop song: the unity of bass and drums; the deft insertion of lead guitar, backing harmonies, a rock-steady drum sound. The greatness is built on the songwriting genius of Lennon and McCartney, it was also how George Martin altered and improved that Beatle sound, rather than Wally Ridley, Norrie Paramour or Ron Richards…

In fact, thanks to George Martin's astute perseverance, those early Fab 45s transcend nostalgia. They rock and are buoyed by a pulsating sense of liberating joy. Personally, on their single releases during late 1964 and much of 65, I think they sagged. It was understandable given the pressure they were under, however, 'I Feel Fine', 'Ticket to Ride' and 'Day Tripper' are, to me, perfunctory releases to fill in spaces. More Oasis than Beatle.

I remember the delights revealed with the introduction of compact discs (how long ago that seems). First off, there was the opportunity to skip 'Revolution #9'. Then appreciate all that stuff you sort of knew was there, but was revealed in all its true hi-fi glory: the strumming intro to 'Eight Days a Week'… the lovely little four-note organ run at the end of 'Lucy in the Sky…' … the flamboyant flamenco ushering in 'Bungalow Bill'… However, with the introduction of the iPod (how long ago *that* seems), there remain fewer pleasures than when, unexpectedly, a Beatle song appears on shuffle, followed by another one, out of sequence, and you marvel again – all this from *one* band? In only eight years.

There remains something compelling and compulsive about Beatle music; just today I suddenly thought how many copies of *The White Album* have I owned? My original scratched vinyl (Mono, No. 0054050, with the long-forgotten phone number 567 6655 someone had written in biro on the back); the clunky original CD; the 30th anniversary 'Limited Edition' CD; the 2009 CD remaster… Finally (finally?) the 2018 box set which included the Blu-Ray, but alas I do not have the equipment to play it on. Not much wonder Apple are coining it. Mind you, in fairness, from the *Past Masters* releases they have picked up the golden baton and run with it. Only latterly have the Rolling Stones paid anything like due attention to their back catalogue.

Look at the way Apple have handled the Beatle legacy compared with their archrivals. Jagger and Co. have a line in the sand: the pre-Allen Klein material (the glory years) and then, basically, the Rest. Finally archive releases with bonus tracks did surface, notably *Sticky Fingers* and *Some Girls*. But ABKCO's handling of anniversary reissues of *Beggars Banquet* and *Their Satanic Majesties Request* was shocking: they might as well have had a cover sticker boasting 'Contains NO bonus material… NO extra tracks… Frankly Absolutely Nothing Different from the original vinyl release of half a century ago".

In comparison Neil Aspinall and the current occupants of the Apple boardroom have, I believe, served us well. Then the contents of the 6CD *Let It Be* box set were revealed. Now, to my mind, this is the first time that Apple have truly and comprehensively dropped the ball when it comes to the reason for their existence. Of the six CDs two are different mixes of effectively the same LP. And with a CD's playing time of 80 minutes, a four-track EP was short-changing the loyal fans. Surely something else, rather than a sparse two CDs of 'Rehearsals and Jams', could have been collated from the widely-reported 140 *hours* of audio?

In September 2015, while talking up interest in the new series of *Doctor Who*, the Doctor (Peter Capaldi) plus companion, and a couple of Daleks, were captured on the Abbey Road zebra crossing. The 2024 Doctor found himself at Abbey Road in February 1963. The Beatles, of course, famously appeared briefly in the show in 1965, in an episode called 'The Chase' on the Doctor's 'Time & Space Visualiser'. They are seen performing 'Ticket to Ride'; asked by the Doctor's companions if she knows who the Beatles are, she replies: "Of course, I have visited their Memorial Theatre in Liverpool". (A line which would have provided viewers' gasps of incredulous laughter.) The scriptwriters' original plan was to have the group made up as old men, appearing at their 50th anniversary show in the future, but Epstein vetoed the plan.

As for *that* zebra crossing… It has played host to everyone from the Red Hot Chilli Peppers to the Simpsons; the Power Rangers to Prime Ministers. It became Grade II listed in 2010. A webcam displays just who is parodying that 1969 album cover, online, 24 hours a day. Due to the lack of footfall, the coronavirus crisis of 2020 was an opportunity to literally brush up the crossing.

It is estimated that the crosswalk attracts 400,000 visitors a year, yet the adjacent studio remains behind closed doors. I took Kevin Kane, a huge Beatles fan, to the sacred spot. Kevin runs the Memphis Convention & Visitors Bureau, so on his watch is Graceland, Stax and Sun Studios, all of which have duly catered to millions of eagle-eyed visitors. Having undertaken the photo opportunity crossing the road, he made his way to the gates until I pointed out that the Abbey Road studios were closed to the general public. "Do you mean", he asked, incredulously, "that EMI are making so much money they don't *need* to open Abbey Road?" Finally, grudgingly, after decades of inactivity, in October 2012, Abbey Road opened up a merchandising store next to the world-famous studio.

Those simple black and white painted stripes are the bane of the drivers of the bus route from Camden to White City. The foreseeable delay always comes along Abbey Road, there are always crowds criss-crossing at what is now London's 17th most visited tourist attraction. Not as frustrating for the dozen or so people who, most days, visit the Dockland Light Railway's Abbey Road station in Newham, East London, which was opened in 2011. Transport for London now display a helpful poster at the station: "Feel like you've been here, there and everywhere and on a magical mystery tour? Then don't pass me by. Unfortunately, you are at the wrong Abbey Road. However we can work it out and help you get back to the correct location… Passengers need a ticket to ride".

So immediately recognisable had that familiar invention for road safety become, that in 2003, the traffic police in Calcutta used the *Abbey Road* cover in a safer crossing campaign under the headline, 'If they can, why can't you?' Again, that LP cover was endlessly photoshopped in 2020 and was widely seen on the internet during the Covid-19 pandemic to emphasise self-distancing.

It was in 2010 that the actual Abbey Road Studios were granted a Grade II listed building status. The National Heritage List of England deemed the building as "of special interest, warranting every effort to preserve it".

Along with 3 Savile Row, it is the most visited London Beatle location. It is only one of the many locations Richard Porter takes fans to on his walks. Richard has been doing them for over 30 years, leaving nearly 200,000 footsore but contented fans.[28]

From across the world they come to pay homage, and of all the conquered territories, Leslie Woodhead's book on the Beatles and their impact on the USSR (*How the Beatles Rocked the Kremlin*) makes for fascinating reading. In the pre-Beatles Soviet Union, jazz was not discouraged, but the ageing Soviet leadership could not abide rock & roll, and none of it was officially issued. There *was* something occurring in many of the Soviet bloc countries: state-sanctioned rock & roll. For example, the Politburo allowed Dean Reed to function as the USSR's Elvis – a YouTube clip of him performing 'Ghost Riders in the Sky' to Yasser Arafat is worth seeking out.

For the real thing during the 1960s, Samizdat copies of Beatle music from radio broadcasts were pressed on 'Grandma's bones', that is, medical X-ray films. As the Beatles were heard illegally, Soviet youth tried to emulate them, fashioning electric guitars from wood, with electric pickups stolen from public phone boxes. It was not until 1967 that a Beatle record was officially released in Russia – 'Girl' appeared on a record released by the state record label. On the LP *Musical Kaleidoscope*, it was listed as "an English folk song".

Some progress toward greater freedoms had been made during the Kruschev era but, following his fall in 1964, the state put the pressure back on, and pulled the strings. Pop groups were sanctioned, with authorised set lists based on ideology rather than rock & roll. 'Organising The Activities Of Vocal Instrumental Ensembles & Improving The Ideological Levels Of Their Repertoires' was only one of the diktats. Cover groups in the USSR could occasionally get away with performing Beatles songs by claiming, for example, that 'Can't Buy Me Love' was a comment on prostitution, or that 'Taxman' was a protest song about the exploitation of taxi drivers in the Capitalist West.

While the Beatles set the rest of the world on fire, the Politburo poured scorn on them, calling them capitalist pigs "performing on stage just wearing swimming trunks with toilet seats on their necks". Their success was solely due to meeting a "London fairy [who] understood that these gifted guys could be real cash earners".

For the occupants of the USSR, the group became as mythic as Russian folk legends – Muscovites are convinced they saw John Lennon incognito during the 1960s, shopping in a Moscow street market… That the Beatles appeared before the Politburo at a special concert in Siberia… That on their way to Japan in 1966, the Beatles had landed in Minsk, and performed an impromptu concert on the plane's wing.

It had been Leslie Woodhead who, as a young Granada TV employee, had shot the first ever TV footage of the Beatles, at the Cavern in 1962. He was back on the track in 2003 when Paul McCartney played Red Square. "The music that had shifted my guts all those years ago in a Liverpool cellar", he wrote 40 years later, "had become this thing, vast and remote and untouchable, sealed behind barriers, summoned by oligarchs, pumped around the planet like gas or oil".

As for the Beatles and their Russian impact, Woodhead astutely noted: "In the capitalist west, rock & roll had been bred among the underclasses of Memphis or Detroit

---

28 Details at www.beatlesinlondon.com

or Liverpool, but in Moscow … I was finding a different story… It was … evidence of how the Beatles revolution was made by bourgeois kids in the Soviet Union, the ones with parents who could travel and had tape recorders and cameras".

Simon Napier Bell's account of trying to organise Wham!'s 1985 dates in Communist China included an account of a meeting with the country's *only* record label. He pulled out a Wham! LP to be told, "I never hear of Wham! How about Beatles? I think Beatles would be better concert". "They broke up". "Oh really… I thought Beatles is very good for England. Why government let them break up?" "In England people can do as they want. How could a government keep a pop group together if they wanted to break up?" "Maybe put them in jail?"

The Beatles had initially described Apple as a kind of "western Communism", but the two ideologies were at odds until the era of Glasnost, as I discovered when I visited Bulgaria in June 1993, as part of a British Council tour, accompanying Jimi Hendrix's longest-serving drummer, Mitch Mitchell.

The capital, Sofia, was a fascinating mix of rococo and Stalinist brutal architecture. But what was overwhelming was the population's *enthusiasm* for music, it was like going back to the 1960s. Preceding the collapse of Communism in 1989, the focal point for protest in the capital had been the Lennon Wall. Following his murder, two 15-year-old schoolgirls sprayed 'Lennon We Love You' and were promptly arrested, which caused a wave of outrage, and the spot became the rallying point for dissent. It was strangely touching to see the graffiti still added to. They were not particularly eloquent statements ('Make Love Not Hate') but by writing them *in English* at a time when this was the language of the enemy was a counter-revolutionary act. "English may be the language of Shakespeare", one Soviet general was quoted as saying at the time, "but it is above all the language of our class enemy".

As in Russia, under Soviet rule, rock & roll was state-sanctioned in Bulgaria. The Grasshoppers were 'the Bulgarian Beatles' from 1964 to 1970. As the group's music grew increasingly accusatory towards the system, the authorities tired of arresting the band, and on one occasion the police tried to arrest the entire audience. By the end they were writing material which openly criticised the government, so to shut them up, the group were all drafted into the army.

As with all countries behind the Iron Curtain, the Beatles were an illicit thrill. Our companions in Bulgaria had learned their English phonetically from the group's records. One memorable evening over a meal, in answer to an earnest Bulgarian Beatle fan's enquiry, I found myself explaining that the Charles Hawtrey Lennon references prior to 'Let It Be' was not a guru or avatar… Had he ever heard of the *Carry On…* films?

On our last night we attended an open-air festival where the country's leading bands performed – many included lengthy drum solos in honour of Mitch's presence. Beneath the balmy night sky a man behind me heard me talking English, tapped me on the shoulder and pointed up: "Lucy in the sky… with *diamonds*", he grinned.

*

Throughout the 21st century, barely a day goes by when the Beatles aren't mentioned, cited or referred to. It is with bated breath that we waited for Peter Jackson's re-imagined *Let It Be*. Originally scheduled for September 2020, it was put back until 2021, another victim of Covid-19. Jackson's directorial hand was proven with the epic *Lord of the Rings* trilogy, indeed so closely was the portly New Zealand director associated with Tolkien's saga that I couldn't help but laugh out loud when I saw a set of model figures from the films, and there among the elves, orcs and Hobbits was … Peter Jackson himself.[29]

What gave Beatle fans hope was the flair, skill and authority Jackson brought to his 2018 documentary *They Shall Not Grow Old*. All were familiar with those stilted, black and white films of the Great War, 1914–18. What Jackson and his team did was to painstakingly bring those long-dead figures alive. It was not just the colourisation, the real jolt came with Jackson getting lip-readers in and employing actors to give those victims voices from beyond the grave. If he could do that with 100-year-old footage, just imagine what wonders he might conjure up with the Beatles from 1969. In July 1970, *Rolling Stone* reflected, "The unedited *Let It Be* film, running to some 800 hours of film … will perhaps some day be donated to the National Trust where scholars will delve into its meaning".

We got a tantalising glimpse when Jackson released a five-minute taster just prior to Christmas 2020: it was a joy, the quality of the print, the vivid colours and the skylarking. With all the features, books and documentaries celebrating the misery evident on that troubled LP and film, what a delight it was to see the Beatles so evidently *enjoying* themselves. What tantalised even further was Jackson's mouth-watering account of a first cut of 18 *hours*.

When Jackson's six-hour version was screened during December 2021, the praise was unanimous. Many lighted upon the way it re-wrote Beatle history – that they weren't at each other's throats *all* the time… That there was a genuine sense of camaraderie, that there was a willingness to find, as the decade ended, a way to continue as the Beatles. For all the evident bonhomie though, while watching it, I still sense that underlying *tension*. Paul's pleading with John for some more new songs… George's palpable lack of interest when he is required to supply backing vocals to a McCartney composition.

If there was criticism, it was that, did we really need six hours of fly-on-the-wall documentary to chronicle what was, the general consensus, the weakest Beatles LP? And after watching all six hours, I felt that *Get Back* was … compellingly boring. All those versions of 'Don't Let Me Down'; the tedious in search of the lost chord; the endless 'Will We' 'Won't We' go up on the roof. George tries out 'Something'… John and Paul do an *Educating Archie* (ask your grandparents) on 'Two of Us'… And then, before your very eyes, Paul puts together 'Get Back' and 'Let It Be'… It was like looking over Mozart's shoulder.

I bought a Blu-Ray player for the occasion and settled down one afternoon for a six-hour trawl. Basically, *Get Back* is McCartney – in the words of Chuck Berry – motorvatin'

---

29 One can only imagine the response of the gentlemanly George Martin when Lightning Boltz put a 'George Martin Action Figure' on the market. Apart from the tie, the 3.75 inch figure bore little resemblance to the urbane record producer.

the Beatles into action. John's disinterest is manifest. George struggles to maintain his commitment. For all the talk of the 'joy' of the Jackson documentary, how they weren't at each other's throats during the sessions, there is undeniably, an underlying discontent. Lennon and Harrison are chafing at the bit; even Ringo you sense is keen to get onto the set of *The Magic Christian*.

Of all the mountain of press the documentary series attracted, I felt one of the best appreciations of it came from Richard Williams. Writing in *Uncut*, the ex-*Melody Maker* journalist appreciated that "it seems clear that the focus was less on the actual music than on negotiating some sort of collective dynamic". In his note on the box set, Giles Martin felt the final LP was, "An attempt at a reconciliation through trying to find the spark that had never previously failed to ignite their unsurpassed musical creativity... They loved the sound that only they could generate with one another".

I loved the full 42-minute Apple rooftop gig when I saw it at the East Dulwich Picturehouse in February 2022. There was criticism that the 60-minute film still included the comments from the passersby; I thought that was one of the strengths. A Snapshot of London as it was: mini-skirted dolly birds and crusty old bowler-hatted types complaining about the noise. As a sign of the times, when *Get Back* finally made it onto Blu-Ray, the sleeve warned, "Contains tobacco depictions". Watching 'the last time', again, there was a real poignancy as Paul quit the roof, took a look over his shoulder, and the caption came up, "This was the last time the Beatles played together".

Peter Jackson himself confessed his trepidation at tackling the whole project. Apparently one un-named director had unbelievably turned the documentary down. Apple, impressed with the technical and emotional power of *They Shall Not Grow Old* approached the Kiwi.

"I said, 'Can I look at all the footage first? And then I'll let you know.' Because I was thinking, I'd love to make a Beatles film, but I don't want to make the Beatles-breakup film. That's the one Beatles movie I would never want to make", Jackson told Joe Hagan. "What I found is that I was laughing continuously. I just was laughing. I was laughing and laughing and laughing, and I didn't stop."

It led to a meeting with McCartney in 2017, which again indicates just how these projects gestate: "I could see on his face he was imagining the worst. I just said to him, 'Look, I've got to say, it surprised the hell out of me because I was expecting it to be a miserable experience for you. I expected to have to witness a rather bleak moment – but it's actually the exact opposite. It's incredibly funny. It's incredibly lively. It shows you guys having a great time.' And he couldn't believe it. He said, 'What? What? Really? Really?' And it certainly surprised him. Because he has never seen this stuff, even though he lived through it. It's a long time ago, and subsequent events, I think, just muddied the whole memory of this thing".

Talking to Dylan Jones three solid months before the rest of the world got to see the six-hour documentary on Disney+, Jackson was buoyant about the upbeat nature: "The moment when George is arguing with Paul ... is actually the worst of it... I've tried to use nothing at all from *Let It Be*, so *Get Back* is completely different. I didn't want to usurp the original film, so this is a companion piece. But the one area we did break that rule is that little exchange between George and Paul, I didn't want to be accused of sanitising the films by not having that, because that's the bit everyone remembers.

"But we've given people the context of the interaction by showing the full six-minute conversation so it no longer feels like an argument. It no longer feels like Paul is getting on George's nerves. You understand what Paul's trying to achieve".

As with all Beatle projects, Jackson's *Get Back* required a full commitment from Paul, Ringo, Yoko Ono and Olivia Harrison. But Jackson marvelled at how much they trusted him: "They're very hands-off. They gave me the footage. I disappeared to the other side of the world with it and I've never been back to Britain since".

"We don't do things by half with The Beatles," Orla Lee-Fisher, Universal Music Group International's SVP of marketing told *Music Week*. "They are global superstars and they resonate everywhere, but the advantage of having the Disney+ three-part series is it gives us an elongated campaign. We will have a sustained campaign through 2021; it will be wall-to-wall Beatles from now until the end of the year, which is really exciting and gives us lots of opportunities to keep driving new consumers to The Beatles".

That is a key point to underline; as their original fans die off, Apple and UMG are keen to keep the furnaces stoked with material which will appeal to an audience reared in a world of Adele, Ed Sheeran and Kanye West. It seemed to have worked in Disney's favour; after only four days on the channel, *Get Back* registered over 500,000,000 minutes of streaming.

And after the world got to see and hear what must, arguably, have been the most keenly-anticipated, unrealised Beatle project since *Anthology*... What next? Well, the De-Luxe *Revolver* box set of 2022 picked up the usual critical plaudits. With the delicacy of craftsmen painstakingly restoring masterpieces, Giles Martin and Sam Odell nip and tweak oh-so familiar recordings. I found something calmly reassuring hearing the voice of George Martin steering the group towards just the *right* decision. How they did it still compels and fascinates after all these years, but the detail can occasionally make the eyes glaze over. In the *Revolver* box book engineer Ken Townsend explained, "It dawned on me that if I took the sync output from the Studer and fed it into the BTR and ran that machine at 30ips..."

Following the 60th anniversary of the release of 'Love Me Do', what could Apple have up their sleeves to commemorate subsequent 60th occasions? Double-pack CDs of mono and stereo versions of the original UK and US LPs? A Best Of ... Zapple? Re-, *re*-remastered CD versions of each original (UK and US) album with a bonus disc of alternate takes? I believe there will be a market for any such physical format releases. As the demographic ages, they (I) prefer things they can touch. They (we) prefer magazines and books we can hold, we like LPs and CDs, not invisible purchases plucked out of the ether, like streaming and Bitcoin.

Surely the real Beatle gold had been mined for the 6CD *Anthology* releases and subsequent box sets? Presumably the best alternate takes were included. What remains must surely be fool's gold. If 'Carnival of Light' is eventually released, it will hardly stack up alongside 'A Day in the Life'. The fact that the entire Apple rooftop gig was excluded from the 2021 *Let It Be* box suggests that it is being held in abeyance for, when, 2029?

On the 75th Anniversary of VE Day, coincidentally, I found myself watching Volumes I & II of the *Anthology* DVDs. It seemed an appropriate date – they were, after all, children of the most destructive war in history. Children who grew up on an island reeling from that war, labouring under rationing and its parochial class attitudes. From there they went on to change the world.

And there is something *still* so affecting, so redeeming watching their story unfold. So much of it is our island's story too. So many elements and angles sprang out. Just looking at photos of them in their Beatle boots, and remembering that, no way would my 2/6d weekly pocket money stretch to a proper pair (75/11d). But, bless her, my mum pointed out that there were some cheaper Wellington boots that *almost* looked like Beatle boots… And I was grateful that my straight hair, much to my dad's disapproval, could, during the school holidays, be combed into an approximation of the Beatle fringe.

I can now pore over Mark Lewisohn's pioneering *The Beatles Live!*, so I can read just how close they came to me in south-east London… Tooting, Lewisham, Croydon, so near, yet so far away. Or spend far too long on Facebook, intrigued by never-before-seen photos – the four Beatles relaxing in an East End pub during the 'Penny Lane' shoot… Paul's 1966 passport photo… Al Aronowitz ushering Bob Dylan past Neil Aspinall into the Delmonico Hotel prior to turning on… Or going down the rabbit hole on YouTube, trawling through out-takes of never-before-seen Fab film footage. Those live performances which burst out of the screen, they positively *pulsate*… Those head-shaking harmonies as Paul and George cluster together… Those blissful early years, when live performance and mob hysteria was something to be savoured rather than resented. They exude charm, confidence, revelling in the excitement.

When I spoke to Paul in 1985, he could finally duck under the Sword of Damocles which had hung permanently over his head for so much of his adult life: "I do hark back to the Beatles… but it was a great time. I mean, I love loving the Beatles. I love loving what we did. But to be frightened of ever doing it again is a bit silly… Because of the *pain* of the separation, of the Beatle breaking up, there was inevitably going to be that little time when you hated any mention of it, but that was always going to be vying with your natural nostalgia. The further you get from that period, the more you can look at it and say, 'Cor, did we do that?' Course we did; wait a minute, we can *still* do that".

One day, at a hotel near the McCartney family home in East Sussex, MPL asked me to sit in on a day of interviews Paul was doing for European press. They were interested if any of the questions appeared to interest *him*. After a couple of hours, even I was bored with the inevitable questions about the band he was in before Wings, and the questions everyone asked since 1980 about a Beatle reunion. During lunch I asked him if it wasn't overwhelming?

"As long as you get into that past thing… I think in a way, if you're gonna be locked in the past, like people who have little railway collections and put on guards' hats and uniforms… It's fine to be in the 'Age of Steam', or to be in the 'Age of Beatle', but you've got to be having a good time in it. It's a pity if you think, 'It's gone, and I'm sad'. You should think, 'It's gone, but I'm glad it *was*', and get on with that knowledge".

On another occasion, while I was setting up the tape, I'd read that it was the anniversary of some Beatle event, and asked him if he'd remembered it. His response was along the lines of: if you look at those Day-By-Day books you'll see how busy the Beatles were, and whole years were a blur. Indeed, 1963 to 1966 are testament to their workload. He said he always felt there would be a response to the *big* anniversaries – Royal Variety, Ed

Sullivan, *Sgt Pepper* – "but not every fucking *day*".

In his biography of Lawrence of Arabia, Michael Korda reported on a young boy about to meet T.E. Lawrence. He is told he should make allowances because he is an extraordinary person.

"I don't want to make allowances... I want him to be a hero".

"Ah, yes", his Aunt Gwen replied, "One does, and that's his great problem. It's the problem all heroes have to cope with – when you've made your gesture you've got the rest of your life to live".

"Do you think it's very difficult for him being a hero?"

"Oh yes, it's very hard work wearing a halo – or any other mark of distinction for that matter".

Funnily enough, Lawrence had another Beatle link: in 2006, I was invited to a preview of an exhibition commemorating Lawrence of Arabia at the Imperial War Museum. It was fascinating and rewarding. At the end I was chatting to the curator who wanted to know what I'd thought. Very satisfactory I confirmed, and I had spotted only one mistake. I'm not saying his face grew ashen, but he *was* curious. "Well", I said, "I'd forgotten Lawrence was on the cover of *Sgt Pepper*, but you've got its release date down as 1987, that was the year of the CD release..." Barely before I'd finished speaking he scuttled off with the Tipp-Ex.

And in the end... after all the forensic examinations, following all the exhumations and analysis, what will survive of the Beatles is their Love. The love which went into that joyous, timeless music. Those finely tuned LPs, EPs and 45s, all recorded during that phenomenal burst spanning the 60s. Songs which endure. Songs which will last and be heard as long as there is electricity to power them. Songs which defy nostalgia but which seem to strike a didactic chord with every fresh generation.

In *The Independent*, Tom Nicholson found Generation Z (born between 1996 and 2010) latching onto the group. Those whose lingua franca is memes and fancam edits, broadcast on TikTok. Typical was 20-year-old Lucy West: "It's like something out of a novel...", her enthusiasm fanned by reissues, box sets, anniversaries, books and documentaries. "It almost doesn't matter that they're not still a band that's still recording albums now, and because there's still a lot to explore". Skylar Moody (24) first saw *Hard Day's Night* in a music class and was captivated: "We can all come together in one agreement that we loved the Beatles... It's so easy to go to social media and find a fan community of people to talk to that will understand you".

For one last time, I was determined to see Paul McCartney in a venue with a roof and, thanks to MPL, duly did so in December 2018 at the O2 Arena. Who could not thrill to be in the same room listening to the man performing the songs he wrote – 'All My Loving', 'Blackbird', 'Eleanor Rigby', 'Lady Madonna', 'Back in the USSR', 'Let It Be', 'Hey Jude'...? And as a Christmas treat, encoring with 'Get Back' featuring Ringo on drums?

And of course, I turned to my companion Colin (who missed seeing the Beatles in 1964 as his Dad wouldn't let him off the Bromyard farm) and mouth, "That's *half* the Beatles". And trying to disguise our quivering, manly bottom lips as we wallowed, and wept, and were swept along.

The idea that large sums of money in the 21st century would be paid to see an act whose first No.1 had been over half a century before might seem preposterous to those reared on Arctic Monkeys or Wolf Alice. But with one eye on surviving Beatles, and as the Rolling Stones limbered up for their 2024 tour, Steve Van Zandt argued that "The rock generation changed the concept of chronicles of time…"

Those who are left, who were there, are understandably overwhelmed by it all. But they have learned to cope. When I spoke to Paul McCartney in 1985 (we go back a long way, I knew him before he was knighted) he was in nostalgic mode and smiled: "I just heard a tape from the Cavern… you realise just what a good little band we were. Really just popping, not bad at all!"

No one would surely begrudge McCartney his place in history, or his role in the Beatles (25% of the quartet, 50% of their songwriting duo). Some still carp at what they see as his seizing the mantle. He, above all, is surely entitled. As he enters his ninth decade, Paul seems happy enough to balance a solo career with a strong reliance on the Beatle years. 2023 saw the National Portrait Gallery host his photographic evidence of those years of Beatle madness, aptly titled *Eye of the Storm*.

It was as if that were a testament to his standing in the national consciousness. How did the world's oldest portrait gallery celebrate its three-year, multi-million-pound reopening? An exhibition of Julia Margaret Cameron photographs? Bloomsbury group portraits? Images of … Peter Jay & the Jaywalkers? No, it was unseen photos of another pop group who had broken up 53 years before.

Later that year, as Ringo called them, "my old group" were on the front page again. 'New Beatles Single' were the worldwide headlines during the Autumn of 2023. Tried out in 1995, 'Now and Then' had been abandoned. But with the technology Peter Jackson and his team had perfected for the *Get Back* film, two decades on, John's vocal and piano could be separated. Rather sweetly, the **M**achine **A**ssisted **L**earning was in homage to Mal Evans, longstanding Beatle insider. That degree of separation allowed new bass, guitar and string parts to be added and fleshed out to give us a new – and final! – Beatles single.

The reviews were generally favourable, the general consensus being "not as bad as we'd feared". Much was made of the forensic detail of creating the single, and one sensed 'Now and Then' was as much a triumph of technology as was any musical merit. In fairness, that technological breakthrough registered around the world, "crying my eyes out"… "speechless"… "in tears"… "puddle of tears"… "joy and sadness at the same time". Liam Gallagher was evocative: "biblical, celestial, heartbreaking, heartwarming". Then reverted to more familiar scally reflection: "The Beatles could shit in my handbag and I'd still hide my Polo mints in there". With a nice sense of symmetry, 'Love Me Do' (the Ringo version) was included on the B-side. So there was the beginning, and the final – *final*? – end. Some did cavil at the price of £17.99 – for a single!

As someone now with both feet firmly inside the Apple tent, Peter Jackson was asked to fashion a promo video. "I just needed a little time to figure out a good reason for turning the Beatles down", the director joked. He of course relented, and fashioned a well-received little film. It was genuinely moving to see Beatles 67 jigging alongside the survivors' 2023 version. It would not perhaps be an overstatement to say that with war raging in the Ukraine, NHS waiting lists now into eight figures, the Middle East in turmoil, Taiwan under threat, the unknown menace of AI… a new Beatles single did provide a ray of sunshine. And while 'Now and Then' may not replace 'Hello Goodbye' or 'Help!' in people's memories, it was, apart from the cover, not a bad way to go out.

Even with physical sales dwindling, the song was soon happily at No.1. Much media mileage was extracted from queues outside HMV Liverpool to be the first to obtain a copy. First in line was 'John Lennon' (name changed by deed poll). Its success made Liverpool boast that with 59, they were now the city with the most Number Ones. 'Now and Then' raced to the UK No.1, its 40,000 physical sales trebling that of the No.2. The single achieved another record – the longest gap between No.1 records.

I was surprised to see the last UK Beatles No.1 had not been 'Get Back' or 'Let It Be', but 'The Ballad of John & Yoko'. Just think of all the changes which had been changed since *then*…

A further avalanche followed – I find it unbelievable just how this stuff gets out there. A 2CD 'Now and Then' bootleg compilation included the original solo Lennon demo, plus tracks such as 'Paul, slide guitar solo' and 'Ringo drum sessions, Takes 1–5'.

Then, happily just in time for Christmas, 6LP, 3CD versions of the *Red* and *Blue* collections, rejigged to include the new single, but mysteriously without 'Free As a Bird' or 'Real Love'. The inclusion of 'If I Needed Someone', 'Within You Without You' and 'I Me Mine' suggested some heft from the Harrison camp had been applied. Many were disappointed by the rejigged track listings, *The New York Times* felt that they were "diluting the canon". In the UK, history repeated itself – both the *Red* and *Blue* were denied the No.1 – in 2023 it was the all-conquering hand of Taylor Swift. In 1973, David Bowie's *Aladdin Sane* had kept them off the pole position.

And in the end… And at the end… There is no end. It will never end. As I was finishing this book, my brother-in-law rang to talk about the sale of his mother's apartment. He was talking to his accountant and somehow the subject of what I did for a living came up. Robert said I was writing a book about the Beatles. "Oh yes", said Jacqui, "my dad used to be in the Beatles".

"And… sorry, is your surname Lennon or McCartney?"

Turned out her father was Chas Newby (1941–2023). That would be the Chas who played bass with the group at four gigs during December 1960. So – how cool is this? – my accountant's father used to be in the Beatles. A fifth Beatle, yes, but at a time when the line-up *was* five Beatles.

So, one dingy afternoon in January 2021, here I was talking to the Beatles' *other* bass player. Chas was a mate and schoolfriend of Pete Best, it was his experience with the Blackjacks that led to those four momentous dates. Chas was on bass for that historic Litherland Town Hall date on New Year's Eve 1960 (the one Beatle gig which Mark Lewisohn told me he'd love to have witnessed).

"We were part of a blessed generation|", Chas told me, looking back on his brief career as a Beatle. "We had proper food, good education, the National Health Service and no National Service". Chas was enlisted because Stuart Sutcliffe was staying behind in Hamburg, and the group needed a bass player. And so Chas, formerly a rhythm guitarist with Pete's group, borrowed a bass from the Casbah's house band the Djangobeats.

"There was never a plan for a career, we were kids. In Liverpool at the time it was Rory Storm, the Bluegenes and Cass & the Casanovas who were the professional groups.

But with the Beatles back, and advertised 'Direct From Hamburg', I remember Billy J. Kramer telling me that he thought they spoke very good English!

"I was only there as a temporary replacement, until Stuart came back from Hamburg". Wasn't there any bitterness that he didn't stay with the group longer? "No regrets. None whatsoever". He re-emphasised a sentiment I'd heard many times from those who were there, the nearly Beatles: "we were *kids*". John did ask Chas to accompany them back to Hamburg, but to keep his parents happy, Chas returned to college, got his degree and went on to a career in chemical engineering.

You can imagine the conversation, with all the conviction of a teenager: "Actually Mum and Dad, I've decided to jack in the prospects of a good career with a pension and join a bunch of unemployed teddy boys in a pop group to play some dates in Germany…"

The way the wheel comes full circle is that Chas – like 'Duff' Lowe – became an honorary Quarryman. "It is amazing – the intensity of interest in the Beatles", Chas told me. "The Quarrymen played a gig in Germany to commemorate what would have been John's 80th birthday. It was very emotional, and the next morning over breakfast, this German guy started singing at us in English. I looked baffled. It wasn't a Beatle song. But remember, I was at the Collegiate School with Pete, but this guy knew all the words to the Quarry Bank school song!"

As long as there is a suitable format, it is those Beatle songs that will be heard. They remain the condition to which every group aspires to. In their years at Abbey Road, the Beatles fashioned the most influential body of work in the history of rock & roll, and in doing so, left an indelible mark on the 20th century. They were a product of their class, time and environment. For popular music, they are *Das Kapital* and *Origin of the Species* combined. No one will ever, *ever* match that arc, from the release of 'Love Me Do' to *Sgt Pepper* in just five years.

So ingrained is their music, that one sometimes overlooks just how good it was. It is. 'Let It Be' came to mind. Perhaps it was the clips of the Peter Jackson documentary, the 27-year-old, doe-eyed Paul looking very grown-up behind his beard, staring at the camera as he sang his lament to "mother Mary". After half a century, you forget just how poignant a song it is; its appeal, heartfelt and unforgettable. A song not just addressed to the mother whose love he was denied when only 14, but a song to see us all through "times of trouble". While never the best-loved Beatle LP, even with all the tweaks and remasters, maybe Paul's plaintive ballad is a suitable place to Let It Be.

No need for a 'new Beatles', there's nothing wrong and everything right with the old one. They are now so firmly entrenched in *Our World* it is literally unimaginable to imagine a world without them. They are 'The Act You've Known For All These Years'. But if, for one fleeting moment, the memory falters, there is that inevitable Anniversary Waltz. God willing, I'll be around for the 60th. But as the 70th anniversaries begin in 2032 (EMI audition, debut single); 2033 (Beatlemania); 2034 (conquest of America, first film…). Then, the centenaries 30 years later beyond that. Everyone who made those records, or listened to them on release, will be long dead. But as the cliché goes, the music lives on. And as long as there is power for whatever device it is heard on, their music will continue to enchant, delight and fascinate for all eternity.

Nobody, not even Mark Zuckerberg or Elon Musk, really knows what the future holds. The latest threat is how Artificial Intelligence will impact on popular music. The industry is facing its biggest threat since Napster opened the floodgates at the end of the 20th century. In theory, with just the most minute strand of musical DNA, anything is possible. With such a wealth of material, the Beatles offer a rich palette. By early 2023, we have already had John singing Paul's 'Junk'. Paul McCartney sings 'Imagine', while, all together now, the entire group can be heard on 'Watching Rainbows', a scrap from the *Get Back* sessions. Paul admitted to utilising AI for the 'last' Beatles song, John's 'Now and Then'. The genie is out of the bottle. Record companies soil themselves as they watch their precious copyrights float upwards like smoke from a Guy Fawkes bonfire.

Across the 22nd-century metaverse, will it be Coldplay and Taylor Swift dominating, their music beamed out of the cold, dead eye of a HAL 9000? I genuinely wish I'd be around to know in 50 years if the Beatles will still hold the high ground. If they remain, as they appear to have always been, the line in the sand … the benchmark by which all others are measured. Will theirs be the music which lasts and which will be pored over as assiduously as Shakespeare plays down the echoing centuries? It would be nice to think so, as theirs was the music which brought so much joy, so much harmony, so much positivism, so much *love* to so many.

In August 2023 I finally made the journey to Liverpool for the city's Beatle Week. The Adelphi has its own history – Roy Rogers stayed there with Trigger, who rode up the hotel's main staircase. It was at the Adelphi that Brian Epstein entertained London journalists who had made the perilous journey north, hoping to impress them with the hotel's faded grandeur. It has long been rumoured that Adolf Hitler worked in the kitchens immediately prior to the Great War. His half-brother, Alois *did*, living in Liverpool with his wife and son, the unfortunately named William Patrick Hitler. Ironically the Hitler family home in Toxteth was destroyed in the last raid of the Liverpool Blitz in 1942.

It was under happier circumstances I stayed at the Adelphi. I mean, I *like* the Beatles. I have spent years writing a book about them, a lifetime listening to them. But this weekend was … *overwhelming*. It was like living in a city under occupation. Trying to find a quiet spot in the Adelphi, we were assailed from one room by bands thumping through 'I Saw Her Standing There' while 'Don't Let Me Down' pounded out from a room opposite. A trawl among the merchandise stalls – all that tat your mum made you throw out now going for eye-watering prices. Here was a rock & roll Lourdes – shavings of the true Cross? Certainly sir… Phial of Christ's blood? Just hang on a sec, madam.

If you needed a break, why not 'Live Like a Beatle' and spend the night at George's family home, 25 Upton Green? Or take a trip down Matthew Street's Cavern Quarter. The Beatles Story… The Cavern Club… The Casbah… The Grapes… The Magical History Beatles Museum. Have your photo taken by the Beatles statue – said to be the most photographed statue in the country. A Gerry Marsden ferry 'cross the Mersey provided a breath of fresh air. But even then we were reminded that the Beatles played four times on the Royal Iris during Cavern-hosted Riverboat Shuffles.

Over breakfast to the last knockings, Beatles music was beamed down. The American Bar, just off the main lobby, was the one place which offered sanctuary. But by then I was beginning to get Beatle-d out; hearing 'Rebel Rebel' I paused and tried to remember if David Bowie had been in the Beatles.

Riding the lifts I was struck by the veritable United Nations of accents. If you offer them a sanctuary, they will come. This was the religious gathering. But, still – just – a living history. My friend Jeremy Taylor had spent much of Saturday at the re-opened Casbah Club ("somewhere not familiar with current Health & Safety regulations…"). Chancing upon Roag Best, Jeremy was introduced to his brother, Pete. "Pete Best! It was like meeting, I don't know, Lee Harvey Oswald. Someone from *history*…"

My friend John Sugar was in reflective mood: "You know, our parents had their Golden Age. It was Hollywood, all those fantastic stars. We had our Golden Age. It was the Beatles".

In their time together they had all the love they needed. It was a love they shared. By the time the group itself sundered, they had been shown everywhere, they had seen the seven wonders, and tomorrow never knew… John Winston Lennon, James Paul McCartney, George Harrison, Richard Starkey may not have known. But *they* did. The Beatles did. The Beatles knew.

THE END

BIBLIOGRAPHY

Keith Badman: *The Beatles Diary, Volume 2* (Omnibus, 2001)
Rob Baker: *High Buildings, Low Morals* (Amberley, 2017)
The Beatles *Anthology* (Cassell, 2000)
Christopher Booker: *The Neophiliacs* (Fontana, 1970)
Michael Bracewell: *Roxy Music* (Faber, 2007)
Craig Brown: *One Two Three Four, The Beatles In Time* (4th Estate, 2020)
Roy Carr: *The Beatles at the Movies* (UFO, 1996)
Ray Coleman: *Brian Epstein: The Man Who Made The Beatles* (Penguin, 1990)
Ray Coleman: *McCartney: Yesterday & Today* (Boxtree, 1995)
Ray Connolly: *Born at the Right Time* (Malignon, 2023)
Peter Cowie: *Revolution!* (Faber, 2004)
Martin Creasy: *Beatlemania! The Real Account of The Beatles UK Tours 1963–1965* (Omnibus, 2010)
Hunter Davies: *The Quarrymen* (Omnibus, 2001)
Paul Du Noyer: *Conversations with McCartney* (Hodder & Stoughton)
Geoff Emerick & Howard Massey: *Here, There & Everywhere* (Gotham, 2006)
Pete Frame: *The Restless Generation* (Rogan House, 2007)
Robert Freeman: *The Beatles: A Private View* (Mitchell Beazley, 1990)
Debbie Geller & Anthony Wall: *The Brian Epstein Story* (Faber, 2000)
Charlie Gillett: *The Sound of the City* (Sphere, 1971)
Jonathan Gould: *Can't Buy Me Love* (Piatkus, 2007)
Colin Hall: *The Songs the Beatles Gave Away* (Great Northern Books, 2022)
Bill Harry: *The Beatles Encyclopedia* (Virgin, 2000)
Max Hastings: *Bomber Command* (Michael Joseph, 1979)
David Hepworth: *Abbey Road* (Penguin, 2023)
John Higgs: *Love & Let Die* (Weidenfeld & Nicolson, 2022)
Patrick Humphries*: Lonnie Donegan and the Birth of British Rock & Roll* (Robson Press, 2012)
Lesley-Ann Jones: *Who Killed John Lennon?* (John Blake, 2020)
Larry Kane: *Ticket to Ride* (Penguin, 2004)
Mark Kurlansky: *1968: The Year That Rocked the World* (Vintage, 2005)
Spencer Leigh: *The Best of Fellas: The Story of Bob Wooler* (Drivegreen, 2002)
Spencer Leigh: *Twist & Shout! Merseybeat, The Cavern, The Star Club and The Beatles* (Nirvana, 2004)
Spencer Leigh: *The Cavern: The Most Famous Club in the World* (SAF Publishing, 2008)
Shawn Levy: *Rat Pack Confidential* (4th Estate, 1998)
Mark Lewisohn: *The Beatles Live!* (Pavilion, 1986)
Mark Lewisohn: *The Beatles: Complete Recording Sessions* (Hamlyn, 1988) – This is the one crucial book crying out for a reprint.
Mark Lewisohn: *The Beatles, Volume 1, Tune In* (Little, Brown, 2013)
Michael Lindsay-Hogg: *Luck & Circumstance* (Knopf, 2011)
Alan Mann: *The Teacher: The Tony Sheridan Story* (AMPS Books, 2013)
Barry Miles: *Many Years from Now* (Secker & Warburg, 1997)
Barry Miles: *In the Sixties* (Rocket 88, 2017)
Richard Morton Jack: *Galactic Ramble* (ISBN 9787195027425, 2020)
Philip Norman: *Shout! The True Story of The Beatles* (Pan, 2004)
Philip Norman: *John Lennon: The Life* (HarperCollins, 2008)
Simon Parkes (with J.S. Rafaeli) *Live at the Brixton Academy* (Serpent's Tail, 2014)
Rob Sheffield: *Dreaming The Beatles* (Dey Street Books, 2017)
Graham Simpson: *The Judith Durham Story* (Virgin, 2003)
Bob Spitz: *The Beatles: The Biography* (Aurum, 2006)
David & Caroline Stafford: *Cupid Stunts: The Life & Radio Times of Kenny Everett* (Omnibus, 2013)
Alexander Walker: *Hollywood England: The British Film Industry in the Sixties*, (Harrap, 1986)
Bruce Welch (with Howard Elson): *Rock & Roll: I Gave You the Best Years of My Life* (Penguin, 1990)
Ian Whitcomb: *Rock Odyssey: A Chronicle of the Sixties* (Hutchinson, 1984)
Ruth Winstone: *Events, Dear Boy, Events: A Political Diary of Britain 1921 to 2010* (Profile Books, 2014)
Leslie Woodhead: *How The Beatles Rocked The Kremlin* (Bloomsbury, 2013)

THANKS

First off, of course, Paul, George and Ringo for the time I spent in their company, and John, who I missed, and is missed.

It is literally unimaginable to consider a book on the Beatles without consulting the works of Mark Lewisohn. From his first, a comprehensive chronicle of those live performances, to Volume I of his magnum opus, *Tune In*, his dedication to the group is legendary. Mark's forensic attention to detail is mind-boggling. With every book or presentation, Mark makes you look at the group with fresh eyes. I am also lucky to count him as a friend. Roll on Volume II (and III).

For all things Liverpool, and beyond, Spencer Leigh has been an invaluable source, as well as a valued colleague for many years. If he ever finds time to write it, Spencer's history of Merseybeat will be the definitive volume.

I first visited Liverpool to see my friend Mark Seaman at university, who took me to the Kop, and down Matthew Street. Half a century on Mark's unwavering support has seen me down a long, and winding, road.

To Tim Seaman, who valiantly scanned.

Bill Brooke, went to university in Liverpool because he so loved the Beatles. He still does… As do Tom, Ellie and Laura, drip-fed in utero…

Paul's PR Geoff Baker was always very kind to me over a long period, allowing me access to the great man. I wish him well… It was during my brief spell in music PR that Bernard Doherty got me into the world of MPL and Paul McCartney. A good friend over the years, thanks again Big BD.

Mal Peachey and Martin Townsend commissioned the features which allowed me access to George and Ringo all those years ago. I thanked them then. I thank them now.

Over the years John Sugar made a number of diverting radio documentaries highlighting lesser-known aspects of the group's career. I value them, but more so his friendship after all these years.

John Williamson in Glasgow and Karl Magee in Stirling provided fascinating background on the Musicians' Union's relationship with the Beatles. Andrew Gustar was most helpful concerning the group and *Desert Island Discs*. His website www. musichistorystats.com

is a fascinating treasure trove, but be warned, it's like going down the rabbit hole…

Thanks to Victoria Shaffer, and Joe Chambers for the copy of the 1963 Beatles letter to the Crickets. When in Nashville, make sure you go to www.musicianshalloffame.com

Stax historian Tim Sampson was most helpful when it came to finding out more about the group's intention to record at the legendary Memphis studio. www.staxmuseum.com

Adam 'Mr Motown' White tracked down the telegram from the group to Tamla.

My brother-in-law Rob Parr's introduction, allowing me the opportunity to use the line, "My accountant's dad used to be in the Beatles".

Patricia Dolan, for alerting me to the Daniel Farson 1963 *Beat City* documentary.

Barry Monks, David Bedford and John Bezzini were the navigators who steered me through the febrile world of the Beatles online.

At school in 1963, Lawrence Morphet was convinced of the group's greatness. His belief has never faltered. Nor his valued friendship.

I first met Alec Cormack in a record shop in 1968. Since then he has proved a loyal friend and invaluable guide through the highways and byways of, phew, rock & roll…

In later years, a shake of the hair to all having their ears bent by me when it came to the Fab Four… Louis Barfe, Steve Blacknell, Tony Bramwell, Rob Crossan, Colin Davies, Susannah Goodman, Peter Hogan, Mick Houghton, Andrew Jarvis, Neil McArthur, Paul McGuire, Tom Mitchelson, Richard Porter, David Stark, Roger Stormo, Jeremy Taylor, Rick Wilson.

Chris Welch gave me hours of endless pleasure when I used to read him every week as 'The Raver' in *Melody Maker*. I am now delighted beyond measure to count him as a friend (and thanks for that Meccano link…) Thanks too for Chris contacting Jon Newey on my behalf, who supplied the fascinating detail of just who the UK got while America welcomed the Beatles.

Over the years Ken Hunt has proved a valued friend and colleague; his bi-monthly posts provided just the sort of detail I treasure.

The eagle eyes of Richard Wallis went through the manuscript. Thanks, mate; and for those Fab Zoom calls.

"Well, well, well, you're feeling fine…" Thanks to our GP, Dr Anne Stephenson.

Saira Quli gave me some lovely first-hand memories of growing up in Liverpool.

Paul Williams was invaluable when it came to uncoiling the complex issues of copyright and music publishing. His specialist knowledge also spotted quite a few howlers. Any that remain are my own.

Philip & Mary Morton were erstwhile supporters, and, indeed, flamin' groovy… It was Philip's late sister Margaret Morton who snapped a delighted John and Paul signing autographs in 1963 (though apparently she'd rather have met Peter Jay, with or without his Jaywalkers).

Many years ago, Ulf Kruger took me round the Beatles' Hamburg…

For Part III, I am particularly grateful to Hilary Kay who shared her personal memories of organising the first Rock & Roll auction at Sotheby's in 1981. Katherine Schofield from Bonham's offered a revealing insight into the way the group dominates the auction houses of the 21st century.

Craig Brown's acclaimed and diverting Beatle book was published while I was writing mine. I deliberately didn't read it until I had finished my own first draft. We obviously drew from the same well when it came to sources, although might I blow my own trumpet by mentioning – again – that I did actually interview three of the Beatles?

Sadly, over the years this book has taken, a number of friends died who I'd like to pause and remember: my old chum Alan Houlden from the Department of the Environment; you, Paul and I will always have The White Horse & Bower… Propping up the bar at The Hope Bruce Hawkins, Paul Mason, Suzy Butler, Tom Dobson, Gael Whelan, Jerry Duggin, David Ferguson, Steve Cross… From *Melody Maker* Colin Irwin and Carol Clerk… Annie Bristow, a BBC radio producer who gave me the beginning of a radio career at the World Service… Johnny Rogan kept himself to himself, but when we did meet, all too infrequently, his enthusiasm was contagious… Sean Body at Helter Shelter in Denmark Street… Dear old Fred Dellar died a few days before his 90th birthday. I knew 'Uncle Fred' when I began freelancing for *NME* in the 1970s, then on to work alongside him at *Vox*. He was a lovely gentle man, a gentleman with a devotion to popular music which was unmatched… Then only a month later, Alan Lewis, another *Vox* compadre whose dry and laconic wit livened up many an editorial conference… Missing at the other *Vox* office, the Stamford Arms, founding Editor, the incomparable Roy Carr, along with Norma Martin, Barry Lazell and Neil Slaven.

On and on – colleagues Bob Fisher… Pete Makowski… Judy Totton… and Simon Wells, who was such a help on all things 60s that I'd forgotten. Old friends Andy Whitfield and Steve Cross, cousins Adrian Lee and Roger Lusk taken.

Thanks to Cathy Hawkes at Apple for letting me 'Get Back'… Sheldon Hall was instructive on the Beatles' film screenings on UK television.

Paul Bond helped rid us of a bee infestation and was happy to share his memories of being behind the camera on *Let It Be* half a century before.

Theo Jones at the Society of Authors has always provided sound counsel. If you write, then you are an author, and you should belong: info@societyofauthors.org

My dear wife Sue Parr said she "always preferred Wings", but has come round to like the music Paul's group made before them. I thank her for 40 years of a mysterious, magical tour through life and love.

A heartfelt thanks to Hlotoshisine Moy, our dear Lottie, who came into our lives in September 2020 and helped carve out time for me to write this book. And a whole lot more. And to Emma Lindley who ably covered. Graham and William helped make me more mobile.

Needless to say all thoughts, opinions and errors are I Me Mine.

Patrick Humphries, south-east London, back in the house where I first heard the Beatles, March 2024.

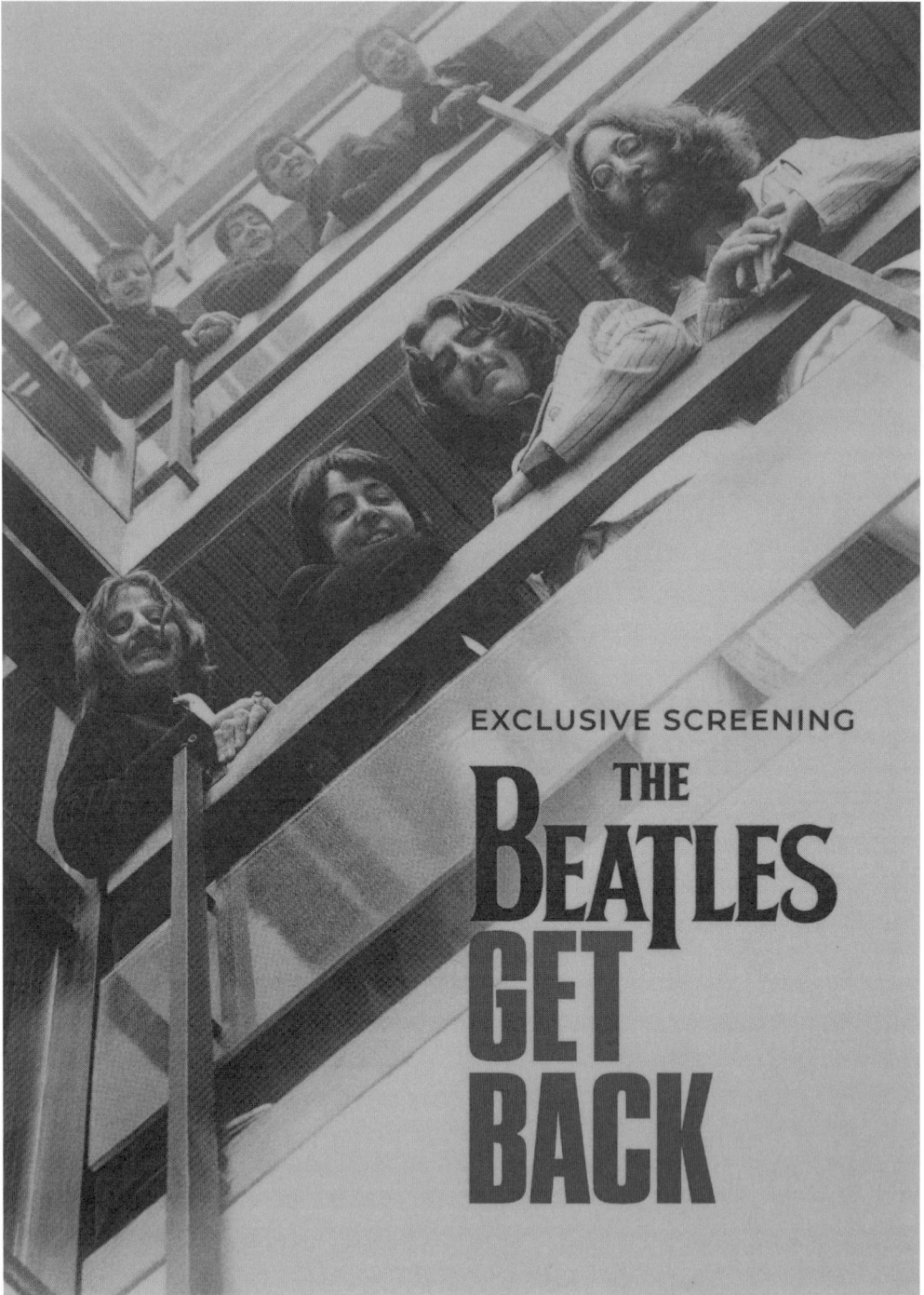

Get Back poster

York
the Beatles hit

VOICE OF FLOWER POWER
SCOTT McKENZIE SPEAKS ON PAGE 8

Melody Maker

MORE MONKE
TV – SEE PAGE

BEATLES

POP
BEATLES

ATLES
PE MONKEES

LAUGH O
BBC BAN

'IT MIGHT
HELP THE LP'

THE BEATLES are back on the early Beatles
at the top! Their formula.
"All You Need Is "All You Need Is
Love" climbed to Love" is the song that
number one this week 400 million people
dislodging the Mon- round the world
kees, the group based watched the Beatles

working on in the
studios as part of the
Our World TV pro-
gramme.
A spokesman for
Nems told the MM on
Monday: — Apart from

Is it
all a big
Beatle
joke?

PAUL IN SECRET SESSION

A MILLION-POUND dream
group was assembled by
Paul McCartney and Graham
Nash of the Hollies for a top
secret experimental recording
session in London last week.
The proceedings were so hush-
hush that no one concerned
would comment.

McGear.
The session featured Liverpool
poet Roger McGough, who is
also a member of the Scaffold.
He was backed by an all-star
group beyond the financial
reach of any commercial producer.
Paul played a Mellotron, with
Graham, Spencer and Dave
Mason on guitars and Gary on
tenor sax.

'DEAD' BEATLE
MANIA MOUN

BEATLES
DOU

DISC
and MUSIC ECHO 1s
USA 20c
JANUARY 4, 1969

Beatles plan
five new LPs
– one 'live!'

BEATLES are to record
their first-ever special
album, and a special
package of FOUR sepa-
rate LPs each one the
individual choice of John,
Paul, George and Ringo.

The Brilliant, the
ad and the Ugly

forthcoming Beatles double album as one
significant landmarks in their recording
Me Do." The 30 tracks do not possess
a "Sergeant Pepper," and neither
the compelling unreality of that
into the mind.

ecial by ALA